WITHDRAWN

Beyond Isabella

Beyond Isabella

Secular Women Patrons of Art in Renaissance Italy

Edited by
Sheryl E. Reiss and David G. Wilkins

Sixteenth Century Essays & Studies
Volume LIV

Truman State University Press

Copyright © 2001 Truman State University Press
Kirksville, Missouri 63501

Library of Congress Cataloging-in-Publication Data

Beyond Isabella: secular women patrons of art in Renaissance Italy /
edited by Sheryl E. Reiss and David G. Wilkins.
       p. cm. – (Sixteenth century essays and studies ; 54)
   Includes bibliographical references and index.
   ISBN 0-943549-78-7 (cloth) – ISBN 0-943549-88-4 (pbk.), v. 54
     1. Women art patrons—Italy. 2. Art patronage—Italy—History. 3.
Art, Italian. 4. Art, Renaissance—Italy. I. Reiss, Sheryl E. II. Wilkins,
David G. III. Sixteenth century essays & studies ; 54.

N5273 .B47 2000
707'.9'45—dc21   00-046674

Text is set in New Caledonia

Cover design: Teresa Wheeler

Book design: David Alcorn,
Alcorn Publication Design, Graeagle, California

The paper in this publication meets or exceeds the minimum requirements
of the American National Standard for Permanence of Paper for Printed
Library Materials Z39.48 (1984).

For Paul and for Ann

Contents

Illustrations   viii

Prologue   xv

Acknowledgments   xxi

Frequently Cited Sources and Abbreviations   xxii

Introduction: Recognizing New Patrons, Posing New Questions   1
David G. Wilkins

Fina da Carrara, née Buzzacarini: Consort, Mother, and Patron of Art in Trecento Padua   19
Benjamin G. Kohl

Controlling Women or Women Controlled? Suggestions for Gender Roles and Visual Culture in the Italian Renaissance Palace   37
Roger J. Crum

The Women Patrons of Neri di Bicci   51
Rosi Prieto Gilday

Caterina Piccolomini and the Palazzo delle Papesse in Siena   77
A. Lawrence Jenkens

Renaissance Husbands and Wives as Patrons of Art: The *Camerini* of Isabella d'Este and Francesco II Gonzaga   93
Molly Bourne

Widow, Mother, Patron of Art: Alfonsina Orsini de' Medici   125
Sheryl E. Reiss

Two Emilian Noblewomen and Patronage Networks in the Cinquecento   159
Katherine A. McIver

Dutiful Widows: Female Patronage and Two Marian Altarpieces by Parmigianino   177
Mary Vaccaro

Vittoria Colonna and the Commission for a *Mary Magdalene* by Titian   193
Marjorie Och

Bronzino in the Service of Eleonora di Toledo and Cosimo I de' Medici: Conjugal Patronage and the Painter-Courtier   225
Bruce L. Edelstein

A Medici Miniature: Juno and a Woman with "Eyes in Her Head Like Two Stars in Their Beauty"   263
Gabrielle Langdon

A Widow's Choice: Alessandro Allori's *Christ and the Adulteress* in the Church of Santo Spirito at Florence   301
Elizabeth Pilliod

Matrons and Motives: Why Women Built in Early Modern Rome   317
Carolyn Valone

About the Contributors   337

Illustrations

Introduction: Recognizing New Patrons, Posing New Questions

David G. Wilkins

1. Nicola di Maestro Antonio d'Ancona, detail of patron (?), *Madonna and Child with Donor and Saints Leonard, Jerome, John the Baptist, and Francis*, 1472. Pittsburgh, Carnegie Museum of Art (photo: University of Pittsburgh) ... 2

2. Nicola di Maestro Antonio d'Ancona, *Madonna and Child with Donor and Saints Leonard, Jerome, John the Baptist, and Francis*, 1472. Pittsburgh, Carnegie Museum of Art (photo: University of Pittsburgh) ... 3

3. Circle of Bernardo Daddi (?), Votive Panel, 1335 (?), Florence, Museo dell' Opera del Duomo (photo: Alinari/Art Resource, N.Y.) ... 7

4. Florentine, mid-fourteenth century, *Lamentation from San Remigio*, ca. 1350, Florence, Galleria degli Uffizi (photo: Alinari/Art Resource, N.Y.) ... 8

Fina da Carrara, née Buzzacarini: Consort, Mother, and Patron of Art in Trecento Padua

Benjamin G. Kohl

1. Baptistery, Padua, exterior, rebuilt 1260 (photo: courtesy Judith Kohl) ... 25

2. Giusto de' Menabuoi and assistants, frescoes on the west wall of the Baptistery, Padua, 1376–78 (photo: courtesy Ministero per i Beni Culturali ed Ambientali, Soprintendenza Beni Artistici e Storici, Veneto) ... 27

3. Giusto de' Menabuoi and assistants, *Polyptych with Madonna Enthroned, Scenes from the Life of Saint John the Baptist and Saints*, 1376–78, Padua, Baptistery (photo: courtesy Ministero per i Beni Culturali ed ambientali, Soprintendenza Beni Artistici e Storici, Veneto) ... 38

4. Giusto de' Menabuoi and assistants, *The Birth of Saint John the Baptist*, 1376–78. Padua, Baptistery (photo: courtesy Ministero per i Beni Culturali ed ambientali, Soprintendenza Beni Artistici e Storici, Veneto) ... 30

5. Giusto de' Menabuoi and assistants, *The Birth of Saint John the Baptist*, detail of *Fina Buzzacarini and Her Three Daughters*, 1376–78, Padua, Baptistery (photo: courtesy Ministero per i Beni Culturali ed ambientali, Soprintendenza Beni Artistici e Storici, Veneto) ... 30

Controlling Women or Women Controlled? Suggestions for Gender Roles and Visual Culture in the Italian Renaissance Palace

Roger J. Crum

1. Florentine, late fifteenth century, *The Assembly of a Domestic Inventory*, Florence, San Martino del Vescovo (photo: Scala/Art Resource, N.Y.) ... 39

The Women Patrons of Neri di Bicci

Rosi Prieto Gilday

1. Neri di Bicci, *Assumption of the Virgin*, 1456, Ottawa, National Gallery of Canada (photo: National Gallery of Canada, Ottawa) ... 52

2. Neri di Bicci, *Annunciation,* 1455, Florence, Santa Maria Novella   53
   (photo: Alinari/Art Resource, N.Y.)

3. Neri di Bicci, *Trinity,* 1463, formerly Florence, San Niccolò Oltrarno   55
   (photo: Alinari/Art Resource, N.Y.)

Caterina Piccolomini and the Palazzo delle Papesse in Siena

A. Lawrence Jenkens

1. Palazzo delle Papesse, Siena, Via di Città, begun ca. 1460 (photo: author)   78

2. Palazzo delle Papesse, detail, ground floor (photo: author)   79

3. Palazzo delle Papesse, detail, *piano nobile* (photo: author)   79

4. Reconstruction of Pius II's proposed intervention in Siena: (A) Palazzo   81
   Piccolomini; (B) Loggia dei Papa; (C) enlarged Piazza Piccolomini (drawing:
   Wolfgang Jung)

5. Loggia del Papa, Siena, 1460–62 (photo: author)   81

6. Giacomo Piccolomini's Palazzo Nuovo (now Palazzo Piccolomini), Siena,   82
   Banchi di Sotto, begun 1469 (photo: author)

7. Andrea Piccolomini's Casamento Vecchio (now Palazzo Piccolomini), Siena,   82
   Piazza del Campo, late fifteenth century (photo: author)

**Renaissance Husbands and Wives as Patrons of Art: The *Camerini* of
   Isabella d'Este and Francesco II Gonzaga**

Molly Bourne

1. Attributed to Andrea Mantegna, *Portrait of Francesco II Gonzaga,* ca. 1500,   94
   Dublin, National Gallery of Ireland (photo: National Gallery of Ireland)

2. Castello di San Giorgio, Mantua, showing the Torretta di San Nicolò   96
   (photo: author)

3. Plan of Castello di San Giorgio, Mantua, *piano nobile* (from Sylvia Ferino-   96
   Pagden, ed., "La Prima Donna del Mondo": *Isabella d'Este, Fürsten und
   Mäzenatin der Renaissance,* exh. cat. [Vienna: Kunsthistorisches Museum
   Vienna, 1994], p. 14, fig. 27)

4. View of Isabella's Grotta in the Castello di San Giorgio, Mantua (photo: author)   97

5. View from Sala delle Cappe in the Castello di San Giorgio, Mantua, of the   97
   hallway (on left) leading to Isabella's Studiolo, and the entrance (on right)
   leading down to Grotta (photo: author)

6. Six ceramic floor tiles from Isabella's Studiolo, Milan, Museo di Castello   98
   Sforzesco (from Sylvia Ferino-Pagden, ed., "La Prima Donna del Mondo":
   Isabella d'Este, Fürsten und Mäzenatin der Renaissance, exh. cat. [Vienna:
   Kunsthistorisches Museum Vienna, 1994], p.189, cat. no. 175)

7. Lorenzo Costa, *Allegory of the Court of Isabella d'Este,* ca. 1506, Paris, Musée   98
   du Louvre (photo: RMN)

8. "Sala del Sole," apartments of Francesco II on ground floor of Castello di San   99
   Giorgio, Mantua (photo: author)

9. Gabriele Bertazzolo, *Urbis Mantuae Descriptio,* Mantua, 1628 (photo: author)   100

10. Gabriele Bertazzolo, *Urbis Mantuae Descriptio,* Mantua, 1628, detail of area around Palazzo di San Sebastiano (in circle) (photo: author)   101

11. Porta Pusterla, Mantua, view ca. 1900 from Te island, showing waterway and bridge leading to Te island (photo: Archivio di Stato, Mantua, authorization 28/99)   101

12. Palazzo di San Sebastiano, Mantua, distant view ca. 1900 from Te island, showing city walls, Porta Pusterla, and bridge leading to Te island (photo: Archivio di Stato, Mantua, authorization 28/99)   102

13. Palazzo di San Sebastiano, Mantua, view ca. 1900 from Te island, with Porta Pusterla visible at right (photo: Archivio di Stato, Mantua, authorization 28/99)   103

14. Schematic plan of Mantua (photo: Carpeggiani and Pagliari, 1983, p. 35)   104

 A-B = Gonzaga axis   d = Church and convent of San Sebastiano
 a = Ducal Palace-Castello complex   e = House of Andrea Mantegna
 b = Cathedral of San Pietro   f = Palazzo San Sebastiano
 c = Church of Sant'Andrea   g = Palazzo Te

15. Palazzo di San Sebastiano, Mantua, modern view of south façade (photo: author)   104

16. Palazzo di San Sebastiano, Mantua, modern view of walled-in arcade on north façade (photo: author)   105

17. Palazzo di San Sebastiano, Mantua, "Camera del Crogiolo" (photo: author)   105

18. Plan (1994) of the ground floor of Palazzo di San Sebastiano with room labels indicating author's reconstruction; dark shading shows original walling (plan: courtesy Arch. A. Guastalla, Mantua)   106

19. Plan (1994) of the *piano nobile* of Palazzo di San Sebastiano with room labels indicating author's reconstruction; dark shading shows original walling (plan: courtesy Arch. A. Guastalla, Mantua)   106

20. Palazzo Ducale, Mantua, Stanza di Giuditta, wooden ceiling with gilded stucco crucible decorations, ca. 1506, originally in the Sala di Triumphi, Palazzo di San Sebastiano (photo: courtesy Giovetti)   107

Widow, Mother, Patron of Art: Alfonsina Orsini de' Medici

Sheryl E. Reiss

1. Francesco Allegrini, *Alfonsina Orsini,* after G. Allegrini, *Chronologica series simulacrorum regiae familiae Mediceae,* Florence, 1761, no plate nos. (photo: Harry Ransom Humanities Research Center, University of Texas, Austin)   126

2. G. B. Paggi, *Piero di Lorenzo de' Medici, Called "The Unfortunate,"* Florence, Galleria degli Uffizi (photo: Soprintendenza, Florence)   127

3. Attributed to Sandro Botticelli, *Portrait of a Woman* (Alfonsina Orsini de' Medici?), ca. 1488, Florence, Galleria Pitti (photo: Alinari/Art Resource, N.Y.)   128

4. Maerten van Heemskerck, *View of Palazzo Madama,* Rome, 1532–36, Berlin, Kupferstichkabinett, 79 D 2, vol. 2, fol. 48r (photo: Kupferstichkabinett, Staatliche Museen zu Berlin PK)   129

5. Palazzo Medici-Lante, Rome, begun ca. 1516, courtyard (photo: author)   130

6. Palazzo Medici-Lante, Rome, begun ca. 1516, captial with arms of Alfonsina Orsini de' Medici and spandrel with Medici diamond ring and feathers (photo: author)   130

7. Letter of Alfonsina Orsini to Lorenzo di Piero de' Medici, 2 September 1514,   131
ASF, MAP, 114, 156 (photo: Archivio di Stato, Florence)

8. Giorgio Vasari, *Entrata of Pope Leo X,* Florence, Palazzo Vecchio, Sala di   131
Leone Decimo, beg. 1555 (photo: Alinari/Art Resource, N.Y.)

9. *Dying Amazon,* Roman copy of Hellenistic original, Naples, Museo Nazionale   132
Archeologico (photo: Alinari/Art Resource, N.Y.)

10. *Dying Persian,* Roman copy of Hellenistic original, Naples, Museo Nazionale   132
Archeologico (photo: Alinari/Art Resource, N.Y.)

11. Maerten van Heemskerck, *View of Palazzo Madama,* Rome, 1532–36, Berlin,   133
Kupferstichkabinett, 79 D 2, vol. 2, fol. 5r (photo: Kupferstichkabinett,
Staatliche Museen zu Berlin PK)

12. Giuliano da Sangallo and Antonio da Sangallo the Elder, plan for a Medici villa   134
in the Via Laura, Florence, ca. 1515, Florence, Galleria degli Uffizi, Gabinetto
dei Disegni e delle Stampe, U 282A (photo: Soprintendenza, Florence)

13. Justus Utens, *Villa Medici at Poggio a Caiano,* late sixteenth century, Florence,   136
Museo Topografico "Firenze com'era" (photo: Alinari/Art Resource, N.Y.)

14. Raphael, *Portrait of Pope Leo X and Two Cardinals,* ca. 1518, Florence,   137
Galleria degli Uffizi (photo: Alinari/Art Resource, N.Y.)

15. Tomb of Alfonsina Orsini de' Medici, 1520s, Rome, Santa Maria del Popolo   138
(photo: author)

16. Giovanni Antonio Sogliani, *Martyrdom of Saint Arcadius* (Achatius?), 1521,   139
Florence, San Lorenzo (photo: Alinari/Art Resource, N.Y.)

Two Emilian Noblewomen and Patronage Networks in the Cinquecento
Katherine A. McIver

1. Biagio Rossetti, Palazzo dei Principi, Correggio, ca. 1507 (photo: author)   162

2. Nicolo dell'Abate, Ceiling Octagon, Camerino dell' Eneide, Rocca Nuova,   166
Scandiano, 1540s (photo: author)

Dutiful Widows: Female Patronage and Two Marian Altarpieces by Parmigianino
Mary Vaccaro

1. Parmigianino, *Vision of Saint Jerome,* 1526–27, London, National Gallery   178
(photo: National Gallery, London)

2. Parmigianino, *Madonna of the Long Neck,* ca. 1534–40, Florence, Galleria degli   179
Uffizi (photo: Alinari/Art Resource, N.Y.)

3. Parmigianino, preparatory drawing for the *Madonna of the Long Neck,* ca.1534,   182
Parma, Galleria Nazionale (photo: Soprintendenza, Parma)

4. Correggio, *Madonna and Child with Saints Jerome and Mary Magdalen,* ca.   184
1526–28, Parma, Galleria Nazionale (photo: Soprintendenza, Parma)

Vittoria Colonna and the Commission for a *Mary Magdalene* by Titian
Marjorie Och

1. Titian, *Mary Magdalen* (Pitti type), ca. 1530–35, Florence, Galleria Pitti (photo: Alinari/Art Resource, N.Y.) 194

Bronzino in the Service of Eleonora di Toledo and Cosimo I de' Medici: Conjugal Patronage and the Painter-Courtier
Bruce L. Edelstein

1. Agnolo Bronzino, *Eleonora di Toledo and her Son, Giovanni de' Medici,* ca. 1545, Florence, Galleria degli Uffizi (photo: Soprintendenza, Florence) 226

2. Agnolo Bronzino, *Eleonora di Toledo and her Son, Francesco de' Medici,* ca. 1550, Pisa, Museo Nazionale di San Matteo (photo: Soprintendenza, Pisa) 227

3. Agnolo Bronzino, *Garzia de' Medici,* ca. 1551, Lucca, Pinacoteca Nazionale (photo: Soprintendenza, Pisa) 229

4. Agnolo Bronzino, *Giovanni de' Medici,* ca. 1551, Oxford, Ashmolean Museum (photo: Ashmolean Museum, Oxford) 230

5. Agnolo Bronzino, Chapel of Eleonora, frescoes ca. 1541–43; replica of altarpiece (fig. 6 here), ca. 1553–54, Florence, Palazzo Vecchio (photo: Soprintendenza, Florence) 231

6. Agnolo Bronzino, *Lamentation,* 1545, Besançon, Musée des Beaux-Arts et d'Archéologie (photo: Ch. Choffet, Besançon) 232

7. Agnolo Bronzino, *Cosimo I de' Medici in Armor,* ca. 1543, Florence, Galleria degli Uffizi (photo: Soprintendenza, Florence) 233

8. Sala de' Dugento with *Story of Joseph* tapestry cycle installed, Florence, Palazzo Vecchio (photo: Alinari/Art Resource, N.Y.) 234

9. Agnolo Bronzino, *Crossing of the Red Sea,* ca. 1541–42, Florence, Chapel of Eleonora, Palazzo Vecchio (photo: Soprintendenza, Florence) 235

10. Agnolo Bronzino, *Saints Francis, Jerome, John the Evangelist, and Michael the Archangel,* ca. 1541 (or ca. 1543–45?). Florence, Vault of the Chapel of Eleonora, Palazzo Vecchio (photo: Soprintendenza, Florence) 236

11. Agnolo Bronzino, *Adoration of the Brazen Serpent,* ca. 1542(–43?), Florence, Chapel of Eleonora, Palazzo Vecchio (photo: Soprintendenza, Florence) 236

12. Agnolo Bronzino, *Moses Striking the Rock and the Gathering of the Manna,* ca. 1543 (1542–43?), Florence, Chapel of Eleonora, Palazzo Vecchio (photo: Soprintendenza, Florence) 237

13. Jan Rost, tapestry after Agnolo Bronzino, *Joseph in Prison and Pharaoh's Banquet,* 1546 (cartoon, 1545–46), Rome, Palazzo del Quirinale (photo: Segretario Generale della Presidenza della Repubblica Italiana, Servizio Patrimonio) 238

14. Anonymous Italian (?), eighteenth century, Plan of the Second Floor of the Palazzo Vecchio, Florence, Prague, Hapsburg Family Archive (photo: Kunsthistorisches Institut, Florence) 239

A Medici Miniature: Juno and a Woman with "Eyes in Her Head Like Two Stars in Their Beauty"

Gabrielle Langdon

1. Alessandro Allori, *Eleonora ("Dianora") di Toledo di Pietro de' Medici*, 1571,   264
   Pendant with two miniatures, front, Lugano, Thyssen-Bornemisza Foundation
   (photo: Thyssen-Bornemisza Collection)

2. Reverse of fig. 1, *Juno, Protectress of Brides, with Nymphs of the Air and*   264
   Serenità delle Notte (photo: Thyssen-Bornemisza Collection)

3. Anonymous, *Eleonora ("Dianora") di Toledo di Pietro de' Medici*, 1587 (post-   265
   humous), Vienna, Kunsthistorisches Museum (photo: Kunsthistorisches
   Museum, Vienna)

4. Anonymous, *Eleonora ("Dianora") di Toledo di Pietro de' Medici*, after 1574,   268
   (posthumous), Baltimore, Walters Art Gallery (photo: The Walters Art Gallery)

5. Alessandro Allori, *Portrait of Anna di Francesco de' Medici(?)*, 1582, Poggio a   269
   Caiano, Villa Medici (photo: Alinari/Art Resource, N.Y.)

6. Giorgio Vasari, *Juno* float for the *Mascherata della geneologia degli dei gentili*,   272
   1565, Florence, Biblioteca Nazionale Centrale, C.B.3.53I, c. 113v–114r (photo:
   BNCF)

7. Alessandro Allori, *Iris*, for the *Mascherata della geneologia degli dei gentili*,   272
   1565, Florence, Biblioteca Nazionale Centrale, C.B.3.53I, c. 115r (photo:
   BNCF)

8. Alessandro Allori, *Rain*, for the *Mascherata della geneologia degli dei gentili*,   273
   1565, Florence, Biblioteca Nazionale Centrale, C.B.3.53I, c.116r (photo:
   BNCF)

9. Alessandro Allori, *Snow*, for the *Mascherata della geneologia degli dei gentili*,   273
   1565, Florence, Galleria degli Uffizi, Gabinetto dei Disegni e delle Stampe,
   2834F (photo: Soprintendenza, Florence)

10. Alessandro Allori, *Fog*, for the *Mascherata della geneologia degli dei gentili*,   274
    1565, Florence, Galleria degli Uffizi, Gabinetto dei Disegni e delle Stampe,
    2835F (photo: Soprintendenza, Florence)

11. Alessandro Allori, *Eleonora ("Dianora") di Toledo di Pietro de' Medici*, 1571,   275
    Vienna, Kunsthistorisches Museum (photo: Kunsthistorisches Museum Vienna)

12. Alessandro Allori, *Hercules Crowned by the Muses*, 1568, Florence, Galleria   277
    degli Uffizi (photo: Alinari/Art Resource, N.Y.)

13. Attributed to Alessandro Allori, *Portrait of a Young Nobleman*, 1570–75, front,   278
    private collection (photo: courtesy Bob P. Haboldt and Co.)

14. Reverse of fig. 13, *Love and Fidelity* (photo: courtesy Bob P. Haboldt and Co.)   278

A Widow's Choice: Alessandro Allori's *Christ and the Adulteress* in the Church of Santo Spirito at Florence

Elizabeth Pilliod

1. Alessandro Allori, *Christ and the Adulteress*, 1577, Florence, Santo Spirito,   302
   Cini Chapel (photo: Alinari/Art Resource, N.Y.)

2. Alessandro Allori, study for *Christ and the Adulteress*, 1577, Florence, Galleria   304

degli Uffizi, Gabinetto dei Disegni e delle Stampe, 10332F (photo: Soprintendenza, Florence)

3. Alessandro Allori, study for *Christ and the Adulteress*, 1577, Paris, Musée du Louvre, inv. 10111 (photo: RMN) — 305

4. Anonymous, *Paliotto with Saint Jerome*, ca. 1565(?), Florence, Santo Spirito, Cini Chapel (photo: author) — 306

5. Diana Scultori, *Christ and the Adulteress*, 1575, etching (photo: New York Public Library) — 308

6. Jan Saenredam, engraving after Hendrik Goltzius, *The Woman Taken in Adultery*, late sixteenth century (photo: Rijksmuseum, Amsterdam) — 309

Matrons and Motives: Why Women Built in Early Modern Rome
Carolyn Valone

1. Giovanni Francesco Romanelli, *Dido Showing Aeneas Her Plans for Carthage*, Barberini cartoon, ca. 1630–35, Pasadena, Norton Simon Museum (photo: The Norton Simon Foundation, Pasadena, Calif.) — 319

2. Simon Vouet, *Artemisia Building the Mausoleum*, ca. 1643, Stockholm, Nationalmuseum (photo: Statens Konstmuseer) — 320

3. Portrait bust of Vittoria della Tolfa, ca. 1585, Rome, Santa Maria in Aracoeli, Chapel of the Ascension (photo: Giandean) — 322

4. Coat of arms of Vittoria della Tolfa, ca. 1585, Rome, Santa Maria in Aracoeli, Chapel of the Ascension (photo: Giandean) — 322

5. Coat of arms of Lucrezia della Rovere, ca. 1550, Rome, Trinità dei Monti, Chapel of the Assumption (photo: Cynthia Stollhans) — 323

6. Daniele da Volterra, *Assumption of the Virgin*, ca. 1550, Rome, Trinità dei Monti, Chapel of the Assumption (photo: ICCD, Rome, G46600) — 323

7. San Bernardo alle Terme, Rome, interior, right side, 1595–1600 (photo: ICCD, Rome, G20952) — 324

8. San Bernardo alle Terme, Rome, portal inscription, 1600 (photo: Cynthia Stollhans) — 325

9. *Crucifixion of Saint Andrew*, from Louis Richeôme, *Le peinture spirituelle*, 1611 (photo: by permission of the Folger Shakespeare Library) — 326

10. San Vitale, Rome, interior, ca. 1605 (photo: ICCD, Rome, E21219) — 326

11. Francesco Zucchi, *Madonna, Saint James, and the Donor, Vittoria della Tolfa*, ca. 1590, Rome, San Giacomo degli Incurabili, Sacristy (photo: Morton Abromson) — 329

Prologue

Since the late quattrocento, Isabella d'Este, marchioness of Mantua (1474–1539), has been praised for her patronage and collecting of art.[1] Indeed, not only has she been exalted as a female patron, she has also been singled out as the great exception, a nearly unique example of woman as artistic patron.[2] In a review article of 1995 entitled "The Progress of Patronage in Renaissance Italy," the historian Kate Lowe encouraged a reexamination of this assumption:

> Perhaps, as a coda, it may be worthwhile to consider new directions in studies on patronage, which have not been represented by the books under review. Not one of them addresses directly the issue of female patronage.... Generally, authors mouth platitudes on Isabella d'Este in lieu of giving serious attention to this utterly neglected field. A huge body of material is available for a consideration of the physiognomy of female patronage, and new studies of it would certainly add greatly to our understanding of gender relations and the place of women in society, as well as to our comprehension of the [patronage] process.[3]

The present study is among the first to provide the serious attention and nuanced interpretation called for by Lowe, and along with other publications of the past decade, it suggests that women—lay and religious—were far more active as patrons in Renaissance Italy than has been previously recognized.[4] We have chosen to focus here on secular women like Isabella d' Este because until recently more attention had been paid to the art patronage of female religious than to that of other women.[5] This particular focus enables us to pose new questions and to provide considerable evidence for a class of women whose patronage of visual culture has, to a large extent, been neglected.

Beyond Isabella d'Este then, who were other female secular patrons in Renaissance Italy? What were their relationships with other women and with men, including kinsmen and the artists and architects whose works they commissioned? To what social classes did these women belong and how were they able to finance the undertakings they sponsored? What types of works did they request? What were the personal, familial, and societal motivations for their patronage? Did the character of patronage by women differ from that of men and what were the mechanisms of their patronage in a male-dominated culture? These are some of the many questions we asked ourselves when formulating an Italian Art Society session on secular women patrons in Italy that we jointly chaired in 1993 (at the 28th International Congress on Medieval Studies, at Western Michigan University in Kalamazoo). Six of the papers collected here (those by Roger Crum, Rosi Gilday, Katherine McIver, Marjorie Och, Mary Vaccaro, and Carolyn Valone) were presented at the Kalamazoo conference, while our own contributions originated as "poster papers" associated with the session. As we began to prepare a publication based on these papers, we became aware of other scholars working on the patronage of secular women in Renaissance Italy, and we invited Molly Bourne, Bruce Edelstein, Lawrence Jenkens, Benjamin Kohl, Gabrielle Langdon, and Elizabeth Pilliod to contribute to this volume.

We have arranged these essays chronologically, beginning with trecento Padua and ending with Rome of the late cinquecento. This sequence reveals that the scope and character of patronage by women expanded significantly in the sixteenth century. In addition to several studies dealing with Florence and Rome, this volume contains essays concerning Siena, Mantua, Padua, and the Emilian region. While none of the essays in this book explore the art patronage of women in Naples, Bologna, Milan, and Venice, we wish to underscore the importance of those major centers not studied by our contributors.[6] It must be emphasized that in the period under consideration there was great diversity among the various Italian courts and city-states, and the experiences and autonomy of women differed from place to place. It should come as no surprise, moreover, that most of the women discussed here were cultural elites with the financial means that permitted them to extend commissions.[7] Some of our authors, however, do present important evidence for patronage by women of other social classes.[8] While most of the papers are case studies of individual women, others look at networks or groups of women in order to reach more general conclusions about the nature of female patronage in Renaissance Italy. Collectively, the essays demonstrate how resourceful women—both aristocratic and bourgeois—found manifold ways to express themselves through patronage, despite the limitations of a highly structured patriarchal society.[9]

It is a fundamental premise of this volume that the study of women's patronage of art provides an important lens for examining female identity and agency in the past.[10] That gender is socially constructed and must be historically and locally situated are basic tenets of gender theory.[11] The essays in this book are predicated on these ideas: the women discussed here functioned within the specific cultural milieu of their time and place.[12] Stanley Chojnacki has posited a useful configuration of gender that involves "two sets of relationships, one between men and women, and one between individuals of each sex and the cultural norms governing gender."[13] The late medieval and early modern female patrons examined here negotiated these sets of relationships in their patronage of art and architecture, which must be understood both in terms of their relations with men and of prevailing cultural constructions of gender. While some of our authors demonstrate how women used patronage to manipulate or subvert the male-dominated structures and institutions in which they operated, others show how some women extended commissions in order to sustain and further patriarchal aims and ambitions.[14]

It is not our purpose here to formulate new theoretical models for gender roles in Italian Renaissance society, although we do hope that the evidence presented and interpreted by our authors will be used by others in the formulation of what Joan Scott has called a "synthesizing perspective."[15] Instead, our primary goal is to participate in the ongoing project of recovering and interpreting female contributions to male-defined societies by exploring specific examples of how women were involved in the shaping of visual culture in Renaissance Italy.[16] We must emphasize that there is still a great deal of historical material to be examined and assessed in this essentially new area of inquiry, and it would be a mistake to construe these essays as simply harking back to the early stages of women's studies.[17] Contributions such as those presented here, which illuminate how Italian Renaissance women acted as patrons within the restrictions of their sociocultural milieu, are much needed to provide a solid, historical foundation for the theoretical reframing of the period we study.[18]

The individual papers employ a variety of approaches and interpretative strategies, ranging from archival, statistical, and iconographic studies to close readings of texts and individual works. A number of the contributions analyze the familial, social, and religious motivations that inspired female patrons. Several themes, to be discussed at greater length in David Wilkins's introduction, unify this volume. These include the significance of role models for female patrons, the dynamics of conjugal patronage, the importance of networks of female patrons, and the patronage of widows, who often enjoyed greater freedom and had greater access to the funds necessary for commissioning works after their husbands' deaths. While piety and commemoration were frequent motivations for patronage by Renaissance women in Italy, the manner in which some female patrons used art and architecture for political and dynastic purposes is particularly noteworthy.[19] The papers gathered here prove dramatically that Isabella d'Este was by no means a unique example and that this area of investigation is full of promise. It is our hope that this volume will encourage scholars to move yet further "beyond Isabella" in their assessment of women's patronage of art and architecture in Renaissance Italy and, in so doing, significantly broaden our understanding of late medieval and early modern patronage patterns in general.

Sheryl E. Reiss and David G. Wilkins

1. In a recent general work, Paola Tinagli, *Women in Italian Renaissance Art* (Manchester: Manchester University Press, 1997), 11, the author says of Isabella d'Este: "Without any doubt, she must be considered the most important woman patron in fifteenth-century Italy, for the range and scope of her commissions and for the amount of information we have about her taste and her dealings with artists." The bibliography on Isabella d'Este's patronage of art is vast. Work with additional references includes Rose Marie San Juan, "The Court Lady's Dilemma: Isabella d'Este and Art Collecting in the Renaissance," *Oxford Art Journal* 14 (1991): 67–78; Sylvia Ferino-Pagden, ed., *Isabella d'Este: Fürsten und Mäzenatin der Renaissance: "La Prima Donna del Mondo,"* exh. cat. (Vienna: Kunsthistorisches Museum, 1994); Clifford M. Brown, "A Ferrarese Lady and a Mantuan Marchesa: The Art and Antiquities Collections of Isabella d'Este Gonzaga," in *Women and Art in Early Modern Europe: Patrons, Collectors, and Connoisseurs*, ed. Cynthia Lawrence (University Park: Pennsylvania State University Press, 1997): 53–71. See also the comments of Molly Bourne in this volume.

2. For example, the bibliography in Tinagli, *Women in Italian Renaissance Art*, 192, lists eight citations under the rubric "Isabella d' Este as Patron," but only two under "Women's patronage (191–92). Jaynie Anderson, "Rewriting the History of Art Patronage," *Renaissance Studies* 10 (1996): 129, calls Isabella a "superwoman."

3. Kate Lowe, "The Progress of Patronage in Renaissance Italy," *Oxford Art Journal* 18 (1995): 149. Our volume was already in progress when Lowe's review article was published. As early as 1975, David Wilkins, "Woman as Artist and Patron in the Middle Ages and Renaissance," in *The Roles and Images of Women in the Middle Ages and Renaissance*, ed. Douglas Radcliff-Umstead, (Pittsburgh: Center for Medieval and Renaissance Studies, 1975), 115, remarked upon the absence of studies on the specific roles women may have played as patrons. See ibid., 117, for remarks on the closely related topic of collecting.

4. Other studies of female patrons in Italy that have appeared in the past decade include Catherine King, "Medieval and Renaissance Matrons, Italian-Style," *Zeitschrift für Kunstgeschichte* 55 (1992): 372–93; Carolyn Valone, "Roman Matrons as Patrons: Various Views of the Cloister Wall," in *The Crannied Wall: Women, Religion, and the Arts in Early Modern Europe*, ed. Craig A. Monson (Ann Arbor: University of Michigan Press, 1992), 49–72; Carolyn Valone, "Women on the Quirinal Hill: Patronage in Rome, 1560–1630," *Art Bulletin* 76 (1994): 129–146. See also the four essays on Italian late medieval and early modern female patrons in *Renaissance Studies* 10 (1996), edited by Jaynie Anderson, and the four contributions in Lawrence, *Women and Art*. In addition, see Catherine King, *Renaissance Women Patrons: Wives and Widows in Italy ca. 1300–1550* (Manchester: Manchester University Press, 1998); Beth Holman, "*Exemplum* and *imitatio*: Countess Matilda and Lucrezia Pico della Mirandola at Polirone," *Art Bulletin* 81 (1999): 637–64. See now the introduction to and essays in "Committenza artistica feminile, edited by Sara Matthews-Grieco and Gabriella Zarri in a special edition of *Quaderni Storici* 35/104 fasc. 2 (2000), which were pub-

lished too recently to be considered in detail in this volume.

5. It may well be that the attention historians have paid to nuns and to female mysticism has tended to obscure the contributions of secular women, including lay female religious. For discussions see *The Crannied Wall*; Margaret L. King, *Women of the Renaissance* (Chicago: University of Chicago Press, 1991), chap. 2, "Daughters of Mary: Women and the Church"; Merry E. Wiesner, *Women and Gender in Early Modern Europe* (Cambridge: Cambridge University Press, 1993), 179–85, 195–203. Work on the patronage of nuns and other female religious in Italy includes Maureen Pelta, "Form and Convent: Correggio and the Decoration of the Camera di San Paolo" (Ph.D. diss., Bryn Mawr, 1989); Caroline Bruzelius, "Hearing is Believing: Clarissan Architecture, ca. 1213–1340," *Gesta* 31 (1992): 83–91; Ann M. Roberts, "Chiara Gambacorta of Pisa as Patroness of the Arts," in *Creative Women in Medieval and Early Modern Italy: A Religious and Artistic Renaissance*, ed. E. Ann Matter and John Coakley (Philadelphia: University of Pennsylvania Press, 1994), 120–54; Jeryldene M. Wood, "Breaking the Silence: The Poor Clares and the Visual Arts in Fifteenth-Century Italy," *Renaissance Quarterly* 48 (1995): 262–86; Jeryldene M. Wood, *Women, Art, and Spirituality: The Poor Clares of Early Modern Italy* (New York, 1996); and Mary-Ann Winkelmes, "Taking Part: Benedictine Nuns as Patrons of Art and Architecture," in *Picturing Women in Renaissance and Baroque Italy*, ed. Geraldine A. Johnson and Sara F. Matthews Grieco (Cambridge: Cambridge University Press, 1997), 91–110. For the period just after that covered in this volume, see Marilyn Dunn, "Nuns as Art Patrons: The Decoration of S. Marta al Callegio Romano," *Art Bulletin* 70 (1988): 451–77; Marilyn Dunn, "Spiritual Philanthropists: Women as Convent Patrons in Seicento Rome," in Lawrence, *Women and Art*, 154–88. See also Karen-edis Barzman, "Devotion and Desire: The Reliquary Chapel of Maria Maddalena de' Pazzi," *Art History* 15 (1992): 171–96, for the reception of church decoration by nuns in late-sixteenth-century Florence.

6. For Venice, see Peter Humfrey, "Veronese's High Altarpiece for San Sebastiano: Patrician Commissions for a Counter-Reformation Church," in *Venice Reconsidered: The History and Civilization of an Italian City-State, 1297–1797*, ed. John Martin and Dennis Romano (Baltimore: Johns Hopkins University Press, 2000), 365–88. For Naples, see Adrian S. Hoch, "Sovereignty and Closure in Trecento Naples: Images of Queen Sancia, alias 'Sister Clare'," *Arte medievale* 10 (1997): 121–39. Maria Conelli is studying women as patrons of Neapolitan Jesuits foundations in the late cinquecento. The recent essays by Sabina Brevaglieri, Bruce Edelstein, and Caroline Murphy in "Committenza artistica feminile," ed. Matthews-Grieco and Zarri, deal with patronage by Venetian, Neapolitan, and Bolognese women respectively.

7. Cf. The comments by Cynthia Lawrence in Lawrence, *Women and Art*, 3–4.

8. For the patronage of nonaristocratic women, see the contributions by Gilday and Pilliod to this volume.

9. Joan Kelly exposed the patriarchal underpinnings of Renaissance culture in a classic essay of 1977 entitled "Did Women Have a Renaissance?" She answered her own question emphatically in the negative, stressing that changing social, political, and economic factors that reduced the autonomy of women in the fourteenth, fifteenth, and sixteenth centuries. The essay was first published in *Becoming Visible: Women in European History*, ed. Renate Bridenthal and Claudia Koonz (Boston: Houghton Mifflin, 1977), 137–64, reprinted in Joan Kelly, *Women, History, and Theory: The Essays of Joan Kelly* (Chicago: University of Chicago Press, 1984), 19–50. For a more flexible and nuanced discussion of patriarchy see Stanley Chojnacki, "Comment: Blurring Genders," *Renaissance Quarterly* 40 (1987): esp. 746 ff., and Stanley Chojnacki, "'The Most Serious Duty': Motherhood, Gender, and Patrician Culture in Renaissance Venice," in *Refiguring Woman: Perspectives on Gender and the Italian Renaissance*, ed. Marilyn Migiel and Juliana Schiesari (Ithaca: Cornell University Press, 1991), 133–54; Natalie Tomas, *'A Positive Novelty': Women and Public Life in Renaissance Florence*, Monash Publications in History 12 (Clayton, Australia: Department of History, Monsah University, 1992), esp. chap. 1, "Renaissance Florence as a Gendered Society." Tomas and other scholars have begun to investigate the degree of autonomy women exercised

within the patriarchal constrictions of specific Italian centers. See, for example, Elaine G. Rosenthal, "The Position of Women in Renaissance Florence: Neither Autonomy nor Subjection," in *Florence and Italy:Renaissance Studies in Honour of Nicolai Rubinstein*, ed. Peter Denley and Caroline Elam (London: Westfield College, 1988), 369–81, and Thomas Kuehn, "Understanding Gender Inequality in Renaissance Florence: Personhood and Gifts of Maternal Inheritance by Women," *Journal of Women's History* 8 (1996): 58–80. We are grateful to Lawrence Jenkens for this reference.

10. The nature of women's (and men's) agency and sense of individualism in the Renaissance is the subject of lively scholarly debate. See the introduction by Thomas C. Heller and David Wellbery to *Reconstructing Individualism: Autonomy, Individuality, and the Self in Western Thought*, ed. Thomas C. Heller, Morton Sosna, and David Wellbery (Stanford: Stanford University Press, 1986), esp. 1–4. For Jacob Burckhardt's role in codifying individualism as a fundamental aspect of Renaissance culture see Stephen Greenblatt, "Fiction or Friction," ibid., 35, and Natalie Z. Davis, "Boundaries and the Sense of Self in Sixteenth-Century France," ibid., 53–63, who argues "that the exploration of self in sixteenth-century France [especially in the case of women] was made in conscious relation to the groups to which people belonged" (53). Similarly, Kuehn, "Understanding Gender,": 59–62, posits an anthropological model of agency that is relational instead of individualistic in a modern, Western sense. This model is useful for understanding agency in terms of lineage and kinship, as defined by F. W. Kent and others. See F. W. Kent, *Household and Lineage in Renaissance Florence* (Princeton: Princeton University Press, 1977). For goals similar to ours in identifying women's historical agency and self-expression through the patronage of visual culture, see Lawrence, *Women and Art*, 2, 17–18.

11. Helpful discussions of gender theory in anthropology and sociology include the introduction to *Sexual Meanings: The Cultural Construction of Gender and Sexuality*, ed. Sherry B. Ortner and Harriet Whitehead (Cambridge: Cambridge University Press, 1981), 1–27, and the preface and introduction to *The Social Construction of Gender*, ed. Judith Lorber and Susan A. Farrell (Newbury Park, Calif.: Sage Publications, 1991), 1–11. For the application of gender theory to historical inquiry, see Joan W. Scott, "Gender: A Useful Category of Historical Analysis," *American Historical Review* 91 (1986): 1053–75. For gender theory and Renaissance studies in general see the introductions to Margaret W. Ferguson, Maureen Quilligan, and Nancy J. Vickers, *Rewriting the Renaissance: The Discourses of Sexual Difference in Early Modern Europe* (Chicago: University of Chicago Press, 1986), and Wiesner, *Women and Gender*, with extensive bibliography. For Italy, see the introductions to *Refiguring Woman*; Tomas, *Positive Novelty*; and Judith Brown, introduction to *Gender and Society in Renaissance Italy*, ed. Judith C. Brown and Robert C. Davis (Harlow, Essex: Addison Wesley Longman, 1998), 1–15. For gender theory and the history of art see Lisa Tickner, "Feminism, Art History, and Sexual Difference," *Genders* 3 (1988): 92–128, and Karenedis Barzman, "Beyond the Canon; Feminists, Postmodernism, and the History of Art," *Journal of Aesthetics and Art Criticism* 52 (1994): 327–39, both of whom insist upon local and historically specific understandings. For a summary of feminist theory that rejects a relational, gender based approach, see the preface and introduction to *The Expanding Discourse: Feminism and Art History*, ed. Norma Broude and Mary D. Garrard (New York: Icon Editions, 1992), esp. x.

12. While many of the contributions to this volume are indebted to aspects of gender and feminist theory, we emphasize that on occasion that theory is applied arbitrarily and ahistorically in a manner that does not enhance our understanding of gender roles in the past. For a similar expression of caution, see Tinagli, *Women in Italian Renaissance Art*, 8–9: "At times, however, problems arise when theory is applied ruthlessly and insensitively to historical evidence. In some cases, standards and anachronistic preoccupations which belong to our own culture are imposed on the culture and society of the past."

13. Chojnacki, "Blurring Genders," 135.

14. This volume presents evidence for both "oppositional" and "relational" behavior by women in late medieval and early modern Italy. Evidence that both models were at work suggest that greater

flexibility is needed in our considerations of how women operated within the socially constructed boundaries of the period. Tomas, *Positive Novelty*, esp. 7–8, and Kuehn, "Understanding Gender," both discuss how women's actions sustained the political and economic interests of their male relatives. Patricia Simons, quoted in Lawrence, *Women and Art*, 17, suggests that such actions constituted collusion "with patriarchal definitions."

15. Scott, "Gender," 1055.

16. For an overview of women and visual culture in Renaissance Europe, see Sheila ffolliott, "Women and Gender in the Renaissance Visual Field," *Women in the Renaissance* 5 (1996): 2–7. See also Wiesner, *Women and Gender*, 142–43, 148–55; Anderson, "Rewriting the History; and the introduction to Lawrence, *Women and Art*. For Italy specifically, see the introduction to Johnson and Matthews Grieco, *Picturing Women*, and Karen-edis Barzman, "Gender and Cultural Production in Early Modern Italy," in Brown and Davis, *Gender and Society*, 213–33. We are grateful to Professor Barzman for sharing her manuscript with us prior to publication.

17. For discussions of various approaches to women's history see Gerda Lerner, "Placing Women in History: Definitions and Challenges," *Feminist Studies* 3 (1975): 5–14, esp. 5–6, for "compensatory history" (the history of what Natalie Davis terms "women worthies") and "contribution history" (the history of women's contribution to and status in male-defined society). The contributions to this volume embody aspects of both approaches, but are also informed by thinking about women, gender, and society. See also Joan W. Scott, *Gender and the Politics of History* (New York: Columbia University Press, 1988), esp. 15–27.

18. Cf. Lawrence, *Women and Art*, 2 and n. 4, for the importance of case studies of female patrons both for patronage studies and for art history in general. While the interpretation of historical texts—published and unpublished—is unfashionable for some art historians, we feel no need to apologize for reliance here on empirical evidence. See Caroline Elam's editorial "In Praise of Positivism," *Burlington Magazine* 138 (1996): 299, and Paul Barolsky "Art History and Positivism," *Source* 18 (1998): 27–30, who underscores the need for "more nuanced positivism," arguing that "even the most skeptical scholars, even those who reject or despise positivism, readily avail themselves of what positivism offers them—a body of information, however flawed or limited, which is the common ground of interpretation." We are grateful to Professor Barolsky, who shared his manuscript with us prior to publication.

19. See Lowe, "Progress of Patronage," 149: "Women seem to have found a particular outlet as patrons of architecture, both as nuns … and as members of the ruling elite who paid for new buildings of hospitals or churches or lodgings. Why was this?" For contributions that address this issue see the essays by Lawrence Jenkens, Sheryl Reiss, and Carolyn Valone in this volume. See also the collection of essays edited by Helen Hills, *Gender, Architecture, and Power in Early Modern Europe* (Aldershot: Ashgate, forthcoming).

Acknowledgments

It is a great pleasure for us to acknowledge the institutions and the many individuals who have assisted and encouraged us during the preparation of this book. We have each thanked the scholars who aided with our own contributions in our respective essays, and we wish to express here our gratitude to those who helped with the book as a whole. First and foremost, we are grateful to the contributors, whose exciting scholarship comprises this volume. Our contributors have endured with patience an array of unexpected circumstances during the course of this project. All of the contributors have offered helpful advice and welcome assurance. We wish to express particular gratitude to Roger Crum, Carolyn Valone, and Bruce Edelstein for their extensive contributions. Thanks are due to Cornell University and the University of Pittsburgh for institutional support and for the use of their fine libraries, which greatly facilitated the research for and editing of this volume. We also owe thanks to Peter Humfrey and to the second reader of the manuscript (who wishes to remain anonymous), both of whom offered many helpful suggestions that improved the manuscript significantly. Paul Evans, Gerhard Gruitrooy, Richard Oram, Linda Pellechia, Anna Maria Petrioli Tofani, and Gianni Tofani must be thanked for providing much-needed assistance in obtaining photographs and permissions. We are deeply grateful to Raymond Mentzer, general editor of Sixteenth Century Essays and Studies series, who has been unflaggingly supportive of this project from the outset. We are also most grateful to Paula Presley, Nancy Reschly, Mindy Butler-Christensen, and Michala Oestmann at the Truman State University Press and to its former director, Robert Schnucker.

We would like to thank a number of colleagues and friends who have offered constructive criticism, guidance, and moral support at various stages of this project. We are both indebted to Craig Felton, who introduced us many years ago. We are especially grateful to Larry Silver, John Paoletti, Konrad Eisenbichler, and Paul Barolsky, who offered sage advice at a critical moment. For fruitful discussions, wise counsel, and much-appreciated encouragement, we wish to acknowledge our gratitude to Patricia Fortini Brown, Caroline Elam, Stephen Edidin, Dagmar Eichberger, Sheila ffolliott, Sara Matthews Grieco, Kenneth Gouwens, Ann Sutherland Harris, Ingo Herklotz, Beth Holman, Pamela Jones, Julius Kirshner, Peter Lynch, Louisa Matthew, Barbara McCloskey, Jacqueline Musacchio, W. David Myers, Alexander Nagel, Maureen Pelta, David Posner, Patricia Rucidlo, Beatrice Rehl, John Shearman, David Summers, Natalie Tomas, William Wallace, Saundra Weddell, and Lilian Zirpolo. For good advice and editorial comments, David wishes to thank Rebecca Wilkins, Katherine Wilkins, and Tyler Jennings, as well as his many students who have discussed patronage issues with him over the years. Sheryl wishes to express special thanks to friends, colleagues, and students now and formerly at Cornell, including Karen-edis Barzman, Amy Bloch, Jennifer Hallam, Cate Mellen, John Najemy, Kathleen Perry Long, Danuta Shanzer, and Margaret Webster. Sheryl's thanks are also due to members of Cornell's Renaissance Colloquium, especially Carol Kaske and William Kennedy. Finally, and most importantly, we wish to thank our families for their seemingly boundless patience with us during the long gestation of *Beyond Isabella*. Paul F. Goldsmith and Ann Thomas Wilkins, our spouses, have provided continuous support and good will, and it is to them that we dedicate this book.

Frequently Cited Sources and Abbreviations

Frequently Cited Sources

DBI = *Dizionario biografico degli italiani*. 49 vols. Rome: Istituto della Enciclopedia Italiana, 1960–97.

Vasari-Milanesi = Vasari, Giorgio. *Le vite de' più eccellenti pittori, scultori, ed architettori...* (1568). Ed. Gaetano Milanesi. 9 vols. Florence: Sansoni, 1878–85.

Abbreviations

The following abbreviations for the citation of archival sources have been employed:

b: busta
c.: *carta*
doc.: document
f.: *filza*
fasc.: *fascicolo*
fol.: *folio*
ins.: *inserto*
MS: Manuscript
r: *recto*
v: *verso*

Names of frequently cited archives, libraries, and manuscript collections, arranged alphabetically by location, have been abbreviated in the following manner. Some collections, if located in museums or referred to infrequently, have not been abbreviated.

Florence

ASF = Archivio Storico
        CA = Carteggio d'artisti
        Cart. Strozz. = Carte Strozziane
        Corp. Rel. Soppr. = Corporazioni Religiose Soppresse dal Governo Francese
        GM = Guardaroba Medicea
        Goro Gheri = Copialettere Goro Gheri
        MAP = Mediceo Avanti il Principato
        MdelP = Mediceo del Principato
        Operai = Reppublica, Operai del Palazzo
BNCF = Biblioteca Nazionale Centrale

Mantua

ASM = Archivio di Stato
        AG = Archivio Gonzaga
BCMan = Biblioteca Comunale

Modena

ASMod = Archivio di Stato
  AG = Archivio Gambara
  CDuc = Cancelleria Ducale Estense
BEMod = Biblioteca Estense

Padua

ASP = Archivio di Stato
  AN = Archivio Notarile

Parma

ASPr = Archivio di Stato

Reggio in Emilia

ASRE = Archivio di Stato

Rome

ASR = Archivio Storico

Scandiano

ASScan = Archivio Storico

Siena

ASS = Archivio di Stato

Vatican

ASV = Archivio Segreto Vaticano

BAV = Biblioteca Apostolica Vaticana
  Ottob. Lat. = Ottoboni Latini
  Urb. Lat. = Urbinati Latini

Introduction: Recognizing New Patrons, Posing New Questions

David G. Wilkins

A pious woman, or—such is the power of images—a woman who wished to be recognized as pious, is represented kneeling in the foreground (fig. 1). She is in profile and at first glance seems proud and prim. She is wearing a sumptuous white overdress with wide hanging sleeves, a narrow blue hem, and a blue and white brocade panel in the front. A red and white chemise is visible at the wrists, while a decorated red belt and pearl necklace complete her outfit. Her elaborately arranged blond hair is adorned with pearls. This emphasis on fashion and elegance is countered by the humility of her kneeling pose and by the position of her hands, which are raised in a traditional Christian gesture of prayer.

This elegantly dressed woman may well be the person who commissioned the altarpiece in which we find her portrait (fig. 2), for she has assumed a place traditionally identified with the patron and/or donor during the Renaissance.[1] The large tempera painting on wooden panel is dominated, however, by the enthroned Virgin and Child and Saints Leonard, Jerome, John the Baptist, and Francis; the woman is in miniature, kneeling at the feet of Jerome. She is positioned on the left side of the painting, a position that in the Renaissance was generally reserved for the man when both husband and wife were represented in such a context. Although the large figures dominate because of their scale, the gazes and gestures of Mary and Christ return our attention to the woman; Mary is represented as if praying with and for her, while the child blesses her. Despite her size, then, it could be argued that at one time this contemporary woman was the most important figure in the altarpiece. In terms of history, the holy figures are more important than she, but to her friends and acquaintances, her appearance here and the notice she is granted by Mary and Christ must have made her loom large in their eyes. While her contemporaries would have understood why she was so prominently presented, some may not have liked it or accepted it without complaint. She looms large for us too, for she is shown without a male companion and in the location usually taken by the man when contemporary figures were presented in an altarpiece. Her unexpected presence raises questions that reveal the breadth of our topic. A study of her role in this altarpiece, painted by a minor, derivative artist working outside the innovative urban centers of the period, urges us to revise our standard of what is worthy of investigation. To understand more fully the roles possible for Renaissance women, we need to cast our net as broadly as possible.

Exactly what constitutes a patron is, of course, an appropriate question at this point. The study of patronage traditionally was understood as the identification and investigation of the person or group who ordered and subsequently paid for a work. To advance our discussion, let me propose that we also consider as patrons a person or group of persons who were assumed by the artist to be potential buyers and users. An artist who responds to the needs or wishes of a particular person or group of persons could then be considered to have a patron,

Wilkins Fig. 1. Nicola di Maestro Antonio d'Ancona, detail of patron, *Madonna and Child with Donor and Saints Leonard, Jerome, John the Baptist, and Francis,* 1472. Pittsburgh, Carnegie Museum of Art (photo: University of Pittsburgh)

even if the work was not specifically commissioned. While this broad interpretation blurs the distinctions among patron, donor, and audience, I would argue for its usefulness. Such a thesis recognizes that whenever an artist creates a work with a specific audience in mind, even if that prospective audience is a group instead of an individual, the artist is accommodating the work to the needs of a patron. It also suggests that the individual or group who pays for a work should not automatically be accepted as the sole patron or even as the most important patron. This extended concept of patronage is in part inspired by the provocative paper by Roger Crum in this volume, and is further discussed below.

This broad definition of patronage opens the possibility of discussing patronage in the altarpiece now at the Carnegie Museum of Art, even though the woman represented is anonymous and is not certainly the patron. While a number of studies have begun to lay a foundation for the study of Renaissance patronage,[2] this altarpiece demonstrates how an undocumented work is useful in raising questions about patronage. The historical circumstances of the Renaissance suggest that many instances of patronage by women are unlikely to have been recorded in documents; while many female patrons will thus remain anonymous, perhaps their achievements can now be recognized. Their activity as patrons during a period when such behaviour was neither expected nor encouraged deserves our close attention. But to help set the stage for our anonymous woman and to further our discussion, an analysis of the rich information offered in this volume about documented women patrons and their activities is in order.

New Evidence for "What Secular Women Did"

In her contribution to this volume, Carolyn Valone asserts that "We need to discover what women did, not what men said." Most of the contributions in this volume respond to this request by offering specific examples of what secular women did in securely documented examples of patronage dating from the fourteenth through the sixteenth centuries. These studies of particular acts of patronage bring us into intimate contact with specific women and their lives and activities. The end result is a gathering of individuals and acts of patronage that expands our understanding of the patronage of secular women during the Renaissance and makes possible some broad generalizations about their activities.

It is clear from the evidence presented, for example, that Italian Renaissance women were often continuing a tradition or were inspired by earlier or contemporary women who had commissioned art. Valone points out, for example, that women patrons interested in architecture had models from the ancient world. Other women looked back to the immediately preceding generation: Veronica Gambara, for example, modeled her patronage on that of her predecessor in Correggio, Francesca of Brandenburg, as discussed by Katherine McIver; Gabrielle Langdon suggests that Dianora de' Medici was motivated by the model of her aunt, Eleonora di Toledo. Molly Bourne suggests that Isabella's inspiration may have been her mother, Eleonora d'Aragona, duchess of Ferrara. Connections between women almost certainly played a role in encouraging patronage. Vittoria Colonna, who plays the key role in Marjorie Och's paper, was the aunt of Dianora da Toledo, whom Langdon proposes as the patron of the Thyssen-Bornemisza miniature (Langdon fig. 1). Veronica Gambara of Correggio corresponded with Colonna and sent her two of her own devotional poems. One important Renaissance model was, as we might expect, Isabella d'Este. McIver demonstrates that both Silvia Sanvitale and Veronica Gambara were encouraged by Isabella's example and that Gambara specifically modeled her *Studiolo* and other activities on those of Isabella.

Isabella d'Este's significance as a model receives a new interpretation in Molly Bourne's paper on the relationship between Isabella's patronage and that of her husband, Francesco II Gonzaga. Bourne's suggestion that Francesco's activities as a patron were in part motivated by a rivalry between Francesco and Isabella is supported by a letter from Isabella to her husband that refers to his new rooms as "beautiful, and even more because Your Excellency has learned from the example of my room, although I must confess that you have improved upon it."[3] Bourne analyzes the gendered nature of the programs husband and wife developed in their rival *camerini*, and questions the traditional assumption that Isabella's commissions overshadowed those of her husband. Bourne's case history offers a rare documented example of a female patron whose commissions served as inspiration and models for a man's activities as a patron.

Wilkins Fig. 2. Nicola di Maestro Antonio d'Ancona, *Madonna and Child with Donor and Saints Leonard, Jerome, John the Baptist, and Francis*, 1472. Pittsburgh, Carnegie Museum of Art (photo: University of Pittsburgh)

A second common factor is based on research demonstrating that Saint Jerome, his writings, and his female followers all served as models for women patrons; Valone demonstrates that this is especially true for widows in Rome at the end of the sixteenth century.[4] Two of the papers offered here expand our understanding of the significance of Jerome for educated women.[5] He figures in two altarpieces by Parmigianino commissioned by widows, for example, as discussed by Mary Vaccaro (Vaccaro figs. 1, 2). Vaccaro also draws attention to Correggio's *Madonna and Child with Saints Jerome and Mary Magdalen* (Vaccaro fig. 4), which was commissioned by the widow Briseide Colla for her husband's burial chapel. Katherine McIver points out that Veronica Gambara commissioned Correggio to paint a *Saint Jerome*, now lost, for her chapel in San Domenico in Correggio. While the importance of Jerome for women at the end of the sixteenth century had been established previously, papers by McIver and Vaccaro demonstrate that Jerome was a significant factor for women patrons during the first half of the century. While every appearance of Jerome cannot be associated with his importance for women, the appearance of Jerome in two specific quattrocento works made for women is worth noting; the altarpiece now at the Carnegie (fig. 2) and the *Assumption of the Virgin* commissioned by India Salviati and her brother Bernardo from Neri di Bicci, as discussed in Rosi Gilday's paper.

Carolyn Valone observes that Jerome's works were especially important in supporting women—especially widows—when they commissioned works of architecture. She demonstrates that women's patronage of architecture was not a new phenomenon by tracing documented examples beginning in the Hellenistic period and concluding with a group of monuments commissioned by Roman widows in the second half of the sixteenth century. Valone cites three motivations for these activities: commemoration, religion, and social welfare. The motivations for some other women, instead, seem to have been dynastic and, on occasion, politicized. Lawrence Jenkens's research elucidates the role played by Caterina Piccolomini, sister of Pope Pius II, in the commissioning and construction of the Palazzo delle Papesse in Siena (Jenkens figs. 1–3). Jenkens suggests that Piccolomini may have been the first fifteenth-century woman to build such a residence. Similarly, Sheryl Reiss demonstrates how much of Alfonisna Orsini's attention was focused on secular architecture, especially the Palazzo Medici-Lante in Rome and the completion of the Medici villa at Poggio a Caiano. Both authors associate these women's building activities in terms of their relationships to male members of their families.

A third factor discussed in several papers is the importance of the erection and/or decoration of the family burial chapel, which often became the responsibility of a widow after the death of her husband. Mary Vaccaro discusses two sixteenth-century women who were active building or decorating chapels for their husband's burial: Maria Bufalini, who decorated a burial chapel in San Salvatore in Lauro in Rome to honor her husband and his father, and Elena Baiardi, who commissioned Parmigianino's *Madonna of the Long Neck* (Vaccaro fig. 2) for her husband's burial chapel in Santa Maria de'Servi in Parma. Katherine McIver discusses Veronica Gambara, who built a chapel dedicated to Saint Jerome for her husband at San Domenico in Correggio.[6]

Some of these women ignored the specific directions left by their husbands. Carolyn Valone points out, for example, that Marchesa Vittoria della Tolfa took the 17,000 scudi her husband had earmarked for a grand family chapel in the Lateran and used it to found a Franciscan nunnery; later, in her own will, Vittoria left the comparatively modest sum of 2,000 scudi for a burial chapel for herself and her husband in another church, the Aracoeli. Livia Muri, also discussed by Valone, chose to bury her husband not in one of the churches he had specified in his will, but in an alternative location.

The altarpiece by Alessandro Allori (Pilliod fig. 1) discussed by Elizabeth Pilliod was created for a chapel that the head of the family, Girolamo di Cino Cini, stipulated should be dedicated to his patron saint, Jerome. The titular saint, however, was relegated to the altar frontal (Pilliod fig. 4), and Anna di Michele Videmon, Cini's widow, chose the virtually unprecedented subject of Christ and the Adulteress for the chapel's altarpiece. Girolamo married Anna, a German woman who was the mother of his children, only on his deathbed; her choice of the adulteress theme is explained by Pilliod in light of her personal history.

As Rosi Gilday points out in her paper, widows often had more autonomy than single or married women, and the death of a husband often required a woman to be more active outside the home than expected or possible when the husband was living.[7] Of the ten documented secular women patrons of Neri di Bicci examined in Gilday's survey, five are widows, while one was married, and the status of the other four is uncertain; four of the widows commissioned altarpieces, and the fifth commissioned a *tondo* intended for a church.

The rich documentation presented here also helps to elucidate other activities undertaken by secular women, making it clear that patronage should be studied within the broad context of women's lives. Isabella d'Este, Eleonora di Toledo, Veronica Gambara, and Silvia Sanvitale, for example, all assumed rulership when their husbands were away from court or had died. Even when their husbands were present the women generally were responsible on a day-to-day basis for behind-the-scenes management of their courts and official public and private entertaining. Veronica Gambara met Pope Leo X and hosted both King Francis I of France and Emperor Charles V in Correggio. In her contribution, Sheryl Reiss details Alfonsina Orsini's role in the planning and staging of ceremonial display at the time of Leo X's Florentine *entrata* of 1515 and the second *nozze* in 1518 of her son Lorenzo and Madeleine de la Tour d'Auvergne. The patronage of women for such events that is documented in the papers by McIver and Reiss suggests that this may be a fruitful avenue for further research. Silvia Sanvitale ruled Scandiano between 1553 and 1560 with the approval of Ercole II d'Este, duke of Ferrara. Silvia and her husband, Boiardo, count of Scandiano, entertained the Este family at their townhouse in Ferrara and in Scandiano; they also hosted a pope, cardinals, princes, and other important individuals. Veronica Gambara and Vittoria Colonna, among others, were active as poets. The fresco discussed by Roger Crum (Crum fig. 1) reveals the seldom-recognized behind-the-scenes roles played by women.

In several cases documents bring to light the difficulties that women faced during the Renaissance. Elizabeth Pilliod's discussion of Anna di Michele Videmon suggests the difficulties this German woman suffered in Florence before and after her husband's death. Probably the most poignant example discussed here is Dianora de' Medici who, as Gabrielle Langdon argues, commissioned Allori's portrait miniature (Langdon figs. 1, 2) as a gift for her husband, Pietro de' Medici. The allegory on the back is a panegeric for marital harmony, but Dianora's story ended tragically when Pietro strangled her five years after their marriage.

Documentation also reveals that women often demonstrated a special concern for the situations of other women, as indicated in the will of Fina da Carrara, with its many provisions for the women of her household, including dowries to help her legatees find husbands after Fina's death. As Ben Kohl points out, Fina even left a legacy to an illegitimate daughter of her husband being raised in Fina's household. Maria Bufalini, discussed by Mary Vaccaro, was generous in her legacies to the women of her patrilineal family.

Despite extensive documentation, the patronage practices of secular women can be difficult to trace for a number of reasons. Sometimes the works women commissioned have not played important roles in the literature simply because they are lost, as is the case with Correggio's *Saint Jerome*, commissioned by Veronica Gambara. In discussing Roman religious buildings that were supported by women during the sixteenth century, Valone emphasizes that these women's advocacy of radical religious reform meant that their buildings were intentionally modest, an innovative development that has not drawn the attention of historians. While contemporary men commissioned structures representative of the extravagant late Renaissance style, the radical style supported by women is characterized by restraint and moderation.

Even cases with ample documentation can prove difficult to interpret. Documents suggest that Federigo II Gonzaga commissioned Titian's remarkable *Magdalen* in the Pitti (Och fig. 1) as a gift for Alfonso del Vasto, but Marjorie Och, through a close reading of the same letters and documents, proposes that it was Vittoria Colonna who originated the commission.

One additional problem concerning the patronage of secular women is brought out by Roger Crum, who discusses the difficulty of isolating women's activities as consumers of art during a period when it was often difficult for a married woman to act on her own. For widows the evidence is usually more complete and less difficult to interpret—but even widows were often required to use a male legal representative, known as a *mundualdus,* in contractual situations, as seen in Rosi Gilday's investigation of the patrons of Neri di Bicci. Contributions by Roger Crum, Bruce Edelstein, and Katherine McIver examine the problem of isolating a woman's commissions when she chose or was required to work through her husband. Crum also discusses the problem of isolating a wife's activities and expenditures within the household context. His argument that documentary evidence of a husband's payment for a work may be nothing more than an expenditure for a work requested by his wife and intended for her use encourages and supports the broader interpretation of patronage formulated in this introduction.

Bruce Edelstein uses a reading of the documentary evidence to suggest an expanded role for Eleonora di Toledo in the official portraiture of the Medici realm. He argues that she played a major role in commissioning portraits intended as diplomatic gifts and emphasizes that the duchess controlled which costume was worn in certain portraits, depending on the intended recipient. Edelstein also argues that passages in letters and Vasari's *Vite* reveal Eleonora's role in commissions at the ducal court, while he simultaneously points out that analyses of the information found in ducal account books and other financial records are seldom helpful in determining who in the household instigated the creation of a particular work. Katherine McIver emphasizes the role of Silvia Sanvitale of Scandiano, who worked in tandem with her husband in the decoration of the Camerino dell'Eneide (McIver fig. 3); documents reveal that Sanvitale picked the theme, selected the artist, and even paid some of the bills from her own accounts. The papers by Bourne, Crum, Edelstein, and McIver all shed light on the difficulties of untangling conjugal patronage during the Renaissance.

Another case in which a woman took a role in defining and controlling a project is discussed in Ben Kohl's chapter on Fina da Carrara, who played the central role in remodeling the Paduan Baptistery as a burial chapel for herself and her husband. Evidence suggests that she controlled the iconography of the frescoes, with their profusion of female saints and Carrara family portraits. In his analysis of life at the Carrara court, Kohl recreates the distinctly gendered living spaces used by Fina and her husband.

The documentation that surrounds the patronage activities of Alfonsina Orsini de' Medici, as discussed by Sheryl Reiss, reveals an exceptionally active woman with a clear agenda. Alfonsina was less interested in her role as a widow than in her activities as a mother determined to provide opportunities for her children. She married her daughter Clarice to Filippo Strozzi, and through her political machinations her son Lorenzo was married to a niece of King Francis I of France and made duke of Urbino. Alfonsina also collected antiquities, and the fact that her activities in general were considered exceptional for a woman is suggested by a letter written to Lorenzo by Filippo Strozzi: "[Alfonsina] exercises that authority which for any other woman would be impossible and for few men easy."[8] As Reiss points out, it seems to have been Alfonsina's activities, including her patronage of secular architecture, that led to her being "reviled as a woman who usurped male roles and prerogatives."[9]

The number of named women brought forward here supports the validity of our approach. Some of the secular women, such as Fina da Carrara, Isabella d'Este, Elenora di Toledo, Caterina Piccolomini, and Vittoria Colonna, are perhaps as well known today as they were during their lifetimes. But Veronica Gambara, Silvia Sanvitale, Alfonsina Orsini de' Medici, Briseide Colla, Maria Bufalini, Elena Baiardi, and Dianora de' Medici will be new to many scholars. Still other women have been drawn to our attention because of a single commission, including the unforgettable Anna di Michele Videmon from Dinkelsbühl; Angiola de' Rossi da Parma, who commissioned a baby crib from Parmigianino; and the eight otherwise unknown secular women patrons of Neri di Bicci. These eight women entered history with the publication of Neri's account books, but Gilday's emphasis on their activities as patrons provides precious evidence for our topic and their names deserve to be recognized: Caterina Bagnesi, Andrea di Barberino, Lionarda del Pescaia, Maria Tinciavegli, Cavallina di Mugello, Checa di Bertoldo, India Salviati, and Agniesa Neroni. Their activity as patrons remains, at the present time, their only claim to fame. Carolyn Valone's research elucidates the main activities—often interrelated—of a group of noteworthy Roman widows in the second half of the sixteenth century: Livia Muti, Marchesa Vittoria della Tolfa, Lucrezia della Rovere, Caterina de'Nobili Sforza, Giovanna d'Aragona, Isabella della Rovere, Caterina Cibo, Fulvia Conti Sforza, Portia Massimi Salviati, Maddalena Orsini, Francesca Baglioni Orsini, Marchesa Giulia Rangoni, Francesca Montioux, and Francesca de Gourcy. Some of the family names listed here will be familiar because of the activities of male members of the family; other names will be new to us. In both cases our attention is focused explicitly on the patronage of women. This roster of named and documented secular women patrons provides an impressive addition to our understanding of women's activities in Renaissance Italy.

The papers gathered here provide new evidence for what secular women did, especially in the better-documented sixteenth century. At this stage, perhaps the most significant query is: "How distinctive were the works patronized by or intended for secular women?" The following discussion of two paintings from the fourteenth century, a period when there is little documentary evidence of patronage practices, suggest that in at least two cases, works that show a particular relationship to secular women were indeed distinctive.

What Secular Women Did in the Trecento

The respectful formats and stock iconography of most trecento panel paintings, the fact that most are unsigned, and the traditional art historical interest in connoisseurship led earlier scholars to devote their energies to compiling catalogue lists of trecento paintings

Wilkins Fig. 3. Circle of Bernardo Daddi (?), Votive Panel, 1335 (?), Florence, Museo dell' Opera del Duomo (photo: Alinari/Art Resource, N.Y.)

sorted by *comune* of origin, by artist or workshop, and by date. Exceptional works became isolated because they did not fit easily into established categories. The two trecento panels discussed below prove worthy of further investigation precisely because each contains a representation of a secular woman.

A painting by Bernardo Daddi or his workshop in the Museo dell'Opera del Duomo in Florence (fig. 3) is unusual because the central figure represents the Virgin Mary *without* the Christ child.[10] Kneeling in close proximity are two women and a boy holding a large candle. It has been suggested that all three be identified as patrons, but it seems more likely that the boy is a server whose candle is meant to indicate devotion to the person and image of the Virgin.[11] The woman on our right, who seems the older of the two, is dressed in black, her hair is completely covered, and she wears a wimple; she is either a nun or a widow.[12] The younger woman wears a richly patterned plaid dress and is clearly secular. The figure of the Virgin is enclosed within a window like frame, and her hand extends out over the lower edge in the direction of the older woman, toward whom she is also looking. A half-length figure of Christ Blessing appears in the gable above, and to the sides stand Saint Catherine of Alexandria and Saint Zenobius, a bishop saint who is a patron of the city of Florence.[13] While disparity in scale between figures is not uncommon in the trecento, a hierarchy of figures in four distinct sizes in a single representation is notable.

An important clue to function is the book held by the Virgin. While it is not unusual for Mary to hold a book, it is rare for it to be held so that we can make out a legible text. Here the text reads: "Most Sweet Virgin Mary of Bagnolo, I ask you to pray to him [God], that he, by his charity and power will grant me dispensation from that for which he has made me responsible."[14] That the book is held toward the older woman is another indication of her importance. The text reveals that the representation of the Virgin here is a copy of a devotional work at Bagnolo, a village in the Val di Greve near Impruneta.[15] Apparently, the original Bagnolo Virgin is lost, but our panel, with what seems to be a copy or version of that image, bears the date 25 February 1334 (Florentine style; 1335 modern style); this precise date suggests that the panel was offered in response to a specific event, perhaps a vow made on or an incident that occurred on that date.[16] Format, iconography, and inscription all support the identification of the Daddesque panel as a votive image requesting assistance from the Virgin of Bagnolo. The supplicator must be one or both of the women shown, but how the two are related to each other and to the need for assistance is still unclear.[17] This is one of the most tantalizing of trecento panels because of the unresolved functional, social, and gender-related issues it raises.

Two women are also represented in the *Lamentation* from the Florentine church

Wilkins Fig. 4. Florentine, mid-fourteenth century, *Lamentation from San Remigio*, ca. 1350, Florence, Galleria degli Uffizi (photo: Alinari/Art Resource, N.Y.)

of San Remigio and now in the Uffizi (fig. 4). This painting has raised scholarly interest in the past mostly because of the question of its attribution. Vasari gives the panel to one "Tommaso di Stefano, nicknamed Giottino," and while this undocumented artist has remained the attribution of choice, scholars have proposed alternative attributions, including the Master of the San Remigio Lamentation.[18] The panel is dated to the mid-fourteenth century on stylistic grounds.

This large altarpiece has been admired for the representation of powerful expressions of grief within an unexpectedly informal composition; the naturalistic nature of the grouping in a unified space emphasizes the individualized emotional responses of the participants. Writers have also commented on the evocative quality of the expansive gold background and the starkness of the cross. The shape of the painting, with its elaborate ogée arch, is uncommon for this time. The altarpiece is also extraordinary in type, for in Florence at this time it was unusual for a large-scale altarpiece to represent a narrative subject.

For our purposes, it is the presence of two women that demands investigation. That they share the same space with the holy figures is exceptional; they even seem to be kneeling on the white cloth spread beneath the body of Christ. They are smaller in scale—but only slightly—than the biblical figures, and each is accompanied by a saint who places his hand on her head. The woman to the left, a Benedictine nun, kneels in front of Saint Benedict. The second woman wears her long hair down and loose, suggesting that she may be no more than a girl; the attention given to her portrait, which is one of the most convincing representations of a specific individual from the trecento, suggests her importance. She is introduced into the scene by a bishop saint traditionally identified as Remigio.[19]

The wealth of the young woman is suggested by her elaborate dress, which has the low, squared neckline popular at this time, but to our eyes such elegance is unexpected in this devotional, meditative context. The dress is black with elaborate bands of golden decoration around the neck, down the front and the sleeves, and on the cuffs; the sleeves have multiple small spherical buttons. She wears a wide, low-slung belt, gold and apparently enameled, which has a large buckle. Our attention is also drawn to her by the vivid yellow-to-green *cangiante* fabric of the garment of the bishop saint behind her.

As in other images discussed here in which contemporary women are represented (Wilkins figs. 1–3), the women are shown in attitudes of prayerful attention; in the altarpiece from San Remigio, however, there is a distinction in focus and gesture between the two women. The nun's hands are raised in a traditional gesture of prayer and she looks toward the girl. The girl, in turn, looks toward the figures of Mary and Christ, the emotional center of the lamentation grouping, and crosses her arms on her chest.[20] The difference in the two gestures almost certainly had a specific intent when the work was created, but this meaning has yet to be reconstructed. The emotion expressed by the two contemporary women seems measured when compared to the anguish and brooding intensity communicated by the biblical women, but whether this emphasis on female emotional response is related to the presence/patronage of the two contemporary women is uncertain.[21]

That the girl is closer to the holy figures and the cross suggests that she is the more important of the two, a conclusion supported by the manner in which the nun's attention is focused on her instead of on the Virgin and Christ, the emotional and devotional core of the subject. The girl may have been the patron of the altarpiece, although other possibilities have to be considered, such as the patronage of her parents or other family members, her joint patronage with the nun, or patronage by the nun alone. The contrast between the powerful emotionalism expressed by the biblical women and the controlled restraint of the two contemporary women is surely intentional and is perhaps an indicator of and model for the kind of behavior expected of women during this period. What need or occasion prompted this commission can only be speculated.

Internal evidence suggests that the two trecento paintings discussed here were made for, if not at the request of, women. Although these women remain anonymous and we know nothing about the exigencies that led to the creation of these works, the paintings provide a historical record that would otherwise be unavailable. Each work is remarkable in format, in iconography, and, above all, in the presence of portraits of contemporary women. In each case at least one of the women represented is secular. In a period when repetitive, conservative principles conditioned the production of panel paintings, these works reveal that when women, including secular women, played important roles—whether as traditional patrons or as recipients—the results are exceptional.

The Anonymous Woman in the Carnegie Altarpiece

Although in the history of Italian Renaissance art, the Carnegie Altarpiece (figs. 1–2) is not unprecedented, it provides a useful test case for assessing the state of our knowledge and for testing our ability to investigate the issues that surround the representation of a secular woman. Whether the kneeling woman was the patron is less important here than determining what the painting reveals about her and about Italian Renaissance women in general. To clarify the following discussion, I use the term *woman* to refer specifically to her, and *patron* to refer to the person(s) who commissioned the work, although they may be one and the same.

The scholarly tradition of Renaissance art history provides a number of approaches useful in studying the altarpiece. Fortunately the work is signed, by "Nicola di Maestro Antonio d'Ancona," and it bears a date of 1472.[22] This is Nicola's only known signed and/or dated work, and little is known about him beyond a few other, less significant works, compiled by connoisseurs on the basis of this signed altarpiece.[23] The date of 1472 is incontrovertible, but what it means is unclear, for the year when a painting was completed would hardly have been a noteworthy fact at this time. The dates found on Renaissance paintings, sculptures, and even buildings more likely refer to an event, a dedication, or a vow than to the moment of a painting's completion or the patron's final payment.[24] Nevertheless, in most cases there was probably some chronological connection between the inscribed date and the creation of the work, and in this case the style of the painting suggests that a date of circa 1472 is not inappropriate. The provenance of this painting is uncertain, but it is probably the work listed in 1821 in the church of San Francesco delle Scale in Ancona, a city on the Adriatic coast of north Italy.[25] We can establish a tentative date and a possible location for the altarpiece, and thus a potential period and site for the anonymous woman as well.

The frame is not original and the painting offers no coats of arms or other information that might identify the woman; this should not prevent us from speculating about her. Her presence as a secular woman without a husband or other family member is seldom paralleled in surviving works.[26] That the altarpiece is large and impressive suggests that she was part of a wealthy elite. A shared bond between the woman and the Virgin Mary is suggested by their fashionable attire and aristocratic demeanor. The Madonna is pale and her eyebrows and forehead are plucked in the late quattrocento fashion. A thin, chiffonlike *veletto* with a beaded edge both covers and exposes her high forehead. The Virgin's long belt with its elaborate buckle, the laced bodice, and the open, laced, brocaded velvet sleeves that show the fine pleated chemise underneath all reflect up-to-date fashion.[27] The stars traditionally found on the forehead and shoulder of the Virgin's robe in Byzantine icons have been translated into elaborate bejeweled brooches in the Renaissance style.

The composition is a type that became popular in Florence in the first half of the quattrocento and the style suggests Nicola's emulation of the illusionistic manner developed there during the same period. He demonstrates an interest in representing anatomical details in the emaciated figure of John the Baptist, and the revival of antiquity is evident in the design and decoration of the throne, with its colored marble inlays and reliefs of boxing putti, and in the ancient Roman-style lettering of the signature and date. Trompe l'oeil details include the fly that seems to have settled on the base of the Virgin's throne and the manner in which the apple and vase of flowers seem to be precariously close to the edge of the base of the throne. One of the foreground tiles of the Virgin's platform looks as if it is cracked, and a piece of paper lettered with the word "ANCONA"—the clever completion of the artist's signature—seems at first to be a real piece of paper attached to the surface of the painting. That Nicola may have set out to trick an unsuspecting priest or sacristan to remove the scrap of paper, swat the fly, or shove the apple or the vase of flowers back to a safer position is suggested by the fact that some of these trompe l'oeil elements still have the power to fool contemporary visitors to the Carnegie Museum of Art.[28] While our sophisticated understanding of visual phenomena prevents us from being tricked by the representation as a whole, it is possible that in Ancona circa 1472, the fashionable illusionistic mode seen here may have been a revolutionary, modern statement. From the viewpoint of that public, and in the eyes of Nicola and the woman and/or patron, this may have been the most up-to-date and sophisticated painting in town. Perhaps this altarpiece functioned as only one of several public expressions of the woman's and/or the patron's wealth and sophistication. Because the woman, the Madonna, and the altarpiece can be characterized as fashionable, it is possible that this quality may be the result of the woman's (and/or patron's) intervention in the creation of the work. Whether the woman or the patron (or, if they are not one and the same, perhaps both) played an instrumental role in encouraging the use of the fashionable style we will never know; perhaps the choice of artist was enough to guarantee that this style would dominate the work.

As late-twentieth-century connoisseurs of Renaissance developments, we can easily point to elements that seem not quite right. The foreshortening of John the Baptist's feet is satisfactory, but that of his left arm is unconvincing and even grotesque, as is Nicola's emphatic treatment of certain anatomical details. While Masaccio used cast shadows based on a single light source to set his forms within a convincing spatial envelope, Nicola uses shadows selectively, muting the overall spatial effect. Florentine artists seldom represented figures in the act of conversing, but here Nicola attempts to engage his saints through gestures and open mouths. The use of a continuous gold background was largely passé in Florence by 1472, but Nicola has maintained a gold surface over much of the background; in keeping with his interest in illusionism, it has been tooled, using a template, to transform it into a gold brocade curtain. He enhances this illusion when he seems to lift it slightly to allow a view of a deep and particularly Marchigian landscape. The conflict that results between curtain and landscape and, therefore, between tradition and innovation, surface and illusion, is curious. It suggests an attempt to satisfy two different expectations; perhaps this reflects some kind of disagreement between or among some of the parties involved—the artist, the woman and/or patron, and perhaps a member of the clergy. Nicola's use of flat gold halos behind the heads of the holy figures is also conservative by the standards of Florence where, by the 1470s, foreshortened halos and translucent, luminous effects were standard. We can judge, then, that from a strictly Florentine point of view the picture is inconsistent and *retardetaire*.

The relationship of our painting to Florentine developments is not our only area of certainty; we can also be sure about much of the iconography. The saints—Leonard, Jerome, John the Baptist, and Francis of Assisi—can be identified by attributes and dress. It seems reasonable that these saints were chosen by the woman and/or patron and that they somehow refer to the woman's personal saint and to the patron saints of the particular altar, the family chapel, the church, the city, or perhaps to other individuals, events, qualities, and/or institutions important to her or to the patron.[29] We can also identify the symbols in the altarpiece.

Mary wears a coral necklace, and the flowers in the up-to-date Venetian glass bottle are the thornless red and white roses symbolic of virginity. [30] The fruit may carry a double meaning: the promise of new life encoded in the Resurrection and the roles of Christ and the Virgin as the new Adam and Eve. The only iconographic uncertainty is the fly, a theme which has been identified variously as an indication of transience, a representation of the devil in the world, a talisman to prevent other flies from despoiling the painting's surface, a simple trompe l'oeil device, or an ancient topos. [31] The role assumed by the woman (and/or patron) in this iconographic program is uncertain, but it seems unlikely that these details were left to the imagination of the artist.

This lengthy exposition on a Marchigian altarpiece is calculated to demonstrate how a little known work can be significant for our understanding of the history of women and the practices of patronage. It is also intended to highlight the state of research in this well-studied period: in iconography we are well grounded, and we are able to interpret stylistic progress from a Florentine perspective and to thereby locate a work within a qualitative, geographic hierarchy. But in the area of patronage we are uncertain how to approach the work because the woman is unidentified and her patronage is by no means assured. Nevertheless, it is clear that clues about her role and significance are encoded in the work. Anonymity, we can conclude, should never be an excuse that prevents us from asking questions about women and patronage.

Expanding the Base for Gender and Patronage Studies

As the previous discussion emphasizes, we cannot be sure that the woman represented at the feet of Saint Jerome was the patron of the work. There is the possibility that someone else—her parents, a brother, a sister, a husband, a son or daughter—commissioned the work to honor her and, perhaps, to assert or celebrate her piety. The painting may even have been commissioned to honor her after her death. Whether her small scale within the context of the representation is significant in determining her role remains uncertain. [32] While we would like to identify the person(s) who paid for the work, we should not be frustrated that in most cases we will never be able to do so. And when querying an undocumented work that includes representations of contemporary figures as devotees, this work reminds us that we must be wary of automatically identifying these persons as the patrons. At the same time, however, we must recognize that such representations help us raise questions about the roles men and women, both secular and religious, played in the complicated social and artistic world of fourteenth-, fifteenth-, and sixteenth-century Italy.

This investigation challenges the traditional approaches to patronage. My examination of the Carnegie Altarpiece supports Roger Crum's proposal that we must expand the theory of patronage to encompass those who requested and/or needed the work, as well as those who were intended to use it. Crum argues that no matter who paid for works of art intended for the home, documentation supports that these works were trusted to the care of the wife and were often, in addition, intended for such wifely duties as the religious training of the children. If an object fulfilled a need experienced by a woman and if she was its primary user, Crum argues, is it important that she neither signed the document of commission nor made the payments? When this idea is appended to my proposal that the broader audience for whom painters created works at least be considered within the study of patronage, a new, more comprehensive approach to patronage can be forwarded. This expanded view provides a means for bridging the problematic chasm between documentation and practice in the study of patronage.

If we base the study of patronage on this larger view, it becomes profitable to conclude—or rather to begin—with a series of questions. We might ask, for example, how a particular work or type of work might have been activated by a single man, a single woman, a couple, a family, a nun, a monk, a religious community, a confraternity, a guild, or a *comune*. How did the patronage of art relate to an individual's or group's other investments and activities, both pious and secular? Were men more important as the patrons of public works, while women played a greater role in needing, requesting, and/or using works in the home? Were certain types, subjects, materials, or functions more likely to be patronized/needed by one group than another, and why? How is patronage typical or atypical of certain classes, professions, or organizations? Did patronage patterns differ from one area of Italy to another, and if so, how and why? When one or more portraits are found in a work, who was chosen to be represented and why? If the great majority of Italian Renaissance works were commissioned, why is it that patrons appear so infrequently, and what does it mean when they do? How can we begin to study the undocumented and largely untraceable impulses that encouraged artists to create works in response to a broad public interest and need? If we could know the identity, the class, the occupation, and the family relationships of all patrons of all works, what patterns would emerge? What likelihood is there that the patterns that we can determine from the relatively few documented instances of patronage would resemble the broader practices of patronage during the Renaissance?

It is clear that the patronage of art by secular women in the Renaissance, so richly documented by specific examples in this volume, can be more fully understood only when studied within the broadest possible context.

Notes

For good advice I owe special thanks to Sheryl Reiss, Ann Thomas Wilkins, Katherine May Wilkins, and Roger Crum.

1. The painting is 60 ¼ x 78 ½ inches. See *Catalogue of Painting Collection*, Museum of Art, Carnegie Institute (Pittsburgh: Museum of Art, Carnegie Institute, 1973), 125–26, and *Carnegie Museum of Art Collection Highlights* (Pittsburgh: Carnegie Museum of Art, 1995), 20. I would like to dedicate this essay to the memory of Leon Arkus, the director of the Carnegie Museum of Art, who acquired this painting for the collection.

2. For general monographs on patronage in the Italian Renaissance see *Patronage, Art and Society in Renaissance Italy*, ed. F. W. Kent and Patricia Simons (Oxford: Oxford University Press, 1987), and Mary Hollingsworth, *Patronage in Renaissance Italy From 1400 to the Early Sixteenth Century* (London: J. Murray, 1994). Important articles on the subject include Catherine King, "Women as Patrons: Nuns, Widows and Rulers," in *Siena, Florence and Padua: Art, Society and Religion, 1280–1400*, ed. D. Norman, 2 vols. (New Haven, Conn.: Yale University Press, 1995), 2:249–54, and Tracy E. Cooper, "*Mecenatismo* or *Clientelismo*? The Character of Renaissance Patronage," in *The Search for a Patron in the Middle Ages and the Renaissance*, ed. David G. Wilkins and Rebecca L. Wilkins (Lewiston, N.Y.: Edwin Mellen Press), 19–32. For studies that go beyond Renaissance art in Italy, see Wilkins and Wilkins, *The Search for a Patron,* and the papers in *Renaissance Studies* 10, no. 2 (1996), edited by Jaynie Anderson. For a study reestablishing the role of the artist in the patronage system, see Creighton E. Gilbert's brilliant and thoughtful "What Did the Renaissance Patron Buy?" *Renaissance Quarterly* 51 (1998): 392–450; Professor Gilbert kindly allowed me to read his manuscript prior to publication.

3. See the essay by Molly Bourne in this volume.

4. See Carolyn Valone, "Roman Matrons as Patrons: Various Views of the Cloister Wall," in *The Crannied Wall: Women, Religion, and the Arts in Early Modern Europe*, ed. Craig A. Monson (Ann Arbor, University of Michigan Press, 1992), 49–72, and Carolyn Valone, "Women on the Quirinal Hill: Patronage in Rome, 1560–1630," *Art Bulletin* 76 (1994): 129–46; also Marilynn Dunn, "Piety and Patronage in Seicento Rome: Two Noblewomen and Their Convents," *Art Bulletin* 76 (1994): 644–63.

5. On Jerome see Eugene F. Rice, Jr., *Saint Jerome in the Renaissance* (Baltimore: Johns Hopkins University Press, 1985).

6. Not all widows were buried in their husband's chapels, even though they were usually responsible for the construction and/or decoration of these sites. Veronica Gambara was buried in a chapel she had founded in San Francesco, Correggio, as discussed by Katherine McIver in this volume. Maria Bufalini's will requested that she be buried in one of her family's chapels instead of with her husband; see Vaccaro's essay in this volume.

7. For a recent study of widows and their roles, see Catherine E. King's *Renaissance Women Patrons: Wives and Widows in Italy, 1300–1550* (Manchester: Manchester University Press, 1998).

8. As quoted in the essay by Sheryl Reiss in this volume.

9. See Sheryl Reiss's essay in this volume.

10. For a study of the painting and earlier bibliography see Richard Offner and Miklós Boskovits, *A Critical and Historical Corpus of Florentine Painting: Florentine Painting, the Fourteenth Century, Bernardo Daddi, His Shop and Following*, secs. 3, 4 (Florence: Giunta Barbera, 1991), 191–200. There it is called the "Florence Votive Panel" and it is stated:"The form of the panel is rare and the representation unique among paintings on wood in the region and the period of its origin." (191). They assign the painting to "Close Following of Daddi" (191). For a discussion of Daddi's life and work that focuses on his stylistic development, see G. Damiani, *DBI*, 31:622–27. The

painting is discussed in some detail in Luisa Becherucci and Giulia Brunetti, *Il Museo dell'Opera del Duomo di Firenze*, 2 vols. (Venice: Electa, n.d.), 2:281–82.

A second, dismembered version of this work, without patrons/donors, by the Daddi shop is now divided between the Pinacoteca Vaticana, Rome, and the Kunstmuseum, Berne; see Offner-Boskovits, *Corpus*, 201–12. A third version, without patrons/donors, is owned by the J. Paul Getty Museum in Los Angeles; see John Walsh and Deborah Gribbon, *The J. Paul Getty Museum and Its Collections: A Museum for the New Century* (Los Angeles: J. Paul Getty Museum, 1997), 110. The Getty attributes its high quality panel not to the shop, but to Bernardo Daddi himself.

11. Becherucci and Brunetti, *Museo dell'Opera*, identify the boy as a "donatore."

12. The meaning of different types of costumes in the trecento is, to the best of my knowledge, still unresolved. In discussing the two women, the 1943 Mosta Giottesca catalogue states that the older one is "in abito monacale or vedovile." Giulia Sinibaldi and Giulia Brunetti, *Pittura italiana del Duecento e Trecento: Catalogo della Mostra Giottesca di Firenze del 1937* (Florence: Commissione della Mostra Giottesca, 1943), 527–29.

13. The saints are identified in the inscription across the bottom of the panel.

14. Offner-Boskovits, *Corpus*, transcribe the text on the book as: "Dolcissima Vergine Maria da Bangnuolo priegoui che preghiate lui per la sua charita et per la sua potenzia me faccia grazia di ciò che mi fa mestiere" (192). Thanks to Dennis Looney, of the French and Italian Department at the Univesity of Pittsburgh, for his help with this translation; an alternate translation for *charita* would be "divine love." Looney pointed out to me the difficulty in translating the word *mestiere*, which can refer to one's occupation.

15. Offner-Boskovits, *Corpus*, 192.

16. The date on the frame reads: ANNO DNI M CCC XXX IIII DIE XXV FEBRUARII; because the Florentine year began on March 25, the date is 1335 modern style. Offner-Boskovits, *Corpus*, 192.

   Another example of a painting with an exact date is Daddi's Bigallo triptych; see David Wilkins, "Bernardo Daddi's Triptych in the Bigallo," *Italian Studies* 6 (American Association for Italian Studies, 1985): 31–41.

17. Offner-Boskovits, *Corpus*, says that painting was apparently "commissioned by the compagnia di Santa Maria Vergine e di San Zenobio," which owned "an altar on a pilaster of the Cathedral" (192), but the presence of the two women and the nature of the inscription would seem to render this an unlikely confraternity offering. For documentation that refers to the confraternity's *tabernacolo*, see Offner-Boskovits, *Corpus*, 192. In a symposium on 17 October 1998 at the National Gallery of Art, Washington, D.C., Lars Jones suggested that perhaps this work copies the *compagnia* painting.

18. On the painting see Luisa Marcucci, *Gallerie nazionali di Firenze: I dipinti toscani del XIV secolo* (Rome: Libreria dello Stato, 1965), 88–90, and *Gli Uffizi: catalogo generale* (Florence: Centro di, 1979), 295 (where the work is dated 1360–65). John White, *Art and Architecture in Italy 1250–1400*, 3rd edition (New Haven, Conn.: Yale University Press, 1993), 422, identifies the artist as "Unknown Florentine" and dates the painting to the second quarter of the fourteenth century. For a discussion of Giottino and the painting, with an attribution to "The Master of the San Remigio Lamentation," see Brendan Cassidy, "Giottino," in *Dictionary of Art* (London: Grove, 1996), 12:681.

19. The painting is first documented at San Remigio in the 1550 edition of Vasari; Vasari-Milanesi, 1:627–28. Kaftal identifies the bishop saint as Remigius, but this is based on Vasari's identification of the painting at San Romeo (Remigio) in 1550; George Kaftal, *Iconography of the Saints in Tuscan Painting* (Florence: Sansoni, 1952), 890.

20. On gesture, see Moshe Barasch, *Gestures of Despair in Medieval and Early Renaissance Art*, (New York: New York University Press, 1976), esp. 57–86, and *Giotto and the Language of Gesture* (Cambridge: Cambridge University Press, 1987), as well as Andrew Ladis's cautionary review of the latter in *Art Bulletin* 74 (1992): 159–61. Barasch's discussions of gesture do not provide an

explanation for the difference in the two gestures in this panel. Both gestures were used in the liturgy, and their use here seems ritualistic. On gesture see also Dirk Kocks, "Die Stifterdarstellung in der italienischen Malerei des 13–15 Jahrhunderts" (Ph.D. dissertation, University of Cologne, 1971), which was unavailable to me.

21. The two female saints with uncovered heads and long reddish hair, both of whom are represented in a highly emotional state, could both be identified as the Magdalen; neither has the ointment jar that would make a specific identification possible.

22. OPUS NICOLAI MI ANTONII DE ANCONA, MCCCCLXXII. On the artist see Bernard Berenson, "Nicola di Maestro Antonio di Ancona," *Rassegna d'arte* 15 (1915): 165–74; Pietro Zampetti, *Painting from the Marches: Gentile to Raphael* (London: Phaidon, 1971), 192–97; Roberto Longhi, "Calepino Veneziano VII: Gl'inizi di Nicola di Maestro Antonio da Ancona," *Arte Veneta* 1 (1947): 185–86; Federico Zeri, "Qualcosa su Nicola di Maestro Antonio," *Paragone* 107 (1958): 34–41; "Nicola di Maestro Antonio di Ancona," *Dictionary of Art*, 23:107–8.

23. At present the name on this altarpiece is the only documented record of his and his father's existence. Zampetti cites a reference in Amico Ricci, *Memorie storiche delle arti e degli artisti della Marca di Ancona* (Macerata, 1834), 1:234, and notes that in 1451 a medalist named Maestro Niccolò di Antonio of Ancona was authorized to mint silver at Macerata. Zampetti agrees that there is no sure way to connect this medalist to our painter.

24. See Wilkins, "Bernardo Daddi's Triptych." An examination of the appearance and function of dates on works of art is long overdue.

25. Alessandro Maggiori, *Le pitture, sculture e architetture della città di Ancona* (Bologna: Forni, 1821), 166. The picture dated 1472 that is documented there is listed as by "Antonio d'Ancona," but this is may be an error in transcription. San Francesco delle Scale in Ancona, built in 1323, was renovated in the eighteenth century and closed in 1852; the Carnegie altarpiece is first documented in 1854, in the Alexander Barker Collection in London. For further provenance see *Catalogue of Painting Collection*, 126.

26. For other examples see King, *Renaissance Women Patrons*.

27. On Renaissance dress of this period see Elizabeth Birbari, *Dress in Italian Painting 1460–1500* (London: J. Murray, 1975); Jacqueline Herald, *Renaissance Dress in Italy 1400–1500* (London: Bell & Hyman, 1981); and Jane Bridgeman, "Dress, V, Fourteenth to Sixteenth Centuries," *Dictionary of Art*, 9:260–64. See also Michele Polverari, *Gli abiti di Carlo Crivelli*, exh. cat. (Ancona: Pinacoteca Comunale, 1990).

28. When I guided my daughter's fourth-grade class through the museum some years ago, I had to prevent a student from hitting at the fly after I had said, in an attempt to rouse interest, "Oh, there's a fly on the painting!" On another occasion an observant adult questioned my statement that the painting is in good condition by pointing to "that crack in the surface" which is only the illusion of a crack painted in one of the marble floor tiles.

29. If the 1821 reference that lists a painting by "Antonio d'Ancona" in San Francesco delle Scale in Ancona refers to the Carnegie Altarpiece, then the figure of Saint Francis would be an obvious reference to the church.

30. The bottle is an important early example of the swirled pattern (*retortoli*) using clear and milky (*lattimo*) glass in the *latticinio* technique, a style usually dated later, to the end of the fifteenth and the beginning of the sixteenth century; see Paola d'Alconzo, "Venice, III, Glass," in *Dictionary of Art,* 32:101.

31. For a discussion and bibliography on the interpretation of the fly, see Maryan W. Ainsworth, *Petrus Christus, Renaissance Master of Bruges*, exh. cat. (New York: Metropolitan Museum of Art, 1994), 27–28 and nn. 10–12. The ancient topos is found in both Pliny's *Natural History* and the writings of Philostratus the Athenian. In discussing the fly in Petrus Christus's 1446 *Portrait of a Carthusian*, Julien Chapuis writes that because the fly is a short-lived insect it is a "traditional symbol of the

transience of life," and he then proceeds to suggest that it "may have been intended as a reminder that this portrait would survive the death of both the sitter and the painter; it would, then, contitute a visualization of the saying 'ars longa, vita brevis.'" See Julien Chapius, "Early Netherlandish Painting: Shifting Perspectives," in *From Van Eyck to Bruegel: Early Netherlandish Painting in The Metropolitan Museum of Art*, ed. Maryan W. Ainsworth and Keith Christiansen, exh. cat.(New York: Metropolitan Museum of Art, 1998), 19 and 21, n. 84. A reasoned conclusion is offered by James Hall, who, while championing the protective talisman theory, argues that the fly can have little symbolic significance because "the subject matter of the paintings on which it appears is widely varied, though usually religious." James Hall, *Dictionary of Subjects and Symbols in Art* (New York: Harper & Row, 1979), 126.

32. On the scale of portraits of women, see King, *Renaissance Women Patrons*, 129–83.

Fina da Carrara, née Buzzacarini: Consort, Mother, and Patron of Art in Trecento Padua

Benjamin G. Kohl

On 7 May 1345, the morning after Giacomo II da Carrara murdered his distant cousin Marsilietto Papafava dei Carraresi to claim the lordship of Padua, he married his eldest son, Francesco, to Fina Buzzacarini, daughter of Pataro Buzzacarini. The marriage probably came as no surprise to the people of Padua, for it was part of Giacomo's policy to win support for his new rule. This included the dismissal of Marsilietto's unpopular vicar, Pietro da Campagnola, the release of clergy and laity unjustly imprisoned by the previous lord, the encouragement of the return of exiles to Padua, and gifts of land, clothes, money, and horses to powerful would-be supporters.[1] Fina Buzzacarini functioned as a trophy consort, uniting an aspiring branch of the Carrara dynasty with a local noble family of wealth and standing. In the early years of marriage, Fina gave birth to four healthy offspring, three daughters and eventually in 1359 a son and heir, Francesco Novello. Finally, her deep piety and hope for memorialization made Fina a major art patron, who converted Padua's Baptistery into a mausoleum for herself and her husband, and for which she commissioned major fresco cycles by Giusto de' Menabuoi with a depiction of Paradise in the dome, scenes from Genesis on the drum, and moments from the lives of John the Baptist, Christ, and the Virgin to adorn its walls.[2]

Consort

Giacomo had claimed the lordship as son of the disfavored Niccolò da Carrara, who had died in exile in 1344, and he badly needed the prestige and stability that the marriage of his son into a powerful (and favorable) local family would bring. Fina was the granddaughter of the loyal and astute Dusio Buzzacarini, whose support of the Carrara regime stretched back to their first election as lords of Padua in 1318. Moreover, the Buzzacarini had overcome criticism of base origins and ill-gotten wealth voiced by such conservative Paduan historians as Giovanni da Non and Albertino Mussato. Their magnificent palace in the *contrada* of San Urbano was now the showpiece of one of the major families of Padua's legal profession. Da Non's jibes at the family as tavern singers, skinners, and gamblers rang hollow when confronted with the Buzzacarini's achievements as magistrates, jurists, and diplomats.[3]

Dusio Buzzacarini had been podestà of Rovigo in 1310, of Bassano in 1319, and of Treviso in 1320. His secretive and deceitful ways and his willingness—even eagerness—to attach his fortunes to any rising star, Dusio had chosen his patrons well and was knighted, along with his crony Marsilio da Carrara, by Cangrande della Scala in 1328 when the lord of Verona assumed the lordship of Padua. Dusio's unswerving loyalty to the Carrara cause eventually paid off. In the treaty concluded between Venice, Florence, and Marsilio da Carrara in 1337, which spelled out the conditions for the reconquest of Padua from the now much-hated Scaliger lords.[4] Marsilio's cousin and heir, Ubertino da Carrara, was to succeed him if he were killed or incapacitated during the siege of the city, and Dusio was named one of councillors appointed to advise Ubertino at his accession.[5] In March 1338 Marsilio did die—from exhaustion, not wounds—and Dusio's place in Paduan politics was secure under Ubertino. By then Dusio had removed from his smaller house near San Tommaso to the Buzzacarini palace at San Urbano, and in 1340 tithes granted by the vicar of the bishop of Padua continued to enrich Dusio's rural holdings, especially in the villages of Arzercavalli and Brugine. Ubertino da Carrara honored Dusio by naming him one of the ambassadors to conclude a treaty of extradition with Venice early in 1345,[6] and in May the new Carrara lord Giacomo II appointed him one of the ambassadors sent to Venice to renew the treaty of 1337.[7] Two years later, probably at the behest of the lord of Padua, the bishop's vicar rewarded Dusio with extensive lay tithes in the eastern Padovano previously held by the deposed chancellor Pietro da Campagnola.[8] As death approached in 1350, Dusio would have had occasion to view the marriage of his granddaughter Fina to the heir apparent to the lordship of Padua, Francesco da Carrara, as the crowning achievement of a career spent in the service of the Carrara lords.

As bride of Francesco da Carrara, Fina soon entered the courtly society created in the Carrara Reggia by her popular and chivalric father-in-law, Giacomo II da Carrara. In the 1340s Ubertino da Carrara had begun the construction of a new court, a complex of palaces, offices, refectories, and living quarters for courtiers, soldiers, and servants on the site of the older Scaligeri residence just to the north of the Duomo and west of the seat of the communal government. Ubertino hired the painter Guariento di Arpo to decorate the walls of this new palace.[9] Guariento decorated the Sala di Cimieri, the waiting room on the ground floor that led to the reception hall, with individual coats of arms, while the Sala dei Carri, the reception hall, was covered with the family's distinctive arms, the cart (carro). On the floor above, Guariento frescoed the family's private chapel with angels and scenes from the Old Testament. Other rooms were decorated with scenes from ancient myth or history, with the legends of Hercules, Camillus, and Nero, and with an ancient naval victory of Thebes. By 1347, Giacomo II had begun the construction of a second palace, the Palazzo di Levante, on the eastern edge of the complex, overlooking the square in front of the church of San Clemente, the present Piazza dei Signori. It was probably here that Francesco da Carrara moved with his bride, Fina da Buzzacarini, to begin their family.[10]

By this time Francesco il Vecchio was deeply involved with the tasks of governing: at the age of twenty-five, he had been propelled into the lordship of Padua by the assassination of his father on 19 December 1350. On that day Francesco and his uncle Giacomino had been hunting hares on family estates in Camposampiero to the north of Padua; to ensure an orderly succession and the safety of his daughter, his son-in-law, and himself, Fina's father Pataro Buzzacarini rode hard to fetch Francesco back to Padua to claim his birthright. Three days later Francesco and his uncle Giacomino took oaths to serve Padua and its commune as their lords.[11] Pataro was soon drawn into the Carrara lords' circle of councillors, and in 1354 accompanied his son-in-law to greet the future Emperor Charles of Bohemia on his first descent to Italy. To reward Francesco, who was by now imperial vicar, Charles dubbed the Carrara lord as his vassal, and Francesco in turn knighted several of his followers, including Pataro. By now Francesco had eclipsed his uncle Giacomino in prestige and leadership, and tensions arose between the two lords. Their wives, too, fell to quarreling over the rights of their children to the succession. Giacomino's wife, Margherita Gonzaga, had already produced a male heir while Fina, though married for a decade, had not. Finally, Giacomino decided to assassinate his popular nephew, but the plot was discovered; Giacomino was imprisoned in the Rocca at Monselice, and Margherita and their young son were sent home to Mantua.[12] Thereafter, Fina was the consort of the sole signore of Padua.

Pataro profited from his son-in-law's success. Francesco il Vecchio's alliance with King Louis of Hungary brought a new opportunity for territorial expansion when Louis received the hill towns of Belluno and Feltre from the dukes of Austria and soon gave them over to his new ally, the lord of Padua. In November 1360 Pataro Buzzacarini was appointed his son-in-law's agent to receive lordship over these two small cities from Hungarian officials.[13] Returning to Padua in poor health and mindful of his own mortality, on 31 January 1361, Pataro made a *donatio inter vivos* of 5,634 lire to Fina, who used the gift to purchase parcels of land, mainly arable, hedged with vines and fruit trees, in Arzercavalli and nearby Ponte Casale from Manfredino Conti and his son Engolfo. The purchase also included seven farmsteads with sheds and barns on more than 150 Paduan campi.[14] Fina already held considerable property in this village, and she wisely used the gift to purchase parcels contiguous with her own property and thus develop large blocks that could be cultivated more efficiently. That same year saw the death of her father and her uncle Salione, a canon at the cathedral chapter. From Pataro, Fina received half of the lay tithes in Arzercavalli and from her uncle income from several parcels on Via Nova in the Paduan campanea.[15]

Venice's continuing cultivation of the support of the Carrara family prompted the signoria, in December 1363, to confer full Venetian citizenship on Francesco da Carrara, Fina and their descendants, and on Fina's brother, Arcoano Buzzacarini, already a military captain and councillor in the Carrara regime.[16] Fina's interest in Venice matured when some years later she appointed a proctor to buy her a town house there.[17] In January 1371, the commune of Florence cemented its alliance with its Guelf ally, Padua, by granting Florentine citizenship to Francesco, Fina and their descendants, and again, to Fina's brother Arcoano.[18] This honor was followed by Fina's loan of 10,000 florins to Florence on 16 June 1371—a loan that would not be repaid until November 1376, after some strains between the two Guelf powers.[19]

The chief source of Fina's wealth (and potential for personal independence and agency) lay in her ownership of extensive rural estates. This interest was centered in three villages to the east and south of Padua: Noventa, Brugine, and Arzercavalli. Here Fina increased and consolidated her holdings through purchases or exchanges with husband and brother. In 1368, for example, she received from Francesco il Vecchio nearly 1,000 campi in 156 parcels and a mill in Noventa in return for granting him 2,000 ducats and 1,014 campi in 158 parcels in Arzercavalli and Braida.[20] Additional purchases were made in 1370: on 8 June Fina bought for 303 lire more than twenty-five campi in three parcels in Noventa, and the same day she gave four parcels in Villa Rusta to her brother Arcoano in exchange for two large parcels in Noventa.[21] On 4 July 1370 Fina bought two more parcels in Noventa from one Bartolomeo, a constable (*preco*) of the commune of Padua. On Christmas Day 1370, she advanced nearly 150 lire to her sharecroppers in Arquà for seed for the spring planting, and on 26 January 1371, she leased for five years a house in Padua near the Benedictine convent of Santa Agata to a linen worker, Biago Scadelato, and his son for an annual rent of 40 lire and gifts of wax and pepper at Christmas.[22] On 30 January 1371 she received from her husband the donation of many parcels that he had purchased for her, and on 1 March she enlarged her holdings in Noventa by purchasing for 2,329 lire more than forty campi with house and barn from one Simone da Noventa, residing in Padua.[23] In May 1371 Fina, acting through her agent the notary Alberto Figario, took possession of all the parcels bought or exchanged in Noventa; in June she bought for 2,410 lire sixteen parcels of arable land in Piove di Sacco, and in March 1372, she consolidated several farmsteads in Brugine by purchasing four campi from one Caterina of contrada Santa Giuliana in Padua.[24] When the outbreak of the border war between Padua and Venice that summer brought an end to her acquisitions of real estate, Fina was probably the wealthiest woman in Padua.

Mother

Despite her Venetian town house, her citizenship in two of the greatest cities of Italy, her enormous loan to Florence (undoubtedly made for political reasons), and her creation of large rural estates, Fina's greatest interests resided in her family and her religion. By midcentury, the new Palazzo di Levante constructed on the eastern edge of the city center was being used to shelter the women of the court from the hazards of court life. The Palazzo di Levante may well have been the first "gendered space" in the Italian courts of the early Renaissance, constructed probably as a nursery for the offspring of the two consorts, Margherita Gonzaga and Fina Buzzacarini, and providing a safe residence for their servants and ladies-in-waiting. Certainly by the middle of the next century, separate households for the women of the signorial and ducal courts, such as the Este of Ferrara, the Gonzaga of Mantua, the Malatesta of Rimini, and the Sforza of Milan, were the norm.[25] A document of 1351 mentions the palace of the lords, Francesco and his ill-fated uncle Giacomino, across from "where reside the wives of the said lords (ubi habitant domine ipsorum dominorum)."[26] It was probably in the Palazzo di Levante that Fina gave birth to her three daughters and only son. Gigliola, born in about 1347, was married to Wencelaus, Duke of Saxony, on 29 January 1367. Caterina, born probably at midcentury, married Stefan Frankapan, count of Veglia and lord of Segni, on 22 June 1372. A third daughter, Lieta, born in about 1355, married Frederick, count of Ortenburg, in 1382. Last born was the heir apparent, Francesco Novello, on 29 May 1359. Fina bore four children in about thirteen years, but after the birth of a male heir, as she approached thirty-five, she had no more children. Francesco il Vecchio had already forsaken the bed of his wife for liaisons with women of the city; he sired a number of Carrara bastards, who were given posts in his army and the Paduan church in the last third of the century.[27]

In what surviving notarial documents call the *camera dominarum* or the *palacium dominarum*, Fina soon developed a female space for her daughters, their nurses and servants, and young noblewomen from the Carrara elite.[28] An accounting of the regime's household expenses made in 1357 provided a separate "account of the ladies (*ratio dominarum*)."[29] This invaluable document of the household government lists five large grants, including purveyance (11,054 lire), soldiers (4,954 lire), and administration (21,000 lire) and ten smaller accounts, disbursing, for example, 595 lire for falcons, 1,501 lire for wine, 887 lire for horses, 151 lire for leather and furs, and 1,216 lire for arms. By contrast, the *ratio dominarum* paid out 4,585 lire for the maintenance of Fina, her children and her household in 1357. Thus, Fina, as consort and mother, commanded a significant part of the expenditures of 60,000 lire for the Carrara regime that year.

As we have seen, Fina's two older daughters left their mother's household for marriage in 1367 and 1372, with only Lieta remaining at home. But even in her later years, Fina's miniature court in the Palazzo di Levante, composed of loyal servants and young noblewomen serving as ladies-in-waiting, afforded companionship in a space that was her exclusive domain. Even so, young friends left to marry, as did Dasia, daughter of the noble Bartolomeo Engleschi, on 15 April 1378, to the young jurist Alessandro Dottori with a dowry of 1,000 lire as Fina's gift.[30] Now in failing health, Fina began to consider making her testament. She wanted to make bequests to churches, clerics, and her married daughters, and Fina asked her husband for dispensation from Paduan statutes which forbade bequests to clergy, religious corporations, and those (such as her married daughters) who were not inscribed in the communal *estimo*. This she received on 15 August 1378.[31] Five weeks later Fina made her last will and testament.

On 22 September 1378, in her own palace, surrounded by her husband's officials, including his treasurer and general factor, in a room decorated with frescoes depicting the

Genealogical Table for the Buzzacarini of Padua

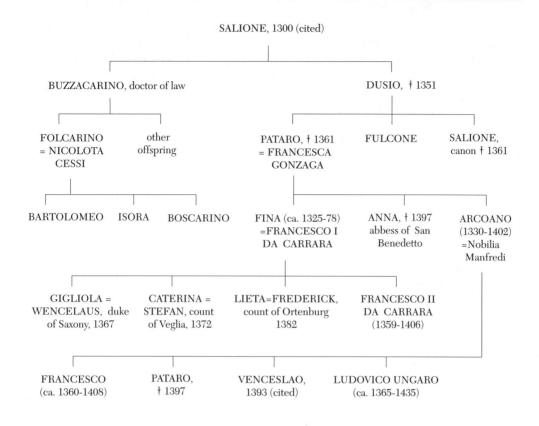

Four Virtues, Fina dictated her will to the Carrara court notary Bandino Brazzi.[32] From this revealing document it is possible to reconstruct the composition of Fina's household at the time of her death and assess her patronage of the Baptistery. Assuming that the young women and servants mentioned in the will were residing in Fina's palace, when she died her household was composed of eleven young women and six servants. By contrast, in 1384 the contemporary Gonzaga court in Mantua listed twenty-nine serving girls and ladies-in-waiting in the household of the lord's wife.[33] In life Fina had provided a comfortable residence for these young women, of whom some were orphans, of the Carrara affinity. Now in death, in an act of gendered patronage, she generously provided them with dowries so that as her household was closed down they could find husbands and marry. The largest dowry, one of 400 ducats (or 1,400 lire), was granted to an unnamed wife of the jurist Ubertino Arsendi, whose father Argentino Arsendi had been a major diplomat in the service of the Carrara regime. She is probably Bartolomea di Federico Ubaldini, who as Ubertino Arsendi's wife made her own will a quarter of a century after Fina's bequest.[34] Dowries of 1,000 lire went to Caterina, daughter of the knight Pietro Capodivacca, from a family prominent in the Carrara affinity, and to Caterina Tergola, daughter of Gerardo, who married a widower, the famous Paduan scientist Giovanni Dondi dall'Orologio in 1379.[35] Two women, both named Margherita of the Dotti family, major supporters of the Carrara regime, received dowries of 1,000 lire each.

One of these Margheritas was the granddaughter of Paolo Dotti, the regime's first factor general, the daughter of Antonio da Giudecca, and the niece of Francesco Dotti, another major servant of the Carrara regime. The other Margherita Dotti was the daughter of Antonio detto Negro di Giovanni, who was apparently a close friend of Fina's brother Arcoano, who had received from Negro in 1375 the gift of a ten-year-old Tartar slave girl. Negro Dotti was also a second cousin of Francesco Dotti and was later named Francesco's residuary heir if the first universal heir, Francesco's nephew Giacomo, predeceased the testator.[36] Fina further left dowries of 600 lire each to Anastasia, daughter of Ser Lucchese of Pisa, and Caterina, daughter of the deceased Marchiano Festucci. Dorotea, daughter of the deceased Antonio Pavanello and perhaps kinswoman of the regime's accountant, received a modest dowry of 200 lire. In recompense for *maleablati* (any unknown misdeeds), Fina bequeathed a dowry of 1,000 lire to the unnamed daughter of Giovanni Monfumo, probably Maria, with the provision that if she or her sister did not marry, the dowry was to go to another young noble maiden of Padua.[37] The bequest of a small house in the Buzzacarini complex in *contrada* San Urbano, 200 lire, and clothing went to Caterina, daughter of Bartolomeo Zabarella.[38] Gifts of 200 lire each went to two sisters of the Costabile family, one of whom was a nun in the convent of San Benedetto where Fina's sister Anna was abbess. Gifts of 200 lire went to the female servant Pulzeta and of 400 lire to her manservant Bartolomeo Celegino of Perugia. Fina's four other serving women, including Lieta's old wet nurse, were to receive the clothes on their backs and room and board for life. The strangest small bequest—of 200 lire—went to one of her husband's illegitimate children, Margherita da Carrara, born of Francesco's favorite paramour, Giustina Maconia, who was also the mother of his oldest natural son, the able condottiere Conte da Carrara.[39] Evidently Francesco had placed his own illegitimate daughter in his wife's household for care and upbringing after her mother's death. Thus, Fina provided generously for members of her household, granting her beloved *fanciulle* ten dowries totaling 8,000 lire and some property, 400 lire as entry gifts for two nuns, and minor bequests of 600 lire, clothing, and lifetime maintenance to her six servants.

Fina's largess also extended to the stewards (*gastaldi*) of her rural villages: she willed 400 lire each to Domenico, steward of Brugine, and Antonio, steward of Noventa, for the express purpose of providing dowries for their daughters. Fina also bequeathed 200 lire each to the villages of Noventa, Brugine, and Arzercavalli for restitution for damages from any debts that she might have left unpaid.

Continuing her program of gendered patronage, Fina provided generously for her own daughters. Her married daughters, Gigliola, duchess of Saxony, and Caterina, countess of Veglia, were each to receive income from property valued at 6,000 ducats. If the daughters bore children and thus continued her bloodline, the entire legacy was to go to Fina's grandchildren. But if either daughter died without living offspring only half was to go to that daughter's heirs and the other 3,000 ducats were to go to her son, Francesco Novello. In addition, the daughters were to receive a residence at San Urbano in case they were widowed and decided to return to live in Padua. Fina made a similar bequest of 6,000 ducats to her unmarried daughter, Lieta, and also left her a house with garden near the Oratory of San Michele.

To her brother Arcoano, Fina left her dwelling in the Buzzacarini complex in contrada San Urbano, then inhabited by her distant but prized cousin Boscarino di Folcarino Buzzacarini. The cousin was a valuable servant of her husband's regime; he had fought in 1373 in the border war against Venice, and in March, 1374, Francesco il Vecchio appointed him as his representative to welcome the new bishop of Padua, Raimondo Gaminberto, and escort him in procession to the Duomo.[40] All other property, which must have included thousands of *campi* of farmland, went to Fina's only son, Francesco Novello. While her husband was named executor of the estate, he received nothing.

Patron of Art

Fina's pointed generosity to the next generation was probably more a part of a strategy of rewarding her family, her friends, and the dynasty's supporters than any calculated affront to her husband. After all, for some years Fina had been involved in providing a fitting burial place for herself and Francesco il Vecchio in Padua's Baptistery. By the time Fina made her will in the autumn of 1378, this major project of artistic patronage was in its final stages of the completion.

Fina's selection of the Baptistery (fig. 1) as her mausoleum depended on several considerations. Though there was, in Christian architecture, a longstanding tradition of the use of baptisteries as burial sites, this adaptation reappeared in Italy only in the fourteenth century. The close connection of burial and resurrection and baptism and spiritual rebirth was not lost on Fina and her advisers in the creation of the Paduan baptistery.[41] There was the further model of the construction of doge Andrea Dandolo's tomb in the baptismal chapel of San Marco in the late 1350s. And, in about 1370, one of Francesco il Vecchio's most trusted and prestigious advisers, Bonifacio Lupi, marchese of Soragna, attempted to persuade the authorities to permit him to decorate the walls of Florence's Baptistery with mosaics in return for the right to build his tomb there. According to one source, the Florentine commune turned down Lupi's request because burials conflicted with the "reverenza del Battesimo." Rejected in Florence, Bonifacio Lupi appropriated the old Rossi burial chapel in the shallow south transepts of the Basilica of Sant'Antonio in Padua for his magnificent funerary chapel. Early in 1372 Lupi made a contract with the Venetian sculptor Andriolo de' Santi for the remodeling and architecture of a new chapel in this space, and work on the frescoes was already well advanced when Fina began to consider the construction of her own mausoleum.[42] By this time, the traditional burial church for both the Buzzacarini and Carrara families, the Dominican convent of Sant'Agostino, had limited space for major new tombs since the elaborate sarcophagi of Ubertino and Giacomo II in the apse already claimed the most prestigious area of the church. Since the two mendicant churches, which had assumed the character of a Pantheon of the local elite, were not available, Fina hit upon the bold plan of adapting the Baptistery for her tomb. In this she was aided by the new bishop of Padua, the Benedictine diplomat and churchman, Raimondo Gaminberto, whom her husband had handpicked for the post in 1374.[43] The adaptation was facilitated by the fact that the Baptistery was underutilized. Changes in canon law and parochial organization required that newborns were now to be baptized within eight days of birth, often in local churches by the parish priest. These new rules coupled with the decline of episcopal prestige meant that many baptisms took place outside the Duomo.[44] The original baptistery, dedicated in 1281, was undecorated and in a bad state of repair.

Kohl Fig. 1. Baptistery, Padua, exterior, rebuilt 1260 (photo: courtesy Judith Kohl)

To transform the Baptistery into a frescoed mausoleum, Fina made a number of interventions, closing a door and some windows on the south wall and perhaps raising the dome to make space for mural paintings.[45] To pay for this major undertaking, early in 1376 Fina, with her consort's permission, recalled the loan of 10,000 florins she had made to Florence five years earlier. In the midst of the War of the Eight Saints with the papacy, Florence's signoria pleaded for an extension, but at the prodding of the lord of Padua, Florence's representatives eventually repaid the loan, with interest, in November 1376.[46]

Fina's choice for this important commission fell on the Tuscan painter Giusto de' Menabuoi, who had arrived in Padua from Milan in 1369, perhaps to aid the aged Guariento and the young Altichiero with the frescoes in the new Carrara reception hall, known as the Sala Virorum Illustrium.[47] By late 1370 Giusto undertook decoration of the funeral chapel in the Eremitani for Tebaldo Cortelliero, the Carrara's regime diplomat who had died recently on a mission to Rome. Trained in civil law at the university, Cortelliero had started as a judge of communal courts but soon attracted the attention of the Carrara lord, who appointed him judge delegate in 1360 and ambassador to Venice in 1362. Entrusted with an embassy to the papal court of Urban V at Rome in the summer of 1370, Cortelliero died there on 20 August at the age of about forty-five, perhaps of the plague. Cortelliero's grief-stricken mother, the widowed Traversina Cortellerio née Curlo, constructed a chapel with frescoes depicting the figures of the Liberal Arts and the Virtues, which were probably part of a larger composition of the Triumph of Saint Augustine. The deceased was depicted in a votive painting to the right of the altar above a Latin inscription commemorating his life and premature death.[48] Significantly, Giusto's first patron in Padua was a noblewoman of the Carrara elite.

Three years later, Giusto received another commission for a funeral chapel in the Eremitani from a member of the Carrara circle, the German mercenary Heinrich Spisser, who had died in September 1373 as a result of wounds received while serving as constable in the cavalry in the Carrara army in the recent war with Venice. On his deathbed, Spisser had appointed two other mercenaries, a Florentine and a German, to oversee the construction and decoration of a tomb in the Eremitani that would be appropriate to his status and dignity. The executors hired Giusto for the frescoes of a *Madonna Enthroned with Saints*, and commissioned the Carrara court sculptor, Andriolo de' Santi, for the stone over Spisser's grave.[49] By 26 April 1375, Francesco il Vecchio had awarded Paduan citizenship to Giusto, who was living in contrada Salone, perhaps a hundred meters from the Duomo; by January 1376, he was residing near the Duomo in a house he later purchased from a member of the Capodivacca family. By then Giusto was probably already at work on the major artistic achievement of his career, the decoration of the Baptistery of Padua.[50] Over the next two years, Giusto adorned the Baptistery with one of the most remarkable fresco cycles of the Trecento (figs. 2–5).

The earliest attribution of this work to Giusto was made by Michele Savorarola in the middle of the quattrocento:

> Giusto de' Menabuoi painted the large chapel which the Paduans call their Baptistery, because in that sacred place on the appointed day the clergy of Padua perform baptisms and the children of the city are baptized there. The very pleasant appearance of the figures painted there is wrought with such great skill that those who enter find it difficult to leave. Moreover, scenes from the Old and New Testaments are depicted with the greatest accomplishment.[51]

But Fina's role in the commission was probably so well known at the time that it was noted in Paduan histories only in the late sixteenth century.

The Baptistery cum mausoleum where Fina was to be buried is a square building topped by a drum and surmounted by a cupola. The principle door on the west side led to the cloister of the cathedral canons, while the public entered from the Piazza del Duomo on the east. The eastern side also contained a small apsidal chapel, joined by a small space where liturgical vessels used in the daily mass were stored, thus serving as a sacristy. The drum and walls teem with scenes from Genesis, and the lives of Mary, Christ, and John the Baptist in a manner similar to the earlier mosaic program in the Baptistery of Florence. The cupola displays a hierarchical Paradise with a massive Pantocrator at the center. Below is the "Virgo orans" in a mandorla, an intercessory figure standard in early Christian funerary art, flanked by rows of individuated saints. The drum depicts scenes from Genesis, starting with the creation of the world, and moving to the story of Adam and Eve and their expulsion, of Noah and the flood, of Abraham and Isaac, of Jacob, and continuing with Joseph sold into slavery, a clear foreshadowing of the sacrifice of Christ. The south wall contains scenes from the life of Christ, the north from the life of John the Baptist. The west wall held Fina's tomb surrounded by scenes from the life of the Virgin, and the east wall scenes of the Crucifixion and Resurrection. The apsidal chapel, with its altarpiece depicting scenes from the life of John the Baptist, is decorated with scenes from the Apocalypse of Saint John. The whole is suffused with the themes of death, resurrection, and personal salvation.

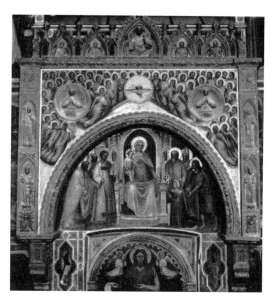

Kohl Fig. 2. Giusto de' Menabuoi and assistants, frescoes on the west wall of the Baptistery, Padua, 1376–78 (photo: courtesy Ministero per i Beni Culturali ed Ambientali, Soprintendenza Beni Artistici e Storici, Veneto)

Fina's precise intentions and role in this project can only be surmised from her will of 22 September 1378.[52] She ordered that her body be buried "in the Chapel of Saint John the Baptist which is today called the Baptistery," and there be "made an honorable tomb according to her station, taking into account the status of the aforesaid Lord, and of her magnificent son, Francesco [Novello] da Carrara, with attention and respect to the wishes of the said testatrix [*attentis et respectibus dicte testatricis*]." The Latin phrase implies Fina's desire for agency, directing the placement of her tomb over the main entrance (from the cloister) just below her donor portrait (fig. 2), where she is shown kneeling before the Virgin Mary, presented by John the Baptist, with attending saints. Thus, Fina's tomb was placed on the same wall with scenes from the life of the Virgin and Christ. The top register depicts the Presentation of Mary in the Temple, the Annunciation, and Visitation in three separate scenes. The elaborate donor portrait is flanked by scenes of the Massacre of the Innocents and Christ's Dispute with the Doctors, while the tomb itself was surrounded by adumbration of the Christ's death and passion: the Entrance into Jerusalem and the Last Supper. Her tomb canopy is adorned with female saints, perhaps to offset the male saints in the votive portrait. Thus, the placement of the tomb on the wall subtly celebrates the Virgin's role as Mother of God. The whole Marian context for the tomb emphasizes the role of bride and mother, and thus Fina's own status as consort and genetrix of the Carrara dynasty.

Though the author(s) of the Baptistery program cannot, of course, be known for certain, Claudio Bellinati has suggested that given the biblical and iconographic complexity

Kohl Fig. 3. Giusto de' Menabuoi and assistants, *Polyptych with Madonna Enthroned, Scenes from the Life of Saint John the Baptist and Saints*, 1376–78, Padua, Baptistery (photo: courtesy Ministero per i Beni Culturali ed ambientali, Soprintendenza Beni Artistici e Storici, Veneto)

of the ensemble, Petrarch was the *mens* (mastermind) of the theological frame of the Baptistery.[53] Perhaps Petrarch did have some role in the initial planning of the frescoes, but he died in July 1374 before Giusto started his work. The possibility, rather, that Fina had some role in the iconography of the Baptistery is suggested by another of her bequests. In this clause, she bequeathed "all her silver and all her clothing in her possession at the time of her death for decorating and adorning the chapel and its altar [*ad ornatum and pro ornamento ipsius Capelle et altaris in ea existentis*]." Since, as Anna Maria Spiazzi points out, the painting of the walls was no doubt far advanced when Fina made her will, her household belongings were probably sold shortly after her death to pay for these furnishings and the chapel's magnificent altarpiece in which Giusto again depicted scenes from the life of John the Baptist.[54]

The numerous Paduan and female saints depicted both in the Paradise in the dome and on the polyptych above the altar suggest a donor both interested in female sanctity and imbued with Paduan hagiology. Of 107 saints and biblical figures represented in the Paradise, twenty-six are female. On the Virgin's left are found a rare grouping of six biblical matriarchs (Anne, Elizabeth, Sarah, Rebecca, Rachel, and Leah), as well as holy virgins, the sisters of Lazarus (Martha and Mary), and virgin martyrs from the Early Church (Agnes, Barbara, Lucy, Ursula, and Catherine of Alexandria). In another part of heaven (on the Virgin's right) are found a number of local saints, including the patron saints of Padua (Prosdocimo, Justina, Daniel, and Anthony), as well as two early bishops (Massimo and Fidenzio), and local martyrs. Catherine King rightly stresses the privileging of chaste female saints and biblical matriarchs in Fina's dome, while Claudio Bellinati correctly underlines that Fina wanted an authentic "sanctilogium patavinum" above her tomb.[55]

The case for Fina's active role in the decoration is strengthened by the same mixture of local male intercessors (Prosdocimo, Daniel, and Anthony) in the votive portrait, with the female saints (Mary Magdalene, Catherine, Lucy, and Justina) sculpted on the pilasters of the canopy above her tomb. A strong Paduan orientation is also evident on the base of the polyptych narrating the life of John Baptist. The lowest register depicts twelve Paduan saints, the city's patrons (Anthony, Justina, Prosdocimo, and Daniel) early bishops (Massimo and Fidenzio), and more recent local *beati* (Anthony the Pilgrim, Compagno of Porciglia, Giordano Forzatè, Crescenzio da Camposampiero, Arnaldo, abbot of San Giustina, and Beatrice d'Este). Thus, the decoration of the altarpiece that was paid for from the sale of Fina's silver and clothing celebrated Padua's liturgical calendar. Virtually all the local saints in "the use of Padua," whose feast days were recognized in the municipal statutes, are depicted on the polyptych. Fina's role in conceiving the altarpiece is further confirmed by the coats of arms of the Carrara and the Buzzacarini families on its *predelle* (fig. 3).[56]

Fina's Baptistery was meant to convey some of the most dramatic moments of Christian history and the message of Christian salvation. Although as noted, baptism now often took place in parish churches, baptisms were still probably performed there on certain feast days. Catherine King states:

> The theme of salvation is partly narrative, but it is also demonstrated through typological links that show the way the events of the Old presaged those in the New Testament. Interwoven with this grand theme, the decoration also provides the appropriate accompaniment to the celebration throughout the liturgical year of the major feasts and fasts of the calendar.... [T]he decoration was designed to act as an appropriate backdrop to the blessing of the baptismal water for the whole diocese which took place here at Easter and Pentecost, when the greater litany of the saints, who had been so meticulously detailed on the dome above, was sung.[57]

Thus, the Baptistery functioned as mausoleum, with two priests appointed to say masses for Fina's soul and two nuns from her sister Anna's convent of San Benedetto deputed to read through the Psalter every year.[58] To these private liturgical acts were added the great public events of baptism on Easter Saturday and the Vigil of Pentecost.

In the Baptistery's frescoes Fina also found a means to commemorate herself, her family, and illustrious members of the Carrara circle. Since Giotto's famous donor portrait of Enrico Scrovegni, painted in the first decade of the century, votive portraits had been common in Paduan mural painting. In his new Sala Virorum Illustrium, which was constructed and frescoed a decade before Fina undertook the decoration of the Baptistery, Francesco il Vecchio celebrated the valor and exploits of ancient Roman heroes. His concern with the active life, military valor, and secular political leadership stands in stark contrast to his consort's more spiritual and religious concerns, represented on the walls of the Baptistery. The Paduan lord had his court painters, the aged Guariento and the younger Altichiero and Giusto depict the major deeds of the dead heroes of ancient Rome, defined and elaborated according to Petrarch's *De viris illustribus*.[59] As their reward Petrarch (and his amanuensis, Lombardo della Seta) earned their own immortalization in portraits on those same walls.

In decorating the nearby Baptistery with hidden portraits, Giusto de' Menabuoi, acting at his patron's behest, engaged in the newfound Paduan art of portraiture. As with Altichiero's commissions at the Santo, Giusto often painted the faces of Petrarch, Francesco il Vecchio, and perhaps Fina herself in several crowd scenes in the lives of Christ and John the Baptist. Though the Renaissance portrait was not fully developed in the fresco art of late Trecento Padua, Giusto had mastered the genre of the individual portrait, defined, in Margaret Plant's

Kohl Fig. 4. Giusto de' Menabuoi and assistants, *The Birth of Saint John the Baptist*, 1376–78. Padua, Baptistery (photo: courtesy Ministero per i Beni Culturali ed ambientali, Soprintendenza Beni Artistici e Storici, Veneto)

Kohl Fig. 5. Giusto de' Menabuoi and assistants, *The Birth of Saint John the Baptist*, detail of *Fina Buzzacarini and Her Three Daughters*, 1376–78, Padua, Baptistery (photo: courtesy Ministero per i Beni Culturali ed ambientali, Soprintendenza Beni

wry phrase, as "the art of painting the recognizable face."[60] In addition to a votive painting showing Fina kneeling before the Madonna Enthroned with Saints, Fina appears most conspicuously with her three daughters as onlookers at the birth of John the Baptist.[61]

Thus, Fina created in Padua an image of herself and her daughters as witnesses to one of the most intimate scenes in a woman's life, the lying-in after childbirth, attended only by other women (fig.4). The aged Elizabeth is comforted by a younger Virgin Mary, while another woman approaches with a golden pitcher and basin, followed by two women presenting a cooked chicken.[62] Below the bed, three women minister to the needs of the infant John the Baptist: one unwinds his swaddling clothes, a second fills his bath in a wooden tub, and a third holds the baby behind his head, while looking up at the Buzzacarini women. They, in turn, gaze with dignified elegance upon the scene, with the middle daughter, Caterina, extending her outstretched hand in an announcing or welcoming gesture.[63] Giusto has made Fina's portrait

unmistakable, depicting her prominent nose and clothing her in the same sumptuous beaded russet robe that she wears in the donor portrait. The daughters are equally naturalistic, with the older married ones wearing the headdresses of matrons, while Lieta, unmarried in her late teens, is depicted bareheaded and with the countenance of a young maiden. The whole composition displays a quiet celebration of motherhood and documents the refined elegance of life at Fina's miniature court (fig. 5).

Portraits of Fina Buzzacarini appear elsewhere in the Baptistery. According to Claudio Bellinati, Petrarch stands between Fina and Francesco il Vecchio in the depiction of Christ working miracles on the south wall and, according to Margaret Plant, she is an onlooker with her husband in the scene she identifies as Christ before Pilate. There are perhaps others members of the Carrara court portrayed in the crowds at the Crucifixion and the much restored Christ before the Sanhedrin.[64] Thus were immortalized for the first time in hidden portraits the leaders, political and cultural, of Carrara Padua. This vogue for hidden portraiture of the Carrara elite culminated a few years later in the representation of the Council of King Ramiro in the Chapel of San Giacomo in the Basilica of Sant'Antonio, where Altichiero depicted King Louis of Hungary as Ramiro, and his patrons Bonifacio and Caterina Lupi, Petrarch and Lombardo della Seta, and the Carrara lords among the king's councillors. Thus, Bonifacio Lupi joined Fina Buzzacarini in providing (in Margaret Plant's felicitous phrase) "patronage within patronage."[65] Here Giotto's Paduan followers used their powerful naturalistic art to represent (and immortalize) famous contemporaries as onlookers in scenes from Christian history and hagiography.

A decade after Giusto completed his last commission in Padua, the Carrara court tutor Pier Paolo Vergerio wrote a series of letters to his protégé, then a student of literature in Florence, Ludovico Ungaro Buzzacarini. After recommending history as the proper study for the statesman, Vergerio turned to the subject of the formation of the orator. Repeating the humanist nostrum that Cicero should be the model for prose as Virgil should be for poetry, Vergerio disagreed with Seneca's view that an author should strive to create a new style out of many models. Rather the orator should choose a single writer and imitate the best model, by implication Cicero. To clinch his argument he drew a contemporary analogy: "So one should do what the painters of our own age do, who though they may look with attention at famous paintings of other artists, yet follow the models of Giotto alone."[66] In making this judgment, Vergerio was ratifying the artistic Ciceronianism he had found in the frescoes of Giusto and Altichiero. He was reminding the nephew of the two greatest patrons of the city, Francesco da Carrara and his consort Fina, creator of the remodeled Baptistery, who was himself named for Louis of Hungary, immortalized as King Ramiro, that Giotto's narrative power had been instrumental in creating the possibility of a new genre at Padua, the Renaissance portrait.

Notes

1. Giacomo's policy of reconciliation following the bloody coup d'etat is recorded in Guglielmo Cortusi, *Chronica de noviatibus Padue et Lombardie,* ed. Beniamino Pagnin, Rerum Italicarum Scriptores, new ed., vol. 12, pt. 5 (Bologna: N. Zanichelli, 1941), 112.

2. The basic monograph on Giusto's frescoes in the Baptistery was Sergio Bettini, *Giusto de' Menabuoi and l'arte del Trecento* (Padua: Le Tre Venezie, 1944), updated in his *Le pitture di Giusto de' Menabuoi nel Battistero del Duomo di Padova* (Padua: Neri Pozza, 1960). The extensive restoration of the frescoes, completed in the 1980s, led to the publication of the major collaborative volume, *Giusto de' Menabuoi nel Battistero di Padova,* ed. Anna Maria Spiazzi (Trieste: LINT, 1989), which contains the important studies of Claudio Bellinati, "Iconografia e teologia negli affreschi del Battistero," 41–82, and Anna Maria Spiazzi, "Giusto a Padova, la decorazione del Battistero," 83–127, as well as Benjamin G. Kohl, "Giusto de' Menabuoi e il mecenatismo artistico in Padova," 13–30. Catherine King provides sketches of Fina's "matronage" in "Medieval and Renaissance Matrons, Italian-Style," *Zeitschrift für Kunstgeschichte* 55 (1992): 376–80, and idem, "Women as Patrons: Nuns, Widows and Rulers," in *Siena, Florence, and Padua: Art, Society, and Religion, 1280–1400,* ed. D. Norman, 2 vols. (New Haven, Conn.: Yale University Press, 1995), 2:249–54. Cordelia Warr, "Painting in Late Fourteenth-Century Padua: The Patronage of Fina Buzzacarini," *Renaissance Studies* 10 (1996): 139–55, explores aspects of Fina's artistic patronage.

3. On the Buzzacarini in communal Padua, see John Kenneth Hyde, *Padua in the Age of Dante* (Manchester: Manchester University Press, 1966), 150–53, 278. A. Mussato, *De traditione Patavii ad Canem Grandem,* Rerum Italicarum Scriptores 10 (Milan, 1726), cols. 756–58. Giovanni da Non's depiction of the Buzzacarini is to be found in Padua, Biblioteca del Seminario, MS 11, *De generatione aliquorum civium urbis Padue,* fol. 49v.

4. Vittorio Lazzarini, "Storia di un trattato tra Venezia, Firenze e i Carraresi (1337–1399)," *Nuovo Archivio Veneto* 18 (1899): 245–46, 279.

5. In a census of 1320 Dusio was residing with his sons Pataro, Fulcone, and Salione near San Tommaso: see the appendix to Antonio da Tempo, *Delle rime vulgari,* ed. G. Grion (Bologna, 1867), 271. In an act of 9 December 1339, Dusio was recorded as living in contrada San Urbano: Achivio di Stato, Padua (hereafter ASP), Archivio Diplomatico, busta 64, perg. 7078. For the grant of tithes, see Padua, Archivio della curia vescovile, Libri feudorum, reg. 5, fol. 217r, 1 September 1340.

6. On Dusio's role in the treaty of extradition, see Gioacchino Beda, "Un trattato di estradizione fra Padova e Venezia," in *In memoria di Oddone Ravenna* (Padua, 1904), 33–34.

7. On Dusio's role in the renewal of the treaty of 1337, see Lazzarini, "Storia di un trattato," 259–60.

8. See *Libri feudorum,* reg. 5, fol. 221v, June 2, 1347.

9. On Guariento's frescoes in Ubertino's palace, see the standard monograph of Francesca Flores D'Arcais, *Guariento* (Venice: Alfieri, 1965).

10. On the development of the Carrara Reggia, see the fundamental study of Cesira Gasparotto, "La Reggia dei Da Carrara, il palazzo di Ubertino e le nuove stanze dell'Accademia Patavina," *Atti e memorie dell'Accademia Patavina di scienze, lettere ed arti, classe di scienze morali, lettere ed arti* 79 (1966–67): 1:71–116; Giovanni Lorenzoni's synthesis, "L'intervento dei Carraresi, la Reggia e il Castello," in *Padova, Case e Palazzi,* ed. Lionello Puppi and Fulvio Zuliani (Vicenza: Neri Pozza, 1977), 29–44, and Diane Norman, "Splendid Models and Examples from the Past: Carrara Patronage of Art," in *Siena, Florence and Padua,* 1:155–75. Of continuing value in documenting the rooms and palaces of the complex is Andrea Gloria, *Documenti inediti intorno al Petrarca con alcuni cenni della casa di lui in Arquà e della Reggia dei Da Carrara* (Padua, 1878), 12–13, 35–37.

11. On the assassination of Giacomo II and its aftermath, see Andrea, Galeazzo, and B. Gatari, *Cronaca carrarese,* ed. Antonio Medin and Guido Tolomei, Rerum Italicarum Scriptores, new ed., 17 (Bologna, 1902–33), 29, and Cortusi, *Chronica,* 128–29.

12. Gatari, *Cronaca carrarese,* 30–31, and Cortusi, *Chronica,* 138, 140–41.

13. See Vittorio Lazzarini, "Il principio della dominazione carrarese a Feltre e a Belluno," *Archivio storico di Belluno, Feltre e Cadore* 1 (1929): 1–4.

14. ASP, AN, reg. 256, fols. 268r–70r, 31 Jan. 1361. A Paduan *campo* equals .954 acres or .38 hectares.

15. Libri feudorum, reg. 7A, fols. 19r–20r, 1 November 1361.

16. Riccardo Predelli, ed., *I libri commemoriali della Repubblica di Venezia, Regesti,* Monumenti della R. Deputazione veneta di storia patria, ser. 1, vol. 3 (Venice, 1883), 23, no. 115.

17. Padua, Biblioteca Civica, MS B.P. 928, *Documenti per servire la storia dei Carraresi,* compiled by G. B. Papafava, vol. 5, fols. 114–15, 16 December 1369.

18. Padua, Accademia Patavina, Archivio Papafava, Codex 35, perg. 3, 8 February 1371, and Pietro Ceoldo, *Albero della famiglia Papafava* (Venice, 1801), 59–60.

19. The date of the original loan is given in record of repayment in ASP, AN, reg. 34, fol. 431r–v, 10 November 1376.

20. ASP, AN, reg. 257, fol. 266r–v, 4 May 1368, fols. 271v–72r, 4 December 1368.

21. ASP, AN, reg. 258, fol. 164v, 8 June 1370.

22. ASP, AN, reg. 258, fols. 165r, 175r, and 176v, 4 July, 25 December 1370, and 26 January 1371.

23. Andrea Gloria, *Monumenti della Università di Padova, 1318–1405,* 2 vols. (Padua, 1888; reprint, Bologna: Forni, 1975), 2:86, no. 1314, 30 January 1371, and *Documenti per servire la storia de Carraresi,* ed. Papafava, vol. 4, fols. 352–53, 1 March 1371.

24. ASP, AN, reg. 258, fols. 177r–78r, 184r–85r, 200r, 11 May and 23 June 1371, and 1 March 1372.

25. See Sergio Bertelli, "L'universo cortigiano," in *Le Corti italiane del rinascimento,* ed. Sergio Bertelli and others (Milan: A. Mondadori, 1985), 8–9. On gendered spaces, see the chapter by Molly Bourne in this volume.

26. See Gloria, *Documenti inediti,* 35.

27. On Francesco il Vecchio's bastards, see Benjamin G. Kohl, *Padua Under the Carrara, 1318-1405* (Baltimore: Johns Hopkins University Press, 1998), 296–300.

28. See Gloria, *Documenti inediti,* 36, 1370, "camera dominarum," Gloria, *Monumenti,* 2:81, no. 1301, 1 March 1370, "ante portam palacii habit. dominarum ipsius domini," and ibid., 2:85, no. 1315, 30 January 1371, "Padue in palaciis habit. dominarum de Carraria." For a detailed discussion of the Carrara household and Fina's place in it, see Kohl, *Padua under the Carrara,* 136–37, 145–47, 152–54.

29. ASP, AN, reg. 256, fols. 61r–62r, 1357.

30. Gloria, *Monumenti,* 2:129, no. 1442, 15 April 1378.

31. ASP, AN, reg. 35, fols. 90r–92r, 15 August 1378, where Francesco il Vecchio, acting on his power to abrogate communal statutes granted him at his election in 1350, exempted Fina from a statute of 1226 prohibiting clergy and ecclesiastical corporations from inheriting property, and one of 1366 prohibiting persons who did not pay communal taxes from inheriting property in Padua and its district. The statutes are to be found in Padua, Biblioteca Civica, MS B.P. 1237, *Codex statutorum carrariensis,* fols. 111v, 324v–25v.

32. The original Latin text is in ASP, AN, reg. 35, fols. 95r–98v, published in a partial edition in Benjamin G. Kohl, "Giusto de' Menabuoi e il mecenatismo artistico in Padova," 24–26, doc. 8, and an English translation in *Major Problems in the History of the Italian Renaissance,* ed. Benjamin G. Kohl and Alison Andrews Smith (Lexington, Mass.: D. C. Heath, 1995), 337–42.

33. See M. Cattini and M. Romani, "Le corti parallele: Per una tipologia delle corti padane dal XIII al XVI secolo," in *La corte e lo spazio: Ferrara estense,* ed. Giuseppe Papagno and Amedeo Quondam, 2 vols. (Rome: Bulzoni, 1982), 1:57.

34. On Argentino Arsendi's career, see A. Abbondanza's entry in *DBI*, and for Ubertino's wife, see Gloria, *Monumenti*, 2:414, no. 2230, May 8, 1403, where Bartolomea Ubaldini is named "uxor Ubertini de Arsendis."

35. See ASP, AN, reg. 36, fol. 245r, 12 October 1384, for record of Caterina Capodivacca as married, and Gloria, *Monumenti*, 2:138, no. 1470, 30 July 1379, for payment of Fina's dowry of 1,000 lire to Giovanni Dondi dall'Orologio.

36. On the Dotti and the Carraresi in general, see my entry on "Dotti, Francesco," in *DBI* 41: 538–40; for the gift of the slave, ASP, AN, reg. 31, 283v, 5 November 1375, and for Dotti as possible residual heir in Francesco Dotti's first will, ASP, AN, reg. 100, fols. 109r–11r, 12 October 1381.

37. By 1384, a Maria Monfumo, daughter of the deceased Giovanni, had married Parisio Todeschini of Treviso; see Gloria, *Monumenti*, 2:177, no. 1586.

38. On 11 November 1381, Caterina di Bartolomeo Zabarella sold a small house in contrada San Urbano to Arcoano Buzzacarini, see ASP, AN, reg. 35, fols. 298r–99r.

39. See G. B. Verci, *Storia della Marca trevigiana e veronese*, 20 vols. (Venice, 1786), 10:137.

40. See Gatari, *Cronaca carrarese*, 107, and F. S. Dondi dall'Orologio, *Dissertazione ottava sopra l'istoria ecclesiastica padovana* (Padua, 1815), 241, doc. 74.

41. See Richard Krautheimer's classic essay, "Introduction to an Iconography of Medieval Architecture (1941)," reprinted in his *Studies in Early Christian, Medieval, and Renaissance Art* (New York: New York University Press, 1969), 115–50, esp. 133–39.

42. On Lupi's attempts to place his tomb in Florence's Baptistery and eventual choice of the Santo in Padua, see Sarah Blake McHam, "Donatello's Tomb of Pope John XXIII," in *Life and Death in Fifteenth-Century Florence*, ed. M. Tetel et al. (Durham, N.C.: Duke University Press, 1989), 163–64, and Maria Chiara Billanovich, "Un amico del Petrarca: Bonifacio Lupi e le sue opere di carità," *Studi petrarcheschi*, new ser., 6 (1989): 259–78, esp. 261–63.

43. On Bishop Raimondo, see Laura Gaffuri and Donato Gallo, "Signoria ed episcopato a Padova nel Trecento," in *Vescovi e diocesi in Italia dal XIV alla metà del XVI secolo*, ed. G. De Sandre Gasparini et al., 2 vols. (Rome: Herder, 1990), 2:947–51.

44. See Enrico Cattaneo, "Il battistero in Italia dopo il Mille," in *Miscellanea Gilles Gerard Meersseman*, 2 vols. (Padua: Antenore, 1970), 1:191–94, and Paolo Sambin, *L'ordinamento parrocchiale di Padova nel Medioevo* (Padua: CEDAM, 1941), 71–74, which cites a Paduan synodal statute of 1339 requiring that infants be baptized within eight days.

45. For various views on the nature and extent of architectural change under Fina's direction, see Lionelli Puppi, "Il battistero," in *Padova, basiliche e chiese*, 2 vols. (Vicenza: Neri Pozza, 1975), 1:105, and Giovanni Lorenzoni, "Il battistero," in *Giusto de' Menabuoi nel battistero di Padova*, 30–39.

46. The letters of negotiation are in ASF, Lettere missivi della prima cancellaria, reg. 16, fol. 61r, 11 January 1376, fols. 61v–62r, 13 January 1376, and reg. 17, fol. 42r, 3 July 1376, with final payment from Florence to Fina, made with her husband's permission, recorded in ASP, AN reg. 34, fol. 431r–v, 10 November 1376.

47. On artistic patronage in Carrara Padua, see, in addition to the synthesis of Diane Norman, "Splendid Models and Examples from the Past: Carrara Patronage of Art," in *Siena, Florence and Padua*, 1:155–75, Margaret Plant's major study, "Patronage in the Circle of the Carrara Family: Padua, 1337–1405," in *Patronage, Art, and Society in Renaissance Italy*, ed. F. W. Kent with Patricia Simon and J. C. Eade (Oxford: Clarendon Press, 1987), 177–99.

48. On the decoration of this chapel, largely destroyed by Allied bombardment in 1944, see Bettini, *Giusto de' Menabuoi e l'arte del Trecento*, 58–60, 112–21, and Spiazzi, "Giusto a Padova," 92–94.

49. See Vittorio Lazzarini, "Un'altra cappella di Giusto pittore agli Eremitani di Padova," *Archivio veneto*, ser. 5, 8 (1930): 78–81.

50. On Giusto's career in Padua, see Claudio Bellinati, "Giusto de' Menabuoi: Scheda biografica," in *La cappella del beato Luca e Giusto de' Menabuoi nella Basilica di Sant'Antonio* (Padua: Edizioni Messaggero, 1987), 171–77, and Benjamin G. Kohl, "Giusto de' Menabuoi," 13–15, with documents on 25–27.

51. Michele Savonarola, *Libellus de magnificis ornamentis regie civitatis Padue*, ed. Arnoldo Segarizzi, Rerum Italicarum Scriptores, 24, pt. 15 (Città di Castello: E, Lapi, 1902), 44. Fina's patronage was noted for the first time in Bernardino Scardeone, *De urbis Patavii antiquitate* (Basel, 1560), col. 363.

52. See text in Kohl, "Giusto de' Menabuoi," 24–26, and English translation in Kohl and Smith, *Major Problems in the History of the Italian Renaissance*, 337–42. Catherine King analyzes some key provisions in "Medieval and Renaissance Matrons," 376–78.

53. See Bellinati, "Iconografia e teologia negli affreschi del Battistero," 49, 58–59, which emphasizes Petrarch's interest in Holy Scripture and hidden portrait in the scene depicting Christ's miracles.

54. See Spiazzi, "Giusto a Padova," 94.

55. See King, "Women as Patrons," 253, 254, and Bellinati, "Iconographia e teologia," 49.

56. Descriptions of the altarpiece are provided in Bettini, *Giusto de' Menabuoi*, 134–35, and Bellinati, "Iconografia and teologia," 79–81. Padua's liturgical calendar in the trecento was defined in the *Codex statutorum carrariensis* (cited in n. 31), fols. 101v–105r, which I have edited and discussed in an unpublished paper, "Competing Saints in Late Medieval Padua."

57. King, "Women as Patrons," 253–54.

58. See text of will in Kohl, "Giusto de' Menabuoi," 25.

59. In addition to the classic essay on Francesco il Vecchio's Hall of Illustrious Men (Theodor E. Mommsen, "Petrarch and the Decoration of the Sala virorum illustrium [1952]," in *Medieval and Renaissance Studies*, ed. E. F. Rice [Ithaca, N.Y.: Cornell University Press, 1959], 130–74), see the studies of Maria Monica Donato, "Gli eroi romani tra storia ed exemplum, I primi cicli umanistici di Uomini Famosi," in *Memoria dell'antico nell'arte italiana*, ed. Salvatore Settis (Turin: G. Einaudi, 1985), 2:103–8 and 114–24; and Diane Norman, "Splendid Models and Examples from the Past: Carrara Patronage of Art," in *Siena, Florence, and Padua,* 1:155–75.

60. M. Plant, "Portraits and Politics in Late Trecento Padua: Altichiero's Frescoes in the San Felice Chapel, San Antonio," *Art Bulletin* 63 (1981): 408.

61. This identification was made first in 1989 by Anna Maria Spiazza, "Giusto a Padova," 106, in her description of "la raffinata eleganza delle vesti e dei copricapi di Fina e delle figlie"; and again in 1995 in "Women as Patrons," 253, Catherine King calls them by name. In his brief discussion of the panel in "Iconografia and teologia," 58, Claudio Bellinati does not mention the hidden portraits of the Carrara women.

62. See Jacqueline Marie Musacchio, "Pregnancy and Poultry in Renaissance Italy," *Source* 16, no. 2 (Winter 1997): 3–9.

63. On the speaking gesture of the "announcing hand" in trecento art, see Moshe Barasch, *Giotto and the Language of Gesture* (Cambridge: Cambridge University Press, 1987), 22–27.

64. See Bellinati, "Iconografia e teologia," 58–59, 67; Spiazzi, "Giusto a Padova," 110; Plant, "Patronage in the Circle of the Carrara Family," 190.

65. Plant, "Patronage in the Circle of the Carrara Family," 189.

66. Michael Baxandall, *Giotto and the Orators* (Oxford: Oxford University Press, 1971), 43–44: "Faciendum est igitur quod estatis nostre pictores, qui, cum ceterorum claras imagines sedulo spectent, solius tamen Ioti exemplaria sequuntur."

Controlling Women or Women Controlled? Suggestions for Gender Roles and Visual Culture in the Italian Renaissance Palace

Roger J. Crum

"Men do two important things in this life: the first is to procreate, the second is to build."[1] So claimed Giovanni Rucellai, a fifteenth-century Florentine, father of seven children, and notable patron of art and architecture. Perhaps Rucellai's wife, Iacopa, shared her husband's opinion concerning *bambini*, but what might she and other Renaissance women have thought about buildings, paintings, statues, decorative objects, and other examples of visual culture? To go beyond the artistic patronage of Isabella d'Este was the objective of the conference session for which an earlier version of this paper was written. In the initial stages of composing that paper, my interest was to think of other, lesser-known Renaissance women whose patronage scholars had either not identified or extensively discussed. But in thinking about women's patronage, particularly in relation to the Italian Renaissance palace, I began to ask fewer questions about specific individuals than about women as a group and about the dynamics and gender politics of artistic patronage generally.[2] Eventually my research came to center on three principal questions: first, what kind of documentation might constitute proof of artistic patronage in the Renaissance? Second, how is the study of women's patronage influenced and possibly limited by an adherence to the traditional patriarchal models for the Renaissance patron, which do not encourage an awareness of areas of control that women may have exercised over the patronage process? And third, did Renaissance women participate in artistic patronage with some degree of independence, or did male members of the family always control such actions? In suggesting answers to these questions my aim is to insert an element of positive uncertainty and to locate a new and more expansive place for women in conventional discussions of artistic patronage in the Italian Renaissance. I also consider ways in which this volume's discussion of secular women patrons relates to the evolution of feminist art history.

The Problem of Documentation

As for my first question, I think many would agree that when a document of commission surfaces, the matter of patronage is satisfactorily solved. Linked by a document, one patron, one artist, and one work of art constitute an indivisible whole, a trinity of sorts, that comfortably defines the parameters of patronage.[3] Since the commissioning person in the Renaissance was often male, we have a certain amount of information concerning the history of male patronage. But what does this history really tell us about patronage? Are the documents telling the whole story? With regard to men, women, and the Renaissance palace, I propose initially to explore these questions by modern analogy.

Let us imagine that five hundred years from now a historian discovers my father's checkbook. Therein he or she would find entries for the house, furniture, carpet, drapes, appliances, china, paintings, and other goods and services, all entered in my father's hand. If we suppose that such documentation is sufficient and self-evident, it might seem an incredible find; with just one document, the portrait of a turn-of-the-century patron could theoretically emerge. But for me, writing at the present time, that piece of documentation is far too limited, since I am closer to the historical moment and to the circumstances and extent of my father's "patronage." The truth is that my mother chose the house and everything in it, and her will is supreme—if not exclusive—when renovations are made, a chair recovered, or a painting selected for purchase or removal. My father is far from being a twenty-first-century patron; he just pays the bills. Patronage for my parents is a process, not a solitary act; it involves them differently, and my mother is involved to an extent that is equal to and usually greater than that of my father.

This modern situation points directly to the limitations of documents and to the problems of relying upon a single source for historical reconstruction. As is the case with my parents' home and my father's accounts, the task of reconstructing a balanced, nuanced image of Renaissance patronage may not be achieved by asking who commissioned, collected, or signed for an object; we also need to ask who was in charge of its preservation, daily use, and perhaps its display. In large measure these and other activities went undocumented because in Renaissance society, as in twenty-first century America, they often existed outside the bounds of financial accountability or legal strictures. In reference to the Renaissance economy, Lauro Martines observes that Florentines "clearly relied very much upon the work of women, not only domestic work but also work that the record easily conceals from view and is often presumed to have been carried out by men."[4] Similarly, women at home performed roles with respect to material possessions that were traditionally shadowed or concealed behind the financial acts and documented patronage of men.[5] In order to examine these roles, we must consult other sorts of contemporary documents and literary sources.

Before addressing these sources we might consider the importance to this discussion of a relatively unknown Florentine fresco of the late quattrocento in the oratory of San Martino del Vescovo (fig. 1). Painted in a style close to that of Ghirlandaio, this fresco is one of a series commissioned by the confraternity of the Buonuomini di San Martino to commemorate their charitable activities.[6] The work represents members of the Buonuomini taking inventory of domestic possessions, perhaps in connection with a legacy given to the confraternity; as three men examine a storage chest, a fourth sits to the side compiling a list of its contents. While ostensibly these men act on the agency of their confraternity, in actuality it would seem that they dispatch their duty on the guidance of the woman who stands between them. Joined by two other women in a doorway, who assist in designating this space a "women's environment," this woman turns toward the compiler with her hand and finger extended, as if to direct his notations.[7] In a culture in which few women other than the Virgin Mary, female saints, or biblical and historical women occupied the center position in pictorial imagery, contemporaries could not have failed to notice the prominence accorded the women in this fresco.[8] The woman in the center is shown dictating to a male scribe, a demonstration of feminine power over information that was probably rare in the male-dominated written culture of the Renaissance. Clearly an important message of this fresco is that the palace interior was the province of women and that the goods contained therein were entrusted to their care. This pictorial definition of a woman's environment and locus of control over material goods is supported in contemporary written sources.

In the dialogue that constitutes Alberti's *Della famiglia*, one of the speakers tells of giving his young bride a tour of his palace, acquainting her with his various goods and treasures and where each thing has its place:

Crum Fig. 1. Florentine, late fifteenth century, *The Assembly of a Domestic Inventory*, Florence, San Martino del Vescovo (photo: Scala/Art Resource, N.Y.)

> After my wife had been settled in my house a few days, and after her first pangs of longing for her mother and family had begun to fade, I took her by the hand and showed her around the whole house. I explained that the loft was the place for grain and that the stores of wine and wood were kept in the cellar. I showed her where things needed for the table were kept, and so on, through the whole house. At the end there were no household goods of which my wife had not learned both the place and the purpose. Then we returned to my room, and, having locked the door, I showed her my treasures, silver, tapestry, garments, jewels, and where each thing had its place.... I wanted none of my precious things to be hidden from my wife. I opened to her all my household treasures, unfolded them, and showed them to her.[9]

Was this information imparted only for safe housekeeping or was the Renaissance bride to be more extensively involved with these and other possessions in her husband's house?[10]

Leaving aside for the moment the more costly goods, it seems that certain Renaissance women were encouraged to make use of religious statuettes and paintings for the proper education of themselves and their children. Such practice had its origin in rituals associated with materials that the bride brought with her at the time of marriage from the house of her parents. Christiane Klapisch-Zuber focuses attention on certain small dolls or figurines, usually representing the Christ child, that were given to Florentine women by their mothers as part of their trousseaux. Klapisch-Zuber discusses how brides were probably encouraged to attend to these "holy dolls" in a role-playing ritual of expectation tied to fertility and mother-hood.[11] As expectation led to realization, this ritual seems to have become a point of departure for the proper education of children. In this regard, it is instructive to turn to the writings of Fra Giovanni Dominici who, in the early fifteenth century, addressed his *Regola del governo di cura familiare* to Bartolomea degli Alberti, the wife of the Florentine Antonio degli Alberti. On the education of children, Dominici writes:

> The first regulation is to have pictures of saintly children or young virgins in the home, in which your child, still in swaddling clothes, may take delight and thereby may be gladdened by acts and signs pleasing to childhood. And what I say of pictures applies also to statues. It is well to have the Virgin Mary with the Child in arms, with a little bird or apple in His hand. There should be a good representation of Jesus nursing, sleeping in His Mother's lap or standing courteously before Her while they look at each other. So let the child see himself mirrored in the Holy Baptist clothed in camel's skin, a little child who enters the desert, plays with the birds, sucks the honeyed flowers and sleeps on the ground. It will not be amiss if he should see Jesus and the Baptist, Jesus and the boy Evangelist pictured together; the slaughtered Innocents, so that he may learn the fear of weapons and of armed men. Thus it is desirable to bring up little girls in the contemplation of the eleven thousand Virgins as they discourse, pray and suffer. I should like them to see Agnes with her little fat lamb, Cecilia crowned with roses, Elizabeth with roses in her cloak, Catherine and her wheel with other such representations as may give them with their milk love of virginity, a longing for Christ, a hatred of sin; make them despise vanity, avoid bad company and begin through the consideration of the saints the contemplation of the Supreme Saint of Saints. For this reason you should know that representations of the angels and saints are permitted and intended for the instruction of the unlearned.[12]

Dominici places Bartolomea, and presumably other women, at the center of the religious and social education of children, where pointed use of works of art for instructional purposes is to be made.[13] The matter of artistic patronage, taken in its traditional sense of the male commissioning act, would seem to hold little concern or consequence for him. The author takes for granted the commissioning and ownership of religious images and chooses instead to place his emphasis on the importance of these to the proper rearing of children. In this context, men, money, and the commissioning initiative recede as the Renaissance woman advances as mother, educator, and sustained manipulator of images.

Together with the ritualized use of "holy dolls," this icon-centered education is part of a feminine continuum that passes from one family to another and across generations from mother, to child, to grandchildren, female and male alike. It could thus be argued that the education of Renaissance boys (and eventual patrons) began not with an independent and documented act but with a more open-ended process that was identified primarily, if not exclusively, with women. Only later would they act alone, or in concert with their fathers, brothers, or other male associates, in the more visible and traditionally sanctioned form of artistic patronage. For the education of Renaissance girls, this patronage process also meant their participation in giving, receiving, and using objects such as "holy dolls" that provided familial, moral, and religious models of a completely female origin and perpetuation. In contrast to the world of record keeping and documentation—the traditional sign of the Renaissance patron to which boys would eventually accede—Klapisch-Zuber notes that participation in this undocumented practice of doll ritual constituted a means for the establishment of a common feminine identity.[14] It would seem that for a moment in childhood these two different male and female points of contact with the visual arts sprang from a common source. Yet despite this convergence of boys' and girls' education through works of art and the agency of the Renaissance mother, Giovanni Dominici clearly believes that even in childhood the sexes are to be educated differently. Centuries before the advent of Barbie and G. I. Joe, sex-specific instruction and social acculturation was embodied in representations of the contemplative femininity of eleven thousand virgins who "discourse, pray, and suffer," or the rugged masculinity of John the Baptist who enters the desert, plays actively with birds, sucks nourishment from flowers, and sleeps on the ground.

It would appear that women's involvement with works of art extended beyond play acting with "holy dolls" or educating their children by matching hagiographic knowledge and iconographical nuances to a desired virtue and behavior. Women were also involved with decisions concerning the advisability of exposing children to objects of special material value. Dominici continues his advice to women:

> Refrain from having gold and silver decorations so as not to make [children] idolaters rather than Christians; since, seeing that more candles are lighted, more heads uncovered and more reverences made before the gilded figures and those adorned with precious stones than before those blackened with age, they may only understand that honor is being given to the gold and jewels, and not to the figures or, more properly, to the personages represented by the same.[15]

If such costly and exquisite things were to be guarded from the eyes of children, what are we to make of the custodial role that Alberti's speaker, Giannozzo, assigns to his wife in *Della famiglia*? We know from written accounts and many Renaissance paintings that goods such as those mentioned in the dialogue did not remain permanently under lock and key. Rather, they were brought out and displayed on such ceremonial occasions as weddings, banquets, and diplomatic visits.[16] In reference to these cases, we might ask whether women were somehow involved in the act of ceremonial display. As in the case of my mother's role at home, the necessary evidence for this involvement in the fuller patronage process is hard to come by and may never surface in satisfactory abundance.[17] Given this situation, we should not conclude that women played no role in the orchestration of such display. While it is wise to base discussions of Renaissance patronage on the documentary record, we must also question the limitations and gender-specific orientation of the available documents.

The Problem of the Patriarchal Model for Patronage

This brings me to my second question concerning women and the traditional patriarchal model for Renaissance patronage. Women in the Renaissance may often have initiated the patronage process, but their financial position and society's dictates for their roles may have prohibited them from drafting and signing relevant documentation. Much as Linda Nochlin exposes the limitations of traditional art historical questioning in producing an understanding of women artists, scholars of Renaissance patronage will have to adjust their frames of reference to become more sensitive to the historical position of women and to their socially circumscribed relationship to the "traditional" patronage act.[18] Records of commission certainly do not record the entire patronage process, which may have involved women to a considerable, though undocumented, degree in activities such as the stewardship and display of objects. As historians, we must always ask questions of what we do not know as well as of what we do; we must also at times be content with and enriched by the questions themselves in the absence of documentary evidence and iron-clad answers. The act of questioning is undeniably a valuable product of historical research. It may even serve to preserve (or at least suggest) the multidimensionality of a matter that might otherwise be ahistorically restricted by an adherence to traditional sources of information and overly narrow standards of scholarly verification.

Despite the clear value of researching women as patrons in the Renaissance, such an investigation may unwittingly elevate the male-centric act of patronage and actually undervalue the involvement of certain women with works of art. In other words, if men dominated the commissioning act, and women entered the field only rarely, we are likely to shape a discourse on women's roles in artistic patronage within a set of masculine instead of feminine parameters. Certainly we use terminology with masculine overtones, since the Latin roots for patron and patronage are *pater* and *paternitas*. In 1972, Ann Gabhart and Elizabeth Broun's exhibition, "Old Mistresses: Women Artists of the Past," alluded to the linguistic assumption that art is created by men. As these scholars comment, "The term 'Old Master' has no meaningful equivalent; when cast in its feminine form, 'Old Mistresses,' the connotation is altogether different."[19] A similar shift in meaning seems to be produced if we translate the discussion from Renaissance patrons to Renaissance matrons.[20]

But it may be that such a translation is not as incongruous for the Renaissance as it now seems from a purely linguistic—and modern—standpoint. Alberti gives unequivocal testimony in *Della famiglia* of a kind of Renaissance 'matronage' in the management of works of art and valuable possessions that persisted beyond the preliminary and usually male acts of commissioning and paying for these things. Since Alberti clearly composes his dialogue as a primer on how to run a family and household, the matter of the familial and wider societal significance of such matronage assumes greater interest.

Women and the "Darker Side" of Artistic Patronage

My third question delves deeper into the matrix of matronage, gender politics, and the position of women in Italian Renaissance society. All three intersect in the text of Alberti's dialogue and in the context of the Renaissance palace; but what remains unclear is the motivation or mechanism that drove their relationship. Did Renaissance women always generate their own, unmitigated interest in the management and use of works of art, or was their interest at times a reflection of their husbands' concern for the material well-being of family and estate?[21]

At this point I would like to cast a glance at the "darker" and perhaps more coercive side of women's involvement in the patronage process for the Renaissance domicile. To this end I would address women's spectatorship or management of works of art and domestic goods in relation to iconographies that prescribed or proscribed specific gender roles and attitudes, the importance of valuable objects to the composition of family wealth and reputation, and the unstable, often transient position of women in the Renaissance household.

According to classic reception theory in literature, a text is never complete until it is received, or concretized, by a reader who brings a certain "horizon of expectation" to bear on the work.[22] The particular form that reception takes results in a negotiation between the reader's expectations and those of the author that are encoded in the text. The same is true for the visual arts, and a central facet of patronage for the Renaissance palace was that a work that was commissioned and encoded by an artist (typically working on the commission of a male patron) was eventually received and concretized by women through their particular "horizons of expectation." Among others, Klapisch-Zuber demonstrates that women in the Italian Renaissance were acculturated to see their lives almost exclusively through a patriarchal lens; a great part of their identity was shaped first in relation to their fathers' and eventually their husbands' needs and by the expectations that they should be humble, obedient, chaste, and dutiful daughters and spouses.[23] In view of these expectations, we can recognize a strong propensity among patrons for the palace interior to invest in works of art with iconographic themes that encode prescribed behavior for women. For example, abundant references in inventories and hundreds of surviving examples attest to the popularity of domestic devotional images of the Madonna of Humility.[24] Doubtless such works were intended to function as models of appropriate feminine deportment as much as they served purposes of domestic devotion; located in bedrooms and, more rarely, private chapels, these visual primers and devotional objects were certainly the frequent focus of women's gaze and contemplation.

Other works of art located in the Renaissance bedchamber, such as *cassone* chests and *spalliere* panels, seem also to have been directed in part toward the conditioning of feminine behavior. Often ornamented with scenes depicting the triumphs and tragedies of virtuous women of the Bible, ancient history and myth, or medieval legend, these works carried strong messages of appropriate feminine behavior and societal responsibility.[25] Having been raised in their father's house to regard works of art as instructional aids (or so Alberti's dialogue would suggest), women entered their marriages with a "horizon of expectation" that prepared them to continue their education as spouses through the agency of humble Madonnas and historiated *cassoni* and *spalliere* panels. Since these pieces of furniture and art were normally commissioned by the husband in the course of outfitting the wedding chamber, there is little ambiguity as to which party held the power to encode and manipulate works of art with gender-guiding messages.[26]

As for references to how works of art might serve to proscribe women's behavior, there is a revealing example in Alberti's *Della famiglia*. Once again Giannozzo is the speaker, and the topic of conversation is women and how to curb an excessive use of make-up. Giannozzo's strategy is to direct his wife's attention to a valuable silver statue:

> Thus I spoke to my wife. To convince her still more fully of the danger, as well as of the shame, in a woman's covering her face with the powders and poisons which the silly creatures call make-up, see…what a nice lesson I gave her. There was a saint in the room, a very lovely statue of silver, whose head and hands alone were of purest ivory. It was set, polished and shining, in the center of the altar, as usual. "My dear wife," I said to her, "suppose you besmirched the face of this image in the morning with chalk and calcium and other ointments. It might well gain in color and whiteness. In the course of the day the wind would carry dust to it and make it dirty, but in the evening you would wash it, and then, the next day, cover it again with ointments, and then wash it again. Tell me, after many days of this, if you wanted to sell it, all polished and painted, how much money do you think you would get for it? More than if you had never begun painting it?"[27]

Giannozzo's wife quickly comprehends the thrust of her husband's analogy and responds "correctly" that in fact one would receive much less for the sale of such a "besmirched" statue. Giannozzo's analogy is of interest for at least two reasons. On the one hand, he clearly makes use of a work of art to proscribe behavior of which he disapproves in his wife. But on the other hand, Giannozzo counts on his story taking effect because his wife understands the material value of the statue and the possibilities for its lucrative resale. With such knowledge lies another aspect of the woman's proper stewardship of valuable objects that husbands could employ to control their wives.

From the text of Alberti's dialogue, it is clear that women were engaged with works of art and precious possessions on a custodial level that far exceeded mere spectatorship. Additionally they were entrusted to appreciate and guard their value. This fact is far from inconsequential, for in managing such objects women were placed at, or at least near, the material goods that constituted an important concentration of the family's financial well-being. Richard Goldthwaite has observed that over the course of the fifteenth century, Renaissance Italians increasingly invested a greater share of their money in filling their homes with costly material possessions. In explanation for this developing "empire of things," Goldthwaite regards demand for material goods and art as a phenomenon that resulted from a substantial amount of surplus money in the Italian economy.[28] Material possessions in abundance were at once a by-product of a strong economy and a visual indicator of a family's participation and share in it. Nonetheless, Goldthwaite is quick to emphasize that the accumulation of these possessions was more than a matter of crass conspicuous consumption, taking his cue from Alberti's *Della famiglia*. As noted above, Alberti discusses the importance of household possessions, which as a group he refers to as *"masserizia."* This term, as Goldthwaite observes, was originally used in reference to money stored or hoarded away, but by the fifteenth century it had come to signify objects, most especially household furnishings. According to Goldthwaite,

> *masserizia* is a form of wealth that is to be preserved and is therefore central to household management, as if the household possessions of a family were the material core of its identity and existence, the foundation of the reputation of the family; it consists not of money but of those material goods that assure the solidarity of affection and the bonds of blood, honor, and virtue. The word came to signify wealth with two specific qualities: first, it is constituted by material possessions; and secondly, these possessions have a strong moral quality about them. Household goods, in short, were a form of capital that represented family solidarity and honor.[29]

This was precisely the manner in which the Florentine Palla Strozzi regarded his domestic possessions. In fact, his attachment to his "empire of things" was so strong that he indicated in his will that his *masserizia* was to be preserved in his family and not sold after his death.[30]

Of course Florentines were also concerned with the proper management of their *masserizia* during their lifetimes, and this brings us back to *Della famiglia* and to the role that Alberti, through his speaker Giannozzo, assigns to women. In the following passage Giannozzo underscores that his wife should learn not only the proper storage of possessions but also their wider significance to the long-term well being of the family:

> When my wife had seen and understood the place of everything in the house, I said to her, "My dear wife, those things are to be as useful and precious to you as to me. The loss of them would injure and grieve you, therefore should you guard them no less zealously than I do. You have seen our treasures now, and thanks be to God they are such that we ought to be contented with them. If we know how to preserve them, these things will serve you and me and our children. It is up to you, therefore, my dear wife, to keep no less careful watch over them than I.... This property, this family, and the children to be born to us will belong to us both, to you as much as to me, to me as much as to you. It behooves us, therefore, not to think how much each of us had brought into our marriage, but how we can best maintain all that belongs to both of us. I shall try to obtain outside what you need inside the house; you must see that none of it is wasted."[31]

Through the voice of Giannozzo, Alberti is at pains to emphasize the equality of men and women, at least as far as the ownership and management of domestic objects are concerned. References to "treasures" that belong to "us both" and admonitions "not to think of how much each" had contributed to the union but how best to "maintain all that belongs to both of us" seem oddly projected into the world of liberated modernity; as these words suggest an equality of union soured by the specter of waste and familial ruin, our first inclination is to locate them somewhere between a masculinist Renaissance marriage and a betrothal by escape-clause that characterizes the contemporary prenuptial contract. I would suggest, however, that Giannozzo in no way articulates a position of marital liberation before its time but one which cleverly makes use of women's stewardship of valuable objects to strengthen male dominance and the survival of the family.

At the root of Giannozzo's concern, if we consider him typical of his age, may have been a sensitivity to the severe financial and familial problems that could arise if women, once widowed, left the household of their spouse and children. This was a serious problem in the Renaissance, as Klapisch-Zuber discusses in an essay devoted to the subject of "cruel mothers"—a contemporary designation that referred to those who severed ties with their family of marriage upon the death of their spouse.[32] Because Renaissance men tended to marry late and to take young wives, they often died and left a spouse who was still of marriageable age. Legally the widow's family of birth could force her to abandon her husband's household, reclaiming her dowry in anticipation of making a second marital union. In this market of political marriage alliances and lucrative dowries, women were clearly caught in a difficult position between the demands and desires of two families and between the ties of affection and those of obligation. All too often women abandoned (or were forced to abandon) the children of their first marriage. What resulted for Renaissance families was a compound tragedy, not least on account of the financial problems that resulted from the removal of the dowry. According to Klapisch-Zuber, contemporary sources indicate that the "'cruel mother' was the woman who left her young children, but it was above all the mother who 'left with her dowry.'"

The alternative model was that of the "good mother," a widow who, as Giovanni Rucellai opined in fifteenth-century Florence, refused to remarry "so as not to abandon her children … in order not to lead them to ruin," and was both "a father and a mother for her children."[33] Being both father and mother to her children meant providing an element of stability and security, which, as Klapisch-Zuber observes for Renaissance Florentines, meant the "transmission of material goods, without which there was no family."[34] Among these goods, we may assume, were precisely those objects that a new bride was encouraged to value and manage, to use in the education of her children, and to behold on the walls and furniture of her new home.

Since the palace was the symbol as well as the repository of a family's material wealth, women's participation in artistic patronage and their stewardship of valuable goods placed them at the center of an important source of a family's economic strength. This behavior may have been not only a means of controlling relationships between husbands and wives and between women and children; it could also have been a matter of sound economic strategy. In view of the threat of a ruinous "cruel mother," I suggest that Renaissance husbands may have involved women in the patronage process, the stewardship of material goods, and the education of children through works of art to involve them directly in the family's material wealth and to engender lineage-sustaining loyalty to the marital family. This message would have been reinforced by the themes of humility, chastity, obedience, and dutiful motherhood that characterize the greater part of Renaissance *cassoni*, *spalliere*, and domestic devotional works that these women beheld on a daily basis. And, of course, all of these goods were introduced into and helped to shape a palace environment that was itself highly gendered in terms of space, function, and communication.[35]

Of course occasions other than the death of a spouse could arise in which proper management of works of art provided an opportunity for women to distinguish themselves as "good mothers." In his *vita* of Pontormo, Vasari tells of Giovan Battista della Palla's intent to purchase the paintings of Pier Francesco Borgherini's bedroom for the king of France. Having retired to Lucca as a result of the siege of Florence (1530), Borgherini was not at home to protect his interests and his paintings. These were protected by his wife, Margherita, who sternly refused the envoy in the following manner:

> So you make bold, Giovan Battista, you vile slop-dealer, you little two-penny pedlar, to strip the ornaments from the chambers of noblemen and despoil our city of her richest and most honored treasures, as you have done and are always doing, in order to embellish with them the countries of foreigners, our enemies.... This bed, which you would seize for your own private interest and for greed of gain,... this is the bed of my nuptials, in honor of which my husband's father made all these magnificent and regal decorations, which I revere in memory of him and from love for my husband, and mean to defend with my very blood and with life itself. Out of this house...Giovan Battista, and go to those who sent you with orders that these things should not be removed from their places, for I am not the woman to suffer a single thing to be moved from here.[36]

In her refusal to release the contents of her nuptial chamber, at a time when her husband is away and Florence is under siege from foreign forces, Margherita is for Vasari "a courageous woman" who does her share in protecting both her home and her homeland, the patriarchy of her husband and his father as well as the *patria* of besieged Florence itself. It was by virtue of her actions, Vasari concludes, "that those gems are still preserved in that house."[37] In general Renaissance writers paid less attention to "gems" of interior decoration than to the monumental palaces in which they were housed. For these writers the construction of a palace and other works of architecture served simultaneously to establish the magnificence of a patron (implicitly male) and to enhance or preserve the magnificence of the city. It appears that just as Giovanni Rucellai had claimed, in Renaissance Italy, men's principal achievements in this life were to procreate and to build. But of course the former is biologically impossible without women, and the latter—interpreted broadly to mean both the construction and maintenance of a home and family—was socially unthinkable, even ruinous, without them. From an anecdote in Vasari, embedded deep within a narrative that is primarily celebratory of male achievement, we can appreciate that Margherita Borgherini, like other Renaissance women, played a part in architectural magnificence. Her achievement, like that of other Renaissance women, seems to have been less in the patronage act than in the broader, usually undocumented but exceptionally important, patronage process.

Women, Renaissance Patronage, and the Feminist Critique of Art History

In the foregoing essay, I ask questions about Renaissance women and artistic patronage more than I have inquired of these women as patrons of art in the traditional sense. On a related methodological note, the matter might be raised as to how the discussion of women patrons in this volume takes a position in relation to the evolution and present state of feminist research in the history of art.

Ann Gabhart and Elizabeth Broun's exhibition *Old Mistresses* of 1972 was a pioneering moment in the development of a feminist approach to art history. It was followed four years later by *Women Artists: 1550–1950*, by Ann Sutherland Harris and Linda Nochlin.[38] These two shows, their catalogues, and a growing body of scholarship on women artists, did much to redress the exclusion of women from the traditional art historical canon. Yet however important this scholarship was, it shied away from what Griselda Pollock calls a necessary confrontation with mainstream (and masculinist) art historical ideologies and practices.[39] By practicing an additive method of bringing women into the existing disciplinary structures of art history, this scholarship did little to question the nature of those structures. Eventually, in the late 1970s and early 1980s, the feminist critique of art history moved strongly toward a deconstruction of the principles and practices of the discipline itself. In 1981 Griselda Pollock and Rozsika Parker argued that what contemporary scholarship needed was "not a history of women artists, but an analysis of the relations between women, art, and ideology."[40] Not surprisingly, this call for a new direction, which has been ably answered by Pollock, Parker, and others, corresponds to a similar revolution in mainstream historical studies. "As feminist historians have undertaken to produce new knowledge," observes Joan Scott, "they have necessarily called into question the adequacy not only of the substance of existing history, but also of its conceptual foundations and epistemological premises."[41]

As I have outlined in brief, the feminist approach to art history has seen a development in two generations.[42] Might we project a similar development in the study of Renaissance women and artistic patronage? Just as the first generation of feminist art historians began by assessing women artists together with their male peers, the present collection of essays stands to initiate much the same process with regard to women patrons. But as we look to the future of scholarship in this area, we should think critically and imaginatively about invitations to go "Beyond Isabella." Initially, I think such invitations ought to be interpreted narrowly to encourage a search for other women patrons whose activities would inform the established history of Italian art and architectural patronage. But we must not limit our studies to this "additive" perspective; we must also reexamine Renaissance patronage itself, question the dominance of a patriarchal model, and ask whether patronage was a solitary act or a process that involved women to a considerable, though often undocumented, degree. In soliciting contributions to the present volume, Sheryl Reiss and David Wilkins stressed that their concern was more with "the many directions in which this topic might be developed than in discussions of single examples." In the end, the editors' invitation has indeed been extended for us to think "Beyond Isabella" to a second generation of patronage studies.

Notes

1. "Due cose principali sono quelle che gl'uomini fanno in questo mondo: La prima lo 'ngienerare: La seconda l'edifichare." This passage is cited from Rucellai's book, the *Zibaldone*, cited by F. W. Kent, "The Making of a Renaissance Patron of the Arts," in F. W. Kent and others, *Giovanni Rucellai ed il suo Zibaldone*, II: *A Florentine Patrician and his Palace* (London: Warburg Institute, 1981), 13.

2. For an excellent discussion of how various aspects of the creation and consumption of art were gendered in late medieval Italy, see Diana Norman, "Women as Patrons: Nuns, Widows and Rulers," in *Siena, Florence and Padua: Art, Society and Religion, 1280–1400*, ed. Diana Norman (New Haven, Conn.: Yale University Press, 1995), 2:243–66.

3. This is the underlying assumption of many documentary-based patronage studies and general compilations of documents. See, for example, the several volumes in the series Sources and Documents in the History of Art, ed. Horst W. Janson (New York: Prentice-Hall); David S. Chambers, *Patrons and Artists in the Italian Renaissance* (Columbia: University of South Carolina Press, 1971).

4. Lauro Martines, "A Way of Looking at Women in Renaissance Florence," *The Journal of Medieval and Renaissance Studies* 4 (1974): 17. For the financial position of women in the Renaissance, see Thomas Kuehn, "*Cum consensu mundualdi*: Legal Guardianship of Women in Quattrocento Florence," *Viator* 13 (1982): 309–33; Elaine G. Rosenthal, "The Position of Women in Renaissance Florence: Neither Autonomy or Subjection," in *Florence and Italy, Renaissance Studies in Honor of Nicolai Rubinstein*, ed. Peter Denley and Caroline Elam (London: Committee for Medieval Studies, Westfield College, 1988), 369–81; Anthony Molho, *Marriage Alliance in Late Medieval Florence* (Cambridge: Harvard University Press, 1994).

5. Judith Brown supports the methodological approach of the present essay. See Judith C. Brown, "A Woman's Place Was in the Home: Women's Work in Renaissance Tuscany," in *Rewriting the Renaissance: The Discourses of Sexual Difference in Early Modern Europe*, ed. Margaret W. Ferguson, Maureen Quilligan, and N. J. Vickers (Chicago: University of Chicago Press, 1986), 206–24, esp. 208: "Although [women's] work was economically significant both to their households and to the economy as a whole, its value was reflected only indirectly in the income earned by the males they helped. Their contribution to the productivity of their households is impossible to measure because it left few traces in the historical record, but this is not to say that it had no value."

6. Adriano Agnati, ed., *Guida d'Italia: Firenze e Provincia*, 7th ed. (Milan: Touring Club Italiano, 1993): 195–96. For the Buonuomini di San Martino, see Dale Kent, "The Buonomini di San Martino: Charity for 'the glory of God, the honor of the city, and the commemoration of myself,'" in *Cosimo "il Vecchio" de' Medici, 1389–1464: Essays in Commemoration of the 600th Anniversary of Cosimo de' Medici's Birth*, ed. Francis Ames-Lewis (Oxford: Clarendon Press, 1992), 49–67.

7. On the idea of gendered, female spaces, see Benjamin Kohl's chapter in this volume.

8. An important exception, where women are prominently represented at or near the center of pictorial narrative, occurs in Ghirlandaio's Tornabuoni-Tornaquinci frescoes in the church of Santa Maria Novella, Florence. See Patricia Simons, "Patronage in the Tornaquinci Chapel, Santa Maria Novella, Florence," in *Patronage, Art, and Society in Renaissance Italy*, ed. F. W. Kent, Patricia Simons, and J. C. Eade (Oxford: Clarendon Press, 1987), 221–50.

9. Leon Battista Alberti, *The Family in Renaissance Florence*, ed. and trans. Renée Neu Watkins (Columbia: University of South Carolina Press, 1969): 208–9. For discussion of Alberti's dialogue, architecture, and questions of gendered space that go beyond the scope of this article, see Mark Wigley, "Untitled: The Housing of Gender," in *Sexuality and Space*, ed. Beatriz Colomina (Princeton: Princeton Architectural Press, 1992), 327–89. For domestic responsibilities (similar to those assigned by Alberti to women generally) assumed by Margherita, the wife of Francesco di Marco Datini, see Iris Origo, *The Merchant of Prato* (Harmondsworth, Middlesex: Penguin, 1963), 172–80.

10. In this essay I concentrate on women and the question of their stewardship of valuable objects and works of art. The next logical step would be to approach the question of gendered spaces, specifically those identified with women, in the Renaissance palace. Alberti, in his discussion of the country house, recommends linked but distinctly separate rooms for husband and wife, and some reflection of this is found in Florentine palaces of the fifteenth century. See Leon Battista Alberti, *On the Art of Building in Ten Books*, trans. J. Rykwert, N. Leach, and R. Tavernor (Cambridge, Mass.: MIT Press, 1994), bk. 5, chap. 17, p.149. For gendered space in the Medici Palace, see Wolfger A. Bülst, "Uso e trasformazione del Palazzo Mediceo fino ai Riccardi," in *Il Palazzo Medici Riccardi di Firenze*, ed. Giovanni Cherubini and Giovanni Fanelli (Florence: Giunti, 1990), 98–129, esp. 114. For a more elaborate discussion of women's spaces in the Roman Baroque palace, see Patricia Waddy, *Seventeenth-Century Roman Palaces: Use and the Art of the Plan* (Cambridge, Mass.: MIT Press, 1990), 25–30.

11. Christiane Klapisch-Zuber, "Holy Dolls: Play and Piety in Florence in the Quattrocento," in *Women, Family, and Ritual in Renaissance Italy*, trans. L. G. Cochrane (Chicago: University of Chicago Press, 1985), 310–29.

12. Giovanni Dominici, *Regola del governo di cura familiare*, parte quarta: *On the Education of Children*, trans. A. B. Coté (Washington, D.C.: Catholic University of America, 1927), 34. It is important to bear in mind that Giovanni Dominici's writing about women, as with other works from the Renaissance, may at times be more prescriptive than descriptive of actual situations and activities of women. This valuable point is made by Joan Kelly, "Did Women Have a Renaissance?" in *Becoming Visible: Women in European History*, ed. Renate Bridenthal and Claudia Koonz (Boston: Houghton Mifflin, 1977), 137–54.

13. Dominici was not alone among Renaissance writers in stressing that women, in addition to being the caretakers of the material welfare of the family, were important as guardians of religious and moral values. See Brown, "A Woman's Place," 215–16.

14. Christiane Klapisch-Zuber, "Images without Memory: Women's Identity and Family Consciousness in Renaissance Florence," in *Imaging the Self in Renaissance Italy* (Boston: Isabella Stewart Gardner Museum, 1992), 37–43.

15. Giovanni Dominici, *Regola*, 35.

16. For the display of valuable plates and other items in Renaissance society, see Peter Thornton, *The Italian Renaissance Interior 1400–1600* (New York: Abrams, 1991).

17. For exceptions, see the papers by McIver and Reiss in this volume.

18. Linda Nochlin, "Why Are There No Great Women Artists?" in *Women in Sexist Society*, ed. Vivian Gornick and Barbara Moran (New York: Basic Books, 1971), 480–510; reprinted as Linda Nochlin, "Why Have There Been No Great Women Artists?" in *Women, Art, and Power and Other Essays* (New York: Harper and Row, 1988), 145–78. Influenced in part by Nochlin's work, Joan Kelly similarly examines historical circumstances and institutional constraints of the period under discussion and asks the important question, "Did women have a Renaissance?" See Joan Kelly, *Women, History & Theory: The Essays of Joan Kelly* (Chicago: University of Chicago Press, 1984), esp. 19–50.

19. As cited in Griselda Pollock, *Vision and Difference: Femininity, Feminism, and Histories of Art* (London: Routledge, 1988), 21.

20. For an article that employs a similar shift in terminology, see Carolyn Valone, "Roman Matrons as Patrons: Various Views of the Cloister Wall," in *The Crannied Wall: Women, Religion, and the Arts in Early Modern Europe*, ed. Craig A. Monson (Ann Arbor: University of Michigan Press, 1992), 49–72.

21. As the other essays in this volume demonstrate, there is now an emerging body of evidence that strongly supports the former position, that is, we must acknowledge the practice of autonomous patronage by secular women of the Renaissance.

22. See Terry Eagleton, *Literary Theory, An Introduction*, 2nd ed. (Minneapolis: University of Minnesota Press, 1996), 47–78.

23. See esp. Klapisch-Zuber, *Women, Family, and Ritual*, passim.

24. See the extensive discussion of these inventories and their contents in John Kent Lydecker, "The Domestic Setting of the Arts in Renaissance Florence" (Ph.D. diss., Johns Hopkins University, 1987).

25. For these works, see Annie B. Barriault, *Spalliera Paintings of Renaissance Tuscany, Fables of Poets for Patrician Homes* (University Park: Pennsylvania State University Press, 1994). For *cassone* painting, now see Cristelle L. Baskins, *Cassone Painting, Humanism, and Gender in Early Modern Italy* (Cambridge: Cambridge University Press, 1998). For the Renaissance bedchamber in general, see Lydecker, "Domestic Setting," 165–83.

26. For Renaissance males commissioning bedroom suites, see Richard Goldthwaite, *Wealth and the Demand for Art in Italy* (Baltimore: Johns Hopkins University Press, 1993), 224–43, esp. 228.

27. Alberti, *The Family*, 214.

28. Goldthwaite, *Wealth*, passim; and Richard Goldthwaite, "The Empire of Things: Consumer Demand in Renaissance Italy," in *Patronage, Art, and Society in Renaissance Italy*, ed. F. W. Kent, Patricia Simons, and J. C. Eade (Oxford: Clarendon Press, 1987), 153–75.

29. Goldthwaite, *Wealth*, 210–11.

30. Goldthwaite, *Wealth*, 211.

31. Alberti, *The Family*, 210–11.

32. Christiane Klapisch-Zuber, "The 'Cruel Mother': Maternity, Widowhood, and Dowry in Florence in the Fourteenth and Fifteenth Centuries," in *Women, Family, and Ritual*, 117–31. For a more far-reaching discussion of the impact of women on the domestic economy of Renaissance Italy, see C. Freccero, "Economy, Woman, and Renaissance Discourse," in *Refiguring Woman: Perspectives on Gender and the Italian Renaissance*, ed. M. Migiel and J. Schiesari (Ithaca: Cornell University Press, 1991), 192–208. The problems associated with women, Florentine families, and dowries receive a much fuller treatment by Anthony Molho in his *Marriage Alliance*. For Renaissance attitudes toward women as "corruptible" and therefore needing to be "controlled," a matter highly relevant to the present essay, see esp. 140 ff.

33. Klapisch-Zuber, "The 'Cruel' Mother," 128.

34. Klapisch-Zuber, "The 'Cruel' Mother," 128.

35. See Wigley, "Untitled: The Housing of Gender."

36. Vasari-Milanesi 6: 262–63. My translation is taken from Vasari, *Lives of the Most Eminent Painters, Sculptors, and Architects*, trans. Gaston Du C. de Vere (New York: Abrams, 1979), 2:1523–24.

37. Vasari-Milanesi 6: 262–63; my translation from *Lives*, trans. de Vere, 2:1523–24. For Pontormo's Borgherini panels, see Peter Francis Lynch, "Patriarchy and Narrative: The Borgherini Chamber Decorations" (Ph.D. dissertation, Yale University, 1992).

38. Ann Sutherland Harris and Linda Nochlin, *Women Artists 1550–1950*, exh. cat. (Los Angeles: Los Angeles County Museum of Art, 1976).

39. Pollock, *Vision and Difference*.

40. Rozsika Parker and Griselda Pollock, *Old Mistresses: Women, Art and Ideology* (New York: Routledge and Kegan Paul, 1981), xix.

41. Joan W. Scott, "Women's History," in *New Perspectives on Historical Writing*, ed. Peter Burke (Cambridge: Polity, 1991), 60.

42. For a thorough discussion of these two generations, complete with an extensive bibliography, see Thalia Gouma-Peterson and Patricia Mathews, "The Feminist Critique of Art History," *Art Bulletin* 69 (1987): 326–57.

The Women Patrons of Neri di Bicci

Rosi Prieto Gilday

Neri di Bicci's *Ricordanze* can be considered a microcosmic model of artistic patron-age in fifteenth-century Florence.[1] This record of his clients' commissions for paint-ings between 1453 and 1475 reflects a cross section of professions, classes, and economic levels in Florentine society. His patrons came from virtually all walks of life, from members of the Signoria to artisans such as bakers, cobblers, and tailors. In many cases the text mentions the cost of each commission, the subject matter, the material specifications, and often the destination of the finished product. It also reports a variety of Neri's personal transactions, including his rental of property, the induction of assistants into his workshop, and the purchase of clothing for his children. The document is unusual not only because it is voluminous, but also because it records the activities of a number of female patrons.

Neri lists twenty-four commissions from women. These patrons can be categorized into two groups: religious and secular. Fourteen of these requests were from nuns, whose patronage is outside the scope of this paper.[2] The remaining ten orders were from lay women who can be further classified: five were widows, one was married, and four are listed without marital status. Most, but not all, of these women sponsored paintings jointly with a *mundualdus*—a court-appointed male guardian who helped a woman conduct legal transac-tions.[3]

This paper analyzes the commissions of Neri's ten secular female patrons to eluci-date the patronage practices of fifteenth-century Florentine lay women. The work requests are examined in terms of the women's marital status, social class, and spending patterns, which are then compared with various aspects of Neri's commissions from secular men.

Neri's commissions from secular women are listed in chronological order below and are abbreviated for clarity. Extant information regarding these commissions from sources other than the *Ricordanze* are included in each citation.

1. Bianca degli Spini

On 28 March 1455, a group of executors commissioned an altarpiece on behalf of the late Bianca degli Spini. They requested from Neri a painting depicting the Assumption of the Virgin with the twelve apostles (fig. 1).[4] The work was to measure approximately six *braccia* tall by five long;[5] it was also to have a classicizing frame, and three scenes from the life of the Virgin in the *predella*. Perhaps the executors at some point requested changes in the commis-sion, as the painting has an old-fashioned Gothic frame and angels in the *predella*. Bianca's altarpiece, which cost 480 lire (96 florins)[6] and was to be paid for in installments, is found today at the National Gallery of Canada in Ottawa. It was originally ordered for the Spini family chapel at Santa Trinita, which, according to Neri, Bianca founded.

Gilday Fig. 1. Neri di Bicci, *Assumption of the Virgin,*
1456, Ottawa, National Gallery of Canada (photo:
National Gallery of Canada, Ottawa)

Bianca's altarpiece, which Neri placed in the chapel on 28 August 1456, was perhaps the last item necessary to finish the decoration of the chapel. Sometime before mid-1453, Neri had decorated the chapel with frescoes of the life of Saint John Gualbert. Although it is unclear whether this chapel was dedicated to this saint, his importance at Santa Trinita is well known. Saint John Gualbert, a native Florentine, was founder of the Vallombrosan order, the same order as the church.[7] Some of his relics are also housed at the church, as is the crucifix that supposedly spoke to him upon his forgiveness of his brother's assassin,[8] and two other frescoes by Neri depicting the saint's life. The *Ricordanze* only alludes to this part of the commission, which was probably listed in a previous volume of this document.[9] The only fresco to survive from this commission is that of the Annunciation at the entrance of the Spini chapel.[10]

The Spini family were members of the chivalric class. In 1293 they and other noble families were excluded from holding political offices; however, between the fourteenth and sixteenth centuries many members of the Spini became prominent in Florentine politics.[11] Their family palace, which is the oldest surviving family residence in Florence and which faces Santa Trinita, is said to have been built in the thirteenth century by the knight Geri degli Spini.[12]

2. Caterina Bagnesi

Caterina, widow of Cristofano Bagnesi, and her *mundualdus*, Ormannozzo Deti, commissioned a large Annunciation on 1 September 1455 (fig. 2).[13] It was to have a classicizing frame in gold leaf measuring four *braccia* tall by three and one-half *braccia* wide, with a *predella* depicting three unspecified scenes and the family coat of arms. The cost was set at 25 florins and it was to be delivered on 20 December 1455 to the church of San Romeo in Florence. A painted curtain and a dossal ordered at the same time cost an additional two florins.

Gilday Fig. 2. Neri di Bicci, *Annunciation,* 1455, Florence,
Santa Maria Novella (photo: Alinari/Art Resource, N.Y.)

Caterina's *Annunciation* is today in the north aisle of Santa Maria Novella.[14] Unfortunately only the main panel of this commission is known to survive; the original frame and the *predella*, curtain, and dossal are apparently lost. The same is true of the three following altarpieces discussed here. The original frames of these paintings probably resembled the surviving frame on a *Nativity* by Neri's father, Bicci di Lorenzo, now at the church of San Giovannino dei Cavalieri in Florence.[15] The loss of these additions limits our understanding of this and other commissions not only in terms of iconography, but also in terms of ritual practice and altar decoration. The custom of commissioning these furnishings as part of a total complex was not restricted to Tuscany; it also seems to have been prevalent in other parts of Italy. A Venetian example is found in Giacomo Dolfin's will of 1505, in which he endowed a chapel in the church of San Francesco della Vigna.[16] It has been suggested that chapel curtains and dossals usually depicted religious scenes that related to the themes of the altarpiece or to the altar's or chapel's titular saint.[17] In this entry, Neri failed to describe Caterina's curtain and dossal, making any analysis of subject matter impossible.[18]

Originally Caterina's altarpiece stood in the Bagnesi chapel in San Remigio, which was then called San Romeo.[19] Dedicated to the Virgin Annunciate, the Bagnesi chapel is the first on the right as one enters the church. In the seventeenth century, Neri's panel was replaced with another of the same subject by Francesco Morosini.[20] This second painting was removed in the nineteenth century and is now missing.[21] What remains is a wooden reliquary and a plaque stating that the chapel was founded by Caterina and enlarged and redecorated in 1629 by descendants of the Bagnesi.[22]

The Bagnesi were important patrician patrons of San Romeo. According to the eighteenth-century historian Giuseppe Richa, this powerful and wealthy family began their patronage here in 1265.[23] In the *Ricordanze* of Senator Giuliano Bagnesi, an entry for the same year states that it was Rinieri de Bagno who assigned the new rector. The apparently exclusive patronage of the church by the Bagnesi lasted approximately a century; by the quattrocento sponsorship was split between the Pepi, Bagnesi, and Alberti families, whose coats of arms can be seen on the church walls.[24]

3. Andrea di Barberino

On 27 January 1457, Andrea, wife of Barberino the tailor, requested a painted curtain depicting Tobias and the archangel Raphael.[25] The curtain, which cost one florin, is now lost; it had a decorative border, a golden crown, and measured approximately two *braccia* long by one and one-half *braccia* wide. This object might have been used in the home or, more likely, to cover an altarpiece in a church.[26] The richness of this furnishing commissioned by a working-class patron suggests it was meant for an ecclesiastical setting.

A few words should be said here regarding hangings that covered altarpieces during the Renaissance. These objects protected paintings from dust, moisture, and light; they also covered them on weekdays and during Lent (although a curtain as ornate as Andrea's probably would have been inappropriate during the period of penance). Apparently, curtains such as Andrea's formed part of a mechanism similar to modern roller blinds: the curtain was wrapped around a wooden cylinder and was raised or lowered by a system of strings connected to the cylinder.[27] These curtains can be related to the cloth that hung between the columns in Solomon's temple that separated the sanctuary where the Ark of the Covenant was kept from the rest of the building. In New Testament writing this veil came to signify the darkness that obscured the human mind before Christ's Passion. Before His sacrifice, the meaning of holy scripture was concealed; however, just as the veil of Jerusalem's temple was torn down at the moment of the death of Jesus, so were the altar hangings removed on Holy Saturday to disclose God's Word. As the words *"Gloria in excelsis"* were heard during the mass of Holy Saturday, the veils and curtains that covered altars were removed so that the truth of the Law exemplified in Christ's sacrifice could be seen (this tradition was common until the Second Vatican Council).[28] I suggest that the unveiling (*svelare*) of altarpieces at Easter or during mass might have been interpreted in the Renaissance as revealing (*rivelare*) the Word of God to the populace.[29]

4. Lionarda del Pescaia

On 19 August 1463 Lionarda del Pescaia commissioned an altarpiece depicting the Trinity in a throne of seraphim with John the Baptist and Saint Lawrence on the left, and Saints Francis and Leonard on the right (fig. 3).[30] Its background was to be in fine gold and the cost was to be 128 lire (25.6 florins); it was also to include a *predella* with half-length figures and the family coat of arms on the frame. Lionarda's *mundualdi* were Nofri the shoemaker, Piero Dalla Volta the ironworker, and Giovanni the fringemaker (*frangiaiuolo*). The painting was destined for the Pescaia chapel in San Niccolò Oltrarno. Details of the Pescaia chapel's foundation are outlined in church documents. This chapel had been established by Lionarda's late husband, Lorenzo di Francesco di Michele del Pescaia. Dedicated to the Trinity, the chapel was to be furnished after Lorenzo's death with an altarpiece of the same subject. Lorenzo, a notary belonging to the merchant class, assigned Lionarda as executrix of his testament on 12 September 1461, and ordered her to build and furnish the chapel after his death.[31]

Finding the original location of the Pescaia chapel is difficult. A nineteenth-century manuscript states that Lorenzo erected the chapel of the Trinity at the altar of Abraham.[32] One of the problems at San Niccolò is that its chapels were redecorated in the sixteenth century with classicizing altars of *pietra serena*, as at Santa Croce and Santa Maria Novella. Because these monuments do not always correspond to earlier chapels, it is unclear how

Gilday Fig. 3. Neri di Bicci, *Trinity,* 1463, formerly Florence, San
Niccolò Oltrarno (photo: Alinari/Art Resource, N.Y.)

many chapels existed in the fifteenth century and where they were located.[33] In the 1950s
Walter and Elizabeth Paatz noted that a *Sacrifice of Isaac* by Alessandro Allori, datable to ca.
1590–1600, hung on the church's inner façade wall, left of the portal.[34] This painting, which is no
longer there, hung above the altar of the Falconi family. Perhaps the Pescaia chapel was rededi-
cated to Abraham as it passed into new hands. I suspect that at some point there might have
been simultaneous references to or images depicting the Trinity and Abraham's sacrifice of
Isaac at the chapel. This would have impressed upon the viewer the parallelism of these themes.

The lack of specifics regarding the Pescaia chapel prevents us from knowing when
Neri's altarpiece was removed from its intended location. As early as 1862 the painting could
be seen to the right of the altar in the sacristy, a position it occupied until the flood of 1966.
After the flood, the painting was removed to the Soprintendenza, where it apparently still
awaits restoration.[35]

If the date of the original removal of the altarpiece cannot be known, iconographic
details of the painting can be deciphered. The saints in the altarpiece represent the patrons of
Pescaia family members. Saint Leonard most likely commemorates Lionarda, Saint Lawrence
memorializes her husband, Lorenzo, and Saint Francis honors his father, Francesco. John the
Baptist may have paid tribute to another family member or, perhaps, stood as the patron saint
of Florence. Standing to the right of Christ, Saint Lawrence occupies the privileged location
usually reserved for husbands in donor portraits, while Saint Leonard, to Christ's left, occupies that for wives.

5. Maria Tinciavegli

On 14 May 1464, Maria, widow of Niccolò Tinciavegli, ordered an altarpiece with an enthroned Madonna and Child flanked by unnamed saints. She requested the use of good colors, including fine gold and German blue, and a *predella* with half-length figures. The painting was delivered, as specified, on 27 November to the brothers at San Donato a Scopeto. The painting, which is now lost, cost Maria 12 florins.[36] Maria probably belonged to a family of wealthy merchants.[37]

6. Nanna Amati

On 10 April 1465, Neri undertook a commission for a narrative painting (*istoria*) from Abbott Iacopo on behalf of the late Nanna Amati, Neri's maternal grandmother.[38] The scene represented Saint Benedict "giving the oracle"—apparently a reference to the miracle in which Benedict foretells his own death to his followers. The painting depicted monks dressed in white on the right (while Saint Benedict was presumably on the left), apparently in front of a monastery; the scene was framed with friezes and other ornamentation. The narrative, which was probably painted in fresco, was placed in an upper region of the cloister of the Abbey of Camaldoli.[39] Its cost of 16 lire (3.2 florins) was to be deducted from rents received for Nanna's house, which the abbey controlled at the time.[40]

Nanna's painting does not survive, and the reason for its commission can only be surmised. Perhaps Abbott Iacopo found the theme appropriate, as the Camaldolese adopted the rule of Saint Benedict.[41] Perhaps Nanna or her executor chose it because it is a scene appropriate to the time of death.

7. Cavallina di Mugello

Cavallina di Mugello and her *mundualdus*, Michele di Pino, commissioned an altarpiece depicting an enthroned Madonna and Child with Saints Ambrose, Catherine, Francis, and Margaret, which is now lost.[42] It measured four *braccia* square and cost 90 lire (18 florins). The patrons specified the use of good colors in general, with the Madonna's mantle in German blue, and a gilt background and frame. The painting, ordered on 4 October 1465, was completed on 29 January 1466. Unfortunately, Cavallina did not state its intended location, and when the painting was finished, the couple collected it from Neri's shop without allowing him to install it. Its large size suggests it was destined for a church or convent. Cavallina, who lacks a surname, was probably a member of the artisan class.[43]

8. Checa di Spigliato

Checa, the widow of Spigliato di Bertoldo, ordered a Coronation of the Virgin flanked by Saints Peter, Augustine, Lawrence, John the Baptist, Nicholas, and Catherine for the monastery of Santa Maria dei Candeli.[44] The commission, which originated on 10 [?] July 1466, calls for the use of fine colors, with abundant gold and ultramarine, the family coat of arms at the sides of the frame, and a *predella* with scenes from the lives of the saints. Checa agreed to pay the painting's cost of 105 florins in installments; should her death occur before the final payment, however, the monastery would owe the balance. Neri also negotiated some payments in wheat. He guaranteed to provide a painting of appropriate value, one with which she would be happy; upon completion, it was to be appraised by Neri's disciple, Francesco Botticini.

Checa's *Coronation of the Virgin* is found today on the main altar of the small parish church of San Bartolo a Cintoia, in the southwestern outskirts of Florence.[45] Unfortunately, little evidence survives to reconstruct the circumstances of its commission for Santa Maria dei Candeli. According to Richa, many of the church's documents have been destroyed by wars, fire, and floods.[46] While he notes that the church of this Augustinian convent was decorated with paintings by Fra Filippo Lippi and Andrea del Sarto, he fails to mention Neri di Bicci's work, suggesting that it might have been removed before the eighteenth century. Richa omits any specifics on church chapels or patrons, which may have been unavailable to him. He affirms, however, that by the seventeenth century the church had been much renovated, especially the main altar. Paatz and Paatz note that a *Coronation of the Virgin* in a stone tabernacle by Matteo Rosselli from 1624 (which now seems to be lost) was transferred from an unstated location to the nuns' choir of the Candeli in 1703.[47] Perhaps this second *Coronation* replaced Checa's altarpiece.

The iconography of Checa's painting is problematic because there is so little information regarding the commission. It is unclear whether any of these saints commemorate Checa's late husband, Spigliato, and it is unknown whether Saint Catherine might be Checa's protector; perhaps Checa was a nickname for Catherine. Saint Peter apparently commemorates Checa's father, whom Neri indicates was an armorer named Piero di Giovanni; similarly, John the Baptist may honor her grandfather, Giovanni.[48] Saint Augustine, the founder of the convent's order, is the only member of the retinue whose presence can be understood with certainty. The reasons for the selection of Saint Nicholas, who is said to have provided dowries for three young, destitute noblewomen, and Saint Lawrence, who was reputed to have dispersed the treasure of the church among the poor, are unclear.[49]

Checa requested her family coat of arms on the altarpiece, suggesting that this daughter of an artisan had aspirations or pretensions of nobility.[50] Perhaps she intended to raise her social status in the community through commissioning this altarpiece. The painting's cost of 105 florins seems to make it the second most expensive work mentioned in the *Ricordanze*.[51]

Neri makes it clear why he charges such a high cost for this painting. He must be paid for "oro, cholori e magistero della sopradetta tavola"—that is, for the gold, the (high-quality) colors, and for his skill.[52] The value of many Renaissance paintings was determined by their frames; often the material and labor of these opulent objects exceeded the cost of the image.[53] This does not seem to be the case with Checa's commission, as the description of the frame is similar to those of less expensive paintings, such as those of Caterina Bagnesi and Cavallina di Mugello. The high cost of Checa's painting was for the panel itself. The entire background is covered in gold, and two figures, including Christ, wear dark blue mantles, which Neri says are of expensive ultramarine (some of the other paintings examined here were made with German blue [azzurro di 'Magnia], which was a carbonate of copper that created a cheaper grade of blue).[54] It is unclear, however, what Neri means when he charges for his "skill." He probably means that this painting is mostly or wholly an autograph work to which he has applied his mastery of the medium. As Michael Baxandall has pointed out, patrons of the second half of the fifteenth century became "conspicuous buyers of skill"; this was a shift away from the statement in earlier contracts that requested gold and ultramarine as a measure of a painting's worth.[55] In working out a pact with Neri, Checa, who might have lived long enough to see both practiced, requested both excellent materials and workmanship for her painting.

9. India Salviati

India Salviati and her brother, Bernardo, commissioned an Assumption of the Virgin with Saints Thomas, Peter, Jerome, John, and Francis on 1 June 1467.[56] The siblings requested the use of good colors, a classicizing frame with the family coat of arms, and a *predella* with half-length figures. This altarpiece cost 110 lire (22 florins).

India's painting was made for the church of San Leonardo in Arcetri. It can still be seen on the left side of the choir's triumphal arch, but it is unknown whether its present location was original because no pertinent documents survive. When Richa visited San Leonardo in the eighteenth century, he listed its various chapels and coats of arms and read the surviving inscriptions on gravestones, none of which survive today.[57] He does not, however, mention Neri's painting or a chapel for the Salviati.

The Salviati were one of the illustrious families of Renaissance Florence. From 1297 to 1525 they were members of the Florentine Signoria.[58] In the course of the Renaissance, the family provided sixty-two priors, twenty gonfaloniers of justice, and five cardinals of the church.[59] Cambio di Salvi, a doctor, was the first family member to hold public office. Forese Salviati, who was probably Bernardo and India's grandfather, was elected gonfalonier of justice in 1391, 1396, and 1400. In 1389, during the threat of war from Milan, he was one of the Ten of War.[60] Later, in the early sixteenth century, Jacopo Salviati, brother-in-law to Pope Leo X (Giovanni de' Medici), served as the pope's advisor. Jacopo, head of a large bank with branches in Rome and Lyons, was also an important figure in returning the Medici to power in Florence.[61]

Of all the family members, only India seems to be represented by a patron saint on her altarpiece. Saint Thomas, who kneels at the Virgin's right (a privileged position), must have served as India's intercessor. Thomas was pierced by a dagger or spear on an evangelical mission to India.[62] The patron seems to have chosen this saint through his association with the distant land, the name of which she bears. No other saints on the altarpiece appear to be family namesakes;[63] perhaps they were of special importance to India herself. India's brother is represented by his patron saint, Bernard, in an altarpiece he had commissioned in 1461 from Neri di Bicci. This painting, which once stood on the main altar of San Leonardo, depicts the Coronation of the Virgin.[64] The presence of these personal onomastic saints—Bernard and Thomas—on the two altarpieces suggests that these commissions were individual ones, each meant to honor the patrons separately.

10. Agniesa Neroni

On 30 September 1467 Agniesa Neroni requested a large *tondo* of the Madonna and Child for the church of Santa Maria della Scala, which is now lost.[65] The Madonna's mantle was to be in German blue and the frame was to be gilt. Neri made a pact with Agniesa for 40 lire (8 florins); no *mundualdus* is listed. Agniesa, the widow of Bartolomeo Neroni, was a patrician.[66]

Agniesa's *tondo* was of a shape unusual in church settings of the Renaissance. Most *tondi* seem to have been found in personal chambers at the time, according to Florentine household inventories, *ricordanze*, and estate books (*libri d'eredità*).[67] An example of this is a *tondo* by Fra Angelico and Fra Filippo Lippi depicting the Adoration of the Magi found today in the National Gallery of Art, Washington, D. C., which may be that listed in the Medicean inventories of 1492 as housed in the "camera grande di Lorenzo."[68]

Conclusion

A detailed comparative analysis of the five surviving paintings—Bianca's *Assumption*, Caterina's *Annunciation*, Lionarda's *Trinity*, Checa's *Coronation*, and India's *Assumption*—is difficult because so little information survives regarding these works and their patrons. When considered collectively, however, these paintings yield slightly better results, especially in regards to the saints beholding and attending the subject scenes. Lionarda's *Trinity* and India's *Assumption* both depict these women's patron saints; as such, they were intended to protect and honor those patrons. Lionarda's painting commemorates various kinsmen and may even have served as a family memorial. In contrast, India's altarpiece seems to be for her benefit alone; her brother's commission in the same church appears likewise. It is difficult to know whether Bianca's *Assumption*, Checa's *Coronation* and Caterina's *Annunciation* made reference to their patron saints or those of family members; they are not present in the main scenes, but perhaps appeared in the lost *predellas* or curtains. The manner in which each of the five paintings demonstrates a relationship to the patron varies from India's highly personalized *Assumption* to Caterina's *Annunciation*, which today bears no clear reference to her. Portraits of the patrons do not appear in any of these works.

If iconographic analyses of these five paintings are disappointing, demographic factors pertaining to Neri's women patrons are more encouraging. When considered together, these factors allow us to make some observations about the activity of secular women patrons in quattrocento Florence.

The ten entries of Neri's *Ricordanze* considered here show that marital status seems to have been an important factor in laywomen's patronage. Widowhood in particular appears to have been a point in life that encouraged such an endeavor, and, as will be seen, the sponsorship practices of this group are homogeneous.[69] In the *Ricordanze*, five of the ten lay female patrons are widows. Four of them (Caterina Bagnesi, Lionarda del Pescaia, Maria Tinciavegli, and Checa di Spigliato) might have commissioned paintings to commemorate their late husbands. The other widow, Agniesa Neroni, ordered a *tondo* for Santa Maria della Scala.

Widowhood was prevalent in Renaissance Florence because of the age gap common between husbands and wives at the time.[70] Men generally married around age thirty for a first marriage; in contrast, women were often wed by sixteen or younger. The relatively low life expectancy also shortened the marriages of Florentines.[71] The *catasto* of 1427 shows that widows were much more numerous in Florence than widowers (25 percent and 4 percent, respectively), and that the women were generally widowed at a younger age than the men and were less likely to remarry than men.[72] Moreover, widows were the heads of 15 percent of Florentine households in this period.[73]

Unlike the patronage patterns of widows in Neri's *Ricordanze*, those of his other women patrons show fewer similarities. India Salviati and Cavallina di Mugello, who apparently were unmarried, commissioned altarpieces for unknown reasons. Andrea di Barberino, the only woman listed as married in the *Ricordanze*, requested a curtain that probably covered a church altarpiece. The smallness of the sample makes it difficult to generalize about the patronage of married and single women; it does, however, confirm the suspicion that such activity was sparse in fifteenth-century Florence. There are fewer patrons in this category than in the widowed group because married and single women generally enjoyed less autonomy than widows.

In addition to marital status, social class was another important factor in these women's patronage. As expected, most of the patrons belonged to the patrician (Bianca degli Spini, Caterina Bagnesi, India Salviati, and Agniesa Neroni) and merchant (Lionarda del Pescaia and Maria Tinciavegli) classes. Only four women from the laboring class are listed in the *Ricordanze* as having commissioned art (Andrea di Barberino, Nanna Amati, Cavallina di Mugello, and Checa di Spigliato), but the existence of patrons from this sector of society was in itself contrary to my expectations.

An unexpected finding of this admittedly small sample is that the working-class women spent more on their commissions than their more affluent counterparts. The average costs of the commissions are as follows: 38.25 florins for patrician women, 12.5 florins for the merchant-class women, and 31.8 florins for women of the laboring class. As has been noted, Checa, who commissioned the most expensive of the paintings, seems to have been a wealthy armorer's daughter who may have been attempting to improve her social standing through her sponsorship. Cavallina and Andrea might also have attempted a similar feat. Neri's description of their commissions makes it clear that they purchased luxurious items.

These women, however, were the exception to the rule. In general, working-class fe-males could not afford such luxuries due to their declining participation in the workplace in the course of the fourteenth and fifteenth centuries.[74] Whereas large numbers of working women are mentioned in documents of the late thirteenth and early fourteenth centuries, few are re-corded over the next two hundred years. Instead, women exercised certain traditionally female occupations, such as midwifery, wet-nursing, and domestic service, which paid low wages.

In contrast to working-class women, their male counterparts purchased a consider-able variety of art objects. Demand for works of art accelerated with the increased construc-tion of homes and family chapels, and artists filled this demand in part with more affordable works made of inexpensive materials—such as glazed terracotta, gilt gesso, and painted stucco—which opened up a wider market for their wares.[75] Vasari mentions sales by Andrea del Sarto and Pontormo to merchants, tailors, and other craftsmen.[76] Neri di Bicci recorded a number of sales to artisans.[77]

Returning to Neri's female patrons, one finds that regardless of social class or marital status, nearly all of them placed commissions with the assistance of a *mundualdus*. The word-ing of the entries suggests that in some instances the institution was of trivial importance. Sometimes the *mundualdus* is mentioned in the first sentence of the entry, as in the commis-sions of Caterina Bagnesi, Lionarda del Pescaia, Cavallina di Mugello, and India Salviati. In these cases, it appears as if the guardians were physically present at Neri's shop when the commissions were placed. At other times, the *mundualdi* are mentioned in the last (and often vaguely worded) sentence, which suggests their absence. This is evident in the commissions of Andrea di Barberino and Checa di Spigliato. In Maria Tinciavegli's case, the *mundualdus* is mentioned only after the delivery of the painting. In Agniesa Neroni's entry, no reference is made to a guardian at all.[78] The reasons for these inconsistencies are unclear. It also should be noted that none of these examples are joint commissions. This is often made clear in the titles of Neri's entries, which almost exclusively list the women's names. Even when men are in-cluded in the entry title, the woman's sole patronage is made clear in the text. In India Salviati's case it is clear that her brother served solely as a *mundualdus* and not as a joint patron be-cause there is no reference to him on her altarpiece; rather, he was honored by his own altarpiece by Neri at the same church.

Having explored laywomen's patronage in Neri's *Ricordanze*, it is instructive to com-pare it with that of their male counterparts. The appendix at the end of this essay lists and categorizes Neri's commissions from laymen requesting works of art for their homes, work-shops, or private chapels. Neri recorded 142 commissions from these male patrons, which can be classified as follows:

> 63 are for domestic settings
> 54 are for ecclesiastical settings
> 21 have no clear destination from their description
> 2 are for workshops
> 1 is for a castle chapel
> <u> 1 is a street tabernacle</u>
> 142 total commissions

In contrast, the commissions of secular women can be broken down thus:

> 9 are for ecclesiastic settings
> <u>1 is probably for an ecclesiastical setting</u>
> 10 total commissions

An important difference between the commissions of men and women is their intended destinations. According to the above numbers, women overwhelmingly requested art for ecclesiastical settings, whereas men seem to sponsor works of art for the home and the church with almost equal frequency. Renaissance men typically purchased art and furnishings for the home in preparation for marriage.[79] Most bought Madonnas, which are ubiquitous in the household inventories of the fifteenth century, even of artisans.[80] Neri's *Ricordanze* lists a number of men who purchased such Madonnas, many of which were made of inexpensive gilt gesso.[81] It is unclear how frequently women purchased works of art for the home, but it should be remembered that men often used their wives' dowries to furnish the household.[82]

Many of Neri's commissions from men that did not specify a destination were probably for the home.[83] Their descriptions are often similar to works of art that Neri states are for the home. These items generally have short descriptions and low prices, as if Neri considered them minor or routine assignments. In contrast, Neri allotted the largest price tags and lengthiest descriptions to church altarpieces, as in Checa di Spigliato's commission. Although one cannot be entirely certain that paintings without a clear destination are for the home, one can probably assume that many were for such a location.

Another distinction between men's and women's commissions is their cost. Men's purchases averaged 10.65 florins, whereas those of women averaged 31.78 florins (although this figure is skewed by Checa's expensive altarpiece).[84] This discrepancy exists in part because Neri generally charged more for ornate church altarpieces than for domestic objects.

The biggest difference between the men's and women's commissions is, of course, frequency. Only about 7 percent of Neri's secular patronage came from women. This leads one to ask whether fifteenth-century Florentine women commissioned works of art from the many other artists in the city. The journals of other quattrocento artists confirm the presence of women patrons, but these records are problematic. Unfortunately, none of these documents is as complete as those of Neri di Bicci. Those that survive are much briefer than Neri's manuscript; most consist of only a few pages.[85]

One such document is the *bottega* (workshop) book of Apollonio di Giovanni. This text enumerates 173 commissions, almost all of which are for *cassoni*, Apollonio's specialty.[86] Unfortunately, the work exists only in an incomplete copy in the form of a list that simply mentions the intended recipients of his *cassoni* and their prices. Apparently the copy was made in 1670 by an archivist whose main interest was genealogy and who may have omitted information not associated with his search.[87] In its shortened version, Apollonio's *bottega* book lists only one commission by a woman for a *cassone*, although others may have appeared in the original manuscript.[88]

The journal of the sculptor Maso di Bartolommeo lists two women as patrons for his works.[89] Like Apollonio's *bottega* book, this short compilation of work requests must be considered incomplete. One woman requested a bell and later canceled the commission. Another asked for a *telaio*—apparently a frame for a hanging textile covering an open door.[90]

Unfortunately, these artists' documents are too sparse to provide a clear picture of patronage in general or of women's sponsorship in particular. Alesso Baldovinetti's *Ricordi*, which mentions no secular patrons, is a case in point.[91] On the average, this document lists one transaction per year, only a few of which can be considered long-term projects. Unlike Neri di Bicci, Alesso recorded some, but not all, of his transactions in this document. Like Neri's *Ricordanze*, Lorenzo Lotto's sixteenth-century *Libro di spese diverse (1538–1556)* lists extensive personal and professional transactions.[92] Disappointingly, Lotto lists only one commission from women: in 1549 Piera da Monaco and other ladies of Ancona requested a large altarpiece with Saints Roch, Sebastian, and Cyriacus, and a smaller altarpiece with Saints John the Baptist and Francis for the church of San Rocco in Posatora near Ancona; both paintings appear to be lost.[93] Returning to the quattrocento, a more extensive *bottega* book remains to be published—that of Bernardo di Stefano Rosselli, a pupil of Neri di Bicci—which hopefully will provide more information on women patrons.[94]

In contrast to these documents, Neri's extensive *Ricordanze* demonstrates patterns that might be representative of Florentine patronage in general. My survey of his text reveals that widows were more likely to sponsor art than married or single women. Patrician and working-class women each form 40 percent of his lay female sponsorship, whereas middle-class women constitute 20 percent. Commissions from women form only 7 percent of Neri's secular sponsorship.[95] And whereas women generally bought art for the church, most men (probably in excess of 50 percent) purchased art for the home. Moreover, because women's commissions were generally more public than those of men, they also tended to be more expensive. While these results are tentative because of the limited amount of evidence available, they provide welcome new insight into the activities of secular women in quattrocento Florence.

Appendix

Men's Commissions in Neri di Bicci's *Ricordanze*

The following is a list of the commissions in Neri di Bicci's *Ricordanze* by private laymen that seem to have been for personal consumption. Work requests from the church, the Signoria, and confraternities are neither tallied nor examined. Canceled and incomplete entries are also omitted. Each commission includes an entry number, its destination, its cost, and its equivalent in florins (according to Richard Goldthwaite, *The Building of Renaissance Florence*, 301, 5 lire were worth approximately 1 florin ca. 1460). An average cost in florins is also included. Orders for regilding or retouching old works of art are those noted by an "x" under the "Refurbishing" column.

Count	Entry No.	Cost	In Florins	Destination	Refurbishing
1	2	£. 15	3.0	church	
2	12	£. 147	29.4	street tabernacle	
3	15	£. 100	20.0	church	
4	22	£. 560	112.0	church	
5	23	£. 70	14.0	church	
6	24	?	?	home	
7	26	£. 28	5.6	home	
8	28	£. 100	20.0	church	
9	29	£. 6	1.2	home	
10	30	£. 5	1.0	church	
11	35	£. 20	4.0	?	
12	47	F. 3 £.15	6.0	home	
13	56	£. 20	4.0	home	
14	78	£. 32	6.4	home	

Count	Entry No.	Cost	In Florins	Destination	Refurbishing
15	79	F. 32	32.0	church	
16	95	F. 30	30.0	church	
17	12	£. 19	3.8	home	
18	21	£. 75	15.0	church	
19	136	£. 5	1.0	home?	
20	137	£. 100	20.0	church	
21	148	F. 10	10.0	church	
22	153	F. 4	4.0	home	
23	181	£. 43	8.6	church	
24	186	£. 8	1.6	home	
25	210	£. 30	6.0	home	
26	211	£. 30	6.0	home	
27	212	£. 22	4.4	home?	
28	217	£. 12	2.4	home	
29	221	F. 1	1.0	home?	
30	223	£. 27	5.4	?	
31	225	£. 25	5.0	home	
32	227	£. 13	2.6	home	
33	228	£. 14	2.8	home	
34	229	£. 24	4.8	home	
35	230	£. 13	2.6	?	
36	235	?	?	church	
37	238	£. 15	3.0	home	
38	239	F. 4	4.0	?	
39	242	F. 2 £. 3	2.4	home	
40	243	£. 40	8.0	home	
41	244	F. 8	8.0	home	
42	247	F. 1	1.0	?	
43	249	F. 4	4.0	?	
44	255	F. 13.5	13.5	home	
45	256	£. 4	0.8	?	
46	257	£. 16	3.2	?	
47	262	F. 1	1.0	?	
48	263	£. 1	0.2	?	
49	272	F. 3	3.0	church	
50	278	F. 5	5.0	?	
51	284	£. 164	32.8	church	

Count	Entry No.	Cost	In Florins	Destination	Refurbishing
52	285	£. 119	23.8	church	
53	298	F. 5	5.0	home	
54	303	F. 4	4.0	home	
55	308	£. 22	4.4	home	
56	321	£. 245	49.0	church	
57	325	£. 11	2.2	home	
58	327	?	?	church	
59	328	?	?	church	
60	329	£. 6	1.2	home	
61	331	F. 9	9.0	church?	
62	333	£. 14	2.8	?	
63	343	£. 80	16.0	?	
64	345	F. 4	4.0	?	
65	351	£. 154	30.8	church	
66	355	F. 4	4.0	?	
67	356	F. 4	4.0	home	
68	359	F. 6 £. 7	7.4	home	
69	360	£. 100	20.0	church	
70	368	F. 5	5.0	home	
71	369	£. 30	6.0	home	
72	374	F. 2	2.0	?	
73	380	£. 144	28.8	church	
74	382	F. 6	6.0	church	
75	385	£. 14	2.8	home	
76	386	F. 3	3.0	home	
77	387	£. 19	3.8	home	
78	393	F. 30	30.0	church	
79	401	F. 25	25.0	church	
80	403	?	?	church	
81	405	£. 87	17.4	?	
82	406	£. 30	6.0	home	
83	416	£. 2	0.4	church	
84	418	F. 30	30.0	castle chapel	
85	420	F. 3	3.0	home	
86	427	£. 150	30.0	church	
87	431	F. 40	40.0	church	
88	432	£. 41	8.2	?	

Count	Entry No.	Cost	In Florins	Destination	Refurbishing
89	434	£. 60	12.0	church	
90	436	£. 190	38.0	church	
91	437	F. 8	8.0	home	
92	439	F. 7	7.0	home	
93	440	£. 19	3.8	?	
94	441	£. 20	4.0	home	
95	446	£. 140	28.0	church	
96	453	£. 72	14.4	church	
97	454	£. 8	1.6	church	
98	459	F.2 £. 8	3.6	home?	
99	462	£. 10	2.0	home?	
100	463	£. 15	3.0	home	
101	464	£. 3	0.6	?	
102	465	F. 4	4.0	home	x
103	470	F. 3	3.0	church	
104	474	£. 45	9.0	home	
105	485	F. 36	36.0	church	
106	512	£. 14	2.8	home	
107	542	F. 8	8.0	home	
108	550	F. 15	15.0	church	
109	556	£. 19	3.8	home	
110	568	F. 1	1.0	?	
111	572	?	?	church	
112	576	£. 6	1.2	home	
113	590	F. 3	3.0	home	
114	593	F. 3	3.0	home	
115	594	F. 3	3.0	home	
116	604	£. 8	1.6	workshop	
117	614	£. 152	30.4	church	
118	627	£. 60	12.0	church	x
119	629	£. 155	31.0	church	
120	647	£. 4.5	0.9	home	
121	656	F. 5	5.0	home	
122	662	£. 80	16.0	church	
123	664	F. 5	5.0	church	x
124	665	F. 4	4.0	workshop	
125	671	F. 10	10.0	church?	

Count	Entry No.	Cost	In Florins	Destination	Refurbishing
126	677	F. 7	7.0	church	
127	683	£. 25	5.0	home	
128	684	F. 2	2.0	home	
129	698	F. 85	85.0	church	
130	700	?	?	church	
131	720	F. 1	1.0	church	
132	730	F. 8	8.0	home	
133	742	£. 4	0.8	church	
134	745	£. 25	5.0	church	
135	749	£. 12	2.4	home	
136	759	£. 13	2.6	home	
137	761	F. 36	36.0	church	
138	762	F. 4.5	4.5	home	
139	763	F. 1	1.0	home	
140	784	£. 28	5.6	church	
141	787	F. 14	14.0	church	
142	789	£. 15	3.0	home	

Average Cost   10.65 Florins

Notes

I am grateful to Professor Whitney Chadwick for reading and commenting on an earlier draft of this paper.

1. Neri's *Ricordanze*, which has been preserved since 1785 at the Biblioteca della Galleria degli Uffizi (MS 2), has recently been published in its entirety: Neri di Bicci, *Le ricordanze*, ed. Bruno Santi (Pisa: Edizioni Marlin, 1976). In the early twentieth century, Giovanni Poggi published excerpts of the text; see "Le ricordanze di Neri di Bicci," *Il Vasari* 1 (1928): 317–38; 3 (1930): 133–53, 222–34; and 4 (1931): 189–202. As Poggi noted, the surviving work was probably not the only one that existed. This manuscript, the cover of which is marked with the letter "D," was seemingly the fourth of a series, of which all other volumes are lost; see Poggi, "Le ricordanze," 1, 317). Neri himself mentions "Ricordanze C" in entry number 13 of Ricordanze D. The extant volume may not have been the final one. The records of the Opera of Santo Spirito list the sale of a painting by Neri on September 1475—five months after the final entry in the *Ricordanze*. At that time Neri sold a *tavola di nostra donna* to Giovanni di Mariano, which was paid for by the Mellini bank, the Opera's cashier; see Richard Goldthwaite, *The Building of Renaissance Florence* (Baltimore: Johns Hopkins University Press, 1980), 404, n. 12. This suggests that a fifth, and probably last, volume once existed.

2. The commissions from nuns, of which only two are known to survive, are as follows: entry no. 232, a *tavola* with the seated Santa Monica surrounded by nuns and saints for the Amantellate nuns of Prato; entry no. 233, a frescoed Crucifixion for the monastery of Faenza; entry no. 299, an altarpiece depicting the Crucifixion for the monastery of Santa Monica; entry no. 320, a tabernacle for the monastery of Santa Monica; entry no. 357, a fresco of the Last Supper for the refectory of the monastery of Foligno; entry no. 575, an Assumption of the Virgin for the abbess Francesca at San Michele of Prato (now in the Johnson collection of Philadelphia's Museum of Art [cat. no. 27]; see note after entry); entry no. 728, a dossal for the nuns at Santa Monica; entry no. 729, *agnioli* (carved angels?) for the monastery of Candeli; entry no. 736, a Madonna for the monastery at Sant' Apollonia (now at the Soprintendenza alle Gallerie di Firenze [cat. no. 3463]; see note after entry); entry no. 738, candle holders for the Monastero del Portico; entry no. 771, a Coronation of the Virgin for the nuns at Sant' Apollonia; entry no. 780, two *viti da vangelo* (holders for the gospel?) for the same location; and entry no. 791, an altarpiece for the nuns at the monastery of San Niccolò. I include the commission from the *pinzochera* Antonia da Pescia for a small painting of San Bernardino (entry no. 185) in the category of religious patronesses. *Pinzochere* were semireligious women who lived alone or in small groups striving to live a life of chastity and poverty, but, unlike nuns, did not take vows of poverty, chastity, and obedience. Joyce Pennings, "Semi-Religious Women in Fifteenth-Century Rome," *Mededelingen van het Nederlands Instituut te Rome*, n.s. 12 (1987): 115. It is unclear whether various entries such as entry no. 416 (for a small Madonna) and entry no. 700 (for an altarpiece) are commissions from nuns or gifts to them from other people.

3. Without the consent of a *mundualdus* few legal actions by a woman were valid. He might be a brother, a father, or anyone else, provided he was male, but he had to be appointed or confirmed by a judge. This tradition originated in Lombardy and was adopted in Tuscany only by the Florentines. The patrimonial power (*mundium*) it bestowed upon a male could be treated like any right in property; it could be sold, given away, or passed on in inheritance. The holder of such a power had to be someone capable of acting as a guardian. In theory the purpose of a *mundualdus* was to see to a woman's welfare; he was not required to be an expert in the law. His function was to consent to a woman's legal transactions, as it was believed that women were incapable of handling such duties on their own. Depending on the circumstances, however, some women were able to have the *mundualdus* more or less reduced to a formality; see Thomas Kuehn, "*Cum consensu mundualdi*: Legal Guardianship of Women in Quattrocento Florence," in *Law, Family and Women: Toward a Legal Anthropology of Renaissance Italy* (Chicago: University of Chicago Press, 1991), 212–37.

4. "Richordo chome detto dì io Neri di Bicci dipintore ò tolto a dipigniere da meser l'abate Bartolomeo…e da Salvestro iSpini e da Giovanni del Pechorella iSpini e da Giovanni di Scholaio iSpini 1ª tavola d'altare, la quale à ' stare in Santa Trinita alla loro chapella, la quale lasc[i]ò mona Bancha degli Spini; e' sopradetti ne sono aseghutori….Riza'la [tavola] in sul'altare di detta chapella in detta chiesa a dì 28 d'aghosto 1456…," Neri di Bicci, *Ricordanze*, 25-26, entry no. 50.

5. The Florentine *braccio* was approximately two feet (58.36 cm) long; Goldthwaite, *Building*, xv.

6. Values in lire have been converted to florins throughout for simplicity. Circa 1460, five lire were worth approximately one florin. Goldthwaite, *Building*, 301.

7. Giuseppe Richa, *Notizie istoriche delle chiese fiorentine*, 10 vols. (Florence: Pietro Gaetano Viviani, 1754–62), 3:154.

8. Ibid.; George Kaftal, *Iconography of the Saints in Tuscan Painting* (Florence: Sansoni, 1952), cols. 576-77.

9. Two entries regarding the chapel mention promise of a (partial?) payment for the frescoes and Neri's return of wooden planks that he had borrowed from a woodworker, probably to use as scaffolding there: "Richordo chome il sopradetto dì [12 May 1453] Domenicho di Chante lina[i]uolo e chonpagni mi promisono per munistero di Santa Trinita…e per Giovanni iSpini e Salvestro, l. trentadua per danari avevo da…avere d'una chapella a loro dipinta…. ," Neri di Bicci, *Ricordanze*, 3–4, entry no. 6. "Richordo ch'el detto dì [26 June 1453] rendei a Tano legniaiuolo…piane 5…, le quali m'aveva prestato…pella chapella di Santa Trinita…" Ibid., 8, entry no. 13. See also Bruno Santi, "Dalle *Ricordanze* di Neri di Bicci," *Annali della Scuola Normale Superiore di Pisa* 3 (1973): 177–79.

10. The *Annunciation* fresco is reproduced in Santi, "Dalle *Ricordanze*," plate 3, after 315. See also Walter and Elisabeth Paatz, *Die Kirchen von Florenz: Ein kunstgeschichtliches Handbuch*, 6 vols. (Frankfurt am Main: V. Klostermann, 1952–55), 5:301.

11. Giovanni Battista di Crollalanza, *Dizionario storico-blasonico delle famiglie nobili e notabile italiane*, 3 vols. (Bologna: A. Forni, 1965), 2:556.

12. Leonardo Ginori Lisci, *I palazzi di Firenze nella storia e nell' arte*, 2 vols. (Florence: Giunti, 1972), 1:127.

13. "Richordo chome detto dì io Neri di Bicci dipintore tolsi a dipigniere da Ormanozo di Guido Deti 1ª tavola d'altare quadra e da mona Chaterina donna fu di Xstofano Bagniesi; al'anticha, di brac[i]a quatro altra [*sic*] e largha 3 ½, chon predella da pie'…cholonne da lato, architrave, freg[i]o, chornic[i]one e foglia, nella quale ò a fare una Nunziata cho l'angelo e inchasamento e nella predella tre istorie e l'arme mesa d'oro fine e.lla Nostra donna d'azuro fine e bene ornata e richa…la quale à stare in Sa[n] Romeo di Firenze…." Neri di Bicci, *Ricordanze*, 32–33, entry no. 63. Giuliano da Maiano, collaborated on this painting; see ibid., 33–34, entry no. 64. Ormannozzo Deti was a jurist who, Thomas Kuehn argues, was sympathetic to female inheritance claims; Kuehn, "*Cum consensu mundualdi*," 252–54.

14. This painting was identified by Giovanni Poggi as a work by Neri di Bicci; Poggi, 'Ricordanze,' (1930): 143–44.

15. Bicci di Lorenzo's painting is reproduced in Bruce Cole, *The Renaissance Artist at Work: From Pisano to Titian* (New York: Harper and Row, 1983), 148.

16. "Voglio et ordeno che…sia fato uno altar con la sepoltura davanti come se quelo da cha grimani et sopra dito altar sia posta la mia pala over ancona la qual al presente me fa messer Zuanne Belin [Giovanni Bellini] con li sui adornamenti et cum la cortina davanti *come se rechiede*"; "I request and order that an altar be made with the tomb in front, such as the one for the Grimani, and above said altar should be my altarpiece (which Giovanni Bellini is presently making) with its adornments and with the curtain in front, *as is required*." Venice, Archivio di Stato, Notary Cristoforo Rizzo, B. 1228, fol. 205; as quoted in Rona Goffen, "Icon and Vision: Giovanni Bellini's Half-Length Madonnas," *Art Bulletin* 57 (1975): 513; emphasis mine.

17. Barbara Markowsky suggests that dossal figures invariably corresponded to the titulus of the altar or chapel; Barbara Markowsky, "Eine Gruppe Bemalter Paliotti in Florenz und der Toskana und ihre Textilen Vorbilder," *Mitteilungen des Kunsthistorischen Institutes in Florenz* 17 (1973): 140. This theory is difficult to test with Neri's commissions because he seldom mentioned the decorations on dossals in the *Ricordanze*. Markowsky examines several dossals that still survive by Neri and other artists in the church of Santo Spirito.

18. For a surviving dossal from Santo Spirito, see the chapter by Elizabeth Pilliod in this volume (Pilliod, fig. 4).

19. Paatz and Paatz, *Die Kirchen*, 5:10.

20. Richa, *Notizie*, 1:258.

21. Paatz and Paatz, *Die Kirchen*, 5:10.

22. The inscription reads:

D.O.M.
HOC SACELLVM A MAIORIBVS OLIM EXTRVCTVM
ET A CATHERINA RAINERIA CHRISTOPHORI BAGNESI VXORE
POSTEA EXORNATVM POTEQVE AVCTVM
IVLIANVS SENATOR
ET ZANOBIVS BAGNESI
SIMONIS FILII
AD HVIVS TEMPLI DECOREM
IN AVGVSTIOREM HAC FORMAM RENDIGENDVM CVRARVNT
FAMILIAE INSIGNIBVS RESTITVTIS.
AN. SAL. MDCXXIX

Richa, *Notizie*, 1:260. Paatz and Paatz incorrectly state that the altar was erected in 1629; Paatz and Paatz, *Die Kirchen*, 5:10.

23. "Signori ricchi e potenti in quel popolo." Richa, *Notizie*, 1:256.

24. Richa, *Notizie*, 1:256; Paatz and Paatz, Die *Kirchen*, 5:13. Several members of the Bagnesi family served as priors and gonfaloniers of justice of Florence—the city's most important public offices; see Crollalanza, *Dizionario storico-blasonico*, 1:79. Cristofano Bagnesi served as an advisor to the Signoria in 1433; Dale Kent, "The Florentine *Reggimento* in the Fifteenth Century," *Renaissance Quarterly* 28 (1975): 604, n. 133.

25. "Chortina di mona Andrea di Barberino sarto:…feci a mona Andrea di Barberino una chortina drentovi l'angelo Rafaello e Tubia e uno freg[i]o d'atorno; cholorite le dette chose, fu la chortina bracc[i]a dua o più alta e uno e mezo largha…missi la chorona d'oro…di metà.…" Neri di Bicci, *Ricordanze*, 68, entry no. 134; the meaning of the golden crown is unknown to me.

    Since many of Neri's paintings are similar, Andrea's curtain might have resembled some of his known representations of Tobias and the archangel Raphael, such as that on the right side of an altarpiece of the enthroned Madonna and child with saints at the Wallraf-Richartz Museum in Cologne; this is reproduced in Raimond van Marle, *The Development of the Italian Schools of Painting*, 19 vols. (The Hague: Nijoff, 1923–38), 10:532, or that on the left side of an altarpiece depicting an enthroned Saint John Evangelist with Tobias and the angel, Saints Lucy and William which Berenson lists as homeless; Bernard Berenson, *Italian Pictures of the Renaissance: Florentine School*, 2 vols. (London: Phaidon, 1963), 2:plate 922.

    Barberino was a nickname; his real name was Antonio di Jacopo; Neri di Bicci, *Ricordanze*, 135, entry no. 264.

26. Although curtains were sometimes found in the home, these usually hung in doorways (instead of windows) to allow breezes in while keeping flying insects out. A rich example of this type is a curtain (*portiera*) listed in the Medici inventories of 1492 that depicted the Triumph of Fame; see Marco Spallanzani and Giovanna Gaeta Bertelà, eds., *Libro d'inventario dei beni di Lorenzo il*

Magnifico (Florence: Stabilimento Grafico Commerciale, 1992), 9. For an analysis of this Medicean curtain, see my dissertation, Rosi Prieto Gilday, "Politics as Usual: Depictions of Petrarch's *Triumph of Fame* in Early Renaissance Florence" (Ph.D. dissertation: University of Pittsburgh, 1996.) A more quotidian example of these curtains is probably the *telaio* mentioned later in this chapter.

27. Alessandro Nova, "Hangings, Curtains, and Shutters of Sixteenth-Century Lombard Altarpieces," in *Italian Altarpieces, 1250–1550: Function and Design,* ed. Eve Borsook and Fiorella S. Gioffreddi (Oxford: Clarendon Press, 1994), 180, 186.

28. Gulielmus Durantis, *The Symbolism of Churches and Church Ornaments: A Translation of the First Book of the "Rationale divinorum officiorum"* (London: Gibbing, 1906), 72–75.

29. Johann Konrad Eberlein, "The Curtain in Raphael's Sistine *Madonna,*" *Art Bulletin* 65 (1983): 61–77, notes that the curtain in Raphael's Sistine *Madonna* was often interpreted as a "revelation" or as a "vision" in the nineteenth century.

30. "Tavola di mona Lionarda à ' stare in Santo Nicholò:...tolsi a dipigniere da mona Lionarda, donna fu di ser..., una tavola d'altare...nella quale ò a fare 1ᵃ Trinità inn.uno trono di Serafini, e da mano destra Santo G[i]ovanni B[ati]sta e Santo Lorenzo; da mano sinistra Santo Franc[esch]o e Santo Lionardo, c[i]oè dua ginochioni e dua ritte a lato a detta Trinità; la quale tavola ò a lavorare in questa forma...." Neri di Bicci, *Ricordanze,* 204, entry no. 404; delivery of the painting is listed on 213, entry no. 421. The painting was identified by Gaetano Milanesi in Vasari-Milanesi, 2:80.

31. Leonardo Tanci, "Memoriae della chiesa di S. Niccolò Oltrarno in Firenze," 1579, unpublished MS in the archives of San Niccolò Oltrarno, fol. 177r. Lorenzo's profession as a notary is mentioned in "Notizie istoriche dei canonicati, cappelle, ufiziature poste nella chiesa di S. Niccolò Oltr'Arno di Firenze compilate nell' anno 1828, Ricordi 'E'," 1828, unpublished MS in the archives of San Niccolò Oltrarno, fol. 597r. My thanks to Grazia Badino at San Niccolò for bringing these documents to my attention.

32. "Signor Lorenzo...[erige]...una cappella...all' altare di Abramo, sotto il titolo della SS. Trinità." Cited in *"Notizie istoriche dei canonicati,"* fol. 600v.

33. Richa, *Notizie,* 10:269.

34. Paatz and Paatz, *Die Kirchen,* 4:367.

35. Giovanna Damiani, *San Niccolò Oltrarno,* 2 vols. (Florence: Officine Grafiche Firenze, 1982), 1:33.

36. "Tavola di mona Maria de' Tinc[i]avegli:...tolsi a fare da mona Maria donna fu di Nicholò Tinc[i]avegli una tavoletta d'altare quadra al'antica, di bracc[i]a 3 largha e alta bracc[i]a 2 ²/₃, chon predelleta da pie' e cholone e chornic[i]one da chapo, nella quale vole 1ᵃ Nostra Donna a sedere chol Figliuolo in chollo e da.llato dritto 1o Santo e da lato mancho 1° altro Santo e nella predeletta meze fighurette, messa dinanzi d'oro fine e da' lati di cholore e lavorata d'azuri di Magnia fini....Rendemo la detta tavola...e démola a' frati di Santo Donato iSchopeto chome disse detta mona Maria...." Neri di Bicci, *Ricordanze,* 230, entry no. 449. The church of San Donato a Scopeto is not listed in Paatz and Paatz, *Die Kirchen.*

37. In his "Tables on Wealth," Lauro Martines lists the leading taxpayers according to the *catasto* of 1427. Table 7, no. 90, mentions a certain Berto di Guido Trinciavelli, who was probably a relative of Maria's husband. The difference in spelling may be due to an error on the part of Neri di Bicci or the notary, or to the nonstandardized spelling system of the time. Lauro Martines, *The Social World of Florentine Humanists, 1390–1460* (Princeton: Princeton University Press, 1963), 374. I assume that the Tinciavegli were not patricians, as I do not find them listed among the noble or notable families in heraldic encyclopediae.

38. "Lavoro fatto all'abate di Chamaldoli: Richordo ch'el sopradetto dì io Neri di Bicci feci fare all'abate Iachopo abate [*sic*] di Chamaldoli e nella detta badia nel chiostro di sopra, una istoria di Santo Benedetto quando dà l'oragholo, tuti e' monaci vestiti di biancho che sono dalla mano destra e una parte del chasamento in ch'è detta istoria e chosì una parte de' fregi e una parte de' ornami...,delle quale fighure e llavoro mi de' dare l. sedici ... e vole el detto abate ch'el detto prezo si pongha a

chonto del livello della chasa fu di mona Nanna d'Amato...," Neri di Bicci, *Ricordanze*, 240, entry no. 466. Nanna is mentioned as Neri's grandmother in ibid., 435.

39. Perhaps this refers to San Salvatore di Camaldoli, which does not survive; see Paatz and Paatz, *Die Kirchen*, 5:42.

40. Entry no. 490 documents that on 7 October 1465 Neri's family regained control of Nanna's house from the abbey; Neri di Bicci, *Ricordanze*, 254.

41. Kaftal, *Iconography of the Saints*, col. 145.

42. "Tavola della Chavalina di Mugello:...ò tolto a dipignere da Michele di Pino dalla Chavallina di Mugello una tavola d'altare fatta al'anticha, c[i]oè quadra, chon predella da pie', quadro in mezo e chollone [*sic*] da.llato a chanali, di sopra architrave, freg[i]o e chornic[i]one...nella quale vole queste figure, c[i]oè in mezo Nostra Donna in sedia cho Nostro Signiore in chollo; da mano destra Santo Biag[i]o e Santa Chaterina; da mano sinistra Santo Franc[esch]o e Santa Margherita, tute bene ornate e cholorite di buoni e fini cholori e Nostra Donna messa d'azuro di Magnia fine...." Neri di Bicci, *Ricordanze*, 252–53, entry no. 488. Bruno Santi states that the painting was formerly in the Wilstach Collection of the Philadelphia Museum of Art (ibid.) as does Berenson, *Italian Pictures*, 1:157. According to Alison Goodyear of the museum curatorial staff, there is no record that the painting was ever there.

43. See David Herlihy and Christiane Klapisch-Zuber, *Tuscans and Their Families: A Study of the Florentine Catasto of 1427* (New Haven, Conn.: Yale University Press, 1985), 347–52, regarding the use of family names in Renaissance Tuscany.

44. "Ò tolto a dipignere da mona Checha...una tavola d'altare...nella quale tavola vole nel quadro di meze la Inchoronazione di Nostra Donna e dal lato ritto Santo Aghostino e Santo Nicholò e dalla mano sinistra Santo[...], chon ang[i]oli e altre fighure..., messa tutta d'oro fine...e lavorata d'azuro oltramarino..., nella predella 3 istoriette e l'arme ne' chanti della predella,...a uso di buono maestro ...e magistero;...ser Ghuaspare...prochuratore, a detto dì mi pose creditore a libro del detto munistero delle istaia 28 del grano ogni anno dopo la vita di detta mona Checha...e fatta e finita la detta tavola, si deba per dua amici chomuni artefici farla vedere e istimare e quello fia istimata e giudichata, deba ese[re] el suo vero prezo, al quale c[i]aschuno debe esere chontento...fu giudichato per Franc[esch]o di Giovanni [i.e., Francesco Botticini] dipintore del Popolo di Santa Lucia d'Ognisanti, albitro e amicho comune...quello che.ssi veniva d'una tavola, c[i]oè della pitura, oro e chol[or]i....Dove questo presente dì el...Franc[esc]o...(intese) finita di tuto...." Neri di Bicci, *Ricordanze*, 274–75, 286–87, 333–34; entry nos. 523, 543, 628.

45. Checa's painting, which was identified by Santi in Neri's *Ricordanze* (275), is reproduced in Richard Fremantle, *Florentine Gothic Painters from Giotto to Masaccio* (London: Secker and Warburg, 1975), 606. Fremantle lists the painting as at the Museo dell'Ospedale degli Innocenti; this is apparently one of its several stopping points following its restoration after the 1966 flood (cf. Santi's note after entry no. 523, *Ricordanze*, 275).

46. Richa, *Notizie*, 2:288–94.

47. Paatz and Paatz, *Die Kirchen*, 3:181; the church of San Bartolo a Cintoia is not mentioned in Paatz and Paatz.

48. Neri di Bicci, *Ricordanze*, 286, entry no. 543.

49. Kaftal, *Iconography of the Saints*, cols. 756–65, cols. 613–21.

50. Checa is not the only person from a working-class background who requested that Neri include a coat of arms in a work. A certain Zanobi di Manno, who was a cooper, requested from Neri a painted dossal bearing his coat of arms on 18 March 1460 (*Ricordanze*, 139, entry no. 272). Almost two years earlier (16 April 1457), Zanobi had requested an altarpiece, which would have been coupled with the dossal (ibid., 75, entry no. 147). In another instance, a druggist named Antonio di Berto Cardini of Pescia requested that his coat of arms be included on a fresco he commissioned from Neri (ibid., 94, entry no. 181).

51. Entry no. 791, almost eight years later, cost 130 florins. Compare this to the average cost of 10.6 florins for Neri's commissions from men in the appendix. The *catasto* officials set the annual minimum cost of living for a single adult at 14 florins; see Goldthwaite, *Building*, 348. For the Tuscan *catasto*, see Herlihy and Klapisch-Zuber, *Tuscans*.

52. Neri di Bicci, *Ricordanze*, 333, entry no. 628.

53. Richard Trexler, *Public Life in Renaissance Florence* (Ithaca: Cornell University Press, 1980), 92.

54. Michael Baxandall, *Painting and Experience in Fifteenth-Century Italy* (New York: Oxford University Press, 1990), 11.

55. Baxandall, *Painting and Experience*, 14–24.

56. "Ebi…una tavola d'atare [*sic*] la quale tavola ò tolto a dipigniere per lla chiesa di Santo Lionardo fuori dalla Porta a San Giorgio da Bernardo Salviati e da mon'India sua sirochia…c[i]oè quadra al'anticha, predella da pie' e quadro in mezo e cholonne a chanali da lato e di sopra architrave, freg[i]o, chornic[i]one, nella quale ò a dipigniere una Nostra Donna quando va in cielo e San Tomaso da piedi e da mano destra Santo Piero e Santo Girolamo e da mano sinistra Santo Giovanni e Santo Francescho, mesa dinanzi d'oro fine dove achade, da pie' nella predella meze fighure e l'arme, lavorata bene e di buoni cholori.…Rendei la detta tavola finita di tuto a' sopradetti mon'India e Bernardo a dì 22 d'aghosto 1467 e rizàmola al detto Santo Lionardo.…" Neri di Bicci, *Ricordanze*, 299–300, entry no. 567; cf. Vasari-Milanesi, *Vite*, 2:74.

    The Salviati coat of arms can be seen in Leonardo Ginori Lisci, *I palazzi di Firenze nella storia e nell' arte*, 2 vols. (Florence: Giunti, 1972), 2:843. India's painting resembles Neri's *Assumption of the Virgin* at the Museum of Fine Arts in Moscow (although this painting has two kneeling figures, Saints Thomas and Jerome), which is reproduced in Maria Mseriantz, "Two New Panels by Neri di Bicci," *Burlington Magazine* 62 (1933): plate 1A, opposite 222.

57. Richa, *Notizie*, 2:15–18; the church is not mentioned in Paatz and Paatz, *Die Kirchen*.

58. Vittorio Spreti, *Enciclopedia storico-nobiliare italiana*, 8 vols. (Milan: Enciclopedia storico-nobiliare italiana, 1928–35), 6:72–73.

59. Spreti, *Enciclopedia storico-nobiliare*, 6:72–73.

60. Pierre Hurtubise, *Une famille-témoin: Les Salviati* (Vatican City: Biblioteca Apostolica Vaticana, 1985), 34. Bernardo is listed on the family tree but India is not; see 496–97.

61. Richard Ehrenberg, *Capital and Finance in the Age of the Renaissance*, trans. H. M. Lucas (London: Jonathan Cape, 1928), 206.

62. Kaftal, *Iconography of the Saints*, col. 969.

63. Cf. the Salviati family tree; Hurtubise, *Une famille-témoin*, 496–97.

64. The commission is listed in Neri di Bicci, *Ricordanze*, entry no. 321, 162–63. Santi identified this painting, which includes Saint Leonard, the patron saint of the church at the Jacquemart-Andrè Museum in Paris.

65. "Patto di detto cholmo cho mona Agniesa: Richordo che avendo tolto a…dipigniere da m[ona] Agniesa vedova e donna fu di Bartolomeo Neroni uno cholmo grande, tondo di sopra chon una ghocc[i]ola di sotto e uno intavolato d'atorno, nel quale feci in mezo una Nostra Donna chol Figliuolo in chollo e da ogni lato una fighura…el quale cholmo disse volere pore nella chiesa di Santa Maria della Schala di Firenze.…" Neri di Bicci, *Ricordanze*, 306–7, entry no. 578. Santa Maria della Scala has been called San Martino della Scala since 1531; Paatz and Paatz, *Die Kirchen*, 4:133.

66. The Neroni family was rich and powerful; its most prominent member was Dietisalvi Neroni. Dietisalvi, together with Luca Pitti, Agnolo Acciaiuoli, and Niccolò Soderini, plotted to depose Piero de' Medici when he came to power in 1464. Luca Pitti was the sole conspirator to be pardoned, the others were exiled; see Francesco Guicciardini, *The History of Florence*, trans. Mario Domandi (New York: Harper and Row, 1970), 15–18.

67. John Kent Lydecker, "The Domestic Setting of the Arts in Renaissance Florence" (Ph.D. dissertation, Johns Hopkins University, 1987), 64–65.

68. "Uno tondo grande cholle chornicie atorno messe d' oro, dipintovi la Nostra Donna e el Nostro Signore e e [sic] Magi che vanno a offerire, di mano di fra' Giovanni...f. 100," Spallanzani and Gaeta Bertelà, *Libro d'inventario*, 12; see also Fern Rusk Shapley, *Catalogue of the Italian Paintings* (Washington: National Gallery of Art, 1979), 1:10–12.

69. Catherine King, "Medieval and Renaissance Matrons, Italian-Style," *Zeitschrift fur Kunstgeschichte* 55 (1992): 372–93. King's research has uncovered the patronage of several widows and nuns.

   In researching this paper I have found a reverse example of the patronage of Neri's widowed patrons; that is, a widower and sons who endow a chapel in memory of their late wife/mother. Pietro, Nicolò, Benedetto, and Marco Pesaro honored Franceschina Tron Pesaro with the chapel of the Pesaro and Bellini's *Frari Triptych* at Santa Maria dei Frari in Venice in 1478; Rona Goffen, *Piety and Patronage in Renaissance Venice: Bellini, Titian, and the Franciscans* (New Haven, Conn.: Yale University Press, 1986), 30–40. I bring attention to this previously published commission to encourage further research into memorials to women in the Renaissance.

70. Regarding widows, see Herlihy and Klapisch-Zuber, *Tuscans*, 214–22; and Christiane Klapisch-Zuber, "The 'Cruel Mother': Maternity, Widowhood, and Dowry in Florence in the Fourteenth and Fifteenth Centuries" in *Women, Family, and Ritual in Renaissance Italy* (Chicago: University of Chicago Press, 1985), 117–31. For other widows, see the chapters by Marjorie Och, Elizabeth Pilliod, Sheryl Reiss, Mary Vaccaro, and Carolyn Valone in this volume.

71. Herlihy and Klapisch-Zuber, *Tuscans*, 210–15. Although it was believed in the Renaissance that a man should take a wife while she was still in her early teens or even younger, this does not seem to have been always the case. Anthony Molho, "Deception and Marriage Strategy in Renaissance Florence: The Case of Women's Ages," *Renaissance Quarterly* 41 (1988): 193–217. Molho's research on the *catasto* and the *Monte delle Doti* shows that fathers often distorted their daughters' ages, making them seem younger and more eligible for marriage.

72. Klapisch-Zuber, "Cruel Mother," 120.

73. Klapisch-Zuber, "Cruel Mother," 120.

74. Judith C. Brown, "A Woman's Place Was in the Home: Women's Work in Renaissance Tuscany," in *Rewriting the Renaissance: The Discourses of Sexual Difference in Early Modern Europe*, ed. Margaret W. Ferguson and Maureen Quilligan (Chicago: University of Chicago Press, 1986), 209.

75. Richard Goldthwaite, *Wealth and the Demand for Art in Italy* (Baltimore: Johns Hopkins University Press, 1993), expands the discussion of the decorative arts as an economic phenomenon; see also Goldthwaite, *Building*, 400–7.

76. Vasari-Milanesi, 5:23, 6:246.

77. As in entry nos. 210, 228, 242; Neri di Bicci, *Ricordanze*, 108, 117, 124–25.

78. Elaine Rosenthal, "The Position of Women in Renaissance Florence: Neither Autonomy nor Subjection," in *Florence and Italy: Renaissance Studies in Honor of Nicolai Rubinstein*, ed. Peter Denley and Caroline Elam (London: Westfield College, 1989), 377. Rosenthal's research similarly shows that of the 125 legal acts she studied in which women were prime movers, almost 17 percent reveal that the woman acted without an attendant *mundualdus*.

79. Lydecker, "Domestic Setting," 145.

80. Goldthwaite, *Building*, 404.

81. See entry nos. 227, 239, 386; Neri di Bicci, *Ricordanze*, 116, 123, 194.

82. The dowry's function was threefold: it took care of household expenses, then the widow's needs, and then ultimately was returned to the woman's descendants. See Christiane Klapisch-Zuber, "The Griselda Complex: Dowry and Marriage Gifts in the Quattrocento," in *Women, Family, and*

Ritual, 216. Regarding the dowry, see also Julius Kirshner and Anthony Molho, "The Dowry Fund and the Marriage Market in Early Quattrocento Florence," *Journal of Modern History* 50 (1978): 403–38.

Women's art patronage for the home in quattrocento Florence may have been scarce, or at least it has been neglected by scholars in the past. In investigating this paper I have come across three such commissions. One of these is for a Madonna for a woman servant of Niccolò Strozzi. Strozzi lent her a florin in order to sponsor this work from an unnamed artist. Two years later, although she still owed him the florin, the woman left him the painting, which he says, "she left in my house, thinking to give pleasure to the children." Cited in Christiane Klapisch-Zuber, "Holy Dolls: Play and Piety in Florence in the Quattrocento," in *Women, Family, and Ritual*, 321. Another of these acquisitions is listed in the inventory describing the contents of Jacopo di Messer Giannozzo Pandolfini's home at the time of his death in 1503. This document mentions the purchase of a small Madonna on 20 December 1493, by a woman named Lisabetta. See Lydecker, "The Domestic Setting," appendix 3. A third example is listed below.

One of Neri's entries (no. 217, 111–12) alludes to what may be another commission for the home by a woman. Neri took an order for a gesso relief of a Madonna for the home from Tedaldo dalla Casa. Because it would take time to complete this work, Neri lent him a similar relief that belonged to Lionarda di Lionardo Gualtieri. Unfortunately, Neri did not state why he had possession of this woman's *Madonna* or whether the work was his own.

83. Cf. entry nos. 210, 441; Neri di Bicci, *Ricordanze*, 108, 224; Neri usually called these domestic works "cholmo di chamera" or "tabernacholo."

84. This finding challenges the assumption in Catherine King, "Matrons," 380, that women bought cheaper artistic goods. Further research, however, is necessary before any conclusions on the subject can be made.

85. My research was restricted to artists' manuscripts in print. Archival research will likely yield more extensive results.

86. The *bottega* book is printed in Ellen Callmann, *Apollonio di Giovanni* (Oxford: Clarendon Press, 1974), 76–81.

87. Ellen Callmann, "Apollonio di Giovanni and Painting for the Early Renaissance Room," *Antichità viva* 27 (1988): 5.

88. This woman's commission is listed as follows: "No. 173. figliuola di Madonna Caterina da Rimini, a Giovanni di mess. Giovanni Pitti, L. 160." The entry merely lists the intended receiver of the *cassoni*—the daughter of Caterina and intended wife of Giovanni. Caterina, who was probably a widow fulfilling the role of a patrician father, purchased a pair of *cassoni* for her daughter's wedding. See Callmann, *Apollonio*, 81. *Cassoni* are painted wooden chests, which sometimes were commissioned in pairs. Sometimes called *forzieri* in the Renaissance, they were used to transport dowry goods when a couple married, and later served as domestic furniture. Regarding *cassoni*, see Cristelle Baskins, *Cassone Painting, Humanism, and Gender in Early Modern Italy* (Cambridge: Cambridge University Press, 1998).

89. Charles Yriarte, *Journal d'un sculpteur florentin au XVe siècle: Livre de souvenèirs de Maso di Bartolommeo dit Masaccio* (Paris: Rothschild, 1894).

90. The commissions are listed as follows: "Ac. 55. terg. E de dare (Mona la Paccia donna del Bianco di Silvestro del Bene) a di 22 di settembre y otto contanti e per me da per parte di paghamento d'una champana che fuse y 8" and "Betta Donna di Gio. Bartolomeo d Telaio alla Porta della Sagrestia di S. Maria del Fiore per accordo con Michelozzo e Luca della Robia"; Yriarte, *Journal d'un sculpteur,* 68 and 91, respectively. Betta's commission shows that women often requested works of art for important locations.

91. His *Ricordi* are reprinted in Ruth W. Kennedy, *Alesso Baldovinetti* (London: Oxford University Press, 1938), 236–53.

92. Lorenzo Lotto, *Libro di spese diverse 1538–1556*, ed. Pietro Zampetti (Venice: Istituto per la Collaborazione Culturale, 1964).

93. Lotto, *Libro di spese diverse*, 166–69, 346.

94. According to Callmann, "Apollonio and Painting," 7. See A. Padoa Rizzo, "Ricerche sulla pittura del quattrocento nel territorio fiorentino: Bernardo di Stefano Rosselli," *Antichità viva* 26 (1987): 20–27.

95. Jaynie Anderson, "Rewriting the History of Art Patronage," *Renaissance Studies* 10 (1996): 131, reviewed an early draft of this chapter, from which she concluded that women comprised 10 percent of Neri's patronage.

Caterina Piccolomini
and the Palazzo delle Papesse in Siena

A. Lawrence Jenkens

The Palazzo delle Papesse in Siena (fig. 1) is only rarely noted in the literature on Italian quattrocento architecture. It is, however, a remarkable building for it was built, as its name implies, by a woman.[1] Begun ca. 1460 by Caterina Piccolomini, sister of Pope Pius II (1458–64), the Palazzo delle Papesse was intended as a residence for herself and her descendants.[2] Yet although Caterina bought the land upon which the palace was constructed, engaged an architect and workers to design and build it, petitioned the city government several times (to allow the building to encroach on communal property, for tax relief on imported materials, and to take timber from public land), and paid taxes on it when it was finished, she is never numbered among the few females generally discussed as patrons of architecture in the Italian Renaissance. Despite Caterina's clear involvement with the project, the Palazzo delle Papesse is usually considered among Pius's building projects both because it was paid for with papal funds and because, more simply, there has been an assumption that women in the Renaissance period did not build palaces. My purpose here is to establish that Caterina, perhaps the first woman in fifteenth-century Italy to build such a private residence, was indeed the patron of the palace she constructed. In order to make sense of this fact, however, we must also look at why and how she built. I suggest a possible avenue by which we might understand Caterina as palace builder not so much as an anomaly, but rather within the context both of gender relationships and patterns of private patronage in the quattrocento.

It is important first to look at the palace and review what little we know about its patron and building history. The Palazzo delle Papesse was designed in three stories around a central courtyard with octagonal piers. The building's main façade, facing the Via di Città, is rusticated with roughly carved travertine *bugnati* on the ground floor and more finely worked blocks of the same stone above. There are three round-headed arched portals of equal size on the ground floor and five two-light windows, their arched openings slightly pointed, on each of the upper floors (figs. 2, 3). The building is crowned by an *all'antica* cornice of modest dimensions. The Palazzo delle Papesse is among a handful of buildings constructed in a "Renaissance"—that is, a Florentine—style in Siena in the fifteenth century.[3] The Palazzo's appearance links it closely to Pius's architectural projects in Pienza and Siena and reinforces, as we will see below, the idea of a shared dynastic strategy.[4]

Caterina Piccolomini

We know little about Caterina Piccolomini, and the few biographical facts that do exist are somewhat confused in the literature. Caterina was one of three surviving children of Silvio Piccolomini and Vittoria Forteguerri, and she, like Pius and her sister, Laudomia, was born in Corsignano. Ugurgieri tells us, without citing a source, that Caterina married

Jenkens Fig. 1. Palazzo delle Papesse, Siena, Via di Città, begun ca. 1460 (photo: author)

Bartolomeo Guglielmi in 1430, and that Pius appointed his brother-in-law prefect of Spoleto early in his pontificate.[5] Tax records make it clear, however, that Caterina, who had indeed married Bartolomeo Guglielmi, was already a widow by 1453, five years before Pius ascended to the papacy; she is listed in the 1453 lira assessments as "Katherina dona fu di Bartolomeo di Francesco di Ghugliemo."[6] Her tax return indicates that she was living with her stepson, Francesco Guglielmi, who had inherited the bulk of his father's estate.[7] Caterina and Bartolomeo had a daughter, Antonia; by 1453 she was married to Bartolomeo Pieri da Massa, and Francesco still owed his brother-in-law 250 florins of Antonia's 850 florin dowry.[8] It must, therefore, have been Caterina's son-in-law, Bartolomeo Pieri, instead of her husband who was Pius's prefect in Spoleto and to whom the pope gave the privilege of using the Piccolomini family name.[9] Bartolomeo Guglielmi died long before the Palazzo delle Papesse was planned or built, which explains the absence of his name from all records concerning it. We will see below that Caterina and her son-in-law filed a joint tax declaration in 1466 since theirs was a single household; the documents that survive, however, make it clear that Caterina alone was responsible for the construction of the Palazzo delle Papesse.[10]

The records of the Gabelle, or contract tax, tell us that Caterina acquired property in the vicinity of the building site in August 1460.[11] It cannot be determined from the tax records if these purchases were indeed for the palace site; there is no doubt, however, that she was planning her palace at this time. In the same month as these real estate acquisitions, the city government ceded to Caterina "quedam platea comunis Senarum positam Senis in loco dicto Piaza Manetti." The document goes on to spell out both Caterina's intention and the speed with which she hoped to complete her palace, "dicta Domine Caterina intendit facere in dicti loco maiorem edifitium quam sit dicta platea et in tam parvo tempore."[12] The *comune* did not stop with assigning public land to Caterina for her project; it also gave her appropriated private lands. On 8 May 1469, Renaldo di Giovanni di Renaldo Chubecha complained to the Consiglio Generale that the city had taken his house "in strada dinançi ala Piaza Manecti," but also "una piaza la quale fu et è del decto Renaldo."[13] Caterina's palace now stood there and in recompense Renaldo asked the counsel to grant him a salaried vicariate for a year in the Cerna Maggiore, a district in the Sienese *contado*. The document reveals that the Consiglio Generale granted Renaldo's petition but not fully: although they did give him a vicariate, it was in the Cerna Minore and only for six months.

Construction of the Palazzo delle Papesse must have begun very quickly, for in October 1460 Caterina petitioned the city's governing council for relief from the Gabella, in this case regarding import duties on the marble and stone imported for the building. The petition makes Caterina's intention clear. She asks for her exemption given that "la detta Madonna

Caterina intende et vuole fare la detta casa honorattissima et con grande spese ad honore di questa Magnifica Città."[14] The same petition asked for permission to build on public property—that is, on part of a small street beside the palace—noting that this was necessary according to the design for the building made by a *valentissimo* master.[15] Both requests were approved. Caterina brought a second petition before the city government in September 1463, asking to take timber from Piancastagnaio, on the slopes of Monte Amiata, in or-

Jenkens Fig. 2. Palazzo delle Papesse, detail, ground floor (photo: author)

der to finish the palace's roof. In making this last request, the building is described as that which she "à facto fare et edificare…come si vede dove già fu el palazo de Marsilii et reducto lo atale perfectione che non resta se non cuprirlo."[16]

The palace must have been finished shortly thereafter, for Caterina's 1466 tax declaration, filed jointly with her son-in-law Bartolomeo Pieri, makes it clear that she was living in the palace with her daughter and her family even though it was not yet finished.[17] Caterina and Bartolomeo filed only one lira declaration because they maintained a single household; as we shall see below, however, Caterina's obligations with regard to the palace remained hers alone. The 1466 lira declaration also spells out the enormous cost of building such a residence; Caterina and Bartolomeo claimed that 7,000 florins had been spent on the palace by 1466, and list a further building debt of 4,282 florins. An examination of *uscite* of the Teseroria Segreta at the Vatican indicate that the bulk of this money came from papal coffers. The regular payment orders specify, using a variety of formulae, that money was being disbursed to Caterina, the pope's sister, for the palace she was building in Siena.[18] Tax declarations filed subsequently continue to claim expenses to finish and furnish the palace; in 1478, for example, Caterina and Antonia—who was at that time presumably a widow—state that the building still required 2,000 florins worth of work and furnishings.[19] This does not mean that they were not living in the palace, for in June 1473 the duke of Amalfi—Caterina's nephew—and his wife and two sons stayed in the Papesse when they accompanied the daughter of the king of Naples on a visit to Siena.[20]

The Architect of the Palazzo delle Papesse

Returning to the 1466 lira declaration, we find the Sienese architect and sculptor Antonio Federighi listed among Caterina's liabilities; indeed, she claimed to owe him 400 florins.[21] This is not a new obligation; on 1 June 1463 the city council wrote to Caterina concerning monies owed to Federighi and a Magister Andreas, a stone cut-

Jenkens Fig. 3. Palazzo delle Papesse, detail, *piano nobile* (photo: author)

ter.[22] The sum to be paid to the latter was to be determined by one Magister Bernardus, sometimes tantalizingly identified as Bernardo Rossellino, Pius's architect at Pienza, who was likely responsible for the buildings that the pope planned in Siena.[23]

Federighi's documented involvement with the Papesse (and perhaps the involvement of Rossellino) raises the interesting question of the attribution of the palace. Federighi clearly played a major role in the construction of the Palazzo delle Papesse, but did he design it or simply supervise the building site?[24] Unfortunately, the building as we know it today tells us little about its original appearance since, as Sigismondo Tizio reports in his *Historia Senensis*, it was destroyed by fire from the *piano nobile* to the roof in August 1523.[25] Ascanio Piccolomini, archbishop of Siena, restored the building but not until 1588.[26] Although overlooked by modern scholars, the fire and subsequent restoration help explain some of the stylistic anomalies—attributable, it seems, to the late-sixteenth-century reconstruction—that we see in the building. There are several anomalies, but perhaps most striking is the use of round-headed arches for the portals on the ground floor and pointed arches for the windows above. The former, set within a heavily rusticated wall, speaks clearly in the language of fifteenth-century Florence and breaks, both in style and choice of materials, with Sienese building traditions.[27] Ascanio's restoration came some thirty years after Siena had been absorbed into the duchy of Tuscany in 1555. His choice of Gothic windows—an archaic form but one strongly identified with Sienese architecture in the Renaissance and later—may well have been intended to soften the building's Florentine and (therefore foreign) look at a difficult moment shortly after republican Siena had lost its independence.

The sixteenth-century restoration, then, has left us with little visual evidence that might help us identify the palace's original designer. The debate over the architect has focused on the possible roles and relationship of Antonio Federighi and Bernardo Rossellino. One's position on this question depends on how one sees the connection between this building and Pius II's own architectural projects. That linkage has shaped more than just the discussion of Caterina's architect. It has literally been constructed by prevailing views of a patriarchal society in which women were confined to a domestic sphere with no role in the public aspects of their society, no access to resources, and therefore no ability to participate in shaping even their own world.[28] It is here that we must look in our effort to deconstruct this understanding and to arrive at a more accurate picture of the interaction between men and women, at least of an élite class, in a society dominated by men. In order to do this we need to review briefly Pius's architectural activity in Siena.

Pope Pius II and Siena

Shortly after he was elevated to the papacy in August 1458, Pius embarked upon an extraordinary building program in and around his native Siena. Most famous today are the palace, cathedral, and piazza at the heart of Pienza, the village where Pius was born.[29] Yet this project was not the end of the pontiff's building ambitions; as he was remaking Pienza he was also developing a plan for an architectural complex in Siena.[30] There Pius intended a large, freestanding palace and loggia, perhaps around an enlarged piazza just a stone's throw from the Campo, the political heart of the city (fig. 4). This project, more difficult logistically and politically than the building program in Pienza, was not completed in Pius's lifetime; he lived only to see the loggia finished (fig. 5).[31] The palace he envisioned was begun in 1469 (five years after his death) by his nephews Giacomo and Andrea, sons of his sister Laudomia.[32] They eventually divided the building site between them and constructed two separate and very different residences (figs. 6, 7).[33]

Taken together with the Pienza buildings, Pius's intention to build in Siena reveals an extraordinary ambition. Born into a noble family long excluded from governmental office in

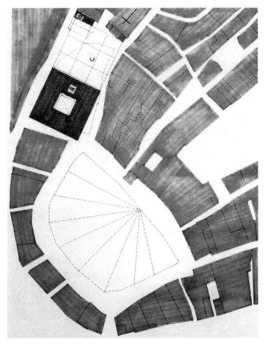

Jenkens Fig. 4. Reconstruction of Pius II's proposed intervention in Siena: (A) Palazzo Piccolomini; (B) Loggia dei Papa; (C) enlarged Piazza Piccolomini (drawing: Wolfgang Jung)

Siena, it was Pius's intention to reinsert his family into the city's political fabric. Yet his architectural program speaks of even greater hopes; together, the family's country seat of Pienza, and the palace complex in Siena, its urban power base, may have been meant to provide Pius's nephews with the necessary architectural trappings for a bid to claim a preeminent if not a dominant role for themselves in the political affairs of the city. Pius was likely acting to secure for his family (and his nephews in particular) a central position in Siena, perhaps hoping to emulate the example of Medici hegemony in Florence.[34]

It seems clear that in this context, Caterina's palace—smaller and less grand than the other, perhaps because she had no male children—was part of the pope's dynasty-building policy. But who then was the patron of the Palazzo delle Papesse? Pius was the prime mover behind the bigger palace; his nephews, who were teenagers at the time, are not documented as playing a public role in the building project until 1469, even though the building site had been purchased in their names. Caterina's role in the construction of her palace was different, for she seems to have been in control: she bought the property, she employed Federighi and others to build her residence, and it was to her that the monies from the papal purse were disbursed. Caterina seems, furthermore, to have acted in her own right. It is true that she and her son-in-law declared the palace as their joint property in 1466, but she alone owed Federighi 400 florins. Tax returns were filed by household, as we saw in Caterina's declarations after 1466;[35] there is no other indication in any document to suggest that Caterina ever shared the responsibility for building her palace.[36] Caterina's freedom to buy property, to petition the city, and to hire an architect and workers—especially given the juristic restrictions placed on Florentine women

Jenkens Fig. 5. Loggia del Papa, Siena, 1460–62 (photo: author)

in the fifteenth century—raises the interesting question of a woman's legal rights in Siena.[37] At this point, though, not enough is known about this issue to be able to judge if Caterina's situation was unique or typical for a Sienese woman of her class and with her resources. One can say that there is no evidence of any other example of female patronage of a building on the scale of the Palazzo delle Papesse in Siena in the quattrocento.

Jenkens Fig. 6. Giacomo Piccolomini's Palazzo Nuovo (now Palazzo Piccolomini), Siena, Banchi di Sotto, begun 1469 (photo: author)

Jenkens Fig. 7. Andrea Piccolomini's Casamento Vecchio (now Palazzo Piccolomini), Siena, Piazza del Campo, late fifteenth century (photo: author)

Women Patrons and Architecture

If we accept that Caterina was the patron of the Palazzo delle Papesse, then we must ask what this means for our understanding of female patronage in fifteenth-century Italy, and of the larger issue of gender interaction within a patriarchal social structure.[38] This is not an easy issue, and we can only here begin to discuss the possible significance of the Papesse in this regard.

When dealing with the question of female patronage in Renaissance Italy, art historians have followed the established model that defines a separation of spheres—the masculine/public sphere and the feminine/private sphere.[39] Women could operate only in the latter, and in those rare instances when they moved beyond it and patronized art, it was through a manipulation or subversion of an accepted social order. In a 1992 article, Catherine King lays out a lucid argument of this kind. She defines three groups of female patrons in the Renaissance—widows, nuns, and the consorts of great rulers—who had both the legal authority and the access to resources which would allow them at least some freedom to commission works of art. King states that "women could take a minor part in only two areas of patronage: that of the family, and that of religious orders." She later specificies that "laywomen, however rich, never commissioned palaces (presumably because they could not be represented as sexually powerful generators of a dynasty)."[40] For King and many others, the relationship between men and women in this period was an antagonistic one.

In a 1996 article, Thomas Kuehn offers a different model for gender relationships that is suggestive for us.[41] Kuehn points to the implicit assumptions about the conception of the self and the experiences of women—imbedded in modern notions of individualism—that underlie arguments like King's. He suggests an alternative: "A broader sense of social personhood as presented by anthropologists points to relationships and social position, not individual freedom and self-determination; and such personhood recasts gender as a matter of contingent differences, not as a matter of absolute opposition."[42] Social inequality has been constructed through sexual difference, but "male solidarity was not an independent variable, rather 'lineage solidarity built on the combination of male and female efficacy suggests an important qualification to assuming the apparent autonomy of male interests.'"[43] According to Kuehn's model, when Caterina Piccolomini built her Palazzo delle Papesse she was operating not simply in her own interests but to benefit her family, just as Pius was doing.[44] Her patronage of this building—seemingly an exceptional case in the history of quattrocento architecture—does not change the fact that women were politically, economically, and legally marginalized in that society. That she built the palace, however, suggests that in this context that same society allowed a woman who had the means and authority to pursue an architectural project. Scholarship of the past few years has shown, furthermore, that Caterina is not a unique example of female patronage of secular architecture.[45]

Kuehn's anthropological model is consistent with recent research on cooperative familial patronage in Florence, especially that of the Medici family.[46] Florence and the Medici provide a powerful point of comparison with the Piccolomini because in both cases in the middle years of the fifteenth century we have private citizens commissioning works of art to further their own dynastic and political ends. In discussing the joint patronage of Cosimo de' Medici and his brother Lorenzo, John T. Paoletti notes that "of special interest in these…commissions is the evolution, if not the codification, of an explicit Medici iconography which asserted the family's prominence within a society where family position and honor were principal motivating forces for both political and artistic activity. Coincidentally this imagery also carries explicit references to dynastic continuity."[47] Pius's and Caterina's buildings can also be interpreted as representing a similar shared dynastic strategy; they were meant as potent and permanent symbols of the presence and political influence of the Piccolomini family. These monuments were likely intended to make a familial statement rather than to express the individual personality of their patrons in any modern sense, and it is in this context that we can begin to understand both how and why Caterina Piccolomini built a palace.

Appendix: Documents Concerning the Palazzo delle Papesse[48]

These documents, arranged by archival font and then chronologically, come from the Archivio di Stato, Siena.

Gabelle:

1. 240, fol. 30r. (Ser Bartholomeus Simonis, notary, 23 August 1460)

Domina Eufrasia relicta Nannis Domenici Feii et Martus Pietri Bortoli Lotti de Senis vendiderunt et cesserunt:

Clarissima domina domina Caterina olim Silvii de Picholominibus de Senis omnia et singula iura que habebant contra hospitale Sancte Maria dela Scala de Senis occasione perpetui afictus et pensionis floreno sex cuiusdam apotece site Senis in compagna Aldobrandini del Mancino infra suos confines pro pretio florenorum centumtriginta de libris iiii ᵒʳ pro quolibet floreno.

2. 240, fol. 30r. (Ser Bartholomeus Simonis, notary, 26 August 1460)

Bartheus olim Guidonis Aluptarius de Senis vendidit:

Domina Caterina supradicta unam domum sitam Senis in terçerio Civitatis et in populo Sancti Johannis infra suos confines pro pretio florenorum trecentorum viginti octo de libris iiii [or] pro quolibet floreno.

Consistoro:

3. 563, fol. 3v, 30 August 1460

Ante dicti magnifici domini et capitaneus populi una cum vexilliferis magistris et offitialibus super ornatu civitatis attendentes qualiter per eorum in offitio precessores fuit concessa quedam platea comunis senarum posita Senis in loco dicto Piaza Manetti magnifice et nobili Domine Caterine de Piccolominibus sorori carnati summi pontificis sub die xviii decembris proxime preteriti cum quibusdam conditionibus. Inter alia de tempore quo dictum edifitium super dicta platea deberet fecisse de quibus omnibus plene patet manu Ser Dei Silvestri tunc notarii concistorii. Et viso quod dicta Domina Caterina intendit facere in dicti loco maiorem edifitium quam sit dicta platea et in tam parvo tempore illud edifitium ut tunc promisit facere non posset quibus de causis servatis servanadis delibaverunt prorogare et solemniter prorogaverunt terminum suprascriptum ad faciendum dictum edifitium ut promisserat usque ad festum Sancte Marie mensis augusti 1462 proxime venturi quibus cunquem incontrarium non obstantibus et hoc omni modo et ceteris.

4. 564, fol. 28v, 29 October 1460
(Approval of Caterina's petitions)

Et in ipso etiam consilio facta proposita super quandam petitionem Nobilissime Domine Chaterine sorori summi pontificis et primo super prima parte ipsius petitionis et super ea redditis consiliis miso partito ad lupinos albos et nigris fuit victum et obtentum per 148 lupinos albos redditos prosic 8 nigris redditis pro non in contrarium non obstantibus. Quod fiat et exequatur in omnibus et per omnia prout in prima parte ipsius petitionis de cabellis conturetur cum eius limitatione obtenta prima deroghatione statutorum per 148 lupinos albos 8 nigris non obstantibus.

Et similiter misso partito super secunda parte ipsius petitionis victum et obtentum fuit per 120 lupinos albos redditos pro sic 36 lupinos nigris redditis pro non in contrarium non obstantibus. Quod fiat et exequatur in omnibus et per omnia prout in ipsa seconda parte continatur obtenta primo deroghatione statutorum per 120 lupinos albos 36 nigris non obstantibus. Que petitione est penes reformationes.

5. 582, fol. 8r, 9 September 1463[49]

Exponsi con ogni dibita reverentia per la devota figliuola della Vostra Magnifica Signoria Madonna Caterina sorella della Santità Nostro Signore che come è noto alla Signoria Vostra e a tucti e ciptadini lei à facto fare e edificare el palazo et hedeficio come si vede dove già fu el palazo de marsilii e reducto lo atale perfectione che non resta se non cuprirlo et che non à potuto fare per non trovare legname adactato al dicto lavoro et ell'è stato recordato che volendo fare cuprirlo et mectervi legname buono et degno a esso lavoro le converrebbe provedere potere avere delli habeti del pigelloto della terra nostra di Piano Castagnaio el quale non si puo havere senza deliberatione secondo l'è stato affermato de vostri consigli per la qualcosa non avendo lei trovato altro legname appropriato recorre alla prefata Vostra Magnifica Signoria quella humilemente pregando consigli fare solennemente provedere ordinare et deliberare et reformare che essa possa et allei sia licito potere fare tagliare in esso pigelloto tucto e legname bisognevole et necessario per lo dicto suo palazo et hedificio el quale legname lei offera volere pagare et satisfare alla ostra Magnifica comunità come parra alla Vostra Magnifica Signoria et benche questa sua domanda le paia assai giusta et ragionevole niente di meno se la reputara a dono et gratia singulare dalla prefata Vostra Magnifica Signoria la quale l'Altissimo feliciti et axalti secondo e suoi desiderii.

6. 1681, fol. 66v, 1 June 1463[50]

Domine Caterine pape sorori scriptum est qualiter Magister Antonius Federici de Ptholomeis assuerit nobis expendidisse certas pecuniam quanititates in rebus aductis pro constructione eius palatii ac etiam cum persona sua valde se exercuit ad dictam constructionem. Quod saltem de denariis extractis de eius marsupio optaret sibi satisfieri. Et quod Magister Andreas de Interanne lapidum ductor assuerit multas pecunias debere habere ab ea. Et quod Magister Bernardus cui erat data commissio declarandi quid ipse Magister Andreas deberet habere recessit et non declaret. Qua propter placeret sibi et dicto Magistro Antonio de dictis denariis expensis facere satis et pro Magistro Andrea conmittere cuicumque sibi visum fuerit dummodo habitet Senis quod declaret et declarato placeat sibi de sua debita mercede satisfacere.

Consiglio Generale:

7. 228, fol. 300v, 15 October 1460[51]

Dinançi da Voi Magnifici et potenti Signori priori governatori del comune et Capitano del Magifica città di Siena.

Supplica humilmente Madonna Caterina de Piccolomini sorella dela Sanctità di Papa Pio ala Signoria Vostra che vi degniate per li vostri oportuni consegli fare solennemente provedere che essa o altri per lei possa mettare in Siena marmi tibertini macigni et qualunque altra generatione di pietro che allei fussero necessarie per la casa da doversi per lei nuovamente edificare cosi per la faccia dinançi come per qualunque altra parte dessa casa sença alcuno pagamento di cabella da pagarsi al comune di Siena / non[…]alcuna leggie statuto di vostra comune che per alcuno modo disponesse incontrario ali quali si degnino le Vostre Magnifice Signori fare solennemente derogare / considerato che la detta Madonna Caterina intende et vuole fare fare la detta casa honorattissima et con grande spesa ad honore di questa Magnifica Citta et dele Vostre Magnifice et ex.se Signori. Item per che la detta Madonna Caterina a facta designare la detta casa da uno valentissimo Maestro dal quale lei ha havuto per consiglio et parere per belleça dela faccia dinançi che allei sarebbe necessario davere quello chiasso di sotto verso el campo a canto ala detta casa nuova. Item per che la via dal canto di sopra dela detta casa volendola lassare tutta libera come era prima sarebbe al quanto mancamento al detto edifitio. Et pertanto supplica la detta Madonna Caterina che vi degniate di fare provedere per li detti consegli che essa possa pigliare del detto chiasso di sotto quello che le fusse bisognevole cioè o tutto o parte secondo el conseglio del detto maestro. Et che essa possa pigliare similmente dela detta via di sopra verso piaça Manetti secondo el parere del detto maestro. Offrendosi pero essa Madonna Caterina in termine di due anni dal di della obtenuta provisione rimettare la detta via in quella largheçça che è al presente non obstante qualunque leggie o statuto che incontrario parlasse. Le quali cose si fara la Vostre Magnifice Signori come spese se lo reputarà ad singularissima gratia da quella.

8. 233, fol. 3v, 8 May 1469[52]

Renaldo di Giovanni di Renaldo del Chubecha vostro minimo servidore con debita reverentia dice et expone che conciò sia cosa che le Magnifice Signori Vostre donassero a Madonna Chaterina sorella che fu de la felice recordatione di papa Pio nel tempo che volse principiare la casa sua in strada dinançi ala Piaza Manecti una piaza la quale fu et è del decto Renaldo dinançi dove era la casa desso Renaldo antichamente dela quali hoggi ateso luogo se n'arebbe cento floreni in circa et questo per errore impero che essendoli confischata la casa et non la piaza ma fu stimato fusse incominciata decta piaza dela quale quando ne dicie niente ala decta Madonna Caterina risponde che li fu donata da li Vostre Magnifice Signori. Et cosi truova esse vero ne'libri del armario dele vostre Riformagioni. Et pero lui ricorre a piei de le Vostre Magnifice Signori quelli humilmente supplicando che in luogo di detta piaza si d…mino fare per li vostri opportuni consigli fare solepnemente dettare et ordinare che sopradetto Renaldo sia et esser s'intenda vicario per uno anno del primo vicariato che vacara dela cerna maggiore con offitio salario et emolomenti consueti la qualcose benche ale Vostre Magnifice Signori sia picciola lui se la repudara grandissima et non solamente ad intero pagamento di detta piaza ma ad gratia singularissima dali Vostre Magnifice Signori ali quali humilmente si racomanda.

Lira:

9. 156 (1466-Città), no folio numbers

Excerpts from lira declaration:

> Madonna Caterina de Picolomini da Siena et Misser Bartolomeo de Picolomini da Massa cittadino di Siena danno le infrascripte loro cose cioè:

> Una casa posta nela città di Siena nel terzo di città nela compagna d'aldobrandino del mancino cole massaritie che anno apartenenti ala detta casa et con panni di dorso loro et della donna sua: et con libri convenienti alui et al suo exercitio. Et con una casetta dietro ala detta casa di valuta fl. 50.

> Trovarsi avere a dare la detta Madonna Caterina et Misser Bartolomeo fl. secento quaranta et due terzi a Ventura d'Antonio et a Francesco di Bartolomeo et a misser Bartolomeo Pecci et a Bartolomeo d'Aghustino di Bettino li quali loro promisero a Petro Turamini et compagni per la detta Madonna Caterina et Misser Bartolomeo.

> Item è debitrice la detta Madonna Caterina a Maestro Antonio Federighi in fl. 400.

> Item è debitrice a Misser Andrea suo nipote in fl. dugento.

> Item è debitrice a più e diverse altre persone cio e Bizone dela Ficarella maestro Andrea da Terni Francesco di Petroccio Filippo di Piero Humido et piu altre persone in fl. cinquecento quaranta sei.

> Item ano di spesa nela detta casa nuova per volerla habitare ancora ducati d'oro due milia a judicio di tutti huomini intendenti.

> Racomandandosi ale Signori Vostre anno paghato da diciotto mesi in qua di debiti per la detta casa fl. quattromilia dugento ottanta due et due terzi et anno speso nela detta casa del lor proprio fl. sette milia annolo fatto per honore et ornamento dela città et per fare questo si sono spogliati di tutto loro beni mobili anno abonificata la citta per la rata loro quanto nissuno altro come si vede furono dannificati nela morte di Papa Pio in ducati tremilia in denari che lassarono a Spoleto et in spese che lo bisogno fare in gente d'arme et in altre spese che fecero per tornare a salvamento. Restarono ad avere per denari serviti et per admonitione dela rocha dala camera apostolica fl. mille cinquecento non speriamo davere niente non lo è rimasto niente se non quanto si vede....

> Item ano di spesa nela detta casa nuova per volerla habitare ancora ducati doro due milia a judicio di tutti huomini intendenti.

Notes

A first version of this paper was delivered at the Renaissance Society of America meeting in Vancouver in April 1997. I am especially grateful to Sheryl Reiss for her immediate and enthusiastic interest in this work and for sharing her own research with me. I want to thank Professors Reiss and David Wilkins for inviting me to participate in this volume. A number of people have read and made useful comments on several drafts of this paper—among them Sheryl Reiss, David Wilkins, Kathleen Weil-Garris Brandt, Brenda Preyer, Linda Pellecchia, Marietta Cambareri, Meredith Gill, and Margaret Kuntz. Catherine Drake has, as always, proved a most constructive editor. Fabrizio Nevola, with the assistance of Dr. Carla Zarilli, Director of the Archivio di Stato in Siena, kindly checked some of the documents cited below. I would also like to thank my colleagues and students at the University of New Orleans for their probing questions when I presented this material to them.

1. The origin of the palace's name—the Palazzo delle Papesse—is not known, although it clearly refers to the fact that it was the residence of the pope's sister and her family. In the late fifteenth century the building was simply referred to as Caterina Piccolomini's palace; the earliest reference I have found to "Palazzo delle Papesse" is in 1548, in the tax declaration of Agostino di Francesco Vescovi. He described a "meza casa in Siena nel Terzo di Città, populo di San Desiderio in tra el Palazzo dele Papesse e la casa de'Figliucci." See ASS, Lira 244, fol. 463r. In the nineteenth century the building was called the Palazzo Nerucci. See Curzio Ugurgieri della Berardenga, *Pio II Piccolomini con notizie su Pio III e altri membri della famiglia* (Florence: Leo S. Olschki, 1978), 299–300.

2. For Caterina Piccolomini, whose date of birth is not known, see Ugurgieri, *Pio II Piccolomini*, 220.

3. The Palazzo delle Papesse has never been treated monographically in the literature. Typical of the palace's treatment, especially by historians, is Ferdinand Schevill's description of it as one of several buildings "all planned either by Florentine architects or by architects under Florentine influence. These splendid structures give the Renaissance touch to Siena which no one would care to miss; nevertheless, they not only represent an artistic importation, but are impotent to drown the mediæval note so formidably struck by the city's ensemble," Ferdinand Schevill, *Siena, The History of a Medieval Commune* (New York: Scribner, 1964), 307. For a somewhat more thorough treatment of this building, see Ruth O. Rubinstein, "Pius II as a Patron of Art, with Special Reference to the History of the Vatican" (Ph.D. diss., Courtauld Institute of Art, 1957), 65–66, and Charles R. Mack, "Studies in the Architectural Career of Bernardo di Matteo Ghamberelli Called Rossellino" (Ph.D. diss., University of North Carolina at Chapel Hill, 1972), 345.

4. A. Lawrence Jenkens, "The Palazzo Piccolomini in Siena: Pius II's Architectural Patronage and Its Afterlife" (Ph.D. diss., Institute of Fine Arts, New York University, 1995), 106–12.

5. Ugurgieri, *Pio II Piccolomini*, 135, 220, 236.

6. ASS, Lira 57, fol. 22v. Caterina Piccolomini is listed as living in the Terzo di Città and the *popolo* of Casato di Sopra.

7. ASS, Lira 136, fol. 13r. Caterina declared "tutti i miei beni mobili et immobili, debiti e crediti" and her dowry of 495 florins which she was still owed by her stepson. She does not declare any property in Siena and is assessed a tax of 750 lire. Francesco, Bartolomeo's heir, is assessed at the substantially higher sum of 5,670 lire. See ASS, Lira 57, fols. 21r, 22v.

8. ASS, Lira 136, fol. 16r. is the tax declaration filed by "Franchesco di Bartolomeo di Franchesco di Guglielmo." Among other things, he declares, "Et più mi truovo debito cho Misser Bartolomeo da Massa mio chongniato per dotte di mea sorela fl. ottociento cinquanta de quali mie padre li lasso una pocisione a Monastero, cioè nela Massa di Siena, e solli tenesse in pengnio per fl.600

et però la deta pocisione no posi in fra i miei si che resto a dare a decto Misser Bartolomeo fl. dugiento cinquanta."

9. Pius himself writes that from 13 November to 16 December 1462, Caterina, her daughter, and her grandson came from Spoleto to visit him in nearby Todi. See Enea Silvio Piccolomini, *I commentari,* ed. Luigi Totatro (Milan: Adelphi, 1984), 2:2009.

10. See below, n. 16.2

11. ASS, Gabelle, 240, fol. 30r. The two transactions recorded here, executed by the notary Bartolomeo di Simone on 23 August 1460, record the purchase of the rights to a shop and the purchase of a house. See appendix, docs. 1, 2.

12. ASS, Consistoro, 563, fol. 3v. See appendix, doc. 3.

13. ASS, Consiglio Generale, 233, fol. 5v. The document was cited and summarized, although not transcribed, in Petra Pertici, *La città magnificata; Interventi edilizi a Siena nel Rinascimento* (Siena: Il Leccio, 1995), 120. See appendix, doc. 8.

14. ASS, Consiglio Generale, 228, fols. 300v–301r. This document has been published in Scipione Borghese and Luciano Banchi, *Nuovi documenti per la storia dell'arte senese* (Siena, Enrico Torrini Editore 1898), 201–2. See appendix, doc. 7.

15. Borghese and Banchi, *Nuovi Documenti*, 201–2. The original text reads, "Item che per la detta Madonna Caterina a facta designare la detta casa da uno valentissimo Maestro dal quali lej ha havuto per consiglio et parere la belleça dela faccia dinançi che allej sarebbe necessario davere quello chiasso di sotto verso el campo a canto ala detta casa nuova." See appendix, doc. 7.

16. ASS, Consistoro, 582, fol. 8r. See appendix, doc. 5.

17. ASS, Lira 156, folios not numbered. I would like to thank Fabrizio Nevola, who in checking this document first brought to my attention the confusion between Bartolomeo Guglielmi, Caterina's late husband, and Bartolomeo Pieri, her son-in-law. See appendix, doc. 9.

18. The documents from the Teseroria Segreta relating to Caterina's palace in Siena have been published by Eugène Müntz, *Les arts à la cour des papes pendant le XVe et le XVIe siècle* (1884; reprint, Hildesheim: Olms, 1983), 1:307–8 and Jenkens, "Palazzo Piccolomini," 2:349–50. The brief entries mention payments to Caterina using formulae such as "per fare murare la sua casa fa fare a Siena," "per lo suo palazzo," and "per lo palazzo di Madonna Caterina."

19. ASS, Lira 174, n.p. Caterina filed another return, alone this time, in 1481 (ASS, Lira 185, fol. 151). In 1483 Antonia filed a single return listing the palace as her residence (ASS, Lira 203, n.p.), suggesting that her mother, who would have been unlikely to take up residence elsewhere, died sometime between 1481 and 1483.

20. Allegretto Allegretti, *Diari scritti delle cose Sanesi del suo tempo*, in Ludovico Muratori, *Rerum Italicarum Scriptores* (Milan, 1733), 23:775.

21. ASS, Lira 156, folii not numbered. "Item e debitrice la detta M.a Caterina a maestro Antonio Federighi in fl. 400." See appendix, doc. 7.

22. This document was published by Gaetano Milanesi, *Documenti per la storia dell'arte senese* (Siena, Onorato Porri, 1856), 2:323. See appendix, doc. 6.

23. Milanesi, *Documenti*, 2:323. Milanesi was the first to identify this Bernardus as Bernardo Rossellino, to whom he attributed the design of the Palazzo delle Papesse. Although we know of no other Master Bernardo active in Siena at this time who would have been asked to evaluate a stone cutter's work, and we also know that Rossellino was usually identified as Maestro Bernardo in the Pienza documents, we cannot be sure that this Bernardus was indeed Rossellino. It seems to have been common practice, at least in Rome, for an architect to assess the work of a craftsman and determine the wage owed him. Furthermore, Bernardo was in Pienza. It is possible that he might have ventured to nearby Siena, which stood on the main road to Florence, on several occasions. For architectural practice in the Renaissance, see James S. Ackerman, *Distant Points: Essays in*

Renaissance Art and Architecture (Cambridge, Mass: MIT Press, 1991), 368–69. Charles R. Mack, *Pienza, The Creation of a Renaissance City* (Ithaca: Cornell University Press, 1987), 36, disagrees, arguing that it would have been strange for the architect of a palace to be called upon to estimate payment for any work on the building.

24. In the 1460 petition to the Consiglio Generale, the building is described as that which "la detta Madonna Caterina a facta designare…da uno valentissimo Maestro." (See above, n. 5.) Unfortunately this "valentissimo Maestro" is not named.

25. Tizio's description of the fire at the Palazzo delle Papesse is quoted in Narciso Mengozzi, "Ascanio Piccolomini quinto Arcivescovo di Siena," *Bulletino Senese della Storia Patria* 19 (1912): 326–27. The text reads "Euisdem vero diei, octava Augusti 1523, vespere, palatium Eneae Piccolominei filii Bartholomei Doctoris Massani, in regione civitatis, tuberosis lapidibus constructum, atque conspicuum, incendio seviente, a medio sursum flamma volitans cum tecto concremavit."

26. Mengozzi "Ascanio Piccolomini," 324. Daniello Leremita, the archbishop's biographer, describes this restoration of the "palazzo fondato da Caterina, sorella del Papa" among Ascanio Piccolomini's notable accomplishments.

27. The choice of such an obviously foreign style for the Palazzo delle Papesse raises the interesting and complicated question of what political statement, if any, Caterina hoped to convey with her building. The palace's style also ties it closely to a small group of buildings erected in Siena at this time, including the Palazzo Piccolomini (begun 1469 but planned earlier) and the Palazzo Spannocchi (begun 1472). This link suggests a style of building that might be closely associated with the Piccolomini and certainly raises the specter of dynastic ambition in the city. See Jenkens, "Palazzo Piccolomini," iv–xvi. For the Palazzo Spannocchi, see Cornelius von Fabriczy, "Giuliano da Maiano in Siena," *Jahrbuch der königlich preussischen Kunstsammlungen* 24 (1903): 320–34. The Palazzo delle Papesse does retain some qualities of traditional palace architecture, especially the three large openings on the building's ground floor. They suggest a commercial use for the space behind them. There is, however, no indication that there were ever shops in the palace or that business was conducted there. Here perhaps the architect was adapting a late medieval palace-type in his design for the Palazzo delle Papesse (similar to the Palazzo Tolomei in Siena or the Palazzo Davanzati in Florence).

28. See Joan Kelly's seminal essay, "Did Women Have a Renaissance?" reprinted in Joan Kelly, *Women, History, and Theory: The Essays of Joan Kelly* (Chicago: University of Chicago Press, 1984), 19–50; Christiane Klapisch-Zuber, introduction, *La famiglia e le donne nel Rinascimento a Firenze* (Rome: Laterza, 1988), v–xix. Since then a number of scholars have sought to demonstrate how women manipulated or subverted social, cultural and even legal mechanisms in order to achieve their ends. See below, n. 39.

29. The literature on Pienza is vast. For bibliographies, see Mack, *Pienza*, and Andreas Tönnesman, *Pienza, Städtbau und Humanismus* (Munich: Hirmer, 1990).

30. For Pius II's architectural projects in Siena, see Jenkens, "Palazzo Piccolomini," 17–101.

31. For the loggia see A. Lawrence Jenkens, "Pius II and His Loggia in Siena," in *Pratum Romanum: Richard Krautheimer zum 100. Geburtstag*, ed. Renate Colella, A. Lawrence Jenkens, and others (Weisbaden: Dr. L. Reichert, 1997), 199–214.

32. Pius's sister Laudomia married Nanni Tedeschini in 1435, and he, like Bartolomeo Pieri, was later adopted by the pope and given the Piccolomini surname. For the Tedeschini family, see Domenico Bandini, "Gli antenati di Pio III," *Bulletino senese della storia patria* 25 (1966–68): 239–51. Laudomia and Nanni had four sons and a daughter. Pius focused much of his attention and, I believe, his ambition on his nephews, making the eldest, Francesco, Cardinal Archbishop of Siena, and marrying Antonio (soon to be the duke of Amalfi) to Maria de Aragona, the illegitimate daughter of the king of Naples. The younger two boys, Giacomo and Andrea, remained to make their careers in Siena, and it was in their names that Pius purchased the palace site in Siena. See Ugurgieri, *Pio II Piccolomini*, 1978, 536–45.

33. Jenkens, "Palazzo Piccolomini," 121–289.

34. Jenkens, "Palazzo Piccolomini," 3–16.

35. See above, n. 20.

36. Ugurgieri, *Pio II Piccolomini*, 299, states—without documentation—that Caterina insisted on having a palace: "Da qualque tempo sua sorella Caterina insisteva per avere in Siena un proprio palazzo. Papa Piccolomini, che raramente sapeva resistere alle richieste dei parenti, acconsentì, le permise di ricorrere all'opera del Rossellino, e al momento opportuno pagò." While his interpretation of the origin of the palace in the relationship between brother and sister is likely incorrect, Ugurgieri does not suggest that Caterina depended on anyone, including her son-in-law, to execute her commission.

37. In the fifteenth century, Florentine women had to obtain the consent of a male guardian or *mundualdus* in order to execute financial or legal transactions. See Thomas Kuehn, "'Cum Consensu Mundualdi': Legal Guardianship of Women in Quattrocento Florence," *Viator* 13 (1982): 309–33. See also Ann Morton Crabb, "How Typical Was Alessandra Macinghi Strozzi of Fifteenth-Century Florentine Widows?" in *Upon My Husband's Death: Widows in the Literature and Histories of Medieval Europe*, ed. Louise Mirrer (Ann Arbor: University of Michigan Press, 1992), 47–68.

38. There is a growing body of literature on this issue, although much of it is being carried out by historians and cultural anthropologists instead of art historians. For a general discussion of gender theory and historical analysis, see Joan W. Scott, "Gender: A Useful Category of Historical Analysis," *The American Historical Review* 91 (1986): 1053–75. For the Italian Renaissance see Catherine King, "Medieval and Renaissance Matrons, Italian-Style," *Zeitschrift für Kunstgeschichte* 55 (1992): 372–93; Thomas Kuehn, *Law, Family & Women: Toward a Legal Anthropology of Renaissance Italy* (Chicago: University of Chicago Press, 1991); Sharon Strocchia, "La famiglia patrizia fiorentina nel secolo XV: La problematica della donna," in *Palazzo Strozzi: Metà millennio, 1489–1989* (Rome: Istituto della Enciclopedia Italiana, 1991), 126–37; Sharon Strocchia, "Funerals and the Politics of Gender in Early Renaissance Florence," in *Refiguring Woman: Perspectives on Gender and the Italian Renaissance*, ed. M. Migiel and J. Schiesari (Ithaca: Cornell University Press, 1991), 155–68; Elaine G. Rosenthal, "The Position of Women in Renaissance Florence: Neither Autonomy nor Subjugation," in *Florence and Italy: Renaissance Studies in Honor of Nicolai Rubinstein*, ed. Peter Denley and Caroline Elam (London: Committee for Medieval Studies, Westfield College, 1988), 369–81.

39. For issues of public and private spaces, see Ann Rosalind Jones, "Enabling Sites and Gender Difference: Reading City Women with Men," *Women's Studies* 19 (1991): 239–49; Hanna Fenichel Pitkin, "Justice: On Relating Public and Private," *Political Theory* 9 (1991): 327–52; Dennis Romano, "Gender and Urban Geography in Renaissance Venice," *Journal of Social History* 23 (1989): 339–53; Linda K. Kerber, "Separate Spheres, Female Worlds, Woman's Place: The Rhetoric of Women's History," *The Journal of American History* 75 (1988): 9–39.

40. King, "Medieval and Renaissance Matrons," 380. Since this article was completed King has published a more complete study on this topic in book form, *Renaissance Women Patrons* (Manchester: Manchester University Press, 1998). Her conclusion remains similar, but she does not write that lay women never commissioned palaces.

41. Thomas Kuehn, "Understanding Gender Inequality in Renaissance Florence: Personhood and Gifts of Maternal Inheritance by Women," *Journal of Women's History* 8 (1996): 58–80.

42. Kuehn, "Understanding Gender Inequality," 59.

43. Kuehn, "Understanding Gender Inequality," 73. Here Kuehn is quoting Marilyn Strathern, introduction, in *Dealing with Inequality: Analyzing Gender Relations in Melanesia and Beyond* (Cambridge: Cambridge University Press, 1987), 6–15.

44. Ugurgieri's description of Caterina's insistence on having a palace is perhaps the most blatant example of an ahistorical interpretation of the patronage of this building (Ugurgieri, *Pio II Piccolomini*, 299; see above, n. 26).

45. See Sheryl Reiss's chapter in this volume. Reiss reaches similar conclusions in her work on Alfonsina de' Medici. Female patronage of religious architecture is a very different case. See King, "Medieval and Renaissance Matrons," 372–93; Carolyn Valone, "Roman Matrons as Patrons: Various Views of the Cloister Wall," in *The Crannied Wall: Women, Religion, and the Arts in Early Modern Europe*, ed. C. Monson (Ann Arbor: University of Michigan Press, 1992), 49–72; Carolyn Valone, "Women on the Quirinal Hill: Patronage in Rome, 1560–1630," *Art Bulletin* 76 (1994): 129–46.

46. See in particular John T. Paoletti, "'ha fatto Piero con voluntà del padre…' Piero de' Medici and Corporate Commissions of Art," in *Piero de' Medici "il Gottoso," 1416–1469*, ed. Andreas Beyer and Bruce Boucher (Berlin: Akademie Verlag, 1993), 221–50; John T. Paoletti, "Fraternal Piety and Family Power: The Artistic Patronage of Cosimo and Lorenzo de' Medici," in *Cosimo "il Vecchio" de' Medici, 1389–1464*, ed. F. Ames-Lewis (Oxford: Clarendon Press, 1992), 195–219. I am grateful to Sheryl Reiss for calling my attention to this work. See also the paper by Carolyn Valone in this collection.

47. Paoletti, "Fraternal Piety," 196.

48. I am most grateful to Dr. Maria Assunta Ceppari for her expertise and patience in checking these transcriptions with me in the Archivio di Stato, Siena. I would also like to thank Dr. Carla Zarilli, Director of the Archivio in Siena, and her staff for their continued kind assistance.

49. This petition was approved.

50. Milanese, *Documenti*, 2:323.

51. Borghese and Banchi, *Nuovi Documenti*, 201–2. The petition was approved.

52. Cited and summarized by Pertici, *La città magnificata*.

Renaissance Husbands and Wives as Patrons of Art: The *Camerini* of Isabella d'Este and Francesco II Gonzaga

Molly Bourne

In September 1506, Francesco II Gonzaga, the marquis of Mantua (ruled 1484–1519), left the city to join Pope Julius II in the papal campaign to expel the Bentivoglio family from Bologna. Shortly after Francesco's departure, his consort Isabella d'Este (1474–1539) inspected the work being done in her husband's absence on the apartments in his new town house, the Palazzo di San Sebastiano, then under construction. In a letter from Mantua dated 5 October 1506, Isabella wrote to Francesco about her impressions, drawing a clear parallel between his new rooms and her own apartments in the Castello di San Giorgio:

> A few days ago I was in Your Excellency's house, and, as I wrote before, thought it most beautiful. You write that I am making fun of you, but this is not true, because if the rooms were not beautiful I would remain silent; but, as they seemed to me to have such a lovely effect, I wrote this to you, and again I tell you that they are beautiful, and even more because Your Excellency has learned from the example of my room, although I must confess that you have improved upon it.[1]

Written in her own hand rather than by one of her secretaries, Isabella's letter reveals an acute sense of mutual awareness between the couple in the use and exhibition of their *camerini*, or private apartments. In the world of the Italian Renaissance court, the decoration of such apartments was carefully designed to convey the status and persona of its inhabitants to those visitors privileged enough to be admitted. While Francesco's San Sebastiano *camerini* are not only no longer extant but have been virtually forgotten, Isabella's Studiolo and Grotta together represent one of the best-studied examples of signorial apartments in the history of art, and, as the product of a woman's initiative, have served doubly to help define our understanding of female patronage and self-representation in the Renaissance.[2] Francesco II Gonzaga and Isabella d'Este represent one of the earliest and certainly one of the best-documented cases of a husband and wife who were both active as patrons. Taken together, a comparison of their apartments provides us with a unique opportunity to examine the patronage relationship between the ruling couple of this important Italian Renaissance court.

Isabella was a long-lived and self-described "insatiable" art collector whose activities are documented in her voluminous surviving correspondence, making it hardly surprising that she stands at the center of most discussions of female secular patronage in the Renaissance. As we learn more about patronage patterns by other women in this period, it is becoming possible to locate Isabella's activities more accurately in the emerging spectrum and to reassess her traditionally paradigmatic status.[3] One area of study in which Isabella continues to rule supreme, however, is the examination of patronage at the Gonzaga court itself. Here, studies have focused on Isabella's creation and decoration of her Studiolo and Grotta, her collecting of antiquities for these spaces, and her sponsorship of literature and music. Scholars have even credited the marchesa for single-handedly orchestrating the cultural resurgence that took place in Mantua after her arrival there in the late fifteenth century. Isabella's gender, unusual for a Renaissance patron, her extraordinary personality, and the wealth of information about her collecting efforts have created the unusual historical phenomenon of a female consort overshadowing her husband.

Francesco II Gonzaga (fig. 1) ruled Mantua as fourth marquis from 1484 until his death in 1519. History has not been kind to Francesco, a mercenary soldier most remembered today for his military accomplishments and for breeding horses, dogs, and hunting falcons. Since the nineteenth century, historians have elected to focus on Isabella, and have constructed an image for Francesco as a virtual barbarian and a convenient foil for his refined wife.[4] The result has been a distorted historiographical legacy which seduces us into viewing Isabella's activities in Mantua in a vacuum, and which all but dismisses the possibility of any cultural con222tribution by her husband. Our knowledge of his contributions is further veiled by the overwhelming interest in his wife's Studiolo and Grotta.

Many art historians would be surprised to learn that Francesco's architectural and artistic projects include work on three major villas outside of the city, while in Mantua itself he built a large city-palace, commissioned the Venetian sculptor Pietro Lombardo to create marble revetments for an important Marian chapel in the cathedral, and built and decorated the church of Santa Maria della Vittoria. The famous altarpiece of this church by Andrea Mantegna, now at the Louvre, depicts the marchese kneeling piously before the Virgin. In many respects, this catalogue of Francesco's projects is more impressive than Isabella's corresponding list, which was limited to the decoration of her private apartments. It is an important indication of the different kinds of patronage opportunities available to a Renaissance ruler as opposed to those possible for his consort.[5]

Bourne Fig. 1. Attributed to Andrea Mantegna, *Portrait of Francesco II Gonzaga,* ca. 1500, Dublin, National Gallery of Ireland (photo: National Gallery of Ireland)

Although Isabella's Studiolo is most often compared to examples in Ferrara, Urbino, Gubbio, and Florence, or to the paintings later collected by her son, Federico II,[8] few scholars have bothered to notice that during the very years in which Isabella was completing the decorations for her first *camerini* in the Castello di San Giorgio, her husband was appointing his own sumptuous apartments in the city-palace of San Sebastiano, which Francesco built and decorated from 1506 to 1512, and which became his primary city residence around 1508. This palace served as an important location for court entertainment and receptions, and was specifically designed to display Andrea Mantegna's famous canvases, the *Triumphs of Caesar*, now at Hampton Court. Although the Palazzo di San Sebastiano is still standing, the room that contained these paintings is much changed, together with most of the other decorations in the palace. Nonetheless, it is still possible to reconstruct the broad outlines of the marchese's apartments and to study them as a parallel to the program Isabella was simultaneously creating in her Castello rooms.[7]

Using their apartments as a focus, this paper seeks to move beyond our "Isabellacentric" perception of Renaissance Mantua by examining the marchesa's patronage in relation to that of her husband. While most studies of patrons are biographical, focusing on the contributions of a single individual, it is here suggested that the dynamic between husband and wife can provide a fruitful and innovative approach to patronage, particularly in the context of the Italian court. Our recognition of Francesco as a significant patron and a reconstruction of his hitherto unknown *camerini* enables us to position Isabella more accurately within the context of the Gonzaga court, and, more importantly, reveals that she was not the sole instigator of cultural activity there, as is conventionally claimed.

As scholarship increasingly points to the importance of family dynamics and *clientelismo* as determining factors in Renaissance society, it is becoming evident that each princely court was not a simple reflection of one ruler's personality, but the product of the numerous and often conflicting agendas promoted by a ruler, his consort, and their many dependents.[8] By examining the relationship between Francesco and Isabella as artistic patrons, we can begin to locate their activities in a framework that studies how rulers and consorts employed art to negotiate the boundaries of gender and dynasty within the social circumscriptions of a Renaissance court. A comparison of Francesco and Isabella's *camerini* also raises questions of taste, gendered space, and conjugal competition, and affords an excellent opportunity to question our traditional assumption of Isabella's cultural monopoly in Mantua. Isabella's *camerini*, as the better known of the two rulers' apartments, are a logical place to begin our discussion.

Isabella's Apartments in the Castello di San Giorgio

Like her husband, Isabella spent a considerable amount of time outside Mantua, traveling or circulating amongst her own villas.[9] Her most elaborate apartments, however, were those located in the city, where they could be shown to select guests during their visits to the Gonzaga court. In 1491, within a year of arriving in Mantua as a young bride, Isabella had begun to decorate the group of rooms in the Castello which were to constitute her urban residence during Francesco's lifetime.[10] Located on multiple levels and communicating by a series of small stairways (*scalette*), these apartments consisted of at least five distinct spaces disposed around the Sala delle Armi on the upper floors of the castle's massive southeastern tower. Isabella spent over fifteen years (from 1491 to about 1508) appointing her *camerini*, the nucleus of which was the Studiolo and Grotta. These were two small rooms, located one above the other in the Torretta di San Nicolò, where the bulk of her collection would be displayed (figs. 2–5).[11] Isabella's mother, Eleonora d'Aragona, Duchess of Ferrara (d. 1493), inhabited comparably disposed apartments in the Ferrarese Castel

Bourne Fig. 2. Castello di San Giorgio, Mantua, showing the Torretta di San Nicolò (photo: author)

Vecchio, and it is possible that these may have provided Isabella with at least a preliminary model for the creation of her own rooms in Mantua.[12]

    Isabella's Studiolo, located above the Grotta, is an intimate room now denuded of original decoration. For this space Isabella acquired paintings of moralizing allegories by some of the leading artists of her day: Andrea Mantegna, Pietro Perugino, and Lorenzo Costa. Prior to the installation of the first paintings in 1496, however, the Studiolo seemed to have presented a predominantly Gonzagan aspect. In fact, in November 1491, in one of Isabella's first orders for the Studiolo, she instructed painter Gianluca Leombeni to decorate the walls with a frieze of arms and devices (*armi e divisi*) containing five subjects which we might more readily associate with her husband, renowned as he was for breeding the famous Gonzaga horses: the *mellega* (maize), *travaglio* (trave), *penarola* (plume), *staffe* (stirrups), and *cavedon* (andiron).[13]

    Similarly, in July 1494, Isabella chose to cover the floor of her Studiolo with maiolica tiles that display not her own Este heraldry

1: Camera degli Sposi
2: Sala delle Cappe
3: Studiolo
4: Sala delle Armi
5: Oratorium

Bourne Fig. 3. Plan of Castello di San Giorgio, Mantua, *piano nobile* (from Sylvia Ferino-Pagden, ed., "La Prima Donna del Mondo": *Isabella d'Este, Fürsten und Mäzenatin der Renaissance*, exh. cat. [Vienna: Kunsthistorisches Museum Vienna, 1994], p. 14, fig. 27)

Bourne Fig. 4. View of Isabella's Grotta in the Castello di San Giorgio, Mantua (photo: author)

or personal *imprese*, but emblems belonging to her husband, including the sun, the glove, the dog muzzle, and the Gonzaga coat of arms (fig. 6).[14] Like any consort, Isabella's allegiances could potentially shift between the dynasty into which she had married and the house from which she came. While we might think that in selecting Gonzaga decorations for her Studiolo floor Isabella was expressing loyalty to her husband, we know that there were more practical considerations behind her choice. The documentary record shows, in fact, that Francesco had commissioned these tiles to decorate the floor of a small but richly decorated room, the *camerino de la maiolicha*, in his countryside villa at Marmirolo. He had the tiles made in Pesaro, one of the finest ceramic centers then available, and when they were delivered to Mantua on the last day of May 1494, he instructed his building superintendent to transport to Marmirolo only as many tiles as were needed for the project, leaving the rest in the Castello. Five weeks later, these leftover tiles were installed in Isabella's Studiolo to solve a recurrent problem of mice nests (*nidi di ponteghi*) under the floor.[15] These circumstances can serve as a cautionary reminder that while princely rulers were acutely concerned with the self-images they conveyed, they were also sensible people. Isabella may have used tiles decorated with her husband's family devices to cover the floor of her Studiolo for no other reason than that they were acceptable and on hand when she needed some in a hurry.

The fact that in the mid-1490s the decoration of Isabella's Studiolo was dominated by Gonzagan emblems is also reasonable when one considers that virtually all Isabella's political power and authority in Mantua derived from her legal union with her husband's family. Beginning around 1496, however, the situation in her Studiolo started to change, as Leombeni's equestrian wall frieze began to be covered by a program of five large-scale allegorical paintings.[16] Although the meanings of these pictures remain difficult to determine with precision, each presents a moralizing theme about female virtue. In one of them, Lorenzo Costa's *Allegory of the Court of Isabella d'Este* (fig. 7), a figure representing Isabella is crowned amidst a group of music-making

Bourne Fig. 5. View from Sala delle Cappe in the Castello di San Giorgio, Mantua, of the hallway (on left) leading to Isabella's Studiolo, and the entrance (on right) leading down to Grotta (photo: author)

courtiers. This painting, which was executed just as Francesco was beginning work on his San Sebastiano apartments, must have impressed the marchese, for he would order a strikingly similar painting from Costa for his own rooms.[17]

Isabella's Grotta, located directly below her Studiolo, is an intimate space that could comfortably accommodate only four or five people (fig. 4). Like the Studiolo, the decoration of this space underwent a similar shift away from Gonzagan motifs toward more personalized ones. At first, the Grotta's barrel-vaulted ceiling was simply adorned with a winged ring painted in fresco on a blue background. This Gonzaga device was later covered up as a result of carpentry work, carried out between 1506 and 1508, to install the spectacular wooden vault that is still in place, which displays the Isabellian *imprese* of lottery tickets and the musical pause.[18] During the same campaign, the Grotta was fitted with wooden cabinets (no longer extant) designed to house the marchesa's growing collection of antiquities.[19] The installation of these cabinets toward 1508 signals another important step in the evolution of her *camerini*, for it was only at this point that Isabella described the Grotta as "finished" and that she began to

Bourne Fig. 6. Six ceramic floor tiles from Isabella's Studiolo, Milan Museo di Castello Sforzesco (from Sylvia Ferino-Pagden, ed., "La Prima Donna del Mondo": *Isabella d'Este, Fürsten und Mäzenatin der Renaissance*, exh. cat. [Vienna: Kunsthistorisches Museum, 1994], p. 189, cat. no. 175)

use it specifically as a repository for her *raccolta di antichità*. The precious objects Isabella kept in her Grotta, together with the moralizing paintings located above in the Studiolo, were displayed to selected guests and served to present Isabella as a virtuous woman of classical erudition and refined taste. While this was a relatively conventional image for an educated noblewoman of the period, Isabella was innovative in *how* she communicated this message: by collecting antiquities, she engaged in an activity unusual for women in the Renaissance,

and one which enabled her to participate in the male-dominated trade in antique gems, coins, medals, and sculptures.[20] Moreover, it was the presence of these antiquities that most distinguished Isabella's *camerini* from those of her husband, and it is possible that she pursued these objects precisely because he did not: despite a well-established tradition amongst male

Bourne Fig. 7. Lorenzo Costa, *Allegory of the Court of Isabella d'Este*, ca. 1506, Paris, Musèe du Louvre (photo: RMN)

members of the Gonzaga family, Francesco did not collect antiquities; Isabella, in doing so, was not competing with him.[21]

In Renaissance courts, it was usual for the ruling couple to keep separate financial accounts, separate households (generally consisting of a large staff), and separate apartments.[22] However, with all the attention given by scholars to Isabella's rooms, it is often forgotten that Francesco's first apartments were located directly below hers on the ground floor of the Castello. Occupied before him by his father Federico I Gonzaga, these were the rooms that Francesco inhabited when he was in Mantua during the first twenty years of his rule. Although we know little about the original layout or appearance of these spaces, it is likely that they were decorated with frescoed Gonzaga devices similar to those which appear today in some of the rooms, such as the sun, dog muzzle, and winged ring (fig. 8).[23] These apartments almost certainly communicated directly with Isabella's rooms above, a common and necessary feature in lodgings of ruler and consort, husband and wife.[24] Although his Castello apartments were often used to house important guests, as was usual in court practice, Francesco does not seem to have made any major alterations to these rooms after assuming power in 1484, possibly preferring to make a bolder statement later in his career with his new apartments at San Sebastiano. It should also be remembered that during the 1490s, when Isabella was beginning to appoint her *camerini* upstairs in the Castello, Francesco was occupied with major projects for additions to two of his countryside residences: the family castle-palace at Marmirolo, located about seven miles northwest of Mantua, and another residence at Gonzaga, south of the Po river.[25] By the early 1500s, these projects were essentially complete, and Francesco turned his sights to the construction of a new city-palace, the Palazzo di San Sebastiano. Erected and decorated between 1506 and 1512, this is where the marchese would create his own urban apartments.

Palazzo di San Sebastiano: Site and Context

In a letter from Mantua to Cardinal Ippolito d'Este on 28 April 1508, the humanist Mario Equicola wrote: "On Easter Monday, Marchese Francesco moved completely to stay day and night in San Sebastiano, and will not return to the Castello."[26] One of the most striking features of Francesco's city-palace is the distance that separates it from the Ducal Palace. Renaissance Mantua was essentially a fortified island encircled by a series of lakes, and the Palazzo di San Sebastiano was situated at its southern edge, just inside the walls next to the Porta Pusterla, one of the city gates (figs. 9, 10). Entering Mantua by the Porta Pusterla, the palace would have been immediately visible on the left, with the house of Andrea Mantegna located just beyond, across the street from Alberti's

Bourne Fig. 8. "Sala del Sole," apartments of Francesco II on ground floor of Castello di San Giorgio, Mantua (photo: author)

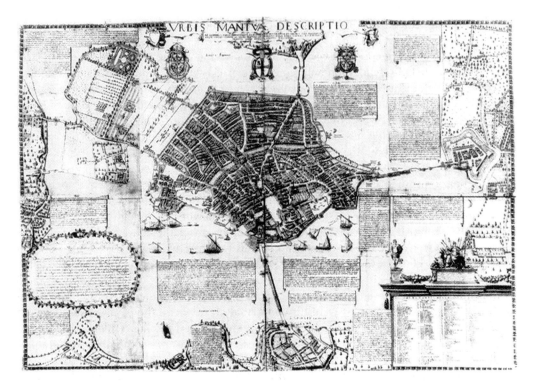

Bourne Fig. 9. Gabriele Bertazzolo, *Urbis Mantuae Descriptio*, Mantua, 1628 (photo: author)

church and convent of San Sebastiano. The road then proceeds through the center of town, passing the main market square and Alberti's second Mantuan church of Sant'Andrea, and ending at the massive Ducal Palace-Castello complex, the seat of Gonzaga rule, on the other side of the city about one mile away (figs. 9, 14). When leaving Mantua by the Porta Pusterla, one immediately crossed a bridge over a waterway to the Te island, where one of the marchese's stables was located (figs. 10–13).[27]

Francesco's acquisition of Mantegna's house in 1502 may have provided the incentive to begin planning his new palace, although serious work was not actually begun until 1506.[28] Construction on San Sebastiano was carried out primarily under the direction of court architect-superintendent, Girolamo Arcari, and Equicola's letter indicates that Francesco had moved in by Easter Monday 1508. Such rapid completion suggests that the palace incorporated preexisting structures, a practice consistent with Francesco's other building projects.[29] Located within the city walls, yet boasting a large garden and easy access to the countryside, Palazzo di San Sebastiano can almost be classified as a *villa suburbana*.[30] The site's proximity to his prized horses and its peaceful, semisuburban surroundings probably contributed to Francesco's decision to build a town house here, while the simple matter of overcrowding in the Ducal Palace may also have encouraged the marchese to create an elaborate new domicile for himself.[31] Finally, it may have been Francesco's declining health which encouraged him to transform San Sebastiano into his primary city residence, where he would eventually die in late March of 1519.[32]

Even if San Sebastiano functioned primarily as a semisuburban retreat and not as an official seat of rule, Francesco's relocation there undoubtedly had a significant impact on

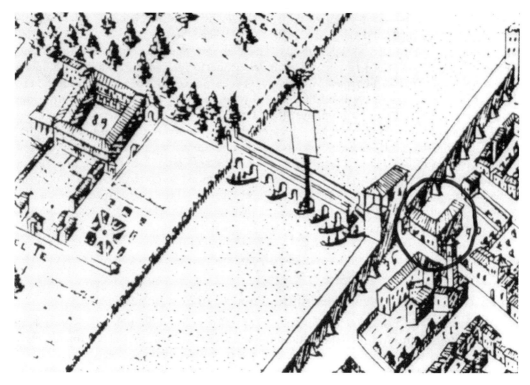

Bourne Fig. 10. Gabriele Bertazzolo, *Urbis Mantuae Descriptio,* Mantua, 1628, detail of area around Palazzo San Sebastiano (in circle) (photo: author)

Bourne Fig. 11. Porta Pusterla, Mantua, view ca. 1900 from Te island, showing waterway and bridge leading to Te island (photo: Archivio di Stato, Mantua, authorization 28/99)

court traffic within the urban fabric of the city, especially since the chancery and other administrative offices continued to be based in the Ducal Palace. Moreover, soon after its completion the town house was already being used to host elaborate court banquets, receptions, and theater productions, such as Terence's *The Andrians*, performed for carnival in 1513 under the garden loggia behind the palace.[33] Francesco's decision to build, reside, and entertain in this part of the city may have been facilitated by the fact that this area had begun to be refurbished in the 1470s under his grandfather, Lodovico II Gonzaga, with projects to build the church and convent of San Sebastiano and with construction of the house of Mantegna, the family's court artist. Francesco's town house thus continued a program of urban renewal by the Gonzaga in this part of the city, one that ultimately culminated in the building of Palazzo Te by his son, Federico II. Spanning three generations of rulers, this series of projects gradually transformed the road between the Ducal Palace and the Porta Pusterla into a ceremonial axis between the two urban nodes of the Gonzaga court (fig. 14).[34] Clearly the construction of Palazzo di San Sebastiano provided Francesco with the opportunity to create his own monument as sovereign in the city. Given the timing of the project, however, one wonders equally whether his desire to make such a mark had been at least partially generated by the recent example of Isabella's apartments.

The Structure and Decoration of the Palazzo di San Sebastiano

Although the Palazzo di San Sebastiano has suffered drastic alterations, it is possible to outline its basic original form and decorative program with the aid of archival documents, early descriptions, and what remains of the building itself.[36] Francesco's palace consisted of an unremarkable two-story rectangular body oriented parallel to the city walls (figs. 12–13, 15). Following local custom, it was constructed of brick and stucco, with smooth façades that may have been painted but were otherwise unadorned. The principal façade, on the more private, north side (fig. 16), opened onto an extensive garden by means of a vaulted, seven-arcade loggia (subsequently walled up) that during carnival season was often used as a stage setting for the classical theater productions Francesco was fond of producing. Originally attached to

Bourne Fig. 12. Palazzo di San Sebastiano, Mantua, distant view ca. 1900 from Te island, showing city walls, Porta Pusterla, and bridge leading to Te island (photo: Archivio di Stato, Mantua, authorization 28/99)

Bourne Fig. 13. Palazzo di San Sebastiano, Mantua, view ca. 1900 from Te island, with Porta Pusterla visible at right (photo: Archivio di Stato, Mantua, authorization 28/99)

the eastern end of the palace, the Porta Pusterla (figs. 11, 13) was torn down in 1902–3, when the waterway that had once separated the palace from the Te island was filled in and paved over to create the busy *viale* that today runs alongside the back of the palace, where the city walls once stood (figs. 12, 14).[36]

The ground floor of the palace was occupied primarily by a row of four large vaulted rooms of roughly equal size, two at each extreme end of the building, with the loggia between (fig. 18). Although one of these rooms was completely destroyed in the nineteenth century by the insertion of a staircase, the other three have more or less retained their original form.[37] One of these, the *camera del crogiolo*, or room of the crucible, at the western end of the palace, displays Francesco's personal emblem of the flaming crucible on the frescoed ceiling while the lunettes around the room's perimeter are adorned with Gonzaga devices (fig. 17).[38] The decoration of the three other rooms was similar to this, each with a different device on the ceiling. In the *camera del sole*, located at the opposite end of the palace, the Gonzaga symbol of the sun is still visible on the ceiling, while we know from documents that the ceilings of the two other rooms each displayed the emblem of an important Gonzaga ally: the coat of arms of the emperor Maximilian and the porcupine of Louis XII, King of France.[39] The Habsburg and French insignias represented the sovereign states of the two most powerful monarchies in Western Europe, and in 1506, when these rooms were being constructed and decorated, Francesco was firmly allied with both.

With the fall of Milan (and his employers, the Sforza) to the French in 1499, Francesco aligned himself with Louis XII, and in August of 1502 he signed a *condotta* in preparation for the ultimately unsuccessful French attempt to recover Naples from the Spanish. That winter, Francesco spent Christmas at Loches castle as a guest of the king, who in July 1503 declared him Lieutenant General of the French army prior to the marchese's march south.[40] Gonzaga relations with the Holy Roman Empire were much older, for it was the emperor Sigismond who, in 1433, had invested the Gonzaga with their title of marquis and to whom they were beholden for their legal title to rule as imperial vicars. More recently, in September of 1501, Emperor Maximilian I had nominated Francesco captain-general of the imperial army in Italy.[41] Francesco's relationships with the French king and the emperor were critical to his survival in the rapidly shifting network of post-1494 Italian politics, and it is entirely logical that he would have wanted to publicize these allegiances. The painted symbols displayed in these four rooms would have been easily recognizable to palace guests, and served to announce San Sebastiano as a space identified not only with Francesco but with the entire Gonzaga dynasty, as well as with the powerful imperial and French monarchies, the legal and temporal sources of the marchese's authority.

The most elaborately decorated rooms in the palace were on the *piano nobile*, and, of these, the most impressive was the long *sala* created to receive Mantegna's *Triumphs*. Visitors ushered up the original staircase at the western end of the palace would have emerged at the end of this great hall—which, according to Mario Equicola, had been built specifically for Mantegna's canvases—and would thus have been encouraged to contemplate its rich imagery while traversing the room to reach Francesco's apartments, located at the other end (fig. 19).[42] Although the *sala* was later

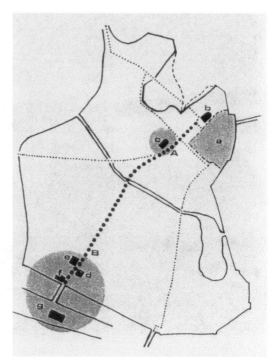

Bourne Fig. 14. Schematic plan of Mantua (photo: Carpeggiani and Pagliari, 1983, p. 35)

A-B = Gonzaga axis
a = Ducal Palace-Castello complex
b = Cathedral of San Pietro
c = Church of Sant'Andrea
d = Church and convent of San Sebastiano
e = House of Andrea Mantegna
f = Palazzo San Sebastiano
g = Palazzo Te

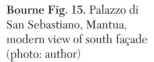

Bourne Fig. 15. Palazzo di San Sebastiano, Mantua, modern view of south façade (photo: author)

Bourne Fig. 16. Palazzo di San Sebastiano, Mantua, modern view of walled-in arcade on north façade (photo: author)

subdivided into smaller spaces and its ceiling lowered, it is possible to calculate that this room originally measured approximately 32 meters long and 7 meters wide, and its wooden ceiling was set a lofty 6.7 meters above the floor. (fig. 19)[43] The *Triumphs* were probably installed above a *spalliera* on the long, originally windowless southern wall, where they would have been illuminated by a row of windows along the opposite side of the room. It is possible that the *Triumphs* were in place here as early as 1506, when special gilded framing elements were being made for them in Venice, although the paintings are not specifically mentioned as being in the *sala* until 1512.[44]

Mantegna's famous paintings have been the primary focus of most discussions of San Sebastiano, but they should, in fact, be interpreted as the centerpiece of a broader decorative program devised for the palace by Francesco. The *Triumphs'* theme of military conquest is entirely consistent with Francesco's self-promoted condottiere image, suggesting that he may have been the original patron of the canvases.[45] At the very least, he was able to personalize the series—often noted as strangely bearing no Gonzagan references—by adding decorations to the *sala*, including the room's elaborate gilt and painted wooden ceiling, which displayed Francesco's unmistakable emblem of the burning crucible (fig. 20).[46] In addition, Francesco commissioned the Mantuan court painter Lorenzo Costa to adorn the two end walls of the *sala* with paintings that, according to Mario Equicola, were necessary to complete the *Triumphs'* iconographical program.[47] Vasari, the only source to actually describe Costa's additions, reported

Bourne Fig. 17. Palazzo di San Sebastiano, Mantua, "Camera del Crogiolo" (photo: author)

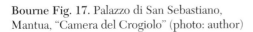

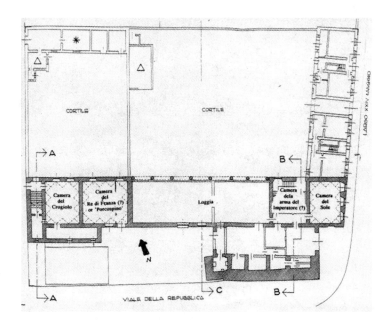

Bourne Fig. 18. Plan (1994) of the ground floor of Palazzo di San Sebastiano with room labels indicating author's reconstruction; dark shading shows original walling (plan: courtesy Arch. A. Guastalla, Mantua)

that the first painting (presumably lost) represented a Sacrifice to Hercules and included portraits of Francesco II together with his three legitimate sons and successors, Federico (b. 1500), Ercole (b. 1505), and Ferrante (b. 1507). The strong dynastic message of this picture was later complemented by the addition at the other end of the room of Costa's second painting, now in Prague. According to Vasari, this painting was "made in oil many years after the first," and commemorated Federico's appointment as captain-general of the papal army.[48] Whether or not the second Costa painting was in place during Francesco's lifetime, it is evident that the decoration of the Sala di Triumphi—and, one might argue, of the entire palace—was the result of a process of selection and assemblage in which certain images already

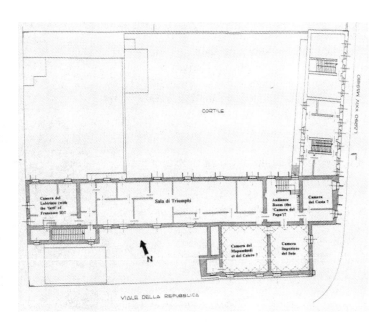

Bourne Fig. 19. Plan (1994) of the piano nobile of Palazzo di San Sebastiano with room labels indicating author's reconstruction; dark shading shows original walling (plan: courtesy Arch. A. Guastalla, Mantua)

Bourne Fig. 20. Palazzo di Ducale, Mantua, Stanza di Giuditta, wooden ceiling with gilded stucco crucible decorations, ca. 1506, originally in the Sala di Triumphi, Palazzo di San Sebastiano (photo: courtesy Giovetti)

established as part of the family iconography were recycled, while new images were added to create a layered visual program that was both legible and personalized to Francesco's needs as a ruler.

We know that this Sala di Triumphi was used for banquets and entertainment, such as the *solemne cena* given in November 1512 to honor the recently reinstalled duke of Milan, which Francesco described as being held "in the room of the triumphs of Caesar, here at San Sebastiano."[49] The Sforza enjoyed a brief return to power in 1512, an event the Gonzaga celebrated in light of their long-standing family and professional ties to the Milanese rulers, particularly since the new duke, Massimiliano Sforza, was Isabella's nephew. Similarly, in August 1512 the Sala di Triumphi had served as an important stateroom during an Imperial Diet held in Mantua. One of the key players at this meeting was Ramon Folch de Cardona, the Spanish general and viceroy of Naples.[50] Cardona was apparently so impressed by the ceiling that he asked Francesco to have drawings of it made and sent to him, together with those of some of the other equally elaborate ceilings in the palace.[51]

Our only account of what appears to have been Francesco's audience room was given by Piero Soranzo, a Venetian ambassador who visited the palace in 1515. He described being received "in a richly decorated room" where Francesco was:

> seated next to a fireplace and…surrounded by three terrible greyhounds and an infinite number of hunting falcons and girfalcons held on the fists [of atten-dants], and on the *spalliera* above were portraits of his beautiful horses and beau-tiful dogs, and there was also a dwarf dressed in gold. Taking leave from his Highness, we went to see the palace. In one room were depicted his victories and deeds, and the baton he had when he was nominated Captain General of our forces.[52]

The marchese's horses, dogs, and hunting falcons represented not only one of his greatest passions as a renowned breeder, but also a major financial investment. Francesco frequently presented examples of these animals as gifts to other sovereigns, and it is logical that he would showcase "portraits" of some of his prized specimens on the walls of his audience chamber.[53]

Two other gilt wooden ceilings have survived from the upstairs rooms at Palazzo di San Sebastiano, one decorated with the motif of a labyrinth and the other clearly bearing signs of a *pastiglia* papal *impresa*, possibly that of Julius II, which it originally bore in the center.[54] Like that from the Sala di Triumphi, these two ceilings probably date to 1506–7, particularly favorable years for Francesco's relations with Pope Julius II.[55] In 1505, the marchese's daughter Eleonora was betrothed to Julius's nephew, Francesco Maria della Rovere, and in December of that year (and not December 1506, as sometimes stated), the marchese's brother Sigismondo Gonzaga was elected cardinal by the pope after two decades of persistent lobbying. The following year Francesco himself was appointed captain-general of the church by Julius II, and in November 1506 he led the papal forces in the expulsion of the Bentivoglio from Bologna. Given the proximity in timing between these political events and the decoration of Palazzo di San Sebastiano, Francesco may have decided to adorn the ceiling of his new audience chamber—probably the same room referred to in the documents as the *Camera del Papa*—with the papal insignia.

We have only relatively scattered information about the other spaces on the *piano nobile* of the palace. The description by Soranzo excerpted above mentions that "in one room were depicted [Francesco's] victories and deeds (*vitorie e fati*)," while a Gonzaga family genealogical tree may have also formed part of the decoration.[56] By the early sixteenth century, the Gonzaga had ruled Mantua for nearly two hundred years in an unbroken line of legitimately born heirs, a feat worth celebrating when one considers the serious problems of succession repeatedly faced by their more powerful contemporaries: the Este, Visconti-Sforza, and Montefeltro families.[57]

Palazzo di San Sebastiano also boasted an *altana* that provided commanding views of the city and surrounding lakes, as well as a room containing a *mappamondo* and a view of Cairo, possibly a reference to the horse-buying expeditions that the marchese frequently sent to this north African city.[58] Francesco had an avid interest in cartography, and in the 1490s collected maps and views of different Mediterranean cities for use in designing frescoed cycles of cities in his country palaces at Gonzaga and at Marmirolo.[59] Like his town house, these palaces also contained transportable cycles of *trionfi*, which were sometimes brought into Mantua for use on festive occasions.[60] The themes of triumphs and cartography—not unrelated subjects—were clearly important elements in defining Francesco's signorial iconography, and their presence in Palazzo di San Sebastiano represents the continuation of the personalized imagery he had established in his countryside residences.

The space in Francesco's city-palace that most closely resembled Isabella's Studiolo, however, was the so-called *camera del Costa*. This intimate room was decorated entirely with paintings by Lorenzo Costa, who had become the Gonzaga court painter upon Mantegna's death in the fall of 1506—the same year Costa assumed responsibility, together with Girolamo Arcari, for supervising the decoration of the palace. Although in 1508 Costa complained that his poor health prevented him from finishing *la camera*, by November 1510 the work was sufficiently complete for Cardinal Sigismondo Gonzaga to describe *la camera del Costa* as "finished and as beautiful as can be," and lacking in only a few final details.[61] Apparently painted in both tempera and oil (*lavorato parte a guazzo e parte a olio*), the only account of this room, now lost, is provided by Vasari, who described the following four pictures: the first portrayed Isabella surrounded by female attendants singing and making music; the second showed the goddess Latona turning peasants into frogs; the third depicted Francesco led by Hercules along a virtuous path up the mountain of eternity; and the fourth portrayed the marchese with his military baton, standing triumphantly on a pedestal and surrounded by a group of jubilant, standard-bearing courtiers.[62] Of these four images, that of Latona is perhaps the most puzzling, and may be related to Mantua's distinctive lake-encircled geography and its fame for frog fishing.[63]

In comparison with the other rooms in the palace, which contained themes of political alliance, military triumph, dynastic legitimacy, and expertise in map collecting and horse breeding, Francesco's *camera del Costa* seems to present a more personal note. In particular, the painting which Vasari describes as showing Isabella surrounded by music-making women appears to have been almost identical to the painting Costa had made a few years earlier for Isabella's Studiolo in the Castello (fig. 7). It is entirely possible that Francesco admired his wife's painting and asked Costa to make a similar one for his own *camerino,* a perfectly logical patronage pattern between ruler and consort.

An important difference exists between the *camera del Costa* and Isabella's Studiolo, namely, that Francesco's room was decorated by a single artist, while in Isabella's room the deliberate confrontation between different artists, or *paragone,* was a fundamental theme. Although this aesthetic choice could be ascribed to differences in taste between the two patrons, practical matters such as speed of execution deserve equal consideration. For example, it should be noted that Isabella's *camerini* in the Castello were decorated over a period of more than fifteen years, giving her time to pursue different artists and to modify the program, while Francesco's entire town house was constructed and decorated in only about five years. As a patron, Francesco can best be described as a builder and decorator of buildings who prized speed of execution above nearly everything else, and whose patronage, in addition to his rooms in Palazzo di San Sebastiano, included numerous architectural projects both within the city and in the *mantovano.* Isabella's involvement in the visual arts was, by contrast, almost exclusively centered around the painstaking appointment of her private apartments with high-quality paintings, antiquities, and *objets d'art.* It should not be surprising that the different needs, social obligations, and personal interests of each ruler are reflected in the individual character of the apartments that each created.

His and Hers Apartments: Functions, Themes, and Parallels

The quotation excerpted at the beginning of this paper provides unusually strong evidence of Francesco and Isabella's close "mutual looking" at each other's *camerini* projects. Although Isabella compliments Francesco by saying that his new rooms "improved" upon hers, she is also careful to point out that the idea or "example" for such a space was hers in the first place.[64] Isabella had been laboring on her own apartments for over fifteen years, and she may have felt threatened by her husband's decision to create his own *camerini,* the very kind of space for which she was beginning to become widely recognized. By the same token, she may have perceived Francesco's project as a complementary gesture made in emulation of her own rooms. Isabella's comment, "you write that I am making fun of you," suggests that Francesco, in turn, may have felt a certain inferiority in embarking upon an artistic project so closely identified with his wife's area of patronage. Could it have been a sense of cultural competition that encouraged Francesco to locate his apartments not in the Castello, but in his new palace on the far side of the city?

Although it was common in the Renaissance for princely couples to spend extended periods of time apart (since one was often away from the state on diplomatic or military missions), it was unusual for rulers to have urban living arrangements that were so geographically separated.[65] By 1506, when construction on Palazzo di San Sebastiano began, Isabella had already given birth to two legitimate male heirs, Federico and Ercole, and by 1508, when Francesco began to spend the majority of his time in his new Mantua town house, a third son, Ferrante, had been born. The Gonzaga succession had been secured, giving the marchese liberty to spend more time in his semisuburban apartments across town. Francesco's motivations for such a removal could have been myriad: to have greater privacy as his health declined, to be closer to his beloved horses stabled on the Te island, or to retreat from what may have been a deteriorating relationship with his wife. Or, in a twist on the usual situation in which the female consort attempted to attain a degree of autonomy by creating her own apartments, Francesco may have felt compelled to carve out his own artistic space at San Sebastiano as a result of Isabella's perceived cultural dominance at the Gonzaga court.

Of all the projects Francesco commissioned during his thirty-five-year rule, it was notably his apartments at Palazzo di San Sebastiano that began to gain prominence as a center of court activity around 1508, precisely the time we begin to see increasing references to Isabella's rooms in the Castello.[66] During this period, Francesco spent increasing amounts of time at San Sebastiano and began to receive visitors there, while at the same time we hear more frequently about guests being shown Isabella's *camerini*.[67] Although we know very little about the marchesa's own activities in her rooms, it has been suggested that she may have used them—particularly the Grotta—for such activities as courtly discussions, letter dictations, or intimate musical concerts.[68] Following a hiatus from August 1509 to July 1510, when Francesco was a prisoner in Venice and Isabella was busy managing state affairs during the crisis, both sets of signorial *camerini* again emerge as important ceremonial foci for the court.[69]

Of particular interest during this period are the carnival celebrations of 1511, which included two banquets hosted by Francesco on successive nights, one at Palazzo di San Sebastiano and one at his new villa, Poggio Reale, located across the lake from the Ducal Palace. These were followed by a party given by Isabella two days later in the Castello courtyard, which had been festively decorated for the occasion.[70] In August 1512, during the Imperial Diet held in Mantua for members of the Holy League, the emperor's envoy, Matteo Lang, paid an official visit to Isabella in the Castello, and the following day was honored by a banquet at the Palazzo di San Sebastiano. Although both Francesco and Isabella attended each event, the courtiers' reports identify the castle with Isabella and the town house with Francesco.[71] For the carnival season of 1513, a classical theater performance was held at San Sebastiano under the garden loggia, and when the duke of Milan visited in December of 1514, he was given a banquet there which was followed by a musical performance and entertainment by Francesco and Isabella's three young sons.[72]

Our examination of Francesco and Isabella's apartments has exposed the gendered nature of their decorative programs: Isabella's *camerini* tended towards didactic moralizing allegories of female chastity and virtue, while her collection of antiquities proclaimed her a discerning and erudite collector. By contrast, Francesco's San Sebastiano rooms employed themes of military triumph, cartography, and heraldry to create a politicized and dynastic program that glorified his house and proclaimed Gonzaga alliances with other sovereigns. Her rooms were small and intimate; his were large spaces designed to accommodate official court functions. Moreover, the absence in Francesco's rooms of objects traditionally associated with male art collecting, such as antiquities or erotic paintings, and the conspicuous presence of antiquities in the *camerini* of his wife, and of eroticizing paintings in the later rooms of his son and successor, Federico, should remind us that art collecting in the Renaissance did not follow strictly gendered or even predictable patterns.

Conclusion

Ultimately, however, our comparison serves to create more questions than answers. How, for example, did Francesco and Isabella view each other's *camerini* projects? Did they perceive themselves as competitors or complements to one another? In the eyes of contemporaries, did the distance between Francesco's San Sebastiano apartments and those of Isabella in the Castello represent a rift between the two rulers, or a grander sense of courtly display, particularly when both sites were used on ceremonial occasions?

While there are no simple answers to these questions, one thing does seem certain: Isabella did not occupy a position similar to that of her father, brother, or son—the figures with whom she is most often compared as a collector. Such comparisons fail to recognize the importance of gender in social positioning—an essential aspect as we begin to determine in what ways her patronage followed accepted norms and in what ways it was truly exceptional. Surprisingly it is an examination of Isabella's cultural activities in relation to those of her husband, the man for whom she served as consort for nearly thirty years, that may prove most illuminating in our attempt to break the tenacious grip Isabella continues to exercise on our perceptions of the Gonzaga court and of female patronage in the Renaissance. Above all, it reveals that Francesco II Gonzaga, long overshadowed by the cultural fame of his wife, was, in fact, a patron worthy of our consideration.

Notes

Research for this article was carried out in part with the support of a Frederick Sheldon Traveling Fellowship from Harvard University. A version of this paper was read at the annual conference of the Renaissance Society of America in Bloomington, Indiana, in April 1996. In addition to assistance and encouragement from editors Sheryl Reiss and David Wilkins, I especially wish to thank Mirka Beneš, Jane Fair Bestor, Clifford Brown, Anthony Cashman, John Shearman, and Elizabeth Swain for their many helpful comments on earlier drafts of this paper.

1.   "Io fui a questi dì in casa de Vostra Signoria, e como li scrissi, mi parse belissima. Vostra Signoria scrive ch'io la delego. Questo non è, perchè io quando non fussero belle taceria, ma perchè me parveno cossì cum effecto, lo feci scrivere a Vostra Signoria, e cossì dico che sono belle, e tanto più belle quanto Vostra Signoria ha pur imparato da la mia camara, l'è ben vero che l'ha poi megliorato[…]" (ASM, AG, b. 2116, c. 262v). At the time of this letter, Francesco was in Cesena, en route from Urbino to Bologna. An English translation of part of the letter was published by Julia Cartwright, *Isabella d'Este, Marchioness of Mantua 1474-1539: A Study of the Renaissance*, 2 vols. (London: John Murray, 1903), 1:289.

2.   On Isabella's Studiolo and Grotta, see esp. Giuseppe Gerola, "Trasmigrazioni e vicende dei *Camerini* di Isabella d'Este," *Atti e Memorie dell'Accademia Virgiliana di Mantova* 21 (1929–30): 253–90; Andrew Martindale, "The Patronage of Isabella d'Este at Mantua," *Apollo* 79 (1964): 183–91; Egon Verheyen, *The Paintings in the Studiolo of Isabella d'Este at Mantua* (New York: New York University Press, 1971); Clifford M. Brown, "'Lo insaciabile desiderio nostro de cose antiche': New Documents on Isabella d'Este's Collection of Antiquities," in *Cultural Aspects of the Italian Renaissance. Essays in Honour of Paul Oskar Kristeller*, ed. C. Clough (Manchester: Manchester University Press, 1976), 324–53; Clifford M. Brown with Anna Maria Lorenzoni, "The Grotta of Isabella d'Este," *Gazette des Beaux-Arts* 89 (1977), 155–71, and 91 (1978), 72–82; J. M. Fletcher, "Isabella d'Este, Patron and Collector," in *Splendours of the Gonzaga*, ed. David Chambers and Jane Martineau, exh. cat. (London: Victoria and Albert Museum, 1981), 51–63; Clifford M. Brown, *La Grotta di Isabella d'Este: Un simbolo di continuità dinastica per i duchi di Mantova* (Mantua: Gianluigi Arcari, 1985); Stephen Kolsky, "An Unnoticed Description of Isabella d'Este's Grotta," *Journal of the Warburg and Courtauld Institutes* 52 (1989): 232–35; Clifford M. Brown, "Purché la sia cosa che representi antiquità," in *Isabella d'Este: I luoghi del collezionismo, Civiltà mantovana* 14–15 (1995): 70–89. The massive Isabellian bibliography has been conveniently collected in Sylvia Ferino-Pagden, ed., *"La Prima Donna del Mondo": Isabella d'Este: Fürsten und Mäzenatin der Renaissance:* exh. cat. (Vienna: Kunsthistorisches Museum, 1994). On decoration and political representation in the context of Italian Renaissance princely courts, see Evelyn Welch, "The Image of a Fifteenth-Century Court: Secular Frescoes for the Castello di Porta Giovia, Milan," *Journal of the Warburg and Courtauld Institutes* 53 (1990), 163–84; on the *camera picta* in Mantua,

see Randolph Starn and Loren Partridge, *Arts of Power: Three Halls of State in Italy, 1300–1600* (Berkeley: University of California Press, 1992), 82–148; Rupert Shepherd, "Giovanni Sabadino degli Arienti, Ercole I d'Este and the Decoration of the Italian Renaissance Court," *Renaissance Studies* 9 (1995): 18–57.

3. For recent scholarship on women and patronage in early modern Europe, see Geraldine A. Johnson and Sara F. Matthews Grieco, eds., *Picturing Women in Renaissance and Baroque Italy* (Cambridge: Cambridge University Press, 1997); Cynthia Lawrence, ed., *Women and Art in Early Modern Europe: Patrons, Collectors, and Connoisseurs* (University Park: Pennsylvania State University Press, 1997).

4. Most influential in this regard has been the work of Alessandro Luzio, who published many of the documents relevant to Isabella's patronage. Despite his nearly infallible archival skills, Luzio's conviction that the marchesa was a faultless heroine and that the "untamed and wild" Francesco II was incapable of cultural contribution led him more than once to attribute to Isabella the initiative for projects that are documented as Francesco's. Scholars have only now begun to call attention to the biases that riddle Isabellian historiography; see Rose Marie San Juan, "The Court Lady's Dilemma: Isabella d'Este and Art Collecting in the Renaissance," *Oxford Art Journal* 14 (1991): 67–78; Stephen Kolsky, "Images of Isabella d'Este," *Italian Studies* 39 (1984): 47–62. Clifford Brown has recently called attention to the need to reexamine Francesco II, showing him to have been a notable patron of the arts. See Clifford M. Brown with Anna Maria Lorenzoni, "'Concludo che non vidi mai la più bella casa in Italia': The Frescoed Decorations in Francesco II Gonzaga's Suburban Villa in the Mantuan Countryside at Gonzaga (1491–1496)," *Renaissance Quarterly* 49 (1996): 268–302; Clifford M. Brown with Anna Maria Lorenzoni, "The Palazzo di San Sebastiano (1506–1512) and the Art Patronage of Francesco II Gonzaga, Fourth Marquis of Mantua," *Gazette des Beaux-Arts* 129 (1997): 131–80.

5. In addition to his architectural projects, Francesco's patronage included the collecting of maps, coins, medals, and illuminated manuscripts, as well as the sponsorship of religious choral music and classical theater productions. Although most of his projects have been lost or altered, contributing to Francesco's neglect as a patron, many can be satisfactorily reconstructed using the same kinds of rich archival material that enable us to document the artistic pursuits of his wife. The broader issue of Francesco as a patron is considered in my doctoral dissertation; Molly Bourne, "Out from the Shadow of Isabella: The Artistic Patronage of Francesco II Gonzaga, Fourth Marquis of Mantua (1484–1519)" (Ph.D. diss., Harvard University, 1998); a brief summary is presented in Molly Bourne, "Al di là di Isabella, un profilo di Francesco II Gonzaga, quarto Marchese di Mantova (1484-1519)," *Quadrante Padano* 19.2 (1998): 65–68.

6. Isabella's Studiolo is most often compared with those of her uncle Leonello, brother Alfonso I d'Este in Ferrara, Federico da Montefeltro in Gubbio and Urbino, and Lorenzo de'Medici in Florence; the erotic paintings Correggio made for Federico II are generally contrasted with the moralizing ones he executed for Isabella's second apartments. Wolfgang Liebenwein provides a survey of Renaissance *studioli* (not, however, including the apartments of Francesco II) in Wolfgang Liebenwein, *Studiolo: Storia e tipologia di uno spazio culturale*, ed. C. Ceri Via (Modena: Panini, 1988).

7. Carla Cerati outlines the construction chronology of the Palazzo di San Sebastiano and publishes many of the pertinent documents in Carla Cerati, *I Trionfi di Cesare di Andrea Mantegna e il palazzo di San Sebastiano in Mantova* (Mantua: Provincia di Mantova, Casa di Mantegna, 1989). Brown, "Palazzo di San Sebastiano," presents much of the documentary evidence for the decoration of the palace. For comprehensive consideration of the palace's construction, decoration, and use as a *luogo teatrale* for the Gonzaga court, see Bourne, "Out from the Shadow," 280–355.

8. F. W. Kent and Patricia Simons provide an excellent discussion of patronage and *clientelismo* in "Renaissance Patronage: An Introductory Essay," in their book, *Patronage, Art and Society in Renaissance Italy* (Oxford: Clarendon Press, 1987), 1–21. On the complexities of court ruler propaganda, see Kristin Lippincott, "The Neo-Latin Historical Epics of the North Italian Courts: An

Examination of 'Courtly Culture' in the Fifteenth Century," *Renaissance Studies* 3 (1989): 415–28; and the series of articles in Ronald G. Asch and Adolf M. Birke, eds., *Princes, Patronage, and the Nobility: The Court at the Beginning of the Modern Age* (Oxford: Oxford University Press, 1991), which problematize Norbert Elias's classic interpretation of the court as a mirror of the prince and an instrument to domesticate the noble classes (as first presented in Norbert Elias, *die höfische Gesellschaft*, 5th ed. [Darmstadt, 1981]). On the importance of family dynamics in court studies, see Elizabeth Ward Swain, "My Excellent and Most Singular Lord: Marriage in a Noble Family of Fifteenth Century Italy," *Journal of Medieval and Renaissance Studies* 16 (1986): 171–95; Jane Fair Bestor, "Kinship and Marriage in the Politics of an Italian Ruling House: The Este of Ferrara in the Reign of Ercole I (1471–1505)" (Ph.D. diss., University of Chicago, 1992).

9. Isabella's suburban residences included a palace in Borgo di San Giorgio (across the Ponte di San Giorgio), and the villa at Porto (across the Lago di Mezzo), both no longer extant. During the Renaissance the villa at Porto was traditionally occupied by the wives of the Gonzaga rulers, including Barbara of Brandenburg (wife of Lodovico II Gonzaga), Margaret of Wittelsbach (wife of Federico I and mother of Francesco II Gonzaga), Isabella d'Este, and Margherita Paleologa (wife of Federico II Gonzaga, Francesco II's successor); see the wills of these women in ASMn, AG, b. 332. On the villa at Porto, see Clifford M. Brown, "'Al Suo Amenissimo Palazzo di Porto': Biagio Rossetti and Isabella d'Este," *Atti e memorie dell'Accademia Virgiliana di Mantova* 58 (1990): 33–56.

10. At some point after Francesco's death in March 1519, Isabella moved her apartments from the Castello to the ground floor of the Corte Vecchia, the other major component of the Ducal Palace complex during the Renaissance. The date of and motivation for Isabella's move are difficult to pinpoint, although scholars agree that she was installed in her second apartments by 1522. Gerola was the first to suggest that Isabella may have begun planning her Corte Vecchia rooms as early as 1514 (Gerola, "Trasmigrazioni," 258–59), thereby introducing a widely accepted theory that has been debunked by Clifford M. Brown, who convincingly demonstrates that there is still no known evidence for Isabella's construction of these apartments until after she became a widow. See Clifford M. Brown with Anna Maria Lorenzoni, "Collecting Greco-Roman Art in Mantua in the Age of Federico II Gonzaga and the Documentation for the Date of Isabella d'Este's Move to the Corte Vecchia," *Quaderni di Palazzo Te,* n.s. 3 (1996): 18–25. Isabella's Corte Vecchia apartments are better documented than those in the Castello, thanks to their detailed description in a 1542 inventory. The relevant portions have been published numerous times, including: Brown, *La Grotta,* 55–67; Daniela Ferrari, "Das Inventar der Grotta von Odoardo Stivini aus dem Jahr 1542," in Ferino-Pagden, *"La Prima Donna,"* 262–88; idem, "L'inventario delle Gioie," in *Isabella d'Este: I luoghi del collezionismo, Civiltà mantovana* 14–15 (1995): 11–33. On Isabella's Corte Vecchia apartments, see also Clifford M. Brown, "'Fruste et strache nel fabricare': Isabella d'Este's Apartments in the Corte Vecchia of the Ducal Palace in Mantua," in *La Corte di Mantova nell' età di Andrea Mantegna: 1450–1550,* ed. Cesare Mozzarelli, Roberto Oresko, and Leandro Ventura (Rome: Bulzoni, 1997), 295–336.

11. It seems that originally the Studiolo and Grotta were completely isolated from one another, with the Grotta accessible only via stairs (now walled up) which led down from the Sala delle Armi, and the Studiolo accessible by the hallway (still extant) that leads in from the Sala delle Cappe. The current entrance to the Grotta (via a short stairway which leads down from the Sala delle Cappe) dates from the 1530s. A useful reconstruction diagram of these spaces is in Brown, "Collecting Greco-Roman Art," figs. 2–3; see also the related diagram of the Grotta's original entrance published by Brown, "Purché la sia cosa," fig. 3.

12. In 1477, Eleonora moved from her apartment in the Corte to a new suite of rooms located in the Torre Marchexana of the Castel Vecchio, presumably because they offered greater security. Although we know far less about Eleonora's apartments than those of her daughter, they appear to have included a balcony, a vaulted chapel, an oratorio with adjacent *camerini*, and, notably, a studiolo with bookshelves. The decoration of the duchess's rooms seems to have been relatively simple, consisting largely of painted arms and devices, and whitewashed walls to receive tapes-

tries. Most interesting was a view of Naples, Eleonora's hometown, which was painted on the back wall of the balcony, a feature that may have inspired Isabella in 1523 to decorate the loggia of her second apartments in the Corte Vecchia with an image of her hometown, Ferrara, together with those of other important cities (see Brown, "Fruste et strache," 326–29); on Eleonora d'Aragona's apartments, see Thomas Tuohy, *Herculean Ferrara: Ercole d'Este, 1471–1505, and the Invention of a Ducal Capital* (Cambridge: Cambridge University Press, 1996), 99–104. It is also worth noting that from the beginning of her tenure as Francesco's consort Isabella did not have to share space or limelight with a dowager marchesa of Mantua, since Francesco's mother, Margaret of Wittelsbach, had died prematurely in 1479. This meant that Isabella could decorate her apartments unencumbered by input from a mother-in-law. The absence of a female consort at the Gonzaga court created by Margaret's death was a major factor in prompting the betrothal of Isabella to Francesco in 1480. For their engagement, see Alessandro Luzio, "Isabella d'Este e Francesco Gonzaga: Promessi sposi," *Archivio storico lombardo* 9 (1908): 34–69. On Margaret of Wittelsbach, see Adele Bellù, "Margarete von Wittelbach," *Zeitschrift für bayerische Landesgeschichte* 44 (1981): 157–200.

13. Isabella d'Este in Ferrara to Gian Luca Leombeni in Mantua, 12 November 1491: "Ne piace che tu sii in dispositione de finire presto el nostro Studiolo […] Quelle divise che volemo nel friso sono le infrascripte: […] La Mellega, Travaglio, Penarola, Staffe, Cavedon." (ASM, AG, b. 2991, libro 1, c. 68). Verheyen, *Paintings in the Studiolo*, 9 n.15, was unable to transcribe these five *divise*, which Brown later published in Brown, "The *Grotta*," 170 n. 7, as maize (*mellega*), trave (*travaglio*), plume (*penarola*), stirrups (*staffe*), and halter (*cavedon*). It is likely, however, that *cavedon* refers not to a horse halter but to an andiron, an obscure Gonzaga device which later appears, for example, in the Camera delle Imprese in Palazzo Te. As in the Studiolo, the first fresco decoration of the Grotta ceiling was of another Gonzaga device: a winged ring on a blue background; Verheyen, *Paintings in the Studiolo*, 12.

14. Critical to understanding the decorative complexes in which they were employed, the numerous emblems used at the Gonzaga court have yet to be treated satisfactorily. See Mario Praz, "The Gonzaga Devices," in Chambers and Martineau, *Splendours*, 65–72; "Isabella's Impresen," in Ferino-Pagden, *"La Prima Donna,"* 77–82; Ugo Bazzotti, "Imprese gonzaghesche a Palazzo Te," in *Giulio Romano: Atti del Convegno Internazionale di Studi su Giulio Romano e l'espansione europea del Rinascimento* (Mantua: Accademia Nazionale Virgiliana, 1991), 155–68; Rodolfo Signorini, "Un albo di imprese gonzaghesche," in *I Gonzaga: Moneta, arte, storia*, ed. S. Balbi de Caro, exh. cat. (Mantua: Palazzo Te, 1995): 457–64; Rodolfo Signorini, "Imprese gonzaghesche," in *La Collezione della Banca Agricola Mantovana*, vol. 2, *Stemmi, imprese, e motti gonzagheschi* (Milan: Electa, 1996), 40–180.

15. On 18 January 1493, Francesco wrote to Giovanni Sforza, Lord of Pesaro, requesting tiles for "uno camerino che havemo facto fare per nostra habitatione qua a Marmirolo," and included with his letter a design detailing the size and devices (*grandeza et arme*) he desired (ASM, AG, b. 2905, libro 147, cc. 3v–4). The marchese was informed of their delivery to Mantua on 31 May 1494 (ASM, AG, b. 2446, c. 199), and the next day wrote to building superintendent Bernardino Ghisolfo: "De quelli quadri de le nostre salegate mandate da Pesaro vogliamo tu faci la discriptione. Et de questi ne andaranno al camarino nostro da Marmirolo, dove tu te transferirai per havere la certeza del bisogno, et quelli retinerai el resto." (ASM, AG, b. 2961, libro 3, c. 21). On 8 July of the same year Isabella was informed that "Hozi si è saligato el studiolo de la Signoria Vostra de li quadri da le divisie del Illustrissimo Signore nostro, quale compare assai bene, et in vero l'è stata una optima provisione et quasi necessaria, perchè sotto quelle asse se li sono ritrovati de molti nidi de ponteghi." (ASM, AG, b. 2446, c. 172). *Ponteghi* are large mice or rats, from *"pontga,"* the Mantuan word for mouse; see F. Arrivabene, *Vocabulario mantovano-italiano* (Mantua, 1882), 588. On the tiles for Isabella's Studiolo, see Maria Rosa Palvarini Gobio Casali, *La Ceramica a Mantova* (Ferrara: Belriguardo, 1987), 155–64; C. Forlani, "I pavimenti ceramici rinascimentali commissionati da Isabella d'Este: Storia di una dispersione," in *Atti XXI Convegno Internazionale della Ceramica: Rivestimenti parietali e pavimentali dal Medioevo al Liberty; Abisola, 29–31 Maggio 1987* (Albisola:

Grafiche Giors, 1991), 223–32; some related documentation is presented by Brown, "Concludo che," 282 n. 33.

16. The most comprehensive treatments of the paintings are those given by Verheyen, *Paintings in the Studiolo*, 30–51; and Sylvie Béguin, ed., *Le Studiolo d'Isabelle d'Este,* exh. cat. (Paris: Musée du Louvre, 1975).

17. The similarity between the two Costa paintings was first pointed out by Brown, "Palazzo di San Sebastiano," 144–45.

18. The winged ring fresco decoration is visible on the Grotta vault underneath the wooden ceiling (Verheyen, *Paintings in the Studiolo*, 12); a somewhat difficult-to-read photograph of fresco fragments on the Grotta vault was published by Brown, "Purché la sia cosa," fig. 7. The lottery tickets and musical pause are both devices that appear frequently in projects commissioned by Isabella. The explanation generally given for the lottery tickets is that they represent the marchesa's attempts to attain peace in her soul, the white tickets having been drawn by lottery (Praz, "Gonzaga Devices," 65). Isabella was a collector of musical instruments, an amateur lute player, and a noted patron of secular music. The musical device on the wooden Grotta ceiling, known as the "impresa delle pause," shows a clef depicting Isabella's own contralto voice, and includes a series of rests and a repeat sign, see Iain Fenlon, "The Gonzaga and Music," in Chambers and Martineau, *Splendours*, 88. Ivy L. Mumford, "Some Decorative Aspects of the *Imprese* of Isabella d'Este," *Italian Studies* 34 (1979): 60–70, discusses both devices. See A. Genovesi, "Due imprese musicali di Isabella d'Este," *Atti e memorie dell'Accademia Virgiliana di Mantova* 61 (1993): 73–102.

19. Some of the documentation for the creation and installation of the Grotta's wooden ceiling and cabinets was presented by Gerola, "Trasmigrazioni," 257–58.

20. See San Juan, "Court Lady's Dilemma." The best discussion of Isabella's collecting of antiquities is Brown, "Lo insaciabile desidero"; see also Clifford M. Brown, "A Ferrarese Lady and a Mantuan Marchesa: The Art and Antiquities Collections of Isabella d'Este Gonzaga (1474–1539)," in Lawrence, *Women and Art*, 53–71. Isabella was not the only woman of her time to engage in this activity, although she may have done so with a higher profile than any woman before her. Isabella's cousin Isabella d'Aragona (d. 1525), wife of Gian Galeazzo Maria Sforza, also pursued antiquities; see Clifford M. Brown, "Little Known and Unpublished Documents Concerning Andrea Mantegna, Bernardino Parentino, Pietro Lombardo, Leonardo da Vinci and Filippo Benintendi," *L'Arte* 6.1 (1969), 140–51. Alfonsina Orsini de'Medici (d. 1520) is another example of a Renaissance woman who collected antiquities: see the chapter by Sheryl Reiss in this volume.

21. Among his immediate relatives, antiquities collecting was pursued by Francesco II's three uncles, Cardinal Francesco Gonzaga (d. 1483); Gianfrancesco Gonzaga, Lord of Bozzolo (d. 1496); and Lodovico Gonzaga, Bishop-elect of Mantua (d. 1511); as well as by his brother, Cardinal Sigismondo Gonzaga (d. 1525). Notably, all but one of these four individuals were clerics, a profession whose members often engaged in the collection of antiquities. On Cardinal Francesco, see David S. Chambers, *Francesco Gonzaga: A Renaissance Cardinal and His Wordly Goods: The Will and Inventory of Francesco Gonzaga (1444–1483)* (London: Warburg Institute, 1992); Clifford M. Brown, "Lorenzo de' Medici and the Dispersal of the Antiquarian Collections of Cardinal Francesco Gonzaga," *Arte Lombarda* 90–91 (1989): 86–103; on Gianfrancesco, see Ann Hersey Allison, "The Bronzes of Pier Jacopo Alari-Bonacolsi, Called Antico," *Jahrbuch der Kunsthistorischen Sammlungen in Wien* 89–90 (1994): 37–310; on Lodovico, see Clifford M. Brown, "I vasi di pietra dura dei Medici e Ludovico Gonzaga vescovo eletto di Mantua (1501–1502)," *Civiltà mantovana,* n.s. 1 (1983): 63–68; and Clifford M. Brown, "Nuovi documenti riguardanti la collezione di oggetti antichi di Ludovico Gonzaga," *Civiltà Mantovana,* 3rd ser., 1 (1991): 41–45; on Cardinal Sigismondo, see Clifford M. Brown, "Cardinal Sigismondo Gonzaga (1469–1525): An Overlooked Name in the Annals of Collectors of Antiquities," *Xenia* 21 (1991): 47–58; on later Gonzaga collectors of antiquities, see Clifford M. Brown and Anna Maria Lorenzoni, *Our Accustomed Discourse on the Antique: Cesare Gonzaga and Gerolamo Garimberto, Two Renaissance Collectors of Greco-Roman Art* (New York: Garland, 1993).

22. See, for example, the discussion of separate household accounts for the duke and duchess of Ferrara, Ercole d'Este and Eleonora d'Aragona, in Tuohy, *Herculean Ferrara*, 39–41. Although the unfortunate destruction in the nineteenth century of nearly all economic registers for the Gonzaga court prevents us from ever obtaining the kind of detailed financial information that survives for the Este court, other kinds of extant Gonzaga documents suggest that the accounting situation in Mantua was at least generally similar to that in Ferrara.

23. Subsequent alterations to these rooms make a reconstruction virtually impossible, although some information can be gleaned from the 1519–23 project of Francesco's son Federico II to redecorate them upon his accession. See Clifford M. Brown, "The Decoration of the Private Apartment of Federico II Gonzaga on the Pianoterreno of the Castello di San Giorgio," in *Guerre Stati e Città: Mantova e l'Italia Padana dal secolo XIII al XIX*, ed. Carlo Marco Belfanti and others (Mantua: G. Arcari, 1988), 315–43. In 1997 the Castello ground floor was serving as storage space for the Museo di Palazzo Ducale, Mantua, and was not generally accessible to the public.

24. In Ferrara the state apartments of Duke Ercole d'Este (d. 1505) were located in the Palazzo di Corte (comparable to the Corte Vecchia in Mantua), and communicated with those of his consort Eleonora d'Aragona in the Castel Vecchio by means of the 'Via Coperta,' a raised passageway about eighty-nine feet long running between the two buildings (Tuohy, *Herculean Ferrara*, 60–62, 98). A spatial relationship similar to that between Francesco and Isabella's apartments is found later in the rooms of Cosimo I de'Medici in the Palazzo Vecchio in Florence, which were located directly below those of his consort Eleonora di Toledo; see Bruce Edelstein, "The Early Patronage of Eleonora di Toledo: The Camera Verde and Its Dependencies in the Palazzo Vecchio" (Ph.D. diss., Harvard University, 1995), 1:135, 199. On royal male and female apartments in sixteenth-century Spain, see Catherine Wilkinson Zerner, "Women's Quarters in Spanish Royal Palaces," in *Architecture et vie sociale: L'organisation intérieure des grandes demeures a la fin du Moyen Age et a la Renaissance* (Actes du Colloque, Tours, June 6–10, 1988), ed. J. Guillaume (Paris: Picard, 1992), 127–36.

25. The country palaces of Gonzaga and Marmirolo, both destroyed in the eighteenth century, have been treated inadequately in the literature. On Gonzaga, see Brown, "'Concludo che,'" and Bourne, "Out from the Shadow," 202–49. The country palace at Marmirolo is usually discussed in the context of the additions and enlargements made by Giulio Romano in the 1520s and 1530s for Federico II Gonzaga; for further references see Amedeo Belluzzi, "Il palazzo di Marmirolo presso Mantova," in Ernst H. Gombrich and others, *Giulio Romano*, exh. cat. (Mantua, Palazzo Te, Palazzo Ducale, 1989), 520–21. Ferrari publishes many of the pertinent documents in Daniela Ferrari, *Giulio Romano: Repertorio di fonti documentarie*, 2 vols. (Rome: Ministero Per I Beni Culturali e Ambientali, 1992), passim, while the earlier contributions made by Francesco II are discussed by Bourne, "Out from the Shadow," 157–201.

26. "Il S. Marchese lunedì di Pasqua totalmente andò ad star dì et nocte in San Sebastiano, et in Castello non torna [....]" (ASMod, Archivio Segreto Estense, Cancelleria Ducale, Ambasciatori, Mantova, b. 1, cc. n.n.). Equicola's letter is one of the first notices of Francesco's move to the palace, and is also important because it provides early documentation for the onset of his syphilis. The letter continues: "Da camerieri in fore [Francesco] ha ordinato che nessuno il vada ad veder o visitare, se non è chiamato. Veramente non se sente bene. Il suo male quale sia precisamente non lo so, ma so che nel principio di Marzo li rende un gran male al membro genitale[....]" Although Francesco's contraction of syphilis is traditionally dated to 1512 (Alessandro Luzio and Rodolfo Renier, "Contributo alla storia del mal francese," *Giornale storico della letteratura italiana* 5 [1885]: 411), Equicola's letter enables us to confirm that the marchese already suffered from the disease by 1508. For more on syphilis during this period, see Anna Foa, "The New and the Old: The Spread of Syphilis (1494–1530)," in *Sex and Gender in Historical Perspective*, ed. Edward Muir and Guido Ruggiero, trans. Margaret A. Gallucci, Mary M. Gallucci, and Carole C. Gallucci (Baltimore: Johns Hopkins University Press, 1990), 26–45.

27. The Porta Pusterla was torn down in the early 1900s, and the waterway that connected the Lago di Paiolo and the Lago Inferiore was subsequently filled in and paved over to create present-day

Viale della Repubblica and Viale Risorgimento. On these and other transformations to the palace after the death of Francesco II and up to this century, see Cerati, *Trionfi*, 69–84. Portions of Francesco's stables on the Te island were later incorporated by Giulio Romano into the north wing of the Palazzo Te, built for Francesco's son and successor, Federico II (ruled 1519–1540). On this, see Amedeo Belluzzi and Walter Capezzali, *Il palazzo dei lucidi inganni: Palazzo Te a Mantova*, exh. cat. (Mantua: Museo Civico and Galleria d'Arte Moderna, 1976), 17–24.

28. Mantegna, who constructed his house on land given to him in 1476 by Lodovico II Gonzaga, appears to have been living there by July of 1496. In January 1502, under pressure from the marchese, the artist ceded his property and house to Francesco II, who may already have planned to incorporate it into the project for his city-palace, which would be located on immediately adjacent property. It may be more than coincidental that the marchese waited until 1506, the year of Mantegna's death after a long illness, to begin construction of Palazzo di San Sebastiano. Relevant portions of the 1502 *permuta* documents have been published by Rodolfo Signorini, "I Domicili di Andrea Mantegna in Mantova," *Civiltà mantovana* 3rd ser. 6 (1993): 26–28. On Mantegna's house, see also Earl E. Rosenthal, "The House of Andrea Mantegna in Mantua," *Gazette des Beaux-Arts* 60 (1962): 327–48; Hans-Pieter Schwarz, *Das Künstlerhaus: Anmerkungen zur Socialgeschichte des Genies* (Braunschweig: n.p., 1990), 152–54; Marie Kraitrovà, "Das Haus von Andrea Mantegna in Mantua und von Piero della Francesca in Sansepolcro," in *Künstlerhäuser von der Renaissance bis zur Gegenwart*, ed. Eduard Hüttinger (Zurich: Waser, 1985), 51–54; Robert Tavernor, "The Natural House of God and Man: Alberti and Mantegna in Mantua," in Mozzarelli and others, *La Corte*, 225–34, esp. 230–33.

29. Cerati, *Trionfi*, 49–50. Building documents indicate that the villa of Poggio Reale, which Francesco was simultaneously building across the Lago di Mezzo, also incorporated structures already on the site. A construction shortcut such as this, which makes sense in light of Francesco's perpetually overextended budget, was common in architectural practice of the period; see Sabine Eiche, "Alessandro Sforza and the Villa Imperiale at Pesaro," *Mitteilungen des Kunsthistorischen Institutes in Florenz* 2 (1985): 248.

30. The Este villa of Belfiore, located just inside the city walls of Ferrara and built by Francesco's father-in-law, Ercole d'Este, as part of his Herculean Addition urban renewal project, may have constituted a model for Francesco's construction of his own comparably sited city-palace. On Belfiore, see Tuohy, *Herculean Ferrara*, 342–52. For some related examples of *ville suburbane*, see Linda Pellecchia, "The Patron's Role in the Production of Architecture: Bartolomeo Scala and the Scala Palace," *Renaissance Quarterly* 42 (1989): 258–91; Linda Pellecchia, "Reconstructing the Greek House: Giuliano da Sangallo's Villa for the Medici in Florence," *Journal of the Society of Architectural Historians* 52 (1993): 323–38.

31. Cramped conditions in the Castello are easy to imagine; in addition to the Gonzaga family, it housed administrative offices and lodgings for members and guests of their extensive court. Crowding in the Reggia Gonzagescha similarly seems to have been the main reason behind the decision of Federico I Gonzaga, Francesco's father, to begin construction in 1480 of a new residence within the walls of the Ducal Palace. This magnificent palace, Luca Fancelli's Domus Nova, was substantially built, but still unfinished, upon Federico's death in 1484. In light of Francesco's severe financial problems following the plague of 1506, it is puzzling that he chose to build a new palace instead of to complete his father's project, particularly when one realizes that in 1508–9 Francesco was building yet another villa, Poggio Reale, on the shores of the Lago di Mezzo. Beverly Brown discusses Poggio Reale, which was destroyed in the eighteenth century, in Beverly Brown, "Leonardo and the Tale of Three Villas: Poggio a Caiano, the Villa Tovaglia in Florence, and Poggio Reale in Mantua," in *Firenze e la Toscana dei Medici nell'Europa del '500* (Florence: Leo S. Olschki, 1983), 3:1053–62, and by Bourne, "Out from the Shadow," 249–79. On the Domus Nova, see Corinna Vasic Vatovec, *Luca Fancelli architetto, Epistolario gonzaghesco* (Florence: Uniedit, 1979), 224–46.

32. Francesco's will, dated 29 March 1519, one day prior to his death, was drawn up "in palatio residentie Sancti Sebastiani" (ASM, Archivio Notarile, Minute di Notaio Leonello Marchesi, Anno 1519,

Pacco 332).

33. The 1513 performance, in which "se representò Andria molto accommodatamente sotto la logia," is described in a series of letters sent to Isabella in Milan, by her secretary, Benedetto Capilupi. See Cerati, *Trionfi*, docs. 34 and 35. Terence's *Andrians* was also a popular choice for theater productions at the court of Ferrara at this time, and later inspired the subject for Titian's painting, the *Bacchanal of the Andrians*, made for the *camerino* of Duke Alfonso I d'Este.

34. On the notion of this "Gonzaga axis" and patterns of urban growth in Mantua, see Paolo Carpeggiani and Irma Pagliari, *Mantova: Materiali per la storia urbana dalle origini all'ottocento* (Mantua: Gianluigi Arcari Editori, 1983); Marina Romani, *Una città in forma di palazzo: Potere signorile e forma urbana nella Mantova medievale e moderna* (Brescia: Edizione Centro di Ricerche Storiche e Sociali Federico Odorici, 1995), esp. 101–21. (Romani mistakenly states [p. 101] that in 1530 Emperor Charles V entered Mantua through the Porta Pusterla, when in fact he entered through the larger and more ceremonially important Porta Pradella: "La quale [l'intrata] fu che primo era stato fatto un porte al Portone dilla Perdella, adornata benissimo"; see, for example, Giancinto Romano, *Cronaca del soggiorno di Carlo V in Italia (dal 26 Luglio 1529 al 25 Aprile 1530)* (Milan: U. Hoepli, 1892), 241:

35. Cerati published many of the pertinent archival documents in Cerati, *Trionfi*, 165–206, with some important additions and a checklist published by Brown, "Palazzo di San Sebastiano," who provides the first comprehensive discussion of the palace's decoration. For the important 1540 Stivini inventory of Palazzo di San Sebastiano, see Daniela Ferrari, "L'inventario dei beni dei Gonzaga (1540–1542)," *Quaderni di Palazzo Te*, n.s. 2 (1996): 107–9. Although this inventory tells us relatively little about the palace's moveable decoration, it provides a useful catalogue of twenty-five rooms and provides clues about their locations within the palace and information regarding the frescoed emblems. Beyond archival documents, references to some of the most important early sources on Palazzo di San Sebastiano are as follows: Piero Soranzo, letter of 6 November 1515, to Marco Contarini, in Marino Sanuto, *I Diarii di Marino Sanuto*, ed. R. Fulin and others (Venice, 1879–1903), 21:cols. 281–82; Giovanni Benivolo (or Bonavoglia), *Gonzagium monumentum*, manuscript of ca. 1522, Mantua, Biblioteca Comunale MS no. 120 (A.IV.26). The extract of Benivolo relevant to San Sebastiano was published by Cerati, *Trionfi*, doc. 40. Other important sources include: Mario Equicola, *Cronica di Mantua* (Mantua: n.p., 1521); Sebastiano Serlio, *Libro quarto di architettura* (Venice, 1537), chap. 10; Vasari-Milanesi, *Andrea Mantegna*: 3:396–99; *Lorenzo Costa*: 3:134–35; *Francesco Bonsignori*: 5:299–300, 303. Brown discusses most of these sources, as well as some others, in Brown, "Palazzo di San Sebastiano." On Equicola's *Cronica*, see also Giovanni Pillinini, "La Cronica de Mantua di Mario Equicola e la sua posizione nella storiografia rinascimentale," in *Mantova e i Gonzaga nella civiltà del Rinascimento* (Mantua: Arnoldo Mondadori, 1977), 145–50; on the Benivolo poem, see Enrico Rostagno, "Il 'Monumentum Gonzagium' di Giovanni Benevoli o Buonavoglia," *La Bibliofila* 1 (1899): 145–68; Alessandro Luzio and Rodolfo Renier, "La cultura e le relazione letteraria d'Isabella d'Este Gonzaga," *Giornale storico della letteratura italiana* 42 (1903): 109–11; on Benivolo, a Mantuan and courtier of the Gonzaga who spent a number of years in Pesaro at the Sforza court, see G. Mazzacurati, "Benevoli, Giovanni," in *DBI* 8:488–89.

36. By the early twentieth century, numerous structural changes had been effected to the palace, which had passed out of the hands of the ruling branch of the Gonzaga in the late 1600s: its roof had been raised and a third story added to the central corpus of the building, much of the original fenestration had been altered, and the partitioning of the building's interior spaces had been significantly modified (Cerati, *Trionfi*, 71–79). Bertazzolo's 1628 map of Mantua depicts Palazzo di San Sebastiano in an extremely schematic manner (see my figs. 9–10) as an L-shaped structure that does not correspond with the palace's present-day L-shape or orientation. The two-story subsidiary wing that today runs along the Largo XXIV Maggio was not constructed until the nineteenth century. (This wing could not, therefore, have been depicted in Bertazzolo's map, as Brown claims, who calls this wing "the L-shaped extension incorrectly oriented" [Brown, "Palazzo di San Sebastiano," 133, fig. 3]). For an introduction to the architectural typology of Renaissance palaces

in Mantua, see Paul Davies, "Quattrocento Palaces in Mantua and Ferrara," in *Mantegna and Fifteenth-Century Court Culture*, ed. Francis Ames-Lewis and Anka Bednarek (London: Royal Academy of Arts, 1993): 72–83; Howard Burns, "The Gonzaga and Renaissance Architecture," in Chambers and Martineau, *Splendours*, 27–38.

37. This staircase was constructed in the 1880s when the palace was converted into a public hospital, or *lazzaretto* (Cerati, *Trionfi*, 76).

38. The crucible was adopted by Francesco as his personal device around 1498, in an effort to promote himself as a loyal condottiere in the wake of accusations to the contrary by his Venetian employers. See Clifford M. Brown, "Gleanings from the Gonzaga Documents in Mantua—Gian Cristoforo Romano and Andrea Mantegna," *Mitteilungen des Kunsthistorischen Institutes in Florenz* 17 (1973): 153–59; Signorini, "Un albo," 462. Francesco II's *imprese* have been treated as a group by Signorini, "Imprese gonzaghesche," 86–99.

39. The "camera del sol," "camera dela arma del Imperatore," "camera dove è l'arma del Re di Franza," and "camera del crusolo." These four rooms are consistently mentioned together in the building documents; see Cerati, *Trionfi*, docs. 9, 11, 14, 16. The room with the French king's arms was also called the "camera del porcospino," the porcupine being an emblem of Louis XII. See Paolo Giovio, *Le Sententiose imprese di Monsignor Paulo Giovio* (Lyons, 1562), 36, which illustrates Louis XII's emblem as a porcupine under a crown. On porcupine imagery and Louis XII, see Guy de Tervarent, *Attributs et symboles dans l'art profane 1450–1600* (Geneva: Droz, 1959), 2:315. The "camera dela arma del Imperatore" was probably decorated with the black eagle, the Habsburg emblem which had been incorporated into the Gonzaga arms in 1433 when they were granted the title of marquis by Emperor Sigismond. See Giancarlo Malacarne, *Araldica gonzagesca* (Modena: Bulino, 1992), 91–93.

40. Documents for Francesco's 1502 *condotta* and his 1503 appointment by the French king are preserved in ASM, AG, b. 386bis, c. 8 and c. 12. On relations between the Gonzaga and the French royal court during a slightly later period, see Raffaele Tamalio, *Federico Gonzaga alla corte di Francesco I di Francia nel carteggio privato con Mantova (1515–1517)* (Paris: Champion, 1994), and Mark Hamilton Smith, "François Ier, L'Italie et le Château de Blois: Nouveaux documents, nouvelles dates," *Bulletin monumental* 147 (1989): 307–23.

41. Giuseppe Coniglio, *I Gonzaga* (Milan: dall'Oglio, 1967), 174. This book provides the best survey of Francesco's military and political career; see 101–249.

42. Equicola's account of the Sala di Triumphi reads: "Nel ultima parte de la città, propinquo alla chiesa di San Sebastiano, [Francesco edificò] palazo superbissimo, edificio e bello, per sicuramente collocare in una sala ad solo questo effecto fabricata, lo triumpho de C. Iulio Cesare, fatiga de molti anni di misser Andrea Mantegna…" (Equicola, *Cronica*, bk. 4, n.p.). Although Mantegna's canvases at Hampton Court number a total of nine, most early descriptions of the Sala di Triumphi at San Sebastiano refer to seven *Triumphs*, suggesting that Francesco may have made a conscious selection for the installation at San Sebastiano. Excerpts of many sixteenth-century accounts of the *Triumphs* at San Sebastiano have been conveniently published by Giovanni Agosti, "Su Mantegna, 4 (A Mantova, nel Cinquecento)," *Prospettiva* 77 (1995): 83 n.129. If there were indeed seven *Triumphs* displayed in the *spalliera* at San Sebastiano, this number would correspond nicely with the eight impresa-decorated pilasters tentatively identified as their original framing elements (see n. 44 below). On the *Triumphs*, see Andrew Martindale, *The Triumphs of Caesar by Andrea Mantegna* (London: Harvey Miller, 1979), esp. 34–37 and 92–96; contemporary descriptions made by visitors to the Palazzo di San Sebastiano suggest that Francesco's own apartments, or *camere*, were located off one end of the Sala di Triumphi; a documentary reconstruction of the entire *piano nobile* is presented in Bourne, "Out from the Shadow," 301–26; see also Brown, "Palazzo di San Sebastiano."

43. Cerati, *Trionfi*, 26–27.

44. Martindale, *Triumphs*, docs. 19, 22A. It is possible that the eight intaglio gilt pilasters decorated

with Gonzaga devices and inscribed with Francesco II's monogram "FMMIIII," now located in the corners of the "Stanza del Labirinto" in the Ducal Palace in Mantua, can be identified with the pilasters which originally framed Mantegna's *Triumphs*, a theory first proposed by Giovanni Agosti, *Le nozze di Perseo* (Milan: Olivetti, 1992), 20–24. Agosti was also the first to furnish dimensions for these *Triumphi* pilasters, which measure approximately 270 x 30 cm each, a height that corresponds perfectly with the 270 cm average height of Mantegna's canvases, and that results in an overall horizontal span for the installed series of 22.0 m (for 8 pilasters and 7 canvases, at an average width for each canvas of 2.80 m), or of 27.6 m (for 8 pilasters and 9 canvases). In light of the fact that the *sala* was originally about 32 m long, either scenario would have been possible, with openings for door(s) accounting for any excess length. Attention was first drawn to the pilasters in the "Stanza del Labirinto" by Renato Berzaghi in 1990, when he published his discovery that the ceiling in this room, and those in the adjacent rooms in the Palazzo Ducale, had been transferred there from the Palazzo di San Sebastiano in the early seventeenth century by Duke Vincenzo I Gonzaga (see n. 46 below). It should be noted, however, that none of the pilasters presently in the "Stanza del Labirinto," nor any of those in the adjacent apartments of Vincenzo I, exactly resembles the six woodcut pilasters published by Andrea Andreasi in 1598–99, and presumed to represent the pilasters used to frame Mantegna's *Triumphs* (the woodcuts are reproduced by Martindale, *Triumphs*, fig. 87).

45. The identity of the original patron of Mantegna's *Triumphs* has been a long-debated subject amongst scholars, and all three generations of Gonzaga rulers—Lodovico II, Federico I, and Francesco II—have been proposed as candidates, although no conclusive proof has yet emerged. A summary of the arguments is given by Charles Hope, "The Chronology of Mantegna's Triumphs," in *Andrea Mantegna*, ed. Jane Martineau, exh. cat. (New York: Metropolitan Museum of Art, 1992), 350–92.

46. This crucible ceiling, together with two other carved ceilings from the *piano nobile* of San Sebastiano, was transferred in 1601 by Duke Vincenzo I Gonzaga to the Palazzo Ducale for installation in his apartments, where they remain today. For this transfer, the crucible ceiling was cut into two roughly equal pieces and installed into the "Stanza di Giuditta" and the "Stanza del Crogiolo," while the other two ceilings, one decorated with a gilded labyrinth and the other with a papal coat of arms, were installed, respectively, in the "Stanza del Labirinto" and the "Camera di Amore e Psiche." See Renato Berzaghi, "Francesco II e Vincenzo Gonzaga: Il palazzo di San Sebastiano e il palazzo ducale," *Paragone* 41 (1990): 62–73.

47. "Parea dicto triumpho trunco & mutilato per non vi essere quella pompa che sequir solea il triumphate, mancavanovi li specatatori, al che puede Francesco prudentemente chiamando alla sua liberalità Lorenzo Costa, homo non solamente in pictura excellentissimo ma amabile & honorato cortegioano, questo oltra le altre laudate opere, con ingegno, arte, & scientia de dicta bellissima sala il capo & fina adorna." (Equicola, *Cronica*, bk. 4, n.p.).

48. "[Costa] dipinse ancora nella sala grande, dove oggi sono i Trionfi di mano del Mantegna, due quadri, cioè in ciascuna testa uno. Nel primo, che è a guazzo, sono molti nudi che fanno fuochi e sacrifizii a Ercole, et in questo è ritratto di naturale il marchese con tre suoi figliuoli, Federigo, Ercole, e Ferrante, che poi sono stati grandissimi signori; vi sono similmente alcuni ritratti di gran donne. Ne l'altro, che fu fatto a olio molti anni dopo il primo, e che fu quasi dell'ultima cosa che dipignesse Lorenzo, è il marchese Federigo fatto uomo, com un bastone in mano come generale di Santa Chiesa sotto Leone Decimo; et intorno gli sono molti signori ritratti dal Costa di naturale." (Vasari-Milanesi 3:135). Martindale has suggested that the Prague canvas may originally have been commissioned by Francesco II but finished after his death by his son Federico II, who inserted his own portrait into the painting (Martindale, *Triumphs*, 95). Signed and dated 1522, the Prague *Triumph of Federico II* measures 2.66 x 6.38 m; it would thus have fit perfectly above a dado on one of the *sala's* approximately seven-meter-long end walls (if one accounts for the space occupied by a doorway). On the Prague painting, see Emil Schaffer, "Der 'Triumph des Federigo Gonzaga' von Lorenzo Costa," *Monatshefte für Kunstwissenschaft* 9 (1908): 763–70.

49. Letter of Francesco II in Mantua to Archdeacon Gabbioneta in Rome on 11 December 1512:

"Quella sera dessimo una solemne cena al Signore Duca di Milano et alli suoi gentilhomini in la sala di triumphi di Cesare qui a Sancto Sebastiano[…]," ASM, AG, b. 2920, libro 225, c. 36, partially published by Martindale, *Triumphs*, doc. 22A. Another excellent and amusing description of these festivities held at San Sebastiano is provided by a letter dated in Mantua on 13 November 1512, written by Gonzaga courtier Lorenzo Strozzi to the young Federico II Gonzaga, who at that time was living in Rome as a hostage of Pope Julius II (ASM, AG, b. 2485, cc. n.n.). Alessandro Luzio publishes a lengthy extract of this letter in Alessandro Luzio, "Isabella d'Este di fronte a Giulio II negli ultimi tre anni del suo pontificato," *Archivio Storico Lombardo* 18 (1912): 139–142, and discussed (with translation) by Bourne, "Out from the Shadow," 349–53.

50. Cardona is usually referred to in the documents as "el Vicerè." He served as viceroy of Naples from 1508, and commanded the Spanish-papal troops during the War of the Holy League at Ravenna in 1512, where his forces lost to the French. He subsequently returned to Naples, where he died in 1522; see *Enciclopedia italiana Treccani* (Milan: Emilio Besetti, 1930): 8:994–95.

51. Full documentation for this episode is presented in Molly Bourne, "A Viceroy Comes to Mantua: Ramon Folch de Cardona, Lorenzo Costa, and the Italian Renaissance in Spain," in *Coming About…A Festschrift for John Shearman*, ed. Lars R. Jones and Louisa C. Matthew (Cambridge, Mass.: Harvard University Art Museums, forthcoming).

52. "Era in una camera forte adornata sentato al focho, con tre ventagi chè non li lassava andar uno pelo adosso, con tre terribilissimi levrieri intorno et infiniti falconi e zirifalchi in pugno li intorno, e su per le spaliere erano quadri che erano retrati li soi belli cavali e belli cani, e li era un nanino vestito d'oro. Tolto licentia da soa signoria, andassemo a veder il palazo. In una camera era depinto le vitorie e fati l'avea fato, e il baston a[v]uto quando fu fato capitano di la Signoria nostra" (Soranzo in Sanuto, *Diarii*, 21:cols. 281–82).

53. Equicola singled out the marchese's knowledge of hunting dogs and birds in his *Cronica*: "Fu de cani perfectissimo conoscitore, peritissimo in la cognitione de ucelli, alli occhi, peso, & colore," and devoted no less than six full pages to a description of Francesco's expertise in horses. On Francesco and the development of the Gonzaga breed of horses, see Giancarlo Malacarne, *Il mito dei cavalli gonzagheschi: Alle origini del purosangue* (Verona: Promoprint, 1995).

54. See n. 46 above; the two ceilings are reproduced by Berzaghi, "Francesco II," figs. 34, 36, 37. The labyrinth ceiling displays the words "FORSE CHE SI, FORSE CHE NO" running continuously throughout the maze decoration; this is the first verse of a *frottola* written ca. 1505 by the leading musician at the Gonzaga court, Marchetto Cara; see Claudio Gallico, *"Forse che si forse che no" fra poesia e musica* (Mantua: Istituto Carlo d'Arco per la Storia di Mantova, 1961). It is difficult to identify the papal impresa on the other ceiling with precision, but it seems possible to make out the crossed oak (*rovere*) branches, the emblem of Pope Julius II's family, the della Rovere.

55. Dating of the crucible ceiling can be deduced from a document of October 1506 which states that "Lorenzo pictor" was preparing "*50 crosoli da meterli*" for the "*sala di sopra*"; presumably these refer to the gilt *pastiglia* crucibles which decorated the ceiling of the Sala di Triumphi (Cerati, *Trionfi*, doc. 13).

56. On the cycle of Francesco's deeds, or *fati*, which are also referred to in later Gonzaga inventories, see Brown, "Palazzo di San Sebastiano," 146–49. Benivolo's description of Palazzo di San Sebastiano in his poem, *Gonzagium monumentum* reads: "Here Francesco painted his ancestors and their predecessors and a whole series of the forebears of the Gonzaga clan." ("Hic et avis, et avorum Atavos: et originis omnem / Gonzagae seriem gentis: maternaque pingi / stemmata: et Augustos Avaiae de sanguine Reges / Iussit, et in patrios advecta trophaea penates.") Benivolo, *Gonzagium monumentum*, c. 85; excerpted in ibid., 177.

57. On illegitimacy as a problem for the house of Este, see Jane Fair Bestor, "Bastardy and Legitimacy in the Formation of a Regional State in Italy: The Estense Succession," *Comparative Studies in Society and History* 38.3 (1996): 549–85.

58. The 1540 inventory lists a *camerino de l'antana* [altana], and a *camera del mapamondi et del caiero*.

On the San Sebastiano *mappamondo*, see Clifford M. Brown, "The 'Camera del Mapamondo et del Caiero' in the Palazzo di San Sebastiano in Mantua: A Fragment of a View of Jerusalem and Vittorio Carpaccio's Letter to Francesco II Gonzaga of 1511," *Journal of Jewish Art* 10 (1984): 32–46.

59. At Marmirolo there was another *mappamondo* and a "camera Graeca," while the "camera dalle città" in the palace at Gonzaga included views of five Italian cities, as well as of Constantinople, Cairo, and possibly even Paris. Francesco's activities as a map collector and the cartographic cycles he commissioned are treated by Molly Bourne, "Francesco II Gonzaga and Maps as Palace Decoration in Renaissance Mantua," *Imago Mundi* 51 (1999): 51–82.

60. Martindale, *Triumphs*, docs. 17, 18, 20.

61. On 2 August 1508, Costa wrote to Francesco complaining of the "grandexemo male" which kept him from "liverare la chamara"; the letter (ASM, AG, b. 2472, c. 585) is published by Clifford M. Brown, "Lorenzo Costa in Mantua: Five Autograph Letters," *L'Arte* 11–12 (1970): 106–7. Sigismondo's November 1510 description of the room as "fenita," was reported by courtier Federico Benale in a letter to Francesco Gonzaga (ASM, AG, b. 2479, cc. n.n.); published by Brown, "Palazzo di San Sebastiano," 173.

62. "Andato poi Lorenzo [Costa] al servigio del signor Francesco Gonzaga marchese di Mantoa, gli dipinse nel palazzo di San Sebastiano, in una camera lavorata parte a guazzo e parte a olio, molte storie. In una è la marchesa Isabella ritratta di naturale, che ha seco molte signore che con varii suoni cantando fanno dolce armonia; in un' altra è la dea Latona che converte, secondo la favola, certi villani in ranocchi; nella terza è il marchese Francesco, condotto da Ercole per la via della virtù sopra la cima d'un monte consecrato all'eternità. In un altro quadro si vede il medesimo marchese, sopra un piedistallo, trionfante con un bastone in mano, e intorno gli sono molti signori e servitori suoi con stendardi in mano, tutti lietissimi e pieni di giubilo per la grandezza di lui, fra quali tutti è un infinito numero di ritratti di naturale...." (Vasari-Milanese 3:134–35). Brown discusses the "camera del Costa" in Brown, "Palazzo di San Sebastiano," 143–45.

63. Ovid (*Metamorphosis* 6:157–381) recounts how Latona ("Leto" in Greek), daughter of the Titans Coeus and Phoebe, after travelling to Delos to give birth to Apollo and Diana without Hera's knowledge (Latona had conceived the twins by Hera's husband, Zeus), was prevented by the Lycian peasants from drinking water there, since they feared the wrath of Hera. Angry and thirsty, Latona asked the gods to turn the peasants into frogs. Although the Latona story is relatively uncommon in the visual arts, it does appear on a maiolica plate made ca. 1525 by Nicolò da Urbino as part of a service for Isabella (pointed out by Brown, "Palazzo di San Sebastiano," 144). For additional examples of Renaissance art objects depicting this story, see J. D. Reid, *The Oxford Guide to Classical Mythology in the Arts, 1300–1990s* (New York: Oxford University Press, 1993), 2:635–36. The Latona myth may also have had special political implications in Mantua because of the story's strong resemblance to the legend of the foundation of the city. According to this story, Mantua was founded by Manto, daughter of the prophet Tiresias, who fled Troy with its treasures and gave birth on the banks of the Mincio river to a future Etruscan king.

64. "Cossì dico che sono belle, e tanto più belle quanto Vostra Signoria ha pur imparato da la mia camara, l'è ben vero che l'ha poi megliorato...." (see n. 1 above).

65. For another example, see the chapter by Benjamin Kohl in this volume.

66. Mario Equicola, who became Isabella's secretary in 1508, may have played a role in making her apartments better known; see Kolsky, "Unnoticed Description," 232–33.

67. According to Mario Equicola, the "Monsignor d'Alegra" visited the palace in May of 1508. In a letter written from Mantua on 10 May 1508 to Cardinal Ippolito d'Este, Equicola writes that the "Monsignor di Alegra ... visitò il S. Marchese in San Sebastiano." (ASMod, Archivio Segreto Estense, Cancelleria Ducale, Ambasciatori, Mantova, b. 1, cc. n.n.). On the accessibility of Isabella's apartments, see Clifford M. Brown, "Public Interests and Private Collections: Isabella d'Este's *Apartamento della Grotta* and Its Accessibility to Artists, Scholars, and Public Figures," in *Akten*

des XXV Internationalen Kongress für Kunstgeschichte (Vienna, 4–10 September 1983; Vienna, 1986), 4:37–41, and Brown, "'Lo insaciabile desiderio,'" 331–32.

68. On 9 May 1498, Isabella penned an autograph letter in the Grotta to Francesco which she signed: "scrita ... in grandissima pressia in la grotta" (ASM, AG, b. 2112, c. 266; Brown, "'Lo insaciabile desiderio,'" 348 n. 45 [but misdated as 9 March 1498]). On music making in Isabella's Grotta, see Iain Fenlon, "Gender and Generation: Patterns of Music Patronage among the Este, 1471–1539," in *La Corte di Ferrara e il suo mecenatismo, 1441–1598,* ed. Marianne Pade, Lene Waage Petersen, and Daniela Quarta (Modena: Panini, 1990), 213–32.

69. In August of 1509, while fighting for the League of Cambrai against his former Venetian employers, Francesco was captured and imprisoned in the doge's palace until July of the following year. On this event and the political aftermath, see Alessandro Luzio, "La reggenza di Isabella d'Este durante la prigionia del marito (1509–1510)," *Archivio storico lombardo* 14 (1910): 5–104.

70. The festivities are described by Gonzaga courtier Amico Maria della Torre in his letter from Mantua of 5 March 1511 to ten-year-old Federico II Gonzaga, then in Urbino: "Hor gli significo che da più de giorni quindeci continui sempre si è ballato et facto festa a San Sebastiano, excepto de giorno dil venere e sabbato, ne li quali la sera lo Ill.mo S.re vostro patre invitava pur a San Sebastiano madama vostra matre cum questi gentilhomini et loro consorti a cena, et una fiata gli dette una cena a Pozo reale […] La Ill.ma madama vostra matre lunì proximo passato fece una bella festa in la Corte propria dil Castello che superbamente da ogni canto era apparata […]" (ASM, AG, b. 2482, c. 173).

71. See, for example, Amico Maria della Torre's description of the events in his letter of 4 August 1512 written from Mantua to Federico II, then in Rome as a hostage of Julius II (ASM, AG, b. 2485, cc. n.n.; partially published by Cerati, *Trionfi,* doc. 29).

72. On the 1513 performance of Terence's *Andrians,* see n. 33 above. The 1514 entertainments are described in a letter written to Isabella by her secretary Benedetto Capilupi on 16 December of that year: "[Il Duca di Milano] ritornò a cena a S.to Sebastiano […] doppo cena andò suso, [e Francesco] fece cantare Marchetto e Ruberto, e fece ballare il Signor Alvise [Ercole Gonzaga] e Signore Ferrando ... Eravi anche S. Federico, il quale molto ha acarezato, e molto gli piaque …" (ASM, AG, b. 2489, cc. n.n.).

Widow, Mother, Patron of Art:
Alfonsina Orsini de' Medici

Sheryl E. Reiss

For centuries the name Medici has been practically synonymous with the patronage of culture in Renaissance Italy. Many members of this illustrious family, including Cosimo il Vecchio, Lorenzo il Magnifico, Popes Leo X and Clement VII, and Cosimo I, Grand Duke of Tuscany, have achieved fame as patrons of painting, sculpture, and architecture. Their varied and widespread building and decorative programs have been the subject of much scholarly inquiry. But what of their wives, widows, and mistresses? And what of their mothers, sisters, and daughters? During the Renaissance, a number of Medici women were involved in the commissioning or realization of paintings, sculpture, architecture, and the so-called *arti minori*. Among Medici women patrons we may list Contessina de' Bardi, Lucrezia Tornabuoni, Ginevra Alessandri, Maddalena Cibo, Lucrezia Salviati, Eleonora di Toledo, and Bianca Cappello. Recently, scholars have begun to pay attention to the patronage activities of these and other Medici women.[1] A particularly intriguing example is Alfonsina Orsini de' Medici, whose patronage of art and architecture I will consider in this essay. Topics I address include Alfonsina Orsini's collecting of antiquities, her activity as a patron of painting and the decorative arts, and especially her patronage of architecture—an area in which other Medici women were also active as patrons.[2]

Alfonsina Orsini de' Medici

On 13 February 1520, Filippo Strozzi, Depositor General of the Apostolic Camera, wrote to a friend with news of the funeral of his mother-in-law, Alfonsina Orsini de' Medici.[3] Strozzi callously jested that, "Alfonsina Orsini, whose death no one and whose life everyone mourned, and whose burial is most pleasant and salubrious to mankind," had been laid to rest.[4] Strozzi's spiteful sentiments are complemented by those expressed in the diary of Bartolommeo Masi, who, in noting Alfonsina's death, said that she died "with little good grace because she cared about nothing but accumulating money."[5] There is abundant contemporary evidence for a rather general loathing of this woman, who was far from the Renaissance ideal of decorousness and dependence.[6] One result of her ambition and avarice, however, was her significant activity as a patron of the visual arts.

Alfonsina Orsini, as seen in an engraving of 1761 by Francesco Allegrini (fig. 1), was born in 1472.[7] Alfonsina was the daughter of the condottiere Roberto Orsini, Count of Tagliacozzo and Alba, and his second wife, Caterina di Sanseverino.[8] Roberto was a member of a Neapolitan branch of the ancient Orsini family and a favorite of Ferrante of Aragon, the king of Naples.[9] In the 1480s, Lorenzo the Magnificent de' Medici pursued a political agenda that maintained peace with Naples.[10] A marriage alliance between the Medici and the Neapolitan Orsini was part of the strategy.[11] The match settled upon was between Lorenzo's

Reiss Fig. 1. Francesco Allegrini, *Alfonsina Orsini,* after Giuseppe Allegrini, *Chronologica series simulacrorum regiae familiae Mediceae,* Florence, 1761, no plate nos. (photo: Harry Ransom Humanities Research Center, University of Texas, Austin)

eldest son Piero (fig. 2), later called the Unfortunate, and Alfonsina Orsini.[12] Lorenzo's ambassador to Naples, his brother-in-law Bernardo Rucellai, described the thirteen-year-old prospective bride as not "particularly good or bad," with a good nose and a slightly heavy mouth that was "not enough to destroy her charms."[13] The dowry settled upon was the very considerable sum of 12,000 ducats.[14]

Alfonsina was married by proxy in Naples in February 1488 and met her husband in May of that year, settling afterwards in Florence.[15] She had two children who survived infancy: a son, Lorenzo, born in 1492, and a daughter, Clarice, born in 1493.[16] With the death of Lorenzo il Magnifico in April 1492, the ever-changing fortunes of the Medici family moved toward disaster under the inept leadership of Alfonsina's husband, Piero.[17] When Piero took it upon himself to deal with the French King Charles VIII, who had crossed into Italy in the autumn of 1494, he offered the final affront to Florentine Republican sensibilities. On 9 November 1494, an angry mob pillaged the Medici palace in Via Larga, a visible symbol of the family's pride and *magnificenza*.[18] Writing in the sixteenth century, Bartolomeo Cerretani described the treatment of Alfonsina and her mother, the countess Caterina of Sanseverino:

> In the palace where Piero lived, at the beginning of Via Larga, there entered, by order of the Signoria, some citizens who took away the wife of the said Piero, and his mother-in-law, both of the Orsini family, and first, having searched them carefully, they pulled all their jewels off their fingers and sent them crying into the monastery of Santa Lucia in Via di San Gallo.[19]

Following this, Piero and his brothers fled the city for Bologna, leaving Alfonsina behind to plead their case with Charles.[20] Alfonsina remained in Florence until September of the following year, when she joined her husband in exile.[21] In 1495 and 1496, a group of Medici partisans (including Baccio Bandinelli's father—the goldsmith Michelangelo di Viviano, who would later work for Alfonsina), attempted to recover Medici possessions that had been seized by the Signoria.[22] Their clandestine activities to recoup medals, vases, gems and other pre-

Reiss Fig. 2. G. B. Paggi, *Piero di Lorenzo de' Medici, Called "The Unfortunate,"* Florence, Galleria degli Uffizi (photo: Soprintendenza, Florence)

cious objects are recorded in the secret ledger ("libretto sagreto") of Francesco di Agostino Cegia, who was beheaded in December 1497 for plotting on behalf of the Medici.[23] The ledger contains numerous references to transactions involving Alfonsina and her mother, who received both liquid funds and movable goods including silver, gold, medals, and works in jasper and mother-of-pearl.[24] After several futile attempts to re-enter Florence, Piero de' Medici drowned in the Garigliano following a battle near Montecassino in 1503.[25] As a widow, Alfonsina resided in Rome and concentrated her efforts on recuperating her dowry (which had been seized in 1494) and on making a suitable match for her daughter Clarice, who was married to Filippo Strozzi in 1508.[26]

With the return of the Medici to power in 1512, and the elevation of her brother-in-law Cardinal Giovanni to the papacy as Pope Leo X, Alfonsina sought unceasingly to advance the political fortunes of her son Lorenzo, whom she wished to be a titled lord.[27] While Alfonsina Orsini is familiar to historians of early-sixteenth-century Florence and Rome as a powerful figure in Medicean politics, her support for the arts has received little scholarly attention.[28] At this point we may turn to her activities as a patron and collector of art, which I will consider in a broadly chronological manner.

Early Patronage and Collecting

The artistic patronage of Piero the Unfortunate is not well defined and it is difficult to say what Alfonisna's role may have been in the early years of her marriage.[29] Even if Ascanio Condivi's famous anecdote about Michelangelo's snowman is untrue, it is clear that the young sculptor did work for Piero after the death of his father Lorenzo the Magnificent.[30] Alfonsina, then, must have known Michelangelo, even if she never offered him a commission. There is, however, some evidence for Alfonsina's early involvement with the visual arts.

The inventory of Lorenzo the Magnificent's properties undertaken at his death in 1492 lists the contents of Alfonsina's apartment at Poggio a Caiano.[31] These included various linens, ribbons, three "libriccini di donna", and five *quadretti*.[32] The same inventory lists a portrait of Alfonsina, painted *al naturale*, in the *anticamera* of Piero's suite in Palazzo Medici.[33] In her compendium of Medici portraits, Karla Langedijk has associated this document with a portrait of a lady in a modest brown dress (fig. 3), sometimes attributed to Botticelli, now in the Palazzo Pitti.[34] While there is no evidence linking Alfonsina to Botticelli, Vasari states that Alfonsina Orsini was Mariotto Albertinelli's first protector and the patron of several paintings by him that she sent to her Orsini relatives in Rome.[35] Vasari says that Albertinelli painted Alfonsina's portrait *di naturale* and this unidentified work may be the likeness mentioned in the inventory of 1492.[36] Vasari notes that because of his close relationship with Alfonsina, Albertinelli thought that he had his fortune made; the revolt of November 1494, however, would bring to an end any work he might have done for Alfonsina Orsini.[37]

There is also some evidence, albeit of a late date, for Alfonsina's patronage of ecclesiastic architecture before Piero's death.[38] According to Giovanni Richa, in the 1480s several women (including Alfonsina, her widowed mother, Caterina, and her mother-in-law, Clarice Orsini de' Medici)

Reiss Fig. 3. Attributed to Sandro Botticelli, *Portrait of a Woman* (Alfonsina Orsini de' Medici?), ca. 1488, Florence, Galleria Pitti (photo: Alinari/Art Resource, N.Y.)

were major benefactors of the Dominican tertiary convent of Santa Lucia in Via Sangallo, where Alfonsina and her mother would flee during the anti-Medicean rebellion of November 1494.[39] Richa states that, at the urging of Savonarola, these women bought up houses and land to enlarge the convent to 120 cells, had rooms and chapels built, and had the convent church rebuilt from its foundations with a large portal on the Via Sangallo.[40] In 1992, Sharon Strocchia drew attention to a document that indicates Alfonsina and her mother had rooms built at Santa Lucia for their personal use "near the street that goes to San Marco."[41]

The remaining evidence related to Alfonsina Orsini's activities as patron and collector dates from after the death of her husband. Scholarship of the past decade has emphasized pious motivations for the patronage of women, especially for widows.[42] For the most part, Alfonsina's actions appear to have been inspired by other considerations, specifically her political and dynastic ambitions.[43] In this context it is noteworthy that Alfonsina, despite her well-documented activity as a patron in other spheres, seems never to have planned for a tomb monument to commemorate her deceased husband, Piero.[44] This stands in contrast to typical patterns of female patronage; recent research has shown that funerary art—including chapels, tomb monuments, and altarpieces—was a particular focus of patronage by secular women in Italy.[45]

In 1504, shortly after her husband's death, Alfonsina received the Castel Sant' Angelo (now Castel Madama), near Tivoli, as part of her Orsini inheritance.[46] Several years later, in

1514, she purchased another property near Tivoli, the Castello di Lunghezza, which was later inhabited by her daughter Clarice and son-in-law Filippo Strozzi, who renovated the structure in the 1520s.[47]

Alfonsina in Rome: Housing Concerns and the Palazzo Medici-Lante

In 1509, while residing in Rome, Alfonsina acquired Palazzo Medici (now Palazzo Madama, the Senate House, fig. 4) from her brother-in-law Giuliano and her son Lorenzo for 11,000 ducats.[48] The palazzo, in the *rione* of Sant' Eustachio, had been the residence of Cardinal Giovanni de' Medici, the future Pope Leo X.[49] The bulk of Alfonsina Orsini's patronage took place after Cardinal Giovanni's elevation to the papal throne in March 1513; soon after that auspicious event she began to look for a new place to live in Rome. On 8 November 1513, Alfonsina wrote to Lorenzo, who was then in Florence, about her housing problems, stressing that she felt herself too removed from the Vatican:

> I think that I shall have to move, me and my entourage, because I remain here with very great difficulty; and also because being far from the papal palace, as you know, turns out to be inconvenient for many reasons. In any case, I am thinking of finding a house in the Borgo.[50]

In December 1513, a month after she complained of her housing dilemma, Alfonsina rented out part of Palazzo Madama to Cardinal Antonio del Monte.[51] In May of the following year, she began to acquire property for construction of a new palazzo; instead of a site in the Vatican Borgo, she chose the Piazza Caprettari near the Dogana (customs house) and not far from the Palazzo Madama.[52] It is likely that this location was chosen because of its proximity to the

Reiss Fig. 4. Maerten van Heemskerck, *View of Palazzo Madama,* Rome, 1532–36, Berlin, Kupferstichkabinett, 79 D 2, vol. 2, fol. 48r (photo: Kupferstichkabinett, Staatliche Museen zu Berlin PK)

grandiose palace on the Piazza Navona planned by Leo X.[53] Alfonsina's acquisition of properties continued with the purchase of new houses on 18 August 1514 and 26 April 1515.[54] Today the Roman palace built for her is known as Palazzo Medici-Lante (fig. 5).[55] The architectural decoration of the palazzo includes Alfonsina's arms (fig. 6), along with those of other members of the Medici family.[56] Significantly, her *scudo accolato* (impaled coat of arms), with the Medici *palle* at the left and the Orsini rose and chevrons at the right, asserts her natal identity within the context of otherwise patrilineal imagery.[57] Christoph Frommel has attributed the design, if not the construction, of the palace to the longtime Medici favorite Giuliano da Sangallo, who died in October 1516.[58] In December 1516, a few months after Sangallo's death, the architect Baccio Bigio was documented in Rome "on account of construction that Madonna Alfonsina wants to do here, near the Dogana."[59] The palace is in a conservative style closer to Florentine quattrocento models than to the antiquarian style formulated in Rome by the Bramante/Raphael circle.[60]

Reiss Fig. 5. Palazzo Medici-Lante, Rome, begun ca. 1516, courtyard (photo: author)

Reiss Fig. 6. Palazzo Medici-Lante, Rome, begun ca. 1516, captial with arms of Alfonsina Orsini de' Medici and spandrel with Medici diamond ring and feathers (photo: author)

Support for an Artist and Collecting Antiquities

On occasion Alfonsina intervened on behalf of artists. In September of 1514, while still in Rome, Alfonsina wrote to her son Lorenzo in Florence recommending an artist named Poggio di Zanobi, whom she called "Poggino n[ost]ro amico vecchio" (Poggino our old friend), for an official position within the Florentine government (fig. 7).[61] As was her custom, Alfonsina signed the letter "Alfonsina Ursina de' Medici."[62] Her follow-up intervention was effective,

for in autumn 1515, this artist, identified as *dipintore di Palazo* (palace painter), worked in the Sala del Papa at Santa Maria Novella and supplied hangings for the papal *baldacchino* used in Leo X's Florentine *entrata* (fig. 8), to which I will return below.[63]

In September 1514 we also hear of Alfonsina Orsini's activities as a collector of antiquities. Her son-in-law Filippo Strozzi wrote to Lorenzo's chancellor, Giovanni di Poppi, that Alfonsina was one of the most fortunate of women, not only because her "God-given" money earned interest through usurious lending, but also because she had come into possession of around five of the most beautiful ancient statues to be found in Rome.[64] Strozzi described the small marble figures as wounded and dead, which were thought by some to represent the Horatii and the Curatii.[65] A few months later, a French visitor to Rome, Claude Bellièvre of Lyons, also noted the statues at Alfonsina's residence.[66] Bellièvre noted six statues and, like Strozzi, thought that they represented the Horatii and Curatii.[67] The antique statuary acquired by Alfonsina has been identified as

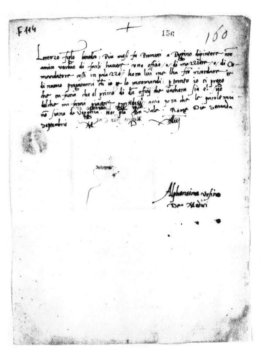

Reiss Fig. 7. Letter of Alfonsina Orsini to Lorenzo di Piero de' Medici, 2 September 1514, ASF, MAP, 114, 156 (photo: Archivio di Stato, Florence)

Reiss Fig. 8. Giorgio Vasari, *Entrata of Pope Leo X,* Florence, Palazzo Vecchio, Sala di Leone Decimo, beg. 1555 (photo: Alinari/Art Resource, N.Y.)

Reiss Fig. 9. *Dying Amazon,* Roman copy of Hellenistic original, Naples, Museo Nazionale Archeologico (photo: Alinari/Art Resource, N.Y.)

Roman copies of the small bronze Attalid dedication group on the Athenian Acropolis.[68] Four of the statues, including a *Dying Amazon* and a splendid *Dying Persian* (figs. 9, 10), are now in Naples in the Museo Nazionale Archeologico.[69] Pieces from the group inspired Raphael on a number of occasions, and figures from it were recorded in a sketch of the antiquities at Palazzo Madama by Maerten van Heemskerck (fig. 11).[70] In Heemskerck's sketch, some of the small statues are just barely visible in the distance on the low garden wall, and another, a wounded Gaul (now in Paris), can be seen in the loggia, in front of the niche. While there is no evidence that Alfonsina shared Isabella d'Este's nearly insatiable craving for ancient art, this account confirms that she did collect antiquities.[71]

Reiss Fig. 10. *Dying Persian,* Roman copy of Hellenistic original, Naples, Museo Nazionale Archeologico (photo: Alinari/Art Resource, N.Y.)

Reiss Fig. 11. Maerten van Heemskerck, *View of Palazzo Madama*, Rome, 1532–36, Berlin, Kupferstichkabinett, 79 D 2, vol. 2, fol. 5r (photo: Kupferstichkabinett, Staatliche Museen zu Berlin PK)

Alfonsina in Florence and the *Entrata* of Leo X

In June of 1515, shortly after the final purchase of properties on the site of her Roman palazzo, Alfonsina moved back to Florence, establishing herself in Palazzo Medici.[72] This allowed her to be closer to her son Lorenzo, the focus and the instrument of her enormous political ambitions. In Florence she sought to achieve near princely status for her son; his marriage to a suitable, and preferably regal, bride was of paramount concern.[73] In one revealing letter Alfonsina told her son that it was not important if a proposed bride was illegitimate because "even Saint Jerome said that love comes from the dowry."[74] In August of 1515, Alfonsina's son-in-law, Filippo Strozzi, wrote to Lorenzo, on the battlefield in Lombardy, of his mother's political activities in Palazzo Medici:

> Her Ladyship is always busy—whether writing to Rome or to you there or giving audiences, because of which the house is always full; such attendance results in good press for the State, encouragement for friends, and dread for adversaries. She exercises that authority which for any other woman would be impossible and for few men easy.[75]

When it was decided in October 1515 that Leo X would return to his native city on the way to meet Francis I in Bologna, hurried preparations were begun for a ceremonial *entrata* of extraordinary splendor, richness, and variety (fig. 8).[76] Alfonsina Orsini was much involved in the plans surrounding this event, which has been studied by John Shearman, Anthony Cummings, and Ilaria Ciseri.[77] Ciseri brought together a number of important documents, many of them unpublished, that augment our knowledge of Alfonsina's artistic patronage at the time of Leo's *entrata*, which took place on 30 November 1515; these include a papal brief of 4 November, in which Leo made her responsible for the preparations for the event.[78] On 3 November, Alfonsina, in Florence, wrote to her son Lorenzo in Milan: "And now I find myself in the midst of a great confusion what with provisions of food supplies for a court, lodgings and decorations, and a thousand other things that would be impossible to describe briefly."[79] Earlier in the letter Alfonsina had already referred to plans for the decorations, including the great triumphal arches that would punctuate the pontiff's ceremonial route.[80]

In this letter and others Alfonsina refers to work on gold and enamel horse trappings (*fornimenti a cavallo*) being prepared by a goldsmith identified as "Michelagnolo"—almost certainly Michelangelo di Viviano, who had aided Alfonsina and other members of the Medici family to recover possessions in 1495 and 1496.[81] Several days earlier, on 25 October, Alfonsina had stressed to Lorenzo that the work was going slowly, as was customary with the *orafo* (goldsmith).[82] This letter expresses interesting aesthetic judgments; apparently Alfonsina was dissatisfied with the objects and wrote to her son that the fittings were not pleasing with enamels.[83] In her opinion, the "old fashioned" sort of brass *fornimento* that was made in Rome was more beautiful.[84] Alfonsina, who seems to have had an opinion on everyone and everything, sharply reminded Lorenzo in the letter that Florence was not the only beautiful city in Italy.[85] In another letter of 17 October 1515 she wrote to Ser Giovanni di Poppi about what gifts Lorenzo should present to Francis I and members of his entourage.[86]

In order to accommodate the many visitors, alterations were planned for Palazzo Medici, where Alfonsina lived with her son.[87] The proposed changes are described in a letter of 29 October 1515 to Lorenzo from Alfonsina's secretary, Ser Bernardo Fiamminghi.[88] Alfonsina planned to give Leo the quarters that she and Lorenzo used, with her own *anticamera* serving as the pontiff's bedroom.[89] It is interesting to note that Alfonsina herself had to find other quarters because Leo did not want her in the palazzo.[90] The alterations were undertaken by Baccio Bigio, Alfonsina's architect of choice, and they were paid for by the Operai del Palazzo.[91] The materials were allocated to Bernardo Fiamminghi, who was clearly acting on Alfonsina's behalf, and to her son Lorenzo.[92]

Documents seem to indicate joint patronage efforts by Lorenzo and his mother, a cooperative pattern not uncommon in Medicean patronage and one that we will see again at Poggio a Caiano.[93] The two may have shared patronage on another Florentine architectural project. Linda Pellecchia has suggested that the never realized plan for a vast Medici palace complex off the Via Laura was intended for Alfonsina and her son (fig. 12).[94] Pellecchia points out that the plan is divided into two identical apartments, which she compares to the gendered

Reiss Fig. 12. Giuliano da Sangallo and Antonio da Sangallo the Elder, plan for a Medici villa in the Via Laura, Florence, ca. 1515, Florence, Galleria degli Uffizi, Gabinetto dei Disegni e delle Stampe, U 282A (photo: Soprintendenza, Florence)

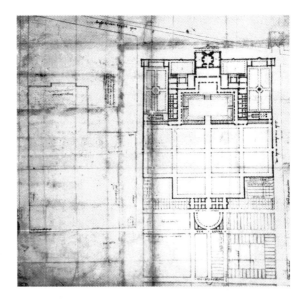

living spaces featured in Greek houses, which were described by Vitruvius.[95]

Alfonsina was also in part responsible for alterations to the Medici parish church of San Lorenzo, which served as the papal chapel at the time of Leo X's visit to Florence.[96] The expenses for the modifications to San Lorenzo, which were first published in the nineteenth century by Domenico Moreni, are recorded in an account book preserved in the Archivio Capitolino di San Lorenzo.[97] Temporary alteration and ornamentation of San Lorenzo included the expansion of the *cappella maggiore* in order to permit more people. The document reads in part:

> And it was pleasing to Madonna Alfonsina Orsini, a woman and our patron, widow of the Magnificent Piero di Lorenzo de' Medici, and to many other honorable men, to take down part of our choir and level it in such a way that it can hold more people because it has been decided that while His Holiness is here in Florence this church will serve as the Papal Chapel.[98]

Interestingly, in the document recording the remodeling, Alfonsina is singled out among *"altri huomini da bene"* and is referred to as *"nostra patrona"* by the chapter of San Lorenzo, a noteworthy instance of the use of gendered language.[99] The spectacular display associated with Leo's return to his native city offended some observers and, in December of 1515, this satirical epigram made the rounds in Florence: "O Florence, after this you've lost your liberty, for the woman of Orsini blood rules you alone."[100]

Poggio a Caiano and Other Building Projects

In the spring of 1516, at the urging of his mother, Lorenzo was declared Duke of Urbino; Alfonsina had the splendid duchy in mind for her son at least as early as November of the previous year.[101] Contemporaries, including Francesco Vettori, Francesco Guicciardini, and Paolo Giovio, mention Alfonsina's role in the usurpation of the duchy of Urbino.[102] Her complicity included the provision of funds to support the Urbino War.[103]

At about the same time, Alfonsina became involved with another major architectural undertaking: the completion of the Medici villa at Poggio a Caiano (fig. 13), where, as a girl bride, she had had her own apartment. It appears that no work had been done at Poggio a Caiano during the eighteen years the Medici spent in exile.[104] During Leo's pontificate, building began anew at Poggio under the aegis of Alfonsina and her son Lorenzo—a pattern of joint patronage we have seen before.

A group of documents, first made known by Philip Foster in his dissertation of 1974, record Alfonsina's involvement.[105] Much of the material cited by Foster is found in a document of 1519 recording Alfonsina Orsini's account with the Opera of Santa Maria del Fiore; the document records several years of transactions concerned with building materials.[106] The earliest transaction records the consignment of 209 wagonloads of wood "for construction at Poggio a Caiano" in March 1516.[107] The Opera del Duomo supplied the wood on the orders of Baccio Bigio, charging the account of Lorenzo, Duke of Urbino.[108] In November of 1516, Goro Gheri informed Alfonsina that Baccio Bigio would soon go to Poggio to take care of matters.[109] In December 1516 and January 1517, nearly a hundred more wagonloads of fir wood were consigned in Alfonsina's name for unspecified construction at Poggio a Caiano.[110] It is almost certain that the building activity was centered on the vault of the great *salone* and the rear portion of the villa.[111]

The funds for construction at Poggio were allocated at the same time as those for building activities at the Lago di Fucecchio, which Alfonsina purchased in 1515, and had drained.[112] She had the existing wall dismantled and had a large moat constructed, which came to be called the Fosso di Madonna.[113] Alfonsina's works there were supervised by Baccio Bigio, who in November of 1516 was dividing his time between Poggio a Caiano and the Lago

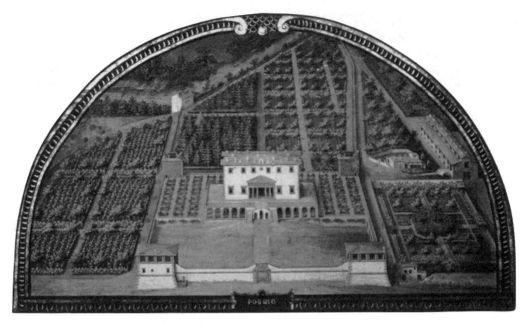

Reiss Fig. 13. Justus Utens, *Villa Medici at Poggio a Caiano,* late sixteenth century, Florence, Museo Topografico "Firenze com'era" (photo: Alinari/Art Resource, N.Y.)

di Fucecchio before leaving for Rome to work on Alfonsina's palazzo in Piazza Caprettari (now Palazzo Medici-Lante).[114] In 1527, seven2 years after Alfonsina's death, her heirs were condemned by the Syndics of the last Florentine republic for her activities at Fucecchio, which were said to have defrauded the Commune of Fucecchio and to have been damaging to local inhabitants and fishermen.[115]

In April of 1519 Alfonsina's account with the Opera del Duomo also records consignments of wood to be used for the *muraglia* at the "garden on Piazza di San Marco," which has recently been identified by Caroline Elam as the site of Lorenzo de' Medici's famed sculpture garden.[116] The document names Baccio Bigio and Baccio d'Agnolo as the architects; presumably they were working on one of the structures at the property, which contained a loggia and a small casino.[117] In August of 1516 Alfonsina supplied trees from the San Marco garden that were used to fashion doors for the new Medici stables on the opposite side of the piazza.[118] There too the architect was Alfonsina's favorite, Baccio Bigio.[119]

In the spring of 1517 there seems to have been a temporary financial setback at Poggio a Caiano: in March, "El Grasso" informed Goro Gheri of the shortage and Gheri asked Leo's datary, Baldassare Turini da Pescia, to inform the pope.[120] The following month, Gheri instructed a subordinate to let Alfonsina know that "there was no more money for construction at Poggio."[121] Nearly a year later, in March 1518, Gheri wrote to Lorenzo in France that Leo had ordered that funds be sent to Alfonsina to help recuperate family possessions and "to complete the construction of Poggio."[122] In July of that year Gheri wrote to Lorenzo that his mother was staying at Poggio, where she had done "a great deal of work and ornamentation."[123]

The Second *Nozze* of Lorenzo de' Medici and Madeleine de la Tour d'Auvergne

In January 1518 Alfonsina's schemes for Lorenzo's marriage bore fruit when he was married by proxy to Madeleine de la Tour d'Auvergne, a niece of Francis I.[124] At some point Francesco Vettori, who had brokered the alliance, suggested that Lorenzo present the villa at Poggio a Caiano to his new bride.[125] In September 1518 Lorenzo and Madeleine stayed at Poggio a Caiano on their way to Florence to celebrate their second *nozze*. According to Bartolomeo Cerretani, on 4 September everyone went to Poggio a Caiano, "which was adorned as if it were a paradise."[126] Since Lorenzo was in France from March until mid-August of 1518, it is likely that Alfonsina was responsible for these decorations at Poggio; she certainly was in part responsible for the temporary decorations at Palazzo Medici for the second *nozze* celebrations, which took place over several days and included the bride's *entrata* and theatrical performances.[127]

According to Cerretani, at the behest of Alfonsina and the heads of state who wished to honor the couple, the Otto di Pratica ordered lavish festivities of the sort customarily staged for the feast of San Giovanni Battista.[128] The Otto ordered the construction of a *palco* (platform) in front of Palazzo Medici with tapestries, awnings and seats; the platform was some three *braccia* high, as wide as the street and as long as the palazzo.[129] Other contemporary observers also described the *palco*, the splendidly dressed company, and the lavish hangings.[130] Cerretani tells us that Alfonsina, along with fifty young women, received the bride on the platform.[131]

The loggias, courtyard, and garden of the Medici palace were also beautifully decorated for the festivities.[132] For the banquet, the garden was paved over with flagstones.[133] Alfonsina herself left an account of the wedding banquet in a letter of 8 September 1518, written to Ser Giovanni Poppi.[134] In her missive, Alfonsina mentioned that her son Lorenzo had Raphael's portrait of *Leo X and Two Cardinals* (fig. 14) placed above the table where the bride sat.[135] She noted that the portrait, which served to represent the pontiff and the two cardinals at the festivities, "brightened everything up."[136] A recently discovered letter suggests that the picture was rushed to Florence to be displayed at this banquet.[137] Since Lorenzo was in France for several months in 1518, Alfonsina may have been involved somehow in the commission of the portrait.[138] While Alfonsina was most pleased with the *nozze*, Cerretani said that the people were little satisfied—in part because of "Madonna Alfonsina's tremendous avarice."[139] No doubt the government's support for such princely display contributed to the condemnation of Alfonsina's greed.

Reiss Fig. 14. Raphael, *Portrait of Pope Leo X and Two Cardinals,* ca. 1518, Florence, Galleria degli Uffizi (photo: Alinari/Art Resource, N.Y.)

The Deaths of Lorenzo, Madeleine, and Alfonsina

Whatever joy Alfonsina took at the marital alliance of her son with a member of the French royal family was short-lived. Soon after the second *nozze*, Lorenzo was taken ill, presumably with tuberculosis and syphilis.[140] In late February of 1519 he settled at Poggio a Caiano to see if a change of air would lessen his infirmity.[141] On 1 March, Alfonsina, already ill enough to be carried on a litter, went to Poggio a Caiano to be with her gravely ill son.[142] It is most unlikely that any building activity was carried on during these months. The dying duke returned to Florence on 7 April, perhaps to attend the birth of his daughter (and Alfonsina's granddaughter) Catherine, the future queen of France, on the thirteenth of that month.[143] Two weeks later, on 27 April, as Lorenzo lay dying in Palazzo Medici, over two hundred more wagonloads of wood were consigned for Poggio a Caiano at Alfonsina's behest.[144] The next day, Madeleine de la Tour d'Auvergne died, followed a week later by her husband.[145]

For Alfonsina Orsini this was, in effect, the end of her world and her access to power and prestige. Her son had been the mechanism through which she manipulated Florentine political structures, and with his death she was spurned and compelled to abandon her behind-the-scenes role in the political life of the city. After Lorenzo's death the project to complete Poggio a Caiano seems to have been taken over by Leo X and his cousin Cardinal Giulio de' Medici, who became the de facto ruler of Florence in May 1519.[146]

In the summer of 1519 Alfonsina returned to Rome where she died on 7 February, 1520 and was buried in Santa Maria del Popolo.[147] Her unusual polychrome marble tomb slab (fig. 15), located in the nave of the church, illusionistically suggests the grave beneath it.[148] The day before her death she dictated a private last testament in which she named Leo her heir, with requests that he provide for her granddaughter Catherine and that he give 6000 ducats to her daughter Clarice.[149] In 1521 Leo provided for two perpetual anniversary masses for the soul of his late sister-in-law.[150]

Reiss Fig. 15. Tomb of Alfonsina Orsini de' Medici, 1520s, Rome, Santa Maria del Popolo (photo: author)

On 11 February 1520 a lavish requiem for Alfonsina was held in Florence at San Lorenzo; the church was filled with candles and the nave was draped with black hangings.[151] Bartolommeo Masi commented with apparent distaste that the splendid ceremony was "like those customarily given for some great lord."[152] Sharon Strocchia has stressed that Alfonsina's requiem (along with that of her daughter-in-law Madeleine de la Tour d'Auvergne) "greatly surpassed the burial honors previously given any woman in republican Florence."[153] Alfonsina's requiem is an indicator of the shift of the Medici's role in Florence from first-among-equals to near-princely status, a shift that Alfonsina herself helped bring about.

An Altarpiece by Sogliani

With the exception of her works at Santa Lucia in Via Sangallo and the alterations to the choir of San Lorenzo at the time of Leo's *entrata*, Alfonsina's patronage of art had been secular in character. There is, however, one further commission that has been associated with her that might indicate a shift, at the end of her life, to pious rather than worldly concerns. This is the commission for Giovanni Antonio Sogliani's altarpiece traditionally said to represent the iconographically rare subject of the *Martyrdom of Saint Arcadius* (fig. 16).[154] The subject has also been identified as the martyrdom of Saint Achatius, one of the ten thousand martyred on Mount Ararat, whose life is seen in the *predella* by Bacchiacca.[155] The painting shows an aged, haloed man with an athletic body, dressed only in a loincloth, nailed to a wooden cross. This is certainly not the martyrdom normally associated with Saint Arcadius who, according to tradition, had his limbs cut off joint by joint, reducing him to a mere trunk.[156] The similarities between the elderly but powerfully built figure and a young, heroic Christ are striking, while the crowns of thorns on the ground further evoke the Passion. The central figure is flanked by two standing, bearded, fully draped male saints embracing crosses; in the foreground kneel two young, beardless, partially nude saints who have not been identified. In the upper corners two *putti* carry palms of martyrdom. The monumental figures and delicate

Reiss Fig. 16. Giovanni Antonio Sogliani, *Martyrdom of Saint Arcadius (Achatius?)*, 1521, Florence, San Lorenzo (photo: Alinari/Art Resource, N.Y.)

sfumato evoke the styles of the Florentine masters Andrea del Sarto and Fra Bartolomeo. At present the only evidence for Alfonsina's patronage of the altarpiece is Vasari's account, included in both the 1550 and 1568 editions of the *Vite*. According to Vasari, Sogliani made the painting for Alfonsina as a votive offering to be placed on the altar of the Chapel of the Martyrs in the Camaldolite church of San Salvatore.[157] The painting was moved in 1550 to San Lorenzo, where it still stands.[158] Sogliani's altarpiece is dated 1521; if the commission was indeed Alfonsina's, the work would have been completed after her death. It is tempting to see this altarpiece as indicative of a shift in Alfonsina's concerns as a patron; however, until conclusive evidence for her patronage is found, such a shift must remain an intriguing possibility.

Conclusion

Throughout her life and for centuries after her death, Alfonsina Orsini de' Medici was reviled as a woman who usurped male roles and prerogatives, a woman whose avarice and ambition were seen as unseemly and threatening. Late nineteenth- and early twentieth-century authors compared her to Lady Macbeth and called her "the evil genius" of the Medici family.[159] At least some of the rhetoric must be understood in terms of Renaissance misogyny, but documents do confirm that she was responsible for some unconscionable acts, in particular the seizure of the throne of Urbino. It seems likely that her feudal heritage and Neapolitan upbringing in some ways contributed to her undisguised political ambitions, which were channeled through her son Lorenzo.[160] We have seen that, for the most part, wifely devotion and piety played little part in Alfonsina Orsini's artistic patronage. For Alfonsina Orsini, as for many of her male contemporaries, patronage of art and architecture served first and foremost to convey familial and personal *magnificenza* rather than spiritual devotion. We have also seen that on occasion Alfonsina obtained funding for her patronage from her brother-in-law Leo and from Florentine governmental sources, such as the Operai del Palazzo and the Otto di Pratica. Most significantly, we have seen that in several instances, most notably the Palazzo Medici-Lante in Rome and the villa at Poggio a Caiano, Alfonsina was the patron of large scale secular architectural projects. This activity is particularly noteworthy, given that as recently as 1993, one author stated categorically that "laywomen, however rich, never commissioned palaces (presumably because they could not be represented as sexually powerful generators of a dynasty)."[161] In her patronage of art, and especially of architecture, Alfonsina manifested her dynastic ambitions for herself and her son. Indeed, I would suggest that her usurpation of traditionally male patterns of secular patronage contributed to the widespread loathing and contempt she engendered.

Notes

I am grateful to the following scholars who provided assistance or read early drafts of this article:Paul Barolsky, Molly Bourne, David Chambers, Anthony Cummings, Esther Dotson, Bruce Edelstein, Laurie Fusco, Julius Kirshner, Lawrence Jenkens, Robert LaFrance, Jacqueline Musacchio, John Najemy, John Paoletti, Linda Pellecchia, Lorenzo Polizzotto, Brenda Preyer, Patricia Rucidlo, John Shearman, T. Barton Thurber, Natalie Tomas, Carolyn Valone, Louis Waldman, and Sandra Weddle. Some of this material was first presented as a "poster paper" at the Twenty-Eighth International Congress on Medieval Studies, held at Western Michigan University in Kalamazoo. Additional material was presented in papers at the Sixteenth-Century Studies Conference in St. Louis, Missouri (1993), and Toronto, Ontario (1994), as well as at the 1994 New College Conference on Medieval-Renaissance Studies, Sarasota, Florida.

1. Useful bibliography includes: Monica Nocentini Nucci, "Giovanni di Bicci e Cosimo Pater Patriae: La committenza medicea negli inventari di arredi della basilica di San Lorenzo," *Rivista d'arte*, 4th ser., 7 (1991): 19–32, for donations by Medici women to San Lorenzo; P. Salvadori, "Le gestione di un catasto; Il carteggio di Lucrezia Tornabuoni dei Medici," *Memoria* 18 (1986): 85–86, for Lucrezia Tornabuoni's works at the baths of Bagno a Morbo near Volterra; Katherine J. P. Lowe, "A Matter of Piety or of Family Tradition and Custom?" in *Piero de' Medici "il Gottoso" (1416-1469)*, ed. Andreas Beyer and Bruce Boucher (Berlin: Akademie Verlag, 1993), 55–69. For Ginevra degli Alessandri and the Villa Medici at Fiesole, see Amanda Lillie, "Giovanni di Cosimo and the Villa Medici at Fiesole," in Beyer and Boucher, *Piero de' Medici*, 195–96. For Eleonora di Toledo as patron, see Bruce Edelstein, review of Janet Cox-Rearick, *Bronzino's Chapel of Eleonora in the Palazzo Vecchio*, in *Art Bulletin* 76 (1994): 171–74; Carolyn Smyth, "An Instance of Feminine Patronage in the Medici Court of Sixteenth-Century Florence: The Chapel of Eleonora da Toledo in the Palazzo Vecchio," in *Women and Art in Early Modern Europe: Patrons, Collectors, and Connoisseurs*, ed. Cynthia Lawrence (University Park: Pennsylvania State University Press, 1997), 72–98; Bruce Edelstein's chapter in this volume.

2. During the quattrocento, several female members of the Medici family were patrons of architecture. Their undertakings were private and public, secular and sacred, and the projects ranged from the building and refurbishing of chapels and convents to the construction and completion of rural villas, fortifications, and bathing establishments. The case of Lucrezia Tornabuoni, wife of Piero the Gouty, is especially interesting. Letters detailing her building activities at Bagno a Morbo, near Volterra, are particularly revealing. Those of her overseer Piero Malegonnelle indicate that Lucrezia Tornabuoni possessed a remarkable degree of hands-on understanding of the minutiae of architectural practice. The building activities she patronized at Bagno were, admittedly, on a small scale. Still, her apparent wish to be apprised of the smallest details of construction would be considered exceptional compared with many male Renaissance patrons. For this correspondence, see Janet Ross, *Lives of the Early Medici as Told in Their Correspondence* (London: Chatto and Windus, 1910), 108–9, 179, 184–86. See also Lucrezia Tornabuoni, *Lettere*, ed. Patrizia Salvadori (Florence: Leo S. Olschki, 1993), no. 102, 150–51.

3. Gaetano Pieraccini, *La stirpe de' Medici di Cafaggiolo* (1924–25; reprint, 3 vols., Florence: Vallechi, 1986) 1:187–88; Melissa Meriam Bullard, *Filippo Strozzi and the Medici: Favor and Finance in Sixteenth-Century Florence and Rome* (Cambridge: Cambridge University Press, 1980), 90, n. 95. The letter to Francesco del Nero is ASF, Cart. Strozz., ser. 3, 110, fol. 160r.

4. I follow Melissa Bullard's translation found in Bullard, *Filippo Strozzi*, 90, no. 95. The text reads, "Alfonsina Ursina cuius obitum nemo vitam deflevunt omnes iocundissimum in humano genere saluberimumque depositum."

5. "È morta con non troppa buona grazia, perché non attendeva ad altro che a comulare danari," Bartolommeo Masi, *Ricordanze di Bartolommeo Masi Calderaio Fiorentino dal 1478 al 1526*, ed. Giuseppe Odoardo Corazzini (Florence: G. C. Sansoni, 1906), 245. Masi continued, "El figlioulo era morto con poca grazia, costei morì conmeno." According to Marcantonio Michiel, Alfonsina left behind "ducati 70,000 et chi diceva molto più." The Venetian diary is cited in Christoph Luitpold Frommel, *Der römische Palastbau der Hochrenaissance*, 3 vols. (Tübingen: Ernst Wasmuth, 1973), 2:227, n. 37a.

6. For Alfonsina Orsini and the negative reactions she elicited from contemporaries, including Francesco Vettori, Paolo Giovio, Bartolomeo Cerretani, and others, see the following: B. Felice, "Alfonsina Orsini, moglie di Piero de' Medici," *Rassegna Nazionale* 150 (1906): 3–25; Yvonne Maguire, *The Women of the Medici* (London: G. Routledge & Sons, 1927), 186–95; Pieraccini, *La stirpe*, 172–88; Emma Micheletti, *Le donne dei Medici* (Florence: G. C. Sansoni, 1983), 61–70. For assessments of Alfonsina's political activities informed by feminist theory, see Natalie Tomas, '*A Positive Novelty': Women and Public Life in Renaissance Florence*, in Monash Publications in History 12 (Clayton, Australia: Monash University, 1992), 62–65; Natalie Tomas, "Negotiated Spaces: Gender, Power, and the Medici Women in Renaissance Florence" (Ph.D. diss., Monash University, 1997), esp. chaps. 4–6. I am most grateful to Natalie Tomas, Honorary Research Associate in the Department of History at the University of Monash, who has generously shared with me the fruits of her research on Medici women and power. For discussions of the negative historical constructions of Alfonsina, see Tomas's unpublished paper entitled "Gendered Power: Contemporary and Historians' Representations of the Medici Women," and chap. 6, part 3 of her 1997 dissertation, cited above. See also Natalie Tomas, "Alfonsina Orsini de' Medici and the Problem of a Female Ruler in Early Sixteenth-Century Florence," *Renaissance Studies* 14 (2000): 70–90.

7. For biographies of Alfonsina, see n. 6 above. No securely identifiable contemporary portraits of Alfonsina have survived (see fig. 3 for a possible candidate). The print is one of the one hundred portraits in Giuseppe Allegrini's *Chronologica series simulacrorum regiae familiae Mediceae* (Florence: Iosephvm Allegrini, 1761), which are discussed in Karla Langedijk, *The Portraits of the Medici, Fifteenth to Eighteenth Centuries*, 3 vols. (Florence: S.P.E.S., 1981–87), 1:215 and 243. For Antonio Selvi's medal of c. 1739 with Alfonsina's likeness, see George Hill, *A Corpus of Italian Medals of the Renaissance before Cellini*, 2 vols. (London: British Museum, 1930), 1:284, no. 1110, and Langedijk, *Portraits*, 1:244. For another medal (apparently once thought to be a work of the cinquecento) in the Museo Civico of Vicenza, see B. Morsolin, "Una medaglia di Alfonsina Orsini," *Rivista italiana di numismatica* 5 (1892): 71–78. The assertive motto, NON NISI PER SPINAS, apparently devised only in the eighteenth century, can be seen as a reference to the prominently displayed Orsini roses, and perhaps as a retrospective allusion to the reputed "thorniness" of Alfonsina's personality. For the formulation of Medici *imprese* in the eighteenth century, see Langedijk, *Portraits*, 3: appendix D, 1558 ff., and esp. 1569 for the motto devised for Alfonsina.

8. On Alfonsina's father, Roberto, see Francesco Sansovino, *L'historia di Casa Orsini di Francesco Sansovino* (Venice: Bernardino and Filippo Stagnini, Fratelli, 1565), pt. 2, c. 67r. See also Felice, "Alfonsina Orsini," 4, and Pieraccini, *La stirpe*, 172–73. An inventory of the possessions of Caterina di Sanseverino is found in the Orsini Family Archive, Special Collection 902, box 231, #2, at the University of California at Los Angeles University Library.

9. On Roberto Orsini as Ferrante's favorite, see Sansovino, *L'historia*, pt. 2, c. 67r. Alfonsina was named either for Ferrante's father or his son, both of whom were named Alfonso.

10. On Lorenzo's politics vis à vis Naples in the crucial years before Alfonsina's betrothal, see Roberto Palmarocchi, *La politica italiana di Lorenzo de' Medici: Firenze nella guerra contro Innocenzo VIII* (Florence: Leo S. Olschki, 1933); H. C. Butters, "Lorenzo and Naples," in *Lorenzo il Magnifico e il suo mondo*, ed. Gian Carlo Garfagnini (Florence: Leo S. Olschki, 1994), 143–51.

11. The marriage also reinforced the Medici relationship with the powerful Orsini. See Palmarocchi, *La politica italiana*, 227, n. 27; Paolo Viti in Philippus Redditus, *Exhortatio ad Petrum Medicem*, ed. Paolo Viti (Florence: Leo S. Olschki, 1989), 64, notes on lines 337–42 of Redditus's text.

Alfonsina's mother-in-law, Clarice Orsini de' Medici, was from the Roman branch of the family. For the political exigencies of her marriage to Lorenzo the Magnificent, see Maguire, *Women of the Medici*. See also Christine Shaw, "Lorenzo de' Medici and Virginio Orsini," in *Florence and Italy: Renaissance Studies in Honour of Nicolai Rubinstein*, ed. Peter Denley and Caroline Elam (London: Westfield College, 1988), 33–42, on Medici-Orsini relations.

12. A copy of the marriage contract is ASF, MAP, 148, 26. See also ASF, MAP 137, 1006.

13. Maguire, *Women of the Medici*, 187. Women could be equally critical in their descriptions of prospective brides. See Lucrezia Tornabuoni's assessment of Clarice Orsini's features in Tornabuoni, *Lettere*, no. 12, pp. 62–63. The letter is also published in Ross, *Lives of the Early Medici*, 108–9.

14. ASF, MAP 148, 26. Alfonsina's uncle Virginio Orsini of Bracciano paid the large dowry. See William Roscoe, *The Life of Lorenzo de' Medici called the Magnificent*, 6th ed., 2 vols. (London: T. Caldwell, 1825), 2:150–51, note b. For the considerably smaller dowries of Lorenzo's own daughters, see Tomas, "Negotiated Spaces," chap. 4, pt. 1. For the average Florentine dowry of 1,430 florins in the years 1475–99, see Anthony Molho, *Marriage Alliance in Late Medieval Florence* (Cambridge, Mass.: Harvard University Press, 1994), 310, table 7-3.

15. Bernardo Ruccellai reported that the proxy marriage was celebrated "in Castello, nella sala grande, presente il Re e tutta la Corte con gran festa e cena." See Pieraccini, *La stirpe*, 173. Maguire, *Women of the Medici*, 188, notes that festivities planned for the couple's arrival in Florence were cut short by the death of Lorenzo's daughter Luigia. In late June a ball was staged in Alfonsina's honor.

16. For a second daughter, Luisa (or Luigia), who died young, see Maguire, *Women of the Medici*, 188; Pieraccini, *La stirpe*, 180. For the "chamera delle balie" in the apartment shared by Piero and Alfonsina in Palazzo Medici, see Wolfger A. Bülst, "Uso e trasformazione del Palazzo mediceo fino ai Riccardi," in *Il Palazzo Medici Riccardi di Firenze*, ed. Giovanni Cherubini and Giovanni Fanelli (Florence: Giunti, 1990), 117. I am grateful to Brenda Preyer for directing me to this reference. For the furnishings of the *anticamera* used as a nursery, see *Libro d'inventario dei beni di Lorenzo il Magnifico*, ed. Marco Spallanzani and Giovanna Gaeta Bertelà (Florence: Stabilmento Grafico Commerciale, 1992), 100–103.

17. On Piero, see Pieraccini, *La stirpe*, 157 ff. Good modern introductions to this period of upheaval include Nicolai Rubinstein, "Politics and Constitution in Florence at the End of the Fifteenth Century," in *Italian Renaissance Studies: A Tribute to the Late Cecilia M. Ady*, ed. Ernest Fraser Jacob (New York: Barnes and Noble, 1960), 148–83, esp. 148–51; Nicolai Rubinstein, *The Government of Florence under the Medici (1434 to 1494)* (Oxford: Clarendon Press, 1966), 229–35. See also Rudolph von Albertini, *Das Florentisnische Staatsbewusstsein im Übergang von der Republik zum Prinzipat* (Bern: Francke, 1955), 3 ff.; J. R. Hale, *Florence and the Medici: The Pattern of Control* (London: Thames and Hudson, 1983), 76–78.

18. On the looting of Palazzo Medici, see Eugène Müntz, *Les Collections des Médicis au XVe siècle* (Paris: Librarie de l'Art, 1888), 98–99 for accounts, including those of Paolo Giovio, Luca Landucci, and Piero di Marco Parenti. See also Masi, *Ricordanze*, 23.

19. "Nel palazo dove abitava Piero in sul primcipio della via Largha v'entrò per ordine della signoria alcuni ciptadini e quali ne trassono la donna di detto Piero et la sua suocera, tutta dua degl'Orsini, et prima trassono loro di dita tutte le gioie e tritamente cerchatole le mandorono piagneddo nel monasterio di Sancta Lucia in via di S. Ghallo." I am grateful to Laurie Fusco for alerting me to this passage, which is now published in Bartolomeo Cerretani, *Storia fiorentina*, ed. Giuliana Berti (Florence: Leo S. Olschki, 1994), 208. The manuscript citation is BNCF, MS II.III.74, fol. 196v.

20. See Felice, "Alfonsina Orsini," 6; Pieraccini, *La stirpe*, 173.

21. Alfonsina, in disguise, fled Florence for Siena. Pieraccini, *La stirpe*, 173, citing Piero di Marco Parenti, states that she was "vestita da monica." Parenti's text simply says "finalmente se la prese nascosamente partì con Averardo de' Medici in compagnia...." See Piero di Marco Parenti, *Storia*

fiorentina I 1476–78, 1492–96, ed. Andrea Matucci (Florence: Leo S. Olschki, 1994), 269. Cf. Luca Landucci, *Diario fiorentino dal 1450 al 1516 di Luca Landucci*, ed. Iodoco Del Badia (Florence: G. C. Sansoni, 1883), 116. It was not common for women to join their husbands and sons in exile. For women and exile in Renaissance Florence see Susannah Foster Baxandale, "Exile in Practice: The Alberti Family in and out of Florence 1401–1428," *Renaissance Quarterly* 44 (1991): 720–56; Ann Morton Crabb, "How Typical Was Alessandra Macinghi Strozzi of Fifteenth-Century Florentine Widows?" in *Upon My Husband's Death: Widows in the Literature and Histories of Medieval Europe*, ed. Louise Mirrer (Ann Arbor: University of Michigan Press, 1992), 47–68; Margery A. Ganz, "Paying the Price for Political Failure: Florentine Women in the Aftermath of 1466," *Rinascimento*, ser. 2, 34 (1994): 237–57.

22. For these dangerous pro-Medici activities, see G. Pampaloni, "I ricordi segreti di Francesco di Agostino Cegia (1495–1497)," *Archivio storico italiano* 115 (1957): 188–234. I am indebted to Laurie Fusco, who made me aware of Cegia's text. On Michelangelo di Viviano, who worked for Lorenzo the Magnificent, see Vasari-Milanesi 6:133–34; Baccio Bandinelli, *Memoriale*, in *Scritti d' Arte del Cinquecento*, ed. Paola Barocchi, 10 vols. (Milan: R. Ricciardi, 1971), esp. 6:1365–67; Kathleen Weil-Garris, "Bandinelli and Michelangelo: A Problem of Artistic Identity," in *Art the Ape of Nature: Studies in Honor of H. W. Janson*, ed. Moshe Barasch and Lucy Freedman Sandler (New York: Abrams, 1981), esp. 224–27.

23. On Francesco di Agostino Cegia (called Cegino), see U. Dorini, "Le disgrazie di un nemico del Savonarola," *Rivista storica degli archivi Toscani* 1 (1929): 186–98; Pampaloni, "I ricordi segreti," 188–96. For Cegia's execution, see Landucci, *Diario*, 160–61. See also the forthcoming study of Lorenzo the Magnificent's collection of hardstones by Laurie Fusco and Gino Corti.

24. Pampaloni, "I ricordi segreti," passim, esp. 198–201, 203–6, 210, 213–18. See, for example, the record of 9 January 1496 (O.S. 1495), ibid., 213–14: "Michelagnolo di Viviano orafo de' dare a dì 9 di giennaio lire 80 piccoli, sono per queste chose aute da me: una cintola di velluto verde piena d'ariento e una cintola d'ariento paghonazza e una cintola nera, più choselline d'ariento e uno chiavachore chon una chatena d'ariento, uno cintolino chon uno nastro, uno chatoncino, 44 bottoni di diaspro e 12 bottoni di madreperla, tutto fé detto Michelagnolo; montassi lire 80, che lire 25 erano della Maria mia donna…e resto a chonto de l'Alfonsina…. " Alfonsina's involvement in the recuperation of *beni* tapers off by early 1496; thereafter Lucrezia Salviati's name is prominently featured.

25. On the ignominious death of the unfortunate Piero, see William Roscoe, *The Life and Pontificate of Leo the Tenth*, rev. Thomas Roscoe, 5th ed., 2 vols. (London: Henry G. Bohn, 1846), 1:211–12.

26. The Archivio di Stato in Florence preserves a large number of documents concerning Alfonsina's attempts to recuperate her dowry. Charles VIII had offered to restore it, but the process dragged on for many years. See Pieraccini, *La stirpe*, 173; Tomas, *'A Positive Novelty,'* 63. On attitudes toward widows, their dowries, and their husband's estates, see Christiane Klapisch-Zuber, "'The Cruel Mother': Maternity, Widowhood, and Dowry in Florence in the Fourteenth and Fifteenth Centuries," in *Women, Family, and Ritual in Renaissance Italy*, trans. L. G. Cochrane (Chicago: University of Chicago Press, 1985), 117–31. Civil law, in fact, protected the dowries of women whose husbands were exiled and those wives could petition to recuperate them. See Julius Kirshner, "Wives' Claims against Insolvent Husbands in Late Medieval Italy," in *Women of the Medieval World: Essays in Honor of John H. Mundy*, ed. Julius Kirshner and Suzanne F. Wemple (Oxford: B. Blackwell, 1985), 275–78; Baxandale, "Exile in Practice," 730–33. I am grateful to Julius Kirshner for these references. For the marriage negotiations between the Strozzi and the exiled Medici, see Melissa M. Bullard, "Marriage Politics and the Family in Florence: The Strozzi-Medici Alliance of 1508," *American Historical Review* 84 (1979): 668–87, and Bullard, "Marriage Intrigues," in *Filippo Strozzi*, chap. 3, 45–60.

27. See, for example, Francesco Vettori, "Sommario della vita di Lorenzo Medici Duca di Urbino," in *La vita e gli scritti di Niccolò Machiavelli nella loro relazione col Machiavellismo*, ed. Oreste Tommasini, 3 vols. (Rome: Ermanno Loescher, 1883–1911), 2:1059, appendix 7: "Et madonna

Alfonsina cominciò a infestare il papa, che dovessi dare uno stato al figliuolo." Cf. Rosemary Devonshire Jones, "Lorenzo de' Medici, Duca d'Urbino 'Signore' of Florence?" in *Studies on Machiavelli*, ed. Myron Gilmore (Florence: G. C. Sansoni, 1972), 308, 313–15; J. N. Stephens, *The Fall of the Florentine Republic: 1512–1530* (Oxford: Clarendon Press, 1983), 99.

28. For Alfonsina's political ambitions and activities, see Pieraccini, *La stirpe*, 174 ff.; Rosemary Devonshire Jones, *Francesco Vettori, Florentine Citizen and Medici Servant* (London: Athlone Press, 1972), esp. 118–21; Stephens, *Fall of the Florentine Republic*, esp. 86–89, 141–42; H. C. Butters, *Governors and Government in Early Sixteenth-Century Florence 1502–1519* (Oxford: Clarendon Press, 1985), passim, esp. 195, 232, 235–37, 270–74, 277–79, 281–82, 290–91, 299; F. W. Kent with Patricia Simons, "Renaissance Patronage: An Introductory Essay," in *Patronage, Art and Society in Renaissance Italy*, ed. F. W. Kent, Patricia Simons, and J. C. Eade (Oxford: Clarendon Press, 1987), 7–8; Lorenzo Polizzotto, "The Medici and the Savonarolans, 1512–1527: The Limitations of Personal Government and of the Medicean Patronage System," in *Patronage*, ed. Kent and others, 146–47; Tomas, *'A Positive Novelty,'* 63–64; and Tomas "Alfonsina de' Medici"

29. For brief discussions of Piero's patronage, see Michael Hirst, "Michelangelo, Carrara, and the Marble for the Cardinal's *Pietà*," *Burlington Magazine* 127 (1985): 155; Caroline Elam, "Lorenzo de' Medici's Sculpture Garden," *Mitteilungen des Kunsthistorischen Institutes in Florenz* 36 (1992): 58–60. Both authors suggest that Piero may have been the patron of Michelangelo's lost *Hercules*; see Janet Cox-Rearick, *The Collection of Francis I: Royal Treasures* (Antwerp: Fonds Mercator Paribas, 1995), cat. no. IX–5, 302–12, with extensive bibliography.

30. For Piero's commission for a snowman, see Asciano Condivi, *Vita di Michelangelo Buonarroti*, ed. Giovanni Nencioni (Florence: S.P.E.S, 1998), 14. The relationship between Michelangelo and Piero is alluded to in a letter of 14 October 1494, which says: "Sapi che Michelagnolo ischultore dal giardino se n'e ito a Vineghia sanza dire nula a Piero tornando lui in chasa: mi pare che Piero l'abia auto molto a male." See Giovanni Poggi, "Della prima partenza di Michelangiolo Buonarroti da Firenze," *Rivista d'Arte* 4 (1906): 34. For the ambiguous wording of the letter, see Elam, "Lorenzo de' Medici's Sculpture Garden," 58. Hirst has shown that Piero even extended a commission to Michelangelo after the 1494 expulsion of the Medici. See Hirst, "Michelangelo, Carrara," 155–56, appendix A.

31. Spallanzani and Bertelà, *Libro d'inventario*, 201.

32. Spallanzani and Bertelà, *Libro d'inventario*, 201. Under the heading "Cose che sono nelle case di madonna Alfonsina" we read of the following: "Dua paia di lenzuola sottile a teli, di br. - il telo/Undici chamicie sottile danne [da donne?]/Sette sciughatoi tra grandi e picholi, che ve n'è uno di fiore grosso et tre da piedo e 3 d'asciughare el capo/Trentuno fazoletto da mano e altro/Più sacchetini, entrovi x grembiuli e sei collaretti di fiore et 9 chuffie tra di panno e di fiore, 7 fra testiere e bende e più pezi di nastro, 5 quadretti, 12 benducci, una chamicia, uno fazoletto con cerri lavorato, uno sciughatoio, 2 lib. di lino sottile, 2 matasse d'accia sottile, 3 paia di forbicie, 3 libriccini di donna, più paniere, schatole, borsotti di raso e altre zachere, tutto monto." For the *donora* or trousseau, and for husbands' gifts to brides, see Christiane Klapisch-Zuber, "The Griselda Complex: Dowry and Marriage Gifts in the Quattrocento," in *Women, Family, and Ritual* 218–24. See also Julius Kirshner, "Li emergenti bisogni matrimoniali in Renaissance Florence," in *Society and Individual in Renaissance Florence,* ed. William J. Connell (Berkeley: University of California Press, forthcoming). I am grateful to Julius Kirshner for sharing his essay with me prior to publication.

33. Spallanzani and Bertelà, *Libro d'inventario*, 94: "Uno quadro, suvi ritratto al naturale la testa di madonna Alfonsina." The inventory for this room also has several items described as "da donna," perhaps belonging to Alfonsina.

34. Langedijk, *Portraits*, 1:21 and 244. Langedijk lists the portrait as an uncertain identification. For a work that accepts this identification, see Anthony M. Cummings, *The Politicized Muse: Music for Medici Festivals, 1512–1537* (Princeton: Princeton University Press, 1992), 100, fig. 30. I am grateful to Patricia Rucidlo, who pointed out that the sitter's dress in the Pitti portrait is in accordance with contemporary Florentine sumptuary laws.

35. See Vasari-Milanesi, 4:219–20. Vasari says that the young Albertinelli "prese servitù con Madonna Alfonsina madre del Duca Lorenzo, la quale, perchè Mariotto atendesse a farsi valente, gli porgeva ognia aiuto." He continues, noting, "alcuni quadri che fece per quella signora, che furno mandati da lei a Roma a Carlo e Giordano Orsini.… " For Albertinelli in Alfonsina's service, see also Ludovico Borgo, *The Works of Mariotto Albertinelli*, Garland Outstanding Dissertations in the Fine Arts (New York: Garland, 1976), 12, who based his account on Vasari's text.

36. Vasari-Milanesi, 4:219–20: "Ritrasse madonna Alfonsina di naturale molto bene."

37. Vasari-Milanesi, 4:218: "e gli pareva avere trovato per quella familiarità la ventura sua. Ma essendo l'anno 1494 che Piero de' Medici fu bandito, mancatogli quell' ajuto e favore.…"

38. Alfonsina's patronage of ecclesiastic foundations can be understood within patterns of patronage established by other quattrocento Medici women. For example, Lucrezia Tornabuoni was especially generous to monasteries and nunneries. She donated objects of *arte sacra* and ex-votos to Florentine churches, including Santissima Annunziata and San Lorenzo. For these activities, see Lowe, "A Matter of Piety," 60–65. It is generally stated in the San Lorenzo literature that in 1465 Lucrezia was the founder of a chapel in the family's parish church of San Lorenzo. See Caroline Elam, "Cosimo de' Medici and San Lorenzo," in *Cosimo "il Vecchio" de' Medici, 1389–1464. Essays in Commemoration of the 600th Anniversary of Cosimo de' Medici's Birth*, ed. Francis Ames-Lewis (Oxford: Clarendon Press, 1992), 175, n. 85. Kate Lowe has challenged this assumption, claiming that the documents do not support Lucrezia's involvement. See Lowe, "A Matter of Piety," 64. Lucrezia was actively involved in the design for some of the ecclesiastic projects she patronized. In a letter of October 1473, Niccolò Michelozzi informed Lucrezia about progress on some of her commissions, "Maxime de' fatti del disegno vostro della cappella in San Marco et di Santa Viviana." Apparently her design for the chapel had been altered and the columns she had proposed were not being carried out. See Tornabuoni, *Lettere*, no. 79, pp. 128–29. I am grateful to Natalie Tomas for this reference. Lucrezia's reply to Michelozzi is found in Tornabuoni, *Lettere*, no. 30, 76–77.

39. Giuseppe Richa, *Notizie istoriche delle chiese fiorentine*, 10 vols. (Florence: P. G. Viviani, 1754–62), 8:348. Saundra Weddle and Natalie Tomas kindly directed me to this passage. If Richa is correct about the patronage of these women, his date of 1484 is inaccurate, for Alfonsina only arrived in Florence in May 1488, and Clarice Orsini died on 30 July of that year. For Santa Lucia, see also Walter Paatz and Elizabeth Paatz, *Die Kirchen von Florenz: Ein kunstgeschichtliches Handbuch*, 6 vols. (Frankfurt-am-Main: V. Klostermann, 1940–54), 2:602–5; Osanna Fantozzi Micali and Piero Roselli, *Le soppressioni dei conventi a Firenze: Riuso e trasformazioni dal sec. XVIII in poi* (Florence: L. E. F., 1980), 182–83. There may have been earlier Medici involvement at Santa Lucia. Pieraccini, *La stirpe*, 1:37 states without documentation that Contessina de' Bardi, wife of Cosimo il Vecchio, "Riedificò il convento di S. Lucia in Via S. Gallo, impiegandovi tutta la sua dote…L'arcivescovo Antonino la coadiuvò nella pia opera." Maguire, *Women of the Medici*, 58, also states (without documentation) that Contessina rebuilt the convent of Santa Lucia in Via Sangallo. For Alfonsina and her mother at Santa Lucia in 1494, see Parenti, *Storia fiorentina*, 125: "Così Piero, mandato prima la donna e la suocera in Santa Lucia, munistero in via di Sangallo." It is worth noting that Savonarola does not encourage widows to build and repair pious foundations in his *Vita viduale*; see Girolamo Savonarola, *Operette spirituali*, ed. Mario Ferrara (Rome: Angelo Berlardetti, 1976), 1:11–62. I am grateful to Konrad Eisenbichler for discussing this point with me.

40. Richa, *Notizie istoriche*, 8:348. Richa states that the group of women included "Clarice del Magnifico Lorenzo de' Medici, Contessina di Giuliano Salviati, Alfonsina Donna di Piero di Lorenzo de' Medici, e la Contessa Caterina di Tagliacozzo Vedova del Conte Orsini."

41. Sharon T. Strocchia, *Death and Ritual in Renaissance Florence* (Baltimore: Johns Hopkins University Press, 1992), 231 and n. 169 for the archival source, ASF, *Acquisti e doni*, 293 (unfoliated). Natalie Tomas has found a document of 1507 that further confirms the support of Alfonsina and her mother for the *muraglia* at Santa Lucia. She is now preparing for publication an article on Alfonsina's patronage at Santa Lucia, in which this document will be published.

42. See Catherine King, "Medieval and Renaissance Matrons, Italian-Style," *Zeitschrift für Kunstgeschichte* 55 (1992): 372–93; Carolyn Valone, "Roman Matrons as Patrons: Various Views of the Cloister Wall," in *The Crannied Wall: Women, Religion, and the Arts in Early Modern Europe,* ed. Craig A. Monson (Ann Arbor: University of Michigan Press, 1992), 49–72; Carolyn Valone, "Women on the Quirinal Hill: Patronage in Rome, 1560–1630," *Art Bulletin* 76 (1994): 129–46; Mary Vaccaro, "Documents for Parmigianino's *Vision of Saint Jerome,*" *Burlington Magazine* 135 (1993): 22–27. See also the chapters by Elizabeth Pilliod, Carolyn Valone, and Mary Vaccaro in this volume (all of which are based on papers presented by these authors at various conferences, including the 1993 session co-chaired by David Wilkins and myself at the 28th International Congress on Medieval Studies, held at Western Michigan University, Kalamazoo, Michigan). For the pious Early Christian widows upon whom Renaissance women modeled themselves, see Bonnie Bowman Thurston, *The Widows: A Women's Ministry in the Early Church* (Philadelphia: Fortress Press, 1989). For widows in medieval and early modern Europe, see Mirrer, *Upon my Husband's Death;* and *Widowhood in Medieval and Early Modern Europe,* ed. Sandra Cavallo and Lyndan Warner (New York: Longman, 1999). For fifteenth- through eighteenth-century Italy, see in Cavallo and Warner the contributions by Isabella Chabot, "Lineage and Strategies and the Control of Widows in Renaissance Florence," 127–44, and Guilia Calvi, "Widows, the State, and Guardianship of Children in Early Modern Tuscany," 209–19. See also Guilia Calvi, "Reconstructing the Family: Widowhood and Remarriage in Tuscany in the Early Modern Period," in *Marriage in Italy 1300-1650,* ed. Trevor Dean and Kate Lowe (Cambridge: Cambridge University Press, 1998), 275–96.

43. See, for example, ASF, MAP 137, 673, a long letter of 12 September 1515 in which Alfonsina urged her son Lorenzo to undertake repairs and ornamentation in one of his territories. She emphasized that such acts would reflect well on the family and earn the gratitude of the inhabitants: "Tale dignita in uno conterraneo loro, che li stima bene per la parte dote, et essendone io certificata de tale cose, parendomi imp[re]sa laudabile et gloriossa, per et la Casa n[ost]ra, ch[e] se fussi obtenuta una tale imp[re]sa honorevile de crear la Cipta dove è terra murata." Later she suggests to Lorenzo that in order to avoid the enmity of the local abbot he should provide "per la loro particular passione, uno ornamento de tale sorte alla terra loro." The locality discussed in this letter is uncertain based on internal evidence.

44. Alfonsina did, however, provide for commemorative masses at San Marco in Florence. I am grateful to Lorenzo Polizzotto for this information. Piero's tomb monument was proposed by Pope Clement VII (Giulio de' Medici) in the 1530s. On Antonio da Sangallo the Younger's plans for Piero's tomb during Clement's pontificate, see Gustavo Giovannoni, *Antonio da Sangallo il Giovane,* 2 vols. (Rome: Tipografica Regionale, 1959), 1:368–75; Langedijk, *Portraits,* 1:11–12, 2:1345–46. On the realized tomb by Francesco Sangallo in the Abbey of Montecassino, see Giovanni Minozzi, *Montecassino nella storia del Rinascimento* (Rome: Opera Nazionale per il Mezzogiorno, 1925), 312–15; Maria Vittoria Marini Clarelli, *Montecassino* (Milan: F. M. Ricci, 1995), xiii, plates 11–14.

45. See King, "Medieval and Renaissance Matrons," passim, for a number of examples. Cf. Valone, "Roman Matrons as Patrons," 55; see esp. Carolyn Valone's chapter in this volume. See also Vaccaro, "Documents," for Maria Bufalini, the patron of Parmigianino's London *Vision of Saint Jerome,* which was commissioned for her husband's funerary chapel in the Roman church of San Salvatore in Lauro. The chapters by Rosi Gilday, Mary Vaccaro and Elizabeth Pilliod in this volume also consider widows as patrons of altarpieces.

46. See Renato Lefevre, "Castelsantangelo (Castel Madama) sotto la signoria dei Medici e di Margarita di Austria nel sec. XVI," *Atti e memorie della Società Tiburtina di storia e d'arte* 40 (1967–69), esp. 9–10. This *rocca* had belonged to the Bracciano branch of the Orsini family and was given to Alfonsina by Giovanni Giordano Orsini at the death of her uncle Gentile Virginio Orsini. For the Bracciano Orsini, see *Bracciano e gli Orsini,* exh. cat. (Bracciano: Castello Odescalchi; Rome: De Luca, 1981).

47. See Renato Lefevre, "Il patrimonio cinquecentesco dei Medici nel Lazio e in Abruzzo," *Archivio della Società Romana di Storia patria* 98 (1975): 98–99. For decorations and furnishings dating

from Clarice de' Medici and Filippo Strozzi's residence at the Castello di Lunghezza, see Elspeth Moncrieff, "The Castello di Lunghezza: A Palpable Sense of History," *Apollo* 134 (1991): 171.

48. See Frommel, *Der römische Palastbau*, 2:224, 227. See also Luisa Marcucci and Bruno Torresi, "Palazzo Medici-Lante: Un progetto medíceo in Roma e il 'raggiustamento' di Onorio Longhi, 1 and 2," *Storia architettura* 5 (1982): 40 and 6 (1983): 34, n. 7. On Palazzo Madama and the Medici, see Domenico Gnoli, "Il Palazzo del Senato già Madama," *Nuova antologia*, ser. 7, 51 (1926): 252–56; Francesco Cossiga and others, *Il Palazzo Madama: I palazzi del Senato*, 2nd ed. (Rome: Editalia, 1984); Gaetano Miarelli Mariani, "Il Palazzo Medici a Piazza Navona: Un' utopia urbana di Giuliano da Sangallo," in *Firenze e la Toscana dei Medici nell' Europea del '500*, 3 vols. (Florence: Leo S. Olschki, 1983), 3:977–93.

49. The future pontiff rented a piece of property and a house near Sant' Eustachio, on the site of the present Palazzo Madama; in 1505 he purchased them in the names of the younger Giuliano and Lorenzo from the bishop of Chiusi, Sinulfo di Castell'Ottieri, for 10,000 ducats. See Cossiga and others, *Palazzo Madama*, 45; Mariani, "Palazzo Medici a Piazza Navona," 980, for this purchase. The Medici library was set up in the Roman palace, and the family's collection of antiques was available for study there. Frommel, *Der römische Palastbau*, 2:227 speculates that Alfonsina resided in the palazzo before she purchased it. He also suggests that she might have lived in one of the Roman Orsini palazzi prior to 1505.

50. "Credo che mi bisognerà mutar casa, perchè qui io stò con grandissima difficultà, io et la brigata che ho con mecho; et anche per essere discosto al palazzo, che come tu sai mi torna molto incomodo per più conti. Credo a omni modo trovare una casa in Borgho." Tommasini, *La vita*, 2:983. For the role of women at the papal court, see Irene Fosi and Maria Antonietta Visceglia, "Marriage and Politics at the Papal Court in the Sixteenth and Seventeenth Centuries," in Dean and Lowe, *Marriage in Italy*, 197–224. It has been suggested that Alfonsina left Palazzo Madama because of Leo's decision to expand the palace that she had purchased five years earlier into a huge complex extending to Piazza Navona. See Lefevre, "Il patrimonio cinquecentesco," 40. For Leo's grandiose intentions, see Gaetano Miarelli Mariani, "Palazzo Medici a Piazza Navona," *Raffaello architetto*, exh. cat. (Rome: Palazzo dei Conservatori, 1984), 88–90, 105, n. 115; Manfredo Tafuri, *Ricerca del Rinascimento: Principi, città, architetti* (Turin: Einaudi, 1992), 97–99.

51. Frommel, *Der römische Palastbau*, 2:227; Lefevre, "Il patrimonio cinquecentesco," 41.

52. On Palazzo Medici-Lante, see Frommel, *Der römische Palastbau*, 2:224–32, cat. no. XIX; Lefevre, "Il patrimonio cinquecentesco," 41–42 and fig. 2 for Alfonsina's purchases beginning 13 May 1514. This document had been previously associated with another Medici property.

53. Cf. n. 50 and see esp. Tafuri, *Ricerca del Rinascimento*, 97 and fig. 18. Tafuri sees the proximity as part of Leo's intentions to establish an *urbs medicea* in the heart of Rome.

54. Frommel, *Der römische Palastbau*, 2:224, docs. 3 and 4; Lefevre, "Il patrimonio cinquecentesco," 41.

55. For the purchase of the palazzo by the Lante family, see Frommel, *Der römische Palastbau*, 2:225; Lefevre, "Il patrimonio cinquecentesco," 49. The palace is also known simply as Palazzo Lante.

56. Frommel, *Der römische Palastbau*, 2:231; Marcucci and Torresi, "Palazzo Medici-Lante," 42. The capitals of the *cortile* feature Leo's yoke and the Medici diamond ring with feathers. Alfonsina's *stemma* is centered front and back.

57. For the use of the *scudo accolato* by women patrons, see Carolyn Valone's contribution to this volume. A *stemma* which may be Alfonsina's appears on fol. 3r of a mid-cinquecento copy of Niccolò Valori's *vita* of Lorenzo il Magnifico in the Biblioteca Riccardiana, Florence, MS 2599, for which see Mario Martelli, "Le due redazioni della *Laurentii Medicei Vita* di Niccolò Valori," *Bibliofilia* 66 (1964): 237 ff.; Paola Pirolo, ed., *Lorenzo dopo Lorenzo: La fortuna storica di Lorenzo il Magnifico*, exh. cat. (Florence: Biblioteca Nazionale; Milan: Silvana, 1992), 50–51, cat. no. 1.20. Despite the impaled Medici-Orsini arms, the dedication, probably copied from an earlier manuscript, is to Lorenzo's daughter Lucrezia Salviati.

58. Frommel, *Der römische Palastbau*, 2:231. Other names that have been suggested in the past include Jacopo Sansovino and Donato Bramante. Lefevre, "Il patrimonio cinquecentesco," 51, also suggests the involvement of Andrea Sansovino.

59. "Per conto d'una muragl(i)a che vuole fare madonna Alfonsina qui presso alla Doghana." See *Il carteggio di Michelangelo*, ed. Paola Barocchi and Renzo Ristori, 5 vols. (Florence: Sansoni, 1965–83), 1:230, for Domenico Buoninsegni's letter of 11 December 1516 to Michelangelo. Buoninsegni said that he thought Baccio Bigio was to be involved with Leo's projects at the *rocca* of Montefiascone, but Baccio said that his work in Rome was for Alfonsina. On Baccio Bigio, see Philip E. Foster, *A Study of Lorenzo de' Medici's Villa at Poggio a Caiano*, Garland Outstanding Dissertations in the Fine Arts, 2 vols. (New York: Garland, 1978), 415–16, n. 362. A group of letters preserved in the *copialettere* of Lorenzo's secretary, Goro Gheri, document preparations for Baccio Bigio's trip to Rome. See ASF, Goro Gheri 1, fol. 147v, letter of 27 November 1516, "E cento ducati per la mancia quod maestro Baldassari li manderò per baccio biggio el q[u]ale partirà Domenica mactina"; fol. 151v, "Baccio Bigio partirà Lundedi insieme col Grasso al quale farrò darli cento ducati per maestro Baldassarri"; fol. 156r, letter of 30 November 1516, "El grasso et baccio bigio partano Domactina sanza mancho et se ne venghano a Roma et Baccio mi dice che ha lassato ordine buono per tutte le muraglie." In his letters to Alfonsina, Gheri generally addressed her as "Illustrissima donna patrona unica." This form of address in a later letter is remarked upon by F. W. Kent with Patricia Simons in the introduction to Kent and Simons, *Patronage, Art, and Society*, 8 and n. 34. For Goro Gheri's relations with the Medici, see K. J. P. Lowe, "Towards an Understanding of Goro Gheri's Views on *Amicizia* in Early Sixteenth-Century Medicean Florence," in *Florence and Italy*, ed. Denley and Elam 91–105.

60. Alfonsina's tastes seemed to be conservative, as evident below in my discussion of her preference for "old fashioned" horse trappings.

61. See ASF, MAP 114, 156, letter of 2 September 1514, in which Alfonsina reminds her son Lorenzo of his promise to the painter: "Più mesi fa promessi a Poggino dipintore, n[ost]ro amico vecchio, di farli havere uno officio/o di mazziere o di comandatore costì in palazzo.… " The letter (slightly mistranscribed) is cited in Pieraccini, *La stirpe*, 1:179. Pieraccini cites this as the only evidence he found for Alfonsina's *mecenatismo*. For Poggio di Zanobi (or Poggino Zanobi), see Vasari-Milanesi, 5:39, 40, 131 and 6:535. See also Dominic Ellis Colnaghi, *A Dictionary of Florentine Painters from the Thirteenth to the Seventeenth Centuries* (London: John Lane, 1928), 216–17. Professor Louis Waldman of the University of Texas, Austin, has generously shared with me the many unpublished documents he has found on this little-studied artist.

62. Alfonsina used both "Ursina de Medici" and "Ursina de Medicis." This assertion of her natal line is in contrast to the practice of Lucrezia Tornabuoni, who signed her letters "Lucretia de' Medici."

63. For Poggino di Zanobi as "dipintori del palazo," see Ilaria Ciseri, *L'ingresso trionfale di Leone X in Firenze nel 1515* (Florence: Leo S. Olschki, 1990), 262. For other payments to him in the fall of 1515, see ibid., 257, 258, 260, 267. Colnaghi mistakenly dated these payments to 1513; Colnaghi, *Dictionary*, 217.

64. Giovanni Gaye, *Carteggio inedito d' artisti dei secoli XIV–XVI*, 3 vols. (Florence: Giuseppe Molini, 1839–40), 2:139, no. LXXXIV. The original is ASF, MAP 108, 118: "Direte anchora al Magnifico che sua madre è la più fortunata donna mai fusse, che li danari che la dà per dio li fruttono più perche se li prestassi a usura." Strozzi continues, "murando a certe monache una cantina vi hanno trovate sino a questo dì circa a 5 figure sì belle quanto ne sian altre in roma." For the discovery of these statues, see Rodolfo Amadeo Lanciani, *Storia degli scavi di Roma e notizie intorno le collezioni romane di antichità*, 4 vols. (Rome: E. Loeschler & Co., 1902–12), 1:162–63; Phyllis Pray Bober and Ruth Rubinstein, *Renaissance Artists and Antique Sculpture: A Handbook of Sources* (Oxford: Oxford University Press, 1986), cat. no. 143.

65. Gaye, *Carteggio inedito*, 2:139: "Sono di marmo di statura mancho che naturale, et sono tutti chi morti e feriti, pure separati. Evi chi tiene che sian la historia delli horatii et curatii."

66. "Apud edem divi Eustachii in una domo mulieris cuisdam Ursinorum familia has sequentes statuas." For Bellièvre's text, see Eugene Müntz, "Le Musée du Capitole et les autres collections romaines à la fin du XVe et au commencement du XVIe siècle avec un choix de documents inédits," *Revue archéologique* 43 (1882):35. On Bellièvre, see Claude Bellièvre, *Souvenirs de voyages en Italie et en Orient, Notes historiques, Pièces de Vers*, ed. Charles Perrat (Geneva: Droz, 1956), xi–xv.

67. "Qui si rem intelligere voles et historiam de pugna, scilicet trigeminorum trium Horatiorum romanorum videlicet et trium Curiatiorum Albanorum, vide Livium decade.... " Müntz, "Le Musée du Capitole," 35. In a marginal note Bellièvre says that a seventh was "ad papam vecta." See Bober and Rubinstein, *Renaissance Artists and Antique Sculpture*, cat. no. 148. This statue is now in the Musei Vaticani, Galleria dei Candelabri VI.

68. On the dedication, see Bober and Rubinstein, *Renaissance Artists and Antique Sculpture*, cat. nos. 143, 148–52. See esp. Beatrice Palma, "Il piccolo donario pergameno," *Xenia* 1 (1981):45–84 with earlier bibliography, 82–83.

69. For the Naples examples, see Enrica Pozzi and others, *Le collezioni del Museo Nazionale di Napoli: La scultura greco-romana, le sculture antiche della collezione Farnese, le collezioni monetali, le oreficerie, la collezione glittica* (Milan: Leonardo, 1989), cat. nos. 14–17 of the Farnese collection of antiquities. See also Palma, "Il piccolo donario," cat. nos. 1, 2, 3, 7. For another example from the original group that is now in the Louvre, see Bober and Rubinstein, *Renaissance Artists and Antique Sculpture*, cat. no. 150. The Venetian cardinal Domenico Grimani also acquired three figures from the group, two of which are not accounted for in the seven noted by Bellièvre. See Bober and Rubinstein, *Renaissance Artists and Antique Sculpture*, 183, cat. no. 149.

70. For Raphael's reliance on the copies of the Attalid dedication group, see Nicole Dacos, *Le Logge di Raffaello: Maestro e bottega di fronte all' antico*, 2nd. ed. (Rome: Istituto Poligrafico e Zecca dello Stato, 1986), 157, 192; Bober and Rubinstein, *Renaissance Artists and Antique Sculpture*, cat. nos. 149–51. For the Heemskerck sketch, see Christian Hülsen and Hermann Egger, *Die römischen skizzenbücher von Marten van Heemskerck im Königlichen Kupferstichkabinett zu Berlin*, 2 vols. (1913–16; reprint, Soest: Davaco, 1975), 1:4–5; Elena Filippi, *Maerten van Heemskerck: Inventio urbis* (Milan: Berenice, 1990), 97–98.

71. On Isabella as a collector of antiquities, see C. Malcolm Brown, "Lo insaciabile desiderio nostro de cose antique: New Documents on Isabella d'Este's Collection of Antiquities," in *Cultural Aspects of the Italian Renaissance: Essays in Honor of Paul Oskar Kristeller*, ed. C. H. Clough (Manchester: Manchester University Press, 1976), 324–53, 497; David S. Chambers and Jane Martineau, *Splendours of the Gonzaga*, exh. cat. (London: Victoria and Albert Museum, 1981–82), cat. nos. 116–17, 119, 122–23; Bober and Rubinstein, *Renaissance Artists and Antique Sculpture*, 473; Rose Marie San Juan, "The Court Lady's Dilemma: Isabella d'Este and Art Collecting in the Renaissance," *Oxford Art Journal* 14 (1991): 75. See Clifford M. Brown in *Isabella d'Este: Fürstin und Mäzenatin der Renaissance: "La Prima Donna del Mondo,"* ed. Sylvia Ferino-Pagden, exh. cat. (Vienna: Kunsthistorisches Museum, 1994), 289–300; see cat. nos. 96–101 for examples of antiquities in her collection. See also Molly Bourne's chapter in this volume.

72. Landucci, *Diario*, 350: "E a dì 4 di giugno 1515, venne in Firenze madonna Alfonsina madre di detto Lorenzo de' Medici."

73. On Alfonsina's ambitions for Lorenzo cf. n. 27 above. For the search for a suitable bride, see Maguire, *Women of the Medici*, 190, 192–94; Devonshire Jones, *Francesco Vettori*, 125–28; Pieraccini, *La stirpe*, 1:175–76.

74. ASF, MAP 114, 57: "etiam S. Hieronimo dice che l'amore viene dalle dote." Cf. Maguire, *Women of the Medici*, 193; Pieraccini, *La stirpe*, 1:176. I have been unable to confirm Alfonsina's remark.

75. "S. Signoria è sempre occupata, o a scrivere a Roma, o costà o a dare udienza, di che ne segue che la casa è sempre piena; e da tal concorso ne risulta riputatione allo Stato, animo agli amici, e timore alli adversi, conclusive fa quello offitio che a altra donna sarebbe impossibile, a pochi huomini facile." This excerpt from a letter of 31 August 1515 is published in L. A. Ferrai, "La giovinezza di Lorenzino de' Medici," *Giornale storico della letteratura italiana* 2 (1883): 85, n. 3.

76. The flurry of excitement preceding the arrival of the Medici pope is sensed in a letter of 15 November 1515 written to Paolo Vettori: "In Firenze non se attende ad altro che a ponerla in ordine, far archi triophali, et altre feste magne per la intrata di N[ostro] S[ignore], la quale sarà il di di Sancto Andrea." See ASF, Cart. Strozz., ser. 3, 220, fols. 140r–v.

77. Few scholars have remarked on Alfonsina's role: an exception is Felice, "Alfonsina Orsini," 14. On Leo's Florentine *entrata*, see esp. John Shearman, "The Florentine *Entrata* of Pope Leo X," *Journal of the Warburg and Courtauld Institutes* 38 (1975): 136–58; Bonner Mitchell, *Italian Civic Pageantry in the High Renaissance: A Descriptive Bibliography of Triumphal Entries and Selected Other Festivals for State Occasions* (Florence: Leo S. Olschki, 1979), 39–43 with bibliography; Ciseri, *L'ingresso trionfale*, which includes a register of published and unpublished documents; Cummings, *Politicized Muse*, chap. 5, "Leo X's 1515 Florentine *Entrata*," 67–82. Professor Eve Borsook generously shared with me the extraordinary array of unpublished material she has assembled on Leo's *entrata*. Some of these documents have been published in Ciseri, *L'ingresso trionfale*.

78. Ciseri, *L'ingresso trionfale*, esp. docs. 12, 23–26, 33. For the brief, see ibid., 32 and doc. 25, 248–49; Tomas, "Negotiated Spaces," chap. 5, pt. 1.

79. Ciseri, *L'ingresso trionfale*, doc. 24, 246. The letter is ASF, MAP 105, 18: "Et hora io mi trovo qui in uno viluppo grandissimo, et di provisioni di vectovagle per una corte, et di allogiamenti, et appararti, et mille altre cose che sarebbe difficile a narratele brevemente."

80. Ciseri, *L'ingresso trionfale*, 246: "et siamo in su disegni di apparati, et archi triomphali.… "

81. Ciseri, *L'ingresso trionfale*, 247: "Circa e' fornimenti ho mandato per Michelagnolo et se si potrà fare quelli gruppi d'oro filato che scrivi et che tornino bene, si farabbo fare, se non si solleciteranno con quelli smalti," et fra X o XII dì et non prima, saranno forniti et subito manderanno." For Michelangelo di Viviano and his partisan activities, see nn. 22, 24.

82. Ciseri, *L'ingresso trionfale*, doc. 26, 249. The letter is ASF, MAP 137, 707: "Li fornimenti che fa Michelagnolo, si sollecitano quanto sì puo, et denari non li mancha, ma come è suo costume, et come ti ho scripto e' vanno adagio.… "

83. Ciseri, *L'ingresso trionfale*, 249: "et anche non riescono molto belli con quelli smalti, et non credo ti habbino a satisfare molto.… "

84. Ciseri, *L'ingresso trionfale*, 249: "et secondo me, è più bello in sé quel fornimento vechio di octone che si fece a Roma, che non sarà questo." For brass *fornimenti a cavallo*, see Benvenuto Cellini, *Opere*, ed. Bruno Maier (Milan: Rizzoli, 1968), 731.

85. Ciseri, *L'ingresso trionfale*, 250: "ti dico che in Ytalia ci è di molte altre cose belle come questa ciptà…perché tutta Italia insieme è più bella tutta insieme che non è Firenze sola." This was in response to Lorenzo's fears that if the meeting between Leo X and Francis I took place in Florence, the French king might try to seize the city because of its beauty. The sharp-tongued Alfonsina once spitefully called Cardinal Bernardo da Bibbiena "quella civecta di Sancta Maria in Portico" because of his anti-Gallic stance as the leader of the imperial party at the papal court. The remark is in a letter of 11 August 1515 (ASF, MAP 137, 652); see Felice, "Alfonsina Orsini," 11; Devonshire Jones, *Francesco Vettori*, 114, n. 30.

86. ASF, MAP 137, 701: "Nostro Signore mi fece intendere a giorni passati che sarebbe ben che Lorenzo donassi a qualche p[er]sonaggio grande qualche gentilezza come peze di drappo/o/ catena/ o simila/ et al Re qualche bello cavallo benguerrito (?)." On the Medici's diplomatic gifts to the French king, see Janet Cox-Rearick, "Sacred to Profane: Diplomatic Gifts of the Medici to Francis I," *Journal of Medieval and Renaissance Studies* 24 (1994):239–58; Cox-Rearick, *The Collection of Francis I*, passim, esp. 75–81, 191–99, 201–23.

87. See Ciseri, *L'ingresso trionfale*, 135–36. Cf. Bülst, "Uso e trasformazione," 119–20, esp. n. 328.

88. Ciseri, *L'ingresso trionfale*, doc. 27. The letter is ASF, MAP 137, 708.

89. Ciseri, *L'ingresso trionfale*, 250–51: "la Signoria di madonna ha pensato che Nostro Signore si servirà de la camera di vostra Signoria Ill. et de le sue…et disegnamo fare uno uscio fra la camera di vostra Illustre Signoria et quella grande di madonna, et si leverà via quelli due lecti che vi sono, et ne l'anticamera di madonna starà el lecto di sua Beatitudine." See also Philip Foster, "Lorenzo de' Medici's Library at the Medici Palace," n. 24, cited as forthcoming in Bülst, "Uso e trasformazione," 119, n. 308.

90. Ciseri, *L'ingresso trionfale*, 136, 251. Fiamminghi wrote: "et madama anchora doverrà trovarse o più presto glene troverero noi una altra casa perché sua Santità disegna che si lasci la casa vuota."

91. Ciseri, *L'ingresso trionfale*, doc. 33. The payments for Palazzo Medici are found in ASF, Operai, 14, and are listed with payments for the work at the Sala del Papa in Santa Maria Novella and other expenses related to the *entrata*.

92. See Ciseri, *L'ingresso trionfale*, 260, for payments for wood. While the *legni d'abeto* allocated to Ser Bernardo "chancielliere della Mangnifica Madonna Alfonsina Ursina de' Medici" is not specified as destined for the Medici palace, the wood allocated to Lorenzo is described as "quali ebe Bacio Bigio loro capomaestro per adoperare in Firenze nel loro palazo."

93. Work on the Medici suggests that members of the family often joined together as patrons. See, for example, Lillie, "Giovanni di Cosimo," 189–90; John Paoletti, "Fraternal Piety and Family Power: The Artistic Patronage of Cosimo and Lorenzo de' Medici," in Ames-Lewis, *Cosimo "il Vecchio,"* 195–219; John T. Paoletti, "ha fatto Piero con voluntà del padre…." Piero de' Medici and Corporate Commissions of Art," in Beyer and Boucher, *Piero de' Medici*, 221–50. See also my discussion of Cardinal Giulio de' Medici's relationship to Pope Leo X in Sheryl E. Reiss, "Cardinal Giulio de' Medici as a Patron of Art 1513–1523" (Ph.D. diss., Princeton University, 1992), 616–18.

94. Linda Pellecchia, "Reconstructing the Greek House: Giuliano da Sangallo's Villa for the Medici in Florence," *Journal of the Society of Architectural Historians* 52 (1993): 338, n. 56. I am grateful to Professor Pellecchia for sharing her ideas on the Via Laura plan with me.

95. Pellechia, "Reconstructing the Greek House," 331 ff. and 338.

96. See Domenico Moreni, *Continuazione delle memorie istoriche dell' Ambrosiane Basilica di San Lorenzo*, 2 vols. (Florence, 1816–17), 2:444–51; Ciseri, *L'ingresso trionfale*, 137–40, for alterations at San Lorenzo.

97. Archivio Capitolino di San Lorenzo, 2471, fols. 305r–307v, published in Moreni, *Continuazione*, 2:444–51; Ciseri, *L'ingresso trionfale*, doc. 12, 213–20.

98. "È piaciuto a Madonna Anfolsina [*Alfonsina*] Orsina, et donna, che fu del Magnifico Piero di Lorenzo de' Medici nostra Patrona, et a molti altri huomini da bene disfare parte del nostro choro, et ridurlo a uno bello piano in modo sia capace di piu genti…a essere Capella di Papa, perchè così fu disegnato in mentre starà Sua Santità in Firenze questa *Chiesa sia Cappella Papale*." I follow the transcription in Ciseri, *L'ingresso trionfale*, 213.

99. In the discussion following our 1993 session at Kalamazoo, (see n. 42) the discussant, Sheila ffolliott, drew attention to the interesting use of the phrase "nostra patrona," which, as we have seen (cf. n. 59), was used as a form of address by some of Alfonsina's correspondents. Molly Bourne informs me that this salutation was also used for Isabella d'Este. For related discussions of gendered language see the chapters by Roger Crum and Marjorie Och in this volume.

100. "Perdita libertas post hoc, Florentie, nam te foemina ab Ursino sanguine sola regit." Francesco Nitti, *Leone X e la sua politica* (Florence: G. Barbèra, 1892), 71; Pieraccini, *La stirpe*, 1:174. See Landucci, *Diario*, 359, for a condemnation of the expense of the celebrations.

101. For the acquisition of Urbino as Alfonsina's idea, see Nitti, *Leone X*, 71–75; Devonshire Jones, *Lorenzo de' Medici*, 313–14. In a letter of 3 November 1515, Alfonsina wrote to Lorenzo that she hoped "per questo mezo noi habbiamo qualche stato, et la mira mia è in su Urbino." The letter (ASF, MAP 105, 18) is published as Ciseri, *L'ingresso trionfale*, doc. 24. See also Ludwig von Pastor, *The History of the Popes from the Close of the Middle Ages*, ed. R. F. Kerr, 3rd ed., 36 vols. (London: Routledge and Kegan Paul, 1924–53), 7:148; Maguire, *Women of the Medici*, 192.

102. See Pastor, *History of the Popes,* 7:148. I am grateful to T. C. Price Zimmermann, who called my attention to Giovio's condemnation of Alfonsina as the instigator of the Urbino War. See Paolo Giovio, *Le vite di Leon decimo et d'Adriano sesto sommi pontefici, et del Cardinal Pompeo Colonna,* trans. L. Domenichi (Florence, 1549), 249. Cf. T. C. Price Zimmermann, *Paolo Giovio: The Historian and the Crisis of Sixteenth-Century Italy* (Princeton: Princeton University Press, 1995), 29.

103. See ASF, MAP 132, fol. 89r for the 7,563 ducats that Alfonsina supplied "causa alla impresa d'Urbino." This inadequately studied account book contains *entrata* and *uscita* records not only for the Urbino War, but also for Lorenzo's household expenses (including clothing, musicians, and silver) from June 1515 through June 1517. See also Tomas, "Negotiated Spaces," chap. 5, pt. 3.

104. Foster, *Study of Lorenzo de' Medici's Villa,* 1:114, 117.

105. Discussed and published in Foster, *Study of Lorenzo de' Medici's Villa,* 1:114–17, 415–19, nn. 361–68.

106. ASF, MAP 149, 27, identified as "conto di legniame d'abeto, dato l'Opera di Santa Maria del Fiore di Firenze alla Illustrissima Madonna Alfonsina Orsina de' Medici per conto di più luoghi cioè Poggio e Lagho e giardino di Firenze.... "

107. "P(er) la muraglia del Poggio a Chaiano.... " Foster, *Study of Lorenzo de' Medici's Villa,* 1:114, 416, n. 362, misdates the debit dated 18 March 1515 in the old Florentine system under which the new year did not begin until 25 March. For this reason the consignment of wood for the *muraglia* at the Lago di Fucecchio dated 24 March 1515 must also be of 1516. See ibid., 1:416, n. 361. This oversight was not corrected in the Italian version of Foster's thesis; Philip E. Foster, *La Villa di Lorenzo de' Medici a Poggio a Caiano* (Poggio a Caiano: Comune di Poggio a Caiano, 1992), 99, 113, nn. 18, 19.

108. Foster, *Study of Lorenzo de' Medici's Villa,* 1:114. Later Clement VII was said to have derided Baccio's work at Poggio a Caiano. See Giovan Francesco Fattucci's letter to Michelangelo of 29 April 1524: "Et quando gli [Clement VII] dissi che avevi menato Bacio Bigio se ne rise, et disse che gli aveva fatto certe cose al Pogio le quale rovinano"; *Il carteggio di Michelangelo,* 3:71.

109. Goro Gheri's letters of 12 November and 15 November 1516 are found in ASF, MAP 142, 304 and ASF, MAP 142, 315. Cf. Foster, *Study of Lorenzo de' Medici's Villa,* 1:115, 417, nn. 363, 364. Foster mistakenly identifies Lorenzo as the author of the latter missive.

110. Foster, *Study of Lorenzo de' Medici's Villa,* 1:114, 417–18, nn. 365, 366. Eighty loads were consigned in December 1516 and another fourteen the next month.

111. Foster, *Study of Lorenzo de' Medici's Villa,* 1:115; Janet Cox-Rearick, *Dynasty and Destiny in Medici Art: Pontormo, Leo X, and the Two Cosimos* (Princeton: Princeton University Press, 1984), 87.

112. Cf. n. 106 for ASF 149, 27 (Alfonsina's accounts for "Poggio e Lagho e giardino di Firenze..."). For Alfonsina's purchase and draining of the Lago di Fucecchio in September 1515, see Emanuele Repetti, *Dizionario geografico fisico storico della Toscana,* 6 vols. (Florence: Giovanni Mazzoni, 1833–46), 2:356; Tommasini, *La vita,* 2:1053, 4:16–17. See also Stephens, *Fall of the Florentine Republic,* 223; Giorgio Galetti and Alberto Malvolti, *Il ponte mediceo di Cappiano: Storia e restauro* (Fucecchio: Edizioni dell'Erba, 1989), 17–19. I am grateful to Louis Waldman for this reference. See also *Il Padule di Fucecchio:La lunga storia di un ambiente naturale,* ed. Adriano Prosperi (Rome: Edizioni di storia e letteratura, 1995). For the *muraglia* at Fucecchio, see Foster, *Study of Lorenzo de' Medici's Villa,* 416, n. 361 for twenty-four wagonloads of "legniami d'abeto...consegniati per lei a Baccio Bigio, disse per conto della muraglia per Lagho di Fucecchio."

113. See ASF, MAP 146, 48, a document of the late sixteenth century, for a description of Alfonsina's works at Fucecchio: "L'anno 1516 mediante la provisione fatta dalla Signoria di firenze fù disfatto il muro del padule di Fuccechi[o] al Ponte à Cappiano da Mad[a]ma Alfonsina Orsina de Medici...si fece un fosso molto largo et patente intorno al padule, che fino à hora si vede.... " See also Giovanni Cambi, *Istorie di Giovanni Cambi cittadino fiorentino...,* in *Delizie degli eruditi toscani,* ed. Ildefonso di San Luigi, 24 vols. (Florence: Gaetano Cambiagi, 1770–89), 23:28; Repetti, *Dizionario,* 4:17.

114. ASF 142, 315, Goro Gheri to Alfonsina, who was then in Rome: "Et lui [Baccio Bigio] martedi anderà al Poggio a ordinare quello che bisogno, di poi anderà al lago, dove mectera tempo fra lu'una et altra cose 12 giorni, secondo mi dice, in modo che fra 15 dì lui se ne verra costà alla alla S[ignoria] V[ostra]." Cf. Foster, *Study of Lorenzo de' Medici's Villa*, 1:417, n. 364.

115. Stephens, *Fall of the Florentine Republic*, 222–24; Tomas, 'A Positive Novelty,' 65; Tomas, "Negotiated Spaces," chap. 5, pt. 3.

116. For Alfonsina's works at the Medici garden, see Elam, "Lorenzo de' Medici's Sculpture Garden," 52, 78, doc. 1.xiv (ASF, MAP 149, 27, which records wood consigned to Baccio d'Agnolo "per conto della muraglia del giardino in sulla piazza di St Marcho...."). See also Caroline Elam, "Il giardino delle sculture di Lorenzo de' Medici," in *Il giardino di San Marco: Maestri e compagni del giovane Michelangelo*, ed. Paola Barocchi, exh. cat. (Florence: Casa Buonarroti; Florence: Silvana, 1992), 166.

117. ASF, MAP 149, 27; Elam, "Lorenzo de' Medici's Sculpture Garden," doc. 1.xiv. See ibid., 46 for the structures on the property.

118. Elam, "Lorenzo de' Medici's Sculpture Garden," 52, 78, doc. 1.xii (ASF, Operai 14, fol. 157r). On the Medici stalls, see Caroline Elam, "Il palazzo nel contesto della città: Strategie urbanistiche dei Medici nel gonfalone del Leon d'Oro," in *Il Palazzo Medici Riccardi*, 52, 54, fig. 78 for a plan of the area.

119. Elam, "Il palazzo," 52, n. 94. In a letter of 15 November 1516 Goro Gheri wrote to Alfonsina: "Così io lo [Baccio Bigio] solleciterò, et per finire le stalle come lui haveva detto questa mactina, ordinai collo Octo della Pratica che facessino provedere qualche ducato...." ASF, MAP 142, 315, published in Foster, *Study of Lorenzo de' Medici's Villa*, 1:417, n. 364. The extent of her involvement with this project is not clear.

120. On 14 March 1517 (1516 o.s.) Gheri wrote to Baldassare Turini da Pescia, "Apresso dite alla Sua Santità che el Grasso dice che per la muraglia dal Poggio non ci sono più danari." See Foster, *Study of Lorenzo de' Medici's Villa*, 1:115, 418, n. 367 for ASF, Goro Gheri 1, fol. 79v and for the possible identification of "el Grasso" as the *legnaiuolo* Filippo d'Andrea. Cf. n. 59 above for "el Grasso's" travel to Rome in connection with construction on Alfonsina's palace in Piazza Caprettari (now Palazzo Medici-Lante).

121. On 19 April 1517 Gheri wrote to Bernardino di San Miniato, "Dite alla Signoria di Madonna che el Grasso mi dice che non c'è più danari per la muraglia del Poggio.... " See Foster, *Study of Lorenzo de' Medici's Villa*, 1:115, 418, n. 367 for ASF, Goro Gheri 2, fol. 144v.

122. ASF, Goro Gheri 4, fol. 136v: "La S[anti]ta di N[ostro] Signore sono circa quattro mesi che fece un breve a Jac[op]o Salviati che pagasse 500 ducati el mese alla S[ignoria] di M[ada]ma perche lei potesse riconperare le possessioni che erano di casa: et etiam finire la muraglia del poggio." I am grateful to John Shearman for this reference. For Alfonsina's involvement in the recuperation of Medici properties, see ASF, Cart. Strozz., ser. 1, 5, fols. 17–20. "Brevis nota bonorum recuperatorum sub nomine heredum magnifici Laurentii quondam Leonis Papa X et Clementii Setimi," published in Tommasini, *La vita* 2:1052–54.

123. "È al poggio et sta benissimo et ha facta uno grande lavorare et acconciare." ASF, Goro Gheri 4, fol. 260v, letter of 23 July 1518. John Shearman generously shared this document with me.

124. See Maguire, *Women of the Medici*, 193–94; Devonshire Jones, *Francesco Vettori*, 125–28, 132–35; Cummings, *Politicized Muse*, 99.

125. Devonshire Jones, *Francesco Vettori*, 132, n. 157; Cox-Rearick, *Dynasty and Destiny*, 87, n. 3.

126. "Addì 4 di septembre n'andarono tutti al Poggio a Caiano dove era adornamenti come d'un paradiso." See Susan McKillop, *Franciabigio* (Berkeley: University of California Press, 1974), 69; Cox-Rearick, *Dynasty and Destiny*, 87; Cummings, *Politicized Muse*, 102 and 218, n. 6. Cerretani's text is BNCF, MS II.IV.19, fol. 50r. It is not entirely clear if the *salone* was vaulted at this time. For conflicting opinions on the chronology of the vault decorations, see Reiss, "Cardinal Giulio de' Medici," 466.

127. For Lorenzo's movements, see Cummings, *Politicized Muse*, 99, 217, n. 43. For the second *nozze* celebrations, see Alessandro Parronchi, "La prima rappresentazione della Mandragola," *La Bibliofilia* 64 (1962): 37–86; Mitchell, *Italian Civic Pageantry*, 43–44, with bibliography; Cummings, *Politicized Muse*, chap. 9, 99–114.

128. For Cerretani's passage of 18 August 1518, see Cummings, *Politicized Muse*, 99, 217, n. 4: "M[adonn]a Alfonsina, con otto capi del governo, pensorono honorarli et grandeme[n]te et dettono questa cura agl'Otto di Pratica, i quali, p[er] loro ministri, ordinorono armeggiere e feste e tutte quelle cose che si solevan fare p[er] San Giovanni."

129. Cummings, *Politicized Muse*, 99, 217, n. 4: "Fecino un palco avanti l'uscio del palazzo largo quanto la via, lungo quanto la casa alto braccia 3, con le tende di sopra apparato con arazerie, e sedie splendidamente." A similar *palco* for dancing had been erected in the street at the time of Lorenzo the Magnificent's wedding to Clarice Orsini. See Pietro Parenti, *Delle nozze di Lorenzo de' Medici con Clarice Orsini nel 1469; Informazione di Piero Parenti Fiorentino* (Florence: F. Bencini, 1870), 9: "e per diverse vie la condussono il Marito, la quale era parata ornatissimamente, e fatto un palco nella via dove si danzassi."

130. See Masi, *Ricordanze*, 235–36; Cambi, *Istorie*, 22:142. Neither Masi nor Cambi mention Alfonsina's involvement. See also Goro Gheri's account of the celebrations, ASF, Goro Gheri 4, fol. 288r.

131. "Avevono a ricivere la sposa in sul palchetto." Cummings, *Politicized Muse*, 217. In her account of the festivities, Alfonsina noted that the *palco* was used for dancing after the guests had feasted: "Andorono fuori su el palco alle XXI hora, dove danzorono fino alle XXIIII hore, et la Duchessa anche lei ballò dua danze.… " See *Le feste celebrate in Firenze nel II giorno delle nozze di Lorenzo de' Medici Duca d'Urbino con Maddalena della Tour d'Auvergne, Nozze* Puccini-Manfredi (Florence: Tipografia dell'Arte della Stampa, 1882), 9.

132. See Cummings, *Politicized Muse*, 217–18, for the suggestion that one of the *logge* mentioned by Cerretani was the *loggia terrena* at the corner of the Medici palace, generally thought to have been closed off in 1517. See also Reiss, "Cardinal Giulio de' Medici," 457–58.

133. Masi, *Ricordanze*, 236: "El convito di dette nozze si fecie nel giardino che era di detta palazzo; che, per fare detto convito, si disfecie e lastricossi tutto con lastre piane commesse come si lastricano queste belle corte.… " Cf. Bülst, "Uso e trasformazione," 120–21.

134. *Le feste celebrate* (*Nozze* Puccini-Manfredi). The text is also available in Tommasini, *La vita*, 2:1010–11; Parronchi, "La prima rappresentazione," 52–53. For an English translation, see Cummings, *Politicized Muse*, 102–3.

135. *Le feste celebrate* (*Nozze* Puccini-Manfredi), 9: "Hovi a dire che la Pictura di N.S. et monsignor reverendissimo de' medici et Rossi el Duca la fece mectere sopra alla tavola, dove mangiava la Duchessa et li altri signori, in mezo.… "

136. *Le feste celebrate* (*Nozze* Puccini-Manfredi), 9, for Alfonsina's remark that the portrait "veramente rallegrava ogni cosa."

137. Richard Sherr, "A New Document Concerning Raphael's Portrait of Leo X," *Burlington Magazine* 125 (1983): 31–32.

138. Bernice F. Davidson, *Raphael's Bible: A Study of the Vatican Logge* (University Park: Pennsylvania State University Press, 1985), 11, draws attention to the pontiff's winter costume and suggests that the portrait was painted in the winter of 1517–18, which would have been prior to Lorenzo's departure for France.

139. "E così fuorono finite le nozze con pochissima satisfatione delle genti et tutto causorono due cose, l'una avaritia grandissima di Madonna [Alfonsina].… " Cerretani in Cummings, *Politicized Muse*, 106, 223, n. 21. I am grateful to Anthony Cummings who reminded me of this revealing passage.

140. For an exhaustive compendium of letters detailing the young man's decline, see Andrea Corsini, *Malattia e morte di Lorenzo de' Medici Duca d'Urbino, studio critico di medicina storica* (Florence: Istituto Micrografico Italiano, 1913), 144–225. Corsini proposes that Lorenzo di Piero died of

tuberculosis, but denies the possibility that the duke was syphilitic, despite the frequency with which this piece of information was recorded by contemporaries (ibid., esp. 91). See also Pieraccini, *La stirpe,* 1:269–79. Pieraccini did believe that Lorenzo suffered from the venereal disease, although he concurred with Corsini that tuberculosis (both intestinal and pulmonary) brought the duke to his death at the age of twenty-seven. An account of Lorenzo's death is found in Ann Carmichael, "The Health Status of Florentines in the Fifteenth Century," in *Life and Death in Renaissance Florence,* ed. Marcel Tetel and others (Durham, N.C.: Duke University Press, 1989), 29–31.

141. "Per vedere se il mutar aria lo poteva fare spelagare di questa infermità." Pieraccini, *La stirpe,* 1:274.

142. Pieraccini, *La stirpe,* 1:184. For Alfonsina's declining health, see n. 147 below.

143. Pieraccini, *La stirpe,* 1:275, 451.

144. Foster, *Study of Lorenzo de' Medici's Villa,* 1:114, 419, n. 368.

145. Pieraccini, *La stirpe,* 1:277, 281.

146. For Cardinal Giulio's role at Poggio a Caiano, see Reiss, "Cardinal Giulio de' Medici," esp. 463–66.

147. On Alfonsina's illness and death, thought to have been due to uterine cancer, see Corsini, *Malattia e morte,* 55–58; Pieraccini, *La stirpe,* 1:181–87; Carmichael, "Health Status," 32. For her funeral, see Filippo Strozzi's letter of 13 February 1520 quoted above in n. 4.

148. For Alfonsina's tomb marker in Santa Maria del Popolo, see Enzo Bentivoglio and Simonetta Valtieri, *Santa Maria del Popolo a Roma* (Rome: Bardi, 1976), 121–26, fig. 43 and plate 48, nos. 117 and 118. See their fig. 44 for a reconstruction of the trompe l'oeil effect. For the now lost inscription, see the various transcriptions in ibid., 121–22, n. 3; Vinenzo Forcella, *Iscrizioni delle chiese e d'altri edifici di Roma dal secolo XI fino ai nostri giorni…,* 14 vols. (Rome, 1869–84), 1:336, n. 1282.

149. On Alfonsina's will, the original of which is ASF, MAP 157, 107, see Lefevre, "Il patrimonio cinquecentesco," 96–97, 129–30, appendix 4, for the "Ragguaglio storico" preceding ASF, MAP 157, which details aspects of Alfonsina's legacy. A copy of her last wishes, part of which is in the vernacular, is found in the Orsini Family Archive, Special Collection 902, box 240, #15, at the University of California at Los Angeles University Library. After Alfonsina's death, Cardinal Giulio de' Medici defrauded Clarice out of a large share of her inheritance. For this unsavory deed, see Devonshire-Jones, *Francesco Vettori,* 147.

150. Bentivoglio and Valtieri, *Santa Maria del Popolo,* 123, 201.

151. Cambi, *Istorie,* 22:158–59: "E addì di detto in sabato mattina si fece un bello asequio quì in S. Laurentio cholla capanna piena di falchole, e co' panni neri per tutta la nave del mezzo della Chiesa."

152. "Come si costuma andara quando si fa le Messe di qualche gran maestro." Masi, *Ricordanze,* 245.

153. Strocchia, *Death and Ritual,* 230.

154. For this beautiful but little-studied altarpiece, see Sydney J. Freedberg, *Painting of the High Renaissance in Rome and Florence,* 2 vols. (Cambridge, Mass.: Harvard University Press, 1961), 1:496. For Sogliani, see Vasari-Milanesi, 5:123–33; Colnaghi, *Dictionary,* 251–53. On the fourth-century North African martyr Saint Arcadius, see *Bibliotheca sanctorum,* 13 vols. (Rome: Istituto Giovanni XXIII nella Pontificia Università lateranense, 1961–70), 2:cols. 346–48.

155. Alfred Scharf first proposed this identification in an unpublished *festshcrift* for Walter Friedländer now in the Kunsthistorisches Institut in Florence. See Paatz and Paatz, *Kirchen von Florenz,* 5:573, n. 231. Scharf's essay was subsequently published in English – see Alfred Scharf, "Bacchiacca: a New Contribution," *Burlington Magazine* 70 (1937): 60–66. See also Howard S. Merritt, "The Legend of St. Achatius: Bacchiacca, Perino, Pontormo," *Art Bulletin* 45 (1963): 258–633. esp. 260, note 6. Freedberg, *Painting of the High Renaissance,* 1:496 identifies the martyr saint as Acasio

(Achatius). For this saint, see *Bibliotheca sanctorum,* 1: cols. 134–36. For Bacchiacca's *predella,* see Lada Nikolenko, *Francesco Ubertini Called Il Bacchiacca* (Locust Valley, N.Y.: J. J. Augustin, 1966), 42, figs. 21–23. I am grateful to Robert LaFrance who has generously shared with me helpful bibliography along with his ideas concerning the origins and dating of the Bacchiacca *predella.*

156. See *Butler's Lives of the Saints,* ed. Herbert J. Thurston and Donald Attwater , 4 vols. (1956; reprint, London: Burnes and Oates, 1981), 1:70–71.

157. "Fece poi per madonna Alfonsina moglie di Piero de' Medici una tavola, che fu posta per voto sopra l'altar della cappella de' Martiri nella chiesa di Camaldoli di Firenze." Vasari-Milanesi, 5:124. On San Salvatore and the Cappella dei Martiri, see Richa, *Notizie istoriche,* 9:142–55, esp. 147– 48; Paatz and Paatz, *Kirchen von Florenz,* 5:41–48, esp. 45; Fantozzi Micali and Roselli, *Le soppressioni,* 244–45.

158. See Richa, *Notizie istoriche,* 5:33; Paatz and Paatz, *Kirchen von Florenz,* 4:503, 573, n. 231.

159. Tommasini, *La vita,* 2:77; Maguire, *Women of the Medici,* 195.

160. For the longstanding Neapolitan tradition of women with political power, see Joan Kelly's classic essay, "Did Women Have a Renaissance?" reprinted in Joan Kelly, *Women, History, and Theory: The Essays of Joan Kelly* (Chicago: University of Chicago Press, 1984), 27, 30–31. See also Armin Wolf, "Reigning Queens in Medieval Europe: When, Where, Why," in *Medieval Queenship,* ed. John Carmi Parsons (New York: St. Martin's Press, 1998), 175–78.; Bruce L. Edelstein, "Nobildonne napoletane e committenza: Eleonora de'Aragona ed Eleonora di Toledo a confronto," *Quaderni Storici* 35/104, fasc. 2 (2000): 295–329.

161. King, "Medieval and Renaissance Matrons," 380. The work of Lawrence Jenkens on Caterina Piccolomini and Bruce Edelstein on Eleonora da Toledo also contradicts King's blanket statement. See their contributions to this volume.

Two Emilian Noblewomen and Patronage Networks in the Cinquecento

Katherine A. McIver

"Wherever courts existed as centers of wealth, artistic activities, and discourse, opportunities abounded for intelligent women to perform in the role as patron of the arts and culture."[1] Margaret King's statement is particularly relevant for north Italian noblewomen, even though modern studies of the patronage of Renaissance women have been dominated by Isabella d'Este of Ferrara.[2] Treated as an exception instead of the rule in modern literature, Isabella has remained "la prima donna del mondo" with regard to patronage issues and the Renaissance woman. Although Isabella pushed the boundaries well beyond the limits imposed on women by Renaissance society, an examination of several women from feudal courts such as Mantua and Ferrara reveals that Isabella was not unique. In the literature of the period, for instance, Veronica Gambara of Correggio was often put on equal ground with Isabella as a woman and as a patron of the arts. Furthermore, in northern Italy during the early sixteenth century, women from feudal courts at Correggio, Fontanellato, and Scandiano had the connections and influence that allowed them to extend commissions to prominent north Italian artists, including Antonio Allegri (called Correggio), Francesco Parmigianino, and Nicolo dell'Abate.

While there were a number of women patrons active in the area now known as the Emilia-Romagna, in northern Italy, the focus of this paper will be on two noblewomen, Veronica Gambara (1485–1550) and Silvia Sanvitale (c. 1512–84). My intent here is to present a preliminary exploration of the systems of patronage in the feudal courts to which these women belonged.

Like Isabella d'Este, Veronica Gambara of Correggio was interested in collecting exotic fabrics and fashionable objects and, as her letters to Ludovico Rossi, her agent in Bologna, suggest, she was concerned with her self-image and with keeping in touch with the latest trends.[3] Of special interest to Gambara was the promotion of the career of Antonio Correggio; through her friend Scipione Montino della Rosa, the artist received commissions in nearby Parma.[4] While Gambara's patronage and attitudes were similar to those of Isabella d'Este, Silvia Sanvitale of Scandiano seems to have worked largely behind-the-scenes in promoting the aspirations of her husband, Count Guilio Boiardo (d. 1553). Sanvitale was instrumental in defining the subject of the frescoes for Boiardo's Camerino dell'Eneide (1540s) in the Rocca Nuova at Scandiano, and documents show that Sanvitale withdrew funds from her private account in Bologna to pay Nicolo dell'Abate for painting the Camerino. Evidence suggests that this commission was a cooperative one between husband and wife. A similar case might also be made for Paola Gonzaga of Fontanellato, whose husband, Gian Galeazzo Sanvitale (1496–1550), is generally credited with commissioning Francesco Parmigianino to paint the so-called *stufetta* in his Rocca in the 1520s.[5]

While the activities of women such as Isabella d'Este and Veronica Gambara as patrons may seem exceptions instead of the rule, it is important to note that the typical woman of the period was seen in contemporary literature as a caretaker best defined and motivated by her responsibilities to the men of her family.[6] As the fifteenth-century Franciscan Saint Bernardino put it, "As the sun is the ornament of the heavens, so the wise and prudent wife is the ornament of the home."[7] In general, women were thought incapable of dealing with business, politics, and war—though many of them did, including Isabella d'Este and Veronica Gambara.[8] At the same time, however, Torquato Tasso, in his *Discorso* of 1562, and other writers suggest that in certain cases status might take precedence over gender. Tasso writes: "In heroic ladies is a heroic virtue that compares with that of a man, and for women gifted with this virtue, modesty is no more appropriate than courage or prudence, nor is there any distinction between their deeds and offices and those of heroic men."[9] Tasso suggests that a noblewoman called by her status to leadership would be required to deny her feminine nature to fulfill her social and political duties. While the exceptional woman of aristocratic birth, such as Isabella or Veronica, might find an individual place in history, more often her leadership qualities would be shrouded in the literary conventions of the day, which typically praised her beauty, learning, culture, and moral virtue. Indeed, the image of Veronica Gambara projected in contemporary writings conforms more closely to traditional rhetoric than to Tasso's exemplar.

Take, for example, Ludovico Ariosto's praise of Gambara in his *Orlando Furioso*, published in 1532:

> Oh what fair, what virtuous ladies, what excellent knights I see gracing the shore, and what good friends, too. I shall be forever indebted to them for the happiness they feel at my return. I can see Mamma Beatrice out on the tip of the pier with Ginevra and other ladies of Correggio. With them is Veronica Gambara, the darling of Apollo and the choir of muses. I can see another Ginevra from the same family, and Julia with her. I see Ippolita Sforza and my lady Domitilla Trivulzio, who was raised in the muses' sacred grotto. I can see you, Emilia Pia, and you Margherita, in company with Angela Borgia and Graziosa. Fair Bianca and Diana d'Este are there with Riccarda and their other sisters.[10]

Ariosto enjoyed the hospitality of Gambara's court in the 1530s, and Veronica established a pension of 100 gold ducats for the poet.[11]

Veronica Gambara of Correggio

Veronica Gambara was born in 1485 in Pratalboino near Brescia, one of the feudal holdings of the Gambara family. Of an ancient, noble, and learned family, Gambara was the daughter of Gianfrancesco Gambara and Alda Pia, whose portrait was painted by Altobello Melone (Milan, Pinacoteca di Brera, c. 1510–16). Veronica married Giberto X, Lord of Correggio, in 1509.[12] She brought to her marriage connections to some of the most illustrious families in north Italy: the Carrara, the Pico, the Estensi, and the Gonzaga. Her mother was the sister of Emilia Pia, whom Castiglione upheld as a model of virtue in his *Book of the Courtier* and whom Ariosto included among his illustrious ladies in *Orlando Furioso*.[13] Giberto distinguished himself as a soldier serving King Ferdinand of Naples and Popes Sixtus IV, Innocent VIII, Alexander VI, and Julius II; after his marriage to Gambara he retired to court life in Correggio.[14] While in Bologna in 1515, Veronica and Giberto were presented to Pope Leo X and King Francis I of France; the king was particularly taken with Gambara's erudite wit, and later he visited the court of Correggio as her guest and friend.[15] At her husband's death in 1518, Gambara became head of the family. She ruled the town of Correggio and in

1538, after repelling the invasion of Galeotto Pico, Lord of Mirandola, staved off famine and sheltered widows, orphans, and refugees.[16]

Today Gambara is ranked, as are Vittoria Colonna and Gaspara Stampa, among the important sixteenth-century Italian poets, but little attention has been given to her activity as a patron of the arts.[17] Gambara received the same education as her three brothers and two sisters; she learned Latin, studied philosophy, and her brother Camillo taught her a little Greek. Although she wrote a commentary on sacred scripture, her greatest love was poetry. Fifty poems survive, as do some 137 letters.[18] Her poems, most of which are sonnets, include love poems addressed to her husband; poems on political issues of the day directed to Charles V, Pope Paul III, and Francis I; and devotional poems, two of which were sent to Vittoria Colonna. She also wrote Virgilian verse in praise of the pastoral countryside around Brescia and Correggio. The most important influence on her poetry was Pietro Bembo; she wrote him for the first time in 1502, at the age of seventeen, and two years later she began sending him her sonnets. Bembo became her poetic mentor and close friend.[19]

Veronica Gambara was not the first woman at Correggio to be distinguished during her lifetime as a *letterata* and patron of the arts. As will become evident in this chapter, several feudal courts in Emilia-Romagna had traditions of learned women who commissioned paintings and architecture. These women, who were often interconnected both to each other and to the Este court through marriage, corresponded frequently and formed a network to promote their own interests and those of their families.

Before turning to a discussion of Gambara's patronage, we must discuss one of her important models, Francesca of Brandenburg (d. 1512), widow of Borso da Correggio (d.1504) and niece of Barbara of Brandenburg, Marchesa of Mantua. In 1504, the year of her husband's death, Francesca commissioned a chapel dedicated to Mary in the monastery church of Corpo del Cristo in Correggio; this was presumably a funerary chapel for her husband.[20] In this instance, Francesca was following a tradition well established at Correggio and elsewhere. Her predecessor, Cassandra Colleoni, daughter of Bartolomeo Colleoni (general of the Venetian republic) and wife of Niccolo da Correggio, had established a family chapel in 1475 at San Francesco in Correggio.[21] As we will see, Veronica Gambara followed in their footsteps and also commissioned a chapel.

About 1507 Francesca of Brandenburg began the construction of the Palazzo dei Principi to the south of the medieval Castelvecchio in Correggio (fig. 1). A cornerstone near the main entrance carries an inscription identifying Francesca as the patron; the design is generally attributed to Biagio Rossetti.[22] Francesca must also have been responsible for the fresco decoration (c. 1508) in two of the rooms, which is attributed to Antonio Bartolotti degli Ancini, a local painter sometimes thought to be the teacher of both Antonio Correggio and Correggio's uncle, Lorenzo; other paintings of the Castel Vecchio have been attributed to Lorenzo Costa.[23] One of the rooms, the Sala Piccola on the ground floor, had a frieze featuring playing *putti* and lunettes with a variety of figures; the ceiling decoration included a balustrade with monkeys, parrots, and other birds.[24] The second room, the Sala Magna, also on the ground floor and across the courtyard from the Sala Piccola, is decorated with a frieze of monochrome grotesque figures; in the center of this frieze on one wall is an inscription that reads *MDIIIIIIII, S.P.Q.R., O.C.N, Erexit Francesca de Brandenburgo*, while in the center of the adjoining wall are the *stemmi* of Borso da Correggio and Francesca of Brandenburg.[25] As will become evident, Veronica Gambara followed Francesca's example.

Considered vivacious, genial, and a brilliant conversationalist, Veronica seems to have been genuinely admired and respected for her intelligence and charm.[26] As Gambara's reputation as a poet and *letterata* grew, her small court attracted learned visitors. Her studiolo in the Castelvecchio in the city and her Casino di Delizie in the country became fashionable

McIver Fig. 1. Biagio Rossetti, Palazzo dei Principi, Correggio, ca. 1507 (photo: author)

settings for cultured nobility; poets, princes, and prelates gathered there to discuss literary and philosophical issues and to dance, dine, sing, and tell stories. Odoardo Rombaldi suggests that by 1511 Gambara had established a literary academy at Correggio.[27] Both the Castelvecchio, with its impressive library, and the Casino were splendidly decorated. In order to better accommodate her illustrious guests, Gambara began as early as 1517 to commission frescoes for the rooms they would occupy; Antonio Correggio was responsible for some of the frescoes in the Casino.[28] Among the circle of friends who met there regularly were Pietro Aretino, Pietro Bembo, Bernardo Cappello, Ercole d'Este of Ferrara, Isabella d'Este of Mantua, Francesco Maria Molza, and Giangiorgio Trissino, to name only a few.[29] In the fall of 1511, Isabella d'Este and her husband Francesco Gonzaga were at the court of Correggio; by November of the same year, Antonio Correggio was recorded at the court of Mantua.[30] Gambara and Isabella, who had begun corresponding in 1503, are described in contemporary literature as close friends.[31] Perhaps it was through Gambara that Isabella became aware of Antonio Correggio.

Beyond governing her deceased husband's territories and raising her two sons, Gambara had a particular interest in promoting the artistic career of Antonio Correggio, who was a close friend to her and her family.[32] On several occasions he acted as a witness in legal matters; on 24 January 1534, for instance, he witnessed the deed of dowry for the marriage of Chiara da Correggio to Ippolito Gambara, Veronica's son.[33] While Correggio's paintings for Gambara and those close to her are unfortunately lost, numerous documents show her involvement with his career.[34] In 1512 Gambara commissioned a *Saint Jerome* from Correggio for her chapel in San Domenico; the painting is known through a description in a now lost letter to her brother, Brunero.[35]

In a letter of 3 September 1528 to Isabella d'Este, Gambara refers to Correggio as "our master Antonio Allegri" and describes a *Saint Mary Magdalen in the Desert* he was painting for Isabella, a work that cannot be identified today.[36] The letter implies a certain intimacy between Correggio and Gambara, who seems to be acting as a kind of mediator for the artist. Perhaps she was responding to an inquiry from Isabella regarding Correggio's progress, or perhaps it was Gambara who had motivated Isabella to commission this work by Correggio for her collection. Panel paintings by Correggio in Veronica's Casino are also mentioned in an undated letter of Luigi di San Giusto that discusses the elegant setting of Veronica's court: "In your casino in Correggio there are marvels of art. By your painter Antonio Allegri are his paintings of the Madonna…."[37] Further evidence suggests that it was through Gambara's friend Scipione Montino della Rosa that the painter received commissions in nearby Parma. These commissions culminated in the decoration of San Giovanni Evangelista, including its cupola with the *Vision of Saint John on Patmos of the Risen Christ* and the frescoes in the apse, the north transept, the choir, the nave, and the del Bono Chapel.[38]

Vasari's *Life of Correggio* does not mention Gambara, but he does refer to two of her correspondents who owned paintings by the artist. In Bologna, the Ercolani owned Correggio's *Noli Me Tangere* (Madrid, Museo del Prado).[39] Gambara's letters to Agostino Ercolani refer to his frequent visits to Correggio, suggesting that he would have had many opportunities to see works by her favorite painter and that Gambara was again promoting him.[40] According to Vasari, Federico Gonzaga, Marchese of Mantua, commissioned Correggio to paint two works, a nude *Leda* (Berlin, Gemaldegalerie) and a *Venus* (now identified with the *Danae* in the Galleria Borghese in Rome).[41] Gambara corresponded with Gonzaga and visited his court on a number of occasions. On this basis we can speculate that it was through his association with Gambara that Gonzaga gained an interest in Correggio's work.[42]

Along with her two sons, Ippolito and Gerolamo, and her brother, Uberto, Veronica Gambara attended the coronation of Emperor Charles V in Bologna in 1530; after meeting Gambara, with whom he had corresponded since 1521, the emperor decided to visit Correggio. On 23 March 1530 he arrived at the Casino di Delizie; he stayed two days, occupying the rooms decorated by Antonio Correggio in 1528. These rooms were surely chosen to provide an appropriately impressive setting for the emperor.[43] Also in attendance for the occasion were Gambara's sons, her nephew Manfredo III, his wife Lucrezia d'Este and their children, as well as other notable families of Correggio.[44] Antonio Correggio, in charge of decorating the town, including the preparation for a pageant and other extravagant celebrations, was functioning in the role of court painter to Gambara.[45] As such he would have been responsible for devising decorative arches, scenery and props for the pageant, and costumes, banners, and other *apparati* for the festivities, all of which, of course, are lost.

In the emperor's honor Gambara built a new, two-mile-long highway leading to the Casino; it was called the Via dell'Imperatore.[46] Charles V's processional entry into Correggio and his journey along the new highway to the Casino must have been similar to his entrance into Mantua, although on a smaller scale.[47] Dressed in gold brocade and mounted on a white horse, he was accompanied by an entourage of cardinals, princes, and soldiers. Moreover, while it was a less politicized event than Bologna, his arrival in Correggio and the accompanying celebrations and procession through the city to the Casino would have been a most significant event for Veronica Gambara as the local ruler. Each time she traveled this highway to her home, she could relive Charles V's procession, re-enacting the event and its imagery of imperial power. She had not only glorified Charles V, but herself and her city as well.[48] Charles V granted Gambara's family various privileges during his visit and told her that he loved her for three reasons: for her renowned virtue, for the nobility of her family, and because she was the sister of Uberto, governor of Bologna, whom he greatly loved.[49] While Charles V's imagery adheres to the traditional rhetoric of the day, Gambara's appropriation of imperial imagery and the exaltation of her image by the emperor's visit relate to the traditional ideals of a male ruler.[50]

Veronica Gambara's letters reveal that she maintained important contacts throughout Italy; after her husband's death, these contacts, essential for any ruler, were also advantageous for her position as Correggio's head of state and for the promotion of her sons' careers. In addition, her letters and sonnets demonstrate that she was profoundly concerned with the political issues of the day. Gambara seems to have wielded a significant amount of power and influence on those around her; such connections could only have benefited the career of her favorite artist, Antonio Correggio.[51]

My focus thus far has been primarily on Gambara's patronage of Antonio Correggio; further evidence indicates that, like Francesca of Brandenburg, Gambara also commissioned architecture—more specifically, two chapels. In the church of San Domenico, Gambara built a chapel dedicated to Saint Jerome as the site for the tomb of her husband, who died in 1518; Gambara also gave financial support to both the church and its convent.[52] It is interesting to note here that Francesca, who lived until 1512, may have had some impact on Veronica, who arrived at Correggio early in 1509. In her will of 1512, Francesca left funds for the completion of the chapel she had dedicated to the Virgin and Saint Jerome in San Domenico; it was Gambara who saw the work to completion and who also donated a painting by an unknown painter of *Christ Handing the Veil to Veronica* (whereabouts unknown) to this chapel.[53]

Gambara's second chapel, dedicated to Saint Anthony of Padua, was located in the church of San Francesco in Correggio. In her will dated 1549, just a year before her death, Gambara established a fund for this chapel and for her tomb there; it was consecrated on 13 July 1550.[54]

Silvia Sanvitale of Scandiano

"La gentile contessa di Scandiano, la parmense e nobile Silvia Sanvitale, donna eletto ingegno e di gran cuore…. "[55] In the Renaissance, the joint patronage of a husband and wife, while particularly difficult to document, seems likely to have been more common than is generally acknowledged.[56] In a patriarchal society where women are relegated to a secondary role, it is often difficult to unravel specific details regarding their patronage. If we are to believe the rhetoric of Alberti, Castiglione, and other writers, the Renaissance woman was to have a public image that submerged her individuality in order to present herself as an image of grace and beauty that would reflect upon her husband's status. Whereas Gambara, like her friend Isabella d'Este, seems to have moved beyond these limitations, Silvia Sanvitale worked within them. Through marriage alliances, networks of communication between families, and financial security, women like Sanvitale from the feudal courts of the Emilian region had a certain independence as well as the means to become patrons of art. Working within societal limits, Sanvitale utilized the patronage systems available to her in at least one cooperative venture with her husband, Giulio Boiardo (d. 1553), Count of Scandiano.

Silvia Sanvitale, the daughter of Gianfrancesco Sanvitale (d. 1519) (the brother of Giangaleazzo Sanvitale, Count of Fontanellato), married Giulio Boiardo in 1523; Silvia's mother, Laura Pallavicina, was the daughter of Federico Pallavicini, Marchese of Zibello, a town outside Parma.[57] Silvia brought to her marriage illustrious connections to the Pallavicini, the Sanvitale, the Lupi of Soragna, and the Farnese of Parma. Laura Pallavicina's niece Virginia was married to Ranuzio Farnese, while Silvia's brother Alfonso (a close friend of Ottavio Farnese, the nephew of Pope Paul III) was married to Gerolama di Galeazzo Farnese. Silvia's mother, Laura, was close friends with Paul III, who visited her on two occasions at Scandiano in 1543. Clearly, Giulio's marriage to Silvia was an advantageous one that brought him a higher social status, a certain amount of financial security, and ties to some of the most prominent families in northern Italy.[58]

From the very beginning, Sanvitale took an active part in the affairs of the court at Scandiano, sometimes in conjunction with her husband and sometimes on her own, as her letters attest. Clearly marrying beneath her, Sanvitale's active role at court brings to mind a passage from Tarquato Tasso's *Il padre di famiglia*, published in 1580:

> When it happens, however, through some accident of fortune that a man marries a woman who is his superior, he ought to honor her—never forgetting that he is her husband—more than he would a woman of his own or an inferior rank.

He should treat her as a companion in love and their daily lives but as a superior in some public acts that are solely for the sake of appearances—in those gestures of honor, for example, that are customarily made to others out of good breeding. For her part, she must think that no difference in rank is as great as the difference in nature between men and women.[59]

Like Veronica Gambara, Sanvitale came from a learned and prominent family and was a well-educated woman with literary interests, including a special fondness for Virgil's *Aeneid*.[60] Also similar to Gambara, Sanvitale received literary tribute; Bernardo Tasso praised her and Lucia Bertani wrote a sonnet in her honor. Lodovico Domenichi's *Dialoghi* of 1562 includes Silvia as a participant in a philosophical dialogue on love.[61] Sanvitale corresponded with Ariosto, Domenichi, Tasso, and others. For a period between her husband's death in 1553 and the death of his brother Ippolito in 1560, Silvia ruled Scandiano with the full approval of Ercole II d'Este, Duke of Ferrara. Until her death in 1584, she maintained control over a variety of territories.[62]

The counts of Scandiano were vassals of the powerful Este family of Ferrara. Giovanni Boiardo (d. 1523), Giulio's father, became count shortly after the death of his cousin, the poet Matteo Maria Boiardo (d. 1494); Giulio's older brother ruled Scandiano briefly until his death in 1528. Giulio, the second son, however, had to wait nearly three years before the Este granted him investiture as Count of Scandiano.[63] Giulio was most likely concerned about his self-image; in collaboration with his wife he commissioned an elaborate fresco cycle for his Camerino that would help define who he was and his place in the world. In 1523, the year of his father's death and his marriage to Silvia Sanvitale, Giulio took up the renovation campaign of the medieval Rocca begun by his father. Together Giulio and Silvia transformed the structure into a Renaissance palace rich with paintings, sculpture, precious objects, and a notable library. In these renovated surroundings, Boiardo and Sanvitale played host to a pope, cardinals, princes, artists, poets, and other worthies.[64] Clearly emulating the Este of Ferrara and the Sanvitale of Fontanellato, they set out to create a court to be respected and envied.

Expanding the campaign begun by his father, Giulio transformed the façade of the Rocca into a symmetrical structure with a pair of matching towers, following the model of the Castello at Ferrara and the Rocca at Fontanellato. We know from documents that the sculptor Bartolomeo Spani and the architect Alberto Pacchioni were actively engaged at the Rocca during this period.[65] While it is difficult to discern the extent of Silvia's involvement in the renovation campaign or how much of her own money she committed to the project, her role was clearly an active one.[66] The majority of documents connected with the Rocca and its renovation and decoration open with the coupled names of Silvia Sanvitale and Giulio Boiardo.[67] One cannot help but think that it was her prestigious family connections that allowed her the authority to make decisions. Women in feudal courts where the importance of landowning was emphasized had a certain amount of financial security; Sanvitale even had private bank accounts in Bologna, as will be discussed below.

Giulio and Silvia did not stop at renovation; their court became one of culture and luxury. The Boiardi, who had a townhouse in Ferrara, frequently participated in Este court functions, and in turn entertained the Este and their court both in Ferrara and at their newly renovated and decorated palace at Scandiano. Their four daughters, who were tutored by the court humanist Sebastiano Corrado, also received musical training. While their musical patronage was not equal to that of the Este, surviving documents list two musicians at Scandiano in the 1540s, Dominus Jugdulus Menon and Minolo. Theatrical productions were performed as well. In 1544, in honor of Giberto Pio of Sassuolo, *Tragidia d'Egisto*, a play by Tommaso Mattacoda, physician and poet of Scandiano, was performed, followed by Matteo Maria Boiardo's *Il Timone*.[68]

As the renovation progressed, Giulio and Silvia's primary interest became their new private apartments on the second floor of the Rocca: the Camerino dell'Eneide, the Salone delle Feste, a bedroom, and a library. Our focus here is the Camerino dell'Eneide, where, ca. 1540, Nicolo dell'Abate was commissioned to paint an innovative decorative program related to Giulio's preoccupation with his self-image—a project in which Silvia had a vested interest and took an active role in promoting. The Camerino, a rectangular room with a fireplace and no windows, was in spatial terms not unlike the *stufetta* at Fontanellato painted twenty years earlier.[69] Nicolo's decoration of the Camerino consists of twelve scenes from Virgil's *Aeneid* disposed above monochrome battle scenes and surmounted by lunettes decorated with landscapes and cityscapes. Female *all'antica* figures adorn the eight pendentives and direct the viewer's attention to the octagon in the center of the ceiling, where Giulio Boiardo, wearing a white plumed hat, looks down upon the viewer (fig. 2). He peers over the right shoulder of his wife, Silvia Sanvitale, who wears a large sleeved dress and holds a book, presumably of music. Over Sanvitale's left shoulder, her mother, Laura Pallavicina, gazes outward. Other members of their court are depicted as well.[70]

Documents of August 1540 and 5 January 1546 refer specifically to the Camerino.[71] The document of 1546 describes the space and discusses Giulio and Silvia's involvement in the decorative campaign. A fragmentary letter from Ippolito Bertolotti mentions the frescoes and other objects in the room, such as sculpture and curios.[72] Noting Sanvitale's erudition and fondness for Virgil, he goes on to say that it was through her influence that the *Aeneid*

McIver Fig. 2. Nicolo dell'Abate, Ceiling Octagon, Camerino dell' Eneide, Rocca Nuova, Scandiano, 1540s (photo: author)

cycle was chosen, and he also credits her with the selection of Nicolo dell'Abate as painter. The document of 1540 is even more interesting because it refers to a payment made by Silvia. Laura Pallavicina, Silvia's mother and a widow since 1519, not only controlled her daughter's dowry (Giulio visited her in Parma in 1542 to discuss financial matters), but also set up bank accounts for her daughter in Bologna. [73] It is from one of these accounts that money was withdrawn to make the 1540 payment to Nicolo dell'Abate.[74] Though this information indicates that it was Silvia who made this first recorded payment to the artist, it does not clarify who was responsible for the original commission. Some speculation may not be out of order here. Nicolo had been working for Gerolamo Pallavicini at Busseto just prior to coming to Scandiano; Laura Pallavicina's uncle ruled Busseto. It is perhaps this earlier connection with the Pallavicini that led Silvia to suggest to her husband that Nicolo be given the commission. An elusive figure throughout the renovation and decorative campaign, Laura Pallavicina seems to have wielded significant power both at Scandiano and Fontanellato. Her involvement at Scandiano goes beyond the simple management of her daughter's dowry. Documents related to her financial dealings indicate that she provided funds for the Rocca project; payment records from 1536, for instance, list the scudi Pallavicina paid for "ornaments" for the Rocca and includes a list of materials.[75] A document of 28 August 1540 discusses negotiations between Giulio, Silvia, and Laura in regards to the Camerino and the use of Silvia's money to pay for its decoration and for its furnishings.[76] Laura Pallavicina seems to have been the motivator behind her daughter, a conclusion that can be symbolically supported by her physical position as she gazes over Silvia's shoulder in the octagon (fig. 2).

The family ties to Fontanellato, with its *stufetta* painted twenty years before by Parmigianino, could have been on the minds of Silvia and Laura when it came time to decorate the Camerino dell'Eneide. What better artist than Nicolo, whose style had affinities with Parmigianino's, and who was already known to the family? Recall too that the choice of the *Aeneid* as the dominant decorative element in the Camerino was Silvia's; it is likely that she consulted the court humanist, Sebastiano Corrado, on the appropriateness of this subject. Concerned with the most effective means of promoting both her husband's self-image and her own, Silvia's choice of the *Aeneid*, which is connected to ideas about the origins of the Modenese region, established Giulio's lineage and linked him and his family to the Este of Ferrara, who claimed descent from Ruggiero.[77]

Once Nicolo was hired, it was probably Sanvitale who encouraged the artist to study Parmigianino's paintings in the *stufetta* at Fontanellato as an appropriate model. While a correlation can be made between Parmigianino's vegetation and figures in the *stufetta* and Nicolo's musicians and singers in the Salone delle Feste, it is the layout of the *stufetta*'s frescoes that is of importance for the Camerino. We know that it was through his patron, Silvia Sanvitale, that Nicolo dell'Abate gained access to Parmigianino's frescoes.[78] It is clear that Nicolo was impressed by the decoration of the rectangular room which, like the Camerino at Scandiano, had a fireplace and was without windows. In both the *stufetta* and Camerino, the illusionistic arrangement of lunettes and pendentives acts as a transition from wall to ceiling. Parmigianino's *putti* stand on platformlike supports in front of the framework that marks the plane along the ceiling cove. With twisting motions of their bodies, they turn in varying degrees into the space of the room. The *putti* posed within their pendentives fulfill a double function: they complement the design of the lunettes and act as directional guides to the ceiling.[79] At Scandiano, Nicolo's adaptation of Parmigianino's *putti* for his female *all'antica* figures attest to his familiarity with Parmigianino's work.

Without a doubt, the motivation for Giulio and Silvia to create a space that would be the crowning achievement of their renovation campaign was connected to Giulio's newly attained position as Count of Scandiano and the desire to impress important visitors who came to Scandiano. Pope Paul III came to visit his friend Laura Pallavicina twice in 1543 and to see the frescoes about which he must have heard so much.[80] As an avid patron of the arts, Paul III would likely have appreciated the complex imagery of the room, and it seems that Nicolo dell'Abate's style would have appealed to the pope's aesthetic sensibilities. Described as a "jewel" in contemporary literature, the Camerino was the centerpiece of the Rocca Nuova.[81] It served as a *studiolo* for both Giulio and his wife, a refuge from the cares of the world, and a place to collect precious objects, listen to music, study, and entertain their closest friends and allies. The Camerino functioned as a space for the most intimate occasions; few would have been allowed in this room. The Salone delle Feste, on the other hand, operated as the formal locale for public events. The large rectangular room found on the same floor as the Camerino was where feasts, assemblies, audiences, receptions and other court celebrations were held.

In looking back to the Gonzaga *stufetta* at Fontanellato, Sanvitale had more than her husband's aspirations in mind. Marrying socially beneath her, Sanvitale could have been inspired to try to create something even more stunning than the *stufetta*.[82] The Camerino dell'Eneide afforded her the opportunity to surpass her relatives at Fontanellato or to put herself at least on equal ground with them. This type of rivalry is well known; take, for example Isabella d'Este's competition with her brother, Alfonso d'Este, in a variety of matters, including the acquisition of art objects and the sponsoring of music and musicians in musical performances.[83] By promoting her husband and his self-image, Silvia was promoting herself in much the same way as Veronica Gambara had when she built the imperial highway for Charles V. Less conspicuous than Gambara, Sanvitale worked behind-the-scenes in a cooperative venture with her husband. Though at times she was eclipsed by Giulio Boiardo's shadow, Silvia Sanvitale clearly took an active role in court life and patronage of the arts at Scandiano. A close examination of the placement of the figures in the ceiling octagon (fig. 2) of the Camerino dell'Eneide and of the documentation presented here suggests that the octagon can be understood as visual evidence of a bilinear family structure (a theme that I have discussed elsewhere).[84] The octagon is a personal statement by which Sanvitale and Pallavicina speak to ideas of a bilinear family, in particular their family and its power and social position in the north Italian court system.

In this chapter we have seen two different types of patrons at work. Veronica Gambara, like her friend Isabella d'Este, independently commissioned works from Antonio Correggio and actively promoted his career. Silvia Sanvitale, on the other hand, presents a clear case of a woman who took an active role with her husband in commissioning paintings, sculpture, and even architecture; she funded at least one project, suggested artists, and also defined the parameters of the commissions, whether for a single painting or an entire room. At the same time, she made a personal statement about herself and her position at court through her dominant role in the ceiling octagon and her active participation in activities at Scandiano. Intimate connections between the two women can be found; both Veronica Gambara and Silvia Sanvitale were widows who never remarried and who ruled their husbands' territories after their deaths. Gambara and Sanvitale were connected through marriage; Giulia Gambara, Silvia's mother-in-law, was a relative, albeit distant, of Veronica. Such alliances suggest the networking available to and important for women, and recommend that we broaden our understanding of the opportunities open to women for patronage. Through further exploration of these and similar networks, a clearer picture of women as patrons will surely evolve.

Notes

1. Margaret L. King, *Women of the Renaissance* (Chicago: University of Chicago Press, 1991), 160.

2. For basic bibliography on Isabella d'Este as a patron see Sylvia Ferino-Pagden, ed., *Isabella d'Este: Fürsten und Mäzenatin der Renaissance: "La Prima Donna del Mondo,"* exh. cat. (Vienna: Kunsthistorizches Museum, 1994); Rose Marie San Juan, "The Court Lady's Dilemma: Isabella d'Este and Art Collecting in the Renaissance," *Oxford Art Journal* 14 (1991): 67–78; *Le Muse e il principle: Arte di corte nel rinascimento padana*, ed. Alessandra Mottola Molfino and Mauro Natale (Milan: F. C. Panini, 1991); Marianne Pade, Lenne Waage Petersen, and Daniela Quarta, eds., *La Corte di Ferrara e il suo mecenatismo: 1441–1598* (Ferrara: Panini, 1987); Giuseppe Papagno and Amedeo Quondum, eds., *La Corte e lo spazio: Ferrara e Estense* (Rome: Bulzoni, 1982); William F. Prizer, "Isabella d'Este and Lucrezia Borgia as Patrons of Music," *Journal of the American Musicological Society* 38 (1985): 1–33; idem, "North Italian Courts, 1460–1540," in *The Renaissance: The 1470's to the End of the Sixteenth Century*, ed. Iain Fenlon (Englewood Cliffs, N.J.: Prentice-Hall, 1989), 133–35; idem, "Isabella d'Este and Lorenzo da Pavia, Master Instrument Maker," *Early Music History* 2 (1982): 87–127. See also Stephen Kolsky, "An Unnoticed Description of Isabella d'Este's Grotta," *Journal of the Warburg and Courtauld Institutes* 52 (1989): 232–35; idem, "Images of Isabella d'Este," *Italian Studies* 39 (1984): 47–62. See also Clifford M. Brown and Anna Maria Lorenzoni, "Isabella d'Este and Giorgio Brognolo nell'anno 1496," *Atti e memorie della Academia Virgiliana di Mantova*, n.s. 41 (1973): 97–122.

3. In addition to the works cited in n. 2 above, see also J. M. Fletcher, "Isabella d'Este, Patron and Collector," in *Splendours of the Gonzaga,* ed. David S. Chambers and Jane Martineau, exh. cat. (London: Victoria and Albert Museum, 1981), 51–63. Isabella d'Este's letters have been published by Alessandro Luzio, *Mantova e Urbino: Isabella d'Este ed Elisabetta Gonzaga nelle relazioni famigliari* (1893; reprint, Bologna: A. Forni, 1976); Alessandro Luzio and R. Renier, "La cultura e le relazioni letterarie d'Isabella d'Este Gonzaga," *Giornale storico della letteratura italiana* 42 (1903): 75–111.

4. On della Rosa, see Ireneo Affò, *Ragionamento del Padre Ireneo Affo… sopra una Stanza dipinta dal Celeberrimo Antonio Allegri da Correggio nel Monistero di S. Paolo in Parma* (1794; reprint, ed. F. Barocelli, Parma: Carmignani, 1969); Umberto Benassi, *Storia di Parma*, 5 vols. (1899–1906; reprint, Bologna: Forni, 1970), 5:69, n. 3.

5. See Odoardo Rombaldi, Roberto Gandini, and Giovanni Prampolini, *La Rocca nuova di Scandiano e gli affreschi di Nicolà dell'Abate* (Genoa: Casa di Risparmio di Reggio Emilia, 1982); Sydney J. Freedberg, *Parmigianino: His Works in Painting* (Westport, Conn.: Greenwood Press, 1971). See Cecil Gould, *Parmigianino* (New York: Abbeville, 1994) for basic bibliography concerning the Camerino dell'Eneide at Scandiano and the *stufetta* at Fontanellato, which Gould believes was a cooperative venture between husband and wife (see n. 69 below). Patronage in Parma is the subject of Valeria Vecchi's article, "Tre donne Sanvitale nel primo cinquecento a Parma," *Aurea Parma* 80.3 (September-December 1996): 287–94.

6. Leon Battista Alberti, *I Libri della famiglia,* trans. Renée Neu Watkins (Columbia: University of South Carolina Press, 1969), 115–16; Bonnie S. Anderson and Judith P. Zinsser, *A History of Their Own: Women in Europe from Prehistory to Present* (New York: Harper and Row, 1988), 1:429. See also King, *Women of the Renaissance*, 157–239; Natalie Zemon Davis and Arlette Farge, eds., *A History of Women: Renaissance and Enlightenment Paradoxes* (Cambridge, Mass.: Harvard University Press, 1993), 9–167. See also Roger Crum's chapter in this volume.

7. Luciano Banchi, ed., *Le prediche volgari di San Bernardino da Siena nella Piazza del Campo l'anno 1427* (Siena, 1880–88), 2:118–20. The translation is from Eugene F. Policelli, "Medieval Women: A Preacher's Point of View," *International Journal of Women's Studies* 1 (May—June, 1978): 287.

8. For Isabella d'Este, see n. 2, and for Veronica Gambara, see her letters published by Pia Mestica Chiapetti, *Veronica Gambara: Rime e lettere* (Florence: G. Barbèra 1879).

9. Torquato Tasso, *Discorso della virtu feminile e donnesca*, in *Le prose diverse di Torquato Tasso*, ed. Cesare Guasti (Florence: Le Monnier, 1875), 2:203–12.

10. Canto 46, 3–4; trans. from Lodovico Ariosto, *Orlando Furioso*, trans. Guido Waldman (Oxford: Oxford University Press, 1983), 557.

11. Riccardo Finzi, *Il Correggio nel suo tempo* (Modena: Aedes Muratoriana, 1957), 35; Rinaldo Corso, *Vita di Giberto III da Correggio, colla vita di Veronica Gambara* (Ancona, 1560), 20–23. Much of the available information on Gambara comes from Corso, who wrote his work in 1554.

12. Riccardo Finzi, *Umanità di Veronica Gambara* (Reggio Emilia: n.p., 1969), 10. They may have married in 1508, but Gambara did not come to Correggio until 1509. Giberto's first wife was Violante, daughter of Antonio Maria Pico, Conte di Mirandola; Violante bore Giberto two daughters, Costanza and Ginevra.

13. Veronica Gambara was connected to the Este family through the marriage of her paternal uncle, Galasso, to Margherita d'Este in the 1460s. Her maternal uncle, Giberto Pio (d. 1500), married Lenora Bentivoglio; their grandson Giberto (d. 1554) married Elisabetta d'Este. Her family was also connected through marriage to the Pico and the Gonzaga. See Odoardo Rombaldi, *Correggio, città e principato* (Modena: Banca populare, 1979), 40, 64; Rinaldo Corso, *Cenni biografici intorno a Veronica Gambara da Correggio* (Ancona, 1566). Gambara's husband, Giberto X da Correggio, was also connected to the Este. His paternal uncle, Niccolo, married Beatrice d'Este, sister of Borso d'Este; their son Niccolo il Postumo da Correggio (1450–1508) was educated at Ferrara and remained in service to the Este (Rombaldi, *Correggio*, 40, 64).

14. Finzi, *Umanità*, 10–11.

15. Unfortunately, we have little information concerning preparations for his visit. Gambara corresponded with King Francis I throughout her life and directed many of her sonnets to him (Rombaldi, *Correggio*, 61–64, 142–43; Finzi, *Umanità*, 16–29; Clementina de Courten, *Veronica Gambara: Una gentildonna del cinquecento* (Milan: Casa Editrice "EST," 1934), 42, 62–82. See also ASMod, Carteggio di principi e signori, Correggio, b. 1146–50, as well as ASPr, Feudi e comunita, Correggio, b. 42–50.

16. She wrote to Ludovico Rossi in Bologna requesting that he buy grain from Romagna and send it to Correggio (Chiappetti, *Rime e lettere*, 180–81). See also Rombaldi, *Correggio*, 62, for a discussion of the rulership of Correggio before and after Giberto's death. Much of this is recorded in Corso's work cited in n. 11; see particularly his *Vita di Veronica Gambara*, 20–23.

17. Richard Poss, "Veronica Gambara: A Renaissance Gentildonna," in *Women Writers of the Renaissance and Reformation*, ed. Katharina Wilson, 47–66 (Athens: University of Georgia Press, 1987); Frank J. Warnke, *Three Women Poets: Renaissance and Baroque* (Lewisburg, Penn.: Bucknell University Press, 1987); *The Defiant Muse: Italian Feminist Poems from the Middle Ages to the Present*, ed. Beverly Allen, Muriel Kittel, and Karla Jane Jewel (New York: Feminist Press at the City University of New York, 1986); Chiapetti, *Rime e lettere*; de Courten, *Gambara*; Finzi, *Umanità*; Giuseppe Toffanin, *Le piu belle pagine di Gaspara Stampa, Vittoria Colonna, Veronica Gambara e Isabella Morra* (Milan: Fratelli Treves, 1935); Luigi Amaduzzi, *Undici lettere inedite di Veronica Gambara* (Guastalla, 1889); Antonia Chimenti, *Veronica Gambara: Gentildonna del rinascimento*, crit. ed. (Reggio Emilia: Magis, 1996). See also Fiora A. Bassanese, "What's in a Name? Self-Naming and Renaissance Women Poets," *Annali d'italianistica* 7 (1989): 104–15; Fiora A Bassanese, "Private Lives and Public Lies: Texts by Courtesans," *Texas Studies in Literature* 30.3 (Fall 1988): 295–319.

18. Finzi, *Umanità*, 8, n. 39. Chiapetti, *Rime e lettere*, publishes 126 of Gambara's letters. These include thirty letters to Lodovico Rossi of Bologna (her friend and purchasing agent), fifty-two letters to Agostino Ercolani of Bologna, thirteen letters to Pietro Aretino, ten letters to Pietro Bembo (Chiapetti also includes twenty-one of Bembo's letters to Gambara), and letters to Francesco Maria Molza, Ludovico Dolce, Cardinal Ridolfi, and others. Many of these are formal letters concerning the education and future of her two sons, Ippolito, named after Ippolito d'Este, and Gerolamo.

Others, personal and friendly, discuss poetry, the acquisition of fabric, food, and so on. Some letters concern political issues, and others, like the one to Molza, thank the sender for sonnets. Amaduzzi, *Undici lettere,* publishes another eleven letters. Most of these are to Ippolito d'Este, Francesco Gonzaga, and Federico Gonzaga concerning the welfare of her two sons. Finzi, *Umanità,* 39, n. 26, mentions a letter to Isabella d'Este dated 1 February 1503, but does not discuss its contents; see n. 29 below. Gould, *Paintings,* 27–28, 186, 190–92, refers to and publishes Gambara's letter to Isabella d'Este (2 September 1528) concerning Correggio's painting of Mary Magdalen, as well as documents concerning Gambara and Correggio.

19. Rombaldi, *Correggio,* 61–64, 142–43; Finzi, *Umanità,* 9–29; Courten, *Gambara,* 12, 42–51; Poss, "Veronica Gambara," 47–49; ASMod, Carteggi di prinicipi e signori, Correggio, b. 1146 and 1147. See also Chiappetti, *Rime e lettere,* for Gambara's letters to and from him.

20. Rombaldi, *Correggio,* 1972, 160; and the notarial records for 1504 in the Archivio Notarile, Biblioteca Comunale, Correggio. The Spanish destroyed San Domenico in 1556, as was Veronica Gambara's Casino; both were located outside the walls of the city.

21. Finzi, *Umanità,* 35–36.

22. Finzi, *Correggio,* 30. "Francesca di Brandenburgo uxor borsi comitis corregiae, qual post abitum viri aulam hanc anno 1507 propriis impensio constuendam curavit." Francesca remained in residence in the Palazzo dei Principi until her death in 1512. Thereafter, the structure replaced the Castelvecchio as the seat of the rulers of the city.

23. Finzi, *Correggio,* 29–30.

24. Finzi, *Correggio,* 27, 29–30. These frescoes survive, but they have been extensively restored.

25. Finzi, *Correggio,* 27, 29–30.

26. Rombaldi, *Correggio,* 61–64; Finzi, *Umanità,* 13–24; Poss, "Veronica Gambara," 49–50.

27. Poss, "Veronica Gambara," 62.

28. Courten, *Gambara,* 42, 46–47. Finzi, *Umanità,* 17, 46, n. 46, refers to Quirino Bulbarini's (1663–1742) "Memorie da cronista correggese," without giving the date of publication or pagination. Rinaldo Corso (1525–82), a *letterato* at the court of Correggio, wrote *Vita di Giberto III da Correggio, colla vita di Veronica Gambara* (Ancona, 1560), *Gli Honori della casa da Correggio con due capitoli in lode delle donne correggi* (Ancona, 1566), and *Cenni biografici intorno a Veronica Gambara da Correggio* (Ancona, 1566). For Gambara's relationship with Correggio, see David Ekserdjian, *Correggio* (New Haven: Yale University Press, 1997), 1, 6, 16, 166, 172.

29. Finzi, *Umanità,* 16, 20–21; Courten, *Gambara,* 62.

30. See Corso, *Vita di Veronica Gambara,* 20–21.

31. See ASMod, Carteggi ambasciatori, Mantova, b. 1, for Gambara's letter to Isabella dated 26 December 1503, as well as a letter from 1500. Isabella was particularly fond of Niccolo il Postumo da Correggio, who was a poet at Ferrara. In 1512 Antonio Correggio was working in Mantua at San Andrea, painting a fresco of the four evangelists in the cupola of the funerary chapel of Andrea Mantegna (Finzi, *Correggio,* 11; Ekserdjian, *Correggio,* 23–27).

32. Her son, Ippolito, was born in 1510; her second son, Gerolamo, was born in 1511. Ippolito pursued a military career, serving first the Venetian Republic and then Charles V. Gerolamo followed a career with the church, serving as papal nuncio in 1538 with Francis I and later with both Charles V and Philip II of Spain. He became a cardinal in 1561 (Finzi, *Umanità,* 11).

33. Gould, *Paintings,* 186, 188, 190–92. Gould publishes the following documents: 5, dated 1 February 1519, mentions Correggio signing documents concerning his family in the palace of Manfredo da Correggio, son of Borso da Correggio; 18, dated 15 February and 18 February, 1525, refers to Correggio as a witness in the presence of Veronica Gambara and Manfredo da Correggio in a

continued examination of the legality of his uncle's gift; 26, dated December 1532, in which Correggio acts as a witness to a deed by which Manfredo da Correggio nominated Paolo Brunori as envoy to Charles V; 37, dated 7 January and 15 January, 1533, in which the painter acts as a witness in Manfredo's palace to the deed of dowry of Chiara on her marriage to Ippolito da Correggio, son of Veronica Gambara.

34. See n. 33 above.

35. Finzi, *Correggio*, 11. The painting, now lost, was at one time recorded in the Grimani collection. The painting is mentioned by Quirino Bulbarini in his "Memorie;" the 1512 letter seems to have been only a fragment and, like the painting, apparently is lost. Corso also mentions this painting and Gambara's letter in Corso, *Vita di Veronica Gambara*, 20–23. In 1514 Correggio was painting for the Confraternity of Saint Maria della Misericordia; Gambara was involved with the confraternity and seems to have acted as a mediator between confraternity and artist.

36. The letter is in the ASMod, AG, Autografi V. Gambara, under the date 3 September 1528. Gould, *Paintings*, 27, 186.

37. See n. 4. "Il suo casino a Correggio era una meraviglia d'arte e di buon giusto. Per lei Antonio Allegri dispense le sue pui belle madonne; gli arazzi del celebre Rinaldo Duro ornarono le sue stanze, che risuonavano di lieti e onesti ragionamenti, di canti, di poesia. Tutto intorno a lei era eleganza e squisitezza; la piccola reggia accoglieva il fiore della nobilita dei natali e dell'ingegno; il marchese di Mantova, l'Ariosto, il Bembo, il Molza e due volte Carlo V convennero intorno a lei." Toffanin, *Belle pagine*, 233. Unfortunately, he gives neither the source nor the date of this document.

38. Rombaldi, *Correggio*, 142–43; Finzi, *Umanità*, 17–18; Toffanin, *Belle pagine*, 233; Poss, "Veronica Gambara," 49; Gould, *Paintings*, 27–28, 186, 190–92.

39. Vasari-Milanesi, 4:116; Gould, *Paintings*, 224–25.

40. Chiapetti, *Rime e lettere*, 189–265. The earliest letter from Gambara to Agostino dates from 1518.

41. Vasari-Milanesi, 1:280; Gould, *Paintings*, 194–95, 270–71.

42. Amaduzzi, *Undici lettere*, 27–29. The possibility that his mother, Isabella d'Este, introduced him to both Gambara and Correggio cannot be ruled out.

43. Unfortunately, we do not have even a description of Correggio's painting for this room, nor do we have descriptions of Charles V's processional entry.

44. Courten, *Gambara*, 42–43; Finzi, *Umanità*, 14, 17–18.

45. Finzi, *Umanità*, 17–18; Courten, *Gambara*, 42–45; Rombaldi, *Correggio*, 61–64.

46. Finzi, *Umanità*, 18, 44, n. 49.

47. See Amedeo Belluzzi, "Battista Covo, Giulio Romano, e Gerolamo Mazzola Bedoli a San Benedetto in Polirone," in *Dal Correggio a Giulio Romano* (Mantua: Casa di Mantegna, 1989): 119–31; Giordano Conti, "L'incoronazione di Carlo V a Bologna," in *La città effimera e l'universo artificiale del giardino*, ed. Marcello Fagiolo (Rome: Officina, 1980), 38–46. Conti's map and itinerary of Charles V's travels through Italy in 1529–30 include both Mantua and Correggio.

48. Amaduzzi, *Undici lettere*, 9, 37, n. 9. See Randolph Starn and Loren Partridge, *Arts of Power: Three Halls of State in Italy, 1300–1600* (Berkeley: University of California Press, 1992), 151–63; Roy Strong, *Art and Power: Renaissance Festivals, 1450–1650* (Berkeley: University of California Press, 1984), 78–86, for a discussion of the imagery of procession. Also of interest are Anthony M. Cummings, *The Politicized Muse: Music for Medici Festivals, 1512–1537* (Princeton: Princeton University Press, 1992); Bonner Mitchell, *Italian Civic Pageantry in the High Renaissance: A Descriptive Bibliography of Triumphal Entries and Selected Other Festivals for State Occasions* (Florence: Leo S. Olschki, 1979); Andrew C. Minor and Bonner Mitchell, *A Renaissance Entertainment: Festivals for the Marriage of Cosimo I, Duke of Florence in 1539* (Columbia: University of Missouri Press, 1968).

49. Finzi, *Umanità,* 16; Courten, *Gambara,* 42–43.

50. This is not unlike Isabella's resolve to take over the government of Mantua during her husband's imprisonment in 1509–10; see Stephen Kolsky, "Images of Isabella."

51. Finzi, *Umanità,* 24–25, 30–31, 48, n. 75. At least two of Gambara's contemporaries can be associated with commissions for paintings by Correggio. Briseide Colla, widow of Orazio Bergonzi, commissioned Correggio to paint the *Madonna of Saint Jerome* (Parma, Galleria Palatina, c. 1525–27). She paid him 400 lira for the work and seems to have been especially pleased with it. In the year of her death, 1528, she donated the painting to her family chapel in San Antonio, Parma (Finzi, *Correggio,* 28). The painting was removed from the chapel in the eighteenth century. See Luigi Pungileone, *Memorie istoriche di Antonio Allegri detto il Correggio* (Parma: Dalla Stamperia Ducale, 1817–21), 183–84; Stefano Bottari, *Il Correggio* (Novara: Istituto Geografico de Agostini, 1990), 76, 193; Gould, *Paintings,* 262; Mary Vaccaro's chapter in this volume; and Ekserdjian, *Correggio,* 193–94. Whether Colla originally intended the work to decorate her husband's funerary chapel or her own is not known.

Ginevra Rangone, poet, writer, and widow of Giangaleazzo da Correggio (d. 1517), is said to have commissioned from Correggio a portrait for her future husband, Marchese Luigi Alessandro Gonzaga di Castelguelfo (St. Petersburg, Hermitage, 1518). This portrait is also sometimes identified as Veronica Gambara; Rangone was praised, along with Gambara, by Ariosto. See n. 10 above.

A third woman, Giovanna Placenza, was clearly a patron of Correggio, as Maureen Pelta shows in her work on the Convent of San Paolo in Parma. Maureen Pelta has worked extensively on Placenza's role as patron of the Camera di San Paolo. The additional examples of these three women suggest that Correggio was widely patronized by women.

52. ASMod, Testamento di Veronica Gambara, 14 August 1548, notary Bartolomeo Zuccardi, Casa e Stato Controversia, b.73. See Katherine A. McIver, "The 'Ladies of Correggio': Veronice Gambara and her Matriarchal Heritage," *Explorations in Renaissance Culture* 26 (2000): 1–20. For other examples of funerary chapels commissioned by widows for their husbands, see the chapters by Elizabeth Pilliod, Mary Vaccaro, and Carolyn Valone in this volume.

53. 11 October 1512. Testamento di Francesca di Brandenburgo, notary F. A. Bottoni. Biblioteca Comunale, Correggio, Archivio Notarile, no. 358 and 6 March 1514. ASMod Carteggi di principi e signori, Correggio, b. 1146.

54. 14 August 1549. Testamento di Veronica Gambara, notary Bartolomeo Zuccardi. Casa e Stato Controversia, b. 74, Archivio di Stato, Modena; Finzi, *Umanità,* 30, n. 75. Unfortunately, we know little about this chapel and tomb. Both were destroyed by the Spanish in 1556; see n. 20. Two other women of the region also commissioned ecclesiastical architecture. Antonia Pallavicini, first wife of Giacomo Antonio Sanvitale, Count of Fontanellato, built a chapel dedicated to San Giovanni Battista in the church of Santa Croce in 1486. His second wife and widow, Veronica da Correggio, sister of Giberto X da Correggio (Gambara's husband), allotted funds for the establishment of a convent, the Sanuario della Madonna, in 1512; she died four months later.

55. This is from a chronicle which is partially published by Aderito Belli, *Storia di Scandiano* (Reggio Emilia: Anonima Poligrafica Emiliana, 1928), 42.

56. Other essays in this volume, especially those by Molly Bourne and Bruce Edelstein, deal with similar issues.

57. Gemiriano Prampolini, "Cronaca di Scandiano al 1543," Biblioteca Municipale Panizzi, Reggio Emilia, MS Turri A113.

58. Rombaldi and others, *Rocca,* 77. The Farnese have an ancient connection to the Parmese region. For an extensive description of family connections see the anonymous "Historia dell'origine et huomini illustri della famiglia Sanvitale," ASPr, Archivio Sanvitale, b. 883B. See also: Biblioteca Palatina, Parma, MS Parma 1193; MS Parma 378.

59. Rombaldi and others, *Rocca,* 77; letter dated 3 October 1538, Carta Mattacodi, Archivio di Stato, Scandiano. "Ma quando pure avenga che per qualch'accidente di fortuna l'huomo tolga donna superiore per nobilità in morglie, dee, non dimenticandosi pero d'esser marito, pui onorarla che non farebbe una donna d'eguale o di minor condizione, e averla per compagna nell'amore e nella vita, ma per superiore in alcuni atti di publica apparenza, i quali da niuna esistenza sono accompagnati: quali sono quegli onori che per buona creanza si soglion fare altrui; ed ella dee pensare che niuna differenza di nobilita puo esser si grande che maggior non sia quella che la natura ha posta fra gli uomini e le donne, per le quali naturalmente nascono lor soggette." Torquato Tasso, *Il padre di famiglia,* in *Tasso's Dialogues: A Selection,* trans. Carnes Lord and Dain A. Trafton (Berkeley: University of California Press, 1982), 82–83.

60. Giovanni Battista Venturi, *Storia di Scandiano* (Modena: G. Vincenzi Compagno, 1821), 104, cites a letter from Silvia full of references to classical and devout literature, and to the *Aeneid* in particular. Venturi cites it as belonging to an otherwise unidentified edition of "lettere di valorose donne," nos. 8, 34, published in Venice in 1548.

61. Ludovico Domenichi, *Dialoghi* (Venice, 1562), 104. See also George Nugent, "Anti-Protestant Music for Sixteenth-Century Ferrara," *Journal of the American Musicological Society* 43 (1990): n. 61.

62. Ippolito seems to have been too infirm to handle the duties of leadership (Rombaldi and others, *Rocca,* 77); he is characterized as "infermo di mente" in contemporary literature. After 1566 the Boiardo holdings shift to Ottavio Tiene, husband of Giulio and Silvia's daughter, Laura Boiardo.

63. Venturi, *Storia,* 100–3.

64. Rombaldi and others, *Rocca,* 78.

65. See the letter of 20 January 1536, which mentions Bartolomeo Spani, and payment records of 1544, which mention the architect, Alberto Pacchioni. The documents and letters concerning the building campaigns are contained in the "Carteggio del reggimento" in the Archivio di Stato, Reggio in Emilia, arranged by date, and ASMod, Carteggio dei Rattori dello Stato, Rebbio, b. 6 and 7 for the years 1531–33. See also ASMod, Archivio per materie ingeneri, Terzo Terzi, b. 6 and 7 for the years 1531–33. See also ASMod, Archivio per materie ingeneri, Terzo Terzi, b. 5 for the years 1535–40, and particularly Giulio Boiardo, 6 August and 7 March 1535.

66. See a series of letters from Silvia Sanvitale to the *fattore* at Scandiano that support the assumption that she took an active role. These letters, dating from 1538 to 1543, are published by Venturi, *Storia,* 55, and are ASScan, "Carte Mattacodi."

67. Rombaldi and others, *Rocca,* 77–80, 100–2. In addition to those cited in n. 65 above, see also the letters and documents concerning Silvia's role in the Archivio di Stato, in Reggio Emilia: see ASRE Archivio Notarile, Deliato Mattacoda, b. 766, 11 November 1535; 4, 8, and 20 December 1536; 28 April 1540; 25 May 1540; atto of 28 August 1540; 3 October and 6 October 1540; b. 767, 16 July 1543; 5 January 1546; and b. 1046, Bertolani Nicolo, 20 January and 20 December 1536. In the ASScan, see Archivi, antico filza 30, "Libro delle corte del comune di Scandiano 1544," which mentions the architect, Alberto Pacchioni.

68. Rombaldi and others, *Rocca,* 79; and ASRE, Archivio Notarile, Deliato Mattacoda, b. 766 for the year 1543, which mentions Menon and Giulio Boiardo. Sebastiano Corrado discusses these activities in the introduction to his *M.T. Ciceronis Epistolas ad Atticum* (Venice 1549), which was dedicated to Giulio Boiardo.

69. In 1523 Parmigianino was commissioned to paint the upper portion of a small room known as a *stufetta* or as the "bagno di Paola," in the Rocca at Fontanellato. Giangaleazzo Sanvitale is generally credited with the commission. It is my contention, however, that the paintings were commissioned by his wife, Paola di Lucovico Gonzaga, whose father was the count of Sabbionetta. Like Silvia Sanviatle, Paola worked cooperatively with her husband. Moreover, the iconographic program of the room is intimately connected to Gonzaga, the loss of her son, and her hopes for future children. Also of significance here is the fact that not only were the Gonzaga and Sanvitale inti-

mately connected through marriage, but Gambara was connected to Fontanellato as well. Her sister-in-law, Veronica da Correggio, was Giangaleazzo Sanvitale's mother and, therefore, Paolo Gonzaga's mother-in-law. Veronica Gambara, Silvia Sanvitale, and Paola Gonzaga were connected through marriage. This is only one of many examples that I have discovered concerning women's networks through marriage alliances. For basic literature on Fontanellato, see Freedberg, *Parmigianino*; Gould, *Parmigianino*; Brown, "Parmigianino at Fontanellato"; Ute Davitt-Asmus, "Fontanellato I: Sabatizzare il mondo. Parmigianinos bildnes des Conte Galeazzo Sanvitale," *Mitteilungen des Kunsthistorischen Institutes in Florenz* 27 (1983): 3–39; Enrico Grassi, *Fontanellato: La famiglia e la Rocca Sanvitale* (Noceto: n.p., 1932); Franco Maria Ricci, *Fontanellato* (Milan: F. M. Ricci, 1994); Luigi Sanvitale, *Memorie intorno alla Rocca di Fontanellato ed alle pitture che vi fece Francesco Mazzola detto il Parmigianino* (Parma, 1857); V. Sgarbi, "Il Bagno di Diana," *FMR* 14 (1983): 49–72; Augusta Ghidiglia-Quintavalle, "Boudoir di Paola Gonzaga, Signora di Fontanellato," *Paragone* 209 (1967): 3–17; Ghidiglia-Quintavalle, *Fontanellato, guida artistica* (Parma: Edizione del Comune, 1977); Ghidiglia-Quintavalle, *Nobilita ed arte di Fontanellato* (Parma: Mario Fresching, 1951); Katherine A. McIver, "Love and Death and Mourning: Paola Gonzaga's Camerino at Fontanellato," *Artibus et Historiae* 36 (1997): 101–8; Marzio dall'Acqua and Mario Calidoni, *Fontanellato: Storia, arte, ambiente di una corte di pianura* (Fontanellato: Commune di Fontanellato, 1998): 73–96. The archives of Fontanellato and Parma are rich with material that may yet yield more facts than those of which we are now aware. See the Archivio di Stato, Parma, Archivio Sanvitale-Gonzaga, buste 2, 4, 24, 43, 55, and in the Archivio Gonzaga, busta 1; in both archivi, documents are filed by dates. I wish to thank Carolyn Valone, who first alerted me to Paola's activities.

70. For bibliography on Nicolo dell' Abate, see Sylvie Béguin, *Mostra di Nicolo dell'Abate*, exh. cat. (Bologna: Palazzo dell'Archiginnasio, 1969); Béguin, "Nicolo dell'Abate" in *The Age of Correggio and the Carracci*, ed. Francis Smith, John P. O'Neill, and Emanuela Spinsanti (Washington: National Gallery of Art, 1986), 45–48; Anton Boschloo, *Il fregio dipinto a Bologna da Nicolo dell'Abate ai Carracci* (Bologna: Nuova Alfa, 1984); Giovanni Godi, *Nicolo dell'Abate e la presunta attivita del Parmigianino a Soragna* (Parma: L. Battei, 1976); Erika Langmuir, "The Early Narrative Cycles of Nicolo dell'Abate" (Ph.D. diss., Stanford University, 1972); Langmuir, "Arma Virumque…Nicolo dell'Abate's Aeneid Gabinetto for Scandiano," *Journal of the Warburg and Courtauld Institutes* 39 (1976): 151–70; Amalia Mezzetti, *Per Nicolo dell'Abate: Mostra di affreschi restaurati* (Modena: Poligrafico Artioli, 1970).

71. See nn. 65–67 above for cited documents. For specific references to the Camerino and Nicolo dell'Abate, see ASMod, particularly Giulio Boiardo, letter of 21 December 1540; ASRE, Archivo del Comune di Reggio, provvigioni, documents for 6 September 1540; 10 March and 2 July 1542; ASRE, Archivio Notarile, Deliato Mattacoda, b. 766: 28 April 1540; 25 May 1540; 3 October 1540; and 16 October 1540.

72. ASRE, Archivio Notarile, Deliato Mattacoda, busta 766, 5 January 1546.

73. Rombaldi and others, *Rocca*, 78. Laura Pallavicina had been a widow for some time; she arranged her daughter's marriage, as well as that of her son, Alfonso. The notary Delaito Mattacoda records many of the documents related to Pallavicina's financial dealings; see ASRE, Archivio Notarile, Deliato Mattacoda, b. 766 for letters from 30 April 1540; 25 May 1540; 3 October and 16 October 1540. Also of interest in the same busta is a document dated 20 December 1536 that records payments in scudi by Laura Pallavicina for "ornaments" for the Rocca, and includes a list of materials. Her involvement at Scandiano seems to go beyond the simple management of her daughter's dowry. Like Veronica Gambara, Laura Pallavicina took an active role in the promotion of the careers of her children, particularly her son, Alfonso, as well as in politics and other activities. Pallavicina never remarried.

74. This payment is ASRE, Archivio Notarile, Deliato Mattocoda, b. 766, atto of 28 August 1540, which discusses negotiations between Giulio, Silvia, and Laura regarding the Camerino and the use of Silvia's money.

75. ASRE, Archivio Notarile, Deliato Mattacoda, b. 766, 4 December and 8 December 1536, and b. 1046, 20 January and 10 December 1536.

76. ASRE, Archivio Notarile, Deliato Mattocoda, b. 766, atto of 28 August 1540.

77. See Katherine A. McIver, "The Room and the View: A New Look at Giulio Boiardo's Private Apartments at Scandiano," in *Fortune and Romance: Boiardo in America*, ed. JoAnne Cavallo and Charles Ross (Tempe, Ariz.: Medieval and Renaissance Texts and Studies, 1998), 281–83.

78. See Prampolini, "Cronaca di Scandiano," and Francesco Morsiani, "Supplemento all cronica di Prampolini," MS Turri C38, both in the Biblioteca Municipale Panizzi, Reggio Emilia. Prampolini states: "La contessa Silvia Sanvitale Boiardo, nota per la sua erudazione e sensibilità artistica, interviene accanto pittore nel ridegere il piano della decorazione della Rocca" (11).

79. Freedberg, *Parmigianino*, 51.

80. The notary Delaito Mattacoda records Laura Pallavicina's presence at Scandiano and the pope's visits on 13 June and 3 July 1543; see ASRE, Archivio Notarile, Deliato Mattacoda, b. 766 under these dates. See also ASMod, Carteggio dei Rettori dello Stato, Reggio, busta 11 for 29 March 1543; 1 and 2 April 1543; 16 July 1543, and ASMod, Carteggio dei Rettori dello Stato, Scandiano, b. 1, 15 April 1543 for further evidence of the pope's visit to Scandiano. Pallavicina had been in correspondence with the pope for years.

81. See the dedication in Corrado, *M.T. Ciceronis Epistolas*, and the notary Deliato Mattacoda in ASRE, Archivio Notarile, b. 766, particularly documents for the years 1542–44.

82. Much of this information is contained in Geminano Prampolini's "Cronica" and in the unpublished manuscript, "Historia dell'origine et huomini illustri della famiglia Sanvitale," ASPr, Archivio Sanvitale, b. 883B.

83. See n. 2 above, particularly the works by Prizer.

84. I wish to thank Carolyn Valone for suggesting that I consider this concept. For bibliography on the bilinear family see David Herlihy, introduction, in Christiane Klapisch-Zuber, *Women, Family, and Ritual in Renaissance Italy* (Chicago: University of Chicago Press, 1985), ix–x; David Herlihy, "Did Women Have a Renaissance? A Reconsideration," *Medievalia et Humanistica* 13 (1985), 11–15; Giulia Calvi, "Diritti e Legami, madri, figli, stato in Toscana," *Quaderni storici* 86 (August 1994): 487–510. See also Giulia Calvi, *Il Contratto morale: Madri e figli nella Toscana moderna* (Bari: Laterza 1994), particularly her introduction and chapter one. Horizontal and cognatic, the bilinear model explores what the wife and her family contributed to the marriage and passed on to their children, as opposed to the patrilinear model, which emphasizes the father's lineage and its transmission to the children. On the bilinear family see Carolyn Valone, "Mothers and Sons: Two Paintings for S. Bonaventura in Early Modern Rome," *Renaissance Quarterly* 53 (2000): 108–32, and Katherine McIver, "Matrons as Patrons: Power and Influence in the Courts of Northern Italy in the Renaissance," *Artibus et Historiae* 43 (2001): 120–45.

Dutiful Widows: Female Patronage and Two Marian Altarpieces by Parmigianino

Mary Vaccaro

Throughout his career Francesco Mazzola, better known as il Parmigianino, worked for female patrons, secular as well as religious, on projects large and small. He painted a room with mythological scenes for a local noblewoman, a baby crib for another Parmese lady, and an altarpiece for Bolognese nuns.[1] Two of his best-known altarpieces were made for secular female patrons. Such a statement is hardly surprising, since sixteenth-century historical sources refer, albeit briefly, to these women. According to Giorgio Vasari, for example, Parmigianino made for a certain "madonna Maria Bufolina da Città di Castello" a painting that corresponds in description to the so-called *Vision of Saint Jerome*, now in the National Gallery in London (fig. 1).[2] Vasari also indicates that Parmigianino later created for the "sorella del Cavalier Baiardo" the altarpiece known today as the *Madonna of the Long Neck*, now in the Uffizi in Florence (fig. 2). A document for the latter painting, published in the mid-nineteenth century, identifies the patron as the Parmese noblewoman Elena Baiardi.[3]

Despite the early mentions of these patrons, little effort has been made to consider them more fully. In this chapter I will focus on the two secular women for whom Parmigianino painted Marian altarpieces. Who were Maria Bufalini and Elena Baiardi, and what was the nature of their commissions? Related archival and biographical information should help elucidate our inquiry. Documents reveal that both Maria and Elena were decorating their husbands' funerary chapels. Each altarpiece should, therefore, serve as an index to uxorial duty— that is, a widow's commemoration of her deceased spouse. But to what extent is each painting an expression of the patron herself? I intend to look first at the specific circumstances of each project, and then I will attempt to discern any patterns that might potentially be significant for the study of secular female patronage in the Renaissance. In particular, both altarpieces invite questions about the relationship of widows to the Virgin Mary and Saint Jerome.

The *Vision of Saint Jerome*

The so-called *Vision of Saint Jerome* is a large altarpiece painted by Parmigianino during his sojourn in Rome between 1524 and 1527. Vasari tells us that during the Sack of Rome in 1527, when imperial troops charged into Parmigianino's studio and found him at work on this painting, they were so impressed by its quality that they left the artist unharmed to continue his business. Even if this story is a topos derived from Pliny, Vasari's account remains important for the factual details it provides about the commission, for he also records that the painting was made for Maria Bufalini to be placed in a chapel in the Roman church of San Salvatore in Lauro.[4]

Two recently discovered documents—the contract for the painting and Maria's last testament—confirm and expand the information given by Vasari.[5] In 1526 Maria Bufalini commissioned Parmigianino (and his uncle) to paint a panel as part of a broader decorative campaign for a chapel in San Salvatore in Lauro. The contract specifies the panel should depict the seated Virgin and Child with Saints John the Baptist and Jerome; it also calls for flanking images (never realized) involving Marian subject matter.[6] The Sack of 1527 did indeed interrupt this project (although perhaps not in the dramatic fashion Vasari reports), since Maria's will of the following year charges her heirs to complete the decoration. Maria's last testament indicates that the chapel in question belonged to her deceased husband, Antonio Caccialupi.[7]

Vaccaro Fig. 1. Parmigianino, *Vision of Saint Jerome*, 1526–27, London, National Gallery (photo: National Gallery, London)

Little is known about Maria Bufalini. She was the daughter of Nicolò Bufalini, an eminent concistorial lawyer from Città di Castello.[8] Both her husband, Antonio (d. 1518), and her father-in-law, Giovanni Battista Caccialupi (d. 1496), were also concistorial lawyers.[9] The dates of Maria's birth and marriage are not recorded, but we may infer from her will that the marriage resulted in no children, or at least none who survived by 1528, and that she never remarried.[10] The document further reveals a clear preference for her patrilineal instead of her marital family.[11] She instituted her Bufalini nephews and grandnephews as universal heirs and provided generously for Bufalini women as well as men. Bequests to her nieces and grandnieces, for instance, ranged from real estate to elaborate silverware.[12] In addition, she endowed a number of religious institutions, stipulating in some cases that commemorative masses be said on behalf of her or her deceased mother, Francesca.[13] She also explicitly requested that she be buried in one of her family's two chapels, located in Rome and Città di Castello.[14]

Although she seems to have had no intention of being buried in her husband's chapel, Maria was nonetheless involved in its decoration. Her husband likely charged her with this duty in his own last testament, which has yet to come to light.[15] When Maria enlisted Parmigianino to paint the altarpiece in 1526, Antonio Caccialupi had already been dead almost a decade. There is reason to believe that both he and his father, Giovanni Battista, were buried in the same chapel. The saints in the lower zone of Parmigianino's altarpiece, which were specified in the contract, support a familial connection, with John the Baptist as reference to the namesake of

Giovanni Battista and Jerome to the erudite legal profession of both father and son.[16] By ensuring the pictorial inclusion of these saints, Maria was paying professional and onomastic homage to her husband and father-in-law.

The patron seems also to have exercised her personal taste in defining the commission. The contract prescribes with diagrammatic clarity that the panel depict the two saints below a seated Madonna with the Christ Child in arms. Such compositional dictates recall Raphael's *Madonna di Foligno*, an image that stood at that time on the high altar of the Roman church of Santa Maria in Aracoeli, and it is tempting to speculate about Maria's predilection for Raphael, several of whose early works were to be found in her native Città di Castello. Certainly she would have known the *Madonna di Foligno*, since her family had a chapel in the Aracoeli that was one of the alternative sites designated by Maria for her burial. The patron may well have suggested this painting to Parmigianino (who was known in his day as Raphael *redivivus*) as a desirable prototype for her altarpiece.[17]

Significantly, Maria's creative share appears also to have extended to iconographic considerations. The contract calls for flanking images representing Anna and

Vaccaro Fig. 2. Parmigianino, *Madonna of the Long Neck*, ca. 1534–40, Florence, Galleria degli Uffizi (photo: Alinari/Art Resource, N.Y.)

Joachim and the Conception of the Virgin. Although never realized, these projected scenes establish a Marian (and Immaculist) context for the chapel. This was probably a private devotional choice on the part of the patron, since it does not appear that the order of San Giorgio in Alga, the canons regular in San Salvatore in Lauro at the time, had a special devotion to the Immaculate Virgin. Maria Bufalini, after all, had the Virgin as a namesake. Furthermore, the Bufalini family chapel in Città di Castello—the other site indicated in Maria's will for her burial—was dedicated to the Immacolata.[18]

The picture that Parmigianino ultimately made for his patron pays elegant tribute to her piety.[19] The Virgin and Child fill the luminous space above, a circular zone demarcated by the upper curve of the frame and a corresponding lower arc of clouds and moon. The Virgin sits with ponderous aplomb atop the clouds, her sandaled foot planted firmly on a rock. She casts her eyes toward a small, half-open book, a common Marian attribute that the Child casually balances on her thigh. The Word has been inscribed not simply on those pages but in the Virgin's very body, through which divinity has assumed human form.[20] Holding a palm in her left hand, she is crowned with a halo, and finely painted rays of light emanate from her body.[21] The picture thus celebrates the Immaculate Virgin and her role in the Incarnation.[22]

While archival evidence greatly expands our understanding of the intended context and Marian content of the altarpiece, it does not immediately explain the curious manner in which Saint Jerome is portrayed. Parmigianino appears to have arrived at this solution only after exploring many poses, including that of an upright and awake Jerome, in the preparatory drawings.[23] The artist finally ascribed to the saint an evocative dream of the Virgin and Child. The contract does not indicate whether such a dream or vision was intended to be the subject of the work, nor do known hagiographic accounts correspond to the scene depicted.[24] Given the rather traditional dictates of the commission (Madonna and Child with accompanying saints), it is revealing that Parmigianino invented a new, more dramatic way to present his subject. Lack of a clear textual source should not lead us to discount the possible significance of Jerome's pose, however, especially since Parmigianino would later return to this invention when working on the so-called *Madonna of the Long Neck*, an altarpiece for another widow.

The *Madonna of the Long Neck*

Parmigianino's most famous work, the *Madonna of the Long Neck*, provides a telling parallel in patronage to that of the *Vision of Saint Jerome*. Upon return to his native town of Parma, the artist began the picture for Elena Baiardi, a local noblewoman. The altarpiece was intended for the church of Santa Maria de'Servi in Parma, as Vasari indicates.[25] A document dated 1534, commonly thought to be the contract for the painting, confirms the details of patronage, but, in contrast to the contract for the *Vision of Saint Jerome*, does not provide any information about the subject matter to be depicted. It does reveal the picture to be part of a larger architectural refurbishment of the chapel, which is explicitly described as the project of Elena Baiardi.[26] The *Madonna of the Long Neck*, left unfinished at the time of the artist's death in 1540, was placed by the patron on its altar in 1542.[27]

Little biographical information is available for Elena Baiardi. A daughter of Caterina Anselmi and the Parmese cavalier and poet Andrea Baiardi, she was born in 1488 and at seventeen married the cavalier Francesco Tagliaferri, also from Parma.[28] The document of 1534 identifies Elena as a widow. Francesco Tagliaferri had died in 1529, and it seems that Elena enjoyed considerable authority over familial affairs after his death. His last testament, dated 19 October 1529, repeatedly stipulates that transactions be subjected to her discretion.[29] It also charges her to decorate his funerary chapel in the Servite church of Parma. Neither an exact monetary sum nor the precise nature of that decoration is specified; instead the will invites her to exercise her judgment when undertaking the task.[30] Such stipulations are common in these wills and, in any case, it is not surprising that Francesco Tagliaferri gave Elena Baiardi, the woman to whom he had been married for over a quarter of a century, legal prerogative over his estate. By 1529 she was forty-one, an age at which a widowed matron would be unlikely to remarry.[31]

Like Maria Bufalini, Elena Baiardi was a widow honoring her uxorial duty, and the chapel for which she had Parmigianino paint an altarpiece belonged to her husband. Whether Elena desired to be buried there herself is unknown, but her patronage reveals an especially close connection to this site. The chapel was evidently dedicated to the Virgin Mary and her Immaculate Conception. A plaque she set up in the chapel when installing the altarpiece read:

> TABULAM PRAESTANTISSMAE ARTIS—SACELLUMQUE A FUNDAMENTIS ERECTUM—HELENA BAIARDI—UXOR EQUITIS FRANCISCI TALLIAFERRI—HONORI BEATISSIMAE VIRGINIS—PRO SUO CULTU IN EAM POSUIT—ANNO MDXLII (Elena Baiardi Wife of Sir Francesco Tagliaferri Placed this Panel Painting of Outstanding Artistry and Erected This Chapel from the Foundation Up in Honor of the Most Blessed Virgin on Behalf of Her [Elena's] Devotion to the Same [BVM]–1542).[32]

This inscription indicates a contemporary Marian dedication, and archival documents, albeit later in date, link the altar and its altarpiece to the Immaculate Conception.[33] While such a dedication would have been typical in a Servite church, given the Marian spirituality of that monastic order, the epigraph suggests a strong personal devotion on the part of Elena Baiardi.[34] Notwithstanding its reference to Francesco Tagliaferri, it declares Elena as the active agent and relates her patronage not to her husband per se but to her wish to honor the cult of the Virgin.

The altarpiece, albeit unfinished, testifies to Elena's pious intention. As Vasari indicates, it shows: "Our Lady with the Child asleep in her arms, and some angels to the side, one of whom holds a crystal urn, in which glitters [*riluce*] a cross that Our Lady is contemplating."[35] The brief description generally accords in ekphrastic detail with the picture, even regarding the cross, which is now much abraded.[36] One apparent discrepancy involves the Virgin, who directs her attention to her Child instead of, according to Vasari, the cross in the urn. She is contemplating instead her infant, who lies with his pronated arm across the urn that is her body. The deathlike sleep of the Child suggests the Crucifixion that will be his destiny. This proleptic Pietà invites the viewer to meditate on the symbolism and final destiny of Mother and Child. The brilliant conceit, with its symbolism of the cross, may also have been intended as a deliberate allusion to Elena's namesake, the holy imperial widow Helen.[37]

Parmigianino's Madonna, that most holy receptacle of the Incarnation, is an avatar of perfect loveliness. Elizabeth Cropper has compared the *Madonna of the Long Neck* to Renaissance treatises on female beauty, demonstrating how the genres of art and literature relate to a broader Petrarchan descriptive tradition in the sixteenth century.[38] A more specific connection exists between the poetic tradition and the picture, however, since Elena's father himself wrote Petrarchan poetry. It seems most likely that both patron and artist would have been familiar with Andrea Baiardi's poems, in which the major topos of female beauty is the very feature that Parmigianino chose here to emphasize—the neck.[39] Such a clever reference to—and, perhaps, at the request of—Elena carries implications of which neither artist nor patron may have been aware. Parmigianino's exquisite vision of Marian beauty invokes, as do the poems of Andrea Baiardi, the Petrarchan culture of (presumably male) desire.

This situation raises important questions about the role of the female patron as beholder. Namely, how should we theorize Elena's affective response to such a construct of perfect beauty, a standard of beauty by which she and women of her social class gauged their own? Would she have necessarily assumed a male point of view, or might she have instead adopted alternative strategies of visual pleasure?[40] Elena's patronage of the *Madonna of the Long Neck*, while not simply the passive execution of her husband's charge, was grounded in the poetic constructs of her father, Parmigianino, and other men.

The earliest preparatory drawings for the *Madonna of the Long Neck* offer some sense of what was probably Elena's general expectation—that is, an enthroned Madonna and Child flanked by Saints Francis and Jerome.[41] These saints remained part of the design process until the end, although their relation to the composition underwent radical change. In the largely unfinished background of the *Madonna of the Long Neck*, dwarfed by an enormous column is a small figure holding a scroll. He looks behind his shoulder as if to address another figure, and the lone foot beside him suggests a companion was indeed intended. Related drawings confirm that the figure shown is Jerome and that Francis was to have been painted in colloquy with him.[42]

Saint Francis was presumably intended to refer to Elena's husband, Francesco Tagliaferri. The inclusion of Jerome, however, resists such a neat onomastic explanation. A number of single-figure studies survive for Jerome, who is almost always shown in the act of reading, either from a book or a scroll, and often with his hand to his head.[43] No such single-figure studies appear to have survived for Francis. While this lacuna might at first seem to be merely a circumstance of chance, the presence of Jerome—and the omission of Francis—in several related drawings that focus on the Virgin and Child group suggest that Jerome may have had a more important symbolic and formal role than Francis.

A drawing in Parma (fig. 3), thought to be an early idea for the *Madonna of the Long Neck*, depicts Jerome with a Madonna *lactans* and Child.[44] Jerome is shown reading a book, with one hand to his head, in front of a block upon which are seated the Madonna and Child. What is curious here, and immediately reminiscent of the saint's portrayal in the *Vision of Saint Jerome*, is his reclining pose. An association appears to have been still vivid in Parmigianino's mind from his work on the earlier picture, notably, Jerome's "imagining" of the Virgin and Child. How might this recurrent visual connection relate to the meaning of the two altarpieces and the intentions of the two patrons? And is there some significance for the study of female patronage in general?

Vaccaro Fig. 3.
Parmigianino, preparatory drawing for the *Madonna of the Long Neck,* ca.1534, Parma, Galleria Nazionale (photo: Soprintendenza, Parma)

The Virgin Mary, the Widow, and Saint Jerome

Both Maria Bufalini and Elena Baiardi were widows decorating their husbands' funerary chapels, each of which bore a dedication to the Virgin Mary. Such an iconographic context is made clear, in the former case, by the contract for the chapel decoration and, in the latter, by contemporary epigraphic evidence. The emphatic presentation of the Madonna in both altarpieces confirms a profound relation between these female patrons and Marian worship. Such devotion seems to have afforded an eminently suitable expression of a widow's piety and respect. Significantly, the plaque Elena placed in the Servite chapel suggests that she considered her altarpiece to be truly worthy of the Virgin.

The inclusion of saints was a means by which a female patron might obviously commemorate her husband and his family. In the *Vision of Saint Jerome*, Saints John the Baptist and Jerome serve as onomastic and professional reference to Maria's husband and father-in-law. While such reasoning may explain the intended presence of Saint Francis in the *Madonna of the Long Neck* (although it is interesting that he is the only figure not completely painted in the picture) the appearance of Saint Jerome remains problematic. The portrayal of the latter saint would seem to require further interpretation.

Studies by Carolyn Valone and Marilyn Dunn have connected Saint Jerome to female patronage practices in early modern Italy.[45] Certain late sixteenth-century Roman matrons deliberately modeled their pious works on the example of aristocratic women applauded by Jerome (a phenomenon that bespeaks a post-Tridentine revival of interest in the Early Christian Church as championed by new reform orders such as the Oratorians). Yet might a tie between Jerome and female patrons have existed even earlier in the century? The altarpieces made for Maria Bufalini and Elena Baiardi invite us to consider the possibility.

Indeed, Jerome's active dialogue with a female audience appears to have been central to the Christian imagination throughout the Renaissance. In the third book of Baldassare Castiglione's *Il libro del cortegiano* (1528), for instance, the Magnifico Giuliano invokes the saint as nothing less than a champion of women. The interlocutor praises the shining example of the Virgin Mary, as well as the many deserving (if less famous) ladies mentioned by Jerome: "How inferior in worth all human creatures are to Our Lady the Virgin…and you can think of many other women also who are less talked about, especially if you will read Saint Jerome, who celebrates certain women of his time with such marvelous praise that it would indeed suffice for the holiest man on earth?"[46] Contemporary behavior manuals for women repeatedly invoke the saint as well. For instance, Ludovico Dolce's *Dialogo della institution delle donne* (1547) remarks on the erudition of the pious women to whom Jerome wrote and recommends these epistles to his own female readers.[47] The final section, devoted entirely to widows, declares: "Have you not heard the names of Marcella, of Salvia, of Paola, of Blesilla, and of the others, whose memory that noble Doctor of the Church Jerome made sacred for all time by dedicating such beautiful and elegant works to them?"[48]

The memory and example of the early Christian women associated with Saint Jerome were very much alive throughout the centuries. The saint had acted as spiritual mentor, urging these women to read and know sacred scripture. He dedicated several of his vulgate biblical translations to female disciples, and wrote many letters to them.[49] The epistles to widows—Paola, Furia, Salvina, and Ageruchia, to name just a few—consistently exhort a life of renewed chastity and piety.[50] The status of widow, which was considered second only to that of a virgin in purity, afforded the freedom to serve Christian ends. A widow was to eschew remarriage, devoting herself instead to Christ, who was considered to be her new bridegroom. Devotion was to be lavished equally on his mother, according to Jerome, for the gift of virginity so richly bestowed on all women had its beginning in her perfection.[51]

Other writings, some apocryphal, further establish the historical Jerome's connection to Marian worship. Author of a treatise on the perpetual virginity of the Virgin, Jerome was widely thought to have translated the pseudo-Matthew gospel about the nativity of Mary.[52] Another text commonly ascribed to Jerome, the so-called Epistle IX, was significant for the worship of the Immaculate Virgin. It was frequently cited in Marian liturgy, including both late fifteenth-century offices for the Immaculate Conception.[53] Believed to have been written to the widow Paola and her daughter, Eustochium, the letter expounds on the Assumption and celebrates the Madonna as the consummate exemplar for virgin and widow alike.

The message of Epistle IX largely concurs with that of Jerome's authentic letters: it instructs women to be the brides of Christ and to worship the chaste Madonna. All of these letters were readily available in Italian vernacular editions and, according to authors such as Dolce, were required reading for the Renaissance woman.[54] Thus Maria Bufalini and Elena Baiardi would likely have known the writings through sermons if not through direct perusal. To these two widows (both older women who evidently did not remarry) the lessons of Jerome may have carried special appeal. In any event, faced with the task of decorating their husbands' funerary chapels, Maria and Elena chose to include Saint Jerome in paintings that honor the Virgin Mary.

The marginal figure of Jerome proves integral to the design and implied narrative of the altarpiece Parmigianino made for each widow. In the *Vision of Saint Jerome*, Jerome appropriates the entire picture as a dream. In the *Madonna of the Long Neck*, the tiny saint with his scroll negotiates a spatial chasm between background and foreground, a visual note explicating the mysteries of the main text. Preparatory drawings reveal just how Parmigianino explored and reworked the imagery for his respective patrons.

At least one preliminary sketch for the *Madonna of the Long Neck* suggests his creative response to a contemporary altarpiece by Correggio (fig. 4), which Parmigianino would

Vaccaro Fig. 4. Correggio, *Madonna and Child with Saints Jerome and Mary Magdalen*, ca. 1526–28, Parma, Galleria Nazionale (photo: Soprintendenza, Parma)

certainly have seen upon his return to Parma.[55] The picture enjoyed considerable popularity in the sixteenth century, as Vasari's biography of Correggio attests:

> In Sant'Antonio in Parma he painted a panel picture showing the Madonna and Saint Mary Magdalene, with a boy nearby in the guise of a little angel, who is holding a book in his hand and smiling so naturally.... This work, which also contains a Saint Jerome, is especially admired by other painters for its astonishing and beautiful coloring, and it is difficult to imagine anything better.[56]

Notably, the composition includes a large figure of the penitent Jerome holding a scroll and offering an open book to the Virgin and Child. The question of the possible impact of this painting on Parmigianino deserves further study, not simply in terms of its *colorito mirabile* celebrated by Vasari, but especially given the circumstances of patronage.

Although Vasari makes no mention of a patron, later sources indicate that a woman commissioned Correggio to paint the altarpiece. Girolamo Tiraboschi alludes to unspecified documents, recorded in the *memorie* of the archive of the church of Sant'Antonio, which disclose that Donna Briseide Colla, wife of a certain Orazio or Ottaviano Bergonzi, ordered the picture in 1523 at the price of 400 lire.[57] Luigi Pungileoni later stated that this pious lady installed the altarpiece in her family chapel in Sant'Antonio in 1528, the year of her death.[58] Recent archival findings permit us now to clarify further the situation: Briseide Colla was the wife of Ottaviano [not Orazio] Bergonzi, who had purchased a chapel in Sant'Antonio for his tomb in 1514.[59] The picture made for Briseide Colla, like those made for Maria Bufalini and Elena Baiardi, was thus destined for the altar of her husband's chapel, although not the result of testamentary patronage, since Briseide's husband appears to have been still alive at the time.[60] In any case, once again Jerome appears in a Marian altarpiece made for a woman, although not a widow in this case, who is decorating her husband's funerary chapel.

A broader and systematic survey of Renaissance imagery and textual sources (such as contemporary sermons) should—and, I suspect, will—further illuminate the connection between the Virgin Mary, Jerome, and women, notably widows. Indeed, the inclusion of the saint in the pictures discussed here suggests that such an iconographic focus would have been in keeping with the behavioral and devotional recommendations made by Jerome to Paola and women in general—especially to dutiful widows, past and present.

Notes

This essay is an expanded version of a paper first presented in May of 1993 at the 28th International Congress on Medieval Studies at Western Michigan University, Kalamazoo, Michigan. Some of the ideas and language of this earlier redaction were used without proper citation by Jaynie Anderson, "Rewriting the History of Art Patronage," *Renaissance Studies* 10 (1996): esp. 136. See the addendum by Jaynie Anderson, *Renaissance Studies* 11 (1997): 160.

1. Vasari-Milanesi, 5:217–42, mentions "una culla di putti che fu fatta per la signora Angiola de' Rossi da Parma" (a lost work) and the panel depicting "una Nostra Donna, Santa Margherita, San Petronio, San Girolamo e San Michele" made for the nuns of Santa Margherita in Bologna (Bologna, Pinacoteca Nazionale). For the altarpiece, see David Ekserdjian, "Parmigianino's *Madonna of Saint Margaret*," *Burlington Magazine* 125 (1983): 542–46. The frescoed room with the legend of Diana and Acteon in the Rocca di Fontanellato near Parma is not discussed in early sources, though its patron is generally assumed to have been Count Galeazzo Sanvitale. Parmigianino may instead have decorated the room for the count's wife, Paola Gonzaga (pictured in the frescoes), using a room painted by Correggio for another female patron (the Camera di San Paolo in Parma) as his prototype. See Augusta Ghidiglia Quintavalle, "Il Boudoir di Paola Gonzaga signora di Fontanellato," *Paragone* 18 (1967): 3–17; Ute Davitt-Asmus, "Fontanellato II: La trasformazione dell'amante nell'amato, Parmigianinos Fresken in der Rocca Sanvitale," *Mitteilungen des Kunsthistorischen Institutes in Florenz* 31 (1987): 2–58. See also Katherine McIver's chapter in this volume and Valeria Vecchi, "Tre Donne Sanvitale nel primo cinquecento a Parma," *Aurea Parma* 80.3 (September-December 1996): 287–94.

2. London, National Gallery, inv. no. 33, oil on panel, 343 x 149 cm. See Cecil Gould, *National Gallery Catalogue: The Sixteenth-Century Schools* (London: National Gallery, 1962), and Cecil Gould, *Parmigianino* (New York: Abbeville, 1994), 186–87. I thank Nicholas Penny and the National Gallery for their generous assistance regarding the painting.

3. Florence, Galleria di Palazzo Pitti, currently on loan to the Galleria degli Uffizi, inv. no. 230 P, oil on panel, 214 x 133 cm. See Sydney J. Freedberg, *Parmigianino: His Works in Painting* (Westport, Conn.: Greenwood Press, 1971), 186–89; Mario di Giampaolo, *Parmigianino, catalogo completo dei dipinti* (Florence: Cantini, 1991), 116–19.

4. Vasari-Milanesi, 5:224–26. The story of soldiers recalls that of Protogenes in Pliny, *Natural History* (35.36). To identify the exact chapel in San Salvatore in Lauro, which is described by Vasari as near the door of the church, is difficult if not impossible. The church burned in 1591 and was rebuilt shortly thereafter; little is known about the appearance and plan of the earlier building.

5. ASR, Collegio Notai Capitolini, vol. 14, Antonius de Alexis, fols. 337 ff. and 353r–354v, 382. The documents were discovered and transcribed by Monsignor Sandro Corradini in "Parmigianino's Contract for the Caccialupi Chapel in San Salvatore in Lauro," *Burlington Magazine* 135 (1993): 27–29. For a preliminary interpretation of the commission based on these documents see Mary Vaccaro, "Documents for Parmigianino's *Vision of Saint Jerome*," *Burlington Magazine* 135 (1993): 22–27.

6. The contract, dated 3 January 1526, requests "unam tabulam cum imagine beatae Mariae virginis sedente cum Filio in brachiis suis, et imagine beati Hieronimi doctoris Ecclesiae et beati Iohannis baptistae in pede Virginis a medietate dictarum Imaginum sanctorum Hieronimi et Io:Baptistae supradicti, necnon imaginem Conceptionis eiusdem beatae Virginis ab uno latere, et imaginem sanctorum Iohachim et Annae ab alio latere in cornicibus cappellae."

7. The pertinent clause in her last testament (dated 15 July 1528) reads: "Item dicta testatrix asseruit dedisse pictori capellae bo: me: dicti quondam d.ni Antonii eius viri ad bonum computum suae mercedis, quae capella est sita in ecclesia S.ti Salvatoris in lauro de Urbe duc. sexdecim auri, mandavit infrascriptis heredibus ut solvant residuum dictae mercedis praefato pictori et procurent quod tabula depicta pro dicta capella ponatur per dictum pictorem in loco suo eiusdem capellae,

et ornetur per eundem pictorem iuxta formam in conventionis factae cum eo, de qua asseruit constare manu mei notarii."

8. For Nicolò Bufalini, see the entry by C. Gennaro in *DBI* 14:802–3. For the Bufalini family in general, see D. Iacovacci, *Repertori di famiglie*, BAV, Ottob. lat. 2548, part 4, fols. 791–96.

9. For Antonio Caccialupi, see Giovanni Carlo Gentili, *De Ecclesia Septempedana* (Macerata: A. Mancini, 1838) 3:162–63; Giovanni Carlo Gentili, *Elogio di Giovanni Battista Caccialupi de'Conti della Truschia, giureconsulto ed advocato concistoriale del secolo XV* (Macerata, 1844), 30. For Giovanni Battista, see the entry by G. D'Amelio in *DBI* 15:790–97.

10. Maria's last testament indicates her status as the widow of Antonio Caccialupi and mentions no children by that marriage. After the death of Antonio, the Caccialupi name was assumed by a nephew (the son of Antonio's sister Francesca) and continued in hyphenated form as Vicoli-Caccialupi. See Vittorio Spreti, *Enciclopedia storico-nobilare italiana* (Milan: Enciclopedia storico-nobiliare italiana, 1929) 2:226–27. Aleandri publishes the Caccialupi family in V. Aleandri, "Il palazzo in Roma, la famiglia e il ritratto di Giambattista Caccialupi Sanseverinate, giureconsulto dal secolo XV," *Arte e storia* 11 (1908): 136–38.

11. For other examples, see the chapter by Carolyn Valone in this volume. On the art patronage of widows, see also Catherine King, *Renaissance Women Patrons* (Manchester: Manchester University Press, 1998), 76–128.

12. The document appoints her nephew Riccomanno Bufalini executor of the will and names him, as well as nephews, Nicolò and Giovanni, and grandnephews, Ventura and Giulio, to be her universal heirs. A few of the Bufalini nieces, notably Bernardina and Maddalena, were each to receive storefront property near the church of San Tommaso in Rome. Silverware is bequeathed to her grandnieces. Nothing is left to Caccialupi relations. A widow's allegiance to her patrilineal instead of marital family was common in the Renaissance, especially in the case of childless widows; see Margaret L. King, *Women of the Renaissance* (Chicago: University of Chicago Press, 1991), 56–62. See also Christiane Klapisch-Zuber, *Women, Family and Ritual in Renaissance Italy*, trans. L. Cochrane (Chicago: University of Chicago Press, 1985), esp. "The 'Cruel Mother': Maternity, Widowhood and Dowry in Florence in the Fourteenth and Fifteenth Centuries," 117–31.

13. The last testament remembers almost a dozen religious institutions, mostly in Rome, with bequests including money and property, and even specifies a few nuns and tertiaries by name (e.g., "Item reliquit sorori Andreae monialibus sive bizocharis monasterii sui domus dictae civitatis ducatos decem similes"). For involvement of Renaissance widows in the conventual community, see P. Renée Baernstein, "In Widow's Habit: Women between Convent and Family in Sixteenth-Century Milan," *Sixteenth Century Journal* 25 (1994): 787–807, with previous bibliography.

14. The place of her death was to dictate the chapel in which she would eventually be buried: "Si ex presente infirmitate ipsam mori contingat in Civitate Castelli mandavit et voluit corpus suum sepelliri in ecclesia S.ti Augustini dictae civitatis et capella Conceptionis, si vero eam mori contigat in urbe Romana voluit sepelliri in ecclesia beatae Mariae de Araceli et capella S.ti Bernardini ac in sepoltura dominorum Bufalinorum."

15. Although D. Iacovacci, *Repertori di famiglie*, BAV, Ottob. lat. 2549, part 1, fol. 8, indicates that Antonio Caccialupi's last testament was drawn up by the notary Benedictus Calligarius on 10 January 1517 and then deposited in the Lateran Hospital archives, this information has not thus far led to the original document, which may not survive. Caccialupi named his wife, Maria, and sister, Francesca, as his heirs.

16. Vaccaro, "Documents," 23–24.

17. Vaccaro, "Documents," 25–26. For the early works by Raphael in Città di Castello, see Alessandro Marabottini and others, *Raffaello giovane e Città di Castello*, exh. cat. (Città di Castello: Pinacoteca Comunale, 1983), and *Raphael Before Rome*, ed. James Beck, in *Studies in the History of Art* 17 (Washington D. C.: National Gallery of Art, 1986).

18. Vaccaro, "Documents," 26–27. According to Vasari, the altarpiece was left in storage for many years after the Sack of Rome and then brought to the church of Sant' Agostino in Città di Castello by a relative named Giulio Bufalini. For mention of the painting in the church, see Francesco Ignazio Lazzari, *Serie de' vescovi e breve notizia di Città di Castello* (Città di Castello, 1963; reprint, Bologna: A. Forni, 1975), 146; M. G. Muzi, *Memorie ecclesiastiche e civili di Città di Castello* (Città di Castello, 1844), 7:191.

19. A standard survey book on Italian Renaissance art describes the altarpiece as nothing less than a "lascivious and perverse" dream in which "Parmigianino has sharply emphasized the [Christ Child's] genitals, just as he has with unprecedented daring shown the Virgin's nipples erect through the tight, sheer fabric of her tunic." See Frederick Hartt, *History of Italian Renaissance Art*, 4th ed. (New York: Abrams, 1994), 564; cf. Giovanni Copertini, *Il Parmigianino* (Parma: Mario Fresching, 1932), 1:82–86; and Freedberg, *Parmigianino*, 70–74.

20. On Marian symbolism in general, see Yrjö Hirn, *The Sacred Shrine: A Study of the Poetry and Art of the Catholic Church*, 2nd ed. (London: Faber and Faber, 1958), esp. 236–48, 303–26; Helen Rosenau, "A Study in the Iconography of the Incarnation," *Burlington Magazine* 85 (1944): 176–79.

21. In the picture, Saint Jerome also holds a palm and a crucifix, establishing a visual and likely symbolic link between that saint and the Madonna with the Christ Child. For the symbolism of palms in Christian art, see Mirella Levi D'Ancona, *The Garden of the Renaissance: Botanical Symbolism in Italian Painting* (Florence: Leo S. Olschki, 1977), 279–89.

22. The *Vision of Saint Jerome*, though not strictly speaking a picture of the Immaculate Conception, was clearly intended as part of such an iconographic context. See Vaccaro, "Documents," 26; Gould, *Parmigianino*, 176; cf. Regina Stefaniak, "Amazing Grace: Parmigianino's *Vision of Saint Jerome*," *Zeitschrift für Kunstgeschichte* 58 (1995): 105–15. For an overview of the theme during the Middle Ages and Renaissance, see Mirella Levi D'Ancona, *The Iconography of the Immaculate Conception in the Middle Ages and Early Renaissance* (New York: College Art Association, 1957); Nancy Mayberry, "The Controversy over the Immaculate Conception in Medieval and Renaissance Art, Literature, and Society," *Journal of Medieval and Renaissance Studies* 21 (1991): 207–44.

23. Vaccaro, "Documents," 24–25. For related drawings, see A. E. Popham, *Catalogue of Drawings of Parmigianino* (New Haven, Conn.: Yale University Press, 1971) 1:7–9, 90, plates 95–112.

24. The dream most commonly associated with Jerome (the so-called Ciceronian dream) involves his chastisement by Christ for being overinterested in Cicero and pagan literature. It is described in his letter to the virgin Eustochium, 22.30. For representation of this subject in Renaissance art, see Eugene F. Rice, Jr., *Saint Jerome in the Renaissance* (Baltimore: Johns Hopkins University Press, 1985), 3–6, 74. Rice convincingly suggests that sleeping or dreaming in Parmigianino's *Vision of Saint Jerome* may be a means of denoting *raptus in spiritu*, and that the "vision" Parmigianino represents evokes the Virgin Immaculate, with whom the historical Jerome is often associated via apocryphal texts such as Epistle 9 (150–51, 252–53). The pseudo-Jerome Epistle IX (discussed below) is also addressed to women.

25. Vasari-Milanesi, 5:231; for Vasari's description of the picture, see below; cf. Giorgio Vasari, *Le vite...nelle redazioni del 1550 e 1568*, ed. Roseanna Bettarini and Paola Barocchi (Florence: Sansoni, 1966), 4:544. Vasari's first edition (1550) tersely identifies the patron as the sister of Cavalier Baiardo, but does not include a discussion of the subject matter or location of the altarpiece. His greatly expanded vita of 1568 curiously drops any reference to the patron.

26. ASPr, Notai di Parma, Andrea Cerati, fol. 761 (1534), first published in Michelangelo Gualandi, *Memorie originali italiane risguardanti le belle arti* (Bologna, 1845), 6:117–22. A more accurate transcription of the document was later published by C. Ricci, "Di alcuni quadri del Parmigianino già esistenti in Parma," *Archivio storico per le provincie parmensi* 4 (1893): 24–25.

This document is not the contract for the picture, as is commonly maintained in the literature, but a slightly later agreement to prepare the chapel for the altarpiece. The chapel has unfortunately been gutted.

27. See Ireneo Affò, *Vita del graziosissimo pittore Francesco Mazzola detto il Parmigianino* (Parma: Filippo Carmignani, 1784), 84, for the text of a plaque (discussed below in n. 32) which was once in the church.

28. E. Scarabelli Zunti, *I Baiardi di Parma* (1844), ASPr, MS 54, esp. genealogical table 6a. For Andrea Baiardi, see entry by R. Ceserani in *DBI*, 5:281–84. For Francesco Tagliaferri, see Umberto Benassi, *Storia di Parma* (Parma, 1899), 1:231.

29. ASPr, Notai di Parma, Antonio Fosia, fol. 1035, with a partial copy of the same in ASPr, Fondo Conventi e Confraternite Soppressi, Serviti di Parma, filza rogiti 5, n. 12, but without a published transcription. Gualandi, *Memorie*, 122, briefly alludes to the last testament of Francesco Tagliaferri and its contents, but provides an erroneous archival reference and date for it. More accurate mention of the document appears in David Ekserdjian, "The Widow's Right," *Times Literary Supplement* (3 November 1995): 21. David Ekserdjian first alerted me to the testamentary nature of this commission.

30. The last testament charges "Item prefatus dominus testator voluit, iussit et mandavit quod prefata domina Elena, uxor sua, possit et valeat de bonis ipsius domini testatoris expendere in ornamento capelle ipsius domini testatoris situate in ecclesia prefata domine Sancte Marie Servorum, omnem illam quantitatem pecuniarum, que et prout eidem domine Elene uxori sue videbitur et placuerit." Since the document invites Elena Baiardi to do as she sees fit with regard to the chapel, I cannot concur with David Ekserdjian's statement in *Correggio* (New Haven, Conn.: Yale University Press, 1997), 312 n. 29, claiming she was "merely fulfilling the conditions of her husband's Francesco Tagliaferri's will."

31. On the administrative competencies of widows, see N. Tamassia, *Il testamento del marito* (Bologna, 1905); *Upon My Husband's Death: Widows in the Literature and Histories of Medieval Europe*, ed. Louise Mirrer (Ann Arbor: University of Michigan Press, 1992). See also the chapter by Carolyn Valone in this volume.

32. See Affò, *Vita*, 84. The plaque was replaced with another by the Cerati family in the early eighteenth century, after the sale and removal of the altarpiece. I would like to thank Ingrid Rowland for her translation from the Latin. The inscription, like all the others recorded in the manuscript sources, is no longer in the church, which has undergone numerous transformations since the Napoleonic suppression of 1805. See Felice da Mareto, *Chiese e conventi di Parma* (Parma: Deputazione di Storia Patria per le Provincie Parmensi, 1978), 273.

33. For these documents, discussed in the context of the sale of the altarpiece, see Mary Vaccaro, "Precisazioni sulla vendita della celebre 'Madonna dal collo lungo' del Parmigianino," *Aurea Parma* 80 (May-August 1996): 162–75.

34. G. Besutti, "Pietà mariana dei Servi nel '500," *Quaderni di Monte Senario: I Servi di Maria nel clima del concilio di Trento* (Monte Senario, 1982), esp. 107–12. On the Servite cult of the Immaculate Virgin, see G. Roschini, "I Servi di Maria e l'Immacolata," *Studi storici dell'ordine dei Servi di Maria* 6 (1954): 29–182; A. Rossi, "Il culto dell' Immacolata presso i Servi di Maria," in *Virgo Immaculata: Acta congressus mariologici* (Rome: Accademia Mariana Internationalis, 1956), 8:80–91. See also Mary Vaccaro, "Parmigianino, the Servants of Mary, and Marian Devotion," in *Studi storici dell'ordine dei Servi di Maria* 47 (1997): 211–23.

35. "La Nostra Donna col Figliuolo in braccio che dorme, e da un lato certi Angeli, uno de' quali ha in braccio un'urna di cristallo, dentro la quale riluce una croce contemplata dalla Nostra Donna," Vasari-Milanesi, 5:231.

36. Vasari's mention of a cross in the crystal urn held by the angel was long thought to be mistaken. See Ute Davitt Asmus, "Zur Deutung von Parmigianinos 'Madonna dal collo lungo,'" *Zeitschrift*

für Kunstgeschichte 31 (1968): 305–13. The picture was cleaned by the late conservator Paolo Gori, who, along with Dott. Alessandro Cecchi, kindly discussed details of the cleaning with me.

37. Regarding the possible reference to Saint Helen in the *Madonna of the Long Neck*, see John Shearman, *Only Connect...Art and the Spectator in the Italian Renaissance* (Princeton: Princeton University Press, 1992), 235–36. For other cases involving female patrons and the iconography of Saint Helen, see Carolyn Valone, "Elena Orsini, Daniele da Volterra, and the Orsini Chapel," *Artibus et historiae* 22 (1990): 79–88; Catherine King, "Medieval and Renaissance Matrons, Italian-Style," *Zeitschrift für Kunstgeschichte* 55 (1992): esp. 373–74.

38. Elizabeth Cropper, "On Beautiful Women, Parmigianino, *Petrarchismo*, and the Vernacular Style," *Art Bulletin* 58 (1976): 374–94.

39. The only printed edition of Baiardi's poems, *Rime del Cavalier Andrea Bajardi Parmigiano*, ed. F. Fogliazzi (Milan: Società Palatina, 1756), is partial and problematic. See B. Basile, "Petrarchismo e manierismo nei lirici parmensi del Cinquecento," in *Le corti farnesiane di Parma e Piacenza*, ed. A. Quondam (Rome: n.p., 1978), 2:71–132; Paola Medioli Masotti, "Letteratura e società a Parma nel Quattrocento," in *Parma e l'umanesimo italiano*, ed. Paola Medioli Masotti (Padua: Antenore, 1986), 231–65. See also Mary Vaccaro, "Parmigianino and Andrea Baiardi: Figuring Petrarchan Beauty in Renaissance Parma," forthcoming in *Word and Image*, 2001.

40. Such questions, though beyond the immediate scope of this paper, merit sustained consideration. For example, the possible relation between the style of Parmigianino's images and their female patronage needs to be more fully explored. The notion of a gender-specific style must be postulated with caution, however. The exquisite sensuality of the *Vision of Saint Jerome* and the *Madonna of the Long Neck*, for example, does not appear to differ conspicuously from the style of works made by Parmigianino for male patrons. It is nonetheless worth considering the very different treatment of drapery found in his *Madonna of Saint Margaret*. One wonders if the patrons, in this case Bolognese nuns, stipulated that the garments of the Virgin and Saint Margaret be heavier and more opaque than those Parmigianino typically painted. Compare the story reported by Vasari about the *Pala Colonna*, in which the patrons, again nuns, evidently insisted that Raphael depict the Christ Child clothed (Vasari-Milanesi, 4:324). On Petrarchan desire and visual subjectivity in Renaissance art, see the excellent remarks by Elizabeth Cropper, "The Place of Beauty in the High Renaissance and Its Displacement in the History of Art," in *Place and Displacement in the Renaissance*, ed. A. Vos (Binghamton, NY: Medieval and Renaissance Texts and Studies, 1994), 159–205, with previous bibliography.

41. Popham, *Drawings*, 1:25–26, plates 345–60; David Ekserdjian, "Parmigianino's First Idea for the *Madonna of the Long Neck*," *Burlington Magazine* 126 (1984): 424–29; and Mario di Giampaolo, "Quattro studi del Parmigianino per la 'Madonna dal collo lungo,'" *Prospettiva* 33–36 (1983–84): 180–82.

42. A drawing in the Ashmolean Museum (Popham, *Drawings*, no. 334r, plate 358) offers three slightly varied arrangements for the two saints, with the group on the far right of the sheet closest to the solution employed, albeit unfinished, in the picture.

43. See, for example, Popham, *Drawings*, no. 661r, plate 345, nos. 242, 719v, plate 357.

44. Parma, Galleria Nazionale, Popham, *Drawings*, no. 553. See Popham, *Drawings*, 1:173–74, and the entry by L. Fornari Schianchi in Diane de Grazia, *Correggio e il suo lascito,* exh. cat. (Parma: Galleria Nazionale, 1984), 468–69.

45. Carolyn Valone, "Roman Matrons as Patrons: Various Views of the Cloister Wall," in *The Crannied Wall: Women, Religion, and the Arts in Early Modern Europe*, ed. Craig A. Monson (Ann Arbor: University of Michigan Press, 1992), 49–72; Carolyn Valone, "Women on the Quirinal Hill: Patronage in Rome, 1560–1630," *Art Bulletin* 76 (1994): 129–46; Marilyn Dunn, "Piety and Patronage in Seicento Rome: Two Noblewomen and Their Convents," *Art Bulletin* 76 (1994): 644–63.

46. "Ma io non voglio ordirvi quanto di dignità tutte le creature umane siano inferiori alla Vergine nostra Signora...molte altre ancor, delle quali tanto non si ragiona, da voi stesso potete vedere,

massimamente legendo san Ieronimo, che alcune de' suoi tempi celebra con tante maravigliose laudi, che ben poriano bastar a qualsivoglia santissimo omo." Baldassare Castiglione, *Il libro del Cortegiano*, ed. B. Maier, 3rd ed. (Turin: Unione Tipografico-Editrice Torinese, 1981), 369. Such remarks belie the complex and conflicting attitudes toward women found in Renaissance texts, including those texts (like Castiglione's) purportedly in defense and praise of women. See Constance Jordan, *Renaissance Feminism: Literary Texts and Political Models* (Ithaca: Cornell University Press, 1990); Pamela J. Benson, *The Invention of Renaissance Woman: The Challenge of Female Independence in the Literature and Thought of Italy and England* (University Park: Pennsylvania State University Press, 1992).

47. Lodovico Dolce, *Dialogo della institution delle donne* (Venice: G. Giolito de Ferrari, 1547), esp. 13–20.

48. "Non havete uditi i nomi di Marcella, di Salvia, di Paola, di Blesilla, e delle altre, le quali quel nobile Dottor della Chiesa Girolamo con si belle e eleganti opere lor dedicate sacrò alla memoria tutti i secoli?" Dolce, *Dialogo*, 66v.

49. *Saint Jerome: Letters and Select Works, A Select Library of Nicene and Post-Nicene Fathers of the Church*, 2nd ser., 6 (New York, 1893). About a third of Jerome's surviving letters were written to women. See Valone, "Women on the Quirinal," 143, and Dunn, "Piety," 659, with previous bibliography.

50. Among Jerome's many letters to widows are letters 54 (to Furia), 79 (to Salvina), and 123 (to Ageruchia). See also letter 108, written to the virgin Eustochium in praise of her recently deceased mother, the widow Paola.

51. Letter 22 (to the virgin Eustochium), esp. 22.21–23, 22.38. In this famous letter Jerome also discusses his Ciceronian dream and the visions that tormented him as he lived as a penitent in the desert (see above n. 25). I hardly intend to cast Saint Jerome as a feminist, especially since his advice to women is predicated on the equivocal if not misogynist assumptions found in patristic writings in general. See Jordan, *Renaissance Feminism*, 71–72. The saint's importance to Renaissance women, however complicit these women might ultimately and unwittingly have been in the social construction of gender difference, must nonetheless be acknowledged.

52. "De perpetua virginitate B. Mariae adversus Helvidium," in *Patrologiae Latinae*, ed. J. P. Migne (1845; reprint, Turnholt: Brepols, 1983), 13:cols. 193–216. For the book of the Virgin's nativity (pseudo-Matthew gospels), see *The Apocryphal New Testament*, trans. Montague Rhodes James, (Oxford, 1924), and Rice, *Saint Jerome*, 46. The popular thirteenth-century *Golden Legend* not only cites this putative translation but also includes a charming story in which the Virgin demands to know why Saint Jerome prays at all the altars in a church except for the one with a Marian image. "Sancta et immaculata virginitas, quibus te laudibus referam nescio," he responds. "Quia quem celi capere non poterant, tuo gremio contulisti." It is interesting to note that Jerome and Matthew are seen together in one of Correggio's pendentives in the church of San Giovanni Evangelista, which also bears soffit decoration alluding to Mary's virginity. This particular pairing may be based on the translation of pseudo-Matthew.

53. "De Assumptione Sanctae Virginis," in *Corpus Christianorum, continuatio medievalis*, ed. Albert Ripberger (Turnholt: Brepols, 1985), 56. For discussion of Epistle 9, see T. A. Agius, "On Pseudo-Jerome, Epistle 9," *Journal of Theological Studies* 24 (1923): 176–83; Rice, *Saint Jerome*, 46, 144–47; E. Ann Matter, *The Voice of My Beloved: The Song of Songs in Western Medieval Christianity* (Philadelphia: University of Pennsylvania Press, 1990), 152–53.

54. An example of Jerome's letters in vernacular edition (including the apocryphal Epistle 9) is *Epistole de San Hieronimo volgare* (Ferrara, 1498). For the diffusion of such religious texts among female readers in the Renaissance, see Gabriella Zarri, "La vita religiosa femminile tra devozione e chiostro," in *Le sante vive: Cultura e religiosità nella prima età moderna* (Modena: Panini, 1990), 21–50; Gabriella Zarri, "Note su diffusione e circolazione di testi devoti (1520–1550)," in *Libri, idee e sentimenti religiosi nel Cinquecento italiano* (Modena: Panini, 1987), 131–54; K. Gill, "Women

and the Production of Religious Literature in the Vernacular, 1300–1500," in *Creative Women in Medieval and Early Modern Italy: A Religious and Artistic Renaissance*, ed. E. Ann Matter and John Coakley (Philadelphia: University of Pennsylvania Press, 1994), 64–104.

55. Parma, Galleria Nazionale, inv. no. 351, oil on panel, 205 x 141 cm. See Cecil Gould, *The Paintings of Correggio* (Ithaca: Cornell University Press, 1976), 262–63; Mario di Giampaolo and A. Muzzi, *Correggio, catalogo completo dei dipinti* (Florence: Cantini, 1993), 114–15. The connection between Correggio's altarpiece and Parmigianino's preparatory studies for the *Madonna of the Long Neck* is especially evident in Popham, *Drawings*, 771, plate 360.

56. Vasari-Milanesi, 4:114: "In Sant'Antonio ancora di qualla città dipinse una tavola, nell qual'è una Nostra Donna e Santa maria Maddalena; ed appresso vi e un putto che ride, ch tiene a guisa di angioletto un libro in mano, il quale par che rida tanto naturalmente… Evvi ancora un San Gerolamo; ed e colorita di maniera si maravigliosa e stupenda, che i pittori ammirano quella per colorito mirabile, e che non si possa quasi dipingere meglio."

57. Girolamo Tiraboschi, *Biblioteca Modenese* (Modena: Società tipografica, 1786), 4:267–68, notes that the patron was so pleased with the work that she offered the artist gifts of wheat, wooden faggots, and a pig.

58. Luigi Pungileoni, *Memorie istoriche di Antoni Allegri detto il Correggio* (Parma: Dalla Stamperia Ducale, 1817–21), 1:184–85, 2:209, refers to the patron's deceased husband variously as Ottaviano or Orazio.

59. For a discussion of the chapel and the church of Sant'Antonio in general, see Piero Paolo Mendogni, *Sant'Antonio Abbate, uno scrigno rococò* (Parma: L. Battei, 1979), esp. 46–54. I would like to thank Dott. Mendogni for generously sharing his bibliography with me. The document of sale of the chapel, dated 11 October 1514, still among the papers of the notary Giovanni Antonio Dal Monte in the Archivio di Stato of Parma, registers the passage of the chapel from Filippo Arcimboldi to Ottaviano Bergonzi and the intention to replace the Arcimboldi coat of arms with that of the Bergonzi. David Ekserdjian transcribes the document in David Ekserdjian, *Correggio*, appendix 2, 297–98; see also his important discussion of the picture on 193–204. Briseide Colla was likely later buried there as well, since she ordered annual anniversary masses for both her husband and herself as part of her testamentary charge to the confraternity of the Steccata in Parma.

60. It should be noted that, in the case of Correggio's picture, the 1514 document of sale of the Bergonzi chapel (see previous note) records the chapel as dedicated to Saint Jerome. The first pastoral visit of Parma (Archivio Vescovile di Parma, Castelli, Visitatio, 1578, fol. 235v.) suggests a subsequent dedicatory shift: it describes the altar as that of the Virgin Mary (and refers as well to anniversary masses celebrated there in honor of Briseide Colla). While the earlier altar dedication might explain Jerome's presence in Correggio's painting (cf. Ekserdjian, *Correggio*, 196), it need not altogether preclude our suggestions about the relationship of female patronage to that saint and to the Virgin Mary. Correggio's picture is not an example of testamentary patronage of a widow acting on behalf of her dead husband and, as David Ekserdjian speculates, Ottaviano Bergonzi may have played some role in the commission. It is Briseide's name, however, that appears invariably in the recorded documents related to the picture; the bequest of the altarpiece to the church in her last testament (notarized by Nicolo Clarimondi, now presumably lost) suggests Briseide's more significant share in its patronage. Of further interest is the presence of a kneeling woman in the background of the picture, perhaps a portrait of Briseide Colla; see King, *Renaissance Women Patrons*, 173-74.

Vittoria Colonna and the Commission
for a *Mary Magdalene* by Titian

Marjorie Och

In 1531 Vittoria Colonna acquired a painting of the Mary Magdalen by Titian that may be the *Mary Magdalen* now in the Palazzo Pitti (fig. 1).[1] The Pitti *Magdalen* is a remarkable image: the penitent saint is represented crying, her reddened and tearful eyes gazing heavenward, her naked body only partially covered by her hair. Unlike the many later paintings of the Magdalen by Titian and his workshop in which the saint appears draped, she is here depicted attempting to cover her nakedness with her long, flowing hair. It is her nudity and what has been interpreted as her eroticism that has been problematic for viewers of both the past and present. Vasari flatly denied the eroticism of Titian's Magdalen, saying, "although she is extremely beautiful, [the painting] does not move the viewer to lustful thoughts but rather to pity."[2] But in denying the eroticism of the Magdalen, was he not calling his readers' attention to it? In any case, twentieth-century viewers are generally more open in their projection of the Magdalen's sexuality as represented by Titian. According to Charles Hope, "The enduring popularity of Titian's *Magdalens*, both lightly clothed and naked, was surely not based on their religious content alone."[3] Such judgments have led many to ask what Vittoria Colonna, the "famous Renaissance bluestocking," would appreciate in this work.[4]

The painting is remarkable for other reasons as well. This was apparently the first of many on the subject of the Magdalen by Titian. In each the Magdalen is placed within a darkened landscape, the walls of her grotto barely distinguishable, with Titian's characteristic blue Venetian sky in the distance. Of Titian's approximately forty paintings of the Magdalen, Harold Wethey identified four main types: the Pitti version is the only one in which the Magdalen is shown nude and without a book; the Naples version is identified by the alabaster or ceramic unguent jar; the Hermitage type is distinguished by the clear glass unguent jar; and finally, in the Escorial type, the Magdalen's book is placed on a small pillow or on a skull facing the viewer, and there is usually a more open distant landscape.[5] The popularity of Titian's representations of the Magdalen for sixteenth-century patrons makes the Pitti painting all the more important for its position of primacy in his oeuvre; moreover, an understanding of the popularity of Titian's Magdalen imagery would seem to require a careful examination of the circumstances under which Titian produced the Pitti version and the interests of the person for whom it was painted. Fortunately, evidence of these circumstances and interests survives in the form of correspondence and has been published.[6] Although these documents feature prominently in every account of Titian's painting, their interpretation has been treated variously, and no account offers the clarification of Vittoria Colonna's participation in the commission that will be presented here.

There are three aspects of this work that can be explored: the singularity of the Pitti version, namely, the naked Magdalen; the popularity and significance of the Magdalen in

Och Fig. 1. Titian, *Mary Magdalen* (Pitti type), ca. 1530–35, Florence, Galleria Pitti
(photo: Alinari/Art Resource, N.Y.)

medieval tradition and sixteenth-century devotions, particularly for women; and finally, the problem of interpreting the documents. I assert that a number of significant factors relating to this painting have not received sufficient attention; its commission has been misunderstood and its visual appeal oversimplified, problems resulting from twentieth-century assumptions regarding both patronage and eroticism. A feminist approach to the historical material here allows for a rereading of Titian's Pitti *Magdalen* and a reattribution of its commission to Vittoria Colonna. My interpretation of the subject matter and documents proposes that Titian's Pitti *Magdalen* was not a gift to Colonna, as it is usually described, but rather a commission of hers made possible by a supportive network within her extended family. Colonna's particular interest in Mary Magdalen as a type of the virtuous woman and as an exemplum of the penitent woman are themes present in Colonna's poetry, letters, and social concerns.

First, I will review the documentation and patronage of Titian's painting and suggest that the initiative for the commission came from Vittoria Colonna. Second, I will examine aspects of the life and myth of Mary Magdalen that led to her popularity in the sixteenth century and her particular meaning for Colonna—a meaning that further substantiates the origin of the commission with Colonna. And finally, I will examine the sensuousness of Titian's *Mary Magdalen* and suggest an interpretation of its eroticism that reestablishes the work within its sixteenth-century context.

The Documentation

The documentation consists of a series of letters dated from March through July of 1531 between Federico II Gonzaga, Duke of Mantua, and his agent in Venice, Benedetto Agnello (see appendix). There are also relevant letters between Gonzaga and Titian and between Gonzaga and Colonna. In Gonzaga's letters to his agent and to Titian, the duke makes known his wish to give a painting of the Magdalen to the Marchese Alfonso d'Avalos del Vasto, who was commander of imperial forces, advisor to Charles V, and cousin of and heir to Vittoria Colonna's husband.[7] In contrast, Gonzaga's correspondence with Colonna points to Colonna's early interest in the painting, although she is never specifically identified as the patron.

Scholars have interpreted these documents variously. Joseph A. Crowe and Giovanni Battista Cavalcaselle who referred only to Federico Gonzaga's letter to Titian of 5 March 1531 (see appendix, letter 1), believed Federico Gonzaga intended to give the *Mary Magdalen* to Alfonso del Vasto.[8] Harold Wethey interprets this same letter to mean that Gonzaga ordered the painting for the Marchese del Vasto to present to Colonna.[9] According to Charles Hope, who mistakenly thought that Vittoria Colonna was the mother of the Marchese Alfonso d'Avalos del Vasto, "[t]he picture was actually for d'Avalos's mother, Vittoria Colonna, but Titian was not informed of this."[10] Monika Ingenhoff-Danhäuser suggests that Gonzaga changed his mind about giving the work to del Vasto, and gave it instead to Colonna.[11] While the letters initially confuse rather than clarify the commission, Gonzaga's correspondence with Colonna seems to suggest that it was Colonna's interest in the painting that activated the commission.

Recent research on women in early modern Europe has highlighted the unconvincing and even inaccurate results of examinations of women's history that do not consider the ways in which the social construction of gender can determine a woman's opportunities and responses. Joan Kelly articulated the question in her 1977 article, "Did Women have a Renaissance?"[12] Social restrictions based on gender consistently denied women access to the political, educational and cultural advances made during the fifteenth and sixteenth centuries.[13] Since Linda Nochlin's "Why Have There Been No Great Women Artists?" of 1971, art historians have begun to recognize the constricting role of society's expectations and the limited realm of offerings available to women with artistic aspirations.[14] Indeed, evaluations of women's contributions to culture in the fifteenth and sixteenth centuries necessitate a reexamination and even a redefinition of our terminology of cultural negotiations. For example, the origin of the word "patron" in the Latin *pater* suggests that patronage is a male-centered activity—hence our expectation that patrons are men, and that the activity of these male patrons defines the norm. Inherent in this male activity is the assumption that the patron or the patron's agent deals with the artist directly; such a system of patronage, however, does not accommodate individuals who acquired works of art through other means, such as through a series of indirect negotiations, as was the case for Vittoria Colonna. With this in mind, it is possible to reread the letters associated with this painting and argue that it was actually Colonna who initiated the commission. These letters also clarify the roles played by Federico Gonzaga and Alfonso del Vasto in Colonna's acquisition of the work. Patronage, here, becomes something other than a client's direct contact with an artist. The manner in which Colonna acquired the *Mary Magdalen* (that is, through the assistance of her extended family) points to a system of women's patronage that may have been more representative of women in the Renaissance than has been previously recognized.

The correspondence begins with Federico's letter to Titian of 5 March 1531 (letter 1) in which Federico states his wish to give the work to Alfonso del Vasto. The duke explains to Titian exactly what he wants the artist to paint:

> I want you to make for me a Mary Magdalen as tearful as you can make her, in a painting as large as this one [referring to a *Saint Jerome* by Titian, which he had just received], or a little larger, and that you take every effort to make it beautiful…supply it as quickly as possible because I want to send it as a gift to the Most Illustrious Signor Marchese del Vasto.[15]

This letter was most likely sent to Venice accompanied by Gonzaga's letter, also of 5 March (letter 2), to Benedetto Agnello, the duke's agent in the city. Among Agnello's duties were the tasks of delivering the duke's correspondence to Titian and, eventually, the painting to the duke. In his brief letter of 5 March, Federico commands his agent to tell Titian of his desire for a painting of the Mary Magdalen, a reiteration of his comments to the artist. Agnello responds to Gonzaga in a letter written 11 March (letter 3) in which he reports that he has given the duke's letter to the artist and that Titian has begun work on the painting.[16] Neither Alfonso del Vasto nor Vittoria Colonna is mentioned in the correspondence between Federico Gonzaga and Benedetto Agnello.

Also dated 11 March 1531 is a letter from Federico Gonzaga to Vittoria Colonna (letter 4) in which he writes that he has heard from a mutual friend, the imperial commander Fabrizio Maramaldo, of her desire to have

> a beautiful picture [of the Mary Magdalen] by the hand of an excellent painter. I immediately sent to Venice and wrote to Titian…to make one most beautiful and as tearful as possible, and to let me have it quickly.[17]

He adds that he hopes to send the painting to her by Easter. That Gonzaga repeated to both Titian and Colonna that the work was to be "most beautiful and as tearful as possible" suggests that this may have been a directive from Colonna that Gonzaga had received from Maramaldo, and that the duke was now assuring her that this would be carried out.[18]

A letter of 19 March from Gonzaga (letter 6) responds to Agnello's of 18 March (letter 5), which indicates that Titian had begun work on the painting. Within a month's time, Titian completed the *Mary Magdalen*, for on 19 April Gonzaga wrote to the artist (letter 12) that he had received the painting and that everyone who had seen it had praised its beauty and the artist's talent. Gonzaga said nothing regarding Vittoria Colonna or Alfonso del Vasto, but Colonna wrote to Gonzaga from Ischia on 25 May (letter 14) to thank him for a painting of the Magdalen: "For the Magdalen, I thank you countless times."[19] Colonna's letter is not particularly effusive; indeed, the brevity of her comments regarding the painting might be considered almost rude from someone who had just received a gift of a Titian painting.[20] The fact that her letter has no words of praise for the painting strongly suggests that Colonna was not the recipient of a gift.

The painting's commission is clarified by a letter of 28 July (letter 15), in which the duke thanks Colonna for two letters he recently received; he notes that one letter was accompanied by a gift of roses, while in the other, "you advised me that you were pleased by the Magdalen that I sent to you," doubtless in response to Colonna's letter of 25 May (letter 14).[21] Again, although roses would seem an unseemly counter-gift for a Titian, they would be entirely appropriate as a thank-you for his assistance in Colonna's effort to acquire a *Magdalen*. In all likelihood, the lost letter that accompanied the roses was written in response to Gonzaga's letter to Colonna in which he informs her that he has written Titian regarding her desire for a painting of the Magdalen (letter 4). Colonna's matter-of-fact acknowledgement of the painting's receipt resembles nothing so much as the successful conclusion of a business transaction.

From this correspondence we know that Titian was at work on a *Mary Magdalen* for Gonzaga by 11 March and that it was finished by 19 April. Finally, we know that Colonna received a *Mary Magdalen* by 25 May 1531. While Colonna's name never appears in the surviving correspondence between Gonzaga and Titian or between Gonzaga and Agnello, it seems to have been Colonna's interest, dictated through Maramaldo and Alfonso del Vasto, that initiated the process; it was Gonzaga who contacted Titian to begin this commission.

Patronage

Why would Vittoria Colonna have turned to Federico Gonzaga instead of communicating directly with Titian? Her reasons could have been both practical and artistic. Vittoria Colonna and Federico Gonzaga, related through the marriage of the duke's sister (Eleanora Gonzaga della Rovere) to Francesco Maria della Rovere (Duke of Urbino and Colonna's cousin), had maintained a steady correspondence since at least 1523.[22] Furthermore, Colonna was the widow of an illustrious imperial commander, Ferdinando Francesco d'Avalos, whose title she retained in her name, Vittoria Colonna, Marchesa di Pescara. And finally, Federico Gonzaga owed her a considerable sum of money. The earliest surviving correspondence between Colonna and Gonzaga is a letter she wrote to him on 8 May 1523 concerning money he owed her husband for a ransom to be paid by the duke in exchange for the freedom of Teodoro Trivulzio, a Venetian captain taken prisoner at Milan in November 1521 and held by Colonna's husband.[23] Letters in April 1535 between Colonna and Fabrizio Peregrino, Federico Gonzaga's ambassador in Rome, indicate that the duke had yet to pay this debt.[24] It is possible that Colonna turned to Gonzaga in 1531 to ask him for assistance in part because of the money he owed her.

Vittoria Colonna may also have sought the duke's advice and help in a transaction in which he was known to excel. With Isabella d'Este as his mother, one could almost say that Federico Gonzaga was born to be a patron. Already by 1524 Gonzaga had lured Giulio Romano from Rome to Mantua where, between 1527 and 1534, the artist was involved in the construction and decoration of the Palazzo del Te.[25] In addition to Giulio Romano's talent, Gonzaga was actively pursuing that of Titian. By 1531 Gonzaga had become one of Titian's major patrons.[26] The duke had already commissioned from the artist several portraits, including one of himself (ca. 1523; Prado, Madrid), as well as the *Madonna and Child with Saint Catherine and a Rabbit* (1528–30; Louvre, Paris), a *Saint Jerome* (delivered March 1531; Louvre, Paris), and a painting described by Titian as "nudes."[27]

Perhaps more important than his patronage of Titian was Federico Gonzaga's ability to serve as a significant contact for the artist. Titian's aspirations for imperial patronage are well known, and it was probably through Gonzaga that Titian first met Charles V.[28] After Charles's coronation as Holy Roman Emperor in February 1530, he was a guest of the Gonzaga in Mantua from March through April. Titian's imperial patronage seems to have developed through the artist's cultivation of his strongest imperial connection, the Gonzaga. Titian's professional interests may help explain the apparent contradictions in the documents relating to the commission for the *Mary Magdalen*, particularly the question of the identity of the ultimate owner of the painting. In his letter to Titian of 5 March (letter 1), Federico Gonzaga makes a point of emphasizing the importance of the person to whom he wanted to give the *Mary Magdalen*: "I want to send it as a gift to the Most Illustrious Signor Marchese del Vasto. Make it of a sort that will be a worthy gift to a Lord such as this Marchese." The Marchese del Vasto, a trusted advisor to Charles V, was high in the command of imperial forces. Federico's statement that he intended to give the painting to the marchese would certainly not have gone unnoticed by Titian; it seems that the duke was alerting the artist of the significance of this commission in the hope that he would create an exceptional work. At a time when Titian was working almost exclusively for the duke, the offer to expand his circle of clients beyond the small courts of northern Italy must have held great appeal to the painter. His success with the emperor and the imperial entourage bound the artist to Federico Gonzaga in gratitude. Indeed, Titian continued to work for the duke until Gonzaga's death in 1540, and even depended on Gonzaga for legal advice.[29] In return for the artist's devotion, the duke facilitated Titian's access to Charles V.[30]

The Marchese Alfonso d'Avalos del Vasto may have also been significant in Titian's rise to favor, although his role in this commission is difficult to plot. In a letter dated November 1531, del Vasto asks Pietro Aretino to arrange for Titian to visit him at his headquarters in Correggio, emphasizing that "the steps of the master would not be taken in vain."[31] From this it is possible to speculate that del Vasto was perhaps as instrumental as Gonzaga in solidifying Titian's imperial patronage. By 1533 del Vasto had certainly acquired the magnificent portrait, now in the Louvre, which is particularly interesting because his pose is similar to that of Charles V in a portrait of 1530.[32] Several years later, Titian was again at work for del Vasto on the *Allocution of the General del Vasto to his Soldiers* (1539–41; Prado, Madrid).[33]

While there is no evidence indicating the marchese knew of Titian's *Mary Magdalen* painted for Colonna, del Vasto and Colonna corresponded with one another and, it seems, discussed art.[34] A letter of March 1533 from Isabella d'Este to Alfonso del Vasto's secretary, Tommaso Tuca (letter 16), indicates that Vittoria Colonna wanted yet another painting of the Magdalen, this time a copy of one owned by Isabella.[35] Unfortunately, it is not clear from Isabella's letter who painted the original or who was to paint the copy. The copy, however, was executed and delivered to del Vasto, as his letter of 4 March 1533 (letter 17) shows.[36] Certainly, Alfonso del Vasto was aware of Colonna's interest in Magdalen imagery at least from 1533, and he may well have known of the 1531 painting by Titian already in Colonna's collection.

It is important to emphasize that while there was no direct contact between Vittoria Colonna and Titian, she succeeded in acquiring this work. I would suggest that both Federico Gonzaga and Fabrizio Maramaldo, and perhaps to some extent also Alfonso del Vasto, acted as Vittoria Colonna's agents, or mediators, in her acquisition of Titian's painting. Her acquisition would, then, have been accomplished through a network of contacts within her extended family. Colonna once again relied on mediation when, in 1533, Alfonso del Vasto acted as Vittoria Colonna's intermediary when he assisted in her acquisition of a second *Mary Magdalen*.[37]

Working through such a network was a common Renaissance way of getting things done, and social historians have shown that this was frequently a legal requirement for unmarried or widowed women.[38] As the legal and social status of women shifted from broader personal rights and liberties in the fifteenth century to fewer in the sixteenth, restrictions increased. One control placed on unmarried or widowed women at this time was the requirement that they work through a male sponsor or *mundualdus* in business matters. While historians have examined this with regard to the exchange of goods and lands, it is possible that as patrons of art, women were also, on occasion, expected to work through a similar legal system.[39] Such a requirement would distinguish the process of women's patronage from that of men and raise a number of questions about specific commissions and patrons, including: What does the originator of the commission, the patron, really know about art? What options does this patron have in choosing the artist? How dependent is this patron on the taste, even whims, of the individual(s) who assist her?

Would Vittoria Colonna have specified to del Vasto, Maramaldo, or Gonzaga that she wanted a painting by Titian? Although Titian is not mentioned by Colonna in any of her surviving letters, it is possible that Colonna could have asked for a painting by this artist. One of her closest friends, Pietro Bembo, was a friend of Titian's, and he may have made her aware of the Venetian's work. Furthermore, we know that Colonna was familiar with Venetian art and that she knew the importance of Giorgione, who is mentioned by Castiglione in *Il Cortegiano*; Colonna received a copy of Castiglione's manuscript from the author by 1520.[40] Moreover, Colonna may have had in her collection an idealized portrait of herself by the Venetian Sebastiano del Piombo, painted ca. 1510 at the time of her marriage.[41] Indeed, one might ask to whom Colonna could have turned for a religious painting at this time. Certainly Italy was not without artists, but Colonna, who traveled between Rome, Naples, and Ischia in the years immediately following the Sack of Rome, would have been aware of the exodus of artists from Rome.[42] Many artists had gone to Venice, and it may have appeared that Venice was becoming the new center for art.[43] It is possible that Alfonso del Vasto's contribution to the commission can be described as follows: Colonna desired a *Mary Magdalen* while at the same time del Vasto wanted to further his social status and perhaps even his imperial connections by supporting Titian—a prominent artist who had caught the attention of the emperor.

The Magdalen in Literature and the Visual Arts

Mary of Magdala is specifically mentioned with reference to four stories in the New Testament. She is the woman Christ frees of seven demons (Luke 8:2; Mark 16:9); she is one of the women present at the death of Christ (Matthew 27:56; Mark 15:40–41; John 19:25); she is one of the three women who found his tomb empty (Matthew 28:1–10; Mark 16:1–11; Luke 24:10; John 20:1–2); and she is the first person to whom Christ appears after his resurrection (Mark 16:9; John 20:11–18). In each case, Mary of Magdala is described as one of the followers of Christ. Two other New Testament women, however, have come to be associated with her. One, an unnamed "woman in the city, which was a sinner," comes to Jesus in the house of Simon the Pharisee; she washes Jesus's feet with her tears, dries them with her hair, and anoints them with perfume (Luke 7:36–50). Although this sinful woman is converted, the nature of her sin is never stated.[44] A third Mary, the sister of Martha, "sat at Jesus's feet, and heard his word" while Martha busied herself with the housework (Luke 10:38–42). From this narrative, Martha and Mary came to symbolize the Active and Contemplative Lives in the Christian church. This Mary, sister of Martha and Lazarus, was identified by John as Mary of Bethany, the woman who anointed Jesus's feet with perfume when Jesus and his disciples were at the house of Lazarus before Passover (John 11:1–2 and 12:1–8).

In the Eastern church, these three women, Mary of Magdala, Mary of Bethany, and the unnamed sinner, maintained separate identities, but in the West they were united to become Mary of Magdala, a converted sinner. It was Pope Gregory the Great who declared that the three Marys were one in his homily on Luke's Gospel delivered in Rome ca. 591. The focus of Gregory's Homily is Mary as an example of conversion and penitence:

> She whom Luke calls the sinful woman…we believe to be the Mary from whom seven devils were ejected according to Mark. And what did these seven devils signify, if not all the vices?…It is clear, brothers, that the woman previously used the unguent to perfume her flesh in forbidden acts. What she therefore displayed more scandalously, she was now offering to God in a more praiseworthy manner. She had coveted with earthly eyes, but now through penitence these are consumed with tears. She displayed her hair to set off her face, but now her hair dries her tears. She had spoken proud things with her mouth, but in kissing the Lord's feet, she now planted her mouth on the Redeemer's feet. For every delight she had had in herself, she now immolated herself. She turned the mass of her crimes to virtues, in order to serve God entirely in penance, for as much as she had wrongly held God in contempt.[45]

The conflation of the Mary stories and the identification of the woman's sins as sins of the flesh resulted in a composite Mary Magdalen who eventually became the penitent saint par excellence.[46] Mary Magdalen became the saint whose body was synonymous with sin; indeed, her body became her most distinctive attribute.

Although the New Testament does not give an account of the life of the Magdalen before her conversion or after the Resurrection of Christ, there is a Mary in the apocryphal books of the New Testament whose identity was merged with that of Mary Magdalen and whose stories further embellish the saint's legends.[47] Born to a royal family, this Mary, again the sister of Lazarus and Martha, was as beautiful as she was rich; while Lazarus owned much of Jerusalem and Martha now held Bethany, Mary owned the castle of Magdala. Characteristic of these accounts is the description of this Mary as a young woman committed not only to her own physical pleasures, but who also draws others into her sinful life. After the death of Christ, however, she is presented as an ideal "widow"; choosing a life of meditation and penitence, she is free to contemplate the death of her beloved, her Christ, her "husband."[48] Other legends concerning this Mary include her miraculous journey to Provence, her baptism of the pagan inhabitants of Marseilles, her thirty years as a hermit near Sainte-Baume, and her miracles. The most popular compilation of medieval Magdalen stories, and perhaps the most influential, was the thirteenth-century account by Jacobus de Voragine in the *Golden Legend*.[49] The Magdalen of the *Golden Legend* is a woman whose life is akin to those of the readers of Jacobus da Voragine—landed nobility with the responsibilities and temptations of wealth—and she is presented for his readers as a model of penitence to follow. The penitent Magdalen was further popularized in trecento Italy by the Mendicant orders, in whose writings and sermons she became the paradigm of penitence.[50] The discovery of her relics in the thirteenth century, much celebrated at the time, promoted her popularity, a popularity that may be seen as symptomatic of a need for a female penitent saint; moreover, new biographies of the saint embellished and moralized the *Golden Legend* account.[51]

The lessons conveyed by the narratives of Mary of Magdala are the bountiful love of Christ for a woman who embodied the evils of womanhood and the salvation offered to the truly penitent. As the woman who had been present at the death of Christ, the individual to whom Christ chose to appear first after his resurrection, and the follower of Christ whom the Early Church called the "Apostle to the Apostles," Mary Magdalen became, after the thirteenth century, the type of the sinful woman redeemed through faith.[52] Her sin was understood as the sin of all women—weakness of the flesh—and a fate she could not deny.[53] The beautiful and decadent young Magdalen merged with the penitent Magdalen to become a powerful, popular image in the Renaissance.

Vittoria Colonna could recognize and find comfort in the life of the Magdalen presented in this tradition. For a widow, an ascetic, and a woman who needed to harmonize her secular and spiritual worlds, the penitent Magdalen was a compelling model. Mary Magdalen thus presented a model of widowhood with which Colonna could identify, and whose feelings toward Christ Colonna could share. In 1525, at the age of thirty-five, Vittoria Colonna had indeed become a widow.[54] In the following years she received several offers of marriage— offers that her brother, Ascanio, encouraged.[55] Colonna steadfastly refused, choosing instead to establish for herself a life in a convent. From 1525 until her death in 1547 Colonna lived in several convents in Rome, Viterbo, and Orvieto. Her life from this point on resembled that of many other widowed noblewomen who chose to live as lay members of religious communities instead of remarrying. In her letters and poetry Colonna referred to these women as her "sisters" and her fellow "brides of Christ."[56] During the 1530s Vittoria Colonna was a prominent member of the Rome-based reform group called the *Spirituali*, and her religious fervor extended beyond thoughts of reform to the mortification of her body, the wearing of hairshirts, and long periods of fasting. We know from a number of sources of Colonna's dedication to an ascetic life in the decade immediately following the death of her husband. Contemporary legend, posthumous accounts, records of the Inquisition, and her own letters suggest that she turned her attentions to the religious life swiftly and with nearly self-destructive force.

When Vittoria Colonna's close friend Pietro Carnesecchi (1508–67) (who was later executed for heresy) was brought before the Roman Inquisition in 1566, he was asked about his acquaintances, including Vittoria Colonna and other members of the *Spirituali* in Rome. All were suspected of heresy, even those who were deceased. In responding to the Inquisitors' demand for information regarding Colonna's views on the controversial debate over Justification by Faith, Carnesecchi replied:

> Before the Signora Marchesa contracted her friendship with the Cardinal [Reginald Pole], she used to afflict herself so much with fasts, sackcloth, and other mortifications of the flesh that she had reduced herself to skin and bone, and this she did, perhaps, because she placed too much confidence in such works, imagining that true piety and religion, and consequently the salvation of one's soul, consisted in these things. But after being advised by the Cardinal that she rather offended God than otherwise by treating her body with such austerity and rigor…the aforesaid Signora began to desist from that very austere mode of life, reducing her mortifications little by little to a just and reasonable mean.[57]

Colonna, herself, had described these religious excesses as "il caos d'ignorantia" in a letter she wrote to Cardinal Giovanni Morone dated 22 December (probably 1542 or 1543).[58] Vittoria Colonna's religious fervor was public knowledge, as one of her contemporaries noted that when Colonna was living at San Silvestro in Capite, she did not "wish to be visited by anyone, and like[d] to go about Rome unrecognized and in the poorest clothes."[59] While the accuracy of this statement can be debated, Colonna's religiosity was notable enough to be recognized as extraordinary.

The Magdalen played a significant role in Vittoria Colonna's spiritual life. In addition to following the Magdalen's ascetic and penitent devotional practices, Colonna was aware of the special position the Magdalen held in the story of Jesus's life. Jesus's instructions to the Magdalen to return to his brothers with news of his Resurrection (Matthew 28:9–10; Mark

16:9–11; Luke 24:10; John 20:11–18) were singled out in her 22 June 1544 letter to Cardinal Giovanni Morone.[60] The Magdalen is isolated by Colonna in another letter to her cousin, Costanza d'Avalos Piccolomini, as "nostra advocata et fedelissima scorta Maddalena."[61] Moreover, Colonna describes the devotions of the Magdalen in an undated poem in which she addresses the Magdalen as 'Donna accesa animosa,' a phrase which would seem to refer to Titian's Magdalen, herself.[62] Finally, Colonna's personal devotion to Mary Magdalen is verified in a letter of 13 March 1537 from Paul III (letter 18), in which he grants her permission to make a pilgrimage to the Magdalen's shrine in Provence.[63] In her decision to follow the Magdalen's intense devotions, as well as in her steadfast refusal to remarry and thus reconnect with the secular world, Colonna may well have been identifying with the similar struggles of the Magdalen.

The Magdalen's significance in the religious life of sixteenth-century women in Italy is also important here. Mary of Magdala had long been held up as an exemplum for Italian noblewomen. One of the most influential of the Magdalen's advocates was Saint Antoninus, Archbishop of Florence from 1446 until 1459.[64] In Antoninus's writings, the Magdalen was praised for her penitence, self-sacrifice, and life of prayer. Antoninus encouraged his contemporaries to adopt the Magdalen as their role model; women, whom he judged to be weak in mind and spirit and thus more likely to succumb to the sins of this world, were particularly urged to follow the example of the Magdalen. Significantly, he did not present the Magdalen as an exemplar only to sinful women (such as prostitutes), although they, too, are urged to follow her. The letters of Antoninus to particular Florentine women like Diodata degli Adimari, suggest that Antoninus was also singling out women of the aristocratic and merchant classes.[65]

For her own part, Colonna was becoming deeply involved in the plight and mission of the Capuchins in Rome in the 1530s. Asceticism and charity, the virtues for which the Magdalen was praised, were the virtues sought by the Franciscans and the motivation behind the Capuchins' eremitic life of prayer and good deeds within their communities. It is likely that the growing interest in Magdalen imagery in the sixteenth century was a response to Capuchin sermons on harmonizing the Contemplative with the Active Life.[66] Indeed, the Capuchins emphasized Magdalen imagery in their early years. The Capuchin Constitutions of 1536, for example, stated that they were to "lead alternately the life of Mary and the life of Martha."[67] This is of particular interest with respect to Vittoria Colonna's patronage of the new order from around 1535. If Colonna found an example in the Magdalen, as I believe she did sometime around 1530, then her response to the Capuchins would have been especially positive because they emphasized the life of the Magdalen in their constitutions and sermons. The fact that so many women, particularly widows, responded to the Capuchins' call for aid raises the possibility that the friars' appeal to these women was, in part, due to the use of Magdalen imagery in their sermons.

The Sensuous Magdalen

Titian's painting of the Magdalen is extraordinary by twentieth-century standards of sensuous beauty, and it offers a sensuousness that is difficult to relate to an understanding of Vittoria Colonna as a "famous Renaissance bluestocking."[68] This apparent contradiction may be resolved by examining the representation of the Magdalen in literature and the visual arts. Following upon the moralizing biography of the Magdalen in the *Golden Legend*, the Magdalen in literature continued to be appealing because, as converted prostitute *and* widow of Christ, she could embody conflicting views of woman. Indeed, the emphasis in the literature of the late Middle Ages is on the Magdalen as a passionate and sensuous woman who simultaneously maintains her role as a penitent saint. Nurith Kenaan-Kedar has suggested that the new focus of the Franciscan piety on the passion of the Magdalen opened the door for new interpretations of her story. In the sermons of Saint Bonaventura (1221–74), for example, the Magdalen is characterized as ablaze with the fire of divine love and burning with a powerful desire. At the same time she is also an example of the Contemplative Life, and an embodiment of the virtues of charity and humility.[69] This Franciscan piety had an important sensual foundation that included an emphasis on burning love and such contrasts as joy and pain.[70] For Kenaan-Kedar, the pictorial equivalent to this Franciscan literary image is Giotto's representation in the Arena Chapel frescoes of the Magdalen as a beautiful and emotional woman at the crucifixion.[71] This is yet more so in the case of Titian, who visualized the saint's body as her most significant attribute—a body symbolic of both feminine beauty and of a woman's sin redeemed.

The sensuality of the Magdalen and the intimacy of her relationship with Christ are the themes of a poem written by Petrarch in the late 1330s—at the time of his pilgrimage to Sainte-Baume, the shrine of the Magdalen in Provence. The poem is in the form of a prayer addressed to the saint:

> Dear friend of God, look kindly on our tears,
> And heed our humble prayers; for our salvation
> Take thought. Indeed thou canst; for not in vain
> Wast thou allowed to touch and bathe His holy
> Feet with thy weeping and to wipe them dry
> With thy sleek tresses and to kiss His soles,
> And on thy Lord's head sprinkle precious scents.
> Nor vainly when He rose up from the dead
> Met He thee first: Christ, King of heavenly
> Olympus, vouchsafed thee to hear His voice
> And see His limbs; so shalt thou ever have
> Undying glory and eternal light.
> He had seen thee cling to His cross without
> Shrinking from dire torments at Jewish hands,
> And taunts and insults of the furious crowd,
> Their tongues as cruel as strokes of the whip.
> But thou, grieved and at the same time intrepid,
> Didst pass thy fingers o'er the gory spikes,
> Thy tears soaking his wounds, thy savage fists
> Beating thy breast, and hands relentlessly
> Tearing thine hair. This, I say, had He seen
> While His stouthearted men fled far and wide,
> Driven by fear. Remembering this, therefore,
> He came back to thee, ere any other,
> To thee alone presented first Himself.
> And then, on leaving earth and to the stars
> Returning, He fed thee for thirty years
> Beneath this cliff, ne'er needing mortal food
> For such a long time, since thou wast content
> With naught but God-sent feasts and wholesome dew.[72]

Petrarch recounts the Magdalen's experiences from the Crucifixion and her visit to the tomb of Jesus through the years of her solitary life. The Magdalen's physical appearance, particularly her nudity, is contrasted with her surroundings in the grotto; these inhospitable surroundings, however, are of little concern to the Magdalen. Petrarch continues:

> This cave thine home, damp from the dripping rocks,
> Gloomy with frightful slime, had yet surpassed

The golden roofs of kings and every comfort
And opulent lands. Here willingly shut in,
Clad in thy long hair, reft of other garb,
'Tis said thou did endure thrice ten Decembers,
Not broken by the frost nor whelmed with dread,
Since hunger, cold, and the hard bed of stone
Were sweetened by the love and hope implanted
Deep in thy breast. Here, to the eyes of men
Unseen, surrounded by angelic hosts,
From thy bodily prison wast thou worthy,
For seven hours of the day upward borne,
To hear responsive hymns of heavenly choirs.[73]

According to Joseph Gibaldi, Petrarch has here transferred the language of the secular love lyric to sacred verse, "anticipating the baroque commingling of the flesh and the spirit,…[Petrarch insists] not just on the beauty of the saint's soul, but on her physical attractiveness, as well; our attention is repeatedly drawn to her shining…hair, her white breast, and her state of undress in the grotto."[74]

In spite of the visual and literary tradition for the Magdalen's beauty, the sensuous nudity of the Pitti *Magdalen* has remained difficult to interpret for both Renaissance viewers and twentieth-century scholars. Evidence suggests, however, that it was less disturbing to Colonna's contemporaries. Titian himself described his 1550 *Penitent Magdalen* in a letter of 1567 to his patron, Cardinal Alessandro Farnese, as "in an attitude of devotion and penitence."[75] In this case, the Magdalen is fully clothed. Her hair, which falls across her shoulders so freely and protectively in the Pitti version of twenty years earlier, is controlled, even tamed. There is less emphasis on the Magdalen's body and more on the landscape setting, as if Titian were intent on making a narrative of this scene. Indeed, Titian may have been responding to a reform environment that dictated clarity and condemned ambiguity in religious paintings.

In describing Titian's *Magdalen* of 1561, Vasari writes:

> Titian painted a work to be sent to the Catholic king [Philip II], a disheveled figure of Saint Mary Magdalen painted down to the middle of her thighs—that is, with her hair falling around her neck down on her shoulders and on her breast, while she raises her head with her eyes fixed towards the sky, showing remorse in the redness of her eyes and, in her tears, sorrow for her sins; this painting would move anyone gazing at it in the most profound manner, and, what is more, although she is extremely beautiful it does not move the viewer to lustful thoughts but, rather, to pity.[76]

Titian's painting of the Magdalen for Philip II is lost, but in what is believed to be a copy, dated 1695 and attributed to Luca Giordano (Escorial, Iglesia Vieja), the Magdalen clutches her hair to her breast with her left hand, while gathering her clothing with her right.[77] Her mouth is more open than in the Pitti version, as if in prayer or song, or as if ready to receive the sacred food delivered to her by angels. The Magdalen's eyes have advanced even further under her eyelids, suggesting a fluttering, as in none of Titian's other Magdalens. Her one exposed breast, and her futile attempt to cover herself, are both sexual and suggestive of the frenzied rapture of religious ecstasy. But this is an ecstasy born of penitence and sorrow—the presence of the skull facing outward reminds both the Magdalen and the viewer of death. This is the only *Penitent Magdalen* composition by Titian in which the skull confronts the viewer in this manner.[78]

Titian's contemporaries continued to puzzle over these *Penitent Magdalens*, and Titian himself was not averse to encouraging a fluidity of meaning. Baccio Valori (1535–1606), a Florentine nobleman, recalled the following discussion with Titian from a visit to his studio:

> There I met Titian, almost immobilized by age who, despite the fact that he was very appreciated for painting from the life, showed me a very attractive Magdalen in the desert. Also I remember now that I told him she was too attractive, so fresh and dewy, for such penitence. Having understood that I meant that she should be gaunt through fasting, he answered laughing that he had painted her on the first day she had entered [her repentant state], before she began fasting, in order to be able to paint her as a penitent indeed, but also as lovely as he could, and that she certainly was.[79]

It is not known which *Magdalen* the two were looking at, although it may have been the Hermitage *Magdalen* of ca. 1560, which was still in Titian's house at the time of his death.[80]

For some twentieth-century viewers, the Pitti *Magdalen* bears an uncanny resemblance to a representation of Venus.[81] According to Charles Hope, "The religious content is a decidedly minor element in the picture's appeal....It is hard to imagine a more overtly sensual treatment of the subject."[82] Hope goes so far as to suggest that Titian may have modified an earlier idea for a *Magdalen* which showed the saint draped, in favor of the Pitti composition of the nude Magdalen. Hope claims that "One could well envisage [Titian] thinking that in this form [the painting] would have a stronger appeal to d'Avalos."[83]

The Christian sincerity of both Titian and Cardinal Farnese, the patron of a late *Magdalen*, continues to trouble art historians. Clare Robertson dismissed Titian's 1567 version of the Mary Magdalen as "hardly likely to inspire devotional thoughts."[84] But should we ignore Vasari who, along with Titian, seemingly recognized the religious honesty of the Magdalen in Titian's paintings? I do not believe that Titian's images of the Magdalen are merely sensual, as Robertson would have it. David Rosand, in his review of Robertson, responded: "The art historian who, like Robertson, dismisses such passages as hypocritical risks missing the very richness and complexity of such images and, more serious still, of the religious sentiment of a culture compelled to reconsider its former commitment to the divinity of human beauty."[85]

Bernard Aikema interprets the eroticism of the Pitti *Magdalen* as a necessary attribute of the saint that should be read within an early sixteenth-century religious context of the Christian faithful confronting temptation. Rather than identifying the Pitti *Magdalen* as the painting once owned by Vittoria Colonna, Aikema has suggested a male patron "who could gain merit by overcoming the temptation of the sensuous depiction."[86] Aikema persuasively argues for an interpretation of the Pitti painting as a moralizing image. However, his conclusion that the Magdalen's eroticism implies a male viewer and hence a male patron—that is, not Vittoria Colonna—would seem to contradict what I take to be Aikema's underlying point regarding the significance of contradiction within early sixteenth-century Christian religious devotion and imagery.

The question remains, how did viewers respond to physical, even erotic beauty in a religious work at a time of Catholic reform? Was the viewer free from temptation, as Rosand might suggest? Or freed by temptation, as Aikema would have it? And how did such a painting fit into the Christian devotions of a woman? Titian's *Magdalen* is the Magdalen of Petrarch and his ideal of female beauty. Her significance, and her attraction to Catholic reformers' eyes, was not in equating beauty with God, but in reminding the viewer, through the Magdalen's own beauty, of God's forgiveness for the sin of the flesh. Indeed, it was the pleasure one found in looking at this beautiful woman that was intended to remind one of penitence.

The youthful Magdalen depicted by Titian is nude; she gathers her hair around her in a self-protective embrace, but her hair does not completely cover her. Hidden yet exposed, the Magdalen's breasts are the embodiment of nourishment and a reference to female sexuality.[87] It is through her very nakedness that Titian highlights the Magdalen's internal struggle against the flesh, communicating not merely an ideal of feminine beauty, but a warning against the dangers of that beauty.

For female viewers, whose own physical beauty was a focus for so many sixteenth-century writers and artists, contemplating the Magdalen as exemplum was particularly complex. Physical beauty was desired and pursued by both women and men.[88] However, as the Magdalen herself demonstrated, there was no joy in this beauty, but a necessary evil if one were to follow the Magdalen. In a sense, Titian's painting was for a male audience, but these were male viewers who could only look through a filter of sixteenth-century notions about female beauty, a construct determining that women, too, saw themselves reflected in that same ideal of physical beauty. Whether Colonna appreciated, enjoyed, or otherwise responded to the appearance of Titian's *Mary Magdalen* may be less significant here than the point that she was expected to see herself, in some manner, as this ideal of feminine beauty. Again we return to what Rosand described as the "richness and complexity" of this period. In seeking an exemplum of penitence, a woman was presented with the most conflicting and dangerous aspect of her own physical being—feminine beauty. Of course, the painting is and was a painting to enjoy. For the devout of the Renaissance, however, the pleasure one found in viewing could be a powerful vehicle for contemplating one's faith and fate.

The visual arts were a significant element in Vittoria Colonna's religious life. Her religious views focused on direct contact with her God, without the intercession of saints or the mediation of priests. The presence of Titian's *Mary Magdalen* in Colonna's life and in her collection would thus not be as intercessor, but as exemplar. Ironically, while this is not an image of intercession, it was through the mediation of her extended family that Vittoria Colonna acquired this work. My proposal suggests new ways of thinking about how women could patronize and how women viewed apparently erotic Christian imagery, both of which may be more representative of Renaissance women and their activities than has been recognized in the past.

Appendix

Letter 1

Federico Gonzaga to Titian
5 March 1531

> Maestro Tiziano. Ho ricevuto il quadro di S. Girolamo che me avete mandato, quale me satisfa summamente, però me è gratissimo, e lo trovo fra le cose mie più care per esser cosa veramente bella et da tenere carissima. Io non so che maggior condizione o laude darli che dire che l'è opera di Tiziano; però sotto questo celeberrimo nome el terrò con quella reputazione che merita: ve ne ringrazio infinitamente. Un altro piacere vorrei da voi, e questo desidero non meno che facessi il S. Hieronimo, quale desiderava summamente; vorrei che me faceste una Sta. Maddalena lacrimosa più che si può, in un quadro della grandezza che è questo, o dua dita più, e che vi metteste ogni studio in farlo bello, il che a voi non sarà gran cosa che non lo potreste farlo altramente, quando ben voleste, sì in fornirlo presto, che verrei [*sic*] mandarlo a donare allo Illmo. Signor Marchese del Guasto, quale è tutto mio, che ve ne priego grandemente, servirmi in ciò, come so che saprete, facendola di sorte chel parà dono onorevole, essendo mandata da me ad un Signore tale come è quel Marchese: et sopra tutto fatemela avere presto, consegnandola, subito che serà fornita, al Magnifico mio Ambasciatore, che me la mandi; che mi farete piacere grandissimo. Me vi offero etd. [*sic*]
> Mantue 5 Martii 1531
> Il Marchese di Montova [*sic*]

ASM, AG, b. 2933, libro 302, fol. 64.
Gaye, *Carteggio inedito*, 2:223.
Ingenhoff-Danhäuser, *Maria Magdalena*, 86.

Letter 2

Federico Gonzaga to Benedetto Agnello
5 March 1531

> Mag. etc. L'alligata, che va a Maestro Tiziano, glie la dareti [*sic*], che è in ringraziarlo del S. Hieronimo che 'l ni [*sic*] a mandato, et pregarlo che 'l ni voglia farme una S.ta Maria Maddalena, la quale finita che sia ce la mandereti [*sic*].
> Mantuae, 5 Marzo 1531

ASM, AG, b. 2933, libro 302, fol. 64.
Ingenhoff-Danhäuser, *Maria Magdalena*, 86.

Letter 3

Benedetto Agnello to Federico Gonzaga
11 March 1531

> 1531, 11 Marzo.
> Ho dato la sua lettera a Mro Ticiano, qual per il desiderio grande che l'ha di servire a V. E. ancho che'l si retrove alquanto indisposto ha gia fatto far la Tavola per far la Sta Maria Magdalena, et credo che hoggi darà principio a lavorarvi, nè

gli mancarà d'ogni diligentia per far una cosa excellente de la quale V. E. ne possi restar sodisfatta. Esso M. Ticiano dice voler fare la detta Sta Ma Magdalena differente da quella che l'ha principato, et che 'l mostrò a M. Vincenzo veneziano per far una cosa più bella, anchor ch'io credo che l'haveria da far assai a poterla migliorare, perchè in effetto quella che l'ha comincio, da quelli che hanno cognitione di pictura è reputata cosa excellentissima.

Da Venetia, alli xi Marzo, 1531.

ASM, AG, b. 1465, libro 302, fols. 82–83.
Crowe and Cavalcaselle, *Life and Times of Titian*, 1:450–51.
Ingenhoff-Danhäuser, *Maria Magdalena*, 86–87.

Letter 4

Federico Gonzaga to Vittoria Colonna
11 March 1531

Ill.ma S.ra come sorella hon. L'amor fraterno, ch'era fra lo ill.mo S.re di Pescara de fe(lice) me(moria) e me, e la stretissima amicitia e domestichezza, che ho con l'ill.mo S.re marchese del Guasto, fa che singularmente ami V. S. congiunta di matrimonio alla dolce memoria dell'uno et de strettissima parentella a l'altro; e questo mio amor verso lei lo fanno anche maggiore le singular virtù sue. Perciò mi è caro havere spesso nuova di quella, et intender il suo ben stare, del che havendo havuto notizia da M. Georgio di Cardi, ne ho havuto piacere molto grande, et tanto maggiore che oltre questa bona nova me ha anche visitato in nome di quella e fattomi le amorevoli et humanissime offerte sue, che me sono state accettissime. Esso me ha anche presentato da parte sua un sacchetto di odoratissime rose, quale si per esser delicato tanto, quanto si possa desiderare, si per venir dalle mani de V. S., m'è gratissimo, e lo tengo molto caro, godendolo in memoria di quella, alla qual vorrei pure far piacere, per il quale fosse certificata del fraterno amore che le porto, se sapessi in che; però la prego di cuore che, desiderando ella di qua cosa alcuna che sia in mio potere, la si contenti di farlomi sapere, che per me non si mancarà di far quello, che ricerca la benevolentia grandissima che è tra noi. E non sapendo per hora in che altro farle piacere, se non in quello che ho inteso dal S. Fabritio Maramaldo, qual me ha detto che ellea desidera d'haver una pittura bella e di mano di pittore excellente d'una figura de S.ta Maddalena, ho subito mandato a Vinegia e scritto a Titiano, quale è instantia a volerne far una bellissima, lagrimosa più che si può, e farmela haver presto; et alla excellentia del pittore e alla instantia ch'io li ne ho fatta, tengo che l'opera serrà perfettissima, et spero d'haverla forsi de que da Pasca, et havutola la inviarò a V. S., alla qual de continuo me racomando.

Da Mantova, alli XI marzo 1531.

ASM, AG, b. 2933, libro 302, fol. 69.
Crowe and Cavalcaselle, *Life and Times of Titian*, 1:451.
Ferrero and Müller, *Carteggio*, 64–66.
Ingenhoff-Danhäuser, *Maria Magdalena*, 89–90.

Letter 5

Benedetto Agnello to Federico Gonzaga
18 March 1531

> M. Ticiano ha dato principio alla S.ta Maddalena et dice che si sforzerà di fornirla
> quanto più presto serà possibile.
> Venegia, 18 marzo 1531.

ASM, AG, b. 1465.
Crowe and Cavalcaselle, *Life and Times of Titian*, 1:451.
Ingenhoff-Danhäuser, *Maria Magdalena*, 87.

Letter 6

Federico Gonzaga to Benedetto Agnello
19 March 1531

> Mi piace che M. Tiziano abbia cominciato la Madalena la quale come piu presto
> lhabbiamo tanto piu ne sara grata ec.
> M. XIX martii MDXXXI.

ASM, AG, b. 2933, libro 302, fol. 76.
Gaye, *Carteggio inedito*, 2:224: as letter of Isabella d'Este to Benedetto Agnello.
Ingenhoff-Danhäuser, *Maria Magdalena*, 87.

Letter 7

Benedetto Agnello to Federico Gonzaga
22 March 1531

> Ticiano lavora gagliardamente dietro la S.ta Magdalena, la quale è già in termine
> che la si può far vedere ad ogni eccellente pictore; et V. Ex. sii certa che serà cosa
> molto degna et di summa excellentia.
> Venetia, alli XXII de marzo 1531.

ASM, AG, b. 1465, fols. 102–3.
Crowe and Cavalcaselle, *Life and Times of Titian*, 1:451–52.
Ingenhoff-Danhäuser, *Maria Magdalena*, 87.

Letter 8

Federico Gonzaga to Benedetto Agnello
8 April 1531

> Dal castellano avemo inteso ch il quadro di s. Madalena ha fatto M. Titiano e
> fornito il ch ne stato gratiss. intendere e volemo ch ringratiate M. Tiziano da
> nostra parte dl studio ch ha messo in servirci bene il ch sapemo che non puo
> essere altramente et presto et perch desideramo d haverlo presto spediamo a
> posta questo cavallaro perch el ce lo porti. Fatelo mo voi intrar in un telaro et
> coprirlo di sorte non si possa guastar di cosa pero piu leggiera ch si puo accio che
> lo possa portar facendo farle quella provision sera de bisogno accio ch alli dazi
> non sia ratenuto ma se sia lasciato portar liberamente.
> Mantuae VIII aprilis MDXXXI

ASM, AG, busta 2933, libro 302, fol. 91.
Gaye, *Carteggio inedito*, 2:225.
Ingenhoff-Danhäuser, *Maria Magdalena*, 87.

Letter 9

Benedetto Agnello to Federico Gonzaga
12 April 1531

> Mando la Sta Magdalena, la quale M. Ticiano ha tenuto ne le mani questi dui dì più contra la promissa che haveva fatto per darli la vernice, ma il tempo l'ha impedito, che per non esser stato il sole ben chiaro non l'ha potuta invernigiare ben a suo modo, pur dice che, così come la sta la si può mandare in ogni loco, affirmando che V. E. non ha havuto cosa alcuna delle sue che sii al paragone di questa et pensa che V. S. ne restera ben satisfacta.
> Da Venetia, xii Aprile, 1531.

ASM, AG, b. 1465, fol. 120.
Crowe and Cavalcaselle, *Life and Times of Titian*, 1:452.
Ingenhoff-Danhäuser, *Maria Magdalena*, 88.

Letter 10

Benedetto Agnello to Federico Gonzaga
14 April 1531

> Non mandai la S.ta Magdalena, si come scrissi alla Ex. V. perchè essendo stata invernigata di fresco M. Titiano dubitava che la non si guastasse; hora, che l'è ben secca, la mando.
> Da Vinegia, 14 Aprile 1531.

ASM, AG, b. 1465, fol. 122.
Crowe and Cavalcaselle, *Life and Times of Titian*, 1:452.
Ingenhoff-Danhäuser, *Maria Magdalena*, 88.

Letter 11

Titian to Federico Gonzaga
14 April 1531

> Tandem ho compito el quadro della Madalena qual v. ex. mi ordino con quella piu prestezza ch mi esta possibile lasciando ogni altra mia facenda ch aveva alle mani nel qual mi ho sforzato d'esprimer in qualche parte quel ch si espetta da questa arte il ch se l abbia conseguito se potra giudicar da altri. Se veramente a li concetti grandi ch aveva nell animo e nella mente le mani col penello mi havessero corisposto penseria de haver potuto sodisfar al desiderio ch ho di servi v. ex. ma ha gran spatio non li son arivato. Et pero quella mi dia perdono el qual accio ch da lei più facilmente el possi impetrar la prefata Madalena mi ha promesso di richiederlo cum le mani al petto et domandargelo in gratia. Altro nò le diro se non ch v. ex. ma tenghi in sta bona gratia e nel numero de suo minimi servitori....
> Venetia 14 april. 1531.

Gaye, *Carteggio inedito*, 1:225.
Crowe and Cavalcaselle, *Life and Times of Titian*, 1:452.
Ingenhoff-Danhäuser, *Maria Magdalena*, 88.

Letter 12

Federico Gonzaga to Titian
19 April 1531

Messer Tiziano. Ho ricevuto il quadro della Santa Maddalena, che ci avete fatto, quale pensavo bene che dovesse essere cosa bella come che de altra sorte non ve ne possa uscire della mani per l'excellentia vostra nella pittura, e tanto più facendola per me, al quale so che vi è caro far piacere. ma la ho trovata bellissima e perfettissima, et veramente de quante cose di pittura ho veduto non mi pare che vi sia cosa più bella; e ne resto più che satisfatto. El simile dice Madama Illma., mia Madre, quale la lauda per cosa excellentissima, e confessa che di quanto opere simili ha viste, che ne ha pur viste assai, e se ne è dilectata, l'agualia a gran pezzo; e questo il medemo dicono quanti altri l'hanno veduta, e più la laudano quelli che più se intendano dell'arte della pittura. dal che conosco che in questa bellissima opera avete voluto exprimere l'amor che mi portate insieme con la singular excellentia vostra, et che queste due cose unite insieme ve hanno fatto far questa figura tanto bella, che non è possibile desiderar meglio; il che non si può exprimer quanto mi sia grato, che certo è che non si possano trovare parole atte ad exprimere l'affetto mio. Ve ne ringrazio, certificandovi che io ho in continua memoria questi e li altri piaceri che me fate, e me vi offero disposto etc.
Mantue 19 Aprilis 1531
Il Marchese di Mantova
A Messer Tiziano.

ASM, AG, b. 2933, libro 302, fols. 1–2.
Gaye, *Carteggio inedito*, 2:224–25.
Ingenhoff-Danhäuser, *Maria Magdalena*, 88–89.

Letter 13

Titian to Federico Gonzaga
29 April 1531

Per una de v. ex. con infinito mio piacere ho inteso che la santa Madalena, che in questi dì passati gli mandai, haverli summamente piaciuta, veramente di tanta mia satisfactione che io non lo potrei dire, che havendo a quel poco o assai de arte, che è in me, impiegato per far opera che dovesse satisfare....Et di questo è cagione la grandezza et liberalitade di v. ex. verso di me, con le quali cose mi si ha così grandemente affezionato e obbligato che io non le saprei dir quanto, benchè, parando a lèi forse piccoli i benefitii a me fatti in comparatione della sua magnanimità, ella cerchi ancora di far si sia più obligato di quello li sono....Non conosco d'aver tanto con lei meritato che dassai più non mi trovi remunerato. Egli è ben vero che per el presente la espeditione del beneficio, cui v. ex. mi fece gratia in persona de mio figliuolo, mi sarebbe di grandissimo contento, nè per ora io potrei da lei aver cosa che più facesse alla quiete dell'animo mio; non dimeno questo sia nell' arbitrio suo. Restami solo a pregar v. ex. de tenermi in soa bona gratia, a la quale humilmente me raccomando, baciandoli le mani.

di Venetia alli XXVIII de aprile MDXXXI
Tiziano.

Gaye, *Carteggio inedito*, 2:226.
Ingenhoff-Danhäuser, *Maria Magdalena*, 89.

Letter 14

Vittoria Colonna to Federico Gonzaga
25 May 1531

Ill.mo et Ex.mo Signor.

Una littera de la Ex.tia Vostra hebbi circa un mese fa, et se sono tardata ad respondere la prego me excusi con la causa che è solo stata per non dupplicar lo error. Rengratio con questa V.ra Ex.tia de la infinita sua cortesia, et per li respecti dice de la felice memoria del Marchese de Pescara, mio signore, et del signor Marchese del Vasto, mio fratello, et per la sua istessa virtù lo ho havuto et havrò sempre in quella estima et reverentia che conviene. Et me dole che Georgio me honorassi cosi poco, che un coscinetto che io non vidi may donasse da mia parta a la Ex.tia V.ra Et essendose dignato immeritatamente satisfarsene, me ha obligata mandarli questi dui, et Dio voglia che non debbia men dolersi Georgio del suo fallo che io de sì scioccamente emendarlo. De la Magdalena la rengratio infinite volte. Sempre che se degnerà commandarme, oltra de farme singolar gratia, serà de me con quella voluntà che farria el dicto signor Marchese del Vasto et con la debita observantia servito. Et Nostro Signor Dio sua Ill.ma et Ex.ma persona guarde con la prosperità che merita et desidero.
Dal castello de Isca, a XXV de magio 1531.
Deditissima servir V. Ill.ma et Ex.ma S.ria
La Marchesa de Pescara.

ASM, AG, b. 1880.
Ferrero and Müller, *Carteggio*, 70–71.
Ingenhoff-Danhäuser, *Maria Magdalena*, 90.

Letter 15

Federico Gonzaga to Vittoria Colonna
28 July 1531

Ill. ma ecc. Doe lettere di V. S. a me gratissime ho ricevuto in questi di passati, una che accompagnava il nobilissimo et precioso dono che la mi mandò di cossinetti di odoratissime rose in un bello et delicato repositorio, l'altra, con che mi avisava de havere havuto grata la S.ta Madalena che le mandai. Di tutto li rendo le maggiori gratie che posso et non manco de lo havere havuto tanto accetto il mio piccolo dono che del havermi mandato a donare cosa tanto degna, la qual veramente non me potria essere stata più grata, sì per esser cosa preciosa da sè, sè per venirmi dal loco che viene. Che V. S. sia stata compiaciuta da me in la S.ta Madalena et che io habbia prevenuto tutti gli altri, che in tale cosa la doveano compiacere, mi piace, perchè havendo ella veduto qualche prontezza in me di satisfarla, spero che la debba tanto più confidentemente ricercarme a farli piacere, quando la vederà di potersi accomodare di me in cosa alcuna da le bande di qua, come la prego di core che la faccia, perchè questo è uno de'grandi desideri che tengo. Volentieri ho fatto sapere al pittore che ha fatto la S.ta Maddalena, quanto V. S. me ne scrive, perchè so di quanto incitamento li serà lo intendere il iudicio ch'ella ha fatto de l'opera sua, dal quale l'haverà da riconoscere de l'aggiungerà cosa alcuna alle perfectione de la sua arte, eccitato de le lode che V. S. li dona. N.

S. Dio conceda a V. S. tutto quello contento che la desidere alla qual, ecc.
Mantova, 28 luglio 1531.

Ferrero and Müller, *Carteggio*, 71–72.
Ingenhoff-Danhäuser, *Maria Magdalena*, 90.

Letter 16

Isabella d'Este to Tommaso Tucca
March 1533

> M. Gio: Thomaso. Io vidi questi dì passati in una lettera che voi scrivevate al mio conte Nicola di Maphei un capitolo sopra il desiderio che tiene lo ill.mo S. Marchese del Vasto d'haver il mio quadro di S.a Maria Maddalena per farne dono a la S.ra Marchesa di Pescara; et perchè non ho cosa al mondo ch'io non vogli che sia parimenti di S. Ex., mi fu di grandissima satisfatione vedere ch'ella havesse tal desiderio, et subito le haverei mandato il quadro, ma perchè ne ho voluto far prima fare un simile, è stato necessario ritenerlo, fra tanto che il pittore se ne sia servito in prenderne l'esempio. Hora che egli l'ha finito, lo mando pel medesimo portatore di questa mia, et lo indirizzo a Voi, pregandovi che in mio nome lo vogliate presentare al p.to S. Marchese, facendo intendere a S. Ex. che mi duole ch'egli non sia assai più bello che non è, benchè piacendo a lei non può essere se non bellissimo; et che quando io habbia alcun'altra cosa di che ella si possa servire et valere, mi par superfluo offrirglielo, ecc.
> Marzo 1533.

Ferrero and Müller, *Carteggio*, 65–66, n. 1.
Cartwright, *Isabella d'Este,* 2:352–53.
Ingenhoff-Danhäuser, *Maria Magdalena*, 91.

Letter 17

Marchese Alfonso del Vasto to Isabella d'Este
4 March 1533

> Ill.ma et Ex.ma S.ra mia,
>
> Ho ricevuto il quadro de la Maddalena che è tale che se mai fui devoto de li soi meriti con la vista di questa imagine che tiene tanto de divinità hora me le son facto devotissimo e essendo di ciò stato causa V. ex. tanto più le rendo gratie de la rarità del dono, poichè con havermi più obligato a li meriti de si gloriosa sancta vengo a ricognoscere da lei il beneficio. Essa sancta sia quella che interceda apresso il Sr. Dio per la longheza de la vita et felicità di V. Ex. che dal canto mio non vedo con che manera de servitio posserle riferir gratie. Et le baso le mani.
> Parmea, IIII martij 1533.
> S.or de V. Ill.ma Ex.ma S.a Marchese del Vasto.
> [Addressed to: Alla Ill.ma et Ex.ma S.ra mis S.ra]

ASM, AG, busta 1880.
Ingenhoff-Danhäuser, *Maria Magdalena*, 91. [No addressee given.]

Letter 18

Pope Paul III Farnese to Vittoria Colonna
13 March 1537

Beloved daughter in Christ, noble woman Vittoria [Colonna], Marchesa di Pescara.

Beloved daughter in Christ receive greetings. The desire of your nobility, expressed to us, to set out abroad, and in addition to the churches of Saint Jacobo in Compostella and of Saint Maximinus in the province of Provence, in which the body of the blessed Mary Magdalen is believed to have been laid, to visit the sacred tomb of our Lord Jesus Christ. [This desire] has greatly enlarged our opinion of your probity, your devotion, and your piety toward Greatest God (if that opinion, which was always the greatest with us concerning you, could in any way be enlarged).

In this matter, that you have put this pilgrimage, laborious indeed and dangerous, before your rest, your wealth, and your comforts, numerous as they are, and that you have not been able to be torn from it by the prayers of your relatives and friends, and that you have set the love of Jesus Christ before all human emotions, you have shown most clearly a manly spirit in a woman's body.

For this reason we, who desire to kindle your fervor rather than to extinguish it in any way, bless you, daughter in Christ, and we ask God that he favor your pilgrimage and that he deem it worthy that you be accompanied on your journey.

Therefore, having listened to your requests, we concede and grant to you by apostolic authority in the spirit of the circumstances, that you be able to visit the tomb, and that you lead with you on this pious effort up to fifteen people. And among them our beloved son Jerome from Monte Politiano, your confessor, of the order of the congregation of the Minor Capuchins, and two other of his companions at the discretion of their superior.

And we order in the virtue of holy obedience to ecclesiastical persons throughout Christianity and even in those parts belonging to the infidels, that they piously show to you and your companions all places, sacred temples, monasteries, and holy relics, and that they receive you and those people, kindly for my sake and for the sake of God…and that they show to you and yours on your journey all the hospitality they can, since they will receive equal gratitude from us, when the time arises.

Rome, 13 March 1537, third year.

Blos.

Ferrero and Müller, *Carteggio*, LXXIX, 131–32.
Translated from the Latin by Elizabeth Klaassen, Bryn Mawr College.

Notes

I would like to thank David Wilkins and Sheryl Reiss for their careful and sympathetic reading of this paper. Thanks are also due to Mary Washington College for providing me with a faculty development grant to complete the research for this paper in Rome during the summer of 1996, and to the scholars and archivists who made my work in Italy so rewarding, particularly Gabriello Milantoni of the Archivio Colonna (Rome), Massimo Ceresa of the Biblioteca Apostolica Vaticana, and the staff of the Archivio di Stato of Mantua. A debt is also due to the faculty members at Bryn Mawr College who have seen my work on Vittoria Colonna through the dissertation stage and beyond: David Cast, my dissertation advisor, Phyllis Pray Bober, Steven Z. Levine, Dale Kinney, and also to Dr. Frederick Ladd, emeritus, Towson State University.

1. It is perhaps impossible to determine if the Pitti *Magdalen* was the painting received by Colonna. However, a date of ca. 1531–35 for the Pitti *Magdalen*, based on stylistic analysis, allows us to consider the possibility that this is, or closely reflects, Titian's *Magdalen* commissioned by Colonna. Moreover, Monika Ingenhoff-Danhäuser, examining X-rays of the Pitti painting, suggests that Titian executed this work quickly. Because documents relating to the Colonna *Magdalen* indicate that it was painted in about a month, Ingenhoff-Danhäuser proposes that the X-rays prove the Pitti painting was Colonna's. See Monika Ingenhoff-Danhäuser, *Maria Magdalena: Heilige und Sünderin in der italienischen Renaissance; Studien zur Ikonographie der Heiligen von Leonardo bis Tizian* (Tubingen: Verlag Ernst Wasmuth, 1984), 80–85. Harold Wethey suggests, and Ingenhoff-Danhäuser agrees, that Colonna may have presented her painting to Eleonora Gonzaga della Rovere. This clarifies the provenance of the Pitti painting, which entered the Medici collection in 1631 in the dowry of Vittoria della Rovere (a descendent of Eleonora Gonzaga della Rovere) upon her marriage to Ferdinando II de' Medici. See Harold E. Wethey, *The Paintings of Titian*, vol. 1, *The Religious Paintings* (London: Phaidon, 1969), 150. If Vittoria Colonna gave Titian's *Mary Magdalen* to Eleonora Gonzaga, then the Pitti *Magdalen* is almost certainly the painting commissioned by Colonna. It is possible that Colonna sent the painting as a gift to Eleonora upon the death of her husband, Francesco Maria della Rovere, in 1538; see below for the significance of the Magdalen for widows. When describing Titian's works in the collection of Francesco Maria della Rovere, Giorgio Vasari claims that a *Mary Magdalen* "con i capelli sparsi, che è cosa rara" was "nella guardaroba" of the duke. However, Vasari visited Urbino in 1546, and his reference may be to the "guardaroba" of Duke Guidobaldo della Rovere, Eleonora Gonzaga's son. Vasari-Milanesi, 7:443–44. Although Vittoria Colonna and Eleonora Gonzaga were friends, there is nothing in their surviving correspondence to suggest that Colonna sent a work of art to Eleanora. Vittoria Colonna and Eleonora Gonzaga were cousins by marriage: Vittoria's mother was Agnese da Montefeltro, daugher of Federigo da Montefeltro and Battista Sforza, and it was Agnese's sister, Giovanna, whose son, Francesco Maria della Rovere, married Eleonora Gonzaga. Upon the death of Guidobaldo da Montefeltro, Duke of Urbino, in 1508, the duchy came into the possession of the della Rovere. As I argue elsewhere, the relationship between Vittoria Colonna and Eleonora Gonzaga della Rovere was likely strengthened through these family ties to Urbino. See Marjorie Och, "Vittoria Colonna: Art Patronage and Religious Reform in Sixteenth-Century Rome" (Ph.D. diss., Bryn Mawr College, 1993), chap. 4, "The Capuchins."

2. Vasari is referring to the *Penitent Magdalen* of 1561. Vasari-Milanesi, 7:454; *The Lives of the Artists*, trans. Julia Conaway Bondanella and Peter E. Bonadella (Oxford: Oxford University Press, 1991), 505.

3. See Charles Hope, *Titian* (New York: Harper & Row, 1980), 76.

4. George Bull, introduction to Baldassarre Castiglione, *The Book of the Courtier*, trans. George Bull (Harmondsworth: Penguin, 1976), 11.

5. Wethey, *The Religious Paintings*, 143–51; figs. 182–86, 189, 235–36.

6. For the documents, see esp. Ermanno Ferrero and Guiseppe Müller, eds., *Carteggio,* 2nd ed. (Turin: Ermanno Loescher, 1892); Giovanni Gaye, *Carteggio inedito d'artisti,* 3 vols. (1840; reprint, Turin: Bottega d'Erasmo, 1968); Joseph A. Crowe and Giovanni Battista Cavalcaselle, *The Life and Times of Titian,* 2 vols. (London: John Murray, 1881); Ingenhoff-Danhäuser, *Maria Magdalena,* 86–91. These letters appear in full in the appendix.

7. Alfonso d'Avalos (1502–46), Marchese del Vasto e di Pescara, was cousin to Vittoria Colonna's husband, Ferdinando Francesco d'Avalos (1489–1525), Marchese di Pescara. Vittoria Colonna and Ferdinando d'Avalos had no children, and upon Ferdinando's death in 1525, the title to Pescara passed to Alfonso. On Ferdinando Francesco and Alfonso d'Avalos, see G. de Caro in *DBI,* 4:612–16, 623–27.

8. Crowe and Cavalcaselle, *Titian,* 1:348. Crowe and Cavalcaselle, followed by Charles Ricketts, believe that the *Mary Magdalen* now in the Pitti was painted by Titian for the duke of Urbino, Francesco Maria della Rovere; in the view of these scholars, Colonna's *Magdalen* is no longer extant. Crowe and Cavalcaselle, *Titian,* 1:350; Charles Ricketts, *Titian* (London: Methuen, 1910), 82.

9. Wethey, *The Religious Paintings*, 143–44, 150. See also Hans Tietze, *Titian, Paintings and Drawings* (Vienna: Phaidon, 1937), 371.

10. Hope does not analyze the correspondence beyond this comment. See Hope, *Titian,* 75–76, 107.

11. Ingenhoff-Danhäuser, *Maria Magdalena,* 81–82. Rona Goffen has agreed that the *Mary Magdalen* was a gift to Colonna from Federico Gonzaga. Rona Goffen, *Titian's Women* (New Haven: Yale University Press, 1997, 177; *Vittoria Colonna: Dichterin und Muse Michelangelos,* ed. Sylvia Ferino-Pagden, exh. cat. (Vienna: Skira, 1997), 336 and 346.

12. Joan Kelly, "Did Women Have a Renaissance?" in *Becoming Visible: Women in European History,* ed. Renate Bridenthal and Claudia Koonz (Boston: Houghton Mifflin, 1977), 137–64.

13. Joan Kelly, in "Did Women Have a Renaissance?," also refers to later periods of renascence, such as the Enlightenment and the French Revolution, which excluded women from social advances characteristic of these periods solely on the basis of gender-specific legal restrictions.

14. Linda Nochlin, "Why Have There Been No Great Women Artists?" in *Art and Sexual Politics: Women's Liberation, Women Artists, and Art History,* ed. Thomas B. Hess and Elizabeth C. Baker (New York: Macmillan, 1973), 1–43.

15. My translation. Vittoria Colonna is not mentioned in this letter. According to Wethey, the *Saint Jerome* was ordered by the duke's mother, Isabella d'Este, in 1523 and delivered only in 1531, as the duke here indicates. Wethey believes the *Saint Jerome* in the Louvre is Isabella's painting; it measures 0.80 x 1.02 m. The Pitti *Magdalen* measures 0.84 m x 0.69 m; see Wethey, *The Religious Paintings,* 133–34.

16. This is an interesting letter, for it would seem that Titian had already begun a *Mary Magdalen,* possibly for Federico or Federico's mother, Isabella d'Este. Nothing is known of this earlier painting.

17. My translation.

18. Alessandro Luzio published documents in support of Federico's claim that Fabrizio Maramaldo informed him of Colonna's desire for a painting of the Magdalen. Luzio cites a letter of 23 November 1530 from Fabrizio to Alfonso d'Avalos in which Fabrizio promises Alfonso that he will visit Mantua in March of the next year; the actual visit apparently occurred in late February 1531. Alessandro Luzio, *Fabrizio Maramaldo: nuovi documenti* (Ancona: A. Guastvo Morelli, 1883), 35–36. Maramaldo's letter has never been brought into the discussion concerning Titian's *Mary Magdalen.* Maramaldo had previously been in Naples, where he would have had the opportunity to visit Vittoria Colonna on Ischia. André Chastel describes Fabrizio Maramaldo as a "captain of

adventure" and a leader of Italian soldiers fighting in the imperial army at the Sack of Rome. André Chastel, *The Sack of Rome* (Princeton: Princeton University Press, 1983), 26.

19. My translation.

20. See Federico's letter to Titian of 5 March 1531 (letter 1) in which he thanks the artist for the *Saint Jerome*; see also the duke's letter of 19 April 1531 (letter 12) in which he expresses his admiration of the *Mary Magdalen*. Colonna's comments stand in contrast to her appreciative remarks to Michelangelo a decade later. To Michelangelo, Colonna wrote: "I would rather wait with a well-prepared mind for some substantial occasion of serving you, praying that Lord of whom you spoke to me with such a fervent and humble heart, on my departure from Rome, that I may find you on my return with his image so renewed and alive by true faith in your soul, as you have so well painted it in my Woman of Samaria." See Maud F. Jerrold, *Vittoria Colonna, with Some Account of Her Friends and Her Times* (London, 1906; reprint, Freedport, N.Y.: Books for Library Press, 1969), 134, where the date 20 July 1542 is given. See also Ferrero and Müller, *Carteggio*, 157:268–69; the letter is here dated 20 July (1542–43).

21. See Wethey, *The Religious Paintings*, 150. My translation.

22. See n. 2.

23. Colonna may be writing this letter on behalf of her husband for the money due him. However, there is a note of both embarrassment and desperation on Colonna's part, for she writes that without this payment, she will have to sell "un castello." From Arpino, she writes: "Li scrivo et li supplico manda pagargli, che certo con grandissima difficultà ho fatto intertenere per vinti dì el vendere un castello." Colonna, *Carteggio*, I, 1–2.

24. Ferrero and Müller, *Carteggio*, 63–65: 96–99.

25. Charles Hope, "Federico Gonzaga as Patron," in *Splendours of the Gonzaga*, ed. David Chambers and Jane Martineau, exh. cat. (London: Victoria and Albert Museum, 1981), 73.

26. On Titian's relationship with the duke, Charles Hope writes:

    His most important patron in the 1530s was Federico Gonzaga. Born in 1500, Federico was several years younger than Titian, which may have led him to behave more deferentially towards the artist than his uncle Alfonso d'Este had done. As a result, Titian himself was somewhat more obliging in completing pictures on time. Federico's decision to employ Titian on a regular basis was marked in the autumn of 1529 by a commission of no less than three paintings and by an offer of help over the purchase of land near Treviso from the Venetian Monastery of San Giorgio Maggiore. The negotiations over the land ultimately came to nothing, but in the following year the duke more than compensated Titian with the gift of the benefice of Medole, near Mantua, for his seven-year-old son Pomponio. Thereafter the artist worked for him continuously for the next ten years.

    Hope, *Titian*, 74. See also Charles Hope, "Titian and His Patrons," in *Titian, Prince of Painters*, exh. cat. (Venice: Palazzo Ducale; Venice: Marsilio Editori, 1990), 77–84. For Wethey's account of Titian's patrons at this time, see Wethey, *The Religious Paintings*, 13–25.

27. Charles Hope has noted the striking resemblance between the shepherd and Federico Gonzaga in the *Madonna and Child with Saint Catherine and a Rabbit* of 1528–30. "This can hardly be accidental since Titian was working on a portrait of the duke at exactly the same time." Hope, *Titian*, 74–75. Hope has also commented on X-rays of this painting which show the Madonna looking toward the shepherd in a gesture that "singled out the shepherd as a donor, rather than just a picturesque accessory." See *Splendours of the Gonzaga*, cat. no. 155, 187. In addition to his own portrait, Federico had portraits by Titian of Girolamo Adorno (possibly the *Man with a Glove* of ca. 1527, Louvre) and of Cornelia Malaspina (by 1530, lost). Wethey, *The Religious Paintings*, 15. Nothing is known of the "nudes," although Wethey's proposal that it was a mythological painting is probably accurate.

28. For Titian's desire for recognition by the emperor, see Wethey, *The Religious Paintings*, 21–22;

Wethey, *Paintings of Titian,* vol. 2, *The Portraits,* 2:18–22; Hope, "Titian and His Patrons." Wethey suggests that Titian initially met the emperor in Bologna in January 1530, and that Titian's first portrait of Charles, now lost, commemorated his coronation as Holy Roman Emperor in Bologna on 24 February 1530. See Wethey, *The Religious Paintings,* 21–22.

29. Wethey, *The Religious Paintings,* 23.

30. Titian, who became one of the emperor's favorite painters, was ennobled in May 1533, when Charles issued a royal decree conferring upon Titian the titles Knight of the Golden Spur and Count Palatine. The rank of nobility was also granted to Titian's descendants. See Wethey, *The Religious Paintings,* 22.

31. See Crowe and Cavalcaselle, *Titian,* 1:349, where the reference is to *Lettere scritte a Pietro Aretino,* 109.

32. This portrait of Charles V is now known only through copies. It is quite likely that del Vasto sought to emulate, even flatter, the emperor through his own portrait by Titian. For illustrations, see Wethey, *Paintings of Titian,* vol. 2, *The Portraits,* 2:22, cat. nos. 9, L-3.

33. For the *Allocution,* see esp. Jean Habert, *Le portrait d'Alphonse d'Avalos par Titien* (Paris: Louvre, 1990). See also Oskar Fischel, *The Work of Titian* (New York: Brentano's, 1913), fig. 89; Erwin Panofsky, "Classical Reminiscences in Titian's Portraits: Another Note on His *Allocution of the Marchese del Vasto,*" in *Festschrift für Herbert von Einem,* ed. Georg Kauffmann and Gert von der Osten (Berlin: Gebr. Mann, 1965), 188–202; and Wethey, *Paintings of Titian,* vol. 2, *The Portraits,* 2:78–80. Alfonso del Vasto appears prominently at the far right on horseback in Titian's *Christ Before Pilate* of 1543 (Kunsthistorisches Museum, Vienna) for Giovanni d'Anna, Flemish merchant and resident of Venice. See Wethey, *The Religious Paintings,* 22, 79–80.

34. Although no letters between the two survive for the period 1530–33, it is clear from Colonna's correspondence with Alfonso's sister, Costanza d'Avalos del Balzo, as well as with Charles V, Eleanora Gonzaga, Claudio Tolomei, Pietro Bembo, and Pietro Aretino that she was in close communication with d'Avalos. This correspondence, as well as surviving correspondence between the two, indicates that their relationship was amicable. For the years 1530–33, see Ferrero and Müller, *Carteggio,* 51:70–71; 57:86–87; 58:88; and 59:89.

35. Clifford Brown alludes to the importance of Mary Magdalen to both Isabella d'Este and her son, Federico Gonzaga; see Clifford Brown, "Documents Regarding Duke Federico II Gonzaga's Interest in Flemish Art," *Source* 11 (1992): 20.

36. Colonna may have intended this second *Mary Magdalen* for a convent of the Holy Claires, which she was planning in the mid-1530s. See Och, "Vittoria Colonna," chap. 5, "Michelangelo." It is probably the construction of this project which was approved by Paul III and which Colonna purportedly discussed with Michelangelo, as recorded by Francisco de Hollanda in his *Four Dialogues on Painting.* See Ferrero and Müller, *Carteggio,* 67:102–4; Francisco de Hollanda, *Four Dialogues on Painting,* trans. Aubrey Fitz Gerald Bell (1548; reprint, Oxford: Oxford University Press, 1928), 10.

37. Yet another example of Alfonso del Vasto acting as intermediary for Vittoria Colonna is the *Noli me tangere* for which Michelangelo provided a cartoon. According to Johannes Wilde and Charles de Tolnay, the *Noli me tangere* was commissioned by the marchese Alfonso del Vasto and the governor of Florence, Nicholas von Schomberg, Archbishop of Capua, on behalf of Vittoria Colonna. An unpublished letter from the Mantuan ambassador in Florence of 19 May 1531 (possibly to Federico Gonzaga) reports that Michelangelo himself provided this information. See Johannes Wilde, *Michelangelo and His Studio: Italian Drawings in the Department of Prints and Drawings in the British Museum* (London: British Museum, 1975), 106; Charles de Tolnay, *The Medici Chapel* (Princeton: Princeton University Press, 1948), 110, 197–98. For this letter, Wilde cites Alessandro Luzio, *La Galleria Gonzaga* (Milan, 1913), 249. For the *Noli me tangere* and a brief account of Titian's *Mary Magdalen,* see Michael Hirst and Gudula Mayr, "Michelangelo, Pontormo und das *Noli me tangere* für Vittoria Colonna," in *Vittoria Colonna,*

exh. cat, ed. Sylvia Ferino-Pagden, 335-46. The commission for the *Noli me tangere* is also known from Vasari's "Lives" of Pontormo and Michelangelo. In his "Life of Michelangelo," Vasari's brief account is included in his discussion of Michelangelo's generosity: "Some have called him miserly, but they are wrong, for in art and in life he showed himself the contrary...For the Marquis del Vasto he did a cartoon of a *Noli me tangere*...excellently painted by Pontormo." For Vasari, this cartoon is evidence of Michelangelo's generosity which manifested itself in the forms of "disegni...cartoni...modegli" and other works which the master presented to friends, pupils, nobles, and princes. See Vasari-Milanesi, 7:276; translation from *The Lives of the Painters, Sculptors, and Architects*, trans. William Gaunt, 4 vols. (London: Dent, 1963), 4:174. In the "Life of Pontormo," Vasari reports that Pontormo's painting achieved some notoriety "for the grandeur of Michelangelo's design and the coloring of Jacopo." As Vasari notes, the *Noli me tangere* was copied several times. See Vasari-Milanesi, 6: 276–77; *Lives of the Painters*, trans. Gaunt, 3:249. The size of this work suggests that it may have been intended for a substantial chapel. Even as early as 1531 Colonna may have been considering an architectural commission for religious women—an establishment into which she herself would enter, as her correspondence with Paul III indicates. See Ferrero and Müller, *Carteggio*, 67:102–4; 75:126–27.

38. See the work of Thomas Kuehn, *"Cum consensu mundualdi*: Legal Guardianship of Women in Quattrocento Florence," in *Law, Family, and Women: Toward a Legal Anthropology of Renaissance Italy* (Chicago: University of Chicago Press, 1991), 212–37, 353–63. See also Rosi Gilday's chapter in this volume for the importance of the *mundualdus* in commissions for paintings.

39. See Merry E. Wiesner, "Women's Defense of their Public Role," in *Women in the Middle Ages and the Renaissance: Literary and Historical Perspectives*, ed. Mary Beth Rose (Syracuse: Syracuse University Press, 1986), 4.

40. Castiglione, *Courtier*, 11, 82. See especially Castiglione's "Dedication," in which he admonishes Colonna for keeping the manuscript for so long and for having it copied by others, contrary to her promise (31).

41. This is Sebastiano's so-called *Wise Virgin* in the Kress Collection, National Gallery of Art, Washington, D. C. In the *Catalogue of the Italian Paintings*, Fern Rusk Shapley proposes that Sebastiano's painting was a wedding portrait of Vittoria Colonna, a suggestion which accommodates a date of ca. 1510, as Colonna was married in 1509. The cleaning of the painting revealed a contemporary inscription below the woman's hand, which is visible under infrared and ultraviolet light: "V. [C]OLONNA." It would appear to be a portrait of Vittoria Colonna as a Wise Virgin. "Such symbolism would have been an appropriate compliment to the nineteen-year-old at the time she was preparing for her marriage in 1509." Fern Rusk Shapley, *Catalogue of the Italian Paintings*, 2 vols. (Washington, D. C.: National Gallery of Art, 1979), 1:421. In his monograph on Sebastiano, Michael Hirst makes no reference to the inscription on this painting, nor to the painting's association with Vittoria Colonna. Michael Hirst, *Sebastiano del Piombo* (Oxford: Oxford University Press, 1981).

42. In his "Life of Perino del Vaga," Vasari writes: "In 1527 disaster fell upon Rome; the city was sacked, many artists fled, many artworks were destroyed or carried away." Vasari-Milanesi, 5:611; translation from A. Chastel, *Sack of Rome*, 3. On the departure of artists from Rome, see Sydney J. Freedberg, *Painting in Italy, 1500–1600*, 3rd ed. (New Haven, Conn.: Yale University Press, 1993), 177, where he discusses the "diaspora of artists that followed on the ruin of Rome." See also Chastel, *Sack of Rome*, introduction.

43. See Wethey, *The Religious Paintings*, 20–21, for a brief discussion of artists who left Rome for Venice after the sack.

44. In both Matthew 26:6–13 and Mark 14:3–9 the tale of this anointing is slightly different: Jesus is in the house of Simon at Bethany, the woman is unnamed, and she anoints Jesus's head, not feet. In all three narratives, the woman has an alabaster jar of expensive perfume, but she is not described as a sinner in either Matthew or Mark.

45. Gregory the Great, Homily 33, PL 76, col. 1239. See Susan Haskins, *Mary Magdalen, Myth and*

Metaphor (New York: Harcourt Brace & Co., 1993), 96.

46. For a history of the cult of the Mary Magdalen, see esp. Haskins, *Mary Magdalen*. See also Helen Garth, *Saint Mary Magdalene in Mediaeval Literature* (Baltimore: Johns Hopkins University Press, 1950); Victor Saxer, *Le Culte de Marie Madeleine en Occident, des origines à la fin du Moyen-Âge* (Paris: Clavreuil, 1959); Marjorie Malvern, *Venus in Sackcloth, The Magdalen's Origins and Metamorphoses* (Carbondale, Ill.: Southern Illinois University Press, 1975); and Sarah Wilk, "The Cult of Mary Magdalen in Fifteenth-Century Florence and Its Iconography," *Studi Medievali* 26 (1985): 685–98. On women in the Early Church, see esp. Elisabeth Moltmann-Wendel, *The Women around Jesus*, trans. John Bowden (New York: Crossroad, 1982); Virginia Burrus, *Chastity and Autonomy: Women in the Stories of Apocryphal Acts* (Lewiston, N.Y.: Edwin Mellen Press, 1987); Stevan L. Davies, *The Revolt of the Widows (The Social World of the Apocryphal Acts)* (Carbondale, Ill.: Southern Illinois University Press, 1980).

47. For the apocryphal gospels, see Edgar Hennecke, *New Testament Apocrypha*, ed. Wilhelm Schneemelcher, trans. Robert McLachlan Wilson (Philadelphia: Westminster Press, 1963), 1:338–44; *The Apocryphal New Testament*, trans. Montague Rhodes James (Oxford: Clarendon Press, 1924). For a discussion of Mary Magdalen in the Apocrypha, see Malvern, *Venus in Sackcloth*, 36–40, and Haskins, *Mary Magdalen*, chap. 2.

48. For the Magdalen as the Bride of Christ, see Haskins, *Mary Magdalen*, 63–67, where the author discusses Hippolytus's commentary on the *Canticle of Canticles*. See also John Dillenberger, "The Magdalen: Reflections on the Image of the Saint and Sinner in Christian Art," in *Women, Religion, and Social Change*, ed. Yvonne Y. Haddad and Ellison Banks Findly (Albany: State University of New York Press, 1985), 115–16.

49. Jacobus de Voragine, *The Golden Legend, or Lives of the Saints*, trans. William Caxton (London: J. M. Dent, 1931), 4:72–89.

50. These orders became so closely associated with the Magdalen that in 1295 the Dominicans were made the guardian of her major devotional sites. See Wilk, "Cult of Mary Magdalen," 687–88.

51. Haskins, *Mary Magdalen*, chap. 4, "The *Grandes Heures* of Vézelay;" Wilk, "Cult of Mary Magdalen," 688.

52. It is Hippolytus, in his *Commentary on the Canticle of Canticles*, who first refers to Mary Magdalen as the Apostle to the Apostles. See Haskins, *Mary Magdalen*, 65.

53. Haskins, *Mary Magdalen*, 228.

54. Alfred Reumont, *Vittoria Colonna, fede, vita e poesia nel secolo XVI*, ed. Giuseppe Müller and Ermanno Ferrero (Turin: Ermanno Loescher, 1892) and Jerrold, *Vittoria Colonna*. For a complete bibliography on Colonna, see Och, "Vittoria Colonna," 207–63.

55. Archivio Colonna, 2 A 29 2, no. 11. In 1996 the Colonna Archives in Rome were transferred to the Biblioteca dell'Abbazia, Subiaco. According to Pietro Ercole Visconti, Vittoria Colonna's brother, Ascanio, hoped to profit by arranging a second marriage for his sister. Pietro Ercole Visconti, *Rime di Vittoria Colonna, Marchesa di Pescara* (Rome: Salviucci, 1840), CXIV..

56. See Colonna's letters to Michelangelo of ca. 1542–43 and to Cardinal Giovanni Morone of 20 May 1545. Ferrero and Müller, *Carteggio*, 157:268–69, and 172:305–07; see also *Il Carteggio di Michelangelo*, ed. Paolo Barocchi and Renzo Ristori, 5 vols. (Florence: Sansoni, 1979), 4:169–70.

57. Translation from Jerrold, *Vittoria Colonna*, 276–77. "La signora Marchesa, avanti che pigliasse l'amicitia del Cardinale, si affliggeva talmente con digiuni, cilicii et altre sorte di mortificationi della carne, che si era ridotta ad havere quasi la pelle in sull'osso, et ciò faceva forse con ponere troppa confidentia in simili opere, imaginandosi che in esse consistesse la vera pietà et religione, et per consequente la salute dell'anima sua. Ma poi che fu admonita dal Cardinale che ella piuttosto offendeva Dio che altrimenti, con usare tanta austerità et rigore contra il suo corpo...la suddetta signora cominciò a retirarsi da quella vita così austera, reducendosi a poco a poco a una mediocrità ragionevole et honesta." See Ferrero and Müller, "Dal Processo di Pietro Carnesecchi dinanzi al

Sant'Uffizio," *Carteggio*, 337. See also Richard Gibbings, *Report of the Trial and Martyrdom of Pietro Carnesecchi, Sometime Secretary to Pope Clement VII, and Apostolic Protonotary* (Dublin: McGlashan and Gin, 1856).

58. "[I]l caos d'ignorantia, ove io era, et il labirinto di errori, ov'io passeggiava sicura, vestita di quell'oro di luce, che stride senza star saldo al paragone della fede, nè affinarsi al fuoco della vera carità; essendo continuo col corpo in moto per trovare quiete e con la mente in agitatione per haver pace." Ferrero and Müller, *Carteggio*, 161:272–73.

59. Jerrold, *Vittoria Colonna*, 207–8, where a letter of Agostino Gonzaga to Isabella d'Este is quoted; the letter is not dated.

60. Ferrero and Müller, *Carteggio*, 277–79.

61. Ferrero and Müller, *Carteggio*, 299–302. Costanza d'Avalos Piccolomini was the sister of the marchese Alfonso d'Avalos del Vasto. Colonna's undated letters to her were published in Venice in 1545 as a group; see *Nuovo libro di lettere de i più rari autori della lingua volgare italiana* (Venice, 1545). See also Ferrero and Müller, *Carteggio*, 292.

62. Rona Goffen refers to this poem as titled "On the Magdalen by Titian Sent to Her by the Duke of Mantua." Rona Goffen, *Titian's Women* (New Haven: Yale University Press, 1997), 179. There is no evidence in Colonna's poem for this title. See Vittoria Colonna, *Rime*, ed. *Alan Bullock (Rome: Gius. Laterza e Figli, 1982), p. 145, n. 121.*

63. In addition to the shrine of Mary Magdalen in Provence, Colonna also desired to visit Santiago de Compostella and the Holy Land. In 1537 Colonna visited Ferrara, where she stayed at the Este court of Ercole II d'Este and Renée of France for ten months. Colonna perhaps intended to embark upon her pilgrimage from Ferrara; instead, she traveled to Bologna, Pisa, Lucca, and Florence before returning to Rome late in 1538. Her decision not to undertake an ambitious pilgrimage may have been due to her health, but it may also have been related to her work with the Capuchins at this time. Her journey to Ferrara was, in part, made to enlist the aid of the Este duke in the plight of the Capuchins. See Och, "Vittoria Colonna," chap. 4, "The Capuchins." In spite of her interest in this pilgrimage, Colonna never made the journey. With regard to Colonna's and Isabella d'Este's mutual interests in the Magdalen, it should be noted that Isabella made a pilgrimage to the Magdalen's shrine at Sainte Baume in Provence. I thank Sheryl Reiss for the information.

64. Wilk, "Cult of Mary Magdalen," 695. See also William A. Hinnebusch, *The History of the Dominican Order* (New York: Alba House, 1973), 2:261–62.

65. At the end of the quattrocento, Florentine women were presented with yet another widow whose pious life was recommended to them. Fra Girolamo Savonarola urged Florentine women to follow the example of the widow Anna, daughter of Phanuel, in her life of solitude, fasting, and prayer (Luke 2:36–38). See Savonarola's *Libro della vita viduale* of 1490 or 1491, written at the request of a group of Florentine women; in *Operette spirituali*, ed. Mario Ferrara, 2 vols. (Rome: Angelo Belardetti, 1976), 1:9–62, 299–329.

66. See Och, "Vittoria Colonna," chap. 4, "The Capuchins."

67. Rule 114, translated by Thaddeus MacVicar, O. F. M. Cap., *The Franciscan Spirituals and the Capuchin Reform*, ed. Charles McCarron (St. Bonaventura, N.Y.: Franciscan Institute, 1986), 89, 136.

68. Bull, introduction to Castiglione, *Courtier*, 11.

69. Nurith Kenaan-Kedar, "Emotion, Beauty and Franciscan Piety: A New Reading of the Magdalen Chapel in the Lower Church of Assisi," *Studi Medievali* 26 (1985): 700.

70. Kenaan-Kedar, "Emotion, Beauty and Franciscan Piety," 702–4. Joseph Gibaldi notes the importance of such contrasts for the Magdalen tradition in literature. See Joseph Gibaldi, "Petrarch and the Baroque Magdalen Tradition," *The Hebrew University Studies in Literature* 3 (1975): 1–19.

71. Giotto's followers continued with their emotionally persuasive imagery in scenes from the life of the Magdalen in the Magdalen Chapel of the Lower Church of San Francesco, Assisi, ca. 1315. Kenaan-Kedar, "Emotion, Beauty and Franciscan Piety," 710.

72. Francesco Petrarch, *Letters of Old Age: Rerum senilium libri I–XVIII*, trans. A. S. Bernardo, S. Levin, and R. A. Bernardo, 2 vols. (Baltimore: Johns Hopkins University Press, 1992), 597.

73. Petrarch, *Letters of Old Age*, 598.

74. Gibaldi, "Petrarch," 5. The Magdalen of quattrocento artists is in sharp contrast to the Magdalen of Giotto and Petrarch. Donatello's mid-quattrocento *Penitent Magdalen* (Museo dell'Opera del Duomo, Florence) presents her as a haggard older woman withdrawn into the life of her inner spirit. This was not the Magdalen that survived into the cinquecento.

75. Crowe and Cavalcaselle, *Titian*, 2:375. See also Wethey, *The Religious Paintings*, 145–46, fig. 183.

76. Vasari, *Lives of the Painters*, trans. Bondanella and Bonadella, 505. "Dopo fece Tiziano, per mandare al re Cattolico, una figura da mezza coscia in su d'una Santa Maria Maddalena scapigliata, cioè con i capelli che le cascano spora le spalle, intorno alla gola e sopra il petto; mentre ella, alzando la testa con gli occhi fissi al cielo, mostra compunzionen nel rossore degli occhi, e nelle lacrime dogliezza de' peccati: onde muove questa pittura, chiunche la guarda, estremamente; e, che è più, ancorchè sia bellissima, non muove a lasciva, ma a comiserazione." Vasari-Milanesi, 7:454. Vasari is referring to the *Penitent Magdalen* of 1561, formerly in the Escorial, Monastery of San Lorenzo and destroyed in London in 1873. This is Wethey's "Escorial type"; see Wethey, *The Religious Paintings*, 148–49.

77. Wethey, *The Religious Paintings*, fig. 190.

78. Wethey considers Giordano's copy to be "the best evidence of the composition of Titian's lost [Escorial] *Magdalen*." Wethey, *The Religious Paintings*, 148, fig. 191. I suggest, however, that Luca Giordano is at least in part fashioning his copy of Titian after Bernini's *Ecstasy of Saint Teresa*, particularly Mary's partially open mouth, upturned eyes, and expanded, nearly palpitating, breast. Giordano would seem to be interpreting the Magdalen according to a late Baroque aesthetic, even likening her experience in the interior of the grotto to Saint Theresa's own ecstasy in her vision. A print by Cornelis Cort may also reflect this lost Escorial painting; see Wethey, *The Religious Paintings*, 148, fig. 191. For Wethey, "[The Escorial version] was similar to that preserved in Cornelis Cort's print dated 1566....It is certain, however, that the painting, shipped in 1561, did not exactly resemble the print in details of setting and landscape." Unlike Giordano's version, but like all others with the skull, the skull here is turned toward the Magdalen. Moreover, if the Magdalen's steadfast gaze is considered, she appears more in control of her emotions; she is more contemplative than ecstatic.

79. "Conobbe qui Tiziano, quasi fermo in casa per l'età, e come che fusse stimato per ritrarre al naturale, mi mostrò una Maddalena nel deserto da piacere; anche mi ricordo hora che dicendoli che era da piacer troppo, come fresca e rugiadosa in quella penitenza. Conosciuto che io voleo dire che devesse con scarna del digiuno, mi ripose ghignando avvertisce [?] che l'è ritratta pel primo dì che rientra, innanzi che cominciasse a digiunare, per rappresentar la pittura penitente sì, ma piacevole quanto poteva, e per certo era tale." English translation and original text from Haskins, *Mary Magdalen*, 245, 459.

80. Wethey, *The Religious Paintings*, 146.

81. Wethey, *The Religious Paintings*, 143.

82. Hope, *Titian*, 75–76.

83. Hope, *Titian*, 76. This comment is surprisingly like his evaluation of Titian's *La Bella*, "Here the sitter was just a pretty girl, presumably meant to be anonymous." Hope, *Titian*, 82.

84. Clare Robertson, *Il Gran Cardinale, Alessandro Farnese, Patron of the Arts* (New Haven, Conn.: Yale University Press, 1992), 149.

85. David Rosand, "Pursuit of Magnificence," *Times Literary Supplement* (20 November 1992): 12. On sixteenth-century responses to Titian's *Mary Magdalen*, see also Goffen, *Titian's Women*, 173.

86. Bernard Aikema, "Titian's *Mary Magdalen* in the Palazzo Pitti: An Ambiguous Painting and Its Critics," *Journal of the Warburg and Courtauld Institutes* 57 (1994): 54.

87. For female breasts as a source of both nourishment and sexual tension in the Renaissance, see Margaret M. Miles, "The Virgin's One Bare Breast: Female Nudity and Religious Meaning in Tuscan Early Renaissance Culture," in *The Female Body in Western Culture, Contemporary Perspectives*, ed. Susan Rubin Suleiman (Cambridge, Mass.: Harvard University Press, 1986), 193–208; and Megan Holmes, "Disrobing the Virgin: The Madonna Lactans in Fifteenth-Century Florentine Art," in *Picturing Women in Renaissance and Baroque Italy*, ed. Geraldine A. Johnson and Sara F. Matthews Grieco (Cambridge: Cambridge University Press, 1997), 167–95. On the sensuality of the Magdalen, see also Goffen, *Titian's Women*, chap: 4.

88. For sixteenth-century discussions of the beauty of women, see esp. Elizabeth Cropper, "On Beautiful Women: Parmigianino, Petrarchismo, and the Vernacular Style," *Art Bulletin* 58 (1976): 374–94 and *Concepts of Beauty in Renaissance Art*, ed. Francis Ames-Lewis and Mary Rogers (Aldershot: Ashgate, 1998).

Bronzino in the Service of
Eleonora di Toledo and Cosimo I de' Medici:
Conjugal Patronage and the Painter-Courtier

Bruce L. Edelstein

Of the many Renaissance women whose importance as patrons has been underestimated in the literature, Eleonora di Toledo represents a particularly remarkable case, given the quantity of surviving documents attesting to her activities in this field. Eleonora's shrewd administrative capabilities were fundamental to her husband, Cosimo I de' Medici, in the establishment of his hegemony over Florence; she frequently acted as head of state for the absent duke and as an invaluable source of capital for him.[1] Nonetheless, the process of recuperating Eleonora's role in artistic commissions, especially for the early years of her reign, is complicated by the surviving court accounts, which do not distinguish works made for the duchess from those made for the duke. Court artists were, in fact, unlikely to have made the same distinctions that modern scholars have been so keen to identify between commissions executed for Eleonora and those executed for her husband. The career of Agnolo Bronzino, who benefited from the patronage of both members of the ducal couple, offers significant evidence in this regard. Bronzino's works also demonstrate that he was a deft courtier whose ability to satisfy the separate desires and the mutual needs of his patrons secured for him his role as principal painter at the Florentine court for more than three decades.

Eleonora di Toledo, Patron of State Portraits

Most of the documents recording commissions from Eleonora to Bronzino are for portraits of herself and her children. These portraits are of great importance, as many were intended for use as diplomatic gifts.[2] In the summer of 1545, for example, one of the secretaries of the ducal court wrote to the majordomo to inform him that, "New commissions from my Lady are to be sent there for pictures and frames, which are said to be requested from Bronzino" (doc. 3). These works were probably commissioned just after the artist completed his famous Uffizi double portrait of Eleonora with one of her sons (fig. 1). On 9 August 1545, Bronzino requested "at least a half-ounce" of ultramarine from the majordomo, which is likely to have been for the deep blue background of this painting. The artist himself wrote, "I do not believe that I could make do with less, because the field is wide and must be dark" (doc. 2). In the 1568 edition of the *Lives*, Vasari identifies Bronzino's portrait of Eleonora with her son Giovanni as having been painted "according to the wishes" of the lady duchess herself.[3]

Eleonora's critical appraisal of Bronzino's talents as a portrait painter is evident from the court correspondence as well. Early in 1547 Eleonora ordered a copy of one of Bronzino's portraits of her son Giovanni from an unidentified Flemish painter (doc. 4), but was clearly dismayed by the result (doc. 5).[4] After March 1547 no known documents refer to portraits ordered by the duchess from anyone other than Bronzino. This is significant, as it suggests that Eleonora's patronage of Bronzino was not merely the result of his availability to her as

Edelstein Fig. 1. Agnolo Bronzino, *Eleonora di Toledo and her Son, Giovanni de' Medici*, ca. 1545, Florence, Galleria degli Uffizi (photo: Soprintendenza, Florence)

one of the court artists; rather, the duchess made a conscious choice to commission her portraits from the painter she considered to be most appropriate for the task.

Eleonora's taste and opinions on portraiture seem to have been considered by Bronzino, not only in relation to works commissioned directly from him by the duchess but also in regard to works commissioned by her husband. One such episode is vividly described in the court correspondence of 20 January 1550. The letter, written by Lorenzo Pagni to Pierfrancesco Riccio, a mere three hours after the secretary's last letter to the majordomo, is a response to a request for a red velvet tunic belonging to the Medici heir, the almost nine-year-old Francesco, and for a red satin overdress belonging to the duchess; these were to be sent to Bronzino in order to complete either a pair of portraits, or, as seems more likely, a double portrait of Eleonora and Francesco.[5] Pagni recorded in Spanish Eleonora's primary concern about the picture, "How could Bronzino paint little Francis's portrait without having it [the tunic] beforehand?"[6] Pagni diplomatically avoided responding to the question by feigning ignorance of artistic practice and noting only that "the portraits were most urgently requested by the Monsignor of Arras," that is, Antoine Perrenot, Bishop of Arras.[7] Upon learning for whom the portraits were being made, Eleonora ordered Pagni to write Riccio with the following orders for Bronzino: Francesco should be depicted in a tunic of red brocade, "the most beautiful he knows and is able to paint," and "a cape lined in marten or sable, as it does not seem to her proper by now that this lord should be portrayed in only a tunic, but with a cape as he was seen in Genoa."[8] As for the duchess's own garb, Bronzino was free to paint any overdress he pleased as long as it was the same color as Francesco's tunic.

Pagni's letter suggests how very important the choice of costume was for the patron of a sixteenth-century state portrait; Eleonora's primary concern was that the heir to the ducal title be portrayed in an appropriately aggrandizing fashion. Francesco had undertaken his first major public role the year before when, at the age of seven, he had been sent to Genoa to greet the prince of Spain, the future King Philip II.[9] The provision of appropriate clothing for Francesco—no doubt to demonstrate not only the luxury of the Florentine court but also the continued high quality of the products of its textile industry—had been a matter of some concern during the preparations for the journey. Eleonora was the person responsible for determining the fashions of the court; as numerous letters from the court secretaries to Riccio demonstrate, the duchess ordered not only her own clothes and those of her children and ladies-in-waiting, but also the livery for the court on special occasions like triumphal entries, and frequently Cosimo's clothes as well.[10] On this occasion, too, Eleonora exercised a decisive role in determining the appearance of the young prince for his first official state mission—that is, his first public appearance outside of Florence and its dominions. In the portrait, Eleonora naturally desired the prince to be portrayed in accordance with his recently established public persona.

By contrast, the duchess seems not to have been the least concerned with her own portrayal, leaving the decision about the garment to Bronzino's discretion. This may well have been a concession on her part to the necessity for speedy delivery of the picture to Perrenot. By 20 January, the portraits must have been long overdue since the urgency of their delivery had already been indicated in a letter from Pagni to Riccio a month earlier:

> Their Excellencies are content that, for the convenience of Bronzino and in order to expedite the dispatch of the portraits of them requested by the most Reverend Monsignor of Arras, the Duchess's garment should not be made of velvet brocade but of some other ornate cloth that would look good. Thus, Your Excellency should order him to begin [the portraits] post-haste, since with every batch of mail they are requested by the Bishop of Forlì.[11]

From this letter it is clear that Bernardo de' Medici, Bishop of Forlì and Cosimo's ambassador to the imperial court, was anxious to present the portraits as a gift to Perrenot.[12] It is also evident that both Cosimo and Eleonora considered it appropriate for her to be portrayed in brocade, and that only the necessity for speedy completion of her portrait would have induced them to make an exception. Since this letter refers only to a pair of portraits of the duke and duchess, it may be concluded that the portraits of Francesco and Eleonora referred to subsequently in the letter of 20 January 1550, were not two independent pictures but one double portrait of Eleonora and her son, probably not unlike the one by Bronzino in Pisa (fig. 2).[13]

Edelstein Fig. 2. Agnolo Bronzino, *Eleonora di Toledo and her Son, Francesco de' Medici*, ca. 1550, Pisa, Museo Nazionale di San Matteo (photo: Soprintendenza, Pisa)

Pagni's letter of 20 January 1550 demonstrates that Eleonora could exercise the privileges of patronage even over works not solely commissioned by her. As gifts from the ducal court—presented by a court official to an imperial minister in recognition of past favors or as part of a program to solicit new ones—such portraits have traditionally been placed under Cosimo's aegis. It is clear, however, that Eleonora took an active interest in such projects, which may be more accurately understood as products of both the duke's and the duchess's patronage. In this case, Eleonora probably did not play a significant role in the initial commission; according to Pagni's letter of 20 January, she clearly displayed surprise to learn that Bronzino had begun a portrait of her son without a sample of his best clothes.[14] Nonetheless, her explicit instructions regarding the garments to be depicted in the painting would undoubtedly have resulted in the single most visible effect of the patron's share in the final appearance of this work.

In late 1550 the duchess ordered Bronzino to join the court in Pisa to execute three portraits: one of herself, one of her second son, Giovanni, and one of her third son, Garzia. Once again, these commissions were linked to diplomatic efforts underway at the Florentine court. On 8 December 1550, court secretary Cristiano Pagni wrote from Pisa to majordomo Riccio in Florence:

> My Lady the Duchess has ordered me to write to Your Lordship that you send Maestro Bronzino here, since she wishes for him to paint a portrait of Lord Don Giovanni to send to the pope, which she wants sent as soon as possible.[15]

By 14 December, Bronzino had arrived in Pisa, and on 16 December, he wrote to Riccio describing his journey there by boat in the company of the sculptor and architect Battista del Tasso (doc. 7). The two were the guests of their friend Luca Martini, whose greetings to the majordomo are duly conveyed by Bronzino in the letter. Naturally, the artist's first obligation on the following morning was to present himself to the duke and duchess, at which time Eleonora commissioned the portrait of her second son, Giovanni, from Bronzino directly:

> Therefore, I sketched the face yesterday and yesterday evening she wanted to see it, and so also did our most Illustrious and most Excellent Patron see it at the same time. The Lady Duchess also ordered that she wished me to make a small portrait of herself and perhaps another of the Lord Don Garzia. And since it would not be easy to have panels made or to have them gessoed here without wasting too much time, finding that the necessary items are there, I am writing so that those things can be sent to me from [Florence]. Therefore I ask Your Reverend Lordship that when those things have been brought [to you] that you send them immediately and with someone who will bring them quickly, because they need to be sized and mastic needs to be applied.[16]

Eleonora's own portrait cannot be plausibly traced or securely linked to any of the numerous known portraits and copies;[17] that of Garzia was probably completed in about six months, and should probably be identified with the type of picture represented by the half-length portrait in Lucca (fig. 3).[18] For one of the three pictures, or perhaps for another unrelated work, a "sheet" of ultramarine was sent to Bronzino from the ducal Guardaroba the following February.[19]

The history of the portrait of Giovanni is the best documented. As Cristiano Pagni noted in his letter of 8 December 1550, the commission was intended from its inception as a gift to the pope and, as such, signals the beginning of an important diplomatic effort to have Cosimo's and Eleonora's second son raised to the cardinalate. A church office, and possibly even the hope that he would one day become pope, was probably intended for Giovanni from

Edelstein Fig. 3. Agnolo Bronzino, *Garzia de' Medici*, ca. 1551, Lucca, Pinacoteca Nazionale (photo: Soprintendenza, Pisa)

his birth; after all, upon his birth he had been given the name of the great Medici pope, Leo X.[20] This has been frequently noted in the literature, but it should also be observed that this was the name of another important church official, Eleonora's powerful uncle, Juan de Toledo, the Cardinal of Burgos.[21] This naturally adds to the probability that such a career would have been expected of a child named John. At some point during the pontificate of Julius III (1550–55), Eleonora is reputed to have said to Diego Laínez, her Jesuit confessor, "What do you think? Should we endeavor to have little don Giovanni made a cardinal?"[22] Since Giovanni Maria del Monte was a fellow Tuscan, Cosimo and Eleonora had probably considered his election as Pope Julius III on 7 February 1550 an auspicious moment to move ahead with such plans for their second son, in spite of the fact that he was not yet seven years old at the time. Although Giovanni was not elevated to the cardinalate until 1560 and did not enter Pisa as its archbishop until 1561, a cardinalate seems to have been promised to him by as early as 19 March 1550, and the episcopal seat of Pisa by 2 May.[23]

According to Luca Martini, Bronzino had completed his portrait of Giovanni "divinely" by 8 January 1551;[24] by the end of July, both it and the portrait of Garzia were probably among the seven portraits of Cosimo and Eleonora's children by "the most excellent Bronzino" sent from Pisa to Florence, referred to again by Martini in a letter to Riccio.[25] In all likelihood, upon its arrival in Florence, the portrait of Giovanni was provided with a frame and dispatched to Rome in less than a week.[26] By 14 August 1551, Averardo Serristori, Cosimo's ambassador at the papal court, wrote the following report to Riccio (doc. 10):

> Your Lordship's letter, written on the fourth of this month, has arrived but not the quantity of wine together with the box containing the portrait of lord Don Giovanni. And, in spite of all the diligence with which I have attempted to find the wagoneer who transported the above mentioned items, it has not yet been possible to discover [his identity] since, if we had not failed in finding some clue to the name of said wagoneer, it would have been possible to have some indication of his circumstances, if he had some accident on the road or for what other reason it has taken him so long to arrive. This situation displeases me greatly, as I know how much those things that are presented to His Holiness from the Duchess, my lady, please him. Assuming that I receive them [the wine and the portrait], I will do that which Your Lordship has instructed me to do.[27]

A subsequent letter from Serristori (doc. 11) seems to indicate that the picture did eventually arrive in Rome.

On 24 October 1551 the Florentine ambassador wrote again to Riccio to inquire whether a new portrait of Giovanni, depicting him tonsured, had arrived in Florence from Rome:

> A few days ago, via Benintendi the wagoneer, a portrait of the Lord Don Giovanni without hair was sent on behalf of Our Lord to the Lady Duchess and it was addressed to Your Lordship, the receipt of which has never been acknowledged, nor that of a medal of His Holiness and another of the Prince of Spain, sent by His Holiness to the Lady Duchess. Similarly, via Gualterotto, she was sent a small cat and a parrot from Lord Baldovino. No news has been received of any of these things from the moment that they left here. May Your Lordship be pleased to find out from Her Excellency if she has received them and to write me something, especially that which Her Excellency thought about the portrait of the Lord Don Giovanni with the tonsure, so that I may report about everything to His Holiness and to Lord Baldovino, who has asked me numerous times what the Duchess said about having Don Giovanni tonsured.[28]

This picture, sent by Balduino del Monte to Eleonora, probably differed only in the rendering of Giovanni's hair, as Karla Langedijk has suggested. Bronzino's portrait of Giovanni in the Ashmolean (fig. 4) is almost certainly of the same type as the one commissioned by Eleonora and sent to Rome in 1551, if not the actual picture given by the duchess to Julius III.[29] Balduino del Monte's gift, then, should be similar to the one in the Ashmolean, but portray Giovanni tonsured. A number of pictures conforming to these criteria exist, the best example probably being the portrait at Bowood, which, if not the actual picture sent by the pope's brother, is likely to be a close copy.[30] Thus, it cannot be assumed that the eight-year-old traveled to Rome in 1551. As far as the portrait is concerned, Bronzino's portrait would have provided an adequate model; hence, Giovanni's presence at the papal court is not a requirement for the production of one there. The tone of Serristori's letter suggests that Balduino del Monte may have sent the portrait to Eleonora as a kind of joke; del Monte seems to have expected the duchess to have been provoked or surprised by the appearance of her son with his new clerical hairstyle. The picture sent by Eleonora was painted by Bronzino before Giovanni was tonsured but probably arrived there after that ceremony had taken place; the portrait sent to Eleonora may then have been a sort of critique of Bronzino's likeness, as the hairstyle no longer reflected the young prince's actual appearance. It may also have

Edelstein Fig. 4. Agnolo Bronzino, *Giovanni de' Medici*, ca. 1551, Oxford, Ashmolean Museum (photo: Ashmolean Museum, Oxford)

been sent as an indirect attempt to curry the duke's favor; just as Eleonora had sent Bronzino's portrait to the pope as the beginning of a long attempt to win a cardinal's hat for Giovanni, Balduino del Monte was seeking to gain Monte San Savino (his home city) as a fief and to be granted a noble title by Cosimo.[31]

Eleonora di Toledo, Patron of the Chapel of Eleonora

The earliest surviving document recording Eleonora's activities as Bronzino's patron is a letter from the bishop of Marsico, Marzio Marzi de' Medici, to the future majordomo of Cosimo's court, Pierfrancesco Riccio. Marzi's letter, dated 31 January 1544, is a response to an earlier one sent by Riccio that includes accounts for Bronzino's work:

> His Excellency [the duke] has seen the accounts of Bronzino and the letter of Your Reverend Lordship, *Verba ad Corinthios*. He offered me no response, and asking him what needed to be written, he said to me, "they should be with the duchess because they are her affair."[32]

While Marzi failed to specify what works Bronzino's accounts were for, there was only one project by the artist underway at the ducal court at the end of 1543 that can plausibly be associated with this brief notice: the Chapel of Eleonora in the Palazzo Vecchio (fig. 5).[33] By early 1544 Bronzino had just completed the fresco cycle of the duchess's private oratory, and the designs for the first version of the altarpiece (fig. 6) and its wings were probably well under way.

Edelstein Fig. 5. Agnolo Bronzino, Chapel of Eleonora, frescoes ca. 1541–43; replica of altarpiece (fig. 6 here), ca. 1553–54, Florence, Palazzo Vecchio (photo: Soprintendenza, Florence)

Edelstein Fig. 6. Agnolo Bronzino, *Lamentation*, 1545, Besançon, Musée des Beaux-Arts et d' Archéologie (photo: Ch. Choffet, Besançon)

Eleonora's personal involvement in the patronage of her chapel is also suggested by close examination of the two versions of Vasari's *Life* of Bronzino. In the first edition of the *Vite*, published in 1550, Vasari provides an outline for his later, more extensive *Life* of Bronzino in the *Life* of Raffaellino del Garbo:

> In order to learn the principles of art, Bronzino, Florentine painter, went to him [Raffaellino] in his youth; he [Bronzino] behaved himself equally well under the guidance of Iacopo da Pontormo, Florentine painter, such that his art has born the same fruit as that of Iacopo his master, as can be ascertained from certain portraits and works by his hand that are in the collection [Guardaroba] of the most illustrious and most excellent lord, Duke Cosimo, and from the chapel executed in fresco for the most illustrious lady duchess; and as he lives and works he [continues to] deserve that infinite praise that everyone gives to him.[34]

As both the painter and the patron of the Chapel of Eleonora were alive when Vasari wrote this description, there is little reason to doubt its veracity. Since one of Vasari's motivations in writing the *Lives* was to ingratiate himself with the duke, it seems unlikely that he would have hesitated to compliment Cosimo on his good judgment in assigning the project to Bronzino had he actually been the chapel's patron.[35]

In the 1568 edition of the *Vite*, Vasari provides further evidence for Eleonora's patronage in her private oratory. He notes that the original side panels on the altar wall depicting *Saint John the Baptist* and *Saint Cosmas* "were put in the Guardaroba when the lady duchess, having changed her mind, had these other two made."[36] This establishes Eleonora as the patron of these later wings—Bronzino's *Archangel Gabriel* and *Annunciate Virgin* (in situ, see fig. 5).[37] Vasari's note may also suggest that Eleonora had commissioned the first set of wings as well; by stating that the duchess "changed her mind" about these panels, Vasari seems to imply that Eleonora had been responsible for choosing them originally.

Cosimo and Eleonora, Conjugal Patrons

Vasari further observes that Cosimo, having recognized Bronzino's excellence in the Chapel of Eleonora and other works, "and especially his ability to paint accurate likenesses with more diligence than can be imagined," commissioned portraits of himself (fig. 7), his consort, and his heir, Francesco. According to Vasari, the duchess was pleased with her portrait and therefore commissioned another, different from the first, in which she was depicted with her son Giovanni (fig. 1).[38] Vasari's comments suggest that the duke considered the portraits important enough to be commissioned from someone who could offer visible proof

Edelstein Fig. 7. Agnolo Bronzino, *Cosimo I de' Medici in Armor,* ca. 1543, Florence, Galleria degli Uffizi (photo: Soprintendenza, Florence)

of his abilities. It may further imply that the Chapel of Eleonora served as a kind of test in deciding what share of the court patronage Bronzino would be given; he allowed the artist to execute a private, although complex and important, work for Eleonora before consigning a major public work to him: the three state portraits, that is, the official images of the duke, the duchess, and the prince.

A revealing pattern may therefore be discerned in Vasari's *Life* of Bronzino. The artist, not yet recognized as the most talented painter in Florence, was initially employed as part of a team of artists in the duke's first official act of patronage—the ephemeral decorations for the arrival of Eleonora as Cosimo's bride in 1539.[39] Bronzino executed two chiaroscuro histories for the second courtyard of the Medici Palace and some fictive bronze reliefs for the base of a statue of the duke's father, Giovanni delle Bande Nere, by Tribolo,

> all of which were the best pictures made on that occasion: therefore, the duke, recognizing the talent of this man, had him put his hand, in the ducal palace, to a not very large chapel for the above-mentioned lady duchess, in truth, among all the women who ever lived, a valorous woman of infinite merits, worthy of eternal praise.[40]

Seeing the positive results of Bronzino's efforts in the chapel, Cosimo then commissioned the first three portraits. Having been pleased by her own portrait, Eleonora commissioned a new one of herself and her son. Finally, late in 1545, Bronzino was given almost exclusive rights to design the cartoons for the first significant series of tapestries to be produced by the newly founded Arazzeria Medicea, a commission originally to have been shared equally with Bronzino's master, Pontormo, and his friend and rival, Francesco Salviati (fig. 8).

Bronzino thus found himself executing works alternately for one member of the ducal couple or the other, or possibly in some cases for Cosimo and Eleonora together. Satisfying one spouse may have been of primary importance but not to the exclusion of the other, who might well have ordered his next major work. Bronzino's situation in Florence was by no means unique. Subsequently, Vasari, who put his hand to renovating the duchess's private apartment in 1560, provides clear evidence in his correspondence that projects at the court proceeded only after consultations with both members of the ducal couple. In a letter from Vasari to Vincenzo Borghini, dated 21 November 1561, Vasari notes that he discussed the problem of the duchess's apartment with the duke "for an hour, and with the duchess perhaps two."[41] This suggests Vasari's skill in confronting the painter-courtier's primary challenge at Cosimo and Eleonora's court; both the duke and the duchess expressed opinions about the commission, but discussions with the duchess, for whose direct use the project was being executed, lasted twice as long. That the duchess was a demanding patron is confirmed by another letter written by Vasari to Borghini, six months later, on 9 May 1562, as the project neared completion: "If I have succeeded in satisfying the duchess," he observed, "it will be no small thing."[42]

Edelstein Fig. 8. Sala de' Dugento with *Story of Joseph* tapestry cycle installed, Florence, Palazzo Vecchio (photo: Alinari/Art Resource, N.Y.)

"Eleonoran" Imagery in Bronzino's Fresco Cycle in the Chapel of Eleonora

The visual evidence of Bronzino's Moses cycle suggests the artist's sensitivity to Eleonora's desires for the chapel decorations; it is tempting to suggest that Bronzino may have had discussions with the duchess of the kind that Vasari did some twenty years later. Of the three Moses stories, the importance of the *Crossing of the Red Sea* is marked by its position on the only wall unbroken by a door or window (fig. 9). This fresco, located opposite what was originally the chapel's window, is better illuminated than the altar wall itself.[43] The *Crossing of the Red Sea* contains an important allusion to the new dynasty founded by Cosimo and Eleonora, specifically, to the birth of a male heir on 25 March 1541. As Janet Cox-Rearick observes, Bronzino's fresco includes a moment in the story of Moses that was normally portrayed in scenes of his Last Acts and Death: Moses Appointing Joshua.[44] Since the figure of Moses was clearly intended as an homage to Cosimo himself (as both a just prince and judge), this scene may well refer to the birth of Francesco, who would continue Cosimo's line; this assured dynastic stability further implies a message of resultant peace and prosperity. Cox-Rearick convincingly suggests that the allusion to Francesco is reinforced by the presence of his name saint, Saint Francis, in the vault compartment directly above Bronzino's fresco (fig. 10).[45] A further reference to Cosimo and Eleonora's heir may be implied by a reading of scenes of the *Crossing of the Red Sea* as a type of baptism. On 1 August 1541, little over a month before Bronzino began painting this fresco, Francesco's baptism had been celebrated with elaborate pomp in the Florentine Baptistery.[46] Eleonora may well have been responsible for overseeing the arrangements on this occasion as she was the acting head of state; her husband was in Genoa, involved in complex negotiations with Emperor Charles V at this time. Cosimo returned briefly to Florence only to take part in these festivities.[47]

Edelstein Fig. 9. Agnolo Bronzino, *Crossing of the Red Sea*, ca. 1541–42, Florence, Chapel of Eleonora, Palazzo Vecchio (photo: Soprintendenza, Florence)

Edelstein Fig. 10. Agnolo Bronzino, *Saints Francis, Jerome, John the Evangelist, and Michael the Archangel*, ca. 1541 (or ca. 1543–45?). Florence, Vault of the Chapel of Eleonora, Palazzo Vecchio (photo: Soprintendenza, Florence)

The birth of an heir would have had particular significance for the duchess. While for Cosimo a male child meant the continuity of his line (and the resultant stability that this implied for his state), the birth meant personal security for Eleonora.[48] During the Renaissance, failure to give birth to a male heir could result in the estrangement of a consort, if not more drastic measures.[49] Most importantly, the existence of an heir insured the duchess of her permanence in Florence; if Cosimo predeceased Eleonora, she would be able to retain her title as regent for the underage Francesco.[50] Eleonora was probably concerned when her first child was born female, although ducal apologists were quick to note that the Medici heirs were typically second children.[51] We can, therefore, imagine her relief upon the birth of Francesco on 25 March 1541.

The allusion to the birth is clearly embodied in the depiction of the pregnant woman at the far right of Bronzino's fresco (fig. 9).[52] While the inclusion of Moses, a necessary component of the narrative, alludes to Cosimo, Eleonora is alluded to in a figure whose complete extraneousness to the scene makes her all the more conspicuous.[53] Cox-Rearick has observed that the much-damaged figure of a man in a blue cloak at the right edge of this fresco is a self-portrait of Bronzino, positioned "next to the figure of Moses, alluding to his patron, Cosimo."[54] This bearded figure, with his blue cap and tunic, may be seen as being equally close to the pregnant woman, who stands directly behind him; the head of this self-portrait is positioned directly over the distended belly of the woman, the single feature that allows us to identify this idealized figure as an allusion to the fecund duchess. We may wish, then, to interpret Bronzino's inclusion of the self-portrait as an indication of his close ties to both Cosimo and Eleonora, since it seems unlikely that court artists would have distinguished between their responsibilities to the one or the other.

The importance of the pregnant woman in the *Crossing of the Red Sea* is reinforced by the abundance of female figures and children in Bronzino's other frescoes; these in turn confirm that the chapel is characterized by a distinctly female and repro-

Edelstein Fig. 11. Agnolo Bronzino, *Adoration of the Brazen Serpent*, ca. 1542(–43?), Florence, Chapel of Eleonora, Palazzo Vecchio (photo: Soprintendenza, Florence)

ductive iconography.[55] Indeed, the Israelites of the *Adoration of the Brazen Serpent* (fig. 11) are primarily women. Particularly noteworthy are the two intricately coifed, fair-haired women, each with a child, among the six who dominate the cluster of figures in the upper left, and the swooning woman supported by another in front of the crucifixlike bronze serpent at the center of the composition. Similarly, while there are a number of important men in the scene of *Moses Striking the Rock and the Gathering of the Manna* (fig. 12), both episodes contain more female than male figures. Again, women with children are readily apparent. In the *Striking of the Rock*, the figure at the center of Bronzino's composition is a woman in orange reaching down with her left hand to dip a bowl into the miraculous spring while

Edelstein Fig. 12. Agnolo Bronzino, *Moses Striking the Rock and the Gathering of the Manna*, ca. 1543 (1542–43?), Florence, Chapel of Eleonora, Palazzo Vecchio (photo: Soprintendenza, Florence)

clutching a crying infant; just behind this woman is another who is already supplying her thirsty child with water. In the *Gathering of the Manna*, a woman in light brown, also at the center of Bronzino's arrangement of figures, raises the hem of her apron to catch the heavenly bread before it falls to the ground; below her, at the far right of the composition, a mother with a magnificent gold vessel filled with manna exchanges a knowing glance with her child, who clutches to his belly a large quantity of the miraculous food wrapped in his toga.

"Eleonoran" Imagery in Bronzino's Designs for the *Story of Joseph* Tapestries

The female and dynastic imagery in the Chapel of Eleonora suggests that the duchess exercised a determining role in Bronzino's commission. The artist's next major project, the designs for a tapestry series, seems more closely aligned with the duke's interests. The chapel frescoes were completed in 1543, the first altarpiece and wings by the summer of 1545. Bronzino then began designing cartoons for the *Story of Joseph* tapestry cycle during the following winter, 1545–46. In striking contrast to the number of women in the Chapel of Eleonora frescoes, each scene is composed almost exclusively of male figures; Bronzino followed the biblical narrative faithfully, including virtually no extraneous women.[56]

One notable exception occurs in what seems to have been Bronzino's first composition for the tapestry cycle: the scene of *Joseph in Prison and Pharaoh's Banquet* (fig. 13).[57] Here, the female figure, positioned prominently by the artist in profile at the center of the tapestry's composition, is not mentioned in the book of Genesis and is likely to be a reference to Eleonora.[58] The physiognomy of Pharaoh's wife is similar to the figure at the center of Bronzino's *Lamentation* altarpiece (fig. 6). This woman, strikingly attired in green velvet, has been identified by Cox-Rearick as Mary of Cleophas, and was almost surely intended as an idealized likeness of the duchess herself.[59] Both figures (Mary of Cleophas and Pharaoh's wife) have the same full chin and elaborate blond coiffure; the rich jewels and pearls depicted by Bronzino as integral parts of their costumes may constitute a further reference to Eleonora, whose extravagant expenditures for these items are well documented. Furthermore, the youthful but bearded and curly-headed figure of Pharaoh resembles Cosimo himself, further sug-

Edelstein Fig. 13. Jan Rost, tapestry after Agnolo Bronzino, *Joseph in Prison and Pharaoh's Banquet,* 1546 (cartoon, 1545–46), Rome, Palazzo del Quirinale (photo: Segretario Generale della Presidenza della Repubblica Italiana, Servizio Patrimonio)

gesting that the identification of Pharaoh's wife with the duke's may well have been intended.[60]

The presence of an allusion to Eleonora in a narrative cycle ostensibly emphasizing parallels to her husband's personal history suggests Bronzino's clear understanding of the way patronage functioned at the Florentine court of the mid-sixteenth century. Nevertheless, the artist may have had even more palpable reasons for including such a reference. In the earliest surviving document referring to the commission for the *Story of Joseph* tapestries, Marzio Marzi de' Medici wrote on 28 August 1545 from Poggio a Caiano to the majordomo in Florence:

> His Excellency wishes [a tapestry series] to be made, and [therefore] measurements should now be taken of the hall where they dine and the large hall where the comedy was performed, and he wishes them to contain the Story of Joseph.[61]

"The large hall where the comedy was performed" can be securely identified as the Sala de' Dugento.[62] This is the space with which these tapestries have traditionally been associated, and their use in this hall is well documented (fig. 8). "The hall where they dined," however, has not as yet been convincingly identified.[63] A great deal of evidence points to this space being the anteroom to Eleonora's private suite, the Salotto (fig. 14).[64] If this hypothesis is correct, then the *Story of Joseph* tapestries may originally have been intended as a joint commission for the use of both the duke and the duchess. Unfortunately, there is no evidence to suggest that the *Joseph* tapestries were ever actually installed in the Salotto; had this in fact happened, only a portion of the series (possibly less than half) could have been accommodated there.

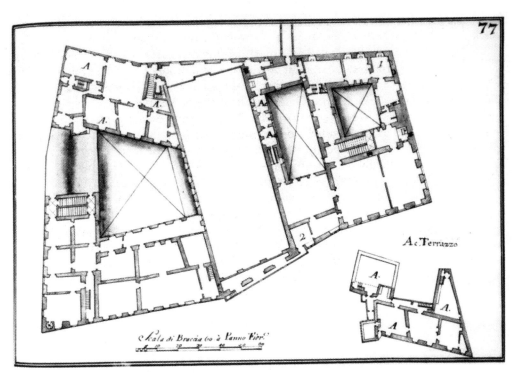

Edelstein Fig. 14. Anonymous Italian (?), eighteenth century, Plan of the Second Floor of the Palazzo Vecchio, Florence, Prague, Hapsburg Family Archive (photo: Kunsthistorisches Institut, Florence)

The Task of the Painter-Courtier

While a large number of account books survive from the reigns of Cosimo and Eleonora, the evidence provided by these documents is ambiguous regarding the patronage of works ordered for the ducal court. Even the artists themselves were often confused about payments for their works. Bronzino, for example, was never paid for two paintings ordered by Eleonora that were probably sent as gifts to powerful Spanish allies; shortly after Eleonora's death in December 1562, two courtiers wrote to the duke on the artist's behalf requesting payment for these works.[65] Although Cosimo seems eventually to have paid the duchess's debt to the artist in April 1564,[66] the duke's original response seems to have been negative, as indicated by the following note written by one of Cosimo's secretaries in the margin of the letter: "Regarding this other affair of Bronzino, as he is paid a regular stipend by us, His Excellency believed that [Bronzino] should have served the duchess as well."[67]

Returning to Marzio Marzi de' Medici's letter of 31 January 1544, we find particularly revealing evidence regarding the nature of conjugal patronage in sixteenth-century court culture. The bishop of Marsico reported that Bronzino's accounts were presented to Cosimo but that the duke refused to examine them, as they were the duchess's "affair."[68] This suggests that artists' accounts were drawn up through the Guardaroba of the ducal court regardless of whether the patron was Cosimo or Eleonora. Thus, while the information provided by account books can be enormously useful for establishing a *terminus ante quem* or a *terminus post quem* for a work of art, this information does not provide incontrovertible evidence for the patronage of that work. The accounts rarely indicate the ultimate source of the funds paid to an artist—that is, whether those funds came from the duke or the duchess.

Marzi's letter of 28 August 1545, recording the commission for the *Story of Joseph* tapestries, serves as a reminder that most artworks were movable furnishings, employed in a variety of ways as the need arose. It may therefore be unnecessarily limiting to consider the sole content of such works, commissioned by the duke or the duchess, as being relevant exclusively to their patron. Between 1539 and 1553 Bronzino executed projects alternately for the duke and the duchess with almost surprising regularity: the wedding ephemera for Cosimo, Eleonora's private chapel, the three state portraits for the duke, the double portrait for the duchess, and finally the tapestry cartoons ordered by the duke but possibly by joint commission. This series of events suggests just how important it was for court artists to consider the desires of Eleonora while executing projects for Cosimo and, conversely, to bear in mind the duke's priorities while working for the duchess. While a simple division of patronage between husband and wife may frequently be impossible because of the way in which the financial records of the court were kept, such a division may not even be desirable, as it is unlikely to improve our understanding of the works of art they commissioned.[69]

Appendix of Documents[70]

Doc. 1: Bishop of Marsico Marzio Marzi de' Medici in Pisa to Personal Secretary, future Majordomo, Pierfrancesco Riccio in Florence, 31 January 1544.[71]

Molto R.do. S.r mio,

S. Ecc.tia ha visto li conti del Bronzino et la carta di V. S. R. *Verba ad Corinthios.* Non mi rispondeva, et domandandole quello havevo a scriver', mi disse "siane con la duchessa che son cose sue." Io glielo dirò, et havendo a fare dentro altro ne avviserò V. S. R.

Sopra le cose del Cavalieri Bandinello per conto de' poderi del Gualterotto, S. Ecc.tia vuol' espettare la lettera di m. Lelio et all'hora si risolverà, quasi parendomi che non ci s'habbi a perder' di speranza.

A quelli che voglion mandar' fuor' quel canto, mandinlo a lor' posta perchè S. Ecc.tia se ne contenta. Et Ciano venda le sue acque saponate in qual giorno, vuole perchè possa a chi n'ha voglia far spender' qualche baiocco per gittarli in aria.

Le lettere che la mi ha inviato gliele ritorno eccetto d'una di Ser Antonmaria Buondini, qual S. Ecc.tia ha data al S.r Campana per trarne d'indi lettere per fuor' del dominio. V. S. R. gli potrà dir' a bocca che S. Ecc.tia approva tutt'e due le cose contenuti in essa. Baciole la mano et me le raccomando quanto posso, dandole nuove del ben esser' delli patroni et della lor corte. Di Pisa li 31 di gennaio 1543 (stile fiorentino).

Le lettere per il commissario di Pistoia la S. V. R. le manderà per uno cavallaro apposto perchè importano.

Servitore,

Martio, vescovo di Marsico

Address: Al molto R.do s.or mio m. Pier Franc.o Riccio intimo secretario di S. Ecc.a

A Fiorenza

Inscribed in second hand:[72] †. 1543 di Mons.r di Marsico di Pisa il 4 di febbraio

Doc. 2: Court Painter Agnolo Bronzino at Poggio a Caiano to Majordomo Pierfrancesco Riccio in Florence, 9 August 1545.[73]

Molto R.do s.or mio osser.mo,

Ho ricevuto l'azurro mandatomi dalla S. V. il quale invero non è tanto a un pezzo, & è tanto poco che non credo sia dua danari. Pertanto V. S. sia contenta, non vi essendo più di quella sorte medesima, me ne mandi di quello che può, tanto che sia almeno mezz'oncia, perchè non credo poter fare con manco, perchè il campo è grande & ha ad essere scuro, talch'io son certo che non ne bisogna manco. V. S. adunque si degni vedere tra quello che venne costì ultimamente di qui del migliore, cioè del più bello, & me ne mandi quel tanto ch'io chieggo, perchè non s'ha adoperare per altri che per S. Ex.tia.

I nostri angeli stanno *aff*atti benissimo & gli adoriamo, parendoci che Iddio ci dia più che humana gratia a poterlo fare. & chosì Iddio sempre a V. S. & a noi gli conservi felici (come speriamo) si Iddio ha cura de' buoni & giusti signori, come si vede che ha.

Circa le campane, vi confesso che m'hanno non manco infastidito scrivendone che costì mi facessino udendole, tant'è che non so quel ch'io mi farò di loro, pure me le sono levate dinanzi.

Duolmi del nostro Barlacchi, Iddio l'aiuti, che in verità ne sarebbe danno grandissimo, perchè, oltre all'essere huomo facetissimo & amorevole, era buona persona & fedelissimo servitore della celeste Casa de' Medici. & certo non sarà un simile a fretta, pure Iddio disponga il meglio.

Altro per hora non mi occorre, salvo ricordare a V. S. che io desidero che quella mi comandi, perchè mi parrebbe, quando quella lo facessi, essere da qualcosa. & senza dire, bacio le mani alla V. S. R.da, pregando nostro S.ore Iddio che quella contenti & conservi.

Dal Poggio alli VIIII d'agosto del XLV per il di V S. R.da

Servitore, il Bronzino Pittore

Address: Al molto R.do s.ore il signor Maiordomo di sua Ec.tia sempre osser.mo

In Firenze

Doc. 3: Court Steward, later Assistant Majordomo Vincenzo Ferrini at Poggio a Caiano to Majordomo Pierfrancesco Riccio in Florence, 14 August 1545.[74]

R.do S.or mio obss.mo,

Io ho fatto come quelli che achozzano la ciena chol disinare nel rispondere alla S. V. perchè io riscevei una di V. S. stamani, et per essere io per astato al rispondere, messo per aggiunto l'altra Vostra per staffetta. E per ora dirò quanto m'ochorre.

Circha le pesche, io ho detto a loro Ex.tie questa mattina che la S. V. à usato diligientia nel fare cierchare delle pesche chotognie, et che per anchora non aveva trovato nemmanco ne pensava trovare per la indispositione dell'annuale. Et horamai ho achoncio loro lo stomacho a patire di frutte per questo anno, talchè se niente di buono per le nostre mane aranno, cie la meteranno a somma diligientia. Vorebbano de' citriuoli piccini, la S. V. ne faccia mandare subito se se ne trova.

Veggho che avessi le misure et che si lavora inposte. Penso che una mattina voi lo vedrete chostà et li darete disinare ma non provedete da ciena perchè io non voglio star qua solo di notte, dipoi lasciateci star qua presso a uno mese.

Confetto debbe essere smaritosi per la via, poichè non è arivato qua. Sono bene venuti e ferramenti sua et, sebbene domani e l'altro non si lavora per essere festa, el Tribolo li arebbe possuto mostrare quello che doveva fare, perchè e' perde tempo ad aspettarlo. E' pura à dell'altre faciende d'inportanza comessoli da S. Ex.tia, la quale sollecita questo giuocho di sorta che domani e l'altro si amattonerà, però mandatelo subito chol-lavoro.

M.o Tribolo à mostro el disegnio delle stalle che la S. V. li comesse a S. Ex.tia, le quale li soddisfano et à conciesso che al prexente se ne facci la terza parte come era parsovi insieme, et ne raguaglierà V. S.

Noi abbian guasto el gusto perchè questo vino non ci piacie, però è forza che o e non reggha nel tramutarsi o l'aria qua lo facci peggiorare, tant'è, poichè non ci è ordine, questi S.ri aranno pazienzia et a chi e non piacie non-ne bea.

À vi si a mandare nuove chomessione di quadri e d'ornamenti per parte di mia S.ra, e quali si diranno a riquizezione del Bronzino.

Pasquino portò li grembiuli datili da m. Pasquino per S. Ex.tia li quali li dovette chonsegniare alle donne.

El ducha à preso stasera lui lo spaccio et l'ànno tramestato di sorta che io non mi posso inmaginare la rachapezzazione, pure per gran' sorta ho auta la di V. S. che la mi scrive perchè il consueto di S. Ex.tia è stato sempre di farmi delle V.e lettere buono servizio. Ora, per choncrudere: la scatola, io non l'ò auta, l'ò ben vista loro tra le mane, et la lettera della duchessa di Mantova. La lettera di m.ro Andrea, io non-ne so niente, benchè la-inporti pocho per me averla vista perchè la doveva essere loro. Et da essa aranno inteso quello ch'è più cholà dimandato era arroto, parendo a m.ro Andrea essere a proposito. Et penso che il chavallaro abbia auto la spedizione per tornarsene.

La quivi aggiunta del Buonanni non l'ò possuto farmela dare nelle mani, bene à detto alla duchessa l'arrivata del grecho a Siena e a m. Cristiano el richapito delle lettere del m.ro del champo. Et sopra ciò non ò che me li dire altro.

Dicie la duchessa che la S. V. hordini delle fiasche di vetricie per enpierle di grecho perchè le vuole mandare chon li marzolini nella Magnia. Non so già quanto, ma penso dua chasse doverrà volerne.

Io ho già speso tutti e mia danari perchè 30 al fornaio, 64 al bechaio, 10 al zegera [*sic*], fa 104 e io n'ebbi ciento, però la S. V. mi faccia rinfondere che oggi è stato venerdì et ne sono soli 4 di questo mese.

El S.or Stefano è stato stamattina qua et ci sono stati tanti forestieri che gli erono 27 a tavola, senza Ser Gio. Conti e Gianmaria Pilli che mangieranno in camera mia e delli altri che si partiranno.

Non dirò altro per ora a V. S., se non che li patroni Ill.mi stanno di buona voglia et mi vi raccomando dal Poggio a-ddì XIIII d'agosto 1545.

Di V. S.

Servitore,

Vincenzo Ferrini

Address: Al R.do s.or mio obss.mo m. Pierfranc.o Riccio maiordomo di s. ex.tia.

In Firenze

Doc. 4: Court Secretary Cristiano Pagni in Bibbona to Majordomo Pierfrancesco Riccio in Florence, 5 March 1547.[75]

Molto R.do s.or mio osser.mo,[76]

Ci accostammo hiermattina alla Cecina, et la trovammo tanto crucciosa, turbida, enfiata et terribile che non fu ordine di passare. Et un cavalleggieri spagnolo che si misse alla prova ci fu por rimanere pur, con la gratia di (Dio), con l'acqua. Finì sopra la sella notando. Il cavallo, doppo d'esser traportato dall'acqua per longo spatio, trovò l'acqua bassa et si condusse a salvamento a riva. Et così loro Ecc.tie, visto questo, dettono volta a drieto et se ne tornarono qui a Bibbona. Et recontrorno per il cammino Don Diego, che ancor esso se ne veniva a Rossignano, per dove questa mattina tutti allegramente si son' partiti, essendo l'acque calate et rasserenato il tempo.

Circa a' XXIII hore, comparse qui il Busino cavallaro con li spacci di v. s., che anch'egli hebbe a aspettar' tre hore o più che le acque laddove son più basse calassino. S'hebbeno tutte l'aggiunte alle di v. s.ria et di esse si rimandano quelle della corte et di Trento per mostrarle a quei S.ri del Consiglio. Mando lo spaccio di Venetia acciò domattina per il procaccio si possa inviare allo Imbasciatore.

La Duchessa mia S.ra dice che V. S.ria ordini al pittore fiammengo che faccia un ritratto del s.or Don Giovanni da quello ch'è già fatto, et che lo spedisca quanto prima potrà.

L'Ecc.e loro son' sane et liete, et così sono li S.ri figliuoli. Bacio la mano a V. S.ria et mi raccomando in sua buona gratia. Da Bibbona.[77] Alli V di Marzo 1546 (stile fiorentino).

Di V. S. molto R.

Affettuosissimo Servitor, Christiano Pagni

Address: Al molto R. s.or mio osser.mo M. Pier Fran.co Riccio Maiordomo di s. Ecc.za.

A Fiorenza

Doc. 5: Court Secretary Lorenzo Pagni in Pisa to Majordomo Pierfrancesco Riccio in Florence, 16 March 1547.[78]

Molto R.do s.or mio oss.mo,[79]

Il Duca nostro s.or m'ha comandato ch'io spedisca a V. S. il presente cavallaro, et li dica da parte sua che per il medesimo subito subito gli invii quello archibuso da uccellare che gli donò il conte di Noceto con quella canna lunga et tonda, che dice S. Ecc.a esser' il più bello che habbi, mandandoli insieme tutto il fornimento suo et comandando al cavallaro che sia qui stasera a ogni modo con ogni cosa.

Li soldati spagnuoli non s'hanno a spesare, anzi hanno a pagare, ma honestamente et come si costuma con li lor' pari.

Ho hauto le lettere di Venetia et lectole a S. Ecc.a insieme con il capitolo, che V. S. mi scrive de' festaiuoli, che se n'ha riso.

Il ritratto del S.or Don Giovanni non è se non piacciuto a S. Ecc.a,[80] per quello che mi disse quando lo scoperse, che ero presente.

Don Diego se n'andrà a Roma subito che sarà comparso Don Francesco di Toledo, et lasserà sospeso il negotio di Pionbino, et nel modo che con la precedente li ho scritto. Lucantonio Cuppano et Marcantonio da Tolentino sono chiamati qua con il traino di Don Diego. Et li soldati spagnuoli restati in Campiglia si licentiano per tornar' costì in Castello.

Queste ex.tie non temano punto del male di Don Pedrico. Così V. S. sarà contenta riferir' da mia parte a m.ro Andrea et a Ser Pasquino, a' quali non posso scriver' per la prestia che S. Ecc.a mi da di spedir' questo cavallaro. Et confidano pienamente nella prudentia et amorevolezza di m.ro Andrea.

Bacio le mani della S. V. et prego Idio che la conservi sana et contente. Da Pisa alli XVI di marzo 1546 (stile fiorentino).

Di V. S.

Servitor,

Lorenzo Pagni

Address: Al molto R. s.r mio oss.mo il S.r Maior[do]mo maggior' di s. Ex.

Firenze

Doc. 6: Court Secretary Lorenzo Pagni at Poggio a Caiano to Majordomo Pierfrancesco Riccio in Florence, 20 January 1550.[81]

Molto R.do et mag.co s.or mio oss.mo,[82]

Parlando con la Duchessa nostra s.ra per haver' il saio di velluto rosso di Don Francesco et una robba di raso del medesimo colore di S. Ecc.a per mandarl'al Bronzino, come V. S. m'ordinava con la carta sua di questa mattina, hebbi da lei questa risposta, in queste, o simili parole, cioè, "Come puede il Bronzino hazer el retratto di Franzischillo, sin haverlo adelante?" Io replicai che non sapevo altro che quel che V. S. mi domandava per dar' fine a' ritratti che con molta instantia domandava Mons.re d'Aras. Allora S. Ecc.a soggiunse ch'io scrivessi alla S. V. facesse intender' a detto Bronzino che, quanto al saio di Don Francesco, ne pingesse uno di tertio pelo[83] rosso, il più bello che sapesse et potesse, ma che l'accompagnasse con una robba foderata di martore o zibellini, non le parendo che questo s.re horamai s'habbi a ritrarre in solo saio ma in una robba come fu visto a Genova. Et circa alla robba che si domandava da S. Ecc.a, mi disse il medesimo che del saio di Don Francesco, cioè che il Bronzino ne pintasse una a suo modo di quel colore. Ho voluto riferir' tutto per sua informatione. Et havendogli scritto 3 hore sono di tutto quello che havevo da dirgli di più, et mandato lo spaccio della Corte, non ho da scriver' altro con questa, se non il ben essere di questi s.ri Ill.mi. Però li bacio le mani, et prego Dio n.ro s.re che conservi lungamente la s. v. sana et contenta come desidera.

Dal Poggio li XX di gennaio 1549 (stile fiorentino).

Di V. S. R. et mag.ca

Servitor',

Lorenzo Pagni

Address: Al molto Rever' et mag.co s.or mio oss.mo il S.or Maiordomo maggior' di S. Ecc.a

In Firenze

Inscribed in second hand:[84] †. 1549 di m. L.zo Pagni del Poggio il 20 di gen.

Doc. 7: Court Painter Agnolo Bronzino in Pisa to Majordomo Pierfrancesco Riccio in Florence, 16 December 1550.[85]

Molto [Ill.e] & [R.do][86] S.re Maiordomo,

Domenica sera, che fummo alli XIIII del presente, arrivammo felic[emente][87] il nostro car.mo Tasso & io in Pisa dove siamo tutti allegri & contenti in casa del V.o & nostro car.mo M. Luca Martini, il quale ha hauto g[rand'] allegrezza di vederci & molto più delle salute dateli in nome di V. S. R.da, la quale ringrazia con tutto il cuore & se le offerisce come buon servitore di quella. Non conto il viaggio per non tediar quella, ma basta che ancoraché per insino al porto ci paresse trovare una dolorosa strada, & che per la barca havessimo di molte balsolate & qualche disagetto come accade, non è però che non ci paia havere hauto un bellissimo tempo, & certo infinitamente più che noi non pensavamo, & il Tasso m'ha fatto ta[nto] ridere che mi s'è hauto ad aprire la testa. Inbarcammoci a un'hora di notte & tutta notte stemmo in berta, & dicemmo & udimmo novelle, a quelli s[ca]faiuoli, & havemmo di matte paure nondimanco di sassi, di ceppi, & di pali, & di pescaie, & di mulini, tanto che andammo conpartendo una novella & una paura, & così di mano in mano insino al gior[no], il quale seguì bellissimo & ci servì fino a sera con piacere nostro grande.[88]

Iermattina parlai a loro Ex.tie Ill.me, & la S.ora Duchessa m'inpose che io[89] cominciassi il ritratto del S.or Don Giovanni. & così ieri li bozzai il [vis]o & iersera lo volse vedere, & così lo vidde ancora il nostro Ill.o & Ex.[o] Padrone. & la S.ora Duchessa m'inpose che voleva che io li facessi un ritrattino di sè & forse un altro del S.or D. Grazia. & perchè quassù non ci sarebbe commodità di far fare quadri o d'ingessarli senza fors[e] troppo tempo, trovandomene io costì che saranno a proposito, scrivo costì che mi siano mandati. Pertanto prego V. S. R.da che quando li saran[no] portati li mandi subito & per persona che li porti presto, perchè hanno bisogno d'incollare & dar di mestica. Altro non mi occorre dire a V. S. Ill.e & R.da, se non che a quella del continuo mi raccomando, come buon servitore di quella, che nostro S.re Iddio sempre la feliciti & conservi. Di Pisa alli XVI di [dicembre][90] del L. Per il vostro humil' servitore,

Il Bronzino[91]

Address: Al Molto R.do s. maior domo M. Pierfranc.o Riccio suo oss.mo

A Firenze

Inscribed in second hand:[92] del Bronzino di Pisa il 14 di X.re

Doc. 8: Superintendent of Pisa Luca Martini in Pisa to Majordomo Pierfrancesco Riccio in Florence, 8 January 1551.[93]

Molto Mag.co et Rev. S.or et Padron mio oss.mo,[94]

L'Ill.mo et Ecc.mo S.or Don Francesco m'ha comandato ch'io mandi a V. R. S. una sua fregatina con tutti li fornimenti, delli quali la nota sarà nella presente, et dice che detta fregatina vuole tenere in Arno. Io l'ho inviata questa mattina al portinario di Signa che l'invii a V. R. S., et la conduca alla sua vaga loggia dove penso starà benissimo et si salverà da ogni cosa, et massime dalle mani de' fanciulli.

Il nostro m.ro Tasso tornò et ha portato seco da far' un nuovo modello, et harà a pieno ragguagliato V. R. S. d'ogni cosa resoluta et come gli sieno passate le cose qua con grandissima satisfazione, però non l'infastidirò con la presente a dirle nulla, salvo che ce lo rimandi presto che S. E. I. lo disidera assai. Il Bronzino ha ritratto l'Ill.o S.or Don Giovanni divinamente, et hoggi si truova a Livorno con loro Ecc.ze Ill.me, et ha condotto là le sue bazziche per lavorar'. Et per non tediar' più V. R. S. farò fine, baciandole humilmente la mano, con pregar' nostro S.re Iddio che le dia ogni felicità et co[n]tento, et mi tenga in sua buona grazia et mi comandi. Di Pisa alli 8 di gennaio 1550 (stile fiorentino).

Di V.ra Rev. S.ria

Servitore, Luca Martini

Address: Al Molto Mag.co et R.do S.or et Padron mio oss.mo il s.or Proposto di Prato, et Maiordò[mo di] Sua Ecc.za Ill.ma

A Fiorenza

Inscribed in second hand:[95] †. 1550 di Luca Martini di Pisa il dì 8 di Gen.o

Doc. 9: Superintendent of Pisa Luca Martini in Pisa to Majordomo Pierfrancesco Riccio in Florence, 31 July 1551.[96]

Molto Mag.co et Rev.e[97] S.or et Padron mio oss.mo ecc.,

Per ordine dell'Ill.ma Duchessa n.ra S.ra, commessomi dal Poggio per lettere di m. Tommaso de' Medici, invio a V. R. S. per Stefano dalla Moriana vetturale una cassa coperta con tela et incerata, diritta a quella in guardaroba, entrovi sette quadri di legniame, entrovi ritratti per il'[98] Ecc.mo Bronzino l'Ill.mi Figliuoli di loro Ecc.ze[99] Ill.me, che due ve ne sono del S.r Don Francesco, uno del S.or Don Giovanni, due del S.or Don Grazia, et due della S.ra Donna Maria. Li quali quella nel cavarli fuora faccia avvertire allo sconficcarli, et al maneggiarli perchè, come vedrà, non hanno adornamenti. Et della riscevuta piaccia a V. R. S. farne dare avviso a loro Ecc.ze Ill.me. Et volendo ancora due teste di mano del medesimo che mi lassorno qui, una d'Homero et una d'Euripide, che invero tenendole, come fo, racchiuse, stanno non troppo bene. Harò caro intenderlo, se le ho a mandare o salvarle qua. Et del porto V. R. S. faccia contentare il vetturale, et la gabella di qua, che è stata l. 16.13.4, l'habbiamo pagata noi. Et per non tediar più V. R. S., baciandole la mano, di cuor' me le raccomando, con pregar nostro S.re Iddio che la mantenga felicissima et me in sua buona grazia. Et quando gli capitano intorno li vertuosi Bronzino et Tasso, gli saluti a mio nome. Et se questa è presuntione la mi perdoni. Et stia sano.

Di Pisa, l'ultimo di luglio MDLI.

Di V.ra Rev.e[100] S.ria

Affezionatissimo Servitor',

Luca Martini

Address: Al Molto Mag.co et Rev.e[101] S.or et Padron mio Oss.mo Il S.or Proposto di Prato et Maiordomo di sua Ecc.za Ill.ma:

A Fiorenza.

Una cassa.

Doc. 10: Florentine Ambassador Averardo Serristori in Rome to Majordomo Pierfrancesco Riccio in Florence, 14 August 1551.[102]

Molto Rev.do s.or mio,[103]

È comparsa la carta di V. S. delli IIII di questo ma non già la somma del vino giuntamente con la casetta del ritratto del s.or Don Gio. Et, con tutta la diligentia ch'io habbi fatta usar' in cercar' del vetturale che portava dette cose, non si è per ancor' possuto rinvenire che, quando si havessi havuto notitia del nome di detto vetturale, facilmente si saria possuto haver' qualche inditio del caso suo, se ha havuto qualche sinistro per via, ovver' perchè egli stia tanto a comparir'. Il che mi dispiace molto, sapendo quanto a S. S.tà piace quel che gli vien' presentato dalla Duchessa mia S.ra. Sempre che mi verranno nelle mane farò quel tanto che V. S. mi scrive. La qual prego a baciar le mani humilmente alla S.ra Duchessa et tenermi in sua memoria. Et a V. S. mi offero et raccomando, pregando Dio che li doni quanto desidera. Di Roma il giorno XIIII d'agosto 1551.

Di V. S.

Servitore,

Averardo Serristori

Address: Al Molto R.do Mons. mio oss.mo il [s.or Prop]osto di Prato Maiordomo di S. E. Fiorenza

Inscribed in second hand:[104] †. 1551 di m. Averardo Serristori di Roma il dì 17 d'Ag.to

Doc. 11: Florentine Ambassador Averardo Serristori in Rome to Majordomo Pierfrancesco Riccio in Florence, 24 October 1551.[105]

Molto Rev.do Mons. mio,[106]

Alli giorni passati per Benintendi vetturale si mandò per parte di N. S.re alla S.ra Duchessa un ritratto del S.or Don Giovanni senza i capelli et s'indirizzò alla S. V., del quale non se n'è mai inteso la ricevuta, nemmanco quella d'una medaglia di S. S.tà et altra del Principe di Spagna, mandatele da S. B.ne alla S.ra Duchessa, come anche per le mani del Gualterotto le mandò il S.or Baldovino un gattino et un pappagallo, nè di tutte queste cose s'è inteso più cosa nissuna, poichè partiron' di qua. Piacerà a V. S. intender' da S. E. se le ha ricevute et scrivemene V. S. qualche cosa, massime del ritratto del S.or Don Giovanni et quel che n'è parso a S. E. così intoso, acciochè di tutto possa dar conto a S. S.tà et al S.or Baldovino, la quale più volte m'ha dimandato quel che la Duchessa diceva del'haver' tosato Don Giovanni. Et se io per la S. V. posso cosa alcuna mi comandi, et mi ami come suole, che N. S.re Dio la contenti. Di Roma, il dì XXIIII d'ottobre MDLI.

Di V. S.

Servitore,

Averardo Serristori

al maiordomo

Address:Al molto R.do Mons. mio Il s.or Proposto [di Pra]to Maiordomo di S. E.

Fiorenza

Inscribed in second hand:[107] †. 1551 di m. Averardo Serr.ri di Roma il dì 24 d'8.re

Notes

This essay depends in part upon material included in my doctoral dissertation, "The Early Patronage of Eleonora di Toledo: The Camera Verde and its Dependencies in the Palazzo Vecchio" (Ph.D. diss., Harvard University, 1995), and subsequent research completed for a talk given at the annual conference of the College Art Association held in Boston in February, 1996. I wish to thank my advisors, John Shearman and Mirka Beneš, for their invaluable criticism and assistance throughout my dissertation and the following colleagues who graciously offered advice regarding the material I presented at CAA: Molly Bourne, Jonathan Nelson, Jeannine O'Grody, Mary Vaccaro, and Mary-Ann Winkelmes. Rab Hatfield, Jonathan Nelson, and Michael Rocke were also kind enough to read various versions of this essay and to offer their comments and suggestions for its improvement.

1. For Eleonora as head of state in Florence and the duchess's financial resources, see Bruce L. Edelstein, "The Early Patronage of Eleonora di Toledo: The Camera Verde and Its Dependencies in the Palazzo Vecchio," 2 vols. (Ph. D. diss., Harvard University, 1995), 1:40–68.

2. For Eleonora's patronage of Bronzino and use of paintings by him as gifts between 1540 and 1553 or 1554 (that is, from the beginning of Bronzino's work on Eleonora's private chapel to the completion of the chapel's second altarpiece), see Edelstein, "Early Patronage," 1:323–61.

3. Vasari-Milanesi: 7:598: "E non andò molto che ritrasse, siccome piacque a lei, un'altra volta la detta signora duchessa, in vario modo dal primo col signor don Giovanni suo figliuolo appresso."

4. See appendix, doc. 5: "Il ritratto del S.or Don Giovanni non è se non piacciuto a S. Ecc.a, per quello che mi disse quando lo scoperse, che ero presente."

5. Bronzino appears to have regularly employed samples from the wardrobe of the ducal couple and their children for the execution of portraits. A Guardaroba *Giornale* cited by Giovanna Lazzi, "Gli abiti di Eleonora da Toledo e di Cosimo I attraverso i documenti di archivio," in *Il costume nell'età del Rinascimento,* ed. Dora Liscia Bemporad (Florence: EDIFIR, 1988), 170, records the consignment on 19 July 1556, of "una veste corta di fianchi di zibellini data al Bronzino pittore per fare uno ritratto di Sua Excellenza."

6. See appendix, doc. 6: "Come puede il Bronzino hazer el retrato di Franzischillo, sin haverlo adelante?"

7. See appendix, doc. 6: "Io replicai che non sapevo altro che quel che V. S. mi domandava per dar' fine a' ritratti che con molta instantia domandava Mons.re d'Aras."

8. See appendix, doc. 6: "Allora S. Ecc.a soggiunse ch'io scrivessi alla S. V. facesse intender' a detto Bronzino che, quanto al saio di Don Francesco, ne pingesse uno di tertio pelo rosso, il più bello che sapesse et potesse, ma che l'accompagnasse con una robba foderata di martore o zibellini, non le parendo che questo s.re horamai s'habbi a ritrarre in solo saio ma in una robba come fu visto a Genova."

9. Although Lorenzo Cantini, *Vita di Cosimo de' Medici Primo Granduca di Toscana* (Florence: Albizziniana, 1805) doubts the occurrence of this voyage due to Francesco's young age, the veracity of this diplomatic mission is confirmed by numerous documents; see appendix, doc. 6. See also the numerous relevant letters written to majordomo Pierfranceso Riccio in Florence in 1548, ASF, MdelP, fol. 1174, ins. 6, e.g.: doc. 13, from Giovanni Francesco Lottini in Livorno, 25 November (recording Cosimo's decision to remain in Tuscany and send Francesco to Genoa in his stead); doc. 14, from il Barbetta in Livorno, 26 November (with specific indications regarding Eleonora's role in the preparation of Francesco's wardrobe on this occasion); doc. 17, from Jacopo Guidi in Livorno, 27 November; docs. 19–20, from Vincenzo Ferrini in Livorno, 28 November (with a complete list of the members of the court who were to accompany the prince to Genoa in a galleon

commanded by Eleonora's brother—who was also Francesco's uncle—García de Toledo); doc. 21, from Mariotto Cecchi in Genoa, 29 November; doc. 22, from Guidi in Livorno, 30 November; doc. 25, from the master of the pages, Camillo degli Elmi, in Genoa, 3 December; doc. 29, from Ferrini in Genoa, 6 December; doc. 30, from Cecchi in Genoa, 6 December; (containing remarks on Francesco's mature compartment) doc. 31, from degli Elmi in Genoa, 7 December; doc. 42, from Guidi in Livorno, 15 December (recording Francesco's return from Genoa); and doc. 43, from Cecchi in Livorno, 15 December (who returned with Francesco from Genoa). Cosimo himself was only thirteen years old when he first met the Holy Roman Emperor in Bologna; Riccio, in a letter to Maria Salviati dated 27 December 1532, published by Cesare Guasti, "Alcuni fatti della prima giovinezza di Cosimo I de' Medici illustrati con i documenti contemporanei," *Giornale storico degli archivi toscani* 2 (1858): 57, notes that Charles V "recognized how prudently Cosimo carries himself."

10.   Stefania Ricci, "Tra storia e leggenda: cronaca di vita medicea," in *Moda alla corte dei Medici: gli abiti restaurati di Cosimo, Eleonora e Don Garzia*, ed. Kirsten Aschengreen Piacenti and Caterina Chiarelli, exh. cat. (Florence: Palazzo Pitti, Galleria del Costume, 1993), 21: "La responsabilità di Eleonora a palazzo era l'abbigliamento del marito e dei figli e l'approvvigionamento dei tessuti e degli arredi per le proprie abitazioni." The ordering of Francesco's wardrobe for his trip to Genoa in 1548 by the duchess is specifically noted by Ricci, "Tra storia e leggenda," 23. Cf. Lazzi, "Gli abiti," 162, and Roberta Orsi Landini, "L'amore del lusso e la necessità della modestia: Eleonora fra sete e oro," in *Moda alla corte*, ed. Aschengreen Piacenti and Chiarelli, 35; regarding Eleonora and court costume, see the excellent article by Giovanna Lazzi, "La moda alla corte di Cosimo I de' Medici," in *Moda alla corte*, ed. Aschengreen Piacenti and Chiarelli, 27–34. Maria Salviati had similarly been responsible for insuring that Cosimo was properly attired when he met Charles V in Bologna in 1532. In a letter to Riccio, dated 29 December 1532, published by Guasti, "Alcuni fatti," 58, Maria instructed her son's tutor and future majordomo on the proper employment of five *braccia* of satin requested for Cosimo's attire: "Si manda il panno roxato che chiedete per Cosimo, et è brazza 5: credo si potrà fare il mantello bondante. Et di poi anco penso gli n'havanzarà per fargli un paio di calze."

11.   ASF, MdelP, f. 1175, ins. 4, doc. 43, court secretary Lorenzo Pagni in Pisa to majordomo Pierfrancesco Riccio in Florence, 21 December 1549: "Queste Ecc.tie si contentano per commodità del Bronzino, et per più celere speditione de' ritratti che desidera di loro Mons.re R.mo d'Aras, che il vestimento della Duchessa non si facci di broccato riccio ma di qualche altro drappo ornato che facci bella mostra. Però la S. V. vi facci metter' mano et li solleciti, che per ogni mano di lettere sono domandati dal Vescovo di Furlì." The text is cited by Gaetano Pieraccini, *La stirpe de' Medici di Cafaggiolo: saggio di ricerche sulla trasmissione ereditaria dei caratteri biologici* (1924–25; reprint, Florence: Nardini, 1986) 2:56, and in part by Lazzi, "Gli abiti," 166. Pieraccini associated this with the famous Uffizi double portrait (fig. 1), although he subsequently (68) dated the same picture to 1546–47, based on the assumption that the child depicted is a five- or six-year-old Garzia. For the problems presented by Pieraccini's interpretation of the text, see Arthur K. McComb, *Agnolo Bronzino: His Life and Works* (Cambridge, Mass.: Harvard University Press, 1928), 14–15.

Orsi Landini, "L'amore del lusso," in *Moda alla corte*, ed. Aschengreen Piacenti and Chiarelli, 42, associates this text once again with the Uffizi double portrait. The author asserts that Eleonora did not own any dresses of the type portrayed by Bronzino, or at least not in those colors, and consequently concludes that the gown is an artistic fiction created from a fabric sample, mistakenly associating this letter with the process. However, not only does the letter fail to indicate that it was accompanied by a sample of brocade, but the text specifically orders Bronzino not to waste time painting the duchess in that complex fabric. That paintings are not photographs and that leeway should always be allowed for artistic license and creativity are points well worth making; nonetheless, since Orsi Landini's evidence suggesting that "black was an infrequent color in [Eleonora's] wardrobe" is derived from Guardaroba records dating not earlier than 1547 (two years after the summer of 1545, when the portrait was most likely painted), her conclusion may not be justified. An extant sample of this fabric in the Carrand Collection, Bargello, Florence (see her fig. 16), attests to its manufacture in sixteenth-century Florence, suggesting the possibility at least that the duchess owned a garment of this type. Janet Arnold, "Cut and Construction," in *Moda alla corte*, ed. Aschengreen Piacenti and Chiarelli, 54, notes that the velvet guards of Eleonora's burial gown may originally have been black, which would seem to negate Orsi Landini's principal objection to Eleonora having owned a gown like the one in the Bronzino portrait since that brocade includes black. At any rate, this exhibition catalogue, esp. Arnold, 53, should finally put to rest the spurious notion that Eleonora was buried in the same dress as that depicted by Bronzino in the Uffizi portrait, reported by several authors, including George Frederick Young, *The Medici* (1909; reprint, New York, 1912), 288–89; McComb, *Agnolo Bronzino*, 30; and Joe A. Thomas, "Fabric and Dress in Bronzino's Portrait of Eleanor of Toledo and Son Giovanni," *Zeitschrift für Kunstgeschichte* 57 (1994): 262–67.

12. For Bernardo de' Medici as Florentine ambassador to the imperial court, see Cantini, *Vita di Cosimo*, 43–44, 64–65. Bernardo later served as ambassador to the French court, when Cosimo attempted to improve relations with the French king and his wife, Cosimo's distant cousin, Catherine de' Medici; see Cantini, *Vita di Cosimo*, 172–74.

13. Karla Langedijk, *The Portraits of the Medici: Fifteenth to Eighteenth Centuries* (Florence: S.P.E.S., 1981–87), 1:697. Another version of the same picture is to be found in the Cincinnati Art Museum; see Edi Baccheschi, *L'opera completa del Bronzino* (Milan: Rizzoli, 1973), 95, fig. 55 b; and Langedijk, *The Portraits*, 1:697, fig. 35,12a (as a copy of the Pisa picture). A third version, formerly in Berlin, seen on the art market in Lucerne, 1969, whose present location is unknown, is mentioned by Baccheschi, *L'opera completa*, 96, cat. no. 55f, and reproduced by Langedijk, *The Portraits*, 1:698, fig. 35,12b (also as a copy of the Pisa picture). Lazzi, "Gli abiti," 166, also connects Pagni's letter of 21 December 1549 (doc. 6) with the Pisa portrait type, although she refers to the version in Cincinnati and the one formerly in Berlin.

14. See n. 6 above.

15. ASF, MdelP, f. 1176, ins. 1, doc. 16: "La Duchessa mia s.ra mi ha commesso ch'io debba scrivere a v. s.ria che la faccia venir' qua M.ro Bronzino, perchè vuol' che faccia un ritratto del S.or Don Giovanni, por mandarlo al Papa, che desidera si spedisca quanto prima far si potrà." See the passage in Anna Baia, *Leonora di Toledo, Duchessa di Firenze e di Siena* (Todi,: Z. Foglietti, 1907), 75; Pieraccini, *La stirpe*, 2: 116; in free translation by McComb, *Agnolo Bronzino*, 17; Detlef Heikamp, "Agnolo Bronzinos Kinderbildnisse aus dem Jahre 1551," *Mitteilungen des Kunsthistorischen Institutes in Florenz* 7 (1955): 133; and Baccheschi, *L'opera completa*, 83. The use of the Spanish "por" instead of the Italian "per" may suggest that the phrase may be a literal quotation of Eleonora's orders; Baia and Pieraccini incorrectly substitute the Italian "per" for "por."

16. See appendix, doc. 7: "così ieri li bozzai il [vis]o & iersera lo volse vedere, & così lo vidde ancora il nostro Ill.o & Ex.[o] Padrone. & la S.ora Duchessa m'inpose che voleva che io li facessi un ritrattino di sè & forse un altro del S.or D. Grazia. & perchè quassù non ci sarebbe commodità di far fare quadri o d'ingessarli senza fors[e] troppo tempo, trovandomene io costì che saranno a proposito, scrivo costì che mi siano mandati. Pertanto prego V. S. R.da che quando li saran[no] portati li mandi subito & per persona che li porti presto, perchè hanno bisogno d'incollare & dar di mestica." The document was first published by Albertina Furno, *La vita e le rime di Angiolo Bronzino* (Pistoia: G. Flori, 1902), 106–7, with minor differences in transcription, and is mentioned by Heikamp, "Agnolo Bronzinos Kinderbildnisse," 133; and Baccheschi, *L'opera completa*, 83.

17. The picture was possibly of the type represented by the portrait in the Wallace Collection (see Langedijk, *The Portraits*, 2:697, cat. no. 11, fig. 35, 11), or the one in the Museum of Arts and Science, Evansville (see Langedijk, *The Portraits*, 698, cat. no. 12c, fig. 35, 12c); for the suggestion that the Wallace Collection picture was executed after Eleonora's death, see John Ingamells, ed., *Wallace Collection: Summary Illustrated Catalogue of Pictures* (London: Trustees of the Wallace Collection, 1979), 37.

18. Heikamp, "Agnolo Bronzinos Kinderbildnisse," 134, following McComb, *Agnolo Bronzino*, 71. See also: McComb, *Agnolo Bronzino*, 17–18; Baccheschi, *L'opera completa*, 99–100; and Langedijk,

The Portraits, 2:937–39. The Prado portrait of Garzia in Langedijk, *The Portraits*, 940, is another possible candidate, and might help to explain the picture's provenance.

19. ASF, MdelP, f. 1176, ins. 9, doc. 4, Mariotto Cecchi, a Guardaroba official in Florence, to major-domo Pierfrancesco Riccio "at the court" (perhaps in Pisa), 11 February 1551: "Mando alla S. V. la scatolina del Bronzino con una delle carte del nostro azzurro oltramarino, et viene inclusa in uno fangotto di camozze a m. Thommaso de' Medici."

20. Other important members of the Medici family had also born the name Giovanni, most notably the patriarch of the two main branches, Giovanni di Bicci, and Cosimo's own father, the popular condottiere, Giovanni delle Bande Nere. Paolo Giovio seems to have presumed that this would have been the name of choice for Cosimo's heir, as is revealed by a letter written to the duke on 3 March 1540, precisely one month before Eleonora gave birth to their first child, Maria. See Paolo Giovio, *Lettere,* in *Opera,* ed. Giuseppe Guido Ferrero, 2 vols. (Rome: Libreria dello Stato, 1956–58), 1:240–41: "V. Ecc.zia speri che la dignissima del tempio, la signora Duchessa il farà maschio: e se sarà femina, pigliasi l'augurio del bon cominciare, come dice el proverbio; e Dio facia io sia a tempo del batesimo per appiccare al Giovanni altro nome che di Romulo." Nonetheless, the choice of the name for a second son would seem to recall more precisely the naming of Lorenzo the Magnificent's second son, Giovanni. Upon Cosimo's birth, Giovanni, as Pope Leo X, had chosen the child's name and served as the godfather at his baptism. Indeed, in a letter to Paolo Giovio dated 20 August 1546, ASF, MdelP, f. 7, c. 281, Cosimo himself observed: "La Santa Memoria di Leone [X] tengo io nel nome di Giovanni mio secondogenito, e se bene sotto il nome di Leone si potette manifestar più al mondo la grandezza del animo suo, non fu però minore la virtù suo sotto questo nome Giovanni poichè con tal nome seppe così ben fare che si fece Papa così giovine in un conclavi dove tutti gli altri colleghi gli potevon per età esser padri."

21. For Juan de Toledo, Cardinal of Burgos, see Antonio Castaldo, *Dell'istoria: ne' quali si descrivono gli avvenimenti più memorabili succeduti nel regno di Napoli sotto il governo del Vicerè D. Pietro di Toledo e de' vicerè suoi successori fino al Cardinal Granvela. Raccolta di tutti i più rinomati scrittori dell'istoria... di Napoli* (Naples, 1769), 6:77; Piero Vettori, *Laudatio Eleonoræ Cosmi Medicis, Floren ac Senens Ducis, Uxoris: Quæ habita est IIII. K. Ian. Florentiæ à Piero Victorio, in æde divi* [stile fiorentino]*Laurentii* (Florence, 1562); Leonardo Ginori Lisci, *The Palazzi of Florence: Their History and Art,* trans. Jennifer Grillo (Florence: Giunti Barbèra, 1985), 1:487. In a letter to Cosimo, dated 10 March 1543, Paolo Giovio (*Lettere,* 1: 306–7) wickedly described the two attributes of Cosimo's and Eleonora's three, soon to be four, children: "Ill.mo et Ecc.mo Signor mio osser.mo, La fretta che si dà Sua Santità in montare l'Appenino è cagion ch'io paia discortese con V. Ecc.zia in non venire lì a basargli la mano con la bocca, come faccio col cuore. In cambio ho visto li tre bellissimi parti de l'Ecc.ma Duchessa, *idest* un'altra Gaia sputata, e il signor Duchino con la fronte del Viceré e la gronda de' sopracigli del signor Giovanni di felice memoria; l'Isabella pare tutta il Cardinale de Burgos: che Dio gli dia fortunatissima allevatura."

22. Mario Scaduto, *L'epoca di Giacomo Lainez,* 2 vols. (Rome: Civiltà Cattolica, 1964–74), 2:38. Laínez, later general of the Society of Jesus after the death of Saint Ignatius, seems to have been repulsed by the duchess's pragmatism about the matter and is reputed to have said in response: "Signora, a me sembra che né le VV. EE. siano tanto povere, né i loro figli siano allevati con tanto sfarzo che non possano mantenerli del proprio mentre sono ancora piccoli; neppura mi sembra giusto che diano loro le rendite della Chiesa fino a che non abbiano raggiunto età, virtù, lettere e volontà per disimpegnare l'ufficio congiunto con quelle. Quando avranno questi requisiti, essendo figli di VV. EE. non mancherà loro la rendita ecclesiastica. Senza questo, si arreccherebbe loro danno." Scaduto, *L'epoca di Giacomo Lainez,* 2:38–39.

23. ASF, MdelP, fol. 1169, ins. 6, doc. 22, Lorenzo Pagni in Livorno to Riccio in Florence, 18 March 1550: "N. S.re par' resoluto (secondo ch'io ho di luogo auctentico) di fare Car.le in Brevi Don Giovanni, et mandargli il Breve senza pubblicarlo, per potersene fare la publicatione ogni volta che paresse expediente. Et il Duca tandem s'è contentato che egli sia di chiesa, che sin qua mal volentieri vi si disponeva." ASF, MdelP, f. 1170a, fasc. 4, c. 621v, Lorenzo Pagni in Pisa to Riccio in

Florence, 2 May 1550: "Oggi col nome di Dio l'arcivescovo di Pisa, per mano mia, ha fatto la procura nel Serristori a renuntiar' l'arcivescovado a Don Giovanni, ovvero a consentir' che N. S.re lo facci suo coadiutor, reservandoli la dignità, collatione di benefitii, l'habito, la denominatione, fructi et regresso." These titles were promised to Giovanni even though he does not yet appear to have been tonsured. Pagni may have been concerned about this since in both instances he warned Riccio to keep this information secret: "V. S. tenga in sè l'aviso del Cardinalato di Don Giovanni per buon rispetto"; "Che V. S. lo tenga in sè." Cf. Pieraccini, *La stirpe*, 2:108.

For Giovanni's elevation to the cardinalate, see Agostino Lapini, *Diario fiorentino dal 252 al 1596*, ed. Giuseppe Odoardo Corazzini (Florence: Sansoni, 1900), 126: "A' dì 30 di detto gennaio [1560], in mercoledì mattina, fu pubblicato in Roma cardinale don Giovanni figlio secondo de' maschi del duca Cosimo, fu fatto da papa Pio IV; e alli 31 detto venne a Firenze la nuova mandata dal vescovo de' Ricasoli che era in Roma." Giovanni's trip to Rome two months later is mentioned by Giorgio Vasari, *Der Literarische Nachlass Giorgio Vasaris*, ed. Karl Frey (Munich: Georg Müller, 1923–30), 1:545–55, 558–68, who accompanied him there; from this correspondence it seems that Giovanni began avidly collecting antiquities at this time. Cf. Giovambattista Cini, *Vita del Serenissimo Signor Cosimo de Medici Primo Gran Duca di Toscana* (Florence, 1611), 443. Upon Giovanni's elevation to the cardinalate, Eleonora provided him with a magnificent gift of textiles; see Orsi Landini, "L'Amore del lusso," in *Moda alla corte*, Aschengreen Piacenti and Chiarelli, 44. Letters from Giovanni to his mother immediately preceding and during his stay in Rome (where he was made a cardinal by Pope Pius IV, Giovanni Angelo de' Medici) are preserved in ASF, MdelP, f. 5922a, c. 185, from Florence, dated 14 March 1560, cc. 189r–v, from Rome, dated 8 April 1560; see also c. 187 for a related letter from a cardinal in Rome to Eleonora regarding the arrangements for Giovanni's arrival, dated 9 March 1560. Regarding Giovanni's entry into Pisa as archbishop on 9 March 1561, see Lapini, *Diario*, 131.

24. See appendix, doc. 8, cited in part by Pieraccini, *La stirpe*, 2:116; McComb, *Agnolo Bronzino*, 17; Heikamp, "Agnolo Bronzinos Kinderbildnisse," 138, n. 28; and mentioned by Baccheschi, *L'opera completa*, 83. Bronzino himself reported having completed the portrait of Giovanni, along with one of Maria, in a letter written from Pisa to Riccio in Florence on 27 January 1551, published by Heikamp, "Agnolo Bronzinos Kinderbildnisse," 137–38. In the same letter Bronzino noted that the portrait of Garzia should be finished within the next day or so and that, as soon as the court returned to Pisa from Livorno, he would begin a portrait of Francesco. The letter is cited in translation by Charles McCorquodale, *Bronzino* (London: Harper and Row, 1981), 90–92, without indication of his source.

25. See appendix, doc. 9; also mentioned by Baccheschi, *L'opera completa*, 84.

26. In his letter of 31 July 1551, Martini makes a specific point of informing Riccio that special care should be taken while unpacking the pictures, as they lacked frames.

27. See appendix, doc. 10: "È comparsa la carta di V. S. delli IIII di questo ma non già la somma del vino giuntamente con la casetta del ritratto del s.or Don Gio. Et, con tutta la diligentia ch'io habbi fatta usar' in cercar' del vetturale che portava dette cose, non si è per ancor' possuto rinvenire che, quando si havessi havuto notitia del nome di detto vetturale, facilmente si saria possuto haver' qualche inditio del caso suo, se ha havuto qualche sinistro per via, ovver' perchè egli stia tanto a comparir'. Il che mi dispiace molto, sapendo quanto a S. S.tà piace quel che gli vien' presentato dalla Duchessa mia S.ra. Sempre che mi verranno nelle mane farò quel tanto che V. S. mi scrive." The document is mentioned by Pieraccini, *La stirpe*, 2:116; and by Heikamp, "Agnolo Bronzinos Kinderbildnisse," 134.

28. See appendix, doc. 11: "Alli giorni passati per Benintendi vetturale si mandò per parte di N. S.re alla S.ra Duchessa un ritratto del S.or Don Giovanni senza i capelli et s'indirizzò alla S. V., del quale non se n'è mai inteso la ricevuta, nemmanco quella d'una medaglia di S. S.tà et altra del Principe di Spagna, mandatele da S. B.ne alla S.ra Duchessa, come anche per le mani del Gualterotto le mandò il S.or Baldovino un gattino et un pappagallo, nè di tutte queste cose s'è inteso più cosa nissuna, poichè partiron' di qua. Piacerà a V. S. intender' da S. E. se le ha ricevute e scrivemene V.

S. qualche cosa, massime del ritratto del S.or Don Giovanni et quel che n'è parso a S. E. così intoso, acciochè di tutto possa dar conto a S. S.tà et al S.or Baldovino, la quale più volte m'ha dimandato quel che la Duchessa diceva del'haver' tosato Don Giovanni." This document was known to Pieraccini, who concluded from Serristori's letter that Giovanni must have traveled to Rome in the fall of 1551 and received his tonsure there; Pieraccini, *La stirpe*, 2:108, note *a*. Pieraccini, 116, further misreads Serristori's letter as an indication that the picture sent by Eleonora in August had just arrived in Rome, rather than its referring to a new portrait being sent to the duchess from Rome; see also Baccheschi, *L'opera completa*, 83; and Langedijk, *The Portraits*, 2:1013, who notes that the new portrait was likely to have been based on the model of Bronzino's picture sent to the pope. Pieraccini, *La stirpe*, 2:58, also bizarrely concludes that Serristori's letter suggests "una specie di zoofilia" on Eleonora's part.

There are no known documents that confirm such an early trip to Rome for the young prince. The evidence, in fact, suggests that Giovanni did not travel to Rome until 1560 and that in 1550 he received his tonsure in the Chapel of the Priors in the Ducal Palace in Florence. Janet Cox-Rearick, *Bronzino's Chapel of Eleonora in the Palazzo Vecchio* (Berkeley: University of California Press, 1993), 37, n. 54, citing a documentary source, reports that Giovanni was tonsured in the Chapel of the Priors on 21 June 1550.

29. Heikamp, "Agnolo Bronzinos Kinderbildnisse," 136, identifies the Ashmolean picture as the actual portrait sent to the pope; Baccheschi, *L'opera completa*, 99, accepts Heikamp's identification. Langedijk, *The Portraits*, 2:1013, more cautiously suggests that they are of the same type but not necessarily the same picture. Heikamp (and Baccheschi following Heikamp) and Langedijk also disagree about the contemporary frame; Heikamp and Baccheschi assert that it is the one that originally belonged with the picture while Langedijk affirms that it is not; Heikamp even hypothesizes that Bronzino himself designed the frame. Given that the picture was unframed when it was sent to Florence on 31 July 1551 and that Serristori was already concerned that the picture might by lost in transit by 4 August 1551, it seems unlikely that, if the picture is actually the one sent to Julius III, such a complicated frame could have been provided in such a short period of time. The picture is sometimes called a portrait of Don Garzia, as it is by McComb, *Agnolo Bronzino*, 17, who rejects the attribution to Bronzino, suggesting instead that it was possibly by Salviati. Another version of the picture in the Museum of Art, Toledo, Ohio, is considered autograph by Langedijk.

30. Collection of Lord Landsdowne; for an image, see Langedijk, *The Portraits*, 2:1015, fig. 54,6. While it is difficult to evaluate Langedijk's attribution to Bronzino solely on the basis of available photographs, the painting seems so similar to the Ashmolean portrait, especially in costume and pose, that it is tempting to hypothesize that it is the picture sent by Balduino del Monte. In Rome at the papal court, the pope's brother would certainly have had access to talented artists and superior copyists who would have been able to imitate Bronzino's style while altering the hairstyle of the original portrait. It may be relevant to note that there are a number of portraits that have been variously attributed to both Bronzino and Salviati, and that Salviati may have executed some portraits of Giovanni. Since Salviati had already returned to Rome by this time, he may be a likely candidate for a reattribution of the Bowood picture.

31. Scipione Ammirato, *Istorie fiorentine con l'aggiunte di Scipione Ammirato il giovine*, ed. Ferdinando Ranalli, 6 vols. (Florence: V. Batelli, 1846–49), 6:304.

32. See appendix, doc. 1: "S. Ecc.tia ha visto li conti del Bronzino et la carta di V. S. R. *Verba ad Corinthios.* Non mi rispondeva, et domandandole quello havevo a scriver', mi disse 'siane con la duchessa che son cose sue.'"

33. Cf. Cox-Rearick, *Bronzino's Chapel*, 68, n. 33, who rejects the possibility that these accounts could be related to Bronzino's work on the chapel. See also Elizabeth Pilliod, review of *Bronzino's Chapel* by Cox-Rearick, *Burlington Magazine* 138 (1996): 334, who similarly links Marzi's letter to Eleonora's patronage.

34. Giorgio Vasari, *Le vite de' più eccellenti architetti, pittori et scultori italiani, da Cimabue insino a' tempi nostri nell'edizione per i tipi di Lorenzo Torrentino Firenze 1550*, ed. Luciano Bellosi and

Aldo Rossi (Turin: G. Einaudi, 1986), 592–93: "Andò ad imparare da costui i principii dell'arte nella sua fanciulezza Bronzino fiorentino pittore, il quale si portò poi sí bene sotto la protezzione di Iacopo da Puntormo pittor fiorentino, che nell'arte ha fatto i medesimi frutti che Iacopo suo maestro, come ne fanno fede alcuni ritratti et opere di sua mano appresso lo illustrissimo et eccellentissimo signor Duca Cosimo nella guarda roba, e per la illustrissima signora duchessa la cappella lavorata in fresco; e vivendo et operando merita quelle infinite lodi che tutto di sé gli danno."

35. See Bruce L. Edelstein, review of *Bronzino's Chapel of Eleonora in the Palazzo Vecchio*, by Janet Cox-Rearick, *Art Bulletin* 76 (1994): 173. As I observe there in n. 12, the changes made by Vasari for the 1568 edition of his *Life* of Bronzino in no way contradict this reading of the 1550 edition of the *Lives* (for the text in the 1568 edition, see the passage cited below, n. 40). One of the characteristics of the 1568 edition of the *Lives* is that projects previously associated with the duchess, such as the Pitti Palace, are reattributed almost exclusively to the duke. This reflects not only an increase in Vasari's flattery of Cosimo, but also what appears to be a change in official policy regarding references to Eleonora after her death in December 1562. This is particularly evident from Vincenzo Borghini's and Vasari's correspondence in relation to the ephemeral decorations to be erected for the wedding *apparato* of 1565; see Piero Ginori Conti, *L'apparato per le nozze di Francesco de' Medici e di Giovanna d'Austria* (Florence: Leo S. Olschki, 1936), 32, n. 47, and 50–55, n. 67. On the nature of the changes made by Vasari for the second edition of the *Lives*, see Patricia Lee Rubin, *Giorgio Vasari: Art and History* (New Haven, Conn.: Yale University Press, 1995), esp. 187–230.

36. Vasari-Milanesi, 7:597: "Quando ne fu levata la prima tavola, erano un San Giovanni Batista ed un San Cosimo, che furono messi in guardaroba quando la signora duchessa, mutato pensiero, fece fare questi altri due [l'Angelo Gabriello e la Vergini da lui Annunziata]."

37. Pilliod proposes a similar reading of Vasari's text in Pilliod, review of Cox-Rearick, 334; as does Carolyn Smyth, "An Instance of Feminine Patronage in the Medici Court of Sixteenth-Century Florence: The Chapel of Eleonora da Toledo in the Palazzo Vecchio," in *Women and Art in Early Modern Europe: Patrons, Collectors, and Connoisseurs,* ed. Cynthia Lawrence (University Park: Pennsylvania State University Press, 1997), 86–87.

38. Vasari-Milanesi, 7:597–98: "Il signor duca, veduta in queste ed altre opere l'eccellenza di questo pittore, e particolarmente che era suo proprio ritrarre dal naturale quanto con più diligenzia si può imaginare, fece ritrarre sé, che allora era giovane, armato tutto d'arme bianche e con una mano sopra l'elmo: in un altro quadro la signora duchessa consorte; ed in un altro quadro il signor don Francesco loro figliuolo e prencipe di Fiorenza. E non andò molto che ritrasse, siccome piacque a lei, un'altra volta la detta signora duchessa, in vario modo dal primo, col signor don Giovanni suo figliuolo appresso." This passage is the source that identifies the child in the Uffizi double portrait (fig. 1) as Giovanni. Robert B. Simon, "Bronzino's Portrait of Cosimo I in Armour," *Burlington Magazine* 125 (1983): 527–39, attempts to employ this passage to establish a chronology for Bronzino's early portraits.

39. On the triumphal entry of Eleonora di Toledo, see Pierfrancesco Giambullari, *Apparato et feste nelle noze dello illustrissimo Signor Duca di Firenze, et della Duchessa sua Consorte, con le sue stanze, madriali, comedia, & intermedij, in quelle recitati* (Florence: B. Giunta, 1539), 5; Ammirato, *Istorie fiorentine*, 6, 257; Luca Landucci, *Diario Fiorentino dal 1450 al 1516 continuato da un anonimo fino al 1542"* ed. Iodoco Del Badia (Florence: Sansoni, 1883), 375; Lapini, *Diario*, 102–3; Giorgio Spini, *Cosimo I e l'indipendenza del principato mediceo* (Florence: Vallecchi, 1980), 136; Anna Maria Testaverde, "Feste Medicee: La visita, le nozze, e il trinofo," in *La città effimera e l'universo artificiale del giardino*, ed. Marcello Fagiolo (Rome: Officina, 1980), 69-100; Anna Maria Petrioli Tofani and Anna Maria Testaverde, "Gli ingressi trionfali," in *Il potere e lo spazio: La scena del principe* (Florence: Officina, 1980), 343–54. See also Andrew C. Minor and Bonner Mitchell, *A Renaissance Entertainment: Festivities for the Marriage of Cosimo I, Duke of Florence, in 1539* (Columbia, Mo.: University of Missouri Press, 1968) for a translation of Giambullari's

description of the *entrata*, the music performed during these festivities, and copious notes regarding the epigrams employed in the ephemeral decorations. On the costumes and stage design for theatrical entertainments, see also Elvira Garbero Zorzi, "La 'festa scenica': Immagini e descrizione," in *Il costume nell'età del rinascimento*, ed. Dora Liscia Bemporad (Florence: EDIFIR, 1988), 189–99; Adriano Ghisetti Giavarina, *Aristotile da Sangallo: architettura, scenografia, e pittura tra Roma e Firenze nella prima metà del Cinquecento; ipotesi di attribuzione dei disegni raccolti agli Uffizi* (Rome: Multigrafica, 1990), esp. "Commentario alla 'Vita di Bastiano detto Aristotile da San Gallo' scritta da Giorgio Vasari," 17–31, and "Scenografia e apparati per feste," 37–50. The music for these performances, primarily by Francesco Corteccia, has been recorded by the Centro di Musica Antica di Ginevra, Studio di Musica Rinascimentale di Palermo and the Schola "Jacopo da Bologna" under the direction of Gabriel Garrido, *Firenze 1539: Musiche fatte nelle nozze dello illustrissimo duca di Firenze il signor Cosimo de Medici et della illustrissima consorte sua mad. Leonora da Tolleto*, 1990.

On the artists involved in the *apparato*, see Vasari-Milanesi, 6:86–89, 441–45, 575–77, and 7:17, 596. See also Henry W. Kaufmann, "Art for the Wedding of Cosimo de' Medici and Eleonora of Toledo (1539)," *Paragone* 21, no. 243 (May 1970), 52–67, who notes that Minor and Mitchell, *A Renaissance Entertainment*, were incorrect in their observation that no art from these festivities survives; among other works, Raphael's famous Uffizi portrait of *Leo X with Cardinals Giulio de' Medici and Luigi de' Rossi* was among those displayed in the courtyard of the Medici Palace. This work had previously been employed at an earlier Medici wedding feast, that of Lorenzo, Duke of Urbino, to Maddalena de la Tour d'Auvergne, in 1518; I thank Sheryl Reiss for this notice, which emerged from her research on Alfonsina Orsini; see her contribution to this volume. Kaufmann further identifies a study by Tribolo for an equestrian monument in the Louvre (inventory 50v) with the ephemeral statue of Giovanni delle Bande Nere that was erected in the Piazza San Marco. The attribution and identification with the wedding decorations were made earlier by Wiebke Aschoff, "Tribolo disegnatore," *Paragone* 18, 209/29 (July 1967): 45–48.

40. Vasari-Milanesi, 7:596: "Che tutte furono le migliori pitture che fussero fatte in quell'apparato: là dove il duca, conosciuta la virtù di quest'uomo, gli fece metter mano a fare nel suo ducal palazzo una cappella non molto grande per la detta signora duchessa, donna nel vero, fra quante furono mai, valorosa, e per infiniti meriti degna d'eterna lode." Regarding Vasari's attribution of the patronage of the Chapel of Eleonora to Cosimo in this edition of the *Lives*, see n. 35 above.

41. ASF, CA, 2, c. 27 (letter 19), previously published by Giovanni Gaye, *Carteggio inedito d'artisti dei secoli XIV, XV, XVI, pubblicato ed illustrato con documenti pure inediti* (Florence: G. Molini 1839–40;), 3:60; Frey in Vasari, *Der Literarische Nachlass*, 1:644: "Ò negotiato stamattina seco un'ora et con la duchessa forse due."

42. ASF, CA, 2, c. 33 (letter 22), previously published by Gaye, *Carteggio inedito*, 3:67–68, and Frey in Vasari, *Der Literarische Nachlass*, 1:676: "Et per fino allora sarà finito di sopra le stanza afatto, che avendo satisfatto alla duchessa, non arò fatto poco."

43. The unity of the two narratives in the *Striking of the Rock and the Gathering of the Manna* (fig. 12) was radically altered when the chapel's original window was converted to a door; see Cox-Rearick, *Bronzino's Chapel*, 130–32. This alteration, along with the creation of the terrace and the Stanza del Lavoro, or so-called Sala del Spioncino, was most likely contemporary with other changes in the chapel decorations made by Alessandro Allori in preparation for its use by Giovanna d' Austria after 1565; Ettore Allegri and Alessandro Cecchi, *Palazzo Vecchio e i Medici: Guida storica* (Florence: S.P.E.S., 1980), 351–52. These are most certainly not contemporary with the last years of Eleonora's residence in the palace, as stated by Cosimo Conti, *La prima reggia di Cosimo I de' Medici nel Palazzo già della Signoria di Firenze: descritta ed illustrata coll'appoggio d'un inventario inedito del 1553 e coll'aggiunta di molti altri documenti* (Florence: G. Pellas 1893), 64.

44. The argument is presented in Janet Cox-Rearick, "Bronzino's *Crossing of the Red Sea and Moses Appointing Joshua*: Prolegomena to the Chapel of Eleonora di Toledo," *Art Bulletin* 69 (1987): 45–67.

45. Cox-Rearick, "Bronzino's Crossing," esp. 62–67.

46. Cox-Rearick, "Bronzino's Crossing," 56–62; Cox-Rearick, *Bronzino's Chapel*, 216–17, 229–30, 305–6, characterizes Bronzino's fresco as an allegory of Cosimo's victory over the Florentine exiles, particularly the Strozzi family rebels, at Montemurlo. I am not completely convinced that contemporary viewers would have interpreted the fresco in this way. If the image of the drowning Egyptians in the left background of the painting (fig. 9) was actually understood to contain such a reference, then it would logically follow that this was intended as another allusion to the infant Francesco, whose baptism was carefully scheduled to occur on the anniversary of the battle of Montemurlo. This would consequently reinforce the fresco's specific imagery, which celebrates Eleonora as *genetrix,* the provider of a male heir, rather than serving as a generic recollection of Cosimo's military prowess.

47. For the events of this period, see Baia, *Leonora di Toledo*, 37, and Spini, *Cosimo I e l'indipendenza,* 202–3. On 25 August 1541, the day after Cosimo's departure for Genoa following the baptism, the elector of Granaiuolo wrote to Eleonora for her approval of the erection of a temporary bridge across the Arno to facilitate the duke's passage to Fucecchio; ASF, MdelP, f. 353, c. 208. See also the letter from Eleonora to the abbess of San Pietro in Pistoia, sent only three days after Cosimo's return to Genoa after the baptism, published by Cantini, *Vita di Cosimo*, 516–17. Cox-Rearick, *Bronzino's Chapel*, 35, publishes a portion of a letter dated 2 September 1541, in which Eleonora states that she has matters of utmost secrecy to communicate to Cosimo that she is afraid to put in writing. This was a reasonable fear, as the frequency with which Cosimo's secretaries transmitted information in code would seem to confirm. Lapini, *Diario*, 104, incorrectly dates Cosimo's return to Genoa one year after Francesco's baptism–that is, 24 August 1542.

48. It was probably with this in mind that Pedro de Toledo closed a letter to his daughter (dated 30 November, during her first pregnancy that resulted in the birth of Maria) by wishing her, "Nro. S. dea v. ex.a tantos hijos i tantos ejitados, que me quiera a mi uno a quien servir," ASF, MdelP, f. 338, c. 292. The *pubblico bene* of Florence was, at any rate, not only associated with Cosimo but with Eleonora and her fecundity as well; see Cox-Rearick, *Bronzino's Chapel*, 290. Public welfare and fecundity remained linked in Medici commissions and in Bronzino's art; see Graham Smith, "Bronzino's *Allegory of Happiness*," *Art Bulletin* 66 (1984): 390–99, esp. 398, regarding the representation of *Felicitas* in the *Allegory of Happiness*. Baccio Baldini,*Vita di Cosimo Medici, Primo Gran Duca di Toscana, discritta da M. Baccio Baldini suo Protomedico* (Florence: 1578), 30, states that Cosimo's principle motivation in marrying Eleonora was to ensure the public welfare of the Florentine state: "Volgeva il Duca continovamente seco varie cose a trovar modo a assicurare del tutto la sua patria & lo stato suo, & d'uno in altro pensiero pervenendo s'avvisò che il prender moglie secondo la voglia & il parere dell'Imperadore fusse per recare grandissima sicurezza alle cose sue, la onde dopo non molto tempo ei tolse per moglie si come piacque a Cesare, la Signora Leonora figliuola del Signor Don Pietro di Toledo all'hora Vicere di Napoli."

49. One need only recall Henry VIII's long succession of wives.

50. Even the emperor's own daughter, Margaret of Austria, had been unable to retain control of the duchy after the assassination of her husband, Alessandro de' Medici, the first duke of Florence, precisely because their union had failed to produce heirs.

51. Such an apology is particularly strange given that this situation appears to have occurred only with the children of Lorenzo the Magnificent, the fate of whose heir, Piero the Fatuous, Cosimo surely did not desire for his own. Jacopo Riguccio Galluzzi, *Storia del Granducato di Toscana* (Florence: L. Martini, 1822), 1:94, explains that the parallel was meant to be with Lorenzo, Duke of Urbino, whose first child was Catherine, later Queen of France. This seems equally unlikely, as Lorenzo produced no legitimate male heirs and the assassination of his illegitimate heir, Alessandro, led to Cosimo's acquisition of the ducal title. The identification of Alessandro's father as Lorenzo, Duke of Urbino, seems now to be generally accepted; see Emilio Grassellini and A. Fracassini, *Profili medicei: origine, sviluppo, decadenza della famiglia Medici attraverso i suoi componenti* (Florence: SP44, 1982), 62. However, see Pieraccini, *La stirpe*, 1:398–403, for a discussion of Alessandro's

paternity and the conclusion that Clement VII was the father of the first duke of Florence.

52. The importance of this figure has been noted by Cox-Rearick, "Bronzino's Crossing," 64; Cox-Rearick, *Bronzino's Chapel*, 316–18.

53. No mention is made of a pregnant woman in either Deut. 31–34 or Num. 27:18–23, the scriptural passages relevant to the Last Acts and Death of Moses, the scene depicted in the part of Bronzino's fresco that includes the pregnant woman.

54. Cox-Rearick, "Bronzino's Crossing," 58.

55. A similar conclusion has been reached independently by Smyth, "An Instance," 97.

56. On this point, see my earlier comments in Edelstein, review of Cox-Rearick, 174.

57. On the tapestry's history, see Nello Forti Grazzini, *Il patrimonio artistico del Quirinale: gli arazzi* (Rome: Lavoro, 1994), 1:29–33, cat. no. 4, with references to the relevant earlier literature. The suggestion that this was both the first tapestry woven at the Arazzeria Medicea after Bronzino's design and the first cartoon provided by him was made by Craig Hugh Smyth, *Bronzino as Draughtsman: An Introduction* (Locust Valley, N.Y.: J. J. Augustin, 1971), 94–101.

58. Forti Grazzini, *Il patrimonio artistico*, 1:32, similarly observes that "la dama seduta a tavola al centro dell'arazzo sarà allora da intendersi come un'allusione alla duchessa, Eleonora di Toledo."

59. Janet Cox-Rearick, "Les dessins de Bronzino pour la Chapelle d'Eleonora au Palazzo Vecchio," *Revue de l'art* 14 (1971): 20; see also Cox-Rearick, *Bronzino's Chapel*, 264–65. None of these idealized blonde types should be considered to be portraits of Eleonora, but rather allusions to her in some of her various roles as duchess, wife, mother, and sometimes head of state; for further comments on these problems, see Edelstein, review of Cox-Rearick, 173; Edelstein, "The Early Patronage," 1:477, n. 185; Smyth, "An Instance," 81.

60. For the identification of the figure of Pharaoh in this scene with Cosimo, see Candace Adelson, "The Tapestry Patronage of Cosimo I de' Medici: 1545–1553" (Ph.D. diss., New York University, 1990), 2:373. See also Forti Grazzini, *Il patrimonio artistico*, 1:32.

61. ASF, MdelP, f. 1170a, fasc. 3, c. 109: "S. Ecc.tia vuole che le [arazzerie] si faccino et se ne pigli adesso la misura per la sala dove si fanno li pasti et per il salone grande dove si fece la commedia, et vuole che vi sia dentro la Storia di Joseph." The document is cited in part by Candace Adelson, "Documents for the Foundation of Tapestry Weaving under Cosimo I de' Medici," *Renaissance Studies in Honor of Craig Hugh Smyth*, ed. Andrew Morrogh, et al., 2 vols. (Florence: Giunti Barbèra, 1985), 2:17, doc. 5. The complete text can be found in Edelstein, "The Early Patronage," 2:645, doc. 30.

62. See Adelson, "Documents for the Foundation," 2:7. For the installation of all twenty tapestries in the Sala de' Dugento and their dimensions, see Adelson in *Palazzo Vecchio: Committenza e collezionismo medicei,* ed. Paola Barocchi, exh. cat. (Florence: Palazzo Vecchio; Florence: Edizioni Medicee, 1980), 50–63.

63. Adelson, "Documents for the Foundation," 2: 8, provides a rather different interpretation of Marzi's letter. She believes that "the hall where they dined" in the Palazzo Vecchio was either the Sala dell'Udienza or the "winter dining room" described by Vasari in Vasari-Milanesi, 7:27, for which Francesco Salviati provided a now lost ceiling decoration. In either case, she presumes that a second set of tapestries, distinct from the Joseph cycle, was to be woven for "the hall where they dine"; she hypothesizes that if the Sala dell'Udienza was indeed intended, then the second set of tapestries was the cycle of grotesque *spalliere* with yellow grounds woven after cartoons by Bachiacca. This hypothesis does not seem to be sustained by the text of Marzi's letter, which apparently refers to a single set of tapestries to be installed in one or both of the two rooms in question.

64. For a complete analysis of the function and furnishings of the Salotto, see Edelstein, "The Early Patronage," 1:259–94. The Salotto of the Quartiere di Eleonora conforms quite closely to the

typology of *salotti* in Roman Renaissance palaces as established by Christoph L. Frommel, *Der Römische Palastbau der Hochrenaissance*, 3 vols. (Tübingen: E. Wasmuth, 1973), 1:70, who notes that these spaces served two primary functions: as a waiting room and usually as a dining hall. Peter Thornton, *The Italian Renaissance Interior, 1400–1600* (New York: Abrams, 1991), 291, similarly notes that *salotti* were generally employed as dining halls. An extremely large trestle table over four and a half meters long that could have accommodated the entire ducal family and their guests for dining is recorded in this room in the inventory of the Palazzo Vecchio compiled in 1553, ASF, GM 28, cc. 10 r–v (transcribed in Edelstein, "The Early Patronage," 1:262); Conti, *La prima reggia,* 62, incorrectly considers this as part of the contents of the Camera Verde rather than the Salotto. Confirmation that the Salotto was a logical place to dine is provided by the fact that the space directly above it, on the attic floor of the palace, was the kitchen; the Salotto and the Cucinone are in fact linked by a spiral staircase hidden in the thickness of the wall, providing servants with perfect access between the two; see Fiorenza Scalia, *Palazzo Vecchio* (Florence: Becocci, 1979), 79; and Allegri and Cecchi, *Palazzo Vecchio,* 10.

65. Payment to Bronzino for the paintings, a portrait of the duchess and a copy after a Madonna by Leonardo, was requested by Giovanni Dini and Carlo de' Medici on 9 February 1563; Gaye, *Carteggio inedito*, 3:94.

66. On 15 April 1564, Bronzino thanked the duke for having paid him what was owed to him for his salary in a letter preserved in the Pierpont Morgan Library, New York, MA 1346 (47), Fairfax Murray Collection of European Autographs. The letter is reproduced in Cox-Rearick, *Bronzino's Chapel*, 87, fig. 45, and transcribed, 342–43 (however, somewhat differently than I would, e.g., "bordino" for "hordinò").

67. Gaye, *Carteggio inedito*, 3:94: "In questo altro del Bronzino, essendo da noi stipendiato, credeva S.E. che servisse anco alla Duchessa."

68. See appendix, doc. 1, cited and discussed above.

69. After this essay had gone to press, Alessandro Cecchi's article, "Il maggiordomo ducale Pierfrancesco Riccio e gli artisti della corte medicea," appeared in the *Mitteilungen des Kunsthistorischen Institutes in Florenz* 42 (1998), 115-43. Cecchi's discussion of artworks created during Riccio's tenure as majordomo naturally includes comments on Bronzino's oeuvre. Our archival sources are largely complementary rather than overlapping, and the reader is referred to his work, esp. 127–33.

I wish to rectify having overlooked a previous publication, cited by Cecchi in his article, of the central portion of the document here published as doc. 6: Gigliola Fragnito, "Un pratese alla corte di Cosimo I: riflessioni e materiali per un profilo di Pierfrancesco Riccio," *Archivio storico pratese* 62 (1986), 70, doc. 12. The portion of the letter transcribed by Fragnito is virtually identical to mine. The reader is also referred to Fragnito's discussion of this document on page 51, esp. n. 73. Cecchi (133, n. 81) also provides a name for the unidentified Flemish painter mentioned in my doc. 5: "Luigi Corto pittor fiammingo." However, he does not identify this artist's work as a copy after a portrait by Bronzino. He also interprets the content of doc. 5 differently, stating that Lorenzo Pagni reported Eleonora's satisfaction with the portrait rather than the opposite, as is suggested here.

70. The documents in this appendix have been edited following the norms established in *Rivista d'Arte* 37, ser. 4, 1 (1984): 393–99. This includes expansion of all abbreviations except for titles, honorifics, and commonly used abbreviations for names; it also includes capitalization of all proper names and place names, and the regularization of punctuation according to modern usage. The use of italics in transcribed documents reflects the use of foreign words or phrases, primarily the use of Latin in Italian texts.

71. ASF, MdelP, f. 1171, ins. 1, doc. 15. The document is cited in part by Cox-Rearick, *Bronzino's Chapel*, 68, n. 33.

72. Possibly by Riccio himself.

73. ASF, MdelP, f. 1170a, fasc. 1, ins. 3 bis, c. 36. The document has previously been published with minor differences in transcription by Gaye, *Carteggio inedito*, 2:329–30, and Cox-Rearick, *Bronzino's Chapel*, 333.

74. ASF, MdelP, f. 1170a, fasc. 3, cc. 60r–61r.

75. ASF, MdelP, f. 1173, ins. 2, doc. 79. The document was previously cited in part by Pieraccini, *La stirpe*, 2:116.

76. Above, in second hand: "5 marzo 1547."

77. Pieraccini, *La stirpe*, 2:116, incorrectly indicates the letter as having been written from Bibbiena rather than Bibbona, which is in fact in the Cecina river valley; see the beginning of Pagni's letter.

78. ASF, MdelP, f. 1173, ins. 3, doc. 108. The document was previously cited in part by Pieraccini, *La stirpe*, 2:116.

79. Above, in second hand: "16 marzo 1547."

80. Pieraccini, *La stirpe*, 2:116, misidentifies the Excellency referred to here as Cosimo.

81. ASF, MdelP, f. 1176, ins. 13, doc. 1.

82. Above, in second hand: "20 Gennaio 1550."

83. Regarding this type of brocade, called *terciopelo* in Spanish, see Adelaide Cirillo Mastrocinque, "Rapporti tra Napoli spagnola e Firenze medicea: la moda e le sue industrie," in *Napoli nel Cinquecento e la Toscana dei Medici*, 193–224 (Naples: Edizione Scientifiche Italiane, 1980), 198, 207; and Florence Lewis May, "Spanish Brocade for Royal Ladies," *Pantheon* 23, no. 1 (January—February, 1965): 8–16.

84. Possibly by Riccio himself.

85. ASF, MdelP, f. 1170a, fasc. 1, ins. 3 bis, c. 38. The document was previously published by Furno, *La vita*, 106–7, with minor differences in transcription.

86. There are losses in the manuscript where these honorifics should be. The presumed address is based on a similar usage at the end of the letter. Furno, *La vita*, 106, records the first honorific as "Ill.mo."

87. The edge of the document has suffered numerous losses. The final "e" of *felice* is clear but there seems to be something after it, including the graphic sign for an ellipsed "m." Unless otherwise noted, square brackets "[ ]" can be presumed to indicate losses at the edge of the page throughout the rest of this document.

88. Furno, *La vita*, 106: "grandissimo."

89. This word is extremely faded in the manuscript but can be clearly discerned under ultraviolet light; Furno, *La vita*, 106, similarly records "io."

90. The left portion of the "X," for the abbreviation "X.bre" is still legible. The reading is confirmed by a partially incorrect annotation in another hand on 39v: "del Bronzino di Pisa il 14 di X.re." The "14" is somewhat unclear but is certainly not "16," the date of the actual letter. As Bronzino refers to 14 December at the beginning of the letter, the author of the note may have taken the date from there.

91. As this corner of the document is lost it is impossible to be certain, but Bronzino's signature may have been followed by an abbreviation for *Pittore*. Furno, *La vita*, 107, in fact, records the signature as "Il Bronzino Pittore."

92. Possibly by Riccio himself.

93. ASF, MdelP, f. 1176, ins. 11, doc. 14. The document was previously cited in part by Pieraccini, *La stirpe*, 2:116; McComb, *Agnolo Bronzino*, 17; and Heikamp, "Agnolo Bronzinos Kinderbildnisse," 138, n. 28.

94. Above, in second hand: "8 Gennaio 1551."

95. Possibly by Riccio himself.

96. ASF, MdelP, fol. 1170a, fasc. 2, ins. 5, c. 12. The document was previously published by Heikamp, "Agnolo Bronzinos Kinderbildnisse," 138, with minor differences in transcription.

97. The superscripted final vowel of the abbreviation is unclear in the manuscript. It may also be an "o"; Heikamp, "Agnolo Bronzinos Kinderbildnisse," 138, transcribes it as such.

98. The "i" of "il" is crossed out.

99. The final "e" of "Ecc.ze" is written over an "a."

100. Heikamp, "Agnolo Bronzinos Kinderbildnisse," 138: "Rev.a."

101. Heikamp, "Agnolo Bronzinos Kinderbildnisse," 138: "Rev.o."

102. ASF, MdelP, f. 1176, ins. 11, doc. 25. The document is mentioned by Pieraccini, *La stirpe*, 2:116; and Heikamp, "Agnolo Bronzinos Kinderbildnisse," 134.

103. Above, in second hand: "14 Ag.o 1551."

104. Possibly by Riccio himself.

105. ASF, MdelP, f. 1176, ins. 11, doc. 27. Cited in part by Pieraccini, *La stirpe*, 2:108, n. *a*, 116.

106. Above, in second hand: "24 ott. 1551."

107. Possibly by Riccio himself.

A Medici Miniature:
Juno and a Woman with
"Eyes in Her Head Like Two Stars in Their Beauty"

Gabrielle Langdon

Giorgio Vasari describes Italian miniatures as a rarified genre of portraiture, seen by few but their owners, and portraying "lords, friends, or ladies beloved by them."[1] To this last category belongs an exceptional miniature from the Thyssen-Bornemisza Collection, Lugano, now exhibited in Madrid, with the portrait of a young woman on its face (fig. 1) and a detailed allegory of Juno as Protectress of Brides on its reverse (fig. 2).[2] The woman is here identified as Eleonora ("Dianora") di Toledo the younger, wife of Pietro di Cosimo de' Medici. She is proposed as patron, and the miniature allegory interpreted as an implicit plea to Pietro for marital accord. Evidence demonstrates that the allegory derives from the Juno float in the *Mascherata della geneologia degli dei gentili* that wound through Florence in February 1566 to celebrate the marriage of Francesco I to Giovanna of Austria. Portrait and allegory can also be linked to wider contexts of Medici imagery and patronage through Vincenzo Borghini, Giorgio Vasari, and Alessandro Allori, the artistic team entrusted with Cosimo de' Medici's programs in the Palazzo della Signoria. Attribution to Alessandro Allori, court portraitist to the Medici at this time, is supported by his extant *Mascherata* drawings, his miniatures, and his style. Most importantly, examination of this work of art exposes a web of ideology at the core of Medici dynastic aspirations that transcends this intimate work of art.

The Sixteenth-Century Miniature

It was in a commentary on his contemporary Giulio Clovio that Vasari noted that the tiny images executed by master miniaturists were luxury items, and that this branch of portraiture was almost exclusively a court genre:

> His [miniatures]…cannot be seen, because nearly all are in the hands of great lords or of men of high rank: I say almost all, because some of these people have beautiful portraits in tiny cases from his hand, of lords, friends, or ladies beloved by them. But such works are not for public viewing, and cannot be seen by everyone, such as paintings, sculpture and architecture by our other artists and artisans.[3]

Miniatures were evidently keepsakes exchanged between the sexes, and spouses and lovers demonstrably did so, as Spanish, English, and Florentine examples attest.[4]

In the sixteenth century, the talismanic power of images made it certain that an aura of intimacy and secrecy would be associated with viewing these minute portraits, as suggested by Bronzino in his *Portrait of Lodovico Capponi*, painted around 1555–60.[5] Lodovico, who is posed in a curtained space, holds a miniature of his love to his heart, visible to him but averted

Langdon Fig. 1. Alessandro Allori, *Eleonora ("Dianora") di Toledo di Pietro de' Medici,* 1571, Pendant with two miniatures, front, Lugano, Thyssen-Bornemisza Foundation (photo: Thyssen-Bornemisza Collection)

Langdon Fig. 2. Reverse of fig. 1, *Juno, Protectress of Brides, with Nymphs of the Air and Serenità delle Notte* (photo: Thyssen-Bornemisza Collection)

from our intrusive gaze.[6] As Bronzino's portrait demonstrates, the miniature as a genre provided a beholder with opportunities for the kind of enthrallment that Leonardo held was the special province of painted portraits:

> If the poet says that he can inflame men with love…the painter has the power to do the same, and to an even greater degree, in that he can place in front of the lover the true likeness of that which is beloved, often making him kiss and speak to it. This would never happen with the same beauties set before him by the writer. So much greater is the power of a painting over a man's mind that he may be enchanted and enraptured by a painting that does not [even] represent a living woman.[7]

Coupled with their potential to captivate the viewer, miniatures exercised powerful esthetic appeal. According to Francisco de Hollanda, miniaturist to the Lisbon court, the virtuosity of drawing on such restricted surfaces won strong admiration, and Vasari suggests that miniature portraits were considered to be a benchmark of excellence.[8] All in all, miniatures were a precious commodity in every sense of the word. The Thyssen-Bornemisza example would have been especially esteemed, as both sides are figured and richly detailed.[9]

The Thyssen-Bornemisza Miniature

For its small size—only 5.5 x 4 cm—and for the complexity of the allegorical scene on its reverse, the Thyssen-Bornemisza work stands as a tour de force of the miniaturist's art. Painted on silver, it is in superb condition and provokes the wonder that Vasari and de Hollanda describe. On the front (fig. 1), a wide-eyed, red-haired young woman, turned slightly to the right, appears to be gently smiling. She is bedecked in costly jewelry. A tiara formed by pairs of large pearls, alternating with rubies or garnets set in gold, crowns her coiffeur, which is dressed with two small pink bows and, over her right ear, a corsage surmounted by a blue lily. Pear-drop pearls decorate her ears. She wears a deep blue gown with a high collar on which the lily motif is embroidered on a yellow ground. On her lavish gold collar large table-cut emeralds and rubies alternate with two pearls; it terminates in a pendant composed of a single ruby and an enormous cabochon emerald.

A vivid, warm presence is conveyed by the slight tilt of the sitter's head, her dawning smile, the fresh rendering of her complexion and through a mutability conveyed by the varied lighting of the irises of her light brown eyes. The artist has succeeded in fulfilling Hilliard's maxim for the miniaturist: to "catch those lovely graces, witty smilings, and those stolen glances which suddenly like lightning pass."[10]

Since the pendant was first published in 1975, several attempts have been made to identify the sitter, but apart from a consensus that this was a Medici woman, her identity seemed elusive.[11] I here suggest that the miniature represents Eleonora ("Dianora") di Toledo (fig. 3), who in 1571 married her first cousin Pietro de' Medici (1553–1604), Cosimo and Eleonora's youngest son. The sitter's light brown eyes and reddish blond hair are identifiable from portraits of Dianora, notably an inscribed miniature panel in Vienna (fig. 3), part of the Ambras Medici set commissioned in 1587. In both works she is dressed in a peacock blue gown.[12] In the Thyssen-Bornemisza miniature her Toledo-Medici links are proclaimed by a twisted-ribbon hair ornament of blue with white and silver (the Toledo colors), and red with green (those of the Medici).[13] In addition, it can be argued that the warm, appealing expression in the Thyssen-Bornemisza portrait reflects contemporary descriptions of Dianora's personality; by all accounts, she was tall, graceful, beautiful, and vivacious.[14]

The Thyssen-Bornemisza portrait holds specific clues to the identity of the sitter.

Langdon Fig. 3. Anonymous, *Eleonora ("Dianora") di Toledo di Pietro de' Medici,* 1587 (posthumous), Vienna, Kunsthistorisches Museum (photo: Kunsthistorisches Museum, Vienna)

Like other portraits of nobility dressed in armorial colors,[15] Dianora wears the dark blue of the *stemma* of her family's Spanish seat, Toledo. The lily motifs on her collar and in her hair proclaim her Florentine Medici connections and marriage, and her jewelry, with its enormous rubies and emeralds, reveals her high rank and the colors of the Medici *stemma*—red and green. The longstanding Medici impresa, the *diamante*, appears on Dianora's right shoulder, as it does on several contemporary portraits of Medici women.[16] Moreover, this Eleonora is linked to her aunt and namesake, the late duchess Eleonora di Toledo, by virtue of the peacock hue of her gown—the *pavonozzo* of Eleonora's impresa, which linked the duchess to Juno and was the color of her personal livery.[17] Finally, Dianora is copiously decked in pearls, the duchess's favorite adornment.[18]

"Dianora" di Toledo

Today we know little of Eleonora ("Dianora") di Toledo,[19] the only daughter of Don Garzia di Toledo and Vittoria d'Ascanio Colonna, niece of Vittoria Colonna the poet. Dianora was born at the Florentine court in March 1553, the year that Garzia (son of Emperor Charles V's Viceroy in Naples and brother-in-law and ally of Cosimo de' Medici) assumed command of the castles of Valdichiana. His tour of duty successfully completed, he returned to Naples with Vittoria. The journey was considered too arduous for their newborn daughter, however, and she was left in the care of Duchess Eleonora, the aunt for whom she had been named. Vittoria died a few months later, and the child, nicknamed Dianora to distinguish her from the duchess, was raised and educated with the younger Medici children, including her cousin and future husband, Pietro. Eleonora di Toledo's death left her motherless again at the age of nine. It seems that Cosimo adored her.[20] Widely described as exceptionally beautiful and vivacious, Dianora served as patron to the Accademia degli Alterati. This Tuscan literary movement was spearheaded by her cousin, Isabella de' Medici Orsini, Cosimo and Eleonora's brilliant daughter.[21] The liberated Isabella's escapades were notorious and gave her legendary status for centuries.[22] Her biographies make it possible to piece together the tragic life of her cousin and sister-in-law, Dianora.[23]

With imperial approval, and reaffirming the longstanding familial and political Medici-Toledo alliance, Cosimo betrothed Dianora to his youngest son, Pietro, in 1568.[24] Dianora's father, Garzia (1514–78), Viceroy of Sicily and later Philip II's commander at Lepanto in 1571, gave her an impressive dowry.[25] Mutual family goodwill, wealth, and acquaintance since birth did nothing to cement this union. On their marriage in April 1571, it was known in Medici circles that Pietro raped his wife to consummate the marriage ("fatto per forza torre in moglie la Toledana").[26] Cosimo's hopes for curbing his unstable son had appalling consequences: Pietro murdered his wife in cold blood at the Medici Villa at Cafaggiolo on 10 July 1576, when she was twenty-three.[27] The diarist Agostino Lapini, who knew her, recorded:

> She was twenty-one years of age [*sic*], beautiful, gracious, genteel, becoming, charming, affable, and above all had two eyes in her head which were like stars in their beauty; there is universal distress by everyone that she was murdered.... She was buried with rites in S. Lorenzo.[28]

Just prior to her death, an admirer, Bernardino Antinori (1537–76), courtier, poet, and Knight of San Stefano, was murdered in his cell by order of Francesco de' Medici.[29] The hotheaded Bernardino had composed love poetry to Dianora from prison (see appendix); the manner in which its neo-Petrarchan mode creates a "verbal portrayal" of the beloved echoes the conventions of the day.[30] Antinori was betrayed by Pierino Ridolfi, a rival admirer, who professed under torture that Dianora had aided and abetted his own escape after an abortive Pucci-led anti-Medicean vendetta; he also implicated Antinori in his escape. Possibly it was this perceived act of treason that cost Dianora and Antinori their lives, but Medici honor was already taxed by rumors of Dianora's and Isabella's "indiscretions."[31] Dianora was taken under guard to the Villa Medici at Cafaggiolo, where Pietro strangled her, apparently with Francesco's tacit approval. Their only child, Cosimino, died a few weeks later.[32]

Dianora's murder is graphically documented by the Ferrarese ambassador to the court, Ercole Cortile, who reported it secretly to Alfonso II d'Este on 29 July 1576.[33] His dispatch also announces the suspicious death of Cosimo's daughter, Isabella, within days of Dianora's murder:

> I advise Your Excellency of the announcement of the death of Lady Isabella [July 16th]; of which I heard as soon as I arrived in Bologna, [and] has displeased as many as had the Lady Leonora's; both ladies were strangled, one at Cafaggiolo and the other at Correto [Guidi]. Lady Leonora was strangled on Tuesday night; having danced until two o'clock [in the morning], and having gone to bed, she was surprised by Lord Pietro [with] a dog leash at her throat, and after much struggle to save herself, finally expired. And the same Lord Pietro bears the sign, having two fingers of his hand injured by [their being] bitten by the lady. And if he had not called for help to two wretches from Romagna, who claim to have been summoned there precisely for this purpose, he would perhaps have fared worse. The poor lady, as far as we can understand, made a very strong defense, as was seen by the bed, which was found all convulsed, and by the voices which were heard by the entire household. As soon as she died, she was placed in a coffin prepared there for this event, and taken to Florence in a litter at six o'clock [in the morning], led by those from the villa, and accompanied by eight white tapers, [carried] by six brothers and four priests; she was interred as if she were a commoner.[34]

A scrawled letter to Francesco from Pietro, apparently written July 11th, refers to his wife's death the previous night:

> Last night at seven an accident occurred to my wife and killed her. Therefore Your Highness be at peace and write me what I should do and if I should go over there or not. Your humble servant and brother, Don Pietro de' Medici.[35]

Francesco dutifully relayed news of the "accident" to his brother, Cardinal Ferdinando.[36]

Although dispatches to Italian and European courts asserted that Dianora had died of a heart attack, the truth was immediately known as far as Spain, where the Florentine ambassador, Baccio Orlandini, registered "enormous disturbance…and infinite torment…[about this news, which] sharply pierced my soul."[37] In Florence, Medici power over legal matters was absolute.[38] Dianora was, however, a ranking Spanish subject, and Francesco was eventually forced to admit to Philip II that Pietro had killed her, for behavior "unbecoming to a lady."[39] As described above by Ercole Cortile, Isabella de' Medici died in mysterious circumstances within days of Dianora's murder, and was widely rumored to have been killed by her husband because she had committed adultery with his cousin, Troilo Orsini.[40]

Dianora and the Thyssen-Bornemisza Miniature

This outline of Dianora's life gives special poignancy to the warm expression she allowed in this portrait, intended, as Vasari suggests, for private reverie in the hand of the recipient. It is the disposition of the frame of the Thyssen-Bornemisza miniature that provides the strongest evidence of Pietro's ownership of the miniature and, by implication, Dianora's role in its commission. Acceptance of her role as patron, and his as recipient, is crucial to our interpretation of the allegory on the reverse.

The frame of the Thyssen-Bornemisza miniature is not original.[41] It may credibly be linked to Pietro de' Medici, however, during his disreputable career in Spain, where he lived in exile from 1577. It is evident from the back (fig. 2) that the jeweled frame is not a good fit and the workmanship is only fair. Of roughly cast silver-gilt, enameled in black, blue, and white, it is crudely secured with ill-placed struts. Each of the box-set, table-cut doublets of green glass imitating emeralds is set in silver-gilt and roughly bolted through the cast frame, with cotter pins visible at the back.[42] Of special interest, however, is the incorporation of blue and green—the Toledo and Medici colors—in these replacement glass sets and the enameled scrollwork of the frame.

Hackenbroch dated the style and crude mounting of this frame to about the end of the sixteenth century, and opined that the miniature's original precious gems had been removed.[43] It has been proposed elsewhere that the frame is Spanish, possibly from the early seventeenth century.[44] The high standard of Medici goldsmiths in this period is well known.[45] Spain, however, was not at the forefront of jewelry design at this time.[46] The crude paste and silver-gilt frame recall the heavy, retardataire settings of Spanish jewelry of the later sixteenth and early seventeenth centuries.[47] The glass settings suggest a reversal of fortune for its owner.

These supposed Spanish associations for the miniature support the proposal that Pietro was its owner. In December 1577, just over a year after he murdered his wife, the Hispanophile Francesco exiled Pietro to the Spanish court "to see if he makes [of himself] a man of this house and rises above the ugliness which vainly consumes the best years of his youth."[48] Pietro's personality continued to be pathologically unbridled and reckless. His outward manners and behavior at court were "*fastidioso*" (irritating),[49] and from Madrid, G. B. Lupi confided to Francesco's secretary, Antonio Serguidi, on 8 October of the same year, "when nature and intellect are of this temper, it is not possible to produce fundamentally more in any event."[50] Pietro's dissoluteness progressed and he was increasingly overwhelmed by debt; he lived out his years as a Spanish grandee, returning only intermittently to Florence to plead for funds.[51] As the miniature was reframed in Spain with glass sets in Medici-Toledo armorial colors around 1600, the original gem-set frame was possibly sold by Pietro in Spain, or was disposed of by his heirs to offset his huge debts after he died there in 1604.[52]

Other evidence supports the likelihood that the miniature was Pietro's property. Dianora's enormous collar of rubies, emeralds and pearls worn in the portrait was probably purchased under the terms of her dowry.[53] Before she died, the collar had been elaborated by an additional third pearl in the divisions between the green and red stones, as evidenced in a posthumous, bust-length *Dianora* (fig. 4). In addition, Medici *diamante* are clearly visible on each shoulder.[54]

In a portrait at Poggio a Caiano (fig. 5), this expanded collar reappears around the neck of a blond Medici girl dressed in fes-

Langdon Fig. 4. Anonymous, *Eleonora ("Dianora") di Toledo di Pietro de' Medici*, after 1574, (posthumous), Baltimore, Walters Art Gallery (photo: The Walters Art Gallery)

tive costume of the late 1570s or early 1580s.[55] She wears an elaborate tiara over a frilled veil, and her bodice is copiously decorated with Medici *diamanti*. This girl strongly resembles Francesco, who in adolescence also had a marked dimple in his chin.[56] Her style of dress and age suggest that she might be one of his daughters—Eleonora (1567–1611), Anna (1569–84), or Maria (1573–1642)—or his half sister, Virginia (1568–1615), daughter of Cosimo and Camilla Martelli. It is most likely Anna, because Eleonora and Maria, like their mother Giovanna of Austria, had strong Hapsburg jaws and show no dimples, while Virginia d'Este bears no resemblance to this portrait.[57]

No likenesses of Anna—who died in 1584 at the age of fifteen—have been identified, but records indicate that three did exist: the first was a portrait completed at the end of November 1578 when she was about ten, the second an adolescent portrait made in 1582 when she was about thirteen, and a posthumous portrait commissioned in 1586, all by Allori.[58] The second, made from life and recorded as one and one-fifth *braccia* high (about 70 cm) would correspond closely

Langdon Fig. 5. Alessandro Allori, *Portrait of Anna di Francesco de' Medici(?)*, 1582, Poggio a Caiano, Villa Medici (photo: Alinari/Art Resource, N.Y.)

to the Poggio portrait, which does not appear to be posthumous in spirit or expression.[59] The resemblance to Francesco, the height of the canvas, Allori's style, and the narrowing of possible sitters to Anna suggest that this may be the lost adolescent portrait; indeed, her identity was once associated with the panel.[60] The reappearance of the jeweled collar on this Medici girl only six years after Dianora's death is interesting for the light it casts on the destiny of such lavish pieces. It would seem that doweried jewelry was the inalienable property of the state, and thus the collar passed not to Pietro, but reverted to Grand Duke Francesco after Dianora's death in 1576.[61] The miniature, on the other hand, would have been Pietro's personal property, and seems to have accompanied him to Spain, where its settings were altered.

Bearing all the circumstantial evidence in mind, it seems likely that the miniature portrait was commissioned by Dianora to commemorate their betrothal or marriage, suggesting a date between 1568 and 1571. It will be argued below that the unusual iconography of the allegory on the reverse was intended to have a special import for Pietro.

The Allegory

The representation on the reverse is a complex scene, and the artist's management of the detailed group of seven figures is impressive (fig. 2). In the center, a nude female figure is posed on an airborne throne. The peacock at her left identifies her as Juno, protector of women and guardian of marriage and childbirth.[62] She and her attendants float above a landscape featuring a walled estate on the shore of a lake or estuary, behind which a pale, dawn light breaks over low hills. Two *putti* personifying wind gods flank the upper scene, each blowing a stream of air.

As *governatrice* of brides and childbirth, Juno appears to have been the most consistent protagonist in sixteenth-century Medici wedding *apparati*. This supports the dating of the miniature to the period encompassing Dianora's betrothal in 1568 and her wedding in 1571. Her aunt's *entrata* and wedding to Cosimo de' Medici in 1539 initiated the chaste, fecund goddess and her peacock as an enduring impresa for Eleonora. The emphasis was dynastic, and references to Juno refer to Eleonora's hoped-for fecundity in establishing a Medici dynasty.[63]

On 21 February 1566, following the marriage of the couple's heir, Francesco, to Giovanna of Austria on 18 December 1565, Juno appeared in an elaborate public procession, the *Mascherata della geneologia degli dei gentili*,[64] where she presided over infelicitous Nymphs of the Air to signify her ability to avert marital catastrophe. This theme emerged again in 1586: Juno cleared the sky of darkness and shadows when she presented felicitations to Virginia de' Medici and Cesare d'Este in the fifth intermezzo of Giovanni Bardi's *L'amico fido* in the inaugural performance for the new Uffizi Theatre.[65] In 1600, in "La contesa fra Giunone and Minerva," Juno and the warlike Minerva competed in an intermezzo enacted during the wedding feast for Maria de' Medici and Henry IV of France.[66] By the end of the century, Juno's role in promoting triumph over marital discord was an entrenched tradition for Medici wedding *apparati*.[67] As Anne Somers-Cocks and Charles Truman demonstrated when they disproved the Thyssen-Bornemisza miniature's links to the 1586 *apparato* for Virginia d'Este's wedding, there were variations in the choice of Juno's supporting players between one Juno wedding *apparato* and another.[68] The departures made in the allegory from its inspirational source reveal the patron's intention to address Pietro.

The nymphs in the allegory match contemporary accounts by Domenico Mellini, Baccio Baldini, and Giovanni Battista Cini that list the attendants associated with Juno's *carro*.[69] This *carro* was the twelfth of twenty-one floats designed for the stupendous *Mascherata della geneologia degli dei gentili* of 1566 in celebration of Francesco de Medici's wedding to Giovanna of Austria:[70]

> Queen Juno, adorned with a superb royal crown and glittering, transparent clothing, passed Vulcan in great majesty in the twelfth [float], not the least of the elaborate carts taking part, which was pulled by two gorgeous peacocks; [its decoration] was divided into five paintings of her deeds.... Following on foot with the cart were to be seen the better part of those impressions which comprise the Air: first among them was seen Iris, believed by the ancients to be the messenger of the gods, daughter of Thaumas and of Electra, beautiful and melting, clothed in red, yellow, blue, and green, signifying the rainbow, [and] wearing two sparrow-hawk's wings on her head to signify her speed. Accompanying her then was Comet, dressed in red and with reddish hair, presented as a young woman, who wore a bright star on her forehead. With them [was] Serenità, appearing virginal because of the enveloping of her face and entire covering [of her body] by large, generous robes, with a white dove on her head signifying the air. But Snow and Fog who together followed them were dressed in tawny robes, above which were many branches on which snow appeared to have settled; and, although it seemed almost formless, it was seen to move as a large white mass; with them came green Dew, depicted with this color because it is usually seen on the green grass; she had a full moon on her head, signifying that when the moon is full, dew falls from the sky onto the green grass in the greatest quantity. Rain followed, dressed in white, albeit somewhat murky, above whose head,

signifying the seven Pleiadi, were seven splendid sections of a dazzling, starry garland, like the seventeen that glittered on her breast, intended to represent the drizzling of Orion. Three virgins of various ages followed adorned in white garments and crowned with olive garlands, representing the three ranks of virgins that used to run [in] Juno's ancient games: finally, last in their group was the goddess Populonia, in rich, matronly clothes, with a garland of pomegranate and bee-balm in her hair, and with a small altar in her hand, to whom all the Airs described crowd to look as she charmingly calls.[71]

The Thyssen-Bornemisza *Juno* corresponds to Cini's description: she wears a crown on her head over a transparent veil, and a decorous strip of blue drapery crosses her lap—surely the magical girdle loaned by Venus to make Juno irresistible to her errant husband, Jupiter. As in the *Mascherata*, she brandishes thunderbolts, his attribute, in her left hand.[72]

Juno's entourage on the miniature is entirely drawn from the Nymphs of the Air in the 1566 *Mascherata*. Iris, first on the left, is clothed as described by Cini but with a complete bird on her head, and she also has a small rainbow above her, details that appear later in Ripa.[73] Each foot is encased in swirling forms. Next on the left, her companion Comet is dressed entirely in red, as Cini narrates, but she holds in her hand a piece of sulfur, an attribute given her by Ripa. Ripa describes her as malevolent and sinister, ever plotting grave mishaps for the world.[74] Snow appears next, at Juno's right elbow, wearing snow-sprinkled branches on her head. Suitably gray and indistinct, Fog appears here separated from Snow, looming beneath the thunderbolts held in Juno's left hand. Beside her, just as Cini describes, Rain is dressed in murky, gray robes and wears a starry, Pleiadian crown, while the seventeen stars on her breast represent the showers of Orion; Ripa's description is identical.[75] Lastly, Dew appears to the right of Rain and, as in Cini's account, is dressed in green and has a full moon over her head. Ripa includes dew-drenched branches mounted on her head—an attribute provided by Baldini.[76] In the miniature these droplets are individually painted with breathtaking illusionistic effect.

The bluish, veiled figure in the foreground is Serenità, a new player, who has been assigned a leading role in the allegory, apparently replacing Populonia, who, with the three virgins from Cini's list, was omitted. The small scale of the work may have been the deciding factor in the exclusion of the three virgins, but Populonia's role would have been redundant in the intimate context of viewing a miniature. Cini and Baldini, after all, were describing a wedding float with enormous dynastic import for the Medici, the first alliance for the Florentine house with a legitimate member of the imperial house.[77] There, a sceptre-carrying Populonia had civic significance appropriate to a public festival: civil obedience and tribute to a ruler are signified by the attributes annotated on Allori's costume drawing for Populonia for the 1566 *Mascherata*.[78] Serenità was accorded no special role in Cini's account of the *Mascherata*, but on the miniature the dark Serenità della Notte—precisely as later described in Ripa's group of Nymphs of the Air, wearing blue drapery and peacock-blue veils—occupies the foreground.[79] Her wide gesture appears to signal that all stormy, inclement elements of marriage may be brought under her control.

Two sets of drawings for the 1566 *Mascherata* survive in the Biblioteca Nazionale, Florence, and the Gabinetto dei Designi e delle Stampe of the Uffizi. Each includes the designs for the twelfth *carro*, for Juno's costume and attributes, and for her attendant Nymphs of the Air.[80] Drawings for the peacock-harnessed *carro* (fig. 6), and personifications of the nymphs (figs. 7–10) are more detailed than the miniature could allow, but they correspond in such essentials as costume, colors, and attributes. Baldini's descriptions of literary sources and symbolism for the latter correspond with annotations found on the Biblioteca Nazionale drawings, the superior group of drawings attributed to Allori.[81] Annotations for *Iride* (meaning "Iris," fig. 7), for example, indicate yellow, red, blue, and green robes. She is shown with large wings on her head—presumably the sparrow hawk's wings described by Cini; in the Thyssen-Bornemisza version, a whole bird appears to adorn her. Swirls of wind about each foot appear in both drawing and miniature; this signifies her speed, according to Baldini.[82] On his drawing for *La Pioggia* ("Rain," fig. 8), Allori notes: "A maiden clothed in murky white…with seven stars on her head…and seventeen stars on her breast…[holding] in her hand a spider who makes its web"; the web is spun on a diviner's rod held by *Pioggia*, apparently Allori's own invention. The spider and web are described in Baldini's account, and make a consistent appearance in every edition of Ripa, suggesting that Ripa was directly inspired by the descriptions of the *Mascherata* of 1566.[83] *La Neve* ("Snow," fig. 9), and *La Nebbia* ("Fog," fig. 10), who, in Cini's account moved together "as a large white mass," are described in Baldini's account as dressed entirely in cotton wool. Although neither Cini nor Ripa record tinted skin for any *Mascherata* personae, Baldini assigns *Cometa* red robes and skin, and describes *La Ruggiada* ("Dew") as "una femmina tutta verde."[84] In the miniature she has green skin, and Comet's skin is red; together they supply the Medici armorial colors.

The larger scale of the Thyssen-Bornemisza *Juno* to the figures around her may also tie the miniature to the *Mascherata* of 1566. Vincenzo Borghini's *invenzione* probably informed the 1566 program, and the floats were the artistic direction of Vasari.[85] The gods in each float were statues, not costumed players,[86] and the Juno of the 1566 procession was probably larger than the live actors personifying her nymphs.

Langdon Fig. 6. Giorgio Vasari, *Juno* float for the *Mascherata della geneologia degli dei gentili*, 1565, Florence, Biblioteca Nazionale Centrale, C.B.3.53I, c. 113v–114r (photo: BNCF)

Langdon Fig. 7. Alessandro Allori, *Iris*, for the *Mascherata della geneologia degli dei gentili*, 1565, Florence, Biblioteca Nazionale Centrale, C.B.3.53I, c. 115r (photo: BNCF)

Langdon Fig. 8. Alessandro Allori, *Rain,* for the *Mascherata della geneologia degli dei gentili,* 1565, Florence, Biblioteca Nazionale Centrale, C.B.3.53I, c.116r (photo: BNCF)

It is not clear from either Cini's or Baldini's descriptions, or from the drawings, if the cortège attending the Juno float formed a tableau, or if more elaborate action explained the roles of each nymph.[87] As Juno's handmaid, however, the figure of Iris is the most consistent attendant in all the *apparati* for Medici weddings described above. On Ammanati's fountain ensemble, Juno—Jupiter's bride—lays aside her thunder-making tambourine on the sculpted rainbow supporting her. In the Thyssen-Bornemisza miniature, Juno's tambourine—visible under strong magnification—rests in Iris's lap.[88] As Juno's assistant, Iris was evidently instrumental in brightening the sky after a storm has subsided.

The references to Juno inevitably recall Eleonora di Toledo and make it evident that the miniature represents an element in a wider web of Medici patronage and visual language. By 1571, the year of Dianora and Pietro's wedding, work was in progress to commemorate the duchess, who died in 1562, on the west "Air" wall of the Studiolo of Francesco I.[89] She presides there costumed in the style of the 1570s—no doubt to suggest a living presence and influence on her son.[90] Similarly, Juno-Eleonora may be perceived on the miniature as a spiritual force in the lives of Pietro and Dianora. For the Studiolo, begun in 1570, Vincenzo Borghini, the prolific Medici fountainhead of *invenzione*, was again the iconographer, while Vasari was artistic director and Allori was the leading artist. Although Borghini's input into the *Mascherata* is not documented, Cini—to whom Borghini some-

Langdon Fig. 9. Alessandro Allori, *Snow,* for the *Mascherata della geneologia degli dei gentili,* 1565, Florence, Galleria degli Uffizi, Gabinetto dei Disegni e delle Stampe, 2834F (photo: Soprintendenza, Florence)

Langdon Fig. 10. Alessandro Allori, *Fog,* for the *Mascherata della geneologia degli dei gentili,* 1565, Florence, Galleria degli Uffizi, Gabinetto dei Disegni e delle Stampe, 2835F (photo: Soprintendenza, Florence)

times deferred on iconographical matters—may have acted on his behalf.[91] While the inspirational source behind the Thyssen-Bornemisza allegory is the *Mascherata*, it is impossible to say if Borghini, Cini, or the miniaturist himself devised the adjusted iconography. During these years, all three were immersed in propagandistic Medici programs.

Among these is the Studiolo, which has links to the allegory. On the left of the "Air" wall, Giovanni Bandini's bronze *Juno* holds a Medici *diamante* in her hand.[92] Opposite her is Elia Candido's *Boreas*, the North wind, which Borghini advised should be distinguished from the West wind, *Zefiro*, in a letter to Vasari of 7 October 1570.[93] Allegorical figures by Allori for *Boreas* and *Zefiro* had appeared in the *Mascherata* of 1566 on the Neptune float, which followed Juno's.[94] On the Thyssen-Bornemisza allegory, *Boreas*, the *putto* to the right and below the Juno figure group, blows a stream of white, frosty crystals. The *putto* opposite, whose breath is less emphasized, and who presides over the mouth of the estuary, must be *Zefiro*, whose western breath comes from across the sea.[95]

As the low hills in the background are typical of the foothills of the Apennines, the estuary in the miniature is surely the Arno west of Pisa. One of Cosimo's gifts to Pietro in the year of his betrothal was the Palazzo da Signore of Collesalvetti, a hamlet south of the Arno at Pisa. A *palazotto rustico* set in wooded hills, it was used as principal resting point for the Florentine court en route to the port of Livorno and as a winter hunting lodge by the younger Medici; it was unique among Medici villas in having westerly views to the sea across a wide plain.[96] In 1571, the year of Dianora's marriage, the abbot of the Badia at Collesalvetti recommended to his community that the monastery's estates—which abutted Collesalvetti's western edge—be deeded in perpetuity to Dianora.[97] The walled area in the miniature may commemorate the Badia's beneficence of 1571, surely a wedding gift to Dianora and now her personal jurisdiction. If so, a *terminus post quem* of 1571 for the miniature is almost certain.

Ammanati's Juno Fountain also has implications for the Thyssen-Bornemisza allegory. Partially installed in the Sala d'Udienza for the 1565 wedding of Giovanna of Austria, the fountain conflates Juno-Eleonora and alludes to her matriarchal role in the new Medici dynasty.[98] Allusions to the elder Eleonora in the miniature are implicit. Its *Juno* allegory invokes the memory of Eleonora as mother and spiritual patroness to the young couple. The Thyssen-Bornemisza portrait also promotes the ancestral emulation that was typical—even imperative—for contemporary portraiture.[99] Dianora wears the Toledan dark blue and copious amounts of pearls, both attributes associated with her aunt, and she is portrayed, in effect, as the second Eleonora di Toledo de' Medici.

Dianora and Eleonora

References to Duchess Eleonora are repeated in a second portrait of Dianora on which the miniature depends or which it inspired. When the Thyssen-Bornemisza miniature appeared in 1975, Detlef Heikamp drew attention to its similarity to the portrait by Allori in Vienna (fig. 11).[100] The brown-eyed sitter with reddish blond hair wears the same coiffure, gown, lily-embroidered collar, and elaborate jewelry as the woman in the Thyssen-Bornemisza miniature. Allowing for the disparity in scale, it is evident that the works portray the same person. This is Dianora, and in the three-quarter-length Vienna portrait, the long arms and neck emphasize her tall stature. There the face is more abstracted, less winsome, and lacks the intimacy of expression of the miniature. Judging from Vasari's description of miniatures and their owners, and Ludovico Capponi's intimate viewing of the miniature of his beloved, these are the differences in decorum that might be expected between miniature and large-scale portraits. In the extended Vienna portrait, associations with Eleonora di Toledo are asserted not only by the *pavonazzo* hue of the silk gown and pearls, but also by the gloves that Dianora holds, which are of a type favored by the late duchess.[101]

Langdon Fig. 11. Alessandro Allori, *Eleonora ("Dianora") di Toledo di Pietro de' Medici*, 1571, Vienna, Kunsthistorisches Museum (photo: Kunsthistorisches Museum, Vienna)

Isabella and Dianora, the daughter and daughter-in-law to whom Cosimo was deeply attached, died violently within two years of the duke's death in 1574. Dianora had been a particular favorite with Cosimo, who was paternal in his protection of his late wife's niece during her short, miserable marriage to his unstable son.[102] The symbolism of the miniature reflects a period when his protection was assured. Cosimo had been deeply involved with Borghini in the 1565 *entrata invenzione*.[103] Iconography addressed to a beloved would imply donation of a miniature to that person—as it does in another Allori double-sided miniature discussed below. The Juno allegory would preclude Cosimo as patron, but his role as iconographic advisor to Dianora cannot be ruled out.

The thunderbolts brandished by the Thyssen-Bornemisza Juno-Eleonora surely refer to the dead Eleonora's guardianship and, as Eleonora had been Cosimo's regent, to Jupiter-Cosimo's too.[104] Significantly, the Thyssen-Bornemisza Juno wears over her bridal veil a radiating crown that is related to the design of Cosimo's crown as grand duke. Cosimo's investiture by Pius V on 5 March 1570, in Dianora's presence, was close to the time the miniature was painted.[105] Eleonora did not live to enjoy this elevation in rank, but a later portrait of her attests that it was granted her posthumously.[106] Replete with Jupiter-Cosimo's grand ducal crown and thunderbolts, the Thyssen-Bornemisza Juno-Eleonora acts as his regent.[107]

Additionally, the conflated Juno-Eleonora celebrates the spiritual patronage of Eleonora di Toledo in the lives of Dianora and Pietro. It also reflects wider contexts of propagandistic Medici commissions of the period; the 1565–66 Medici-Hapsburg wedding celebrations, Ammanati's Juno Fountain, and the Studiolo of Francesco in the 1570s again suggest that Cosimo had input into its allegorical content.

The Attribution of the Miniature to Alessandro Allori

As it has been assumed that there were no extant miniatures by Allori, an attribution to him of the Thyssen-Bornemisza miniature was considered inconclusive.[108] Evidence presented here will suggest otherwise. Firstly, the artist's association with Dianora at this moment may be inferred from Heikamp's identification of the portrait on the miniature with the same woman as the portrait usually attributed to Allori in Vienna (fig. 11).[109] Although attribution of the Thyssen-Bornemisza miniature to Allori has been disputed, by 1571 he had succeeded his master Bronzino as principal Medici court portraitist.[110] Vasari and Hollanda held miniatures in high esteem; a commission by a ranking Medici patron, especially for an occasion as important a betrothal or wedding, would most likely go to Allori if he had mastered the art of *miniatura*. In fact, by 1571 Allori was an established miniaturist.[111] His *Ricordi*, begun in 1579, mention several examples of his activity in this sphere.[112]

Allori's 1561 portrait of Francesco de' Medici shows the prince holding a tiny portrait of his deceased sister, Lucrezia.[113] The tiny portrait matches a miniature portrait of her (probably by Allori) on tin now in the Pitti Palace.[114] His densely populated, small-scale works on copper executed around 1570 provide a logical vehicle for comparison to the Thyssen-Bornemisza Juno allegory, and miniaturization characterizes his contemporary Studiolo panels.[115] Further, his signed *Hercules Crowned by the Muses* (fig. 12), painted in 1568 for Francesco de' Medici, was praised by Vasari and Rafaello Borghini for its miniaturization.[116] Its principal muse, Clio, is similar in pose and figure style to the Thyssen-Bornemisza Juno. In both a small, wedge-shaped head widens at the brow and is set on robust, broad shoulders and upper chest. Limbs are long and smooth but well covered, with knees round and prominent. Clio and Juno demonstrate nearly identical poses for arms, hands, and fingers, and both have Allori's customary large hands, with the index finger pointing and the other fingers curled under.[117] Allowing for the difference in scale, Juno's left arm, with the hand holding thunderbolts, is a slight variant on Clio's as she holds her book. Allori has evidently merged the body

Langdon Fig. 12. Alessandro Allori, *Hercules Crowned by the Muses,* 1568, Florence, Galleria degli Uffizi (photo: Alinari/Art Resource, N.Y.)

of his principal muse, Clio, with the head of Terpsicore to compose the Thyssen-Bornemisza Juno. A second miniature on copper shows that it is not just his style, but an impulse to combine miniature portrait and allegory on recto and verso of a metal ground that links the Thyssen-Bornemisza miniature to Allori at this moment.

Allori's *Portrait of Bianca Cappello*, with the populous *Allegory of Human Life* on its reverse, measures 37 x 27 cm. Painted in the early 1570s, its small-scale portrait and allegory and its intimate associations—Bianca and Francesco were clandestine lovers at this time—suggest that it is a forerunner for or is painted from the same impulse as the Thyssen-Bornemisza portrait and allegory.[118] The two works demonstrate Allori's characteristic figure style, and the Thyssen-Bornemisza landscape, with its pearly, dawn light, is typical of Allori's contemporary *Pearl Fishers*, painted for the Studiolo of Francesco I in 1571.[119] It can be suggested that Allori's *Hercules and the Muses*, the *Allegory of Human Life*, his *Pearl Fishers*, and the Thyssen-Bornemisza miniature were all commissioned during the years of Vincenzo Borghini and Vasari's partnership with Allori. They worked together as the creative and artistic directors to the Medici court for the 1565 *entrata* and the *Mascherata*, as well as for the Studiolo, which was begun in 1569 and finished in 1575. To each of these projects Allori contributed handsomely. In addition, evidence suggests that Allori referred to his own annotated drawings of Juno and her nymphs for the 1566 *Mascherata* costumes as specific sources for the Juno allegory.

Langdon Fig. 13. Attributed to Alessandro Allori, *Portrait of a Young Nobleman,* 1570–75, front, private collection (photo: courtesy Bob P. Haboldt and Co.)

Langdon Fig. 14. Reverse of fig. 13, *Love and Fidelity* (photo: courtesy Bob P. Haboldt and Co.)

Recently, a double-sided portrait miniature on copper (figs. 13, 14) that has been reliably attributed to Allori was sold.[120] The front portrays a young man with a view of Florence in the background. On the reverse Amor slumbers under a peach tree from which a few peaches have fallen; a dog looks up to the tree, presumably to keep watch for the falling peach that will rouse Amor to his task of aiming his bow at a chosen *inamorata.* This opportunity presents itself, for walking toward Amor is a woman who has left a walled city in the background and who is presumably the object of the patron's desire. The iconography confirms that the allegory in this miniature was, like the Thyssen-Bornemisza allegory, intended for intimate viewing by a *persona grata.* The role of patron-donor for the youth portrayed is implied, just as it is for Dianora in the Thyssen-Bornemisza allegory, suggesting that she should be added to the long list of Renaissance women who commissioned their own portraits.[121]

Conclusion

This study of Allori's double miniature of 1571 in the Thyssen-Bornemisza Collection proposes an almost unknown Medici woman, Dianora di Toledo di Pietro de' Medici, as the work's patron. Because of its preciousness and expense, this genre of portraiture flattered both patron and recipient.[122] The allegory of *Juno, Patroness of Brides,* directed to the recipient, Pietro de' Medici, is drawn from the Juno float for the *Mascherata della geneologia degli dei gentili* of February 1566, which celebrated the wedding of Francesco de' Medici to Giovanna of Austria. The tiny portrait exhibits the covert ancestral and familial references usually found in sixteenth-century Florentine court portraiture.[123] Portrait and allegory together confirm that patronage itself deferred to a social hierarchy that radiated from the person of Grand Duke Cosimo, and to a dynastic mythology that accorded the role of dynastic mother and spiritual patroness of marriage to his wife, Eleonora di Toledo.[124] Cosimo's role as affectionate, surrogate father to Dianora suggests that this commission, with its complex messages of ancestry and dynasty, carried his ideas, and that he may even have been involved in its iconography.[125] It is clear that networks of mental attitudes and social linkage can support a powerful client's taste, and that they can also help us understand a work produced in his ambit.[126] Dianora's relaxed decorum belies the fact that, even in so intimate a commission, Allori drew on a central thread of Medici iconography in patron-client relations—the promotion of the dynasty through reference to the Hapsburg-Medici alliance evident on the reverse of the miniature. In the absence of an heir for Francesco and Giovanna, a fruitful union between Pietro and Dianora must also have been greatly desired.[127] Cosimo's fatherly affection for Dianora, his awareness of the instability of his son Pietro, and the need for a Medici heir may all have contributed to the allegorical theme of marital harmony and the miniature's message of protection and patronage.[128] Medici patronage of the new Medici-Toledo union is also implicit. Within two years of Cosimo's death in 1574, however, a fatal fracturing of paternal protection occurred, and the tragic uxoricides of Dianora and Isabella demonstrate how implacable codes of conduct and ferocious justice could be applied to even the most privileged of women in sixteenth-century Florence.

Appendix

Love Poetry from Prison, ca. 1574–76, from Benardino Antinori (1537–76) to Eleonora ("Dianora") di Pietro de' Medici (1553–76)[129]

(In Italian followed by English translation.)

I

Occhi ch'alti miracoli solete

far con i dolci rai del vostro lume

e le potenze interne in quel movete che di mirar vostra luce presume;

con quel poter che i cori altrui prendete,

fate in me d'Elicona sorger fiume,

ch'io dica il bel che in voi chiaro si vede,

e 'l gran valor ch'ogni valore eccede.

II

Oh che goder perfetto! Oh che contento!

Oh che piacere, veder due fidi amanti

mentre ciascuno è ne'begli occhi intento

dell'altro, e scorge in quelli i suoi sembiati!

Oh che soave oblio d'ogni tormento,

quand'escono i visivi spirti santi,

che con miracol sì raro e sì grato

fan trasformar l'amante nell'amato!

III

Testa sostien si bella e si divina
in cui del Cielo il gran valor si scorge,
la delicata gola alabastrina
che dalle larghe spalle dritta sorge
nel bianca petto Amor gli strali affina;

. . . .

La membra ond'ha composta la persona
son con proportion si ben formate
ch'ogni sua parte con l'altra consuona,
e tutte con tal' arte collegate
che si può dir che non fu mai persona.
Ossia delle presenti ovver passate,
che avesse corpo si leggiadre e bello,
cercando il mondo in questo loco e in quello.

IV

Nella candida man pose natura
ogni suo studio per farla perfetta,
E lungo alquanto, senza vene, e pura
qual terso ivorio, poi morbida, schietta,
in cui non par che sia sforzata cura,
ma per se stessa bianca, molle e netta:
sottil le dita, senza nodi e grate,
unghia grandette, pulite, inarcate.

V

Stupisce ogn'uomo ai graziosi gesti
se va, se posa, o balla, o parla, o ride.
Sono i bei modi in un dolci e modesti
co'quai da vita in un tempo e uccide;
gli atti, tutti amorosi e tutti onesti,
fan che onestà da amor non si divida.
Lieta si mostra e grata in ogni parte,
ascosta umil, risponde con grand' arte.

VI

Poi ch'io pur dir nol so, dicalo amore

donna, qual sia maggior mentre vi miro,

o la beltade in voi e in me l'ardore!

VII

Qual si possente e si benigna stella

ornò voi di si pregiati onori

per farvi sopra l'altre altera e bella.

≈

I

Eyes, accustomed to working great miracles

with the sweet rays of your light

you move the inner powers of him who

dares to look at your light;

using that power with which you capture others' hearts

make a river of Helicon spring forth in me

so that I may tell of the beauty that in you shines so clear

and of your great worth exceeding all worth.

II

Oh what perfect joy! Oh what bliss!

Oh what pleasure, to see two trusting lovers

as each, intent on the other's eyes

sees there his own image!

Oh what sweet oblivion of all torment,

when the visible holy spirits go out

and with a miracle so rare and so welcome

transform the lover into the beloved!

III

Holding up a head so lovely and so divine

in which Heaven's great worth is revealed,

the delicate alabaster throat

rises erect from broad shoulders.

In her white breast Love sharpens his darts....

The parts of her body

are so well formed and proportioned

that every part harmonizes with the others

and all are connected so skillfully

that one could say never has there been anyone

past or present

who had a body so light and lovely

though one searched the world over.

IV

Nature took every care

to make her white hand perfect,

uncommonly long, veinless and pure

as polished ivory, and soft, flawless,

so it seems not formed by art

but in itself white, soft, and clear:

slender fingers, not gnarled [but] graceful

with largish nails, clean and curved.

V

Every man marvels at her graceful ways

as she walks, or pauses, or dances, or speaks, or laughs.

These are her lovely manners, at once sweet and modest

with which she at the same time gives life and kills;

her actions, all loving, all chaste,

make virtue inseparable from love.

Happy she appears, and pleasant in every way,

modest, she responds masterfully.

VI

Since I don't know how, let Love say,

Lady, which is greater as I gaze on you,

the beauty in you, or the ardor in me!

VII

What powerful and kindly star

adorned you with such glorious gifts

to make you above all others so exalted and beautiful.

         ❧

For Rachel Nolan

Notes

This paper derives from continuing research for a chapter in a full-length study, *Portraits of Medici Women in the Reign of Duke Cosimo I,* funded by a Postdoctoral Research Fellowship of the Social Sciences and Humanities Research Council of Canada, for which I am grateful. Partial research for it occurs in my dissertation, "Decorum in Portraits of Medici Women at the Court of Cosimo I, 1537–1574" (Ph.D. diss., University of Michigan, Ann Arbor, 1992), chap. 7. I acknowledge continued encouragement by my former advisors, Professors Graham Smith and Marvin Eisenberg. Special thanks are due to Dr. Silvia Meloni Trkulja, Director of Research at the Uffizi, who shared her expertise during my study of the Uffizi's miniature collection; to Signor Andrea Daninos, who shared his knowledge of miniatures and his library; to Mr. Julian Stock of Sotheby's, London and Rome; to Professor Sheryl Reiss for useful bibliography; and to Richard Scorza for fruitful exchanges on Borghini. My greatest debt is to Dr. Edward Goldberg, Director, and his assistants, Drs. Robert Carlucci and Bruce Edelstein, of the Medici Archive Project, <http://www.jhu/~medici>, for tracing elusive letters and unearthing unpublished documents. Susan Scott-Cesaritti refined some of my translations of sixteenth-century texts and translated Antinori's poetry, and Professor Corinne Mandel generously read an earlier draft of this paper. I also thank my editors for many cogent suggestions.

1.   Vasari-Milanesi: 7:568–69. See the passage quoted in n. 3 below.

2.   The miniature, on long-term loan from the Thyssen-Bornemisza family in Lugano, is exhibited in Madrid at the Fundaciòn Coleccion Thyssen-Bornemisza, inventory no. K122-B, oil on silver, in silver-gilt frame, enameled in black, white and light blue, and set with green glass doublets, 5.5 x 4 cm, frame 8 x 6.3 cm. Formerly in the collection of Peter Bodmer, Zurich, it was acquired from Julius Böhler of Munich in 1975. See "Notable Works of Art Now on the Market," *Burlington Magazine* 117 (June 1975): Sale Supplement plates 11, 12; and Detlef Heikamp in Julius Böhler, *Sale catalogue* (Munich, October-November 1975), no. 7.

3.   "De quale ho voluto dare al mondo questa notizia, accio che sappiano alcuna cosa di lui quei che non possono ne potranno delle sue opere vedere, per essere quasi tutte in mano di grandissimi signori e personaggi: dico quasi tutte, perche so alcuni privati avere in scatolette ritratti bellissimi di mano di costui, di signori, di amici, o di donne da loro amate. Ma, communque sia, basta che l'opere di si fatti uomini non sono publiche, ne in luogo da potere essere vedute da ognuno, come le pitture, sculture e fabriche degli altri artefici di queste nostre arti." See Vasari-Milanesi: 7:568–69, describing the art of Giulio Clovio. Alison Eckhardt Ledes, "Portraits in Miniature," *Antiques* 136 (1989): 1244 refers to Nicholas Hilliard's claim that miniature painting "tendeth not to comon mens use…none should medle with limning but gentlemen alone." Ledes notes that these were never intended for public display.

4. Sofonisba Anguissola's life-size *Elizabeth of Valois, Queen of Spain* (Prado, Madrid), that I would date to about 1570, shows her with a painted miniature of Philip II in her right hand. See also Isaac Oliver's miniature ca. 1585 (in the Victoria and Albert Museum, London) of the *Youth Surrounded by Flames*. The flames signify poetic ardor, as the youth extends a miniature worn around his neck, featuring the portrait of a woman. His *déshabille* makes the intimate circumstances of his viewing clear. Bronzino's *Lodovico Capponi* is discussed below. See also John A. Cuadrado, "Portrait Miniatures—Captivating Glimpses into History," *Architectural Digest* 58, no. 4 (April 1991): 42, 46, 54.

5. See Norman E. Land, *The Viewer as Poet: The Renaissance Response to Art* (University Park: Pennsylvania State University Press, 1994), chap. 3; for a husband's experience of viewing, see Land, *Viewer as Poet*, 85. See also Rona Goffen, "Titian's *Sacred and Profane Love* and Marriage," in *The Expanding Discourse, Feminism and Art History*, ed. Norma Broude and Mary D. Garrard (New York: Icon Editions, 1992), 111, 117, who proposes that in the Renaissance the act of beholding a spouse's portrait implied a joining of souls and the promise of physical love.

6. New York, Frick Collection, oil on panel, 116.5 x 86 cm. See Edi Baccheschi, *L'opera completa del Bronzino* (Milan: Rizzoli, 1973), plate 64. Lodovico, secretly betrothed to Maddalena Vettori, married her in 1559; see Charles McCorquodale, *Bronzino* (New York: Harper and Row, 1981), 138–39.

7. Martin Kemp, ed., *Leonardo on Painting*, trans. Martin Kemp and Margaret Walker (New Haven, Conn.: Yale University Press, 1989), 26. See also John Shearman, *Only Connect...: Art and the Spectator in the Italian Renaissance*, A.W. Mellon Lectures in the Fine Arts, 1988; Bollingen Series 35, 37, (Princeton: Princeton University Press, 1992) 118; and Land, *Viewer as Poet*, 81–97, who discusses talismanic properties of portraits described in poetry by Pietro Bembo, Giovanni della Casa, and Pietro Aretino. Castiglione's well-known poem in the voice of his wife, Ippolita, envisages her playing, laughing, and joking in response to Raphael's portrait of the author; Land, *Viewer as Poet*, 85–86.

8. Francisco de Hollanda, *Do tirar polo natural, Lisbon, 1549*, in "Die Manuscripte des Francesco d' Ollanda," trans. and ed. Th. von Fournier, *Jahrbucher für Kunstwissenschaft* 1 (1868): 334–58: "[miniatures] can be done very well, due to the perfection of the drawing being so powerful, even on so small a space" (340). De Hollanda's treatise on portraiture was written following his ten-year stay in Rome, in 1549.

   Vasari, giving high praise to Pontormo's portrait of Alessandro de' Medici, notes that "the works of miniaturists cannot compare with it; since beyond being a good likeness, there is in this head everything that could be desired in a rare painting." Vasari-Milanese 6:278. See Gabrielle Langdon, "Pontormo and Medici Lineages: Maria Salviati, Alessandro, Guilia and Giulio de' Medici," *Revue de l'art canadienne/Canadian Art Revue* 19, no. 1–2 (1992): 28. Malcolm Campbell also notes its *dongiovannesco* decorum, so Vasari's coupling of it with the miniature portrait genre is significant; Malcolm Campbell, "Il ritratto del duca Alessandro de' Medici di Giorgio Vasari: Contesto e significato," in *Giorgio Vasari: Tra decorazione ambientale e storiografia artistica. Convegni di Studi, Arezzo, 8–10 Ottobre 1981*, ed. Gian Carlo Garfagnini (Florence: Leo S. Olschki, 1985), 339–62, 340.

9. Medals, figured on both verso and recto, were produced in multiples, could be worn (but were not covered), and were passed from hand to hand. See Mark Jones, *The Art of the Medal* (London: British Museum, 1979), 7–8, 29; George Hill, *Medals of the Renaissance,* rev. and ed. Graham Pollard (London: British Museum, 1978), 13–14; and Stephen K. Scher, *The Currency of Fame: Portrait Medals of the Renaissance,* exh. cat. (Washington: National Gallery of Art, 1994). The decorative portrait miniature—as opposed to the larger format "cabinet" miniature—was not designed to be exhibited; the former evolved directly from medieval manuscript portraits. See Jill Finsten, "Isaac Oliver: Art at the Courts of Elizabeth I and James I," 2 vols. (Ph.D. diss., Harvard University, 1981), 1: 1–2; George C. Williamson and Percy Buckman, *The Art of the Miniature Painter* (London: Chapman and Hall, 1926), 3–9; Roy Strong and V. J. Murrell, *Artists of the*

Tudor Court: The Portrait Miniature Rediscovered, exh. cat. (London: Victoria and Albert Museum, 1983), cat. no. 61, 163.

Most importantly, the decorative portrait miniature demonstrates the most intimate decorum of all portrait genres. For women sitters this can include a relaxed, direct gaze, very revealing décolletage, even racy dishevelment, especially in English forms; see Finsten, "Isaac Oliver," 2:1–2, 11–14, 59, 91–93, 133–34, and figs. 50, 62, 72, 96, 97. Intended for private viewing (ibid., 1:17–18), it was worn on the person in a covered frame, or kept privately in a box (ibid., fig. 95). See also Strong and Murrell, *Artists of the Tudor Court,* cat. 163. Karla Langedijk, *The Portraits of the Medici: Fifteenth to Eighteenth Centuries,* 3 vols. (Florence: S.P.E.S., 1981–87), 1:cat. no. 12, 35, records "Uno scatolino col ritratto della Granduchessa Bianca" in the estate of Don Antonio, 1621. Copies are rare.

A detailed history of the genre in Italy has yet to appear, but see Silvia Meloni, "The Collection of Miniatures and Small Portraits," in *Paintings in the Uffizi and Pitti Galleries,* ed. Mina Gregori (London: Little, Brown, 1994), 625–28. For Eleonora di Toledo's decorum in Giulio Clovio's miniature of 1551, see Robert B. Simon, "Giulio Clovio's Portrait of Eleonora di Toledo," *Burlington Magazine* 131 (1989): 481–85; Langdon, "Decorum," 1:207, 223, 234, 243–45; and Philippe Costamagna, "A propos du séjour Florentin de Giulio Clovio 1498–1578," in *Kunst des Cinquecento in der Toskana* (Munich: F. Bruckmann, 1992): 168–75.

10. Quoted by Cuadrado, "Portrait Miniatures," 54. Ernle Money, "The Art of the Limners," review of *The English Renaissance Miniature,* by Roy Strong, *Contemporary Review* 244, no. 1417 (February 1984): 108–9, describes how Hilliard insisted that these fleeting expressions be caught; he prescribed the length and number of sittings, six hours in total. Money also features Edward Norgate's advice, as recorded in his *Miniatura* of about 1620: "You must be ready and sudden to catch at and steal your observations and to express them with a quick and constant hand."

11. Detlef Heikamp proposed that the sitter might be Lucrezia di Cosimo, who married Alfonso d'Este in 1558. See Heikamp in Böhler *Sale catalogue.* Heikamp also noted that she was once identified as Anna de' Medici, daughter of Francesco I, who died unmarried in 1584 at the age of fifteen. As the obverse Juno scene suggests a marriage, this identification seems unlikely. Yvonne Hackenbroch, "Un gioiello Mediceo inedito," *Antichità viva* 14 (1975): 31–35, identified the allegory with Buontalenti's set design for the fifth intermezzo of Giovanni Bardi's *L'Amico fido,* performed to celebrate the wedding in 1586 of Virginia de' Medici, the legitimized daughter of Duke Cosimo I and Camilla Martelli, when Juno, borne on a chariot with Iris, was attended by fourteen nymphs, one representing Day, one Night, and twelve others representing the Seasons [*sic*], or more properly, the Months of the Year. Hackenbroch concluded that the miniature portrayed Virginia; see Hackenbrock, "Un gioiello Mediceo," and Yvonne Hackenbroch, *Renaissance Jewelry* (London: Sotheby Publications, 1979), 35–36. Anne Somers-Cocks and Charles Truman challenged the 1586 intermezzo association because three of Juno's attendants, Comet, Rain, and Dew, each recognizable from Ripa's *Iconologia,* did not coincide with the descriptions of Day, Night, and the Seasons in Bardi's intermezzo. They noted too that the style of costume was of the early 1570s, which excludes Virginia, who would then have been a very young child. See Ann Somers-Cocks and Charles Truman, *Renaissance Jewels, Gold Boxes and Objets de Vertu: The Thyssen-Bornemisza Collection,* ed. Simon de Pury (London: Sotheby Publications, 1984), 79. The date also excludes Lucrezia di Cosimo, who died in 1561 at the age of fifteen. I concur with this claim, as the gown's style matches that of the woman in the *Portrait of a Florentine Noblewoman with Her Little Boy,* dated 1574, in the Wadsworth Atheneum Gallery, Hartford, Connecticut. The author hopes to publish findings on this portrait shortly.

12. Anonymous, paper on panel, 13.5 x 10.5 cm, Vienna, Kunsthistorisches Museum, inscribed: "LEONORA / VXOR DI PIERO / MEDIC/CE"; and on the back: "(E)leonora di toled(o) (mo)glie di s do Pie(tro) (M)edicci." See Langedijk, *Portraits,* 1:cat. no. 36,4; a similar three-quarter length version, cat. no. 36,6, attributed to Francesco Brina, is in the Museo Stibbert, Florence. See also Langedijk cat. no. 36,6b, where Dianora appears pregnant, dating the work to very late in 1572.

Dianora's only child, Cosimino, born 10 February 1573, was heir apparent until his death in 1576 (Filippo di Francesco was born in 1577). For Cosimino's birth, see ASF, MdelP 5088, c. 14; not MdelP 642, as stated by Gaetano Pieraccini, *La stirpe de' Medici di Cafaggiolo: Saggio di ricerche sulla trasmissione ereditaria dei caratteri biologici* , 3 vols. (1924–25; reprint, Florence: Vallecchi, 1986), 2:186.

Langedijk also includes a second miniature, cat. 36,7, as Dianora, attributing it as "workshop," Uffizi inv. 1890, no. 8930, measuring 3.2 x 2.7 cm. It bears little resemblance to her secure portraits, and I have not included it here.

13. See Janet Cox-Rearick, *Bronzino's Chapel of Eleonora in the Palazzo Vecchio* (Berkeley: University of California Press, 1993), 276–78, plate 5, fig. 171, describing the combined *stemme* of Eleonora di Toledo and Cosimo de' Medici by Bronzino in the crown of the chapel vault, still partially visible through a superimposed *Trinity*. The Toledo *stemma* is found also in Eleonora's *Book of Hours*, ibid., fig. 24, and in the vault of the Camera Verde, apartments of Eleonora, in the Palazzo Vecchio, ibid., fig. 32. The Toledo-Medici arms appear on Bronzino's design for a tapestry, 1552, now in the Pitti Palace; see Baccheschi, *L'opera completa*, cat. no. 90.

14. Pieraccini, *La stirpe*, 2:186, quoting an anonymous, contemporary diarist: "This Eleonora was a tall young woman, charming and beautiful, of becoming presence and endowed with courtly manners and virtuous habits." (Era la detta Leonora fanciulla di grande statura, di vago e bellissimo aspetto, e di presenza leggiadrissima e ornata di gentili maniere e di virtuosi costumi.)

15. See Graham Smith, "Bronzino's *Holy Family* in Vienna: A Note on the Identity of Its Patron," *Source* 2 (1982): 21–25; Bronzino's *Ludovico Capponi* (Frick Collection, New York) wears his family colors. See Baccheschi, *L'opera completa*, plate 64; *Stefano Colonna* (Palazzo Barberini, Rome), stands before a column and wine-red curtain, the Colonna impresa and color, ibid., plate LV. See Graham Smith, "Bronzino's Portrait of Stefano Colonna: A Note on Its Florentine Provenance." *Zeitschrift für Kunstgeschichte* 40 (1977): 266. For other examples, see Langdon, "Decorum," chap. 7.

16. See Langdon, "Decorum," figs. 26–27. The *Diamante* motif appears also on the sleeve fastenings on the *Eleonora di Toledo with Her Son Giovanni*, Uffizi; and ibid., fig. 40, those of her daughter *Maria de' Medici*, Uffizi, and on the left shoulder and elsewhere on the bodice of a *Dianora*, Walters Art Gallery, Baltimore (fig. 4).

17. Anna Baia, *Leonora di Toledo, Duchessa di Firenza e di Siena* (Todi: Z. Foglietti 1907), 21–23.

18. See Langdon, "Decorum," 1:237–38 for an extended discussion of their import.

19. The principal sources for Dianora's life are Guglielmo Enrico Saltini, "Due Principesse Medicee del Secolo XVI, parts 1–6," *Rassegna nazionale* 121, no. 23 (September—October 1901): 553–571; 122, no. 23 (December 1901): 599–613; 123, no. 23 (February 1902): 618–630; 125, no. 23 (May 1902): 209–220; 127, no. 24 (September 1902): 227–241; 127, no. 24 (November 1902): 169–191; Pieraccini, *La stirpe*, 2:185–214; and Fabrizio Winspeare, *Isabella Orsini e la corte medicea del suo tempo* (Florence: Leo S. Olschki, 1961), 31, 40–41, 80, 91, 115, 133–38, 153–58, 162, 168, 171, 172. See also Francesco Domenico Guerazzi, *Isabella Orsini, Duchessa di Bracciano* (Paris, 1845), who dramatizes Isabella's and Dianora's tragedies, but cites some archival documents. Donna Cardamone graciously shared her unpublished, preliminary study of Isabella's musical career in her paper, "Isabella Medici-Orsini: A Portrait of Self-Affirmation," which was presented at the American Musicological Society Conference in 1996.

20. She delighted in arms and horsemanship; Cosimo would half-heartedly caution her to behave with decorum, concluding, "Tu sé proprio nata in Fiorenza." Saltini, "Due Principesse," part 1:121, no. 23, 562.

21. In August 1575, in her capacity as patron of the Alterati, Dianora asked the academicians to prepare a judgment on Alessandro Piccolomini's Tuscan *Annotazione... nel libro della Poetica d'Aristotele*, published in Venice that year and dedicated to Cardinal Ferdinando de' Medici. The

judgment was delivered on 16 August 1575. See Bernard Weinberg, *A History of Literary Criticism in the Italian Renaissance*, 2 vols. (Chicago: University of Chicago Press, 1961), 1:553. Her role certainly reflects Fantoni's claim that patronage constituted an ideological network of intellectuals, writers, and artists under the control of the duke and his family. See Marcello Fantoni, *La Corte del Granduca: Forma e simboli del potere mediceo fra Cinque e Seicento* (Rome: Bulzoni, 1994), 41–42.

22. Saltini, "Due Principesse," part 3:619–20, quotes the *Diario fiorentino anonimo*, recording that in 1565, Isabella scandalized Florentines by noisy nocturnal junkets with companions in carriages, "sonando, urlando, fischiando, che paravano tanti demoni." Passionate letters to her husband's cousin, Troilo Orsini, signed "Your Lordship's slave forever," confirm the affair that led to her murder by her husband in 1576. See Pieraccini, *La stirpe*, 2:172, citing ASF, MdelP 844. See Bastiano Arditi, *Diario di Firenze e di altre parti della cristianità 1574–1579*, ed. Roberto Cantagalli (Florence: Istituto Nazionale di Studi sul Rinascimento, 1970), 69, 109–10, 164, for other scandals and rumors. See also Emma Micheletti, *Le Donne dei Medici* (Florence: Sansoni, 1983), 126–34.

    On her legendary status, see Lorne Campbell, *Renaissance Portraits* (New Haven, Conn.: Yale University Press, 1990), 222, who cites the plot of Webster's *The White Devil*. (Isabella, faithful to Orsini, kisses his portrait each night, and is poisoned by doing so.) Guarazzi's dramatized biography of 1845, Stendhal's story of Vittoria Accoramboni and Paolo Orsini's affair in his *Italian Chronicles*, and Alexandre Dumas's *Les Médicis*, show that interest in the legends surrounding Isabella did not wane for centuries.

23. See nn. 19, 22 for these.

24. See ASF, MdelP fol. 5028, c. 413, 19 June 1568; see also congratulatory correspondence from Spain, c. 415, 22 July 1568; c. 360 of 22 September 1568 from her uncle Don Antonio; and c. 493 and 494, 12 October 1571, from the duke of Alba. Dr. Edward Goldberg, Director, and Dr. Robert Carlucci of the Medici Archive Project, *Guide to Art Historical Sources in the Medici Granducal Archives*, <http://www/jhu/~medici>, traced these letters.

    Such approval also reflects Cosimo's formal agreement in 1557 that his sons would not contract marriages without the explicit approval of the Spanish crown. See Edward Goldberg, "Artistic Relations between the Medici and the Spanish Courts, 1587–1621: Part 1," *Burlington Magazine* 138 (1996): 105.

25. The dowry amounted to forty thousand ducats of gold, five thousand of which were to provide jewelry for the bride. Saltini, "Due Principesse," part 1:566, quotes ASF, Atti internazionali, without giving the *carta*. See also ASF, MdelP 5023, c. 538. This staggering sum reflects the wealth of the Alba family; the dowry is surpassed, however, by Cosimo's for Isabella de' Medici Orsini in 1558, of fifty thousand ducats of gold, with five thousand for jewelry, Saltini, "Due Principesse," 565.

    Garzia's political stature was expressed in the 1565 *entrata* for Giovanna of Austria, where he appears with Hapsburg rulers on the Arch of Austria. See Randolf Starn and Loren Partridge, *Arts of Power: Three Halls of State in Italy, 1300–1600* (Berkeley: University of California Press, 1992), 172–73. For the Alba family in this period, see William Maltby, *Alba: A Biography of Fernando Alvarez de Toledo* (Berkeley: University of California Press, 1983).

    Cosimo deeded enormous wealth to Pietro in August of 1568, including the Medici villas and *poderi* of Careggi, Trebbio, Castagnola, Fiesole, Livorno, Massa Maremma, Pisa, Collesalvetti, Mugello, Montepaldi; mills and tracts of lands across Tuscany; and the Medici palace in Via Largo. See his creditors' appeals of 1605, ASF, MdelP f. 5127, c. 216–73.

26. Saltini, "Due Principesse," 1:121, no. 23 (October 1901), 570–71, quoting ASF, MdelP 514, c. 11, Simone Fortuna, to the duke of Urbino, where Fortuna caustically refers to Medici proposals to wed Pietro in 1580 to the duke's sister, Lavinia, to secure the succession.

On contemporary meaning for "fatto per forza torre" as bridal rape, see Robert Darnton's review of two books: Robert Darnton, "Sex for Thought," reviews of *L'Enfer de la Bibliotheque Nationale; Romans libertins du XVIIIe siècle*, ed. Raymond Trousson, and Jean Marie Goulemot, *Ces Livres qu'on ne lit que d'une main: Lecture et lecteurs de livres pornographiques au XVIIIe siècle*, in *The New York Review of Books* 41, no. 21 (December 22, 1994): 69. On bridal rape, see also Margaret Carroll, "The Erotics of Absolutism: Rubens and the Mystification of Sexual Violence," *Representations* 25 (1989): 3–30. (I thank Dr. Sheryl Reiss for this reference.)

Pieraccini, *La stirpe*, 187, quotes Pietro's own letter to Francesco on his failure to consummate the marriage. Bridal rape was seen as a serious offense by Duchess Bianca Cappello, who advised against arranging the Urbino alliance referred to by Fortuna in his letter because Pietro had raped his wife, Dianora, and for his great ill-treatment of her. Dianora records his cruelty in her letters to her family, which her brother, Pietro di Toledo, disdainfully presented to the Medici envoy following Francesco's "justification" for her murder; Saltini, "Due Principesse," 190 (see n. 39 below). Pietro's problems were longstanding: Isabella de' Medici reported his intractability to Francesco during her father and brothers' mourning, two months after the loss of their mother and two brothers, when Pietro would have been ten, ASF, MdelP 6366, c. 234, dated 31 January 1563.

27. See Pieraccini, *La stirpe*, 2:185; and esp. Saltini, "Due Principesse," part 6, 127, no. 24, 170–89.

28. Agostino Lapini, *Diario fiorentino dal 252 al 1596,* ed. Giuseppe Odoardo Corazzini (Florence: Sansoni, 1900), 191. For conflicting references to an unceremonious interment, see Ercole Cortile's description, cited in n. 34, and Arditi, *Diario di Firenze*, 107, written in 1576.

Dianora's exceptional beauty was widely admired. In his *Memorie fiorentine*, Settimanni, ferociously opposed to the Medici, described her as "la più bella fanciulla che fosse in Firenze." See Pieraccini, *La stirpe*, 2:186. Contemporary writers singled her out from other young Medici women as especially beautiful. See C. Carnesecchi, "Giovanna d'Austria in pellegrinaggio," *L'illustratore fiorentino* (1909): 51–61, who paraphrases a pamphlet of elegiac stanzas by Felice Faciuta, published in 1573, describing a pilgrimage that year to the shrine of Our Lady of Loreto made by Giovanna of Austria, accompanied by Isabella de' Medici Orsini and Pietro and Dianora de' Medici.

29. See Saltini, "Due Principesse," part 5, 127, no. 24, 228 ff., and part 6, 127, no. 24, 167–87, for Antinori's military career at Lepanto, his escapades, Dianora's attachment to him (and her distress at his trial and exile to Elba in 1574 for killing Ceccino Ginori during a brawl), his letters to her, his forced return for treason, and his death in the Bargello by order of Franceso de' Medici. See also Winspeare, *Isabella Orsini*, 156; and Arditi, *Diario di Firenze*, 105–7.

30. The cataloging of each physical aspect of the beloved occurs in Bembo's, Giambullari's, and Bronzino's Neo-Petrarchan poetry. Antinori's poetry (with its use of Petrarchan, "word-painting" tropes such as "alabaster throat," "hands pure as polished ivory," and the emotive reflection of each lover in the mutual exchange of glances) makes explicit the charged eroticism and the merging of lover-beholder that the mode allows. For a detailed excursus on this, see Amedeo Quondam, "Il naso di Laura," in *Il Ritratto e la Memoria: Europa delle Corti*, ed. Augusto Gentili (Rome: Bulzoni, 1989), 9–44.

31. Saltini, "Due Principesse," part 6, 127, no. 24, 173–87, upholds Antinori's innocence.

Winspeare, *Isabella Orsini*, 159, cites ASF, Cart, Strozz., ser. I, fol. 28. Cardinal Ferdinando de' Medici, responding to pasquinades in Rome vilifying Isabella and Dianora, demanded that Francesco act to uphold Medici honor–his sensitivity no doubt increased by scurrilous lampoons proclaiming his own affair with Clelia Farnese, daughter of Cardinal Alessandro Farnese.

32. See n. 12 above. Settimanni's contention that Pietro poisoned Cosimino is probably spurious. Arditi, *Diario di Firenze*, 108, attributes his death to dysentery. He was sole Medici heir at this moment; there was extreme concern that Francesco and Giovanna had produced only daughters since their marriage in 1565. (Their son, Filippo, was born in 1577, but died in 1582). See Eladi Romero Garcià, *El Imperialismo Hispanico en la Toscana durante el Siglo XVI* (Lleida, Spain: Dilagro, 1986), 121.

33. Saltini, "Due Principesse," part 6, 188–89, quoting ASMod, Cancelleria Ducale, dispacci da Firenze, dispatch dated 29 July 1576, from Ercole Cortile to Duke Alfonso II of Ferrara.

34. "Avisai V.A. per l'ordinario passato della morte della signora donna Isabella; la quale intesi subito che io fui giunto a Bologna, la quale ha dispiaciuto altrettanto come ha fatto quella signora donna Leonora; le quali signore ambedue sono state strangolate una a Cafaggiolo et l'altra al Correto. La signora donna Leonora fu strangolata il martedi notte, havendo ballato fino alle due hore, et dipoi andata a letto, le fu gettato da don Pietro una lassa da cane alla gola, et dopo molta difesa che fece, fu finalmente morta. Et detto signore don Pietro ne porta il segno, avendo due dita della mano maltrattate dal morso di detta signora. Et se egli non chiamava aiuto di due sciagurati romagnoli, che per questo dicono, esser fatti venire aposta, havea egli forse la peggiore. La povera Signora, per quello che s'é inteso, fece grandissima difesa come si vide dal letto, che fu trovato tutto stravolto, et per le voci che furono udite per tutta la casa. Subito morta, fu posta in una cassa, ivi preparata per tale effetto, et fu mandata in Firenze alle sei hore di notte, in una lettica condotta da quelli della villa, che l'accompagnarone con otto torce bianche, con sei frate e quattro preti; et fu sepolta come se fosse stata una privata."

I thank Susan Scott-Cesaritti for refining my translation of this passage. See also Arditi, *Diario di Firenze*, 105–7. "Due hore" and "sei ore" refer to hours after sunset, that is, about 10 P.M. in July. On timekeeping before the end of the seventeenth century in Italy, see Salvatore Battaglia, *Grande Dizionario della Lingua Italiana* (Turin: Unione Tipografico-Editrice Torinese, 1981), 11:1090. I also thank Edward Goldberg for useful discussion on this topic. On Dianora's interment, see n. 28 above.

35. "Serenissi^{mo} signo^{re·}Stanotte a sett'hore e venuto huno acidente a mia moglie et la mort(a) pero V.A. se lo pigli in pace et mi scriva quello che io ho (fare) et se io ho venire costà et quello che facia no altro. humile ser.^{re} et fratello, Don Pietro de Medici." Pieraccini, *La stirpe*, 2:185, fig. 36, quoting ASF, MdelP 5154, c. 86 (but "sett'hore" wrongly noted as "sei hore"). Pietro's handwriting shows extreme distortion, perhaps due to the injuries he sustained. Note the different time "sett' hore" given by him for Dianora's death, possibly due to his own confusion or dissembling.

36. Pieraccini, *La stirpe*, quoting ASF, MdelP 5088, c. 34.

37. ASF, MdelP 4906, fol. 83v, dated 7 August 1576 from Madrid. Orlandini received official confirmation only two days earlier—nearly four weeks after her murder. I am greatly indebted to Edward Goldberg for alerting me to this exchange (fols. 82r, 83v, 84r).

38. See Laura Ikins Stern, *The Criminal Law System of Medieval and Renaissance Florence* (Baltimore: Johns Hopkins University Press, 1994), 237–39.

39. "Sebbene nella lettera vi si dice dell'accidente di Donna Eleonora, avete nondimeno a dire a S. Maesta Cattolica che il Signor Don Pietro nostro fratello l'ha levata egli stesso di vita per il tradimento ch'Ella gli faceva con i suoi portamenti indegni di Gentildonna…. Noi abbiamo voluto che la Maesta Sua sappia il vero…; e con la prima occasione se li manderà il processo ove Ella conoscerà con quanta giusta cagione il Signor Don Pietro di sia mosso." Pieraccini, *La stirpe*, 2:185, quoting R. Galuzzi, *Istoria del Granducato di Toscana*, lib. 4, cap. 2. On receiving the promised records in April 1577, Pietro di Toledo disdainfully responded to Francesco that her death was reprehensible. See Saltini, "Due Principesse," part 6, 191. By 15 May, on the strength of these, the Hapsburg court absolved Pietro of his wife's murder, and preparations were under way to receive him as a courtier and to stand as godfather to Philip's newborn heir. ASF, MdelP 4906, fols. 269r–270r, Antonio Serguidi to Francesco I. Again, I thank Edward Goldberg for revealing these references.

40. See n. 22 above.

41. Hackenbroch, "Un gioello mediceo," 33.

42. Hackenbroch, "Un gioello mediceo," 33.

43. Hackenbroch, *Renaissance Jewelry*, 35–36.

44. Somers-Cocks and Truman, *Renaissance Jewels*, 79.

45. Notably Benvenuto Cellini; for other masters, see C. Willemijn Fock, "Les orfèvres-joailliers étrangers à la cour des Médicis," in *Firenze e la Toscana dei Medici nell'Europa del '500, III: Relazioni artistiche; Il linguaggio architettonico* (Florence: Leo S. Olschki, 1983), 831–45, noting Hans Dômes, Jaques Bylivelt, Eduard Vallet, Jonas Falchi, and Léonard Zaerles.

46. For this retarded development, see Priscilla E. Muller, *Jewels in Spain, 1500–1800* (New York: Hispanic Society of America, 1972), 3–4.

47. See Muller, *Jewels in Spain,* fig. 71, 62, a design for a jeweled cross by Joan Llado that illustrates the taste for table-cut gems in boxlike settings. A similar cross is worn by the Infanta Isabella of Spain in a portrait by Frans Pourbus painted in the last decade of the sixteenth century, now in Stockholm: see Ulf G. Johnsson, *Porträtt, Porträtt: Studier I Statens Porträttsamling på Gripsholm* (Stockholm: Rabén & Sjögren, 1987), fig. 20, p. 77. Donald F. Rowe, *The Art of Jewelry, 1450–1650,* exh. cat. (Chicago: Martin d'Arcy Gallery of Art, Loyola University, 1975), cat. no. 19, notes the Spanish characteristics of a jeweled pendant cross that has, like the Thyssen-Bornemisza frame, enameled scrollwork surrounding table-cut emeralds.

48. "Per vedere ce si faccia huomo da questa Casa et si levi dall'otio, il quale gli consuma vanamente i migliori anni della sua gioventù." Pieraccini, *La stirpe,* 2:189–90, citing ASF, Cart. Strozz, ser.1, fol. 41, c. 261. On his exile, Pietro became hostage to the Spanish crown. See Edward L. Goldberg, "Artistic Relations between the Medici and the Spanish Courts, 1587–1621: Part 1," *Burlington Magazine* 138 (1996): 105–14.

49. See Prospero Colonna's letter from Spain of 3 August 1578 referring to Pietro as the "canaglia" (blackguard) of the Medici. Pieraccini, *La stirpe,* 2:190, citing ASF, MdelP 1181, ins. 12, c. 620.

50. "Quando le nature et i cervelli son di questa tempera, no si può farne fondamento più che tanto." Pieraccini, *La stirpe,* 2:189–90, citing ASF, MdelP 1181, ins. 12, c. 481.

51. Pieraccini, *La stirpe,* 194–96.

52. Following his death in 1604, dozens of creditors' appeals—among them some of the most illustrious names in Florence—appear in the petition prepared by the Pietà della Città di Firenze, dated 13 June 1605; see n. 25 above. (His debts amounted to 148,374 scudi).

53. For her dowry, see n. 25 above.

54. Baltimore, Walters Art Gallery, oil on panel, 46 x 41 cm, inv. no. 37.1112, identified from a portrait inscribed "DNA ELEONORA PETRI DE MEDICES VXOR," Vienna, Kunsthistorisches Museum, inv. no. 4440. See Langedijk, *Portraits,* 3:cat. no. 36, 1a, 1b, 1c (*addenda*), all similar. The wooden expression of this portrait suggests that it was posthumous and made without benefit of a death mask. There was no opportunity to make one, as Dianora was interred within hours of her murder.

55. Florence, inv. Ville 1911, Poggio a Caiano no. 64, 64 x 48 cm. Langedijk, *Portraits,* 1:cat. no. 17,25, rejects the identification as Caterina de' Medici (1519–89), Queen of France, proposing instead Margherita Gonzaga (1591–1632), daughter of Eleonora di Francesco. Margherita, however, would not have been in adolescence until about 1603, when this costume style was outmoded by twenty years.

56. See Bronzino's *Portrait of Francesco de' Medici as a Boy,* Uffizi, Langedijk, *Portraits,* 1:cat. no. 42,24, executed in 1551. See also the preparatory drawing by Allori of the young Francesco, ibid., 1:cat. no. 42,13a, where he holds the miniature of his sister, Lucrezia, c. 1561, ibid., cat. no. 42,23. (The dimple is less pronounced in his portrait.) Filippo, his infant son, was also dimpled, as Domenico Poggini's marble bust shows. See ibid., cat. no. 41,7.

57. See Langedijk, *Portraits,* for Eleonora, 1:cat. no. 33,3; for Maria, 1:cat. no. 86 ff.; and Virginia's, 1:cat. no. 109,1–4.

58. Allori's letter of 27 November 1578 to Antonio Guidi, secretary to Francesco, at Poggio a Caiano informs Guidi that it is not possible to send portraits of Anna and Eleonora with the courier, as the

colors have still not dried thoroughly; Simona Lecchini-Giovannoni, *Alessandro Allori* (Turin: U. Allemandi, 1991), 67. For the two later examples of portraits of Anna, see Langedijk, *Portraits*, 1:cat. no. 4, 1e and 1d (posthumous). Allori's letter to Eleonora of 12 October 1585 records his continuing search for the likeness of Anna made late in her life so that he might paint a posthumous portrait. See Lecchini-Giovannoni, *Alessandro Allori*, 74. In March 1586 Allori informed Eleonora that he had finally found the model for the posthumous *Anna*, which was delivered to Eleonora in June 1586; Langedijk assumes that it was based on Allori's last portrait of Anna from life, made in 1582, measuring about 70 cm high.

59. The Poggio portrait has been slightly trimmed, as the lower edge twice cuts across the fingers of the sitter's right hand. By "completing" the hand pose, I estimate that about one-tenth of the panel is missing; the 64 cm high panel would originally have measured about 70 cm.

60. See Heikamp in Böhler, *Sale catalogue*, no. 7.

61. The first instance of a decree enshrining the reclamation of jewelry by the treasury or crown occurs in letters patent by Francis I of France, dated 15 June 1530. Henceforth, such jewelry reverted to the royal treasury. See Hackenbroch, *Renaissance Jewelry*, 35–36, figs. 64a, 64b, plate I. In Florence this would have been a recent development, as Margaret of Austria, widow of Alessandro de' Medici, took his collections with her to the Farnese when she remarried in 1537. See Anna Maria Massinelli and Filippo Tuena, *Treasures of the Medici* (New York: Vendome Press, 1992), 29. Cosimo I greatly admired Francis, and may have followed his lead in this respect. Possibly this explains the reclamation of jewels bestowed on his mistress, Eleonora degli Albizzi, following Cosimo's death. See ASF, MdelP, 1182, c. 14, in Paola Barocchi and Giovanna Gaeta Bertelà, *Collezionismo mediceo Cosimo I, Francesco I, e il Cardinale Ferdinando* (Modena: F. C. Panini, 1993), 61.

62. See "Notable Works," 1975, plates 11 and 12; Hackenbroch, "Un gioello mediceo," 31–35; Hackenbroch, *Renaissance Jewelry*, 36, figs. 64a, 64b, and plate 2; and Somers-Cocks and Truman, *Renaissance Jewels*, 78–79. See also Detlef Heikamp, "Ammanati's Fountain for the Sala Grande of the Palazzo Vecchio in Florence," in *Fons Sapientiæ: Renaissance Garden Fountains*, ed. Elizabeth MacDougall (Washington: Dumbarton Oaks, 1979), fig. 1; the reconstruction of the contemporary fountain shows Juno with her two peacocks.

63. See Andrew C. Minor and Bonner Mitchell, *A Renaissance Entertainment: Festivities for the Marriage of Cosimo I, Duke of Florence, in 1539* (Columbia, Mo.: University of Missouri Press, 1968): 135–39; and Janet Cox-Rearick, *Dynasty and Destiny in Medici Art: Pontormo, Leo X, and the Two Cosimos* (Princeton: Princeton University Press, 1984), 290 on astrological import for Juno-Eleonora, and for Juno as patron of brides in the 1555–56 frescoes for Eleonora's Juno terrace, as described in Vasari's *Ragionamenti*. See also Corinne Mandel, "Verrocchio's *Putto with a Dolphin*: The Metamorphosis of a Medicean Symbol," in *Italian Echoes in the Rocky Mountains: Papers from the 1988 Annual Conference of the American Association for Italian Studies* (Provo, Utah: American Association for Italian Studies, 1988), 86, 95–97, figs. 8, 12. For Ammanati's ill-starred Juno fountain, parts of which are now in the Bargello, see Heikamp, "Ammanati's Fountain," 117 ff., and Malcolm Campbell, "Observations on the Salone dei 500," in *Firenze e la Toscana*, 3: 819–30. Eleonora's conflation with Juno is also subtly woven through the composition of Bronzino's state portrait, *Eleonora di Toledo with Her Son Giovanni*, of 1545, in the Uffizi. See Langdon, "Decorum," 1:228–29, 243–44. See also Cox-Rearick, *Bronzino's Chapel*, 42–45, 51–53, noting full conflation of Eleonora with the deity by the 1550s.

64. Alois Maria Nagler, *Theatre Festivals of the Medici, 1539–1637* (New Haven, Conn.: Yale University Press, 1964), 27.

65. Nagler, *Theatre Festivals*, 59. See n. 87 for Bastiano de' Rossi's contemporary description of the intermezzo of 1586, where Juno instructs her nymphs; see also Hackenbroch, "Un gioello mediceo," 33.

66. Nagler, *Theatre Festivals*, 65–67.

67. Bardi's intermezzo of *L'amico fido*, set to Alessandro Striggio's music, expresses the essential, recurring theme of Juno's role. (Featured first in Italian followed by the English translation.)

> Restata la pioggia, l'arcobaleno, intorno all bella nugola, apparve naturalissimo, e Giunone, al suono di liuti, d'arpi, e gravicembali, cominciò così a cantare:

> Giunone   Il nubiloso velo

>   Che cuopre, o Ninfe, il dolce sereno

> E le Ninfe al suono degli stessi strumenti e di tromboni, e flauti grossi, cantando, risposero:

> Le Ninfe   Squarciasi il velo oscuro.

✛ ✛ ✛

> The rain stopped, the rainbow, around a beautiful cloud, appeared naturally, and Juno, to the sound of lutes, harps, and gravicembali began thus to sing:

> Juno   The cloudy veil

>   Covers, O Nymphs, the sweet fair weather

> And the nymphs, to the sound of the same instruments and of trombones [and] large flutes,

> responded [and] sang:

> Nymphs   Dispel the dark veil.

See Federico Ghisi, *Feste musicali della Firenza Medicea* (Bologna: Forni, 1969), 25 and 44, who notes that no record of an *apparato* for Lucrezia de' Medici's wedding has been found. This is probably because Lucrezia's wedding to Alfonso II d'Este (on 9 July 1558) took place before the requisite year of mourning for her sister Maria's death (on 19 November 1557) was over.

68. For the 1586 celebration, see n. 11 above. For Eleonora's *entrata* in 1539, Juno appeared on the Porta al Prata, and muses for the *Mascherata* signified celestial harmony. See Claudia Rousseau, "The Pageant of the Muses at the Medici Wedding of 1539," in *Theatrical Spectacle and Spectacular Theatre: Papers in Art History for the Pennsylvania State University* (State College: Pennsylvania State University Press, 1990), 417–23. See also James M. Saslow, *The Medici Wedding of 1589: Florentine Festival as Theatrum Mundi* (New Haven, Conn.: Yale University Press, 1996).

69. Domenico Mellini, *Dell'origine, fatti e costumi e lodi di Matelda* (Florence, 1589); Baccio Baldini, *Discorso sopra la Mascherata della Genealogia degl' Iddei de' Gentili. Mandata fuori dall'Illustrissimo e Eccellentiss. S. Duca di Firenze, e Siena, il giorno 21 di Febbraio MDLXV* (Florence, 1566); and Giovanni Battista Cini, *Descrizione dell'apparato... per le nozze dell'illustrissimo Don Francesco de' Medici... e della serenissima regina Giovanna d'Austria*, erroneously credited to Mellini by Vasari in *Le vite* (Vasari-Milanesi), 8:516–617. For Cini's proven authorship, see Richard A. Scorza, "Vincenzo Borghini and *Invenzione*: The Florentine *Apparato* of 1565," *Journal of the Warburg and Courtauld Institutes* 44 (1981): 57. For further bibliography on *apparato* for the wedding, see Starn and Partridge, *Arts of Power*, 344, n. 64; and Rousseau, "Pageant of the Muses."

70. Nagler, *Theatre Festivals*, 1–2, notes that 392 costumed "actors" created the tableaux.

71. "Ma la regina Iunone, di reale e ricca e superba corona e di trasparento e lucido vesti adorna, passato Vulcano, si vide con molta maestà sul duodecimo, non men di nessun degli altri pomposo carro venire, da due vaghissimi pavoni tirato; dividendo le cinque istoriette de'suoi gesti...venire a piè del carro poi buona parte di quelle impressioni che nell'aria si fanno: fra le quali, per la prima, si vedeva Iride, tenuta dagli antichi per messaggiera degli Dei, e di Taumante e di Elettra figuola, tutta snella e disciolta, e con rosse e gialle e azzure e verdi vesti (il baleno arco significando) vestita, e con due ali di sparviere, che la sua velocità dimonstravano, in testa. Veniva con lei accompagnata poi di rosso abito e di rosseggiante e sparsa chioma la Cometa, che sotto figura di giovane donna una grande e lucida stella in fronte aveva; e con lore la Serenità, la quale in virginal

sembianza pareva che turchino il volto e turchina tutta la larga e spaziosa veste avesse, non senza una bianca colomba, perchè l'aria significasse, anch'ella in testa. Ma la Neve e la Nebbia pareva che dopo costoro accoppiate insieme si fussero; vestita quella di leonati drappi, sopra cui molti tronchi d'alberi tutti di neve aspersi di posarsi sembravano' e questa, quasi che nessuna forma avesse, si vedeva come in figura d'un grande e bianca camminare: avendo con loro la verde Rugiada, di tal colore figurata per le verdi erbe in cui vedere communemente si suole; che una ritonda luna in testa aveva, significante che nel tempo della sua pienezza è massimamente la rugiada solita dal cielo sopra le verdi erbe cascare. Seguitave la Pioggia poi di bianco abito, benchè alquanto torbidiccio, vestita; sopra il cui capo, per le sette Pleiadi, sette parte splendide e parte abbacinate stelle ghirlanda facevano, at come le diciasette, che nel petto gli fiammeggiavano, pareva che denotar volessero il segno del piovoso Orione. Seguitavano similmente tre vergini, di diversa età, di bianchi drappi adorne e di oliva inghirlandate anche'elle, figurando con esse i tre ordini di vergini, che correndo solevano gli antichi giuochi di Iunone rappresentare: avendo per ultimo in lor compagnia la dea Populonia, in matronale e ricco abito, con una ghirlanda di melagrano e di melissa in testa, e con una piccola mensa in mano, da cui tutta la prescritta aeria torma si vedea leggiadramente chiudere."

See Cini in Vasari-Milanesi 8:605–6. For detailed descriptions with iconographical sources, see Baldini, *La Mascherata*, 78–84.

72. The stump held aloft by Ammanati's Juno was probably a clutch of Jupiter's lightning bolts, as in the following works: the Thyssen-Bornemisza allegory (fig. 2), two *Mascherata* drawings for Juno on her cart (see n. 80 below), and Baccio Baldini's description of Juno riding in procession in the *Mascherata* of February 1566—with Jupiter's thunderbolts in her right hand and a tambourine in her left. See Baldini, *Mascherata*, 79–80; and Anna Maria Petrioli, *Mostra di disegni vasariani. Carri trionfale e costumi per la Genealogia degli Dei 1565*, exh. cat. (Florence: Uffizi, 1966), no. 17, fig. 16. These all support Malcolm Campbell, "Observations," 824, who proposes that Ammanati's Juno once held a clutch of thunderbolts. See also the reconstruction of the fountain in Heikamp, "Ammananti's Fountain"; and Ettore Allegri and Alessandro Cecchi, *Palazzo Vecchio e i Medici: Guida storica* (Florence: S.P.E.S., 1980), 223–26.

73. Somers-Cocks and Truman, *Renaissance Jewels*, citing Cesare Ripa, *Iconologia* (Padua, 1611), 355. Scorza, "Vincenzo Borghini and *Invenzione* ," 58, has commented that Borghini, who could claim primacy as the foremost classical scholar of his generation, probably did not refer to Cartari as reference for the 1565 *entrata*. It is possible that Ripa's version of the Nymphs of the Air was inspired by Cini's *Mascherata* description in Vasari's *Vite*. During his Siena sojourns, Ripa would have known Cini to have been Borghini's respected assistant.

74. Somers-Cocks and Truman, *Renaissance Jewels*, citing Ripa, *Iconologia*, 357.

75. Somers-Cocks and Truman, *Renaissance Jewels*, citing Ripa, *Iconologia*, 356. The seventeen stars on her breast, overlooked by the authors, are visible under strong magnification.

76. Baldini, *Mascherata*, 81; and Ripa, *Iconologia*, 356–57.

77. Alessandro de' Medici married Margaret of Austria, illegitimate daughter of Charles V, in 1533. Widowed in 1537, she married Ottavio Farnese shortly after.

78. The verso of *Populonia* in the collection of drawings in the Biblioteca Nazionale Centrale, Florence (BNCF, II, I, 143, no. 117), is annotated to indicate the three sources of her attributes (a honeybee and an altar): Saint Augustine's *City of God*, bk. IV; Horus's *Heiroglyphics*; and Pliny's *Natural History*. Baldini's account of the *Mascherata* explains that the honeybee offers the gather of honey to the sovereign, while the ancients also made sacrifices to this deity. Her other attributes, pomegranate and bee balm, signify concord, see Baldini, *Mascherata*, 87. See also Petrioli, *Mostra di disegni vasariani*, 51, where Baldini's commentaries for these deities are recorded.

79. Ripa, *Iconologia*, 379. Somers-Cocks and Truman, *Renaissance Jewels*, 79–80, citing Ripa, *Iconologia*, 380–81, cautiously identify the leading figure at the center foreground as Pudicitia but note one

missing attribute, her tortoise. Pudicitia did appear in the *Mascherata*, not in the twelfth but in the third (Saturn) float. See Cini in Vasari-Milanesi, 8:594; or Baldini, *Mascherata*, 24–25.

80. BNCF, CB.3.53, vols. 1 and 2. Vol. 2 includes Juno's *carro* (no. 123), *Iride* (no. 114), *Cometa* (no. 115), *Serenità* (no. 116), *Neve* (no. 118), *Nebbia* (no. 119), *Rugiada* (no. 126), *Pioggia* (no. 121), *Tre fanciulle* (no. 122, a single drawing for three identical virgins), and *Populonia* (no. 117). The Uffizi group in the Gabinetto dei Disegni e delle Stampe are found in *Vasariana*, vol. 2: *Carro di Giunone* (no. 2830F), *Iride* (no. 2831F), *Cometa* (no. 2832F), *Serenità* (no. 2833F), *Neve* (no. 2834F), *Nebbia* (no. 2835F), *Rugiada* (no. 2836F), *Pioggia* (no. 2837F), *Tre fanciulle* (no. 2838F, one drawing for three identical virgins), and *Populonia* (no. 2839F).

From detailed examination of both groups of drawings, I concur with Lecchini-Giovannoni, *Alessandro Allori*, cat. no. 22, who attributes the entire BNCF group of 132 annotated costume designs to Allori, but gives the sixteen more detailed *carro* designs to Vasari. She believes the Uffizi group to be more or less faithful workshop copies.

81. See previous note. See also Petrioli, *Mostra di disegni vasariani*, 10–11, commenting on the Uffizi group only; Petrioli assigns the costume designs mostly to Allori.

82. Baldini, *Mascherata*, 80, gives the source as Hesiod's *Teogonia*. For illustrations, see Petrioli, *Mostra di disegni vasariani*, fig. 17, and Lecchini-Giovannoni, *Alessandro Allori*, colorplate 15.

83. Allori's inscription on the drawing (fig. 8) is found on the upper right: "una fanciulla vestita in bianca…ma scura…et in cappo habbia sette stelle…nel petto 17 stelle…in mano un ragnarlo, che facci la tela." On Ripa's probable sources, see n. 73. For concordances of Ripa's *Pioggia*, see Yassu Okayama, *The Ripa Index: Personifications and Their Attributes in Five Editions of the Iconologia* (Doornspick, The Netherlands: Davaco, 1992), 196.

84. Each drawing (Uffizi no. 2834F, *La Neve*, illustrated in Petrioli, *Mostra di disegni vasariani*, fig. 19, and no. 2835F, *La Nebbia*), is massed in with a bistre wash to achieve this effect. *La Ruggiada* is Uffizi no. 2836F. (Baldini's commentaries are given with each of Petrioli's.)

85. Petrioli, *Mostra di disegni vasariani*, 10–11; see also Nagler, *Theatre Festivals*, 24. Although Borghini devised the iconography for the 1565 *apparato*, there is no documentation of his involvement in the *Mascherata*. See Scorza, "Vincenzo Borghini and *Invenzione* ," 58. Vasari and Allori—and indeed the entire intelligentsia of Medicean Florence—were saturated with Borghini's ideation of Medici power. See Paola Corrias, "Don Vincenzo Borghini e l'iconologia del potere alla corte di Cosimo I e di Francesco I de' Medici," *Storia dell' arte* 81 (1993): 169–81. See also Robert Williams, "Borghini and Vasari's *Lives*" (Ph.D. diss., Princeton University, 1988).

86. Nagler, *Theatre Festivals*, 25. Vasari's *carro* drawings (see figs. 6 and n. 79 above) bear this out: each cart has its deity mounted on it; no other figures are included in these drawings.

87. The fifth intermezzo of *L'Amico fido*, in the Uffizi theatre for Virginia de' Medici-d'Este's wedding in 1586, was staged with elaborate deus ex machina for the airborne goddess and her train. Bastiano de' Rossi's *Descrizione* of the 1586 intermezzo helps explain the general theme of the Thyssen-Bornemisza scene, even if the supporting players have changed:

> Presently, when act four came to a close, the fifth intermezzo began, and little by little …the sky darkened, and was seemingly filled with clouds…and with great fury began to flash with lightning, and to thunder…and in a brief space of time, in the middle of these storms a serene cloud appeared, in which there was a chariot drawn by two large, beautiful peacocks [looking] as though real…and in it Juno with Iris, and with their fourteen Nymphs, two of which were Sirens of the Day and of the Night, and twelve had the signs of the zodiac on their heads, [signifying] the four seasons. Juno was seated regnant in the chariot, and beneath her, rank by rank, were all the Nymphs. …She began to sing…[and] the sky was restored, became clear, and shone brightly."

See Bastiano de' Rossi, *Descrizione del magnificentiss. apparato e de'maraviglioso intermedi fatti per la commedia rappresentata in Firenze nelle felicissime Nozze degl'Illustrissimi, ed Eccellentissimi*

Signori il Signor Don Cesare D'Este, e la Signora Donna Virginia Medici. In Firenze, Apresso Giorgio Marescotti. l'Anno MDLXXXV (Florence, 1585), 20–21.

Note that Iris is not listed here as a nymph; she is, however, described as principal nymph in Cini's description of the 1566 *Mascherata* above, as she consistently is by Ripa from 1603. Cini's superior, Borghini (or his circle) again appear to be Ripa's sources for the Nymphs of the Air, as I suggest above. See Okayama, *Ripa Index*, 196.

88. For the annotated costume designs for Iris, see n. 80 above.

89. For the Studiolo program and plan see Walter Vitzthum, *Lo Studiolo di Francesco I a Firenze* (Milan: Fratelli Fabbri, 1965); Scott Schaefer, "The Studiolo of Francesco I de' Medici in the Palazzo Vecchio in Florence" (Ph.D. diss., Bryn Mawr College, 1976), esp. figs. 5a–b; and Cox-Rearick, *Dynasty and Destiny*, 288–90, plate 198.

90. Uffizi, slate, 112 cm diameter, attributed to Allori by Lecchini-Giovannoni, *Alessandro Allori*, cat. no. 190.

91. See Scorza, "Vincenzo Borghini and *Invenzione*," 58.

92. See Schaefer, Studiolo, 1:457–58, plate 12e, 17–21.

93. Borghini corrects his instructions of two days earlier and advises Vasari: "Take note then, that where the statue of Zephyr is, it must be Boreas, and in my writing is otherwise and in error, because the crystals he makes are from across the mountains and not from the sea...it is the person of Boreas who has the other quality from that of Zephyr." ("Avertite ancora, che, dove e quella statua di Zephiro, ha a esser' Borea; et nel mia scritto sta altrimente e per errore, perche i cristalli si fanno alla tramontana et non al marino...che la persona di Borea è d'altri qualità che quella di Zephiro.") Schaefer, Studiolo, 1:460–61, fig. 12b.

94. *Mascherata* drawings for *Boreas* and *Zephyr* are Uffizi 2835F and 2846F, respectively.

95. See Borghini's letter to Vasari, quoted in n. 93 above, in which he differentiates Zephyr's breath from Boreas's, whose frosty breath ("i cristalli si fanno") comes "from across the mountains and not from the sea." (For Boreas as snowy see Okayama, *Ripa Index*, 280; for Zephyr as the west wind see Okayama, *Ripa Index*, 628).

96. It was situated close to the port of Livorno, which had recently been fortified by Cosimo. On Medici villas as a strategic network and means of maintaining rural government, see Saslow, *Medici Wedding*, 12–13, 122, 134.

97. Daniela Mignani, *Le Ville Medicee di Giusto Utens* (Florence: Arnaud, 1993), 17, 98, 99, known from Utens's lunettes for the Villa Artimino, 1599, now in the Museo Topografico "Firenze com'era," Florence. See ibid., colorplate p. 69, detail p. 99. (Mignani confuses this Eleonora di Toledo with her aunt, who had died in 1562 and could not, therefore, have been the recipient of the Badia's largesse in 1571).

Utens's prospect is directly north, with the villa at the base of wooded hills, a walled garden extending north, and the Arno proper beyond. This ancient Medici holding, originally Cosimo the Elder's, had dependencies and a crenellated villa outside its garden walls; the walled estate shown in the Thyssen-Bornemisza miniature, however, is set in open countryside by the estuary, with its enclosure extending east. The estuary's Pisan hills are north, and woods show on the eastern edge, suggesting that the Medici holdings at Collesalvetti were immediately east of the scene.

That the walled area to the left (west) of the scene is the Badia is borne out in an eighteenth-century map of the Medici holding at Collesalvetti, which shows the Badia's footpath leading off from the western side of Collesalvetti, also towards the sea. The river, woods, and the Appenines to the north of the property are also indicated. See Francesco Mineccia, *Da Fattore Granducale a Communità: Collesalvetti 1737–1861* (Naples: E. S. I., 1982), 65. (I thank Professor Franco Angiolini for this reference and Professor William McQuaig for useful exchanges concerning the region today). The hamlet of Collesalvetti, which today incorporates the much-altered former villa and its estates, is one mile from the Ligurian coast west of Livorno, about one and one-half miles south of Pisa. See Laura Alidori, *Le Dimore dei Medici in Toscana* (Florence: Polistampa, 1995), 80.

This territorial jurisdiction in association with a woman's portrait repeats a theme from another well-known portrait of her aunt, Bronzino's *Eleonora di Toledo with her Son Giovanni* of 1545, in the Uffizi. For this, see Langdon, "Decorum," chap. 5; and Langdon, "Bronzino's *Eleonora di Toledo with Giovanni*: A Declaration of Regency, '*Religio regis*,' and Ducal Patronage," unpublished paper delivered at the Renaissance Society of America Conference in St. Louis, Missouri, 1996.

Soon to be Admiral of the Tuscan Fleet, Pietro was domiciled in Pisa, where Cosimo held court in his retirement. See Saltini, "Due principesse," part 2, 607; part 3, 627–60.

98. See Rousseau, "Pageant of the Muses," 419–57; and Cox-Rearick, *Bronzino's Chapel*, 42, 52. The fountain was intended for this location, and its full installation abandoned only after Cosimo's death in 1574. See M. Campbell, "Observations," 822–23, 828.

99. Langdon, "Decorum," 1:176–78. See also Joanna Woodall, *Portraiture: Facing the Subject* (Manchester: Manchester University Press, 1997), 3, who notes that portraiture "articulated the patriarchal principle of genealogy upon which aristocratic ideology was built," the subject being "situated within chains or hierarchies of resemblance."

100. See Heikamp in Böhler, *Sale catalogue*, no. 7. Langedijk, *Portraits*, cat. nos. 85,5 and 76,3, identifies her as Maria di Cosimo, noting earlier proposals for her sister Lucrezia. Maria had gray-blue eyes, as her portrait in the Uffizi demonstrates, and Lucrezia had very dark eyes and black hair, as her miniature in the Pitti attests. Maria died in 1557, Lucrezia in 1561, but this woman is dressed in early 1570s style, as noted by Somers-Cocks and Truman, *Renaissance Jewels*, 78.

101. With regard to the gloves, see Alison Lurie, "Agnolo Bronzino: Portrait of a Young Lady," *Bulletin of the Cleveland Museum of Art* 61, no. 50 (1974): 8.

102. Dianora was promised in the names of both Cosimo and her father, Garzia, before her wedding. Saltini, "Due Principesse," part 1, 566. Cosimo severely admonished his son for adultery and poor treatment of Dianora only months after the couple's wedding, but to no avail. Ibid., part 2, 608, and part 6, 190. See also n. 26 above concerning her letters of complaint to her family.

103. Scorza, "Borghini and the *Apparato*," 58.

104. See Mandel, "Verrocchio's *Putto*," 86, for the Juno-Eleonora conflation in Vasari's lost frescoes for the Terrace of Juno, 1555, and references in Vasari's *Ragionamenti* in Vasari-Milanesi 8:71–76. The Jupiter-Cosimo conflation was well established, as Vasari describes in his *Ragionamenti*; in their writings, Paolo Giovio and Bronzino also refer to the merging of mortal and divine for these two deities and the ducal couple. See Campbell, "Observations," 822.

105. Winspeare, *Isabella*, 115. The title of grand duke, long coveted by Cosimo, was granted in a papal bull of 9 September 1569. See Henk Th. van Veen, "Circles of Sovereignty: The Tondi of the Sala Grande in the Palazzo Vecchio and the Medici Crown," *Vasari's Florence: Artists and Literati at the Medici Court*, ed. Philip Jacks (Cambridge: Cambridge University Press, 1998), 206–10, shows that the *corona radiata* was inspired by that worn by Cosimo in Vasari's central *tondo* on the ceiling of the Salone Grande of the Palazzo Vecchio. Van Veen also documents that its final design is recorded in a detailed miniature that accompanied the text of the bull by which Pius V conferred Cosimo's new title in 1569. See van Veen, "Circles of Sovereignty," fig. 87. A full bibliography for the crown is found in his n. 36. I am indebted to Professor van Veen for generously sharing his unpublished manuscripts. The crown, commissioned from Jacques Bylivert, was received on 15 March 1570 from Pius, thus its form was probably known to Allori and Dianora. For the Bylivert version, see C. Willemijn Fock, "The Medici Crown: Work of the Delft Goldsmith Jacques Bylivert," *Oud Holland* 85 (1970): 199, fig. 8. For the regalia, see Karla Langedijk, "Ritratti granducali a Firenze, una volta all'Ospedale di Santa Maria Nuova, e a Palazzo Pitti," *Prospettiva* 13 (April 1978): 64–67; see also Langedijk, *Portraits*, cat. nos. 27, 7–9 and 27, groups 40, 41, 43, 43a, 48, all posthumous.

106. Langedijk, *Portraits*, cat. no. 35,42. Eleonora is portrayed with her son Francesco, on textile, designed by Jacopo Ligozzi, 1613–21; the crown is on a plinth, to the left of the composition.

107. For Eleonora's documented periods of regency, see Langdon, "Decorum," chap. 5; and Langdon, "A Declaration of Regency," paper delivered at the Renaissance Society Conference in St. Louis, Missouri, 1996. See also Cox-Rearick, *Bronzino's Chapel*, 34–35; Bruce L. Edelstein, "The Early Patronage of Eleonora di Toledo: The Camera Verde and Its Dependencies in the Palazzo Vecchio" (Ph.D. diss., Harvard University, 1995); and Bruce Edelstein's contribution to this volume.

108. The attribution is denied Allori in Lecchini-Giovannoni, *Alessandro Allori*, 301.

109. Heikamp in Böhler, *Sale catalogue*, cat. no. 7. See Vienna, Kunsthistorisches Museum, inv. no. 2583; 114.5 x 89.5 cm, 1973 cat. no. 5 (as *Maria de' Medici* by Allori). Heikamp believed this to be Cosimo de' Medici's daughter, Lucrezia (1545–61). Baccheschi, *L'opera completa*, cat. no. 174, describes the subject of the same Vienna panel as a Medici princess, under "uncertain attribution." The attribution to Allori has been challenged recently by Philippe Costamagna. See Lecchini-Giovannoni, *Alessandro Allori*, 301, who proposes Santi di Tito as its author. Nevertheless, the portrait shows the typically long, heavy forearms and recurring hand pose used by Allori. The latter is discussed below in this text at n. 117; these tendencies are each in evidence in Allori's signed *Portrait of a Florentine Noblewoman with Her Son* of 1574. (See n. 11 above.)

110. For attribution to Allori, see "Notable Works," 1975, citing Heikamp; Hackenbroch, "Un gioello mediceo," 33; Hackenbroch, *Renaissance Jewelry*, 36; and, calling for reappraisal, Somers-Cocks and Truman, *Renaissance Jewels*, 77. Also see Langedijk, *Portraits*, 2:cat. no. 109,6 (as Virginia de' Medici d'Este).

Bronzino, who died in 1572, appears not to have portrayed Cosimo and Eleonora's children in adulthood. See Langdon, "Decorum," chap. 6. Vasari is not a contender: by his own admission he found portraiture unappealing and avoided it whenever possible. See Vasari-Milanesi 7:688.

111. Somers-Cocks and Truman, *Renaissance Jewels*, 79, merely note that there was no documented example of an Allori miniature for comparison with the Thyssen-Bornemisza portrait; however, the double-sided Florentine miniature attributed to Allori and sold in 1991, discussed below, was not available to influence their conclusions.

112. I. B. Supino, *I ricordi di Alessandro Allori, 1579–84* (Florence, 1908), 20. Don Giovanni de' Ricci paid for a tiny oval portrait on silver, 4 July 1583. Other miniatures (perhaps very small panels) of the Medici are recorded, as well as two *tondi* on copper for reliquary boxes, ibid., 23.

113. Francesco appears to be in mourning; Lucrezia died in Ferrara in 1561. For the *Francesco with a Miniature of Lucrezia d'Este* portrait, see Langedijk, *Portraits*, 2:cat. no. 42,23; see also Lecchini-Giovannoni, *Alessandro Allori*, cat. no. 180.

114. See Langedijk, *Portraits*, cat. no. 76,3 ("Bronzino workshop"); and Baccheschi, *Opera Completa*, cat. no. 161, who lists attributions to and against Bronzino. Its style reflects Allori's post-Roman period. For a detailed comparison of the styles of Bronzino and Allori at this time, see Gabrielle Langdon, "A Reattribution: Alessandro Allori's *Lady with a Cameo*," *Zeitschrift für Kunstgeschichte* 52 (1989): 25–45.

115. Richard A. Scorza, "Borghini, Butteri and Allori: A Further Drawing for the 1565 'Apparato,'" *Burlington Magazine* 137 (1995): 175, notes Allori's "highly-wrought miniaturist detail" on the *Pearl Fishers*, 1571–73.

116. Lecchini-Giovannoni, *Alessandro Allori*, fig. 50, cat. no. 23. Allori was paid for a small work on copper in October 1568; this seems to be for his *Hercules Crowned by the Muses*, in the Uffizi.

117. In Allori's *Susannah and the Elders*, oil on panel, 202 x 117 cm (Musée Magnin, Dijon), dated 1561, the large Michelangelesque nude shows all of these characteristics . See Lecchini-Giovannoni, *Alessandro Allori*, fig. 23, cat. no. 18.

118. Lecchini-Giovannoni, *Alessandro Allori*, figs. 426, 427, cat. no. 191. Dr. Silvia Meloni Trkulja has

called my attention to a possible Medici precedent for the double-sided oval miniature from Castello, showing Francesco(?) as a young boy, the reverse of which depicts a male nude who plucks leaves and places them in a large urn (Uffizi 1890, no. 1040, oil on copper, 15.9 x 12.5 cm). Langedijk, *Portraits*, 1:122, cat. no. 42,44, tentatively proposes Carlo Portelli as its author.

119. The Studiolo was commissioned during the winter of 1569–70. Schaefer, "Studiolo," 1:xx. For detailed discussion of the landscape in the Thyssen-Bornemisza miniature and the *Pearl Fishers*, see Hackenbroch, "Un gioello mediceo," 34.

120. Haboldt & Co., Paris, *Tableaux anciennes des ècoles du nord, française et italienne,* sale cat., 1990–91, cat. no. 22, *Portrait of a Young Nobleman*, oil on copper, 4 in. diameter, now in a private collection. It is attributed to Allori by Robert Simon because of its high quality and its similarity to his Studiolo style. It is proposed that its allegory, described as *Love and Fidelity*, implicitly makes the youth portrayed its donor-patron, and the recipient his betrothed. Jane Mitnick of Haboldt and Co., New York, graciously allowed me to publish an illustration of the miniature.

121. Other Medici women commissioned portraits of themselves. Duchess Bianca Cappello's was commissioned from Allori in 1581 (Langedijk, *Portraits*, 1:845, cat. nos: 41,1, A and C). Rubens's cycles eulogizing her life were commissioned by Maria de' Medici, Queen of France, in 1622–25 for the Luxembourg Palace. See Christopher White, *Peter Paul Rubens, Man and Artist* (New Haven, Conn.: Yale University Press, 1987), 161–70. See also the papers by Sheryl Reiss and Bruce Edelstein in this volume.

Earlier instances are known. Giulia Muzzarelli's donor portrait in a *Visitation* for her own memorial chapel was commissioned from Girolamo da Carpi and is mentioned by Vasari; see Catherine Turrill, "Girolamo da Carpi's Muzzarelli Altarpiece," *Studies in the History of Art* 24 (1990): 75–86. I thank Dr. Turrill for this reference and for useful discussion on the topic. Isabella d'Este's unfulfilled hope of a portrait from Leonardo is well documented. For this and others, see Lorne Campbell, *Renaissance Portraits*, 62, 65, 81, 140, fig. 93. It cannot have been unusual for women to commission their own portraits, as implied in Tito Vespasiano Strozzi's poem satirizing a woman named Helen who commissions her portrait from Cosimo Tura; Turrill, "Carpi's Muzzarelli Altarpiece," 140. Margaret of Austria frequently commissioned portraits of herself (ibid., passim, esp. fig. 86, her portrait in Brou by Bernard Van Orley, who was her personal portraitist from 1518–30); Jan Vermeyen was also retained by Margaret from about 1525 (ibid., 126 and passim), and Margaret's successor, Mary of Hungary, had Guillaume Scrots in her service from 1537 until 1546 (ibid., 126). J. K. Steppe, "Mencía di Mendoza et ses relations avec Erasme, Gilles de Busleyden et Jean-Louis Vivès," in *Scrinium Erasmianum*, ed. J. Coppens (Leyden: Brill, 1969), 2:480, documents the commission of her own portrait by Mencía, Countess of Nassau. Lorne Campbell, *The Early Flemish Pictures in the Collection of Her Majesty the Queen* (Cambridge: Cambridge University Press, 1985), xx, xxvi, notes that Catherine Parr commissioned her own portrait in 1547, as did Mary Tudor in 1553. I am indebted to Dr. Campbell for useful bibliography; he also informs me of his findings that Margaret of Burgundy, Countess Dowager of Hainault and Poland, commissioned her portrait from Pierre Henne in 1417–18; Soeur Joye Lachier, the prioress of Hôpital Comtesse, Lille, paid Jean Pillot for another in 1476–77; and Mary of Hungary commissioned one of herself in 1535. Agustín Gonzále de Amezua y Mayo, *Isabel de Valois, reina de Espagña 1546–1568* (Madrid: Gràficas Ultra, 1949), 264, documents Isabel of Valois's commission of her own portrait. Sofonisba Anguissola, lady-in-waiting and retained portraitist to Isabel, painted the queen several times, and was later called on by her daughter, Isabella Clara Eugenia, Queen of the Netherlands, to portray her at Genoa when she was en route to her wedding. See Ilya Sandra Pierlingieri, *Sofonisba Anguissola* (New York: Rizzoli, 1992), 121–26. 190.

122. Martin Wackernagel, *The World of the Florentine Renaissance Artist*, trans. Alison Luchs (Princeton: Princeton University Press, 1980), 8, 295, suggests that along with the patron's instinct for self-elevation, the role of collector and connoisseur stems from awareness by the owner of a work's formal excellence or the individual mastery of certain prominent artists. In this case, Pietro is flattered as the connoisseur. Renaissance taste led especially to the demand for meticulously or-

nate execution of detail, and the art of book illumination, from which the genre of miniature portraiture sprang at the beginning of the sixteenth century, was one of the principal areas where painstaking detail was cultivated.

123. See n. 99 above

124. See Werner Gundersheimer, "Patronage in the Renaissance: An Exploratory Approach," in *Patronage in the Renaissance*, ed. Guy Fitch Lytle and Stephen Orgel (Princeton: Princeton University Press, 1981), 19, on the ambiance of the "Big Man" as patron. For Cosimo as principal artificer of the absolute state, and for creating centrality in the figure of the prince, see Fantoni, *La Corte del Granduca*, 24–29. On works of art in court circles as instruments in exposing propagandistic rhetoric, see Starn and Partridge, *Arts of Power*, 5; and James M. Saslow, "Review of *Arts of Power: Three Halls of State in Italy, 1300–1600*, by Randolf Starn and Loren Partridge," *Renaissance Quarterly* 47 (1994): 1006–7.

On the momentum of family patronage, see Edward L. Goldberg, *Patterns in Late Medici Art Patronage* (Princeton: Princeton University Press, 1983), ix; and Mary Hollingsworth, *Patronage in Renaissance Italy From 1400 to the Early Sixteenth Century* (London: J. Murray, 1994), 1–2. In this context, the comment by Gundersheimer, "Patronage," 20, that the present leader "is part of a great continuum, extending deep into the past and far into the future" is particularly apt.

125. See n. 20 above on Cosimo's delight in her company. Gundersheimer, "Patronage," 19, proposes that the most important links between the "Big Man" and corporate structures are those with their families. It is significant that Cosimo kept a strict eye on iconography generated by his iconographer, Borghini. See Scorza, "Vincenzo Borghini and the *Apparato* of 1565," 58, and Fantoni, *La Corte del Granduca*, 24–29.

126. Gundersheimer, "Patronage," 13, 19–20.

127. In fact, their son Cosimino, born in 1573 (see n. 12), was heir to the dukedom until his death in 1576. Giovanna's and Francesco's son Filippo was born only in 1577. (On the extreme concern about their lack of heirs, see n. 32 above.)

128. Cosimo's close control over expressions of ideology and propaganda is recorded in letters between him and Vincenzo Borghini, via Vasari. See Scorza, "Vincenzo Borghini and the *Apparato* of 1565," 58.

129. Excerpted by Saltini, "Due Principesse," part 6, 173–75, from Domenico Maria Manni, in "Notizie della vita di Agostino…Ubaldini, scultore e poeta," in *Raccolta di opuscoli scientifici e filosifici detta del Cologera* 36 (Venice, 1748), 327–28.

A Widow's Choice: Alessandro Allori's *Christ and the Adulteress* in the Church of Santo Spirito at Florence

Elizabeth Pilliod

Among his late cinquecento contemporaries, Alessandro Allori's (1535–1607) importance must have been obvious, for his paintings and other designs were highly sought after in both Medicean and non-Medicean circles. Yet his astonishing productivity, which was sometimes achieved through the aid of apprentices and assistants, has acted to blind scholars to the sensitivity of many of the individual works of art.[1] In fact, much still remains to be discovered about his career, especially his role in the transformation of Florentine art from the late Renaissance forms of the 1540s to the burgeoning realism of the seicento. What is well known is that Alessandro was the designated heir, both financially and artistically, of his mentor Agnolo Bronzino.[2] Allori ultimately became the premier artist in Florence during the third quarter of the sixteenth century, even dabbling in architecture on several occasions. Alessandro's long career led to his becoming the formative influence on virtually all the significant Florentine Baroque painters of the next generation, including Cigoli, Passignano, and his own son, Cristofano Allori, all of whom received training in his *bottega*.[3]

Alessandro Allori's *Christ and the Adulteress*

Among Alessandro's many altarpieces still to be found in situ is the *Christ and the Adulteress* (fig. 1), located in the church of Santo Spirito at Florence. Although the painting is inscribed with the date 1577, and in two near-contemporary descriptions of the painting the name of the patron appears to be recorded, the painting, its subject, and meaning have remained mysterious. Our lack of information about this altarpiece probably is a result of the relative scholarly neglect of late sixteenth-century Florentine religious painting. Yet the painting rewards the persistent observer, as it is both a moving and intelligent visual statement, one carefully shaped by the special circumstances of the commission and its meaning. Yet, to date, only its elegant style has been singled out; the subject matter of the altarpiece, which is rare for its time and place, has elicited no discussion.[4]

In Allori's lifetime, however, the Santo Spirito painting was mentioned in the two major published accounts of the arts in Florence. Raffaello Borghini's *Il riposo* (1584) and Francesco Bocchi's *Le bellezze di Fiorenza* (1591), both composed within a generation of the installation of the altarpiece in Santo Spirito, contain some highly significant criticism, as well as information regarding the patrons of this chapel and altarpiece—the Cini family.[5] The earlier account of the two, Raffaello Borghini's text, describes the notable works of art to be seen in Santo Spirito: "[By Allori there is] in Santo Spirito…a painting at the Chapel of the Cini family, where the adulteress [is shown] demonstrating remorse for her sin.…" In a second descriptive passage, Borghini repeats that he particularly likes the figure of the "woman caught in sin, who, in addition to being beautifully outfitted, is arranged in such position as to demonstrate shame for her error."[6]

Less than a decade later, Francesco Bocchi also praised the picture, in which he finds all the figures and their actions perfectly expressive of the sacred story—a prerequisite for his Counter-Reformation critical approval. Bocchi particularly emphasizes the gesture of the woman, who partially covers her face with a veil, declaring that the adulteress is "admirably drawn, so that, while on one side there is a veil that covers her face, which is colored with shame; on the other side, she shyly blushes and shows in the presence of the Savior to have repented of her sin."[7]

That was the sum of our information on this commission until the discovery of the documents that will supply the basis for our discussion. These archival sources inform us about the Cini family and its somewhat unusual situation in Florentine society. They also reveal the original intentions for the chapel's dedication and theme, and may suggest a personal motivation for the subsequent alteration of those intentions by one member of the Cini family. As a result of this alteration, the altarpiece's subject was transformed into the present one, Christ and the Adulteress. Why this subject was apposite is the substance of this study.

Pilliod Fig. 1. Alessandro Allori, *Christ and the Adulteress,* 1577, Florence, Santo Spirito, Cini Chapel (photo: Alinari/Art Resource, N.Y.)

Girolamo di Cino Cini and Anna di Michele Videmon from Dinkelsbühl

First, the matter of the proper identity of the Cini who were responsible for this chapel in Santo Spirito should be clarified. Girolamo di Cino Cini, who was born in 1510 and died in 1565, was a successful Florentine cloth merchant whose business operations led him to live for considerable periods of time in Poland and Germany.[8] In 1557 he was recorded as having erected a funerary monument at Cracow to his friend, Galeazzo Guicciardini.[9] Also in Poland, Girolamo acquired a Polish servant who later returned with him to Florence and was provided for in a testamentary bequest. In fact, it is through Girolamo Cini's two wills—the first testament dated 1561, the second dated 1565—that we learn of his long-standing involvement in Germany, specifically in Nuremberg, where he spent a great deal of time for his business.[10] He had purchased and furnished a house in the very center of the city, and is known to have resided there. Records of the Cini house in the city archives at Nuremberg indicate that it was owned by his sons at least through the end of the sixteenth century.[11]

According to Girolamo's earlier will of 1561, he acquired another associate during his stay in Nuremberg; this time he found, as he put it, "a loving and honorable woman," who then became his mistress, and whom he grew to adore. The woman in question was a native German, Anna di Michele Videmon, from Dinkelsbühl, a small town outside Nuremberg. In his testament Girolamo dictates an intimate account, at least by sixteenth-century notarial standards, of their relationship, documenting its beginning six years earlier, when Anna came to live with him in his Florentine house. He reveals that at the time she had already borne him one son, called Pagolo, and, at the moment of the writing of the testament, was pregnant with another child of his. He affirms that neither he nor Anna had ever been married, nor did either of them have any children, save the boy, Pagolo, whom Girolamo had fed, educated, loved, and considered as his true son.

Continuing with Girolamo's testament, we find the declaration that from Anna the testator has received the most extraordinary "solicitude and love." In return, should Girolamo die, he wished to provide Anna with the use of his house and its contents for the duration of her life. His gratitude or affection for Anna is revealed by the elaborate provisions he had the notary record, which cover virtually every conceivable future contingency. Perhaps the most remarkable of these was his stipulation that even if they both had determined to leave one another while he were still alive, she was still to receive a legacy of forty bushels of grain, sixteen barrels of wine, and 30 florins every year so long as she would live, and these items were to be delivered free of taxes by his heirs to her at her new home. Other provisions state that should she decide to marry after his decease, he would have her provided with a dowry of 400 florins. If she wished to continue to live in his house in Florence, she could do so until her death. If she preferred to live elsewhere, she was to receive the same portions of grain, wine and florins as above. If she preferred to become a nun, still other provisions were made.

Girolamo evidently suspected that Anna might not have been entirely comfortable in Florence (or perhaps that after his death she would feel less a part of the city), for he also stipulated that if she should elect to return to Germany, she should receive 300 florins immediately. He furthermore enjoined his only close relative, a brother called Miniato, not to bother her over the family property or the bequests to her. To insure her tranquility in this event, he had listed the jewels, clothes, and furniture she had brought into his house, stipulating that there must be no question that these things had always been her property.

Five years later, shortly before his death in December 1565, Girolamo Cini had a second testament drawn up. It was a brief document in comparison with the previous one. According to its preamble, Girolamo Cini believed himself to be dying, and indeed this was to be the case. Again Girolamo records that Anna had treated him with "maravigliosa sollicitudine et amore" (marvelous solicitude and love).[12] The couple had by that time three children, Pagolo, Elisabetta, and a baby of only a few days, whom they had named after Girolamo's father, Cino. It was a significant christening, as the makeshift "family" of Girolamo and Anna was now about to become a real family. In the second testament, Girolamo announced that, in light of his love for their children, and, in order to "remove the stain of illegitimacy," a death-bed marriage between himself and Anna had been performed.[13] He moreover required of his heirs the legitimization of the children. Before his illness, Girolamo had forged an agreement with his business partner, Antonio Torrigiani, obligating Torrigiani to sell his magnificent double-entrance palazzo in Via Maggio to Girolamo's heirs for 1600 florins.[14] Anna was to have use for life of this palazzo in Via Maggio, her residence situated in the most fashionable street in Florence, and almost across the street from Bianca Cappello's palace. Anna was to share the palazzo with his brother, Miniato, and they were to be served by the trusted Polish retainer who had been for many years with Girolamo, and who was in return promised food and clothing throughout his lifetime. Girolamo's two male children were named his universal heirs, with his brother, Miniato, as next in line. With the Florentine palazzo, country villa, business inventory, and other real and personal property, Cini's estate was in the tens of thousands of florins.

The Cini Chapel at Santo Spirito and Its Altarpiece

In addition to the usual testamentary provisions, and the far from usual personal glimpses into the depth of his love and solicitude for Anna, Girolamo's testament of 1561 contained instructions for the decoration of the funerary chapel he had decided to establish in his parish church of Santo Spirito. The relevant passage in the early will states, "[the testator] commands and charges the said heirs in the two years following his death to have made a picture in which [should be] represented a crucifix and a Saint Jerome…[and this picture should] be placed in the Cini chapel in the church of Santo Spirito at Florence."[15] Although Girolamo had evidently selected the chapel in Santo Spirito, it was actually purchased by his heirs only after his death, by a deed drawn in January 1566.[16]

The Cini chapel lies behind the high altar of Santo Spirito, the second from the left of the four major chapels that would have mirrored Brunelleschi's original plan for four doors to the church. Like the Bardi and Pitti chapels that flank it, the Cini chapel and its altarpiece are now almost completely obscured by the Baroque altar and *baldacchino* constructed in the first years of the seventeenth century. But when Allori's altarpiece was first erected, before the additions of altar and *baldacchino*, the Cini Chapel would have been a prominent one because of its position on a direct line of sight from the main portal of the church to the high altar.

Brunelleschi's sweeping lines of columns, intended to guide the viewer down the nave of Santo Spirito, were apparently imitated by Alessandro Allori in the architectural background of the Cini altarpiece, in which a row of columns behind *Christ and the Adulteress* is shown in dramatic receding perspective (see fig. 1).[17] While the elevated flights of steps that appear immediately behind the two main figures were Allori's creative elaboration, the columns themselves are nearly identical to those of Brunelleschi. In fact, not only the columns, but also the division of the floor according to the quadrants described by the modular plan of the church suggest the interior of Santo Spirito. This identification of the "temple" in the biblical episode, as illustrated in the painting with the actual interior of Santo Spirito, evidently was the end result of some deliberation on Allori's part, since of the two preparatory sketches for the altarpiece, only the second contains columns similar to those in Santo Spirito (fig. 2). This sheet, which was squared for transfer, documents an evolution away from the less specific interior in an earlier sketch (fig. 3), in which Solomonic columns evoked the ancient setting of the meeting of Christ with the woman taken in adultery.[18]

Pilliod Fig. 2. Alessandro Allori, study for *Christ and the Adulteress*, 1577, Florence, Galleria degli Uffizi, Gabinetto dei Disegni e delle Stampe, 10332F (photo: Soprintendenza, Florence)

Pilliod Fig. 3. Alessandro Allori, study for *Christ and the Adulteress*, 1577, Paris, Musée du Louvre, inv. 10111 (photo: RMN)

The Cini altarpiece was signed and dated 1577 by Alessandro Allori.[19] While no contract has been found to establish precise dates for the beginning and completion of the commission, the style of this altarpiece can be comfortably situated just after his securely dated paintings of the early to mid-1570s. One example would be the Bracci altarpiece in Santa Maria Novella of 1575, in which Allori still utilized the slightly heavier figure type associated with his earlier, Roman-influenced mode.[20]

As Girolamo Cini died in 1565, and his heirs purchased the chapel in Santo Spirito only a month later, it is certain that Girolamo himself did not commission the painting. One is led to wonder, then, who did arrange for it? By 1571 all of the guardians and tutors Girolamo Cini had appointed to run the affairs of Anna and their children were deceased.[21] His brother, Miniato, had died as well, and was interred on 11 June 1570 in the chapel founded by Girolamo five years before.[22]

Only Anna herself remained and there seems little doubt that she was the controlling figure behind the altarpiece. Documents reveal the friars at Santo Spirito collected their annual fee for masses directly from her beginning in the year 1571, which strongly suggests that by that date Anna had complete financial responsibility for the Cini chapel.[23] The question of her direct influence and power over the figuration of the chapel's iconography is crucial for any discussion of the resulting altarpiece, for clearly the theme of the chapel was diverted from that of Saint Jerome, her husband's eponymous saint, to the biblical story of Christ and the adulteress. While no document shows her directing Allori to make a picture of this theme, there can be no other reasonable explanation than that it was Anna's decision to focus on the New Testament episode of the adulteress.

Saint Jerome and the Chapel's *Paliotto*

Although the chapel no longer had Saint Jerome as its central image, a Saint Jerome does appear in the chapel, albeit relegated to a secondary, yet complementary, position vis-à-vis the large altar panel. The painted wooden *paliotto* presently in the chapel is decorated with an image of a penitent Saint Jerome (fig. 4), and is almost certainly the chapel's original painted altar frontal, as its condition, shape, and subject matter demonstrate.[24] While indistinct in some of its details, one still can make out a large central laurel wreath about the image of the penitent Saint Jerome in the wilderness. The saint, attired in his traditional red, has doffed his cardinal's hat, and kneels, arms crossed over his breast, to adore the crucifix placed on the ground before him. This *paliotto* has been repainted several times, resulting in a rather clumsy and unfocused central image. However, despite any uncertainty resulting from the

Pilliod Fig. 4. Anonymous, *Paliotto with Saint Jerome,* ca. 1565(?), Florence, Santo Spirito, Cini Chapel (photo: author)

overpainting, it is still possible to observe that the general proportions of the figure of Jerome, as well as the appearance of the background landscape, do not recall Alessandro's hand. Instead, they appear to be the work of a less accomplished artist. We might consider the possibility that the decorated *paliotto* was installed soon after Girolamo's death in 1565. This may be the likely order of events, since Girolamo's will provided for the celebration of masses for his soul at the chapel, and therefore an altar was essential to the proper function of the chapel. If this altar had been erected soon after his death, it also would have appropriately commemorated the deceased and satisfied his testamentary wishes for an image of a Saint Jerome adoring a crucifix.

The Cini Arms

The textile pattern painted on the *paliotto* has been updated along its upper border at the corners with the coat of arms of a subsequent owner of the chapel, possibly the da Bagnano family, who acquired the former Cini chapel in 1653.[25] This relatively recent coat of arms (a rampant stag or some such similar animal) also appears in the extreme right- and left-hand compartments of the *predella*. These representations, it can be shown, actually replaced the Cini family's coat of arms, which appeared in five places throughout the chapel. There is still one surviving example, a carved stone *stemma* immured above the altarpiece: a divided star, blue on the right half on a gold field, gold on the left half against a blue field.[26] A document relative to the sale of the chapel in 1653 details the locations, media, and sizes of each of the original five exemplars of Cini arms in the chapel, thereby coincidentally proving that not only the *paliotto*, but also the gilded frame of the painting, preserve their original format.[27] As this document reveals, the Cini arms were inserted into two compartments of the *predella*, and an additional two were painted on the border of the *paliotto*. Therefore the da Bagnano arms replaced Cini arms precisely at the positions and in the sizes of the lost originals; only the large, immured stone *stemma* was permitted to remain, most likely for practical considerations.

Since family armorials were an integral part of the gilded frame, this implies that the present disposition of the other compartments is likely original. Hence, the tiny full-length portraits of male and female groups in the two oblong compartments of the *predella* probably replaced original panels with portraits of the members of the Cini family. The subjects of the present panels are most certainly to be identified as portraits of the later owners, the da Bagnano family. This is suggested by the distribution of ages and sexes of the figures depicted in the panels, which could not represent the Cini family. While it is possible that these later *predella* panels were painted by Allori near the end of his career (or by one of his assistants) as has been suggested by one scholar, they were obviously not part of the ensemble as it appeared in 1577.[28]

Anna and the Adulteress

While Saint Jerome still appeared in the chapel, it would seem that Anna had appropriated for her own purposes the altarpiece of the chapel her husband had founded, selecting as its subject the biblical episode of the adulteress, told in the Gospel of John, 8:2–11. While Christ was teaching in the temple at Jerusalem, the Pharisees brought before him an adulteress. Under Mosaic law the punishment for the offense was lapidation, but the Romans had deprived the Jews of the power to impose the death penalty. The Pharisees demanded that Christ pronounce her sentence, hoping he could be tricked into offending either their own or Roman law. Instead, Christ knelt, wrote something in the dust and then said, "He that is without sin among you, let him first cast a stone at her." At this, the woman's accusers slunk away, outfoxed and mortified. Christ pardoned the woman, saying, "Go, and now sin no more."

The subject is highly unusual in Florence; in fact, there are no significant local prototypes for it. However, in northern Italian art, the subject was fairly common. There are sixteenth-century renditions of the theme by Jacopo Bassano in the Museum at Bassano del Grappa, by Lorenzo Lotto in the Louvre, and by Tintoretto in the Palazzo Barberini at Rome.[29] Still, none of these examples is particularly close to Allori's image, for while these paintings stress either Christ's mysterious writing in the dust or the hostility of the crowd, neither of these aspects is emphasized in Allori's painting. Allori did at first toy with the idea of including the common iconographical detail of the mysterious writing, as a figure crouches to the far left in the squared preparatory sketch introduced above (fig. 2). However, in his final solution, the crouching figure that strains to read this writing was eliminated, as were the additional members of the crowd behind the adulterous woman.

Allori's composition is a powerful one. Christ and the adulteress are isolated in the foreground, their hushed confrontation emphasized by the symmetrical placement around a central axis. Their psychological distance is underscored by the *pietra serena* cross in the pavement between their feet. A second Latin cross is formed by the intersection of Christ's right hand with the staff held by an old man, who is perhaps an allusion to the chapel's founder, Girolamo Cini, although this can neither be proved nor denied.[30] In any event, the central zone of the painting is filled with images of crosses and columns in a dogmatic underscoring of the instruments of Christ's Passion, through which humanity receives the promise of salvation. At the left, the adulteress quivers, gathering herself into her garments, hiding her face, and covering her body. In contrast, Christ is an open and inviting figure. He advances in her direction, raising his right hand to engage her attention, his left to beckon her to her newfound faith.[31]

Their actions and attitudes signal the final moment of the biblical account: the woman's shame and repentance as Christ charitably pardons and gives her leave to go. While the sinful woman had been judged and condemned by traditional religious authorities, the painting seems to suggest that the infinite mercy of Christianity had arrived at a different conclusion, pronouncing her worthy of salvation. Such a reading is suggested by an unusual iconographical detail in the painting. Directly above the two protagonists hovers a winged figure, which holds both sword and scales, gazing at the bowed head of the adulteress. This figure is an allegory of Justice: although its sword is poised to fall in horrible judgment, a *putto*, symbol of divine love, intervenes to stay Justice's hand.[32] As in the biblical account on which the painting is based, no man weighs judgment on the adulteress; rather, she is freed to live in peace.

While this outcome is derived from biblical passages, it does not seem to have been the focus of previous visual depictions of the story. The inclusion of an allegory of Justice in a representation of the story of Christ and the adulteress evidently is highly unusual, if not unique. Once again, examination of the preparatory sketches reveals that Allori's first version of the composition for the Cini altarpiece lacked this figure (fig. 3). The second, squared drawing (fig. 2) does contain the flying female personification, which brandishes a sword, but, significantly, no *putto* is present to stop her hand.

In Allori's painting we may have a potential record of sixteenth-century standards of interpretable body language and readable gesture. As previously discussed, the attitude of the adulteress in Allori's painting was seen by at least two sixteenth-century observers as one of shame and repentance. In his account, Borghini repeatedly described the figure as exhibiting remorse for her sin. In one of these descriptive passages, Borghini remarked that he particularly likes the figure of the woman caught in sin, who, "is arranged in such a position that [it] demonstrates shame for her error." [33] A second explicit comment in Francesco Bocchi's *Le bellezze di Fiorenza* of 1591, dwelt upon the face and veil of the adulteress, who is "admirably drawn, so that, while on one side there is a veil that covers her face, which is colored with shame; on the other side, she shyly blushes and shows in the presence of the Savior to have repented of her sin…and discovers her soul, conscience and faith."[34] In one case the author perceived her shame in her position, in the other, it is the manner of the color and shadow cast onto her face by the veil. Both her posture and the use of the veil were calculated to express the shame felt by the woman.

The source for the general outlines of the posture of Allori's *Adulteress* would appear to have been the *Venus pudica*, the so-called modest Venus, which supplied the classical inspiration for figures such as Botticelli's well-known *Birth of Venus* in the Uffizi. Earlier this type had also carried connotations of religious virtue in medieval art, as in its use by Giovanni Pisano on the Pisa pulpit as an allegory of Prudence (or perhaps Chastity or Temperance), as Panofsky believed.[35] Allori was not the only artist to utilize the *Venus pudica* position for the figure of the adulteress. Two notable examples of apparently the same iconographic choice for the figure of the adulteress can be found in prints. The first of these is in a print by Diana Scultori (Diana Mantovana) dated 1575, which she drew after an unknown work by Giulio Romano (fig. 5).[36] In the Scultori print, the adulteress, if reversed, would have been close

Pilliod Fig. 5. Diana Scultori, *Christ and the Adulteress,* 1575, etching (photo: New York Public Library)

indeed to that in Allori's painting. The two images are closely comparable in the manner in which they evoke the confrontation between Christ and the woman; we see a quietly intense meeting of the two, who are isolated at the center of the picture.

The second relevant image is a print by Jan Saenredam after the Dutch master, Hendrick Goltzius. The print was evidently part of a series of Women of the New Testament (fig. 6).[37] Based on drawings by Goltzius, this and other similar prints seem to suggest a fairly widespread currency for this representation of the adulteress.

Borghini's claim that the figure exhibits shame by virtue of her position might possibly be connected with the representation of the adulteress as a *Venus pudica*, graphically indicating the source of the woman's shame—the sexual attractions her body affords to men. This would seem to be suggested by the use of the same iconography by Goltzius for both his adulteress and Susanna images. However, it is not really the towering shame of her past acts, but rather her present penitence and concomitant faith, that are the central ideas of Allori's image.

Pilliod Fig. 6. Jan Saenredam, engraving after Hendrik Goltzius, *The Woman Taken in Adultery*, late sixteenth century (photo: Rijksmuseum, Amsterdam)

Bocchi's description of the crucial role her face and veil played in her characterization as "shameful" and "penitent" may lead to a second reference embedded in the altarpiece's central figure. While rarely employed, one type of allegory of Penitence is apposite to Allori's configuration. Particularly in the northern Italian tradition, Penitence could be shown as a woman in mourning, with her head heavily veiled.[38] The notion of Penitence as a female figure in mourning, swathed in heavy drapery, her head covered, would appear to be descended, even if quite remotely, from Roman funerary representations of women.[39] Clearly the connection between the women depicted on Roman funerary stele, and the personification of Penitence as a veiled woman, is the objectification of sorrow, loss, and regret. In the Roman models, these draped women invariably grasp with one upraised arm the selvage of the veil over her head—just as the adulteress does in Allori's image.[40] This gesture had a sterling pedigree in the classical tradition of connoting a wife or widow. These associations naturally would have been entirely appropriate for a funerary monument and commemorative painting that, in the very arrangement of its main figures, recalls the friezelike compositions of the Roman prototypes, with which Allori was most likely familiar from his various sojourns in Rome.

It would appear that Allori adapted these iconographic types, marrying shame with repentance, and incorporating gestures of modesty that alluded to both sexual shame and uxorial funerarial prototypes. Even the color of her veil, a rich yellow tinged with green, was associated with shame and sin. As Borghini put it, "Whosoever wears yellow courts sin."[41] Still, it is the modest and regretful withdrawal that most strikes the viewer of Allori's altarpiece for the Cini family chapel. Both Borghini and Bocchi understood the content of the image in this way.

While a woman, singled out and characterized as ashamed and penitent, is the main and riveting subject of the painting, it is Christ's (and by implication, divine mercy's) forgiveness that was intended to instruct and comfort the contemporary viewer. The hand of Justice is stopped by an emissary of divine love, a *putto*, as Christ reaches out to the penitent sinner. In fact, even the gestures of Christ might have been calculated to convey explicitly his willingness to take back the sinner, for his right hand, raised, with fingers gently curling downward, is a well-known gesture of welcome or invitation.[42]

Given the strong case presented here for the commissioning of this painting by a woman, Anna Videmon Cini, who very likely suffered the shame of being a mistress and unmarried mother for many years before Girolamo made an "honest woman" out of her, this image of concealed shameful femaleness would indeed have corresponded to a certain sinful period in her own past. In the eyes of community and clerical authority, Anna had succumbed to the temptations aroused by her own body, and sinned by contracting a union that was not sanctioned by the church. Hence she, like the adulteress in the biblical account, had been a victim of her own womanhood and weak will. It does not take a great deal of imagination to conceive of the social ostracism and condemnation that would face a foreign woman in Florence, especially one who had sinned as she had. In fact, it was precisely in these years of Counter-Reformation influence that prostitutes and other women of ill repute were banned from the major churches in Florence—including Santo Spirito.

Anna's selection of the story of the adulteress for the altarpiece in the Cini chapel may have been meant to indicate both the nature of her transgression—which we now are able to recognize with the discovery of documents that supply some details of her life with Girolamo Cini—and her belief in her ultimate salvation. As the adulteress was delivered from condemnation at the hands of an outraged and righteous community by her repentance and faith, so was Anna triumphant over her critics. Indeed, the very act of installing such a picture in one of the most visible sites in Santo Spirito must have constituted a defiant response to the supercilious Florentines.

So the chapel dedicated to the penitent Saint Jerome that Girolamo Cini had intended to erect in Santo Spirito was refashioned after his death by his widow, Anna. It was her choice, a widow's choice, to allude to her own salvation in the stunning altarpiece of the Cini chapel. The image of the adulteress, it appears, was to be identified with the repentant Anna herself—a type of allusion that was fairly common practice near the century's end. While in this painting she is delivered by divine justice from her persecutors, in the *paliotto* below, her husband Girolamo continued to perform the acts of penitence, mortification, and devotion that would someday insure his salvation as well. Anna's revamping of her husband's testamentary wishes is a rare instance of a decidedly nonaristocratic woman's point of view finding lasting representation in a what became a de facto public monument. While one might argue that it was her deceased husband's money that made this monument possible, and that her iconographic choices reflect the sad oppression of a woman by male, civic, and clerical authority, it is the brilliant realization of those social mores and deeply felt religious convictions that marks this painting as a masterpiece; one of both Anna's and Allori's devising.

Notes

This study was first presented at the 1989 Sixteenth Century Studies Conference in Minneapolis, Minnesota; then, in a revised form, it was presented at the 1990 Renaissance Society of America meeting in Toronto, Canada. On both occasions many useful reactions and suggestions were offered. It is hoped that those who were so generous with their wisdom will find their names below. I also thank Eric Apfelstadt, and wish to send acknowledgments to Cristelle Baskins and Patricia Simons—even if I could not do justice to their observations.

1. I leave aside here the question of the collapse of his critical fortunes in the wake of modern art history's negative assessment of late sixteenth-century art in general, and late sixteenth-century Florentine painting (as opposed to drawing) in particular.

2. See Elizabeth Pilliod, "Bronzino's Household," *The Burlington Magazine* 134 (1992): 92–100.

3. For references to the fundamental contributions to Allori studies made by Philip Pouncey, Detlef Heikamp, and other scholars, see the extensive entries in Simona Lecchini Giovannoni's monograph on Alessandro Allori. This study provides for the first time a much needed account of Allori's multifaceted career; Simona Lecchini Giovannoni, *Alessandro Allori* (Turin: U. Allemandi, 1991). Some additional information can be found in Elizabeth Pilliod, review of *Alessandro Allori*, by Simona Lecchini Giovannoni, in *The Burlington Magazine* 134 (1992): 727–29. In the United States Allori's work unfortunately is found in few collections, among them find: A *Portrait of a Lady* in the Isabella Stewart Gardner Museum; *The Penitent Saint Jerome* at the Princeton Museum of Art; a *Madonna and Child* in the Detroit Institute of Art; and the *Allegory of Charity* in the Minneapolis Museum. Two panels are found in southern California, a *Venus Disarming Cupid* in the L. A. County Museum of Art, and *The Rape of Proserpina* in the J. Paul Getty Museum. In Europe, and especially in Florence, the prolific range and richness of Allori's career is visible. His work includes graphic production (of which there are over three hundred sheets in the Uffizi Drawings Cabinet alone), portraits, paintings of mythological and religious subjects, and the remains of his architectural projects.

4. Philip Pouncey, "Drawings by Alessandro Allori for the Montauto Chapel in the SS. Annunziata," *Scritti in onore di Ugo Procacci*, 2 vols. (Milan: Electa, 1977), 2:442, surely intends the reader to consider this work when he lauds the "neoclassical elegance" of Allori's mature style. Lecchini Giovannoni notes that this altarpiece has been the most praised of all Allori's works; Lecchini Giovannoni, *Allori*, 240.

5. See the descriptions in Raffaello Borghini, *Il riposo*, ed. Mario Rosci (Milan: Labor Riproduzione e Documentazione, 1967), 114, 203, 625; Francesco Bocchi, *Le bellezze di Fiorenza* (Florence: 1591), 74. In her monograph, Simona Lecchini Giovannoni suggests that the Cini responsible for this commission was Giovambattista Cini (cat. no. 55, 240–1); however, while the family name was indeed "Cini," this specific identification is incorrect, as we shall see below.

6. Borghini, *Il riposo*, 625 and 203, respectively: "Dove l'adultera dimostrante pentimento del suo fallo" and "Adultera d'Alessandro Allori, tavola dove si veggono molte figure con buona dispositione, e convenevoli attitudini, e bei colori, e particolarmente me piace la femina colta in fallo, la quale oltre all'essere benissimo ornata, è acconcia in tal atto che dimostra vergogna del suo errore." In an additional passage related to the painting, Borghini reiterates this sentiment. "A' me sodisfa molto, soggiunse il Vecchietto, e particolarmente cotesta femina, che dimostra vergogna, e pentimento del fallo commesso" (Borghini, *Il riposo*, 114).

7. Bocchi, *Le bellezze di Fiorenza*, 74: "Ma la donna adultera è stata mirabilmente effigiata, perche mentreche da una parte con un panno si cuopre il viso, che è tinto di vergogna, arrossa nell'altro timorosamente, & mostra alla presenza del Salvatore di haver pentimento di suo fallo."

8. For his birth (27 December 1510) and death (buried in Santo Spirito, 24 May 1565), see ASF,

Tratte 443bis (Approvazione d'età), fol. 25v and 444bis, fol. 37v; and Morti della Grascia 7, fol. 157v. For additional information, see ASF, Carte Sebregondi, "Cini," ins. 4 (which records Girolamo's presence on the Consiglio dei Dugento in 1564, as well as the positions held by his father, Cino, brother, Miniato, and sons, Cino and Pagolo). This Cini family came originally from Gaugalandi.

9. Louis Fournier, *Les florentins en Pologne* (Lyon: Brun, 1893), 265–66.

10. The two testaments, with brief codicils following, are found at ASF, Notarile Antecosimiano R328 (Ser Frosino Ruffoli, Testamenti, 1561–69), fols. 1r–7v (10 May 1561); 102r–7v (23 November 1565).

11. Stadtarchiv, Nuremberg, Lochners Norica Register, 546, with references to the "Sini" family of Florence in 1613, 1625, and 1626. The business partners of the Cini, the Torrigiani family, were also present in Nuremberg. See ibid., under "Torrisani," "Dorisani," and other variants of their name.

12. A copy in Italian of this second testament is found at ASF, Dono Torrigiani appendice, Diplomatico cartaceo a quaderno, 23 November 1565.

13. Or, as this is put in Italian, to "levasse via la machia della illegittimità."

14. The unusual two-door façade of this palazzo is explained by the fact that both Antonio and Luca Torrigiani, brothers, inhabited this palazzo. I am grateful to Brenda Preyer, who kindly directed my attention to this rare feature, and explained that it often was evidence of such a duplex living arrangement. The census description of 1561 for this palace leaves no doubt as to its identity. See ASF, Decima Granducale 3780, nos. 1193–95, with the entry for no. 1194 reading thusly: "Antonio Torrigiani una casa in Via Maggio sul canto della Via del Velluti con dua entrate di più nella detta via...." For the only, partial, publication of the history of this palazzo, see Walther Limburger, *Die Gebäude von Florenz* (Leipzig: F. A. Brockhaus, 1910), 108, no. 446, (Via Maggio 9) which lists the following owners: Velluti, Martellini, Rosselli del Turco.

15. Testament cited at n. 10 above, fol. 1v: "Infra duos annos proxime sub seguentes euis mortem fieri faciant unam tabulam in qua sit pictura Crucifixi et unius Sancti Hieronimi."

16. The sale was mentioned in several books of Santo Spirito. See ASF, Corp. Rel. Soppr. 122, 63, fol. 75r, as having been previously owned by Pier di Cosimo de' Medici, then Francesco Frescobaldi, before its transfer per a contract of 16 January 1566, notarized by Ser Lorenzo di Cristofano di Gregorio Guidi. This contract is preserved in ASF, Notarile antecosimiano G819 (vol. 3, 1564–66), fols. 311r–v. According to the contract, the chapel was purchased from the Opera of Santo Spirito for 300 florins by the guardian and tutor of the heirs, as well as Cino's surviving brother, Miniato. For a record of the payment of 300 florins on 8 January 1566, see ASF, Corp. Rel. Soppr. 122, 128bis, fols. 69r, 72v. According to the latter entry, Luca di Raffaello Torrigiani actually handled the transaction for the heirs of Girolamo Cini. The chapel is invariably described as "dietro il coro," between the chapels of the Bardi and Pitti families.

17. It is also possible that the original idea for the vista of columns was supplied by the Venetian example. See Marcia B. Hall, *Renovation and Counter-Reformation: Vasari and Duke Cosimo in Sta Maria Novella and Sta Croce 1565–1577* (Oxford: Oxford University Press, 1979), 78.

18. These two drawings are, respectively, Uffizi 10332F and Louvre 10111. For these and a third possible related drawing, see Lecchini Giovannoni, *Allori*, figs. 100, 101, and cat. no. 55, 240; Françoise Viatte, *Inventaire général des dessins italiens III, Dessins Toscans XVIe–XVIIIe siècles, I, 1560–1640* (Paris: Editions des Musées Nationaux, 1988), cat. nos. 20, 29–30. The third drawing (Uffizi 14957F), which is close to the painting itself, has been considered both a copy after the picture and a *modello*. See Lecchini Giovanni, *Allori*, 240, in which she suggests this was a presentation piece for the patron that was then adopted after being subjected to a few alterations. All three drawings contain a figure of the young Saint John immediately behind Christ, while in the painting this figure became a much older gentleman. This certainly provides support for Lecchini Giovannoni's suggestion that the third drawing, Uffizi 14957F, is indeed by Allori (and not a copy

after the painting). This also raises the question of why this alteration was made, and perhaps suggests reading an allusion to Girolamo Cini himself in the old man.

19. The two-line inscription appears on the lowest riser, immediately to the left of Christ's robe: ALEX•ALL•C•FLO•FAC/A•D•M•D•LXXVII•

20. For this painting, see Hall, *Renovation and Counter-Reformation*, 117–18, plate 90.

21. The tutors and guardians were stipulated in the two testaments and can be seen acting for Girolamo's heirs, as for instance, in the transfer of the palazzo from the Torrigiani to the Cini heirs, and in the purchase document for the site of the chapel.

22. ASF, Morti della Grascia 7, fol. 257r. Miniato's burial place, presumably in the pavement of the chapel, was marked with his name, see ASF, MS 624 (Sepoltuario di Stefano Rosselli), 17, no. 22. No sign of this marker survives.

23. In ASF, Corp. Rel. Soppr. 122, 36 (Memoriale F), fol. 26v, one finds that while Anna promised monies for the recitation of masses at the chapel, she apparently failed to make good on her promises.

24. The Cini *paliotto* is identical in dimensions to the other original *paliotti* that remain in the church. For a discussion that touches upon this, see Alison Luchs, "Stained Glass above Renaissance Altars: Figural Windows in Italian Church Architecture from Brunelleschi to Bramante," *Zeitschrift für Kunstgeschichte* 48 (1985): 177–224.

25. For the replacement of these arms, see ASF, MS 624, c. 17, no. 22: "Cappella della famiglia di Cini....Questa cappella questo present'anno 1653 è stato da' Padroni venduta a Giovanni e Francesco de' Dainelli da Bagnano, che 'anno levate l'arme antica e messavi la loro, per prezzo di scudi 200."

26. The Cini arms are illustrated in ASF, MS 624, c. 15, no. 5, where they are described as "stella azzurra a man destra in campo d'oro, et a man sinistra d'oro in campo azzurro."

27. ASF, Capitani di Parte Guelfa, numeri neri 823, no. 149. This preserves the request of the Cini heirs, pursuant to the sale of the chapel in 1653, for permission from the grand duke to remove their coats of arms from the chapel. The relevant description is as follows: "Che detta cappella è posta dietro al Coro di S. Spirito e che il suo titolo è la cappella dell'Adultera de' Cini, come si legge del Libro della Sagrestia di detta chiesa. Detta cappella ha l'ornamento di legname d'orato e la tavola dell' Adultera si dice parere mano del Bronzino Vecchio. Sono in detta Cappella cinque arme: una di pietra grande b. 1 ½ circa, e l'altre quattro di legname intagliato e colorito grande circa ¾, a parte nel cornicione di detta Cappella, e l'altre due arme sono dipinte nel fregio sotta la tavola." In a letter appended to this report, a clearer description records, "Questa cappella è di legno dorato, con tavola dell'Adultera, pare a noi sia di mano del Bronzino Vecchio. Si veggono cinque armi di detta familiglia con la dicontro impresa [colored drawing in left margin], delle quali una è di pietra colorita e dorata, et è murata sopra la finestra di detta cappella et sarà grande circa a braccia 1 ½. Le altre quattro—due son di legname intagliato, dorato e colorito, e son grandi circa a ¾, e son posti nel cornicione dorato di detta cappella; e le altre due son di pittura e son nel fregio sotta la tavola, son grande circa a ½ braccia. Inscrizione non ve ne sono alcuna." Evidently, the two Cini arms in the frame were carved and gilded (these are now replaced with painted arms); those on the border of the *paliotto* were only painted (as are the present overpainted ones). The sizes given in this document compare closely with those of the present replacement arms.

28. Lecchini Giovannoni, *Allori*, 240, tentatively advances the name of Allori's assistant, Alessandro Pieroni, as the executant of these diminutive family portraits. Finally, no mention is made in any source of either the small compartment at the center of the *predella*, which now contains a painting of the Crucifixion, or the two subsidiary panels below the *predella* and behind the *paliotto*. In the first case, we must assume that the Crucifixion is either original or a replacement for something of precisely the same dimensions. The compartment itself is integral to the frame, and is identical in size to the two flanking compartments that hold the coats of arms. As to the possible

date of the *Crucifixion*, I am unable to make a conclusive determination; the extremely dark panel could be Allori's work. In the second case, that of the two standing figures with inscriptions painted over gold leaf at either side of the *paliotto,* I suspect we are confronted with a later-sixteenth or early- seventeenth-century addition. On the left is a figure representing Charity, with the inscription: CELI ET TERRAE PLENITUDO, a quotation derived from the Sanctus of the Mass. I am grateful to Peter Howard for searching out the source of this quotation. The second figure, a female who holds a flagellum, is paired with the inscription: SECUNDA POST NAVERAGIUM TABULA, a reference to a means of deliverance, as a *tabula ex naufragio* is a plank on which a shipwrecked person saves himself. In this context, the inscription refers to the second chance given to sinners. Regarding the restoration of the fallen in the decrees on Justification of the Council of Trent, see H. J. Schroeder, *Canons and Decrees of the Council of Trent* (St. Louis: B. Herder, 1941), 39.

29. An excellent review of the theme is found in *Reallexikon zur Deutschen Kunstgeschichte,* ed. Otto Schmidt (Stuttgart: Alfred Druckenmüller Verlag, 1958), 4: 791–803.

30. Evidently Allori had some clear purpose in mind in including the old man, for in both preparatory sketches (figs. 2, 3), as well as the possible presentation drawing for the patron (see n. 18 above), this figure was a young Saint John. In the final presentation drawing, the old man made his first appearance, but as a secondary figure tucked behind the young saint. In the painting, the young saint has vanished entirely, and was replaced by the old man. This change of character, as well as the rather obvious importance of the old man's gesture, subtly alters the conception of the scene, possibly providing a role for the deceased Girolamo Cini within the biblical episode of Christ with the woman.

31. Although I have modified his idea somewhat, I am indebted to George Gorse for making the fascinating suggestion that Christ's gestures may have been derived from those of the famous equestrian sculpture known as the Marcus Aurelius, in which the upper hand signifies address, the lower clemency and mercy towards the captured prisoners of war. See below.

32. I thank Richard Betts for bringing this detail and its potential meaning to my attention.

33. Borghini, *Il riposo*, 203, "È acconcia in tal atto che dimostra vergogna del suo errore." Also compare, ibid., 114, "Cotesta femina, che dimostra vergogna, e pentimento del fallo commesso," (that woman who demonstrates shame and repentance for the error [she] committed); and ibid., 625, "L'adultera dimostrante pentimento del suo fallo," (the adulteress demonstrating repentance for her sin).

34. Bocchi, *Le bellezze di Fiorenza*, 74, "Ma la donna adultera è stata mirabilmente effigiata, perche mentreche da una parte con un panno si cuopre il viso, che è tinto di vergogna, arrossa nell'altro timorosamente, & mostra alla presenza del Salvatore di haver pentimento di suo fallo."

35. Erwin Panofsky, *Studies in Iconography: Humanistic Themes in the Art of the Renaissance* (1939; reprint, Boulder, Colo.: Westview Press, 1972), 157. See also John Pope-Hennessy, *Italian Gothic Sculpture*, 2nd ed. (London: Phaidon, 1972), 175–76; Enzo Carli, *Giovanni Pisano* (Pisa: Pacini, 1977), 113.

36. *Christ and the Woman Taken in Adultery*, 1631. New York Public Library Collection. 22 ½ x 16 ½ in. I wish to express my gratitude to Roberta Waddell for her willing assistance in obtaining this material. Stefania Massari sets forth the history of this image and its six known states in Stefania Massari, *Incisori Mantovani del '500: Giovan Battista, Adamo, Diana Scultori e Giorgio Ghisi dalle collezioni del Gabinetto Nazionale delle Stampe e della Calcografia Nazionale,* exh. cat. (Rome: Istituto Nazionale per la Grafica-Calcografia, 1981), cat. nos. 97–98, 150. Massari considers the original of 1575 to be derived from an unknown or lost Guilio Romano image from ca. 1532–35.

37. The date of the original drawings and prints has not been established. See Walter L. Strauss, ed., *The Illustrated Bartsch, Netherlandish Artists: Matham, Saenredam, Muller* (New York: Abaris Books, 1980), 4: 363, no. 47 (237). For the related images, see Caterina Limentani Virdis, Davide Banzato, and Cinzia Butelli, *Da Bruegel a Goltzius: Specchio dell'antico e del nuovo mondo. Incisioni*

fiamminghe e olandesi della seconda metà del Cinquecento dei Civici Musei di Padova (Milan: Electa, 1994), 106–11, which discusses the Old Testament images of Judith, Deborah, and Susanna. The Susanna for the series was also in the *venus pudica* position. For the New Testament scenes, see *Hollstein's Dutch and Flemish Etchings, Engravings, and Woodcuts ca. 1450–1700*, vol. 23 (Amsterdam: M. Hertzberger, 1980), 33–36, nos. 35–40.

38. Rudolf Wittkower first observed this in relation to a painting by Girolamo da Carpi; Rudolf Wittkower, "Patience and Chance: The Story of a Political Emblem," *Journal of the Warburg and Courtauld Institutes* 1 (1937–38): 173–74. See also *Nell'età di Correggio e dei Carracci, pittura in Emilia dei secoli XVI e XVII*, exh. cat. (Bologna: Pinacoteca Nazionale, 1986), 88–89, cat. no. 23. Wittkower identifies this type as well in a print by Girolamo Mocetto after Andrea Mantegna. See *Illustrated Bartsch: Early Italian Masters*, 25 (New York: Abaris Books, 1984), 62, no. 2505.

39. For a standard example, see Guntram Koch, *Roman Funerary Sculpture, Catalogue of the Collections* (Malibu: J. Paul Getty Museum, 1988), 92–94, cat. no. 33. See Leo Steinberg, "Michelangelo's Florentine *Pietà*: The Missing Leg Twenty Years Later," *Art Bulletin* 71 (1989): 490, for the formulation of the general type and a brief survey of its influence upon Renaissance art.

40. Allori seems to have selected a specific subset from the general type of the velation motif. One might observe that in a significant group of funerary reliefs from Byzantine sites, as one arm crosses the woman's body and holds the edge of the veil, her other arm crosses the body at the waist in a line exactly parallel to the upper arm, thus creating the effect of a *venus pudica*. See Ernst Pfuhl and Hans Möbius, *Die Ostgriechischen Grabreliefs, Textband*, vol. 2 (Mainz am Rhein: Van Zabern, 1977), nos. 1728–1736; *Tafelband* 1, nos. 165 and 507.

41. See Borghini, *Il riposo*, 240, "chi porta il giallo vaghegheggia in fallo," which seems to indicate a yellow mixed with green; also ibid., 232. See also Mary Pardo, "The Subject of Savoldo's *Magdalene*," *Art Bulletin* 71 (1989), 71. While yellow was associated with Jews, for two reasons it seems unlikely that Anna was Jewish: her parent's goodness and honesty are repeatedly affirmed in Girolamo's testament; and one of her sons entered the priesthood at Santo Spirito. I wish to thank Barbara Wisch and Catherine Sousloff for alerting me to this possibility.

42. Michael Baxandall, *Painting and Experience in Fifteenth-Century Italy* (Oxford: Oxford University Press, 1972), 67–68, identifies the gesture in relation to Italian Renaissance art. It should be noted that this may be a survival from classical usage, as the gesture Baxandall describes seems to have been derived from the *adventus* gesture of Roman imperial usage, as it bore connotations of "expressed speech, benevolence, and/or greeting." For this, see Richard Brilliant, "Gesture and Rank in Roman Art: The Use of Gestures to Denote Status in Roman Sculpture and Coinage," in *Memoirs of the Connecticut Academy of Arts & Sciences* 14 (1963): 174–76.

Matrons and Motives:
Why Women Built in Early Modern Rome

Carolyn Valone

Giorgio Vasari, in the first edition of *The Lives of the Artists*, includes the biography of only one woman, the Bolognese sculptor Properzia de'Rossi; in effect, she stood for all women artists.[1] Until recently art historians dealing with art patronage in Renaissance Italy have done much the same with Isabella d'Este—they let her stand for all secular women patrons. Happily, this collection of essays and other works in the past ten years demonstrate that it is possible to go "beyond Isabella." If we wish to reconstruct the role played by women patrons in early modern Italy, we must go beyond female tokenism which relegates women patrons to the category of "exceptions" when compared to that historical myth, the "Renaissance Man."

The necessity of reintegrating women patrons into their historical context is particularly important in the area of architecture—that most expensive and visible form of art.[2] The commissioning of a work of architecture is an extremely public act because buildings mold both the physical and cultural environment of a given place. Architectural patronage is an outward expression of ideas, motives, taste, wealth, and status; it is a means of constructing the patron's public persona.

Secular women from antiquity to the early modern period *had* no public persona, if we are to believe philosophers, writers, jurists, statesmen, and clerics from Aristotle to Alberti.[3] The realm of women was the private household, and their role was to serve their husbands and families with obedience and modesty. Nonetheless, running parallel to this male notion of a woman's place was another tradition: that of matron as patron of public architecture. From the Hellenistic world to early modern Italy, women built. They used their own money to commission civic and religious buildings which functioned in the public realm, giving them a public voice, which was recorded by their contemporaries and "heard" by other women in later periods who modeled their own patronage on the matrons of the past.[4] It is only in the modern period that this tradition has been largely overlooked by historians.

To some extent, the neglect of female patrons can be linked to the mistaken assumption that secular women rarely had the economic or legal autonomy necessary for architectural patronage. That approach makes each female patron an exception who, through strength of character or otherwise, managed to overcome the patriarchal system set against her. This image of matron as heroine is appealing, and not altogether false, but it obscures the richness of the tradition of female patronage and prevents us from reintegrating a wide range of women into the historical narrative. It also perpetuates another stereotype: the woman as victim of the male figure—her father or her husband—who controlled her access to her wealth. To be sure, women did have to work within a patriarchal system that denied them equal economic rights. However, few legal codes from antiquity to the seventeenth century completely excluded women from inheritance, not because of any generosity towards women, but because men could imagine situations in which their own ends could best be served by assuring some economic rights for women. This legal stance is particularly prevalent in societies where strong family networks depended on alliances formed through arranged marriages. The purpose of such marriages, after all, was to benefit *both* families, and the law had to protect the wealth of both parties. The rights of the wife (or widow) with regard to inheritance and dowry had to be guarded, if only because the men in her family demanded it.[5] Thus, any search for female patrons must avoid generalities and concentrate on reconstructing the legal and economic options available to women in a given time and place. If possible, that information should be based on actual usage, not on male rhetoric or even the letter of the law.[6] We need to discover what women did, not what men said.

In her important essay, "Women and Wealth," Riet Van Bremen has shown that women in the Hellenistic-Roman world could enter traditionally male spheres of public life because of their new access to wealth.[7] The main source of wealth in the ancient world was land; the urban elite of Asia Minor and imperial Rome depended on their vast estates to finance their status in cities. If a woman could inherit, buy, and sell land, generally she could also administer it, either with or without a male "guardian" whose signature became mostly a formality by late Hellenistic and late Republican times.[8] I would submit that land-based economies were generally more favorable to wealthy women than economies based on commerce; women might not be able to compete in the marketplace, but often they could control land. Land equaled wealth, and wealth often led to patronage, whether we are looking at the urban centers of antiquity and early modern Italy or at the feudal society of the Middle Ages.

What motivated women to build? At one level all patrons are persuaded to spend their money because of a particular personal set of circumstances. Nonetheless, there are certain reoccurring patterns in patronage, and I believe that the architectural patronage of women from the Hellenistic era to early modern Italy often falls into one of the following three categories: commemorative structures such as tombs or family chapels; religious complexes such as temples, churches, convents, monasteries, and novitiates; buildings related to the social good or social welfare such as aqueducts, hospitals, orphanages, and schools.

These categories are not exclusive to women alone, nor are they the only categories within which women worked; they should be used only as indicators of areas where research on women patrons has a high probability of success. For more than two thousand years women were motivated to use architecture as their public voice to speak about the family, the life of the spirit, and social needs.

Ancient Models

Before turning to the focus of this paper—that is, women patrons in early modern Rome—let me illustrate the tradition of matron as patron with some examples from the ancient world, from the fourth century B.C.E. to the fifth century C.E. In the humanist tradition the archetypal female patron was probably Dido: "She had a marvelously beautiful, large, and strong city constructed which she named Carthage; she called the tower and citadel 'Byrsa,' which means cowhide," wrote Christine de Pizan in *The Book of the City of Ladies*.[9] Christine's allegorical city, like Dido's, was "strongly constructed and well founded," built with "durable and pure mortar to lay the sturdy foundations and to raise the lofty walls all around, high and thick, with mighty towers and strong bastions, surrounded by moats with firm blockhouses, just as is fitting for a city with a strong and lasting defense." Lady Rectitude advised Christine, giving her a symbolic instrument to aid in constructing the buildings: "All these are measured by this ruler," she says, in this city "which you have been commissioned to build, and you will need it for constructing the facade, for erecting the high temples, for measuring the palaces,

houses, and all public buildings, the streets and squares, and all things proper to help popu-
late the city."[10] The *City of Ladies* may be allegorical, and Dido's Carthage may be mythical,
but the language about their construction is firmly based on architectural practice, and presumably Christine believed her female readers could appreciate this.

Dido's fame as a builder was still alive in the seventeenth century, when a tapestry
cartoon done for the Barberini by Giovanni Francesco Romanelli again presented her as a
knowledgeable patron, explaining the architect's plan to Aeneas, while the actual business of
construction goes on around her (fig. 1). Of course, few women expected to build on the scale
of Dido, although Zenobia, Queen of Palmyra, invoked her as a role model, and built the
fortress of Zenobia on the west bank of the Euphrates when she consolidated her border
defenses in the third century C.E.[11] Other women pursued more modest goals related to
memory, religion, and social welfare.

The desire to commemorate is best exemplified in antiquity by Queen Artemisia,
whom Pliny credited with the patronage of her husband's great mausoleum at Halikarnassos.
If modern historians have sought to downgrade her patronage to the role of collaborator with
her husband, Mausolus, Christine de Pizan had no doubt that it was Artemisia alone who,
prompted by wifely love, "wished to build a sepulcher to her husband's memory to serve
forever as his memorial."[12] The Artemisia tradition is marvelously depicted in Simon Vouet's
mid-seventeenth-century painting (fig. 2). He captures her swooning grief as well as the close
attention she pays to the plan being presented by the architect, whose ruler and compass will
bring "measure" to her building, as it had to Christine's *City of Ladies*.

More ordinary women also engaged in commemoration and left tangible proof of
their actions. An extant imperial Rome inscription reveals that a "most unhappy mother,"
Marcia Doris, "put up this monument to her best and most devoted daughter, and for herself,
and for her descendants."[13] Eumachia in first-century Pompeii built a tomb outside the city

Valone Fig. 1. Giovanni Francesco Romanelli, *Dido Showing Aeneas Her Plans for Carthage,*
Barberini cartoon, ca. 1630–35, Pasadena, Norton Simon Museum (photo: The Norton Simon
Foundation, Pasadena, Calif.)

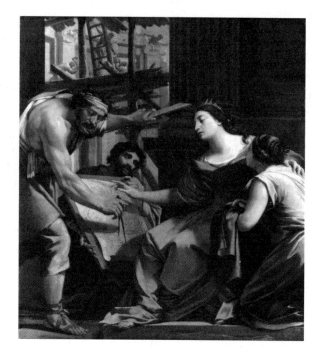

Valone Fig. 2. Simon Vouet, *Artemisia Building the Mausoleum*, ca. 1643, Stockholm, Nationalmuseum (photo: Statens Konstmuseer)

with the following inscription: "Eumachia, daughter of Lucius, built this for herself and for her household."[14] In the second century Caelia Macrina of Tarracina, in memory of her son, ordered in her will that 300,000 sesterces be spent for a building, plus 1,000,000 sesterces be set aside for an endowed alimentary fund to feed annually two hundred deserving boys and girls.[15] We could also place her patronage in the social welfare category.

Religious buildings were also popular among women patrons in antiquity. The Arsinoeion on Samothrace, one of the largest round buildings in the Greek world, was dedicated "to the Great Gods" by Queen Arsinoe II early in the third century B.C.E.[16] Queen Apollonis, wife of Attalos I (who reigned 247–197 B.C.E.), built "at her own expense" the urban sanctuary of Demeter at Pergamon, together with its propylon and stoas.[17] Less exalted patrons are also recorded, such as Euxenia who, according to a second-century B.C.E. inscription from Megalopolis, was remembered for "a sturdy wall around the temple she built for the goddess (Aphrodite), and a house for public guests,"[18] and Epie of Thassos who was honored because she had repaired many temples in her city, particularly the Artemision.[19] One of the greatest patrons among the Roman empresses was the Syrian princess Julia Domna, wife of Septimius Severus. Her buildings extended across the empire and in the Roman Forum she renewed the Temple of the Vestals.[20] Female imperial patronage was continued in the Christian era by Galla Placidia, who restored San Paolo fuori le Mura and Santa Croce in Gerusalemme in Rome, and built San Giovanni Evangelista in Ravenna.[21] Other Theodosian empresses continued the tradition.[22] Numerous Hebrew women in late antiquity also engaged in religious patronage, such as Tation, who, with her own funds, donated a synagogue in Phocaea, Ionia, in the third century C.E.[23]

Under the category of social welfare we can include, in addition to Caelia Macrina mentioned above, Phile of Priene, daughter of Apollonius, wife of Thessalus, who, in the first century B.C.E., dedicated "at her own expense" a cistern and water pipes for her city,[24] and Modia Quinta, who not only adorned a portico with marble paving, coffered ceilings and columns, but also built an aqueduct.[25] Not easily categorized is the munificent patronage of Eumachia who "in her own name and that of her son...built with her own funds" the fine headquarters of the Fullers Guild which faces on to the forum in Pompeii.[26]

Whether we are looking at queens or commoners in antiquity, the oft-repeated assertion found in the inscriptions that women used their own funds to build tells us that women had wealth and that society accepted their role as public patrons. The proof of their patronage is, of course, fragmentary, but the same is true for men. Furthermore, we must guard against the unspoken assumption that buildings with no known patron were paid for by men.

Early Modern Rome

It is the example of aristocratic Christian matrons of late fourth-century Rome that provides the most forceful patronage model for the women of early modern Rome.[27] The Early Christian matrons, particularly Paola and Marcella and the other women who supported the radical religious reforms of Saint Jerome, were well known in Renaissance Rome. This fame is due to the letters of Jerome and to the Early Christian revival which was the basis of Catholic reform in Rome after the Council of Trent, particularly in the circle of Saint Philip Neri and the Oratorians. Jerome's letters praised not only the piety and learning of his female friends, but also the architectural patronage of these women who had sponsored the building of churches, monasteries, and hospitals. The matrons of sixteenth-century Rome imitated Jerome's women, and their contemporaries hailed them as new Paolas and Marcellas, "treading in their steppes, esteeming the service of God above al their temporalities," as Gregory Martin wrote in the late sixteenth century.[28]

The architectural patronage of women in early modern Rome generally was in the service of the Roman Catholic Church, but the matrons did not passively turn their money over to that institution, as we shall see. They continued the tradition of using their own money to build within those suitable categories of commemoration, religion, and social welfare, but they also managed to speak about their own personal motives via the public medium of architecture.

Commemoration

The role of the perfect Christian widow, according to the late sixteenth-century reform bishop of Verona, Agostino Valier, was to serve God completely, once she was freed from the chains of matrimony.[29] This newfound independence would allow her to devote her whole being to contemplating God's goodness and to commemorating His great beneficence towards the human race. One of the chief virtues of the devout widow, he writes, is "la memoria."[30] She should also visit often the tomb of her husband to honor his memory, to pray for his soul (for who knows better his defects? Valier asks), and to remind herself that she too will soon face death. Her love for her husband will be shown by her constant prayers and offerings for masses and offices, and her duty is to remind her children of their obligations to keep alive their father's memory.[31]

Widows in Renaissance Rome were well aware of their duty to commemorate their husbands. Although this duty no doubt motivated them to buy and decorate family chapels, they often did not hesitate to put their own wishes above their husbands' instructions, as two examples from the Franciscan church of Santa Maria in Aracoeli illustrate.[32]

Livia Muti in 1572 commissioned the Chapel of the Transfiguration in memory of her husband, Tomaso Armentieri.[33] In his will of 1565, he had asked to be buried in any one of four churches: three in Rome, one in Piacenza. Livia was unable to obtain space in the Roman churches and she rejected Piacenza because it was too far from Rome; instead she

Valone Fig. 3. Portrait bust of Vittoria della Tolfa, ca. 1585, Rome, Santa Maria in Aracoeli, Chapel of the Ascension (photo: Giandean)

chose to spend 1,400 scudi for a chapel in the Aracoeli. Her choice of this site, close to her palace at the foot of the Capitoline Hill, may have been motivated by wifely devotion or by her desire to make a statement in one of the most visible and frequented Roman churches.

Marchesa Vittoria della Tolfa (fig. 3) was also willing to commemorate her husband, Camillo Pardo Orsini, but again on her own terms. In 1553 her husband died, leaving her a wealthy, childless widow. In his will he left 17,000 scudi to build a grand chapel for himself at Saint John Lateran and to maintain ten chaplains to carry out services there. Vittoria, whose uncle became Pope Paul IV in 1555, chose to ignore Camillo's instructions and instead used the money for quite a different pious work—the founding of a convent and church dedicated to the Annunciation for Franciscan nuns. The convent was to be located on property which she had inherited from her uncle and husband, near the obelisk of San Macuto beyond the Pantheon. Her desire to provide for

Franciscan nuns did not mean she intended to dishonor her husband; in her own will of 1578 she designated 2,000 scudi for a chapel dedicated to the Ascension in the Aracoeli where she and her husband were both to be buried in tombs marked by fine portrait busts (fig. 3). She apparently cared deeply about this location; she literally had to steal half of the large della Valle chapel for her chapel because no other space was available in the Aracoeli.[34] Like Livia Muti, Vittoria preferred to commemorate her husband in the venerable and highly visible Marian church on the Capitoline Hill. She clearly announced her patronage of the chapel with a display of her own coat of arms (fig. 4), an impaled coat of arms, or *scudo accollato*, which shows her father's *stemma* on the left

Valone Fig. 4. Coat of arms of Vittoria della Tolfa, ca. 1585, Rome, Santa Maria in Aracoeli, Chapel of the Ascension (photo: Giandean)

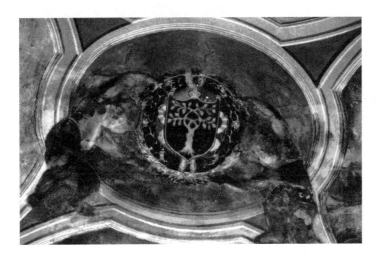

Valone Fig. 5. Coat of arms of Lucrezia della Rovere, ca. 1550, Rome, Trinità dei Monti, Chapel of the Assumption (photo: Cynthia Stollhans)

(sinister) and her husband's on the right (dexter). This does not mean they shared in the patronage; it signifies only that she was the patron. The impaled coat of arms indicates the status of a married woman. It may also be a reminder that Vittoria's husband had lost his own land near Naples due to unwise political choices, and most of his wealth came from her dowry and inheritance.[35]

Some women preferred to pay for burial chapels that did not include their husbands. For example, Lucrezia della Rovere, the niece of Pope Julius II and wife of Marc'Antonio Colonna I, commissioned Daniele da Volterra to decorate a chapel in Trinità dei Monti at midcentury which would house her tomb but not her husband's.[36] In an unprecedented gesture, Lucrezia signified her patronage by using only the della Rovere coat of arms of her maternal lineage (her father had adopted the della Rovere name) on both the floor and the vault of her chapel (fig. 5). This was probably less a statement about her view of her husband than a complaint about her strained economic relations with the Colonna family, which was trying to cheat one of her daughters out of her rightful dowry.[37] Her Colonna marriage *was* acknowledged by the impaled coat of arms on her tomb and perhaps by the Ionic columns that frame the fresco of the Assumption on the main chapel wall (fig. 6), but the marble intarsia della Rovere coat of arms in the floor and the painted stucco *stemma* in the center of the vault clearly tell the sixteenth-century viewer that the chapel was built by Lucrezia, with no help from the Colonna.[38]

Valone Fig. 6. Daniele da Volterra, *Assumption of the Virgin*, ca. 1550, Rome, Trinità dei Monti, Chapel of the Assumption (photo: ICCD, Rome, G46600)

Caterina de'Nobili Sforza combined both commemorative and religious motives (see below) in her munificent patronage of the church and monastery of San Bernardo alle Terme, dedicated in 1600 (fig. 7).[39] The domed interior of the church recalls the Pantheon, and one function of the church was to serve as a pantheon for the de'Nobili family. The sculptural program and five of the six commemorative Latin inscriptions that encircle the church pay homage to Caterina's relatives: her mother, Maddalena, her grandmother Lodovica del Monte, her great uncle Pope Julius III, her father, Vincenzo, her brother Cardinal Roberto, and her son Cardinal Francesco. Her husband, who died in 1575, is commemorated in a single Latin inscription, but he is buried far from Rome in his feudal holding of Castellarquato, near Parma, where Caterina had commissioned a monument to him in 1576. In the inscribed tablet over the main portal of San Bernardo (fig. 8), Caterina identified herself as the wife of Sforza, Count of Santa Fiore, and mother of Cardinal Francesco and of the duchess of Sora, Costanza. After her husband's death, Caterina had been extremely successful in arranging for her children's futures: Francesco was made a cardinal at age twenty-one in 1583 and Costanza was married to the nephew of Pope Gregory XIII. Her daughter also aided her at San Bernardo by endowing one of the side chapels in the church. Caterina's intent at San Bernardo was to glorify her de'Nobili lineage, not her husband's.

The expected duty of women to commemorate their husbands produced a good deal of architectural patronage, but as these few examples have shown, women in early modern Rome were adept at grafting their own more personal motives on to the general one of commemoration. These matrons chose to say things about "family" which Bishop Agostino Valier may not have anticipated.

Valone Fig. 7. San Bernardo alle Terme, Rome, interior, right side, 1595–1600
(photo: ICCD, Rome, G20952)

Valone Fig. 8. San Bernardo alle Terme, Rome, portal inscription, 1600 (photo: Cynthia Stollhans)

Religion

Like the ancient and Early Christian women discussed above, Renaissance women dedicated much of their patronage to the service of religion. Out of dozens of examples, I have chosen a sample of eleven buildings commissioned between 1560 and 1600 to give some insight into why women built. The motive that unites all these women was the desire to support radical religious reform in Rome in the years following the Council of Trent. Women chose to patronize those religious groups that were newly founded or newly reformed in the sixteenth century; of the eleven examples, four were built for men and seven for women, indicating that reform, rather than gender, was the paramount issue.

The Jesuits, from their inception in 1540, were leaders in reform, and three noble-women provided them with some of their most essential spaces in Rome.[40] Marchesa Vittoria della Tolfa, whom we have already met (fig. 3), was persuaded by the Jesuits to transfer her patronage from Franciscan nuns to their own order, and in 1560 the Marchesa founded the first permanent seat of the Collegio Romano on her property near the obelisk of San Macuto after the nuns had been transferred elsewhere. Six years later Giovanna d'Aragona, the duchess of Tagliacozzo and wife of Ascanio Colonna, provided the Jesuits with their first perma-nent Roman novitiate, Sant'Andrea al Quirinale, by giving them land on the Quirinal Hill and an endowment of 6,000 scudi, which also allowed them to build a new and larger church of Sant'Andrea. Although the church has been replaced by Bernini's later one, we know a good deal about it thanks to the description and engravings published in 1611 by the Jesuit Louis Richeôme.[41] He commented at length on Durante Alberti's altarpiece, *Crucifixion of Saint Andrew*, which he reproduced (fig. 9), and particularly on the woman shown kneeling at the foot of Andrew's cross. She is Maximilla, a Christian noblewoman who arranged for the burial of Saint Andrew in spite of the fact that her husband was the Roman proconsul who had ordered Andrew's crucifixion. Her prominent role may well be a reference to the long tradi-tion of Christian women and their courage to support "radical" religion, a tradition in which Giovanna d'Aragona participated by her patronage of the early Jesuits.

LE MARTYRE DE SAINCT ANDRE.

Valone Fig. 9. *Crucifixion of Saint Andrew,* from Louis Richeôme, *Le peinture spirituelle,* 1611 (photo: by permission of the Folger Shakespeare Library)

Although both Giovanna d'Aragona and Vittoria della Tolfa were dedicated believers in the new Jesuit ideals, they were not passive patrons. When the Jesuits refused to allow Giovanna access to Sant'Andrea to hear mass with the novices, she retaliated by leaving the rest of her property on the Quirinal Hill to the Capuchin Poor Clares (see below), and when the Marchesa della Tolfa felt that the Jesuits were failing to give proper respect to her and her husband when the new Collegio Romano was built by Gregory XIII, she showed her dissatisfaction by complaining bitterly to the pope and by cutting the Jesuits out of her will.

The third woman, Isabella della Rovere, wife of Bernardino Sanseverino of Bisignano, rescued the Jesuits some thirty years later when they had outgrown their original novitiate built by Giovanna. In 1598 Isabella became the second *fondatrice* of the combined novitiate of Sant'Andrea and San Vitale (located behind Sant'Andrea on the slope of the Quirinal Hill) by giving the Jesuits the extraordinary sum of 90,000 scudi realized by the sale of her jewels. Thanks to her, the Early Christian titulus of San Vitale was completely restored and embellished with frescoes and fine altarpieces (fig. 10), and the Jesuits were quick to point out the parallel between Isabella and the first builder of San Vitale, an Early Christian matron named Vestina, who sold her jewels to build the church.[42] Isabella's patronage takes on added meaning when we consider that her munificent gift was given while her husband was languishing in debtor's prison in Naples; her actions reveal that her jewels were part of her della Rovere extra-dotal inheritance and thus could not be touched by her husband's creditors.[43]

Valone Fig. 10. San Vitale, Rome, interior, ca. 1605 (photo: ICCD, Rome, E21219)

The austere return to the true rule of Saint Francis is the hallmark of Capuchin spirituality in the sixteenth century and women were the first protectors of the Franciscan rebels who found their order too lax.[44] Caterina Cibo, the Duchess of Camerino, Vittoria Colonna, and her sister-in-law Giovanna d'Aragona were among the first to support the followers of Fra Matteo da Bascio in the 1520s and 30s; they were called "mothers" of the new order by the friars.[45] In 1536 the two Colonna women provided the Capuchins with the church of San Nicola de'Portiis (later San Bonaventura), located at the edge of the Colonna garden, and in 1575 Giovanna became the patron of the female branch, the Capuchin Poor Clares. She built their first church and convent in Rome, Santa Chiara on the Quirinal Hill, and furnished the carriage which brought the first four nuns from the Mother House in Naples to Rome.[46] Twenty-five years later another woman, Fulvia Conti Sforza (the sister-in-law of Caterina de'Nobili Sforza) provided the second house for the Capuchin Poor Clares in Rome by rebuilding the derelict church of Sant'Urbano, located in front of the Forum of Augustus.[47] Fulvia was a great heiress, inheriting all her father's wealth and outliving both her husband and her only son. She was a benefactor of the Oratorians, another radical group, and built Sant'Urbano with the help of Cesare Baronio, the great Oratorian historian. She also joined forces with another Oratorian, the musician Francesco del Soto, to found the first house in Rome for Carmelite nuns following the reforms of Saint Theresa of Avila.[48]

The strict reform and enclosure of Dominican nuns in the second half of the sixteenth century was a catalyst for three pious widows who used their own money to build Dominican convents. The widows also chose the peace of the cloister for their own lives. Portia Massimi Salviati was twenty-two years old when her husband died in 1562, but she rejected a second marriage and took her dowry of 15,000 scudi into the Dominican convent of Santa Lucia in Florence. In 1572 she returned to her home town of Rome to establish the new convent of Santa Caterina a Magnanapoli, "at her own expense," according to her contemporary, Antonio Gallonio, an Oratorian historian.[49] In 1581 Maddalena Orsini followed her example by building a second Dominican convent on the Quirinal, Santa Maria Maddalena.[50] Maddalena, also a young widow, had to engage in a bitter legal battle with her family to gain control of her inheritance of 50,000 scudi left by her husband, Lelio Orsini. She finally settled for 20,000 scudi which she took with her to the convent, and in 1582 she and eleven other nuns opened the new house in Rome, which she also had helped design.[51] A third widow, Francesca Baglioni Orsini, paid 6500 scudi for property near the Trevi Fountain in 1600, and on 7 March 1601, she placed with her own hands the foundation stone of her new Dominican convent called Santa Maria dell'Umiltà. Although she did not take the veil, she retired to the convent and served as a model of piety for the nuns.[52]

Under Pope Sixtus V (1585–90), a group of Cistercians called the Foglianti, led by Jean de la Barrière, entered into a reform so extreme that the papal curia under Clement VIII ordered their disbanding and deprived their leader of all spiritual contact with his followers in Rome.[53] Caterina de'Nobili Sforza, whose wish to commemorate her family has already been noted above, refused to be intimidated by curial displeasure; she took de la Barrière into her own house, and in 1593 embarked on the grand project of building a church and monastery for this austere group, gambling on the belief that they would be vindicated—as they were. She spent more than 10,000 scudi to transform one of the round towers of the Baths of Diocletian into San Bernardo alle Terme (fig. 7).[54] She followed the example of Camilla Peretti, the widowed sister of Sixtus V, who had taken an interest in the female branch of the Foglianti a few years earlier, and had used her money and some of her brother's to renovate the church and convent of Santa Susanna for them.[55] San Bernardo was built across the piazza from Santa Susanna, close to the Acqua Felice built by Sixtus V.

There is no reason to doubt the religious commitment that motivated all these women to support Catholic reform in early modern Rome. However, other considerations also may have come into play. The very fact that women did *not* live in the public spotlight focused on men may have given them the freedom to seek out more radical ideas and to take more chances. Furthermore, the new or newly reformed orders were dedicated to austere simplicity and true poverty and they may have found women to be more sympathetic to their aims, which did not require grandiose structures or patrons with a penchant for self-aggrandizement. Unfortunately, this has worked against the women patrons in the long run; many of their buildings *were* modest, not because women were unable to afford larger buildings, but because women were willing to pay for humble spaces which expressed the new religious ideals.[56] As this rhetoric of humility changed in the seventeenth century, many of the earlier buildings, such as Sant'Andrea al Quirinale, were replaced by grander Baroque ones, eclipsing the sixteenth-century message of both orders and patrons.

Social Welfare

Social welfare, like the other two categories, was not the sole preserve of women in sixteenth-century Rome, but the variety of institutions paid for by women is notable, as three examples will show. In 1593 Marchesa Giulia Rangoni, a devout follower of Philip Neri, joined forces with other women and an Oratorian priest to establish a shelter for women on the Quirinal Hill, near the ruins of the Baths of Constantine. Santa Maria del Rifugio was built to provide a home for poor but honest girls (*zitelle*), fallen women who wished to repent, and needy widows of good reputation.[57] Marchesa Rangoni was doubtlessly following the example of Early Christian widows, but she also had a more immediate patronage model: her sister was Maddalena Orsini, who had built Santa Maria Maddalena al Quirinale (see above). The patronage of these sisters illustrates two common patterns in Rome: women often reinforced each other by building in the same area (ten women built on or near the Quirinal Hill between 1560 and 1630),[58] and related women often contributed to the family tradition of patronage (this extended also to in-laws as in the case of Caterina and Fulvia Sforza). Women were motivated not only by models from their Christian past, but also by their contemporaries.

Hospitals were an obvious place for the patronage of women. Vittoria della Tolfa (fig. 3) exemplifies this: she made two hospitals, Santo Spirito in Sassia and San Giacomo degli Incurabili, her universal heirs.[59] Both these institutions were revitalized in the late sixteenth century, owing in part to the ministries of Philip Neri and Camillo de Lellis who belonged to the new breed of active city saints. Vittoria also commissioned the Chapel of the Pentecost at Santo Spirito and another chapel at San Giacomo. In the latter, Francesco Zucchi's altarpiece (fig. 11) showed the Marchesa as a humble widow whose private devotion and public patronage were both placed in the service of the poor and sick.[60]

Two foreign women came to Rome in 1600 and their patronage would provide a home and education for young women who neither wished to marry or enter a convent. Francesca Montioux, who was from a noble Parisian family, fled her home to escape an unwanted marriage.[61] She intended to travel alone to the Holy Land (following the model of Santa Paola Romana, the friend of Saint Jerome), but in Rome she came under the sway of Philip Neri while staying at the home of one of his followers, Fulvia Conti Sforza, the countess of Santa Fiore (see above). Francesca de Gourcy of Flanders also wished to dedicate her virginity to God, but her noble family insisted on her marriage. Eighteen months later she was widowed and, refusing all further suggestions of marriage, she went on a pilgrimage to Cologne (like Saint Ursula), where for five years she worked with the poor. In 1600 she traveled to Rome for the Holy Year and there met Francesca Montioux. The two

Valone Fig. 11. Francesco Zucchi, *Madonna, Saint James, and the Donor, Vittoria della Tolfa,* ca. 1590, Rome, San Giacomo degli Incurabili, Sacristy (photo: Morton Abromson)

women decided to pool their resources in order to found the Congregation of Saint Ursula, and in 1602 they began to buy up land and buildings in Trastevere near the derelict church of Saints Rufina e Seconda, which Paul V finally gave to them in 1611. They must have chosen the site with care as it was thought to be the location of the house of Rufina and Seconda, two young Roman sister saints of the third century who fled Rome in order to escape unwanted marriages. Upon their capture, they were offered the choice of death in prison or the joys of life and marriage. Claiming that prison represented only temporary pain versus the eternal loss of their souls, they elected virginity and death. Their bodies were later gathered up by the pious Roman matron Plautilla for burial. Like Rufina and Seconda, the two Francescas chose virginity, but created an unusual alternative to the cloistered convent. They built the Collegio di Sant'Orsola around the church of SS. Rufina e Seconda; it was open to honest girls of good families who, according to a seventeenth-century writer, were spirited and talented, with a great wish to serve God. They made no final vows and were not strictly cloistered; they often went out in groups to visit the holy sites in Rome.[62] In many ways their communal life of study and prayer resembled the practice in the houses of Marcella and Paola, the noble friends of Saint Jerome, who gathered like-minded women around them to share in a personal dedication to God which needed no formal vows.

Women in early modern Rome doubtlessly were motivated by the long tradition of matron as patron of architecture, and for the most part they conformed to the categories of commemoration, religion, and social welfare.[63] Nonetheless, within those confines they managed to say a number of personal things in a very public way.

What about the women who originated the tradition in the ancient world? Were commemoration, religion, and social welfare motives for building which they defined for themselves, or were those motives shaped by what men would allow? Once men gave women access to wealth, patronage was sure to follow, but were the categories of women's patronage reflective of female values? Or did men allow women to share only in those aspects of patronage deemed suitable for women—patronage which could increase family status, but which did not actually give women more power in any political or self-determining sense? In the Hellenistic world, Van Bremen writes, "activities requiring action in the form of traveling, deliberating, voting, etc., remained closed to women…and the ever-present ideology of the modest, silent, loving wife" was not disturbed.[64] Ramsay MacMullen softens the blow somewhat. He agrees that women could not speak in public in the Roman world, but "as any reader of Tacitus knows, women had a great deal to say about the decisions that determined the lives and fortunes of the most important people (and 'politics' rarely rose above that courtier level, to the level of what we would call 'policy')."[65] Nonetheless, it seems that men may have set the limits to women's patronage in antiquity, and women may have concurred because some voice was better than none.

Succeeding generations of matrons as patrons either internalized these restrictions and made them their own, or they were subject to the same ideology about what was suitable for women. A thorough discussion of this issue is beyond the scope of this paper, but I would like to close with the following thoughts: there can be no doubt that the world of political and military power was closed to women in the ancient world and in early modern Italy, but defining history in terms of such power has always been a male construct of history. It is possible that the love of family, the belief in religious reform, and the desire to help the needy really do represent female values in the long tradition of matron as patron—values which women have generally understood to be more permanent than the ephemeral honors of state or of military conquest.

Notes

1. Frederika H. Jacobs, "The Construction of a Life: Madonna Properzia de'Rossi 'Schultrice' Bolognese," *Word and Image* 9, no. 2 (1993): 122; Natalie Harris Bluestone, "The Female Gaze: Women's Interpretations of the Life and Work of Properzia de' Rossi, Renaissance Sculptor," in *Double Vision: Perspectives on Gender and their Visual Arts*, ed. Natalie Harris Bluestone (Carnbury, N.J.: Associated University Presses, 1995) 38–64; Fredrika H. Jacobs, *Defining the Renaissance Virtuosa: Women Artists and the Language of Art History and Criticism* (Cambridge: Cambridge University Press, 1997) passim, esp. chap. 4; see also Sheryl Reiss's unpublished paper on the artist.

2. Carolyn Valone, "Women on the Quirinal Hill: Patronage in Rome, 1560–1630," *Art Bulletin* 76 (1994): 129–46; Marilyn Dunn, "Piety and Patronage in Seicento Rome: Two Noblewomen and Their Convents," *Art Bulletin* 76 (1994): 644–63; and articles on the patronage of women in Islamic architecture by Esin Atil, Noha Sadek, Roya Marefat, Ulkü U. Bates in *Asian Art* 6, no. 2 (1993). On secular women as patrons of architecture see the chapters by Lawrence Jenkens, Sheryl Reiss, and Katherine McIver in this volume.

3. Aristotle, *The Politics*, part 1:ii, xii, xiii; part 2:ix; part 3:i–v; Leon Battista Alberti, *Della Famiglia*, trans. as *The Family in Renaissance Florence* by Renée Neu Watkins (Columbia: University of South Carolina Press, 1969). Within the Christian tradition the pronouncements attributed to Saint Paul in I Cor. 7–14 and in I Tim. have also contributed to this notion.

4. Carolyn Valone, "Roman Matrons as Patrons: Various Views of the Cloister Wall," in *The Crannied Wall*, ed. Craig A. Monson (Ann Arbor: University of Michigan Press, 1992), 59–67. On patronage of art by widows, see the chapters by Rosi Gilday, Sheryl Reiss, Katherine McIver, Mary Vaccaro, Marjorie Och, and Elizabeth Pilliod in this volume.

5. For the legal status of women see David Schaps, *Economic Rights of Women in Ancient Greece* (Edinburgh: Edinburgh University Press, 1979); Jane Gardner, *Women in Roman Law and Society* (Bloomington: Indiana University Press, 1991); Susan Treggiari, *Roman Marriage* (Oxford, Clarendon Press, 1991), 323–63, 365–96; Eva Cantarella, *Pandora's Daughters*, trans. Maureen Fant (Baltimore: Johns Hopkins University Press, 1987); Maria Teresa Guerra Medici, *I diritti delle donne nella società altomedievale* (Naples: Edizioni Scientifiche Italiane, 1986); Thomas Kuehn, *Law, Family, and Women: Toward a Legal Anthropology of Renaissance Italy* (Chicago: University of Chicago Press, 1991); Giulia Calvi, *Il contratto morale, madri e figli nella Toscana moderna* (Bari: Laterza, 1994); Louise Mirrer, ed. *Upon My Husband's Death* (Ann Arbor: University of Michigan Press, 1992).

6. Guerra Medici, *I diritti delle donne*, 14, emphasizes the need to examine not only the written law but also the application of the law: "non è sempre agevole stabilire, invero, sino a che punto la legge rifletta le condizioni giuridiche e sociali di una società." Calvi, *Il contratto morale*, 18–32, demonstrates the surprising fact that in early modern Tuscany the guardianship for a young son was not always given to the deceased husband's male kin, but often to the boy's mother, in spite of the rhetoric about patrilinear power structures in the period. Further works which reveal the importance of studying usage are Susannah Baxandale, "Exile in Practice: The Alberti Family in and out of Florence, 1401–1428," *Renaissance Quarterly* 44 (1991): 720–56; Thomas V. Cohen and Elizabeth S. Cohen, *Words and Deeds in Renaissance Rome* (Toronto: University of Toronto Press, 1993); Joanne M. Ferraro, "The Power to Decide: Battered Wives in Early Modern Venice," *Renaissance Quarterly* 48 (1995): 492–512.

7. Riet Van Bremen, "Women and Wealth," in *Images of Women in Antiquity*, ed. Averil Cameron and Amèlie Kuhrt (Detroit: Wayne State University Press, 1983), 223–42. See also Ramsay MacMullen, "Women in Public in the Roman Empire," *Historia* 29, no. 2 (1980): 208–18; and Diana E. E. Kleiner and Susan Matheson, eds., *I Claudia, Women in Ancient Rome* (New Haven, Conn.: Hull Printing, 1996).

8. Cantarella, *Pandora's Daughters*, 139; Van Bremen, "Women and Wealth," 226.

9. Christine de Pizan, *The Book of the City of Ladies*, trans. E. J. Richards (New York: Persea Books, 1982), 94.

10. Christine de Pizan, *City of Ladies*, 10, 12–13.

11. Richard Stoneman, *Palmyra and Its Empire, Zenobia's Revolt Against Rome* (Ann Arbor: University of Michigan Press, 1992), 120–25.

12. Christine de Pizan, *City of Ladies*, 123. For the Mausoleum, see Andrew Stewart, *Greek Sculpture* (New Haven, Conn.: Yale University Press, 1990), 180–82 and 282 for the quote from Pliny's *Natural History*, 36.30–31.

13. *Women's Life in Greece and Rome*, ed. Mary R. Lefkowitz and Maureen Fant, 2nd ed. (Baltimore: Johns Hopkins University Press, 1992), 207.

14. Lefkowitz and Fant, *Women's Life in Greece and Rome*, 160.

15. Lefkowitz and Fant, *Women's Life in Greece and Rome*, 159.

16. Brunilde Sismondo Ridgway, "Ancient Women and Art: The Material Evidence," *American Journal of Archaeology* 91, no. 3 (1987): 407.

17. Ridgway, "Ancient Women and Art," 408.

18. Van Bremen, "Women and Wealth," 223.

19. Ridgway, "Ancient Women and Art," 408. Epie's patronage probably dates to the first century B.C.E.

20. Mary Gilmore Williams, "Studies in the Lives of Roman Empresses," *American Journal of Archaeology* 5 (1902): 261–305.

21. Stewart Oost, *Galla Placidia Augusta* (Chicago: University of Chicago Press, 1968).

22. Kenneth Holum, *Theodosian Empresses* (Berkeley: University of California Press, 1982).

23. Bernadette Brooten, *Women Leaders in the Ancient Synagogue* (Chico, Ca.: Scholars Press, 1982), 141–44, 157–65.

24. Lefkowitz and Fant, *Women's Life in Greece and Rome*, 158.

25. Lefkowitz and Fant, *Women's Life in Greece and Rome*, 160. Projects related to water seem to have a certain appeal to women. In the fifteenth century Lucrezia Tornabuoni de' Medici rebuilt the baths at Bagno a Morbo. For other aspects of Lucrezia's patronage, see Katherine J. P. Lowe, "A Matter of Piety or of Family Tradition and Custom?" in *Piero de' Medici "il Gottoso" 1416–1469,* ed. Andreas Beyer and Bruce Boucher (Berlin: Akademie Verlag, 1993), 55–69. On Lucrezia Tornabuoni, see also Sheryl Reiss's chapter in this volume, nn. 2 and 38.

26. Lefkowitz and Fant, *Women's Life in Greece and Rome*, 159. See also Elizabeth Lyding Will, "Women in Pompeii," *Archaeology* 32, no. 5 (1979): 34–43. This is the same Eumachia who built the tomb outside the Porta Nuceria. See Lefkowitz and Fant, *Women's Life in Greece and Rome,* 160.

27. Valone, "Women on the Quirinal Hill," 141–44. For Early Christian women, see Rosemary Ruether, "Mothers of the Church," in *Women of Spirit*, ed. R. Ruether and E. McLaughlin (New York: Simon and Schuster, 1979), 71–98; and Anne Ewing Hickey, *Women of the Roman Aristocracy as Christian Monastics* (Ann Arbor: University of Michigan Press, 1987).

28. Gregory Martin, *Roma Sancta 1581*, ed. G. B. Parks (Rome: Edizioni di Storia e Letteratura, 1969), 10. The Oratorian historians in late-sixteenth-century Rome referred to Maddalena Orsini as another Santa Paola Romana, and her sister Giulia Orsini Rangoni was also called "la nova Paola." Francesca Baglioni Orsini was compared to both Paola and Marcella by her biographer. For full documentation see Valone, "Women on the Quirinal Hill," 143.

It is beyond the scope of this article to outline the medieval tradition of female architectural patronage, which is particularly rich in the area of convent building throughout Europe, but the following works will indicate the richness of the bibliography: Suzanne Wemple, "S. Salvatore/S. Giulia: A Case Study in the Endowment and Patronage of a Major Female Monastery in Northern Italy," in *Women of the Medieval World*, ed. Julius Kirshner and Suzanne Wemple (Oxford: Blackwell, 1985), 85–102; Caroline Bruzelius, "Hearing is Believing: Clarissan Architecture ca. 1213–1340," *Gesta* 31, no. 2 (1992): 83–91; Constance H. Berman, "Women as Donors and Patrons to Southern French Monasteries in the Twelfth and Thirteenth Centuries," in *The Worlds of Medieval Women*, ed. Constance H. Berman, Charles Cornell, Judith Rice Rothschild (Morgantown: West Virginia University Press, 1985), 53–68; and Jeffrey Hamburger, "Art, Enclosure and the Cura Monialium: Prolegomena in the Guise of a Postscript," *Gesta* 32, no. 2 (1992): 114–17.

29. Agostino Valier, *La istituzione d'ogni stato lodevole delle donne cristiane*, ed. Gaetano Volpi (Padua: Giuseppe Comino, 1744), bk. 3, 17–38.

30. Valier, *La istituzione*, 25.

31. See Sharon T. Strocchia, "Remembering the Family: Women, Kin, and Commemorative Masses in Renaissance Florence," *Renaissance Quarterly* 42, no. 4 (1989): 635–54.

32. See Elizabeth Pilliod's chapter in this volume for other examples of widows "going their own way."

33. Johanna Heideman, *The Cinquecento Chapel Decorations in Santa Maria in Aracoeli in Rome* (Amsterdam: Academische Pers, 1982), 127, 132. The artist Livia employed for the altarpiece was Girolamo Siciolante of Sermoneta.

34. Heideman, *Cinquecento Chapel Decorations*, 68–70, 111–25; Carolyn Valone, "Piety and Patronage: Women and the Early Jesuits," in *Creative Women in Medieval and Early Modern Italy*, ed. E. Ann Matter and John Coakley (Philadelphia: University of Pennsylvania Press, 1994), 157–84. Vittoria had a predilection for Franciscans: she was also a patron at San Francesco a Ripa in Trastevere.

35. Goffredo di Crollalanza, *Enciclopedia araldico cavalleresca* (Bologna: Arnaldo Forni, 1976), 14, 427. Vittoria's dowry included the marquisate of Guardia Grele near Chieti, which provided both a title and income for her husband after he lost his Neapolitan lands and title. See Franca Allegrezza, "Formazione, dispersione e conservazione di un fondo archivistico privato: Il fondo diplomatico dell'archivio Orsini tra medioevo ed età moderna," *Archivio della Società Romana di Storia Patria* 114 (1991): 95.

36. Pompeo Litta, *Famiglie celebri di Italia*, 10 vols. (Milan: Giusti, 1819–83), 2: plate 4. On the final page of the volume is an engraving of her tomb. Lucrezia, whose mother was the sister of Julius II, died in 1552 at the age of sixty-seven. Her husband, who had supported Julius II, switched his military allegiance from the papacy to the French in 1517 and was killed in battle in Milan in 1522. Thus, Lucrezia remained a widow for thirty years. For her tomb inscription, see Vincenzo Forcella, *Iscrizioni delle chiese e d'altri edifici di Roma* (Rome: Berncini, 1873), 3: 116. For the artist see Paul Barolsky, *Daniele da Volterra, A Catalogue Raisonné* (New York: Garland Press, 1979).

37. See Carolyn Valone, "The Art of Hearing: Sermons and Images in the Chapel of Lucrezia della Rovere," *Sixteenth Century Journal* 31 (2000): 753–77.

38. Lucrezia's wealth included her dowry of 10,000 scudi and the properties of Sant'Angelo Romano, Monticelli, and Frascati. For her marriage contract see Colonna Archives, Matrimoni 3. BB. 2, 6. See also Annibale Ilari, *Frascati tra medioevo e rinascimento* (Rome: Edizione di Storia e Letteratura, 1965), 77–90.

39. For full documentation see Valone, "Roman Matrons as Patrons," 53–59. See also Sergio Ortolani, *San Bernardo alle Terme* (Rome: Fratelli Palombi, 1924).

40. For a fuller discussion and documentation of the patronage of the three women, see Valone, "Piety and Patronage," 157–84. On the early Jesuits, see John W. O'Malley, *The First Jesuits* (Cambridge, Mass.: Harvard University Press, 1993).

41. Louis Richeôme, *La peinture spirituelle* (Lyons: Rigualt, 1611), 3–46.

42. Jesuit Curia Archive, Rome (ARSI), Provincia Romana, vol. 162, 1, pp. 166v, 167r–v.

43. Giuseppe Coniglio, *Visitatori del Viceregno di Napoli* (Bari: Società di Storia Patria per la Puglia, 1974), 56–74. Her husband's debts totaled 1,700,000 scudi.

44. Capuchin spirituality in the sixteenth century is also discussed in Marjorie Och's chapter in this volume.

45. Edoardo d'Alençon, *Il terzo convento dei Cappuccini a Roma. La chiesa di S. Nicola de'Portiis San Bonaventura, Santa Croce dei Lucchesi* (Rome: Befani, 1908), 23. The references to women acting as mothers to the new order come from the sixteenth-century chronicles of Mario da Mercato Saraceno, Capuchin General 1567–73, and Bernardino da Colpetrazzo.

46. For the early Capuchins and women , see Bernardino da Colpetrazzo, "Cronica 1525–1593," in *Monumenta Historica Ordinis Minorum Cappuccinorum*, ed. Melchior da Pobladura, 3 vols. (Assisi: Collegio S. Lorenzo da Brindisi, 1939), 2:185–96, 224, 292–95, 302–4, 488–89; d'Alençon, *Il terzo convento*; Valone, "Women on the Quirinal Hill," 131–32.

47. C. Ceschi, "S. Urbano ai Pantani," *Capitolium* 9, 8 (1933): 380–91; Valone, "Matrons as Patrons," 50–53.

48. This convent, called San Giuseppe Capo le Case or alle Frate, was built in 1596–98, and rebuilt in 1628. See Ottavio Panciroli, *Tesori nascosti dell'alma città di Roma* (Rome: Zannetti, 1625), 385.

49. "Fatto a sua spese." See Antonio Gallonio, *Vita del beato p. Filippo Neri fiorentino* (Rome: Zannetti, 1601), 98–99.

50. BAV, Urb. Lat. 1049, 338v. This "avviso" is dated 18 August 1581.

51. Bonaventura Borselli, *Breve narrazione della vita e virtù della ven. Suor Maria Maddalena Orsini* (Rome: Tinassi, 1668), 20–25, 30–40.

52. Francesco Maria Bertucci, *Istoria della vita ed azione di Francesca Baglioni Orsini, fondatrice del monastero di Santa Maria dell'Umiltà* (Rome: Salomoni, 1753), 51, 61, 90–97.

53. Ortolani, *San Bernardo*, 3–8, 16–21.

54. See n. 39 above.

55. For full documentation see Valone, "Women on the Quirinal Hill," 134–36.

56. For example, in the early 1600s Margherita Cavazzi della Somaglia, the wife of Michele Peretti, great-nephew of Sixtus V, wished to honor the Capuchins by enlarging the choir of San Bonaventura and replacing the simple wooden roof with a vaulted one. The Capuchins refused this architectural grandeur, but did accept, a few years later, a new painting, *Madonna in Glory*, for the high altar. See Erina Russo de Caro, "Gli ultimi discendenti di Sisto V e i frati cappuccini di Roma" *Strenna dei Romanisti* 49 (1988): 458–60.

57. Pietro Felini, *Trattato nuovo delle cose maravigliose di Roma* (Rome: Franzini, 1610), 184; Valone, "Women on the Quirinal Hill," 136–37.

58. Valone, "Women on the Quirinal Hill."

59. For her will, see ASR, Archivio del arciospedale di Santo Spirito in Sassia, b. 1139, insert 162. For her Early Christian model, Fabiola, see Martin, *Roma Sancta*, 182–83.

60. This chapel was the first to the left of the portal. The space has been remanaged (and is generally closed), but still contains the original altarpiece by Zucchi. Vittoria's coat of arms and an inscription from her chapel are now found in the second chapel to the left. See Howard Hibbard, *Carlo Maderno* (London: Zwemmer, 1971), 120–21. For a description of the painting, see Giovanni Baglione, *Le vite de'pittori, scultori et architetti* (1642; reprint, ed. Valerio Mariani, Rome: Calzone, 1935), 102. For her chapel at Santo Spirito in Sassia, see Carolyn Valone, "The Pentecost: Image and Experience in Late Sixteenth-Century Rome," *Sixteenth Century Journal* 24, no. 4 (1993): 818–26.

61. Ernesto Iezzi, *Studio storico della chiesa a del monastero delle SS. Rufina e Seconda in Trastevere* (Rome: San Nilo, 1980), 35–62.

62. Carlo Piazza, *Opere pie di Roma* (Rome: Buffotti, 1679), 345–49. This College of Saint Ursula was not connected to the Ursuline order founded by Angela Merici in sixteenth-century Brescia, but the two Francescas apparently found Merici's ideas congenial to their own aims.

63. Women as patrons of palaces and villas still needs to be explored; see the chapters by Lawrence Jenkens and Sheryl Reiss in this volume and Carolyn Valone, "Mothers and Sons: Two Paintings for San Bonaventura in Early Modern Rome," *Renaissance Quarterly* 53 (2000): 121.

64. Van Bremen, "Women and Wealth," 235–37.

65. MacMullen, "Women in Public," 215–18.

About the Contributors

Molly Bourne teaches art history at Syracuse University in Florence, Italy. She received her Ph.D. from Harvard University with a thesis on the artistic patronage of Francesco II Gonzaga and it's relationship to the patronage of his consort, Isabella d'Este. A specialist in the art and architecture of Renaissance Mantua, she has published on topics including villa design and cartography at the Gonzaga court, as well as on cultural exchange between Mantua and Spain. Currently she is editing and contributing to a collection of interdisciplinary essays on art and culture in Renaissance Mantua.

Roger J. Crum received his Ph.D. from the University of Pittsburgh in 1992, and in 2000 was named the Dr. Thomas C. and Janet M. Graul Chair in Art and Languages at the University of Dayton, where he has taught since 1991. A specialist in the art and architecture of Renaissance Florence, he has published articles and reviews in *The Art Bulletin, Art Journal, Artibus et Historiae, Renaissance Quarterly, Renaissance Studies,* and *The Sixteenth Century Journal.* Together with John T. Paoletti, he is presently editing a volume on the spaces of Florentine art, 1300–1600, forthcoming from Cambridge University Press. He has been a Samuel H. Kress predoctoral fellow at the Kunsthistorisches Institut in Florence, a fellow at the Newberry Library in Chicago, and a member of the Institute for Advanced Study at Princeton.

Bruce L. Edelstein currently teaches in Florence for New York University and Florida State University. He received his Ph.D. from Harvard University in 1995 after completing a dissertation on the patronage of Eleonora di Toledo. He has held teaching positions at Syracuse University in Italy and the Harvard University Graduate School of Design, and curatorial and research positions at the Medici Archive Project, the Museum of Fine Arts in Boston, and the Fogg Art Museum. In addition to contributing to the *Dizionario biografico degli italiani,* he continues to research and publish on various aspects of artistic patronage at the Medici court in the sixteenth century. Forthcoming articles treat Agnolo Bronzino's design for the vault fresco in the Chapel of Eleonora, the mid-sixteenth-century appearance and function of the Camera Verde in the Palazzo Vecchio, and the employment of the lost Neapolitan villa of Poggioreale as a model for the hydraulic systems in Medici villa and garden complexes. For the academic year 2001–2, he will be a fellow at Villa I Tatti, the Harvard University Center for Renaissance Studies.

Rosi Prieto Gilday received her doctorate in art history from the University of Pittsburgh. She specializes in Italian Renaissance art and architecture and has focused her research and teaching on political, literary, feminist, and economic issues in Florentine art. Her current research includes topics on Neri di Bicci, Andrea del Sarto, and Andrea del Castagno. Her article, "Contradiction and Ambivalence: Castagno's 'Famous Women' as Female Role Models," is forthcoming. She has taught at San Francisco State University, the University of Pittsburgh, and the University of the Pacific. She teaches at the California State University at Hayward.

A. Lawrence Jenkens is currently associate professor of art history at the University of New Orleans. He received his A.B. from Harvard University and his M.A. and Ph.D. from the Institute of Fine Arts, New York University. His research activities have focused on the architecture of Siena in the fifteenth century; he is the author of several articles on the Piccolomini family and architectural patronage in late fifteenth-century Siena. and is editing and contributing to a collection of essays on the art and architecture of Siena in the Renaissance which will appear in 2001. Professor Jenkens's recent work has been supported by a fellowship from the National Endowment for the Humanities and several research grants from the University of New Orleans, and he is the recipient of a fellowship at the Harvard Center of Italian Renaissance Studies (Villa I Tatti) in Florence for the 2001–2002 academic year.

Benjamin G. Kohl is Andrew W. Mellon Professor of the Humanities at Vassar College, where he has taught medieval and Renaissance history since 1966. He is the coeditor, with Ronald G. Witt, of *The Earthly Republic: Italian Humanists on Government and Society* (1978); co-editor, with Alison Andrews Smith, of *Major Problems in the History of the Italian Renaissance* (1995), and the editor of several humanist Latin texts. In addition to numerous studies on the political, social, and cultural history of early Renaissance Italy, he is the author of a monograph on *Padua Under the Carrar, 1318-1405*, published by Johns Hopkins University Press in 1998. A fellow of the Royal Historical Society, Professor Kohl serves on the Advisory Board of the journal *Renaissance Studies,* and has been a past president and is currently councillor of the American Friends of the Warburg Institute. His current research focuses on Trecento Venice.

Gabrielle Langdon received her Ph.D. from the University of Michigan. She lives in Canada and in Ireland. She currently teaches at University College, Dublin, and has taught in Canada, the United States, and Italy. Her research interests focus on Florentine Mannerist portraiture, especially of the Medici Court, with publications exploring the portraiture of Pontormo, Bronzino, and Allori. A book-length study, "Portraits of Medici Women from the Court of Cosimo I," is nearing completion. She has also published on Matisse's murals for the Dominican Chapel in Venice. A former museum educator, she holds a Dip. Ed. from the Cambridge Institute, England.

Katherine A. McIver is associate professor of art history at the University of Alabama at Birmingham. She has published several articles on the artistic patronage of women in northern Italy in the sixteenth century which have appeared in *Artibus et Historiae, The Sixteenth-Century Journal, Explorations in Renaissance Culture* and *Fortune and Romance: Boiardo in America.* She has received numerous UAB faculty research grants to pursue her work on women patrons as well as a Gladys Krieble Delmas Foundation Grant. In addition to patronage issues, Professor McIver's research interests include Vasari, women artists, and the relationship between the visual arts and music.

Marjorie Och is associate professor of art history at Mary Washington College in Fredericksburg, Virginia. She received her Ph.D. in 1993 from Bryn Mawr College with a dissertation that examined Vittoria Colonna's patronage of art. Her work on Colonna's portrait medals is forthcoming. Currently she is researching interpretations of artists' biographies in the early modern period. She has received grants from MWC Faculty Research, the Kress Foundation, and the National Endowment for the Humanities.

Elizabeth Pilliod is associate professor of the history of art at Oregon State University; she has also taught at the Syracuse University program in Florence, and at Santa Clara University, Rutgers University, and Princeton University. She has received grants from the Kress Foundation, Villa I Tatti, and the National Endowment for the Humanities. Her publications include articles in the *Burlington Magazine, Master Drawings, Princeton Museum Bulletin, Revue du Louvre, J. Paul Getty Museum Bulletin,* and elsewhere. Her book, *Pontormo,*

Bronzino, and Allori: A Genealogy of Florentine Art, will be published by Yale University Press in 2001. A second book on Pontormo at San Lorenzo is forthcoming with the University of Chicago Press.

Sheryl E. Reiss, Senior Research Associate in the Office of the Vice Provost for Research at Cornell University, received her Ph.D. from Princeton University in 1992. Her doctoral dissertation examined the art patronage of Cardinal Giulio de' Medici, the future Pope Clement VII. Her research concerns Italian art and art patronage of the early sixteenth century, particularly that of the Medici family in Florence and Rome. She has published articles in the *Zeitschrift für Kunstgeschichte*, the *Jahrbuch der Berliner Museen*, the *Journal of the Society of Architectural Historians*, and the *Burlington Magazine*. Dr. Reiss, who has taught at Mount Holyoke College, Smith College, and Cornell University, is the caa.reviews Associate Editor for Early Modern Southern Europe and has received awards from the Kress Foundation, the National Endowment for the Humanities, and the Renaissance Society of America.She is currently preparing a book entitled *The Making of a Medici Maecenas: Giulio de' Medici (Pope Clement VII) as Patron of Art* and is co-editing a collection of essays entitled *The Pontificate of Clement VII: History, Politics, Culture*.

Mary Vaccaro is assistant professor at the University of Texas in Arlington. She received her doctoral degree from Columbia University in 1994 and has held fellowships at the American Academy in Rome and, most recently, Villa I Tatti—the Harvard University Center for Italian Renaissance Studies. Her work focuses on sixteenth-century art in Parma, especially Parmigianino. She has just completed a book on Parmigianino's drawings, coauthored with Sylvie Béguin and Mario di Giampaolo (English and Italian editions both published by Umberto Allemandi, Turin, 2000), and edited a volume on plagiarism in art and art history (Visual Resources, 2000).

Carolyn Valone is professor emerita, Department of Art History, Trinity University, San Antonio, Texas. She has been engaged in research and publication on issues related to women as patrons of architecture in early modern Rome for the past twenty years. Her current project is a study of women in the Cesi family from 1500–1700

David Wilkins, Professor of the History of Art and Architecture at the University of Pittsburgh, was educated at Oberlin College and the University of Michigan. He is author of *Maso di Banco: A Florentine Artist of the Early Trecento; Paintings and Sculpture of the Duquesne Club;* and many articles. He has coauthored *Donatello; The History of the Duquesne Club; The Illustrated Bartsch*, vol. 53; and *Art Past/Art Present* (4th edition, 2001). He coedited with Rebecca L. Wilkins *The Search for a Patron in the Middle Ages and the Renaissance* and is now working on the fifth edition of Frederick Hartt's *History of Italian Renaissance Art*.